Studien zur Außereuropäischen Christentumsgeschichte (Asien, Afrika, Lateinamerika)

Studies in the History of Christianity in the Non-Western World

Herausgegeben von / Edited by
Klaus Koschorke & Johannes Meier

Band 17 / Volume 17

2011
Harrassowitz Verlag · Wiesbaden

Jörg Haustein

Writing Religious History
The Historiography of Ethiopian Pentecostalism

2011

Harrassowitz Verlag · Wiesbaden

Bibliografische Information der Deutschen Nationalbibliothek
Die Deutsche Nationalbibliothek verzeichnet diese Publikation in der Deutschen
Nationalbibliografie; detaillierte bibliografische Daten sind im Internet
über http://dnb.d-nb.de abrufbar.

Bibliographic information published by the Deutsche Nationalbibliothek
The Deutsche Nationalbibliothek lists this publication in the Deutsche
Nationalbibliografie; detailed bibliographic data are available in the internet
at http://dnb.d-nb.de.

For further information about our publishing program consult our
website http://www.harrassowitz-verlag.de
Printed on permanent/durable paper.
Printing and binding: Memminger MedienCentrum AG
Printed in Germany
ISSN 1611-0080
ISBN 978-3-447-06528-3

To You

Contents

Preface

I stood and watched as the Pentecostal healing service simply erupted with noise. So far, I had witnessed much singing, testimonies by different people, prayers for healing, violent exorcisms, and a sermon of forty-five minutes. But now, roughly four and a half hours after the meeting had begun, the noise and worship intensity reached an unprecedented level in a simultaneous mass prayer, prompted by the worship leader. As a Western observer, unaccustomed to such long services and tired from sitting on an uncomfortable bench, I had long since grown weary, but not so the people around me. I carefully peeked at my surroundings—a small fraction of the close to 4,000 worshipers that I could observe. A few bowed forward, mumbling prayers in Amharic. Others loudly prayed in tongues, with their heads tilted back and their eyes closed. Still others, as if combating invisible forces, regularly underscored their prayers with a karate-like hand movement and a forcefully uttered *"bä iyäsus śim!"*[1] A number of worshipers around me quivered and shook violently, some lost their balance and fell back onto their benches. One woman not far from me ecstatically rolled her head in fast motion until she lost consciousness. The leader of the mass prayer fueled this atmosphere by repeatedly shouting *"iyäsus geta näw!"*[2] and his cry was echoed by many participants. Nobody seemed to be bothered by the intense noise, not even the babies I saw around me, huddled up to their mothers. As I stood there in the Ketena Hulet Full Gospel Church, observing this energy and vibrancy among the worshipers, I realized that Pentecostalism had come to Ethiopia to stay.

In the terminology of the anthropologist Clifford Geertz, this introduction to my fieldwork might qualify as a "Being There" narrative.[3] In his astute analysis of anthropological writings, Geertz proposes that "Being There" narratives assert the authorship and the authority of an anthropological work by pointing to the writer's physical presence "there" at a given point in time. They "author-ize" a text by visibly inserting the author into the text in distinction to the researched group, they ground his competence in asserting his physical "Being There," and by nonchalantly oscillating between his visual sensations and thoughtful musings they suggest that anyone who would have "Been There," would have seen and felt the same. My opening followed the same pattern. I am visibly present and yet distinguished from those I observe. There are signs of bodily discomfort to assert my physical participation and to hint at the price I paid for "Being There." Moreover, by quoting Amharic phrases and providing their translation, the reader is assured of my basic linguistic capabilities for understanding what is going on. At the same time, my self-identification as a

---

1 "In Jesus' name!"
2 "Jesus is Lord!"
3 See CLIFFORD GEERTZ, *Works and Lives: The Anthropologist as Author* (Standford, CA: Stanford University Press, 1988), 1–24.

somewhat distanced "Western observer" sets up an alliance with readers who would be unfamiliar with the scene, suggesting that they would read the situation in a similar fashion. Finally, the conclusion to my observations, which in its generality can hardly be refuted, assures the imagined audience that a certain reflectiveness is aspired to, which of course is grounded in actually "Being There."

Indeed, I was there. I actually did attend the Saturday healing service at the Ketena Hulet Full Gospel Believers' Church in Addis Ababa on February 21, 2004 from 9:30 a.m. to 1:30 p.m. I sat on those benches, took notes, observed, and thought. However, there are many different forms of representing this past event, all of which shape its content. My observation protocol of that service is a rather dry and phenomenological listing of worship positions, convulsions, sermon arguments, exorcism rites, and testimonies. It also meticulously records the beginning and end times of each service part as well as the number of participants, their clothes, and certain features of the building, perhaps aspiring to some standardization for comparing similar events. My diary entry about the event, on the other hand, is rather short. It reflects the worship noise and intensity with some irony, notes my achievements and difficulties in understanding the Amharic language, and mentions a little encounter with children afterwards, that was omitted in the observation protocol but corresponds well with my diary's interest to reflect the omnipresent poverty. From these two accounts and my vague memories, I have produced a third narrative, my "Being There" account above, authorizing my presence and observations. This account, however, was shaped by a fourth interest, that is, to conform to Clifford Geertz ironic representation of such narratives in order to make a point about the many forms of representing history. Finally, it should be added that the self-transparency and intentionality contained in these prefacing remarks also have an "author" function which I will leave to others to analyze.

This multifariousness of the historic representation is the main topic of my book about Ethiopian Pentecostalism. When I first set out to explore Pentecostal and Charismatic movements in Ethiopia, I quickly realized that they were a vibrant and growing part of Ethiopian Christianity and that there was much primary material available, but almost no comprehensive and academic treatise of its history or theology. Therefore, I began to collect interviews, documents and personal impressions from as many churches as possible, in the rather ambitious hope of writing an overview which would not only detail the genesis and present characteristics of the Pentecostal and Charismatic movements in Ethiopia, but also study how Pentecostal identities are constructed and sustained in the Ethiopian church landscape. However, when I began to scrutinize the history of Ethiopian Pentecostalism, I became intrigued and fascinated by the divergence of my sources, the often irreconcilable differences between two accounts of the same event, the different ways to set up a story, and the political thrust of my informants. This called for a detailed investigation that would move beyond traditional historiography and thereby could account for the many narrative plots, historical arguments and political implications contained in my sources. In the course of writing such a history, I realized that I was in fact studying the production of Ethiopian Pentecostal and Charismatic identities—in their past and present historiographic representations. Thus, by equally considering the historical and the

historiographical sides of oral and written histories, it became possible to show how
Ethiopian Pentecostalism came into "being" as a concept, over and over again.

The resulting monograph is a slightly revised version of my doctoral dissertation,
which was accepted in 2009 by the Faculty of Theology at the University of Heidelberg. Most material for this study was gathered in three field trips to Ethiopia,
conducted in 2003 from September 8 to October 7, in 2004 from February 17 to
April 3, and in 2005 from January 3 to April 1. The largest part of the research
was carried out in Addis Ababa, but in 2005 I also spent about three weeks each
in Awasa and Bahir Dar. Addis Ababa is by far the largest and most hybrid city
of Ethiopia, and almost all denominations have their headquarters there. Awasa is
important for the early history of Ethiopian Pentecostalism and is located in a largely
Protestant area. Bahir Dar, on the other hand, lies in the Orthodox north and is important for understanding the proliferation of Pentecostalism in contexts classically
dominated by the Ethiopian Orthodox Church. During my fieldwork I visited sixty-
six different gatherings in twenty-one different denominations, from Sunday services
and healing programs to small groups and prayer meetings. In Addis Ababa, I was
able to acquire copies of all seminary theses pertaining to the topic of my research,
which were a valuable resource never before explored to this extent. I conducted 115
interviews in Ethiopia, and fifteen more interviews were arranged in other contexts,
partly as telephone conversations with Ethiopian Pentecostal leaders residing abroad.
Altogether there were 140 informants from sixty-four different organizational entities.[4] The typical interview length was roughly one and a half hours, and almost
all were recorded on tape and subsequently digitized. Roughly seventy of these interviews, which were most relevant to the history of Ethiopian Pentecostalism, were
transcribed and indexed for this study, the others were only revisited on occasion.
Since I had guaranteed anonymity to all my informants, the interviews are cited by
unique numbers throughout the book.

In addition to the fieldwork in Ethiopia, I conducted a study tour to Finland and
Sweden in the summer of 2004 during the course of which I gathered a large amount
of archive material from the Finnish and Swedish Pentecostal missions working in
Ethiopia. Another visit was paid to the archives of the World Council of Churches in
Geneva in November 2007. Relevant excerpts of the Finnish material were translated
by Anna-Mari Nikkilä, whom I would like to thank for her diligent and careful work.
All other translations of Amharic, Swedish, Norwegian, Danish, and German material
were provided by me, unless otherwise indicated. The transliteration of Amharic
terms is based on the *Encyclopaedia Aethiopica*,[5] with the exception of proper names,
for which I adhered to the spelling used by the respective persons, and geographic
names, which conform to the transliteration on maps by the Ethiopian Mapping
Authority. Religious terms are employed as they are used by my informants or in
general Pentecostal discourse.

This project would not have been possible without the help and support of many
others. First and foremost, I would like to thank my interview partners, who not only

4   See List of Informants provided on p. 281.
5   See SIEGBERT UHLIG, ed., *Encyclopaedia Aethiopica*, vol. 1 (Wiesbaden: Harrassowitz, 2003),
    xx-xxi.

gave me a significant amount of their time, but also granted me valuable insights into their lives and their faith. I would also like to thank Genet Kebede, Nega Namaga, Solomon Gebremichael and Salam, Daniel Gezahegne, Beyene Dogarso, and Roswitha Schultheiß for providing me with accommodations and logistical assistance. A special thanks also goes out to Paul Baliski and Seleshi Kebede, who facilitated the most important initial contacts for me, and to Bedru Hussein, Debela Birri, and Michael Schultheiß for helping me access the many valuable seminary theses in Addis Ababa. Furthermore, I very much appreciate the support in obtaining archival sources, which was offered by Magnus Wahlström at the Swedish Pentecostal Research Institute in Ekerö, Pauli Runolinna and Rauno Mikkonen at Fida in Helsinki, and Paul Johansson and Joy Niswander of the Elim Bible Institute in Lima, New York. Mukiria Chacha has provided me with invaluable material from his fathers' writings, which so far has not been sighted and gives a unique insight into Chacha Omahe's perception of a central part of Ethiopian Pentecostal history.

I am very grateful for Klaus Koschorke's offer to publish this book in his *Studies in the History of Christianity in the Non Western World*, and for the assistance of Barbara Krauß and Reinhard Friedrich at Harrassowitz. I would also like to thank Carol Waite for her careful proofreading of an earlier draft of this manuscript. All mistakes remain my own.

I am deeply indebted to my Doktorvater Michael Bergunder, who not only coaxed me toward the uncharted waters of this project, but also supported me in navigating them with his advice and patience. Without his encouragement and the academic environment for Pentecostal Studies that he created, this project would not have been possible. The co-appraisal of the dissertation manuscript was written by Friederike Nüssel, and her insightful questions were also much appreciated in the preparation of this publication.

Finally and most importantly, I would like to thank my wife Cheri, whose friendship and support have meant everything to me in this endeavor and beyond.

Heidelberg, April 2011   Jörg Haustein

Abbreviations

Some official church names in this list actually include the word "Ethiopian," i.e. "Ethiopian Gennet Church." This has been omitted in most cases, not only for better readability of the acronym but also because some churches have suffered splits in recent years, in which the label "Ethiopian" pertained to only a part of the original denomination (e.g. Full Gospel Believers' Church, Evangelical Church Mekane Yesus).

AACC   All Africa Conference of Churches

ACE   Apostolic Church of Ethiopia

AG   Assemblies of God

CCCE   Council for the Cooperation of Churches in Ethiopia

CHIC   Calvary Holiness International Church

CRDA   Christian Relief Development Association

ECFE   Evangelical Churches' Fellowship of Ethiopia

EDU   Ethiopian Democratic Union

ECMY   Evangelical Church Mekane Yesus

ELF   Eritrean Liberation Front

EPLF   Eritrean Popular Liberation Front Also called Eritrean Popular Liberation Forces or Eritrean People's Liberation Front.

EPRP   Ethiopian People's Revolutionary Party

EPRDF   Ethiopian People's Revolutionary Democratic Front

EOC   Ethiopian Orthodox Church

EVASU   Ethiopian Evangelical Students' Association

FFFM   Finnish Free Foreign Mission (In 2002 the FFFM united with the aid organization Lähetyksen Kehitysapu (LKA) and changed its name to Fida International.)

FGBC   Full Gospel Believers' Church (This church is also often called by it's Amharic name, *mulu wängel*.)

FGM   Full Gospel Mission

GC   Gennet Church

GDC   Gospel Deliverance Church

GEC   Gubae Egziabiher Church (Assemblies of God)

HBC   Hiwot Berhan Church

HCG   Harvest Church of God

KHC   Kale Heywet Church

MKC   Meserete Kristos Church

PEFA   Pentecostal Evangelistic Fellowship of Africa

PMU   Stiftelsen Svenska Pingstmissionen U-landshjälp (Foundation of the
         Swedish Pentecostal Mission Help for Underdeveloped Countries)

SFM   Swedish Free Mission

SIDA   Swedish International Development Cooperation Agency

SIM   Sudan Interior Mission (Today the organization is called "Serving in
         Mission")

SPCM   Swedish Philadelphia Church Mission

SPTEC   Scripture Publishers To Every Creature

SWIM   Swedish Industrial Mission

TPLF   Tigray People's Liberation Front

TTI   Teacher Training Institute

UBS   United Bible Society

UPC   United Pentecostal Church

WCC   World Council of Churches

1 Introduction: Parameters for a History of Ethiopian Pentecostalism

Ethiopian Pentecostalism has many contexts, stories, and voices. It appeared during the 1950s and 1960s in Imperial Ethiopia, where it soon became the subject of political and legal controversy. As a result, Pentecostals spent the last years of Emperor Haile Selassie's reign as an underground movement, as well as much of the time after the Ethiopian revolution in 1974, before they re-emerged publicly as a vibrant face of Ethiopian Protestantism when the revolutionary regime was ousted in 1991. The movement's origins are linked to European Pentecostal missions, but its national core and early leadership mainly consisted of a young educated elite, who in turn were connected to rural contexts and revivals. Early on, the movement diversified organizationally and began to enter the established Protestant[1] churches and even the Ethiopian Orthodox Church (EOC), thereby creating a fairly complex network of Pentecostal and Charismatic Christians. As a result, the history of Ethiopian Pentecostalism is told from many political, denominational, and ideological backgrounds, creating a multifarious, hybrid, and disputed source archive for historical research.

This introduction to Ethiopian Pentecostal historiography therefore must begin by mapping out these different contexts. The political and legal parameters for religious movements under the different Ethiopian regimes will be discussed in a first section. This is followed by a basic account of the development of the Pentecostal movement in Ethiopia, which will also introduce the central points of historical debate. Finally, a review of available sources will document the many historical and institutional backgrounds from which the histories of Ethiopian Pentecostalism have emerged.

---

1   A number of studies use the term "evangelical" instead of Protestant, see e.g. Gustav Arén, *Evangelical Pioneers in Ethiopia: Origins of the Evangelical Church Mekane Yesus*, Studia Missionalia Upsaliensia; 32 (Stockholm: EFS Förlaget, 1978); Johannes Launhardt, *Evangelicals in Addis Ababa (1919–1991): With Special Reference to the Ethiopian Evangelical Church Mekane Yesus and the Addis Ababa Synod* (Münster: Lit, 2004); Tibebe Eshete, *The Evangelical Movement in Ethiopia: Resistance and Resilience* (Waco, TX: Baylor University Press, 2009). This correlates with the use of the term in a number of church names, such as Evangelical Church Mekane Yesus (ECMY), which probably has to do with the use of the translated German term "evangelisch" by missionaries, i.e. by the Evangelical Lutheran Mission. This study will use the general label of "Protestantism" for the group of Lutherans, Mennonites, and Baptists, in order to avoid confusion with the more specific and established English use of "evangelical" for Methodism and its branches.

1.1 Historical Context: Political and Legal Conditions for Pentecostalism in Ethiopia

1.1.1 Imperial Ethiopia

The modern Ethiopian empire was created by Shewan/Amhara dynasties at the end of the 19th century, who successfully navigated the precarious balance of the three colonial powers in the Horn of Africa (England, France, and Italy) in order to expand their rule and build a modern nation-state conforming to the requirements of the European colonial interests.[2] This Abyssinian colonization of southwestern, southern, and southeastern territories created an empire of considerable religious diversity. The political and military powers as well as the land settler class relied on the ancient Abyssinian alliance with the Ethiopian Orthodox Church (EOC), which in turn gave rise to alternative faiths among the subdued peoples, as is evident by the entrance of Protestantism in western and southwestern Ethiopia as well as the strength of Islam in parts of southern and most of eastern Ethiopia.

The imperial center of the resulting Ethiopian nation-state was inextricably bound up with the EOC, but at the same time the emperors strove to curb the church's influence and sought the modernizing impulse of European Protestant missions.[3] This is especially true of the policies of the last Ethiopian Emperor, Haile Selassie I, who ruled from 1930 to 1974, interrupted by his exile in England from 1936 to 1941 on account of the Italian occupation. Before inheriting the imperial throne, Haile Selassie, then Ras Tafari Makonnen, effectively utilized the alliance of state and Orthodox church when he accused his predecessor and main rival, Lij Iyasu, of leanings toward Islam. This contributed to Iyasu's deposition in 1916 and Haile Selassie's ascendency to the throne, which he finally inherited after fourteen years of co-regency with Empress Zewditu in 1930.

Once he was crowned as Ethiopian Emperor, Haile Selassie sought to strengthen the Imperial center by basing its legitimacy on a legal instead of a religious footing. In 1931 he laid down the first Ethiopian Constitution, which made no reference to

---

2 For an excellent treatment laying out this argument, see BONNIE K. HOLCOMB and SISAI IBSSA, *The Invention of Ethiopia* (Trenton, NJ: Red Sea Press, 1990).

3 For most of the 19th century, Catholic and Protestant missions competed for influence on equal footing, DONALD CRUMMEY, *Priests and Politicians: Protestant and Catholic Missions in Orthodox Ethiopia, 1830–1868* (Oxford: Clarendon Press, 1972), cf. DONALD CRUMMEY, "The Politics of Modernization: Protestant and Catholic Missionaries in Modern Ethiopia," in *The Missionary Factor in Ethiopia: Papers from a Symposium on the Impact of European Missions on Ethiopian Society, Lund University, August 1996*, ed. GETATCHEW HAILE, AASULV LANDE, and SAMUEL RUBENSON, Studien zur interkulturellen Geschichte des Christentums; 110 (Frankfurt am Main: Lang, 1998), 85–99; SVEN RUBENSON, "The Missionary Factor in Ethiopia: Consequences of a Colonial Context," in *The Missionary Factor in Ethiopia: Papers from a Symposium on the Impact of European Missions on Ethiopian Society, Lund University, August 1996*, ed. GETATCHEW HAILE, AASULV LANDE, and SAMUEL RUBENSON, Studien zur interkulturellen Geschichte des Christentums; 110 (Frankfurt am Main: Lang, 1998), 57–70. However, with Italy's growing aspirations to turn Ethiopia into a dependent colony, which were reined in by the battle of Adwa in 1896, Catholic missions in Ethiopia were faced with considerable difficulty and could only expand in the Italian colony of Eritrea, cf. KEVIN O'MAHONEY, *The Ebullient Phoenix: A History of the Vicariate of Abyssinia 1839–1916*, rev. as one book (Addis Ababa: United Printers, 2002), 258–324.

religious matters nor the EOC.[4] Instead, it was inspired by the Japanese Meiji Constitution of 1889,[5] and defined the Emperor as the central institution in an imperial absolutism. The rights of the people, as well as the basic legislative, executive, and juridical bodies were secondary derivatives of the imperial power.

After the Italian occupation and Haile Selassie's reinstatement in 1941 the matter of religion and religious diversity in Ethiopia was taken up by new legislative initiatives. The first instance was the "Regulations Governing the Activities of Missions" from August 1944, often called the "Missions' Decree."[6] These regulations state their intent to "define clearly the policy to be pursued toward Missions so as to effect the closest possible collaboration between this Government and Missions." They also seek to protect the EOC by demanding the missions to concentrate on the "non-Christian elements of the population," and to "not direct their activities toward converting Ethiopian nationals." This was facilitated by the establishment of so-called "open areas" and "Orthodox Church areas" for missions, the boundaries of which were to be determined by a committee on missions, headed by the Minister of Education. Only Addis Ababa was explicitly declared an open area. In the "Ethiopian Church areas" missions were only tolerated in medical, educational, or developmental projects, and only as long as they refrained from proselytization. In "open areas" they were free to offer spiritual ministries and to make converts among Muslims or adherents of African traditional religions. The authority over the establishment of missions was given to the Minister of Education, who had to coordinate his work with the Minister of Interior, and the Minister of Foreign Affairs. With the exception of the ECMY

---

4   See *The Constitution of Ethiopia: Established in the Reign of His Majesty Haile Selassie I, July 16, 1931* (1931), http://www.worldstatesmen.org/Ethiopia_1931.txt (accessed February 20, 2008).

5   The Japanese transition from a feudal country to an industrial monarchy was what Ethiopian intellectuals aspired to, see BAHRU ZEWDE, *Pioneers of Change in Ethiopia: The Reformist Intellectuals of the Early Twentieth Century* (Oxford: James Currey, 2002), 62; BAHRU ZEWDE, *A History of Modern Ethiopia 1855–1991*, 2nd ed. (Addis Ababa: Addis Ababa University Press, 2001), 110; also HEINRICH SCHOLLER and PAUL BRIETZKE, *Ethiopia: Revolution, Law and Politics*, Afrika-Studien; 92 (München: Weltforum Verlag, 1976), 39. For a detailed comparison of the Meiji and Ethiopian Constitutions, see J. CALVITT CLARKE, "Seeking a Model for Modernization: Ethiopia's Japanizers," *Selected Annual Proceedings of the Florida Conference of Historians* 11 (2004): 35–51.

6   A copy of the "Regulations" can be found in AYMRO WONDMAGEGNEHU and JOACHIM MOTOVU, *The Ethiopian Orthodox Church* (Addis Ababa: Ethiopian Orthodox Mission, 1970), 171–174. For more information on the decree and its implementation, see MARGERY PERHAM, *The Government of Ethiopia* (London: Faber and Faber, 1948), 133–136; BRIAN FARGHER, *The Origins of the New Churches Movement in Southern Ethiopia, 1927–1944*, Studies of Religion in Africa; 16 (Leiden: Brill, 1996), 276–278; TIBEBE ESHETE, *The Evangelical Movement in Ethiopia*, 94–97; FRIEDRICH HEYER, *Die Kirche Äthiopiens: Eine Bestandsaufnahme*, Theologische Bibliothek Töpelmann; 22 (Berlin: De Gruyter, 1971), 317; SÆVERÅS, OLAV, *On Church-Mission Relations in Ethiopia 1944–1969: With Special Reference to the Evangelical Church Mekane Yesus and the Lutheran Missions*, Studia missionalia Upsaliensia; 27 (Uppsala: Lunde, 1974), 31–34; ARNE TOLO, *Sidama and Ethiopian: The Emergence of the Mekane Yesus Church in Sidama*, Studia Missionalia Upsaliensia; 69 (Uppsala: Uppsala Universitet, 1998), 127; JOHN H. SPENCER, *Ethiopia at Bay: A Personal Account of the Haile Sellassie Years* (Algonac, MI: Reference Publications, 1984), 170.

all protestant churches remained registered under their respective missions until the Ethiopian revolution and thus worked under the premises of the Missions' Decree.[7]

At the same time, Haile Selassie labored to bring autocephaly to the EOC, which had been under the jurisdiction of Alexandria since its foundation in the fourth century. In 1948 an agreement of future ecclesiastical independence was signed, followed by the ordination of Abuna Basilios as first Ethiopian archbishop in 1951, who in 1959 was crowned as the first patriarch of the EOC.[8] While autocephaly obviously was a prestigious gain for the EOC, it also deprived the church of its "only remaining external source of legitimacy that was beyond the emperor's control" as Haile Mariam Larebo observed.[9]

In 1955 a number of factors led to the revision of the 1931 Constitution, most of all the need to accommodate the more modern Eritrean Constitution in the Ethiopian federation.[10] The Constitution was drafted under considerable American influence,[11] and it was promulgated by Haile Selassie on the twenty-fifth anniversary of his coronation.[12] The Constitution accommodated a number of Western juridical principles,[13] while at the same time remaining clearly affirmative to the old monarchical order. In contrast to the 1931 Constitution, the 1955 Constitution contained a number of provisions about the EOC, closely aligning it with the Ethiopian Empire: the archbishop (later the patriarch) is appointed as a member of the Council of Regency (art. 10),[14] the emperor must be of Orthodox faith (art. 16), the archbishop must take an oath of loyalty to the emperor (art. 20), the emperor pledges to defend the Orthodox faith in the coronation oath (art. 21), the EOC is the established church of the empire (art. 126), and the election of bishops and archbishops is subject to the emperor's approval, who may also introduce legislation pertaining to the church (art. 127).[15] Thus

7 It was not until 1969, i.e. well after the revision of the Constitution and the establishment of a registration procedure, that the ECMY was "declared legally registered" as Evangelical Church Mekane Yesus in Ethiopia, cf. ØYVIND M. EIDE, *Revolution and Religion in Ethiopia: Growth and Persecution of the Mekane Yesus Church, 1974–85*, 2nd ed. (Oxford: Currey, 2000), 37–38.

8 See SEVIR CHERNETSOV, "Ethiopian Orthodox (Täwaḥǝdo) Church: History from the Second Half of the 19th Century to 1959," in *Encyclopaedia Aethiopica*, vol. 2, ed. SIEGBERT UHLIG (Wiesbaden: Harrassowitz, 2005), 421–424.

9 HAILE MARIAM LAREBO, "The Ethiopian Orthodox Church," in *Eastern Christianity and Politics in the Twentieth Century*, ed. SABRINA PETRA RAMET, Christianity Under Stress; 1 (Durham: Duke University Press, 1988), 387.

10 See BAHRU ZEWDE, *A History of Modern Ethiopia 1855–1991*, 206–207; PAUL HENZE, *Layers of Time: A History of Ethiopia* (London: Hurst and Company, 2001), 252–253.

11 The drafting committee consisted of three American advisors and two members of Haile Selassie's government, cf. BAHRU ZEWDE, *A History of Modern Ethiopia 1855–1991*, 206; SPENCER, *Ethiopia at Bay*. It was drafted in English and then translated into Amharic, see HENZE, *Layers of Time*, 252.

12 See HAILE SELASSIE I, "Proclamation Promulgating the Revised Constitution of the Empire of Ethiopia," *Negarit Gazeta*, 2 1955, 3–19.

13 See SCHOLLER and BRIETZKE, *Ethiopia: Revolution, Law and Politics*, 39–40.

14 The Council of Regency is to form an interim government if the emperor is "unable to exercise the imperial Office whether by reason of minority, absence from the Empire, or by reason of serious illness" and the crown prince or presumptive heir is not yet of age or otherwise unable to assume regency, cf. arts. 8–11.

15 Art. 127 led the Orthodox church to comment: "There is no separation of Church and State", see AYMRO WONDMAGEGNEHU and MOTOVU, *The Ethiopian Orthodox Church*, 166.

the Constitution not only explicitly established and protected the EOC in Ethiopian law, it also clearly affirmed its status as the church of the empire. In light of these explicit provisions, there is a rather timid assurance of non-interference in religious practices in article 40:

> There shall be no interference with the exercise, in accordance with the law, of the rites of any religion or creed by residents of the Empire, provided that such rites be not utilized for political purposes or prejudicial to public order or morality.[16]

Contrary to the notion that "religious freedom is assured"[17] here, article 40 does not provide a general assurance of freedom of religion, but merely guarantees non-interference in the "exercise ... of the rites of any religion or creed by residents of the Empire."[18] This provision is limited in two ways. First, the exercise has to be "in accordance with the law," which would enable any legislation to curtail the exercise of religious freedom in any way desired. Secondly, religions essentially have to be unpolitical, and they may not interfere with public order or morality, both of which are highly expandable provisions.

The Civil Code of 1960, which is still in effect in present Ethiopia, quotes art. 40 of the 1955 Constitution (with minor grammatical alterations) in art. 15.[19] It is notable that whereas the preceding and subsequent articles are titled "Freedom of thought" and "Freedom of action", respectively, art. 15 is placed under the simple headline "Religion". Further regulations about religion in the Civil Code provide personal and constitutional rights regardless of "race, colour, religion or sex" (art. 8(2)), forbid discrimination "based on race, religion or social condition" in agricultural communities (art. 1492), and specify the role of religion with regard to marriage (esp. arts. 577, 579, 591, 605, 623–625, 671–672). Of particular importance to the legal state of religious communities are the regulations pertaining to corporate bodies. Here, the Civil Code explicitly declares that the "Ethiopian Orthodox Church is regarded by law as a person," including its dioceses, parishes and monasteries (arts. 398–399). With regard to other religious groups, the Civil Code states:

> (1) Churches, religions, associations other than the Ethiopian Orthodox Church shall be subject to the special laws concerning them.
> (2) Failing such special laws, these groupings shall be deemed to be associations falling under the provisions of this Chapter.[20]

Since special legislation for religious groups never ensued, all churches outside the EOC were considered to be associations, and had to comply with the detailed reg-

---

16 HAILE SELASSIE I, "Proclamation Promulgating the Revised Constitution of the Empire of Ethiopia," Art. 40.

17 AYMRO WONDMAGEGNEHU and MOTOVU, *The Ethiopian Orthodox Church*, 165.

18 The meaning of the formulation "by residents of the Empire" is ambiguous, as it could refer to creeds (held) by residents or to a non-interference by residents. The Amharic version confirms the former interpretation.

19 See TSAHAFE TAEZAZ AKLILU HABTE WOLD, "Civil Code of the Empire of Ethiopia," *Negarit Gazeta*, 2 1960.

20 Art. 407, "Groupings of Religious Character".

ulations in arts. 404–482 of the Civil Code. An "Office of Associations" was to be
established in the capital of every province,[21] which exercised control over the associations. The religious bodies in turn were required to submit their statutes, including
later amendments, decisions taken at general meetings, names of board members,
and yearly balance sheets to the Office of Associations. The Office was entitled to
participate in general meetings, and to legally challenge decisions adopted therein. If
an association continued to carry on its activities after it had been dissolved by the
Office of Association, its leaders and members were declared eligible for punishment
according to the Penal Code.

In September 1966 the Minister of the Interior further specified the application
procedure and control of associations in the "Legal Notice No. 321."[22] Three specific regulations are of special importance to the history of Ethiopian Pentecostalism.
Art. 7 provided that within sixty days after the submission of a given application,
"the Office shall conclude all such measures of examination and investigation as may
be necessary to determine" the accuracy and reliability of the information submitted
as well as their compliance with the legal requirements. Contrary to later Pentecostal
interpretation,[23] this did not entail that the application was considered granted if not
answered within this period. Furthermore, art. 8 gave three reasons for the denial
of registration other than an incomplete application: a) false or misleading information provided in the application or memorandum of the association; b) "unlawful or
immoral" purposes; or c) the association's purposes are "against national unity or
interest." Finally, art. 20 specified the punishment for disobedience to a refused registration by reference to art. 476 of the Penal Code of 1957,[24] according to which
the organization of, participation in, or letting premises to forbidden meetings was
punishable with a fine of up to 500 Ethiopian dollars, while "ringleaders, organizers
or commanders are punishable with imprisonment not exceeding six months."

It is apparent in this legislative development that the Ethiopian Imperial government intended to put its religious policies on a robust legal footing, which was
noticeably inspired by Western legislation and juridical principles. However, while
the status of the Ethiopian Orthodox Church as church of the Empire was legally
fortified in detail,[25] other religious groups were on less firm ground. As was shown
above, the right to freedom of religious practice could in theory be limited by any

---

21 This apparently was not deemed possible by later legislation, which gave the Addis Ababa Office
   a subsidiary role, failing the establishment of registration offices in the capitals of the provinces,
   see TSAHAFE TAEZAZ AKLILU HABTE WOLD, "Legal Notice No: 321 of 1966. Regulations Issued
   Pursuant to the Control of Associations Provision of the Civil Code of 1960," *Negarit Gazeta* 26
   (1 1966): §3(4).
22 See ibid. The Minister of the Interior, Aklilu Habte Wold, was at the same time Prime Minister
   as well as Minister of the Pen, which made him the most powerful figure in the emperor's court.
23 Cf. e.g. TORMOD ENGELSVIKEN, "Molo Wongel: A Documentary Report on the Life and History
   of the Independent Pentecostal Movement in Ethiopia 1960–1975" (Unpublished Manuscript,
   The Free Faculty of Theology, Oslo, 1975), 51; TIBEBE ESHETE, *The Evangelical Movement in
   Ethiopia*, 171f.
24 See TSHAFE TAEZAZ TAFFARA WORQ, "The Penal Code of Ethiopia 1957," *Negarit Gazeta* 16 (1
   1957).
25 Cf. the appendix in AYMRO WONDMAGEGNEHU and MOTOVU, *The Ethiopian Orthodox Church*,
   157-178 which meticulously details all legal provisions pertaining to the church.

legislation. This was of much importance to the emerging Pentecostal movement, since it became the first test case for some of these provisions.

1.1.2   The Ethiopian Revolution

In 1974 the Ethiopian Empire was ended by a revolution that slowly gave way to a Socialist military dictatorship led by Colonel Mengistu Haile Mariam. These tumultuous and far-reaching political developments are well documented by a number of histories from a wide political spectrum and[26] profoundly affected Ethiopia's religions, including the Pentecostal and Charismatic movements.

When the Ethiopian revolution erupted in the beginning of 1974 with a diverse mix of military mutiny, strikes, demonstrations, and urban revolts, religious equality became one of the passionately voiced demands. On April 21, 1974, reportedly 100,000 Addis Ababa residents took part in a demonstration calling for the separation of church and state, which had primarily been organized by the Muslim community but also saw Christian support.[27] The revision of the 1955 Constitution, ordered by the Emperor already in March, apparently heeded these demands and gave more liberty to religious groups outside of the EOC. Though it still mandated the faith of the emperor to be "that of the Monophysite Ethiopian Orthodox Church,"[28] it provided a robust formula for freedom of religion, including the right to form religious associations for the "dissemination of the Christian, Moslem or any other faith."[29]

However, in the midst of the rapidly unfolding events of early 1974 a new political leadership emerged in the form of the so-called "Coordinating Committee of the Armed Forces, Police, and Territorial Army," also called the "Derg,"[30] which began its reach for power on June 28, 1974 by placing the mass media under its control. Within

---

26 See esp. ANDARGACHEW TIRUNEH, *The Ethiopian Revolution 1974–1987: A Transformation from an Aristocratic to a Totalitarian Autocracy* (Cambridge: Cambridge University Press, 1993); CHRISTOPHER CLAPHAM, *Transformation and Continuity in Revolutionary Ethiopia* (Cambridge: Cambridge University Press, 1988); FRED HALLIDAY and MAXINE MOLYNEUX, *The Ethiopian Revolution* (London: Verso Editions, 1981); JOHN W. HARBESON, *The Ethiopian Transformation: The Quest for the Post-Imperial State* (Boulder, CO: Westview Press, 1988); MARINA OTTAWAY and DAVID OTTAWAY, *Ethiopia: Empire in Revolution* (London: Holmes & Meier Publishers, 1978); SCHOLLER and BRIETZKE, *Ethiopia: Revolution, Law and Politics*; PETER SCHWAB, *Ethiopia: Politics, Economics and Society* (London: Frances Pinter, 1985); TEFERRA HAILE-SELASSIE, *The Ethiopian Revolution 1974–1991: From a Monarchical Autocracy to a Military Oligarchy* (London: Kegan Paul International, 1997); MULATU WUBNEH and YOHANNIS ABATE, *Ethiopia: Transition and Development in the Horn of Africa* (Boulder, CO: Westview Press, 1988). Since the following section focuses on the politics of religion, these publications may be consulted for a more general treatment of the Ethiopian revolution.

27 See SCHOLLER and BRIETZKE, *Ethiopia: Revolution, Law and Politics*, 126; ANDARGACHEW TIRUNEH, *The Ethiopian Revolution 1974–1987*, 49.

28 See Draft Constitution of 1974 art. 9, cf. SCHOLLER and BRIETZKE, *Ethiopia: Revolution, Law and Politics*, 155.

29 Art. 24, cf. ibid., 158.

30 "Derg" is the Amharic word for committee and was used as the short name of the "Coordinating Committee". The rule of the Derg in this narrow sense technically ended with Mengistu Haile Mariam's assent to power, but the term "Derg" in popular terminology is usually expanded to denote all post-revolutionary government in Ethiopia until the end of the socialist government in 1991. The origin and members of the group were held in obscurity for quite some time, but it seems to have been an assembly of lower-rank revolutionary leaders in the Ethiopian armed forces, cf. e.g. OTTAWAY and OTTAWAY, *Ethiopia*, 50–52.

three months the Derg undermined and eventually toppled the Imperial Government and the Emperor himself. On September 12, 1974, the Coordinating Committee made its first legislative proclamation, declaring the deposition of Haile Selassie, the suspension of the 1955 Constitution, and the assumption of government powers by the so-called Provisional Military Administrative Council.[31] The 1974 draft Constitution was found insufficient, thereby leaving Ethiopia without fundamental law until the Constitution of 1987. In November 1974 the radical elements of the Derg gained the upper hand, and the revolution took a bloody turn with the assassination of over sixty politicians from the old government and from the Derg itself, which was followed by the declaration of Ethiopian socialism in December.[32] By the end of the year, the Derg launched a massive mobilization effort, sending around 50,000 secondary school and university students on a campaign to the countryside to propagate the revolutionary ideology,[33] which often brought Marxist ideas into conflict with established religion.[34] In 1975 a multitude of socio-economic reforms were initiated by the new government, a number of which also had profound effects on the churches, like the nationalization of health and educational services, and the land reform.

Tensions within the Derg further increased in 1976, eventually leading to a violent shootout on February 3, 1977, out of which the first vice-chairman of the Derg, Mengistu Haile Mariam, emerged as winner, who was to rule Ethiopia as socialist military dictator for the next fourteen years. Mengistu, who hailed from the subdued southern Ethiopia, originally intended to build a new Ethiopian power base, undermining the established Abyssinian-Orthodox dominance by the support of the "hitherto neglected nationalities and religious groups."[35] However, this strategy could not be sustained for two reasons. First, competing liberation movements and Marxist parties, most notably the Ethiopian People's Revolutionary Party (EPRP), Ethiopian Democratic Union (EDU), and the Eritrean Liberation Front (ELF), were already well established in the periphery. When in the infamous Red Terror of 1977 Mengistu violently eliminated the internal opposition to the Derg, he drove the remainder of their camp into diverse ethnic liberation movements and thus further undermined his support in the periphery. Secondly, Ethiopia was attacked by Somalia in the same year when Siad Barre sought to take advantage of Ethiopia's internal weakness and laid claim to the disputed Ogaden region. This frustrated Mengistu's intention to enlist Muslim powers at the expense of the Orthodox Church, the latter of which

---

31 See "Provisional Military Government Establishment Proclamation, No. 1 of 1974", quoted in SCHOLLER and BRIETZKE, *Ethiopia: Revolution, Law and Politics*, 184-185. Ethiopia originally was to remain a monarchy with the crown prince Asfa Wossen as king, who, however, did not trust this proclamation and chose to remain in exile. In March 1975 the nomination of Asfa Wossen was annulled without replacement, effectively ending the monarchy in Ethiopia, see ibid., 133.

32 Cf. ANDARGACHEW TIRUNEH, *The Ethiopian Revolution 1974–1987*, 77–79, 86–89.

33 See CLAPHAM, *Transformation and Continuity in Revolutionary Ethiopia*, 49–50.

34 However, as Donald Donham has observed, in some localities Christians were the primary supporters of the campaigners, since they had called for the modernization of the traditional societies they lived in, see DONALD L. DONHAM, *Marxist Modern: An Ethnographic History of the Ethiopian Revolution* (Berkely, CA: University of California Press, 1999), 45–49.

35 HAILE MARIAM LAREBO, "The Orthodox Church and the State in the Ethiopian Revolution, 1974–84," *Religion in Communist Lands* 14 (2 1986): 152.

he now needed as a nationalistic rallying base. At the height of these internal and external threats, Mengistu managed to switch camp from Ethiopia's long-time ally, the USA, to the Soviet Union, and subsequently achieved decisive military victories over the liberation movements and Somalia through Soviet arms and Cuban military assistance.

These developments had immediate effects on the churches in Ethiopia. Early on, the EOC was forcefully co-opted by Mengistu's government, most visibly in the deposition and arrest of the old patriarch in 1976 and the election of a new one. The religious communities outside of the EOC, the Catholic Church and Islam, however, were increasingly marginalized and suppressed throughout the 1980s, entailing the closure of numerous churches as well as the arrest, torture and even murder of church members and officials.

In the following years, Ethiopia's new political center was consolidated with the formation of the Workers' Party of Ethiopia in 1984 as well as the promulgation of a new Constitution, the proclamation the People's Democratic Republic of Ethiopia, and the election of a national parliament (Shengo) in 1987, all under the undisputed leadership of Mengistu Haile Mariam.[36] The Derg involved the EOC, the Catholic Church, the ECMY, and the Muslim community in the process of drafting the new Constitution, and allowed representatives of these religious communities to serve as members of the Shengo. Moreover, these churches were increasingly needed as channels of foreign aid in the food and humanitarian crisis of 1984/5, with their financial contributions even being drawn in to support the highly controversial and inhumane villagization and resettlement campaigns.[37]

1.1.3   The Rise of the EPRDF

The Derg's inability to adequately deal with the humanitarian crises of the 1980s and the influx of foreign aid significantly contributed to the erosion of the peripheral power base of the Derg and prepared the later advance of northern liberation movements toward Addis Ababa.[38] In the first years of the Ethiopian revolution, the Eritrean liberation movements were engaged in a civil war with one another, allowing Mengistu's forces to control large parts of Eritrea after a massive military offensive in 1978.[39] By August of 1981 the Eritrean Popular Liberation Front (EPLF) had established its hegemony over the Eritrean liberation movements, and in the following years it launched a number of raid attacks against Ethiopian garrisons in Eritrea, while successfully withstanding an attack by Mengistu's forces on its stronghold in

---

36 See TEFERRA HAILE-SELASSIE, *The Ethiopian Revolution 1974–1991*, 274–284.

37 See DAWIT WOLDE GIORGIS, *Red Tears: War, Famine and Revolution in Ethiopia* (Trenton, NJ: Red Sea Press, 1989), 289–308 for the megalomanic resettlement and villagization programs and their haphazard implementation. Teferra Haile-Selassie contends that "[p]erhaps villagisation was a major factor that contributed to the downfall of the government," see TEFERRA HAILE-SELASSIE, *The Ethiopian Revolution 1974–1991*, 270

38 See BAHRU ZEWDE, *A History of Modern Ethiopia 1855–1991*, 263.

39 See HENZE, *Layers of Time*, 303–304; BAHRU ZEWDE, *A History of Modern Ethiopia 1855–1991*, 257–259.

Nakfa.[40] The EPLF's most significant victory over the Derg came at Afabet in 1988, which is generally described as a turning point in favor of the northern liberation movements, since the guerilla warriors not only destroyed and captured an entire division of the Ethiopian army, but inherited a significant amount of heavy military equipment.[41] In the province of Tigray, another liberation movement emerged in 1975 as the Tigray People's Liberation Front (TPLF), which was an isolationist movement with a rural power base, gradually eliminating other rebel groups in the Tigray region until 1980.[42] With a policy of non-interference in religious matters, the TPLF won over the support of the Christian and Muslim communities, even enlisting clergy among their fighters.[43] The TPLF slowly took control of Tigray and northern Welo and signed a military coordination agreement with the EPLF, despite the ideological differences between both organizations which would later play into the Ethiopian-Eritrean war from 1998 to 2000.[44] Together they inflicted another important defeat on Mengistu's army in Sire in February 1989. Around this time, the TPLF leader Meles Zenawi began to build a political power base by integrating a number of regional opposition movements in the Ethiopian People's Revolutionary Democratic Front (EPRDF), which was dominated by the TPLF.[45]

With their growing military success, the EPLF and TPLF gradually gained international recognition, especially as they were quicker than Mengistu to denounce socialist ideology and join the Western camp.[46] Faced with the growing strength of the armed liberation movements, the government called for peace talks. However, while Mengistu previously had refuted the idea of dialog, the liberation movements now were in a position to do so, with their armed forces steadily advancing toward Addis Ababa. At the same time, the collapse of the socialist block pressured Mengistu into announcing his own reforms. These reforms, though often dismissed as "too little and too late,"[47] actually were quite far-reaching. Economy and trade were liberalized, the rights of land use and transfer to legal heirs was restored to peasants, provisions were made for entrepreneurial agriculture, and private investors were allowed back into the real estate market. A reformation of the Workers' Party of Ethiopia was initiated which quite prominently announced religious equality: "This means that the party [...] will embrace all nationals irrespective of their class, and religion, tenets, groups or a follower of this or that faith, who are genuinely committed to Ethiopia's unity and progress, will be represented with a common objective."[48] While these changes, especially the government affirmation of religious equality and private property ownership, allowed Ethiopia's underground churches to re-emerge in some contexts, they

40 See HAROLD G. MARCUS, *A History of Ethiopia* (Berkeley, CA: University of California Press, 1994), 202–203, 209.
41 See TEFERRA HAILE-SELASSIE, *The Ethiopian Revolution 1974–1991*, 286; BAHRU ZEWDE, *A History of Modern Ethiopia 1855–1991*, 264; MARCUS, *A History of Ethiopia*, 211.
42 See esp. BAHRU ZEWDE, *A History of Modern Ethiopia 1855–1991*, 259–261.
43 See HENZE, *Layers of Time*, 293.
44 Cf. ibid., 320–321, 329–338.
45 BAHRU ZEWDE, *A History of Modern Ethiopia 1855–1991*, 265.
46 Cf. TEFERRA HAILE-SELASSIE, *The Ethiopian Revolution 1974–1991*, 284–286.
47 Cf. ibid., 302.
48 See Central Report to the Eleventh Plenum, President Mengistu Haile Mariam, quoted in ibid., 304.

could not improve the Derg's standing internationally, nor did they halt the steady advances of the northern liberation movements. Peace talks were finally scheduled to take place in London on May 28, 1991, but Mengistu was aware of his demise and fled to Zimbabwe seven days before they commenced. The London peace talks thus became a negotiation of Ethiopia's post-Derg future, and focused on the independence of Eritrea, the demilitarization of Addis Ababa, and the composition of the transitional government. The EPRDF took hold of Addis Ababa and formed a transitional government. After parliamentary elections in June 1992 a new Constitution was drafted and adopted in 1994, which fundamentally recast Ethiopia's unity as a conglomerate of regional ethnic groups, as signified by its preamble: "We, the Nations, Nationalities and Peoples of Ethiopia ... ". This line of ethno-regional federalism[49] brought new dynamics to all of Ethiopia's politics, including the churches.

The 1994 Constitution contained clear provisions for freedom of religion and the separation of church and state (art. 27), which, moreover, were upheld in practice by the new executive. Churches are not considered as distinct legal entities in Ethiopian law,[50] but are treated as associations, like non-governmental organizations or labor unions, and they are required to register with the Ministry of Justice, in accordance with the Civil Code (arts. 404ff.) and the regulatory guidelines of 1966.[51] Over 280 religious associations were registered with the Ministry of Justice in 2004.[52]

1.2 Historical Overview: A Synopsis of Pentecostalism in Ethiopia

1.2.1 Earlier Protestant Missions

The origins of Ethiopian Pentecostalism are usually placed with Finnish and Swedish Pentecostal mission initiatives who entered Ethiopia in the 1950s. At the time of their arrival, a number of other Protestant missions were already well-established in the country leading to the foundation of Ethiopian churches in the following decades, most notably the Kale Heywet Church (KHC), the Evangelical Church Mekane Yesus (ECMY), and the Meserete Kristos Church (MKC).

The beginnings of modern Lutheran missions in the Horn of Africa date back to the middle of the 19th century.[53] After unsuccessful attempts by the Hermannsburg

---

49 Cf. CHRISTOPH EMMINGHAUS, *Äthiopiens ethnoregionaler Föderalismus: Modell der Konfliktbewältigung für afrikanische Staaten?* (Hamburg: Lit, 1997); also DAVID TURTON, ed., *Ethnic Federalism: The Ethiopian Experience in Comparative Perspective* (Oxford: James Currey, 2006).

50 MARTA TORCINI CORAZZA, "State and Religion in the Constitution and Politics of Ethiopia," *European Journal for Church and State Research* 9 (2002): 376.

51 See TSAHAFE TAEZAZ AKLILU HABTE WOLD, "Legal Notice No" In an interview with a representative from the ministry of justice, it was confirmed to the author that this law from Imperial Ethiopia still forms the legal base for the registration of associations. The only adjustment made, pertains to the amount of capital assets of associations, interview no. 55.

52 List of registered associations, obtained March 22, 2004.

53 See esp. the meticulous accounts of Gustav Arén in ARÉN, *Evangelical Pioneers in Ethiopia* and GUSTAV ARÉN, *Envoys of the Gospel: In the Steps of the Evangelical Pioneers, 1898–1936*, Studia Missionalia Upsaliensia; 75 (Stockholm: EFS Förlaget, 1999). Arén even traced the beginning of Lutheran missions in Ethiopia to the physician Peter Heyling who worked as a doctor, teacher and Bible translator in Ethiopia from 1635 to 1652, and contends that there is "direct line from Peter

Mission to reach Oromo tribes in southwestern Ethiopia in 1854 and 1858, missionaries of the Swedish Evangelical Mission arrived at Red Sea port of Massawa in 1866 with the same goal.[54] They too failed to reach the Oromo and subsequently remained in the region of Eritrea, where they planted a church and made their first converts, most prominently the freed Oromo slave Onesimus Nesib, who not only translated the Bible into Oromo, but later was instrumental in evangelizing his own people in Welega after the region had been incorporated into the Ethiopian empire.[55] These efforts in western and southwestern Ethiopia were expanded in the 1920s and 1930s by a renewed and successful endeavor by the Hermannsburg Mission, or Evangelical Lutheran Mission.[56]

The work of the American United Presbyterian Mission in Ethiopia began in 1919 with Dr. Thomas Lambie, who founded a medical clinic and a mission station in Seyo in western Ethiopia and from 1922 on built up a hospital in Addis Ababa.[57] Other Presbyterian missionaries soon joined Lambie, and the work was extended by a third clinic in Gore (Ilubabor) in 1924. Lambie wanted to extend the mission work to the southern provinces, but his mission board did not agree. While on furlough in 1926 he left the United Presbyterian Mission and founded the Abyssinian Frontier Mission together with other missionaries, which joined forces in 1927 with the Sudan Interior Mission (SIM), a faith mission established by the Canadian missionary Rowland Bingham with the intent of doing missions in Africa's heartland.[58] The SIM mission efforts in Ethiopia, which began at the end of 1927, were diverted to the southern regions of Hadiya, Woleyita, and Sidama, where nine mission stations were established in the following years. Though the SIM missionaries came from many different countries and denominational affiliations, they developed a common theological profile in their emphasis of conversion, separation of believers from tradition, and the centrality of believers' baptism, which set them apart from the Lutheran and Presbyterian missions.[59] Furthermore, influenced by Roland Allen's mission theology, they immediately formed self-governing local congregations after the first converts had been baptized.[60]

Heyling to the founders of the Evangelical Church Mekane Yesus," ARÉN, *Evangelical Pioneers in Ethiopia*, 34–38, 409–410; ARÉN, *Envoys of the Gospel*, 134–136.

54 See ARÉN, *Evangelical Pioneers in Ethiopia*, 105–148.

55 See ibid., 127–167, 383–385, 412–439; ARÉN, *Envoys of the Gospel*, 287–323. Onesimus' mission efforts had been preceded by previous evangelistic incursions into Oromo territory on the heals of Orthodox expansion and with the help of the converted Orthodox priest Gebre-Ewostateos, see ARÉN, *Evangelical Pioneers in Ethiopia*, 374–412.

56 ARÉN, *Envoys of the Gospel*, 407–452; ERNST BAUEROCHSE, "Die Arbeit in Äthiopien," in *Vision: Gemeinde weltweit: 150 Jahre Hermannsburger Mission und Ev.-luth. Missionswerk in Niedersachsen*, ed. ERNST-AUGUST LÜDEMANN (Hermannsburg: Verlag der Missionsbuchhandlung, 2000), 585–709; LAUNHARDT, *Evangelicals in Addis Ababa (1919–1991)*, 56–64.

57 See ARÉN, *Envoys of the Gospel*, 343–389.

58 See F. PETER COTTERELL, *Born at Midnight* (Chicago, IL: Moody Bible Institut, 1973), 11–21. The term "Sudan" pertained to Africa south of the Sahara and north of the Congo Basin.

59 See FARGHER, *The Origins of the New Churches Movement in Southern Ethiopia, 1927–1944*, 26–33, 41–48, 139–162.

60 See ibid., 49–59, 145. This of course does not mean that the mission did not attempt to remain an influential advisor and theological authority over these congregations.

During the Italian occupation of Ethiopia and the Second World War, the work of the Protestant missions was severely curtailed. The Swedish Lutheran, German Lutheran, and the SIM missionaries were forced to leave Ethiopia at different times, and the years of their absence coincided with a significant growth and expansion in the Ethiopian churches they had initiated.[61] Beginning in 1944, the churches with Presbyterian and Lutheran backgrounds explored the formation of a united Ethiopian Evangelical Church and hosted a series of Conferences of Ethiopian Evangelical Churches, some of which also saw the participation of SIM-affiliated churches.[62] However, the groups could not agree on a common theological platform for a joint denomination. Consequentially the Presbyterian congregations formed the Evangelical Bethel Church in 1947,[63] the Lutherans came together in the ECMY in 1959,[64] and in 1974 the KHC was founded by the SIM-affiliated churches.[65] In 1974 the Evangelical Bethel Church joined the ECMY.[66]

The first Mennonite missionaries arrived in Ethiopia in 1945 and began to operate a hospital in Nazaret, 45 km southeast of Addis Ababa, which was part of the "Orthodox church areas" in accordance with the Missions' Decree of 1944 and therefore only allowed developmental projects for foreign missions.[67] The Mennonites gradually expanded their mission with schools,[68] clinics, and different development projects into the open area of the Harar zone, and Addis Ababa. In these different projects, the Mennonite missionaries made a number of converts and conducted a first water baptism in 1951, which was a violation of the Missions' Decree.[69] The Mennonite mission was severely reprimanded and had to promise not to baptize believers again, but instead left this to the Ethiopians to conduct in secret, which led the way to the foundation of a national church, the Meserete Kristos Church (MKC), established in a longer process from 1959 to 1965. The MKC was not granted legal registration, which also meant that the Mennonite Mission continued as legal owner of much of the church's property.

---

61 See ARÉN, *Envoys of the Gospel*, 453–535; BAUEROCHSE, "Die Arbeit in Äthiopien," 604–617; COTTERELL, *Born at Midnight*, 82–123; LAUNHARDT, *Evangelicals in Addis Ababa (1919–1991)*, 106–107.

62 See ibid., 105–118.

63 See ibid., 146–149.

64 ibid., 142–145. The only Lutheran group which didn't join were the churches founded by the Swedish Mission Bible-True Friends, who became the so-called Lutheran Church Bible-True Friends, see ibid., 145–146.

65 See ibid., 152–154. The churches had previously established an Evangelical Believers' Association.

66 See ibid., 148.

67 For the following, see NATHAN B. HEGE, *Beyond Our Prayers: Anabaptist Church Growth in Ethiopia, 1948–1998* (Scottsdale, PA: Herald Press, 1998), 40–146.

68 The most noticeable school project was a secondary school in Nazaret, the Nazaret Bible Academy, see ibid., 78–85; JAN BENDER SHETLER, "The Nazareth Bible Academy in Retrospect" (Unpublished manuscript, private collection, 1984).

69 The baptism concerned converts from Nazaret, but was conducted in the "open area" of Addis Ababa in hopes of circumventing the "Regulations Governing the Activities of Missions," see HEGE, *Beyond Our Prayers*, 128–131.

1.2.2 Pentecostal Missions

The first Pentecostal missionaries with a long-term presence in Ethiopia, were the
Finnish couple Anna-Liisa and Sanfrid Mattsson who arrived in Addis Ababa in 1951.
After lengthy negotiations they secured a permit to operate a vocational school in
Wolmera, a town approximately 35km west of Addis Ababa. Mattsson's "Scripture
Publishers to Every Creature" functioned as an umbrella organization for all other
Finnish Pentecostal missionaries for many years, but it was structured like a faith
mission, with every missionary securing their own support. In 1956 a work center was
founded in the Addis Ababa Merkato area by the female missionary Helvi Halme,
who also conducted prayer meetings and Bible studies for Ethiopians there.

A number of Swedish Pentecostal mission initiatives commenced from 1959 onward. The most important one for the beginnings of Ethiopian Pentecostalism was
the work of the Swedish Philadelphia Church Mission (SPCM) established in the
southern town of Awasa in 1960. While the main work of the mission there was a
vocational school, the importance of the Swedish mission in Awasa for the early Pentecostal movement in Ethiopia lies in the annual summer Bible conferences that the
mission conducted. These revival meetings lasted several weeks and were attended
mostly by students in their summer break from all over the country.

The Pentecostal movement gained momentum in Ethiopia toward the middle of
the 1960s, with a number of Ethiopians encountering the baptism in the Holy Spirit
and starting local revival groups. An often cited "beginning" in this sense was the
ministry of a Kenyan evangelist in the summer of 1963 who came to the Awasa
Bible conference and the Finnish mission in Addis Ababa. However, a number of
other events also compete for the "real origin" of Ethiopian Pentecostalism: a prayer
movement of High School students in Nazaret in 1964/65, a revival among trainees at
the Teacher Training Institute (TTI) in Harar at about the same time, the formation
of a Pentecostal gathering of university students in Addis Ababa in 1965, and the
separation of some Ethiopian believers from the Merkato Finnish mission. These
initiatives are connected to a number of people, who later emerged as leaders in the
Ethiopian Pentecostal movement, and the plurality and rivalry of their stories and
missionary writings have produced many different ways of telling the beginnings of
Ethiopian Pentecostalism.

1.2.3 The Establishment of Ethiopian Pentecostal Churches

A number of these movements converged in Addis Ababa and eventually conglomer-
ated around the university student gathering, leading to the establishment of a first
national Pentecostal church in 1967, the Full Gospel Believers' Church (FGBC). The
ordination of the first seven elders of this church was conducted with the help of
Swedish Pentecostal missionaries, which led to a serious conflict between the Northern European Pentecostal missions, since the Finnish mission in Addis Ababa had
lost much of their following to the university student movement including some of the
ones now ordained by the Swedish as elders.

A few months later, the FGBC applied for registration as a religious association
in accordance with the Civil Code and the applicable "Legal Notice No. 321" of 1966.
In the fall of 1967 this application was rejected, which also entailed the closure of the

church's meeting places. The FGBC at first relied on private meetings and the use of Swedish mission property in Addis Ababa, but slowly resumed public meetings in homes and rented premises. During this time, the Ethiopian Pentecostal movement encountered its first doctrinal division when one of its evangelists teamed up with Oneness Pentecostal missionaries and subsequently founded the Apostolic Church of Ethiopia (ACE).[70]

From the end of 1971 onward, the political pressure on Pentecostals again increased, culminating in an arrest of approximately 250 worshipers on Sunday, August 27, 1972. The legal and political aftermath of this incident did not turn out in favor of the Pentecostals, even though they had managed to bring their case to the attention of the international press and even found some Lutheran supporters, who sparked an investigation by the World Council of Churches (WCC) regarding the role of the EOC in the matter. The FGBC, which remained underground until the Ethiopian revolution in 1974, was not the only religious group targeted by the government during this time. Alongside the Pentecostals, the government rounded up Jehovah's Witnesses in Addis Ababa, the Oneness ACE suffered severe repressions, especially in Awasa, and even the Finnish mission in the capital was closed for longer intervals. A number of different narratives developed early on, attempting to make sense of the political suppression of Pentecostals in late Imperial Ethiopia.

1.2.4 After the Ethiopian Revolution

Immediately responding to the Ethiopian revolution's promise of religious equality, the FGBC reestablished its national structure and resumed public meetings in the summer of 1974. At about the same time, another division occurred within the church over the issue of the Christian Deliverance doctrine,[71] leading to the subsequent establishment of the Gospel Deliverance Church (GDC). The FGBC's public meeting in Addis Ababa again was closed in 1976 due to a neighborhood riot, but in the beginning of 1977 the church was granted land by the city and immediately embarked on a building project on the site. It was completed in October 1978, despite the difficult conditions in Addis Ababa and elsewhere during the Red Terror. While the FGBC enjoyed a few months of uninterrupted public meetings in the capital, a number of its rural congregations were already shut down with some of their leaders put into prison. The Addis Ababa church was closed and taken over by the Derg in September 1979. Throughout much of the 1980s the FGBC continued and grew by the means of

---

70 On Oneness Pentecostalism in general, see See DAVID ARTHUR REED, "Oneness Pentecostalism," in *The New International Dictionary of Pentecostal and Charismatic Movements*, ed. STANLEY M. BURGESS and EDUARD M. van der MAAS (Grand Rapids, MI: Zondervan, 2002), 936–944. The ACE is a very strong church, especially in southern Ethiopia, and was featured in a number of English Oneness publications, see NONA FREEMAN, *Unseen hands: The Story of Revival in Ethiopia* (Hazelwood, MO: World Aflame Press, 1987); NONA FREEMAN, *Then Came the Glory* (Minden, LA: Nona Freeman, 1994); TEKLEMARIAM GEZAHEGNE, *The Identity of Jesus Christ* (Hazelwood, MO: World Aflame Press, 1989).

71 Deliverance teachers emphasize that spiritual deliverance or exorcism are meant for both, believers and non-believers. This of course leads to the heavily contested issue whether a born-again believer can be inflicted by demonic powers, and if so, to what degree and how. The most prominent advocate of the Deliverance teaching was the evangelist Derek Prince.

house fellowships, while in some regions public meetings resumed toward the end of the Derg.

The Finnish mission at Merkato in Addis Ababa appointed Ethiopian leaders for their work in 1976, who less than one year later notified the mission of their desire to be established as a financially independent national church. In 1978 the Finnish Pentecostal missionaries were forced out of their projects in the provinces of Kefa and Shewa and subsequently decided to leave Ethiopia. A fellowship of Finnish mission related churches was formed in June 1978, which took on the name of Gennet Church (GC), and the pastor of the Addis Ababa congregation was appointed as the representative of the Finnish mission, before the last missionaries departed in July 1978. In 1979 the Addis Ababa GC church was closed by the government and its leaders imprisoned for some months, and a number of other GC congregations were shut down throughout the country. In 1980 the return of the missionaries and a leadership crisis led to a split within the GC, with the former head pastor departing and subsequently founding another church, the Harvest Church of God (HCG). While much of the GC had to rely on house meetings and secret chain programs, its southern branch in the Sidama province flourished and operated publicly throughout the Derg.

The Swedish Philadelphia Church Mission invited Ethiopian representatives from its congregations to the yearly mission meeting in Awasa in 1975, where they agreed to form the Hiwot Berhan Church (HBC), with its headquarters in Addis Ababa. Their application for registration as religious association was not received favorably by the revolutionary rulers. In 1978 the Swedish missionaries were forced out of the Kefa province, and the churches there were closed. One year later the Addis Ababa HBC was shut down as well. The Awasa mission station and church continued until 1983, when they too were closed and the property taken over by the government. The SPCM continued to work in the country, mostly in relief projects, and some local HBC churches managed to stay open throughout the Derg.

The political repression of Ethiopian Pentecostalism also had significant repercussions in the mainline Protestant churches, especially when they too were targeted by the government and the derogatory label "Pente," originally invented for Pentecostals, was applied to them as well, increasingly conflating Protestants and Pentecostals in public discourse. In some instances this caused the mainline churches to distinguish themselves from the Pentecostal movement and put Charismatic groups within these churches in a precarious position. In other cases the common encounter of government suppression facilitated ecumenical contacts, between individuals as well as on official levels. Numerous stories are told about the origin of the Charismatic movements in the mainline churches, but many of them point to the repressions by the Derg as main explicatory reference.

1.2.5 The Development in Recent Years

After the fall of the Derg, the Pentecostal churches and missions were allowed to resume public meetings and managed to reclaim much of their dispossessed real estate. All churches reported significant gains during the Derg time. In the traditionally Orthodox northern provinces, the public re-emergence of Pentecostal churches was a more difficult process accompanied by occasional riots, but the new executive and

judiciary upheld the statutes of religious equality. The provisions of the 1960 Civil
Code and the "Legal Notice No. 321" of 1966 pertaining to the registration of associations, were put into practice, mandating and allowing the official registration of all
religious bodies. A list of registered associations obtained from the Ministry of Justice
bears witness to the mushrooming and fraying of the Christian denominational landscape in recent years.[72] The majority of the approximately 280 religious associations
in this list are Protestant denominations, smaller churches, or ministries, many of
which belong to the Pentecostal/Charismatic spectrum.[73] The most relevant recently
established Pentecostal denominations are the Gubae Egziabiher Church (GEC), the
Bible Army Church, the Gospel Light Church, the Maranata Church, the Evangelical
Praise Church, the Rhema Faith Church, and the Winners' Chapel.

The largest trinitarian Pentecostal denominations are the FGBC and the HBC
with approximately 500,000 members each.[74] The Oneness ACE is comparable in
size.[75] Other Pentecostal churches are considerably smaller with membership estimates in the five-figure-range.

Estimates about the overall size of the Pentecostal community are notoriously
difficult. The figures provided in the World Christian Encyclopedia and its follow-up
project, the World Christian Database, do not seem to come from sources familiar with
the Ethiopian scene.[76] Similarly, the numbers provided by the churches themselves
appear to be of little reliability,[77] which was illustrated by a recent statistical survey,

---

72 See "List of registered associations," Ministry of Justice, Addis Ababa.
73 For an annotated list of the most important Pentecostal and Charismatic churches, see JÖRG
HAUSTEIN, "Pentecostal and Charismatic Churches in Ethiopia" (2009), http://www.glopent.
net/Members/jhaustein/ethiopia/pentecostal-charismatic-churches-in-ethiopia (accessed February 28, 2009). See also GÜNTER SCHRÖDER, "Äthiopien: Religiöse Gemeinschaften, Organisationen
und Institutionen. Ein Überblick" (Unpublished manuscript, private collection, 1997) for a more
exhaustive description of religious associations in Ethiopia containing Pentecostal/Charismatic
churches, which, however, contains a number of inaccuracies with regard to the history of Pentecostal and Charismatic churches.
74 For the FGBC estimates obtained with church leaders in interviews ranged from 500,000 to one
million, interviews no. 1; 131.
75 The church estimates its number of congregations at over 5,000 with altogether 2 million members, interview no. 108. A more conservative estimate by a trinitarian Pentecostal with intimate
knowledge of southern Ethiopia, where the church is strongest, still puts the number at around
600,000, interview no. 69.
76 The World Christian Encyclopedia of 2001 is unaware of the 1984 and 1994 censuses that had
been released by the time it was published, and states that its numbers are based "on a number
of estimates over the years," see DAVID B. BARRETT, GEORGE THOMAS KURIAN, and TODD M.
JOHNSON, World Christian Encyclopedia: A Comparative Survey of Churches and Religions in
the Modern World, 2nd ed. (Oxford: Oxford University Press, 2001), 264. The World Christian
Database in 2006 estimated 6,322,000 "Renewalists," consisting of exactly 1,709,920 "Pentecostals," 3,370,916 "Charismatics," and 1,241,164 "Neocharismatics." These sub-categories are of
very limited applicability in Ethiopia, which is confirmed by the list of denominations assigned to
them. Furthermore, the specificity of the sub-category numbers (single-digit) as opposed to the
main category (rounded by thousands) suggests that they are calculated by some type of formula,
rather than based on actual data. JÖRG HAUSTEIN, "Pfingstbewegung und Identität im Kontext
äthiopischer Migranten in Deutschland," in Migration und Identität: Pfingstlich-charismatische
Migrationsgemeinden in Deutschland, ed. MICHAEL BERGUNDER and JÖRG HAUSTEIN, Beihefte
der Zeitschrift für Mission; 8 (Frankfurt am Main: Lembeck, 2006), Cf.
77 Especially with smaller churches, the estimates in interviews often appeared greatly exaggerated.
A test occasionally applied during research was to also inquire about the number of churches and

conducted by the Evangelical Churches' Fellowship of Ethiopia (ECFE) and financed by Dawn Ministries, a US-American organization promoting strategic church planting. The survey was conducted in 2005 by eighty-six researchers who went to different zones and districts to gather information about the churches there. In comparing the survey results with the estimates the ECFE had gathered from the head offices of its member denominations, the study found a considerably smaller cumulative membership than previously estimated (9.7 million vs. 12–13 million), but almost twice as many local congregations (29,805 vs. 14,300).[78]

The most reliable religious data for Ethiopia is provided by the decennial Population and Housing Censuses conducted by the Ethiopian government in 1984, 1994, and (postponed) in 2007. The census data reveal a significant increase of Protestantism in Ethiopia, indicating a dramatic shift in Ethiopia's confessional landscape. In 1984 about 2.1 million Protestants were counted, which was approximately 5.5 percent of the total population.[79] By 1994 their number had more than doubled to 5.4 million, representing a share of approximately 10.2 percent.[80] The 2007 census revealed unabated growth with Protestants now amounting to 13.7 million or 18.6 percent of the overall population.[81] Most of this increase seems to have come at the expense of the Ethiopian Orthodox Church, whose share declined from 54.0 to 43.5 percent in the same time span, which highlights the ecumenical difficulty of Protestant growth.

---

the size of the largest congregation. These two numbers multiplied with each other would indicate the theoretical maximum of church members overall, and a number of informants exceeded this limit with their guess about the size of their denomination.

78 Interviews no. 114; 33. A detailed list of churches in the different regions, including locations, names of pastors, etc., was presented during one of the interviews. It appears that the results of the survey were not published as previously intended. However, the current web site of the ECFE still quotes the exact number congregations found by the study in 2005, but puts its membership figure at 13 million, see EVANGELICAL CHURCHES FELLOWSHIP OF ETHIOPIA, "Introduction to ECFE" (2009), http://www.ecfethiopia.org/introduction.htm (accessed March 3, 2009).

79 See TRANSITIONAL GOVERNMENT OF ETHIOPIA, OFFICE OF THE POPULATION AND HOUSING CENSUS COMMISSION, *The 1984 Population and Housing Census of Ethiopia: Analytical Report at National Level* (Addis Ababa: Central Statistical Authority, 1991), 60. The census was not published until the Derg was ousted in 1991. The 1984 statistics may under-represent the number of Protestants, since adherents in some regions may have been hesitant to identify themselves as such, due to the suppression of Protestant churches.

80 FEDERAL DEMOCRATIC REPUBLIC OF ETHIOPIA, OFFICE OF THE POPULATION AND HOUSING CENSUS COMMISSION, CENTRAL STATISTICAL AUTHORITY, *The 1994 Population and Housing Census of Ethiopia: Results at Country Level*, vol. 2, *Statistical Report* (Addis Ababa, 1998), 129.

81 See FEDERAL DEMOCRATIC REPUBLIC OF ETHIOPIA, POPULATION CENSUS COMMISSION, *Summary and Statistical Report of the 2007 Population and Housing Census: Population Size by Sex and Age* (Addis Ababa, 2008), 17, http://www.csa.gov.et/pdf/Cen2007_prelimineray.pdf (accessed February 27, 2009). The representative Demographic and Health Survey of 2005 pointed in a similar direction, with 18.9 percent Protestants (weighted), see CENTRAL STATISTICAL AGENCY and ORC MACRO, *Ethiopia Demographic and Health Survey 2005* (Addis Ababa: Central Statistical Agency, 2006), 32. Protestantism is more of a rural than an urban phenomenon: 19.6 percent of the rural population are Protestant compared with 13.5 percent of the urban population. Furthermore, there is a considerable regional variance: from 0.1 percent of the total population in the classical Orthodox region of Tigray and the predominantly Muslim Somali region, to 70.1 percent in the western region of Gambela. In Addis Ababa, Protestants have a share of 7.8 percent. Cf. FEDERAL DEMOCRATIC REPUBLIC OF ETHIOPIA, POPULATION CENSUS COMMISSION, *Summary and Statistical Report of the 2007 Population and Housing Census*, 111-113.

1.2.6   The Charismatic Movements

The census data does not provide sub-categories for Protestants, but their noticeable overall increase is of direct relevance to the study of Pentecostal and Charismatic movements, since most Protestant mainline churches now are Charismatic in practice and theology.[82] It is not uncommon to observe praying in tongues in mainline Protestant churches, even from the pulpit, as well as prophecy, exorcism, and prayers for healing. The structure of services is very similar between all Protestant churches, and pulpit sharing between Pentecostals and mainline Protestant is a common practice.[83] There are only few smaller churches and denominations in the evangelical spectrum that explicitly resist being identified as Charismatic.[84]

The largest mainline Protestant churches, the KHC, the ECMY, and the MKC,[85] are deeply influenced by the Charismatic movement. Though the intensity of the Charismatic influence varies from church to church and region to region,[86] all have centrally accommodated the Holy Spirit revival movements in their theological discussions and regulations. The Doctrinal Statement of the KHC includes a six-page section on the Holy Spirit in its 2004 revision.[87] It defines the terms "baptism in the Holy Spirit" as well as "fullness of the Holy Spirit," lists twenty kinds of spiritual gifts, establishes the origin and aim of these gifts, and regulates in detail the prac-

---

82 There are a number of Charismatic movements within the EOC and the Catholic Church as well; however, they did not have any comparable impact there. Especially in the EOC Charismatic groups remain a contentious issue, not least because Charismatic groups either tend to function as a transit point of Orthodox moving to Protestant churches. Moreover, in the past, whole groups have left the EOC due to conflict and have established an independent denomination in the Protestant fold, the most prominent case being the Emmanual United Church. In Addis Ababa, there are about fifteen different renewal groups in the EOC, but they all keep a low profile in order to avoid conflicts.

83 The first service observed by the author in Ethiopia was in a local FGBC congregation, the sermon was preached by a pastor from the MKC, there was a featured singer from the KHC, and several ECMY members attended according to the information of a local missionary accompanying the visit.

84 Most notably, the Baptist Bible Fellowship (self-estimate 30,000 members), Baptist Evangelical Association (8,000 members); Faith Church of Christ (400 members), Lutheran Church in Ethiopia (25,000 members), interviews no. 15; 11; 133. A number of them admit that they have Charismatic youth movements in their midst anyway.

85 In 2009 the KHC claimed over five million members in 5,740 congregations, whereas the ECMY estimated its membership at 4.8 million (2.3 million communicant), see ETHIOPIAN KALE HEYWET CHURCH, "Mission" (2009), http://www.ekhc.org.et/Mission.htm (accessed March 2, 2009); ETHIOPIAN EVANGELICAL CHURCH MEKANE YESUS, "EECMY Synods" (2009), http://www.eecmy.org/synods.htm (accessed March 2, 2009). The MKC, third-largest mainline Protestant church, counted 219,000 members in 2003 in 311 congregations and 683 "church planting centers", interview no. 37. The ECMY and MKC provided detailed figures for different regions.

86 For the western ECMY, for example, Hermann Domianus reported conflicts within the churches with regard to the Charismatic movement, see HERMANN DOMIANUS, "Die eigene Stimme klingt am schönsten: Das Phänomen des geistlichen Aufbruchs in Äthiopien," in *Mit wachsender Begeisterung: Evangelische Christen in Äthiopien*, ed. HENNING UZAR (Hermannsburg: Missionshandlung Hermannsburg, 1998), 61–72. In Addis Ababa, on the other hand, a number of ECMY congregations have integrated Charismatic elements into their services, while in the young ECMY congregation in Bahir Dar, the services are of considerable more Charismatic intensity than those of the local Pentecostal churches.

87 ETHIOPIAN KALE HEYWET CHURCH, የአመነት አቋም, [Doctrinal Statement.], 3rd ed. (Addis Ababa, 2004), 26–32.

tices of speaking in tongues, prophecy, healing and miracle working, and laying on of
hands.[88] The ECMY is the third-largest Lutheran church worldwide and, according
to a Lutheran observer, "is probably the one which is most heavily influenced by
the charismatic movement."[89] It has held a number of consultations on the Charismatic movement since 1976,[90] and has developed an affirmative but cautious attitude
toward the movement: "The EECMY recognizes Charismatic experiences in her congregations as a blessing to the Church if handled in the right way according to the
Scripture."[91] In 2007 a German Lutheran advisor to the ECMY was asked to revise
the Evangelical Church Mekane Yesus (ECMY) Book on Liturgy and Worship in order
to incorporate not just more Ethiopian worship forms, but also Charismatic elements,
like prophecy, speaking in tongues, healing and exorcism.[92] This revision contains a
four-page section on "Worship Discipline and the Benefit of Spiritual Gifts," which
deals with potential abuses and erroneous applications of spiritual gifts, but overall
affirms the importance of Charismatic gifts and encourages local leadership to value,
guide, and train Charismatic youths.[93] The Mennonite MKC has introduced a fourth
item in its teaching about God, after its treatments of Father, Son, and Holy Ghost,
which is titled "Fullness of the Holy Spirit (Baptism)" and confirms the belief of the
church in the "fullness of the Holy Spirit" and the work of spiritual gifts "today."[94]

The theological alliance between mainline Protestants and (trinitarian) Pentecostals has its organizational correlate in the Evangelical Churches' Fellowship of
Ethiopia (ECFE).[95] This interdenominational fellowship comprises twenty-two denominations, mainline Protestant as well as Pentecostal. It is the only ecumenical
body that the major Pentecostal churches participate in,[96] and it facilitates theologi-

88 With regard to tongues it is especially interesting that there is no explicit prohibition of public
    tongues speaking in the service, but that the doctrinal statement maintains, like Pentecostals,
    that there are two types of tongues, one for the service, and one for private edification.
89 AGNE NORDLANDER, "Charismatic Movement and Lutheran Theology in the Ethiopian Evangel-
    ical Church Mekane Yesus," in *Med Kristus til jordens ender: Festskrift til Tormod Engelsviken*,
    ed. KJELL OLAV SANNES (Trondheim: Tapir Akademisk Forlag, 2008), 193.
90 See KILIAN MCDONNELL, "Lutheran Church – Mekane Yesus, Ethiopia, 1976: The Work of the
    Holy Spirit," in *Presence, Power, Praise: Documents on the Charismatic Renewal*, vol. 2, *Con-
    tinental, National, and Regional Documents Numbers 38 to 80, 1975–1979*, ed. KILIAN MCDON-
    NELL (Collegeville, MN: The Liturgical Press, 1980), 150–182 for a documentation of the first
    consultation in 1976.
91 *Proceedings of the consultation on the Charismatic Movement, held in August 1993*, quoted
    in ALEMU SHETTA, "Reflection Paper to 23rd Meeting of the Committee of Mutual Christian
    Responsibility, January 21–24, 2002" (Unpublished manuscript, private collection, 2002), 4.
92 See EVANGELICAL LUTHERAN MISSION IN LOWER SAXONY, "Annual Report 2008/2009" (2009): 10,
    http://www.elm-mission.net/fileadmin/uploads/I_Finanzen/jahrbuch_elm_2008-laender-1.pdf
    (accessed March 4, 2009).
93 See ETHIOPIAN EVANGELICAL CHURCH MEKANE YESUS, ይቅዳሴና የአምልኮ ሥነ ሥርዓት መጽሐፍ, [Book of
    Liturgy and Worship.], 3rd ed. (Addis Ababa, 2008), 243–247.
94 See MESERETE KRISTOS CHURCH, ed., መሠረተ እምነት, [Foundation of Faith] (Addis Ababa, 1995),
    section 3.2.4, p. 6.
95 For the history of the ECFE, see DANIEL FITE, "The Challenges of Denominational Conflicts in
    the Context of Ethiopian Evangelical Churches" (B.Th. thesis, Mekane Yesus Seminary, 2001),
    17–22.
96 Contrary to LAUNHARDT, *Evangelicals in Addis Ababa (1919–1991)*, 160, the Ethiopian Pentecos-
    tal Churches' Fellowship is only a loose and hardly active conglomerate of very small Pentecostal
    churches.

cal discussions as well as cooperation in evangelism, developmental projects, practical
matters such as burial grounds, and, to some extent, political representation. As
such, it also functions as a platform for Pentecostal and Charismatic theologies. In
February 2005, for example, the ECFE hosted a church leadership conference titled
"The Biblical Use of the Gifts of the Holy Spirit."[97] The conference basically was a
seminar taught by the invited keynote speaker, the British Assemblies of God pastor
Dr. David Petts. Petts laid out a decidedly Pentecostal theology, including a defense
of the doctrine of speaking in tongues as initial evidence of the reception of the Holy
Spirit. However, the most controversial point of his presentation was not so much
his Pentecostal theology, but that when he likened the Holy Spirit reception to water
baptism, he displayed a decidedly Baptist understanding of water baptism, which
drew harsh criticism from the attending Lutherans. The observed group discussion
sessions at the seminar also did not take up the issue of Pentecostal versus Charismatic theology, but mainly focused on problems in the administration of spiritual
gifts.[98]

The theological and organizational convergence of Pentecostals and mainline Protestants therefore broadens the scope of historic research, since a sharp distinction
between Pentecostal and Charismatic movements cannot be applied anymore, especially with regard to the available sources. Histories from the background of mainline
Protestant churches or missions have produced their own account of the Holy Spirit
movement in Ethiopia, in which they either trace the influence of their respective
denominations on the Pentecostal movement, or assert that they too are part of the
wider renewal movement in Ethiopia, which transcends the classical delimitation of
Pentecostalism. The MKC, for example, has absorbed part of the early Pentecostal
revival movement in Nazaret, and thus occasionally presents itself as part of Ethiopian
Pentecostalism from the start.[99] With regard to the ECMY, the missionary Hermann
Domianus, who worked extensively on the Charismatic movement within this church,
noted that many of his informants asserted that the beginnings of the ECMY in the
early 20th century "resembled a charismatic revival" because of the role healing and
exorcism played herein.[100] Likewise, a KHC historian pointed to the importance of
prophecy, exorcism and healing in the missionary foundation of the church,[101] and a
longstanding SIM missionary publicly reflected how his own theological position and

---

97   The author was able to observe this conference.
98   Speaking in tongues, for example, was only discussed in relation to the problem of untranslated
     glossolalia coming from the pulpit.
99   See section 3.1.4, p. 101ff.
100 HERMANN DOMIANUS, "Essay zum TEE-Lehrbuch: The Charismatic Movement within the Ethi-
     opian Evangelical Church Mekane Yesus; A Theological Foundation for an African Lutheran
     Church between Tradition and Revival" (Unpublished manuscript, private collection, 2005), 7.
     Similarly, interviews no. 122; 77.
101 Interview no. 106. According to the informant, the only difference to the present charismatic
     movement was that they did not use tongues or shout when exorcizing demons. See also
     WONDEYE ALI, በመከራ ውስጥ ያበበች ቤተ ክርስቲያን: የኢትዮጵያ ቃለ ሕይወት ቤተ ክርስቲያን ታሪክ, ቅጽ እንድ,
     (ከ1920–1933), [A Church Blooming in Hardship: The History of the Ethiopian Kale Heywet
     Church, vol. 1, 1928–1941] (Addis Ababa: Ethiopian Kale Heywet Church, 1998), 66–76 for the
     role of prophecy in evangelizing the southern areas.

that of his mission changed from cessationist to Charismatic.[102] The perspectives inserted by these histories have considerable weight, since for certain time periods they constitute the majority of available sources, as will be shown in the following section.

1.3 Historical Archive: Sources About Pentecostalism in Ethiopia

1.3.1 Imperial Ethiopia

Histories of Ethiopian Pentecostalism were not produced until after the Ethiopian revolution. Therefore, the relevant sources dating to before the Ethiopian revolution of 1974 consist solely of press articles and personal correspondence held in the archives of the Finnish and Swedish Pentecostal missions.[103] With regard to the Finnish mission, the most important documents are Sanfrid and Anna-Liisa Mattsson's letters, as well as some archival documents dating back as far as 1951. The plurality of the Swedish beginnings, on the other hand, resulted in a somewhat more complex archive, with the most important sources for this research being the extensive correspondence of Karl Ramstrand, Tage Johansson, and Allan Wedin. In addition, the documents collected in the church archives of Jönköping and Valla allow an insight into the politics of mission on the Swedish side. This material on the Swedish missions is complemented by a number of articles and reports in the weekly *Evangelii Härold*.

This fairly voluminous collection of correspondence and articles[104] is a valuable resource for studying the historiography of Ethiopian Pentecostalism, because the complexity of contemporaneous perspectives can be contrasted with later historical narratives. More than any other source, the missionary letters, reports, and minutes reveal the organizational plurality and fragmentation of the Swedish and Finnish mission endeavors, the political precariousness of their presence in Ethiopia, and their at times competitive claims and attempts to influence the Ethiopian Pentecostals. Furthermore, since they do not seek narrative closure to the same extent as subsequent

---

102 See PAUL BALISKI, "Case Studies from the Bible and from History of Non-Biblical Charismatic Practices Which Have Been Divisive in the Body of Christ," in *The Biblical Use of the Gifts of the Holy Spirit: Seminar Convened at Ethiopia Graduate School of Theology, Addis Ababa, 30 October 2004* (Addis Ababa: Unpublished collection, Ethiopian Graduate School of Theology, 2004), 14–19. This document also contains a report about four SIM missionaries who encountered Spirit baptism in 1969 and spoke in tongues, including the field director of the time. This caused heated discussions within the SIM at the end of which all four missionaries had to terminate their work and leave Ethiopia.

103 The Finnish sources were gathered from the Fida archive in Helsinki Finland in August 2004. Swedish archive material was acquired in August 2004 as well, partly in the city archive of Jönköping, which includes the archives of the local Pentecostal church, and for the most part in the Pingströrelsens Informationscentrum in Kaggeholm, Ekerö near Stockholm. The very well organized collection of material on Ethiopia at Kaggeholm was compiled by Gunilla Nyberg Oskarsson's during research for her book about the Swedish Pentecostal missions in Ethiopia, see GUNILLA NYBERG OSKARSSON, *Svensk Pingstmission i Ethiopien (1959–1980)*, [The Swedish Pentecostal Mission in Ethiopia] (Huddinge: MissionsInstitutet-PMU, 1997).

104 Altogether around 3,850 pages of material were acquired, about 650 pages from the Finnish and 3,200 from the Swedish archives. The Finnish material was reviewed and partially translated by Anna-Mari Nikkilä. The Swedish documents were reviewed and evaluated by the author.

histories, events later endowed with much gravity may be reported with less ambition here.

With regard to the political oppression of Pentecostals in the late Imperial Ethiopia, contemporaneous press articles, ranging from Ethiopian press to Western Christian periodicals, allow an insight into the contentiousness of the affair and are a testimony to the publicity efforts of Pentecostals and their allies. Furthermore, the WCC archives in Geneva contain some documents and correspondence elucidating the ecumenical politics surrounding the investigation of the Council into the matter.

1.3.2 After the Ethiopian Revolution

It was immediately after the Ethiopian revolution, that the first histories of Ethiopian Pentecostalism were produced, i.e., works that claim to tell the full story of the revival in Ethiopia from its inception to the present. These histories not only set out to establish the origin of the Pentecostal movement and trace its growth from there, they also seek to define the meaning of the political oppression that Pentecostal groups had encountered in the last years of the Empire, and as such they contain a message for the relatively unstable times of the initial revolutionary years.

The earliest and still most influential of these histories was produced by the Norwegian missiologist Tormod Engelsviken in 1975.[105] Engelsviken had served as a missionary for the Norwegian Lutheran Mission in Ethiopia in 1971–1973, where he taught at the Mekane Yesus Seminary. His stay coincided with the mass arrest of Pentecostals in late August 1972, and in early September Engelsviken visited the detained Christians in prison together with a group of mainline Protestants.[106] At that point, he had already become acquainted with the Pentecostal movement, since he had previously been drafted by the ECMY leadership to investigate the "history and doctrine of the Pentecostal movement in Ethiopia" and had presented his report to the Executive Committee of the church in June 1972.[107] The Executive Committee asked Engelsviken to prepare a revised version of the document and some recommendations for the ECMY general assembly in Yirga Alem to be held in January 1973. This paper, though it raised some concerns, in general was affirmative of the Pentecostal movement. However, Engelsviken's report and recommendations were not favorably received at the assembly. The reasons for this are not entirely clear. While Engelsviken contends that there was a "general aversion and enmity against the Pentecostals among the rank and file members of the church" due to the large influence of Oneness Pentecostals in the south, and that others deemed it imprudent to express solidarity with a movement persecuted by the government, other informants argue that Engelsviken's report went "too far" or that most delegates simply were not yet aware of the Pentecostal movement and considered the matter irrelevant.[108] Whatever the different motivations may have been, it is clear that by this point Engelsviken was more than a distant missionary observer, but an advocate of

---

105   See ENGELSVIKEN, "Molo Wongel."
106   See his report in ibid., 166–168.
107   Ibid., 197.
108   See ibid., 198–199. This was also mentioned in interviews no. 77; 122.

the emerging Pentecostal movement, who, though not uncritical, tried to make way for an ecumenical acceptance of Ethiopian Pentecostals.

Engelsviken originally met the Pentecostal movement through the missionary Knut Sigurd Aasebø, who was the director of the ECMY Youth Hostel in Addis Ababa. The hostel, established in 1966, had a small assembly hall in which a Christian university student group gathered, which became one of the most important meeting places for the Pentecostals after their own premises were closed in 1972.[109] Aasebø was instrumental in facilitating ecumenical contacts to Pentecostals in the aftermath of the 1972 arrests, and he provided Engelsviken with initial contacts to the movement as well as with some interviews he had conducted with Pentecostal leaders.[110] Engelsviken teamed up with Aasebø to support the Pentecostals and began to collect his own interviews as well as internal information and documents pertaining to the ecumenical deliberations about their case.

In 1975, while teaching at the Wartburg Theological Seminary in Iowa, USA, he completed a 225-page manuscript titled *Molo Wongel. A Documentary Report on the Life and History of the independent Pentecostal movement in Ethiopia 1960–1975.* The motivation for the report stated in the preface was two-fold. First, Engelsviken intended to tell the story of the 1972 oppression of Pentecostals. Though he was aware that the political situation had significantly improved,[111] he found it important to write down what he knew in order to "tell the truth about the Ethiopian Pentecostals and by doing so vindicate them morally and religiously in [the] face of false accusations."[112] Secondly, the document was to establish "an important chapter of the history of church and mission in Ethiopia, and in Africa" in that it is "a report on how the Gospel can spread" by indigenous agency. Engelsviken's plans for publishing this manuscript[113] did not materialize, but it was privately circulated and made available to the Mekane Yesus Seminary library in Ethiopia as well as to Western libraries. The scope of the document, its availability in the relevant institutional contexts, and its relative singularity due to the lack of early historical writings made it the single-most referenced source in all histories of Ethiopian Pentecostalism.

The first source referencing Engelsviken was a B.A. thesis submitted to the Department of History at the Addis Ababa University in 1976 by Yosief Kidanewold,

---

109   This is mentioned in a number of publications and interviews, see ETHIOPIAN FULL GOSPEL BELIEVER'S CHURCH, የኢትዮጵያ ሙሉ ወንጌል አመኞች ቤተ ክርስቲያን 25ኛ ዓመት በዓል: ከ1959–1984, [The 25th Anniversary of the Ethiopian Full Gospel Believer's Church: From 1959 to 1984.] (Addis Ababa, 1992), 10; TIBEBE ESHETE, *The Evangelical Movement in Ethiopia*, 162; also interviews no. 77; 87; 21. The FGBC meeting to reestablish its national structure in 1974 also took place in the Youth Hostel, see ETHIOPIAN FULL GOSPEL BELIEVERS' CHURCH, ሙሉ ወንጌል ቤተ ክርስቲያን ከልደት እስከ ... መቻሉ ሰው ጌታ ኢየሱስን ፈልጎ ሲመጣ ተመለስ አይባል!! [The Full Gospel Church from Birth Until ... Well, it is Impossible to Turn Back the People When They Come Wanting Jesus!!] (Addis Ababa, 1978), 28.
110   See ENGELSVIKEN, "Molo Wongel," 8–9; TORMOD ENGELSVIKEN, E-mail to author, 4 March 2009; OGBAZGHI SIUM, E-mail to author, 16 April 2008.
111   See ENGELSVIKEN, "Molo Wongel," 223–225.
112   Ibid., 7.
113   Cf. TORMOD ENGELSVIKEN, Letter to Philip Potter, 2 September 1975, Ethiopia Correspondence, WCC Archives, Geneva.

titled *The History of the Pentecostal Movement in Addis Ababa.*[114] Yosief mentions
that Engelsviken allowed him to read his manuscript and his overall trajectory follows
the *Documentary Report* in large parts. However, he also interviewed over fifteen of his
own informants,[115] which at times allowed him to depart from Engelsviken. Yosief's
ability to recruit these informants, his familiarity with a number of details, and the
introduction of the thesis referencing Acts 2 and the story of Pentecost suggest that
he was part of the Pentecostal student movement. The stated aim of the thesis is
to "present the History of the Pentecostal movement in Addis Ababa from 1963 on-
wards up to 1976,"[116] but its conclusion highlights an apologetic interest as well.
Mentioning that some Pentecostal students encountered difficulties in the mobilization campaigns of early revolutionary Ethiopia, Yosief insists that Pentecostals are
making valuable contributions to the new society and are "concerned both to defend
their faith and to support socialist goals."[117] He ends by noting that "[d]espite the
spiritual and societal contributions and its struggle of over ten years, the Pentecostal
movement [...] is still being persecuted," but that it nevertheless has proven "to be
like an inextinguishable fire."[118]

One year later, a student at the Mekane Yesus Seminary by the name of Taye
Abdissa, wrote his "Thesis for a Degree Course," titled *The Pentecostal Development
and the Rise of [the] Charismatic Movement in Ethiopia.*[119] Taye was a Spirit-
baptized member of the ECMY and aimed to show in his paper how the Pentecostal
movement emerged in Ethiopia and spread to the ECMY. Beginning with the history
of Pentecostal and Charismatic movements in the USA, he traces the emergence of
Pentecostalism in Ethiopia, its spread to the ECMY, especially in western Ethiopia,
and he concludes with the consideration of some doctrinal differences between his
church and Pentecostal groups. Taye does not reference Engelsviken's or Yosief's work
directly, but notes that he interviewed Yosief, who "read through the unpublished
documentary report [...] by Tormod Engelsviken."[120] In addition to information
gathered from Yosief, his account of the early Pentecostal movement is based on
two informants: Merid Lema, the main pastor of the FGBC, and Hiruy Tsige, then
leader of the Finnish mission congregation at Merkato.[121] The overall structure and
a number of details of his story are similar to Engelsviken's report, but it is unclear
whether this is because his two Pentecostal informants basically told the same story
or because of Yosief's recapitulation of Engelsviken's work for him.[122] Taye's account
of the emergence of the Charismatic movement in the ECMY is based on a number

---

114 YOSIEF KIDANEWOLD, "The History of the Pentecostal Movement in Addis Abeba: 1963–1976"
     (B.A. thesis, Addis Ababa University, History Department, 1976).
115 See ibid., iii.
116 See ibid.
117 Ibid., 52.
118 Ibid., 54.
119 See TAYE ABDISSA, "The Pentecostal Development and the Rise of Charismatic Movement in
     Ethiopia" (B.Th. thesis, Mekane Yesus Seminary, 1977).
120 Ibid., 4. He did, however, have access to Engelsviken's 1973 report to the ECMY General
     Assembly in Yirga Alem.
121 Cf. ibid., 4, also notes 30–37.
122 Since Taye does not explicitly cite Yosief Kidanewold in his paper, his influence is difficult to
     ascertain.

of informants from his church, to whom he was closely related through a Charismatic student group at the Mekane Yesus Seminary, and who later became key figures for the revival in their church.[123] His thesis was not only the first history of a Charismatic movement in Ethiopia, but it also linked the mainline church revival to persecution, which became a recurring theme in many later histories.

The last of these early histories was provided in 1978 by the Full Gospel Believers' Church in their jubilee magazine on the occasion of the dedication of the church's first building. The magazine does not refer to previous studies of the history of Pentecostalism in Ethiopia and appears to be based exclusively on sources from within the FGBC. It significantly differs from the other accounts in that it puts most of its emphasis on the Addis Ababa student movement and does not even refer to a number of story elements that were important to Engelsviken's account. Moreover, its political references are more concealed, especially with regard to the 1972 arrests and the surrounding events. However, in its primary apologetic aim the paper converges with the other accounts. In the introduction the authors state that they believe "that for our friends living far from the Evangelical churches, or moreover from the spiritual realm, this magazine will drive out the distorted and baseless gossip heard in society and will reveal the goals and spiritual foundation that the church is laboring for."[124]

These four histories from different contexts all reflect the time in which they were written, namely the short period of relative freedom and political insecurity that followed the Ethiopian revolution. They look back on the Ethiopian empire and the limits it had imposed on Pentecostal groups, they take stock of the past achievements of the revival movements in this environment, and they attempt to lay down their history for the first time, defining the main characters and events. At the same time, they also speak to their immediate political context. All except Taye, who wrote within the safe haven of his church, do not expose any names and are careful to protect their sources. Moreover, their desire to educate the public and other churches about the origin and character of the Pentecostal movement stems from an insecurity about the future political parameters, which in turn is based on the experience of riots and other opposition in revolutionary Ethiopia.[125]

1.3.3 During Socialist Dictatorship

The production of Pentecostal and Charismatic histories that had begun in different contexts was disrupted for about a decade, following the consolidation of Mengistu Haile Mariam's dictatorship and the ensuing political repression of Pentecostals and other Protestants. From 1979 on, there were no relevant publications or even seminary theses pertaining to the history of Ethiopian Pentecostalism until almost the very end of the Derg.[126] There are also no unpublished Pentecostal manuscripts or internal

---

123 For their names and stories cf. section 5.3.4, p. 235ff.
124 ETHIOPIAN FULL GOSPEL BELIEVERS' CHURCH, ሙሉ ወንጌል ቤተ ክርስቲያን ከልደት እስከ . . ., 2.
125 For details, see section 5.2.2, p. 214ff.
126 There were a few exceptions outside Ethiopia, which generally did not leave a mark on Ethiopian histories. Ramstrand's memoirs (KARL RAMSTRAND, *Det heliga äventyret*, [The Holy Adventure] (Stockholm: Den Kristna Bokringen, 1986)) were in Swedish and were not used outside Swedish sources. The account by Rice (MARIE S. RICE, *Sister Bertha, Sister Ruth* (Nashville, TN: Jonathan Publishers, 1984)) pertained to a different period, spoke to an Amer-

documents from this time that could be located during research, or that are mentioned in later publications.[127]

Furthermore, the Finnish and Swedish missionary correspondence and periodicals, which had provided an additional angle on the situation of the Pentecostals in the late Imperial Ethiopia, largely fell silent during the Derg. For the most part the missionaries only reported about their efforts in humanitarian and developmental aid. Due to considerable security concerns, the Ethiopian Pentecostals kept missionaries significantly less informed than before, and they in turn did not have the liberty to share the little they knew. Moreover, their political standing within the country had changed fundamentally. Under Haile Selassie's government, the missions had relied on building good relations to the Imperial family, and saw themselves as advocates for the Pentecostals, a role, which corresponded to their interest of keeping the peace with the authorities. Now, under attack themselves and no longer able to secure a good standing with the socialist government, the missions were in no position to advise the Ethiopian Pentecostals or to intercede for them. The Swedish missionary Tage Johansson, for example, who in his previous correspondence had been rather outspoken and prescriptive about the political conflicts of 1972, apparently no longer saw the opportunity to voice his opinion on controversies in the churches. In one of his letters he mentioned the issue of Christians chanting the required socialist slogans, which was a highly controversial topic in all Protestant churches at the time.[128] Noting that some Pentecostals were arrested for refusing to participate in the chants and explaining the issue at stake, Johansson simply states that this was discussed at a meeting of missionaries from different organizations, where it was decided that "we should leave that to the natives themselves to decide," without offering his own

ican background, and likewise was generally not noticed in the Ethiopian Pentecostal historiography. The history of the ACE provided by Freeman (FREEMAN, *Unseen hands*) has also been ignored due to the ostracization of this Oneness church.

127   Even Tibebe Eshete's account, as yet the best researched and detailed history of the FGBC during the Derg, only references one written source for the persecution years, the short report about Tesfaye Gabbiso's arrest provided in the *Keston News Service*, "Tesfaye Gabiso," January 24, 1985, 22. See TIBEBE ESHETE, *The Evangelical Movement in Ethiopia*, 263–272; cf. TIBEBE ESHETE, "Growing Through the Storms: The History of the Evangelical Movement in Ethiopia, 1941–1991" (Ph.D. thesis, Michigan State University, 2005), 475–487.

128   Most Pentecostals refused to shout socialist slogans, like "Above all, the revolution", since they believed it contradicted their desire to put God above all, see TIBEBE ESHETE, *The Evangelical Movement in Ethiopia*, 247f. EIDE, *Revolution and Religion in Ethiopia*, 247. In the ECMY, on the other hand, the general secretary Gudina Tumsa argued that the slogans were meant to "inspire people in the progress of the Revolution" and are not of religious significance. Therefore "joining with others in reciting them will have no effect on one's Christian commitment," see GUDINA TUMSA, "The Role of a Christian in a Given Society," in *Witness and Discipleship: Leadership of the Church in Multi-Ethnic Ethiopia in a Time of Revolution; The Essential Writings of Gudina Tumsa, General Secretary of the Ethiopian Evangelical Church Mekane Yesus (1929–1979)*, ed. PAUL E. HOFFMAN (Addis Ababa: Gudina Tumsa Foundation, 2003), 8; EZRA GEBREMEDHIN, "The Ethiopian Evangelical Church Mekane Yesus under Marxist Dictatorship," in *Changing Relations Between Churches in Europe and Africa: The Internationalization of Christianity and Politics in the 20th Century*, ed. KATHARINA KUNTER and JENS HOLGER SCHJØRRING, Studien zur außereuropäischen Christentumsgeschichte; 11 (Wiesbaden: Harrassowitz Verlag, 2008), 96–97.

opinion on the matter.[129] The same letter also reported a widespread sentiment that
the mission might not be able to stay much longer, which according to Johansson was
also articulated in prophesies. Thus, while the Pentecostal sources on persecution
were waning in general, the alternative voice of missionary correspondence also largely
disappeared from the historical archive.

In comparison to the scarcity of sources about Pentecostals during the Derg, the
political oppression of the EOC and mainline Protestant churches is fairly well documented in publications of the time. The deposition of the EOC patriarch in 1976 was
taken up by the earliest academic treatments of the Ethiopian revolution, and a number of other scholarly publications.[130] The measures taken against the ECMY, like
the confiscation of central property and the abduction of its general secretary, were
met with official protest notes by the WCC and the Lutheran World Federation.[131]
and were reported by Christian magazines.[132] Though not treated as extensively, the
cases of the MKC and the KHC were also taken up from time to time in the American
evangelical press.[133] While some of these sources also reference the oppression of the
Pentecostal movement, none of them do so in noteworthy detail.[134]

Thus, the oppressive political treatment of Pentecostals had immediate effects on
the production of histories. There is not only a lack of relevant new sources during this
time, but the Pentecostal story of political repressions under the Derg was virtually

129 See TAGE JOHANSSON, Letter to Bo Hörnberg, 18 May 1978, Tage Johansson Collection,
     Pingstarkiv Kaggeholm, Ekerö.
130 See esp. OTTAWAY and OTTAWAY, *Ethiopia*, 172; JOHN BROWN, "Religion and Revolution in
     Ethiopia," *Religion in Communist Lands* 9 (1–2 1981): 50–55; FRIEDRICH HEYER, "Die Ortho-
     doxe Kirche Äthiopiens im zehnten Revolutionsjahr," *Ökumenische Rundschau* 34 (2 1985):
     216–221; SCHWAB, *Ethiopia*, 92–95; MIKAEL DOULOS, "Christians in Marxist Ethiopia," *Religion
     in Communist Lands* Summer 1986 (1986): 143–144; HAILE MARIAM LAREBO, "The Orthodox
     Church and the State in the Ethiopian Revolution, 1974–84"; FRIEDRICH HEYER, "Chancen
     für das orthodoxe Äthiopien?" *Ökumenische Rundschau* 37 (3 1988): 342–345; MULATU WUB-
     NEH and YOHANNIS ABATE, *Ethiopia*, 126–128; PETER COSTEA, "Church-State Relations in the
     Marxist-Leninist Regimes of the Third World," *Journal of Church and State* 32 (1990): 281–
     308.
131 Copies of these protest telegrams can be found in the WCC archives.
132 See *Christianity Today*, "Ethiopian Casualties," April 15, 1977, 57–58; *Christianity Today*,
     "The Campaign to Root Out 'Alien' Religion in Ethiopia," September 7, 1979, 64; TODOR
     SABEV, Cable to the Ethiopian Government, 12 November 1981, Correspondence Member
     Churches: EOC, WCC Archives, Geneva; BRUCE BEST, "Ethiopia: Growing Church Under At-
     tack in Political Struggle," *One World* (74 1982): 5; MANFRED LUNDGREN, "När traditioner och
     relationer satts på prov," [When Traditions and Relationships are Put to the Test.], *Svensk
     Missionstidskrift* 17 (1983): 32–38; WOLFGANG MARWEDEL, "Mitmachen, aber mit kritischer
     Distanz: Evangelium und Sozialismus in Äthiopien.," *Zeitschrift für Mission* 10 (4 1984): 198–
     204.
133 See esp. the magazine Christianity Today, e.g. SHARON E. MUMPER, "Ethiopia Continues
     to Impose Restrictions on the Churches," *Christianity Today*, 14 1985, 70–72; *Christianity
     Today*, "The Protestant Church is Thriving in an Otherwise Dismal Ethiopia," November 7,
     1980, 94; *Christianity Today*, "Mission Agency Launches $8.2 Million Famine Relief Project
     in Southern Ethiopia," March 1, 1985, 43; *Christianity Today*, "New Growth for Ethiopian
     Church," October 6, 1989, 51.
134 The only story reported to some extent was that of the FGBC pastor and popular singer,
     Tesfaye Gabbiso, see *Keston News Service*, "Tesfaye Gabiso"; KESTON COLLEGE STAFF, "Im-
     provements in the Church Situation in Ethiopia?" *Religion in Communist Lands* 14 (1986):
     328–329.

drowned out by contemporaneous sources about similar experiences of the mainline churches, who also had the better international connections. It is not until the last years of the Derg that the writing of Ethiopian Pentecostal and Charismatic history was resumed, most notably in the context of the mainline churches.[135]

1.3.4 After the Derg

In the years after the downfall of the Derg the available sources about Ethiopian Pentecostalism multiplied and diversified. There are, first of all, historical abstracts produced by Pentecostal churches themselves in anniversary magazines, such as celebrating twenty-five or forty years of the FGBC, or the fiftieth anniversary of the GC.[136] They all contain longer historical narratives revealing what the respective churches regard as key events and main actors. Furthermore, the determination of anniversary dates as well as the arrangement of the magazine material are of interest to the study of Ethiopian Pentecostal historiography.

The church histories presented in such jubilee magazines are intimately connected to oral histories told by contemporaneous observers, participants and leaders. Many of them are still available to tell their story, and have been asked to do so during research for this study. Their rich accounts not only provide different historical trajectories, they also illustrate the different claims laid to the origins and developments of Pentecostal and Charismatic movements in Ethiopia.

The Finnish and Swedish Pentecostal missions have also produced histories of their work in Ethiopia in recent years. On the Finnish side, the most important source is the unpublished "Condensed History of the Finnish Mission in Ethiopia," written by the missionary Kyösti Roininen, who, with interruptions, has worked in Ethiopia since 1961.[137] A brief overview is also presented in a book published for the 70th anniversary of the Finnish Free Foreign Mission (FFFM).[138] There are also a number of Finnish missionary biographies and memoirs, most notably an extensive novel about Anna-Liisa Mattsson's life, which allow some insight into the politics of the Finnish Pentecostal foreign missions.[139] The Swedish Pentecostals have financed and

135 See JOHNNY BAKKE, *Christian Ministry: Patterns and Functions Within the Ethiopian Evangelical Church Mekane Yesus*, Studia Missionalia Upsaliensis; 44 (Oslo: Solum-Forlag, 1987), 251–255; BRIAN FARGHER, "The Charismatic Movement in Ethiopia 1960–1980," *Evangelical Review of Theology* 12 (1988): 345–358; SELESHI KEBEDE, "The History of the Guenet Church" (B.Th. thesis, Mekane Yesus Seminary, 1990).

136 See ETHIOPIAN FULL GOSPEL BELIEVER'S CHURCH, የኢትዮጵያ ሙሉ ወንጌል አማኞች ቤተ ክርስቲያን 25ኛ ዓመት በዓል; ADDIS ABABA FULL GOSPEL BELIEVERS' CHURCH, የ40ኛ ዓመት የወንጌል አገልግሎትና የምስጋና በዓል መጽሔት /ሕምሌ 1958–1998 ዓ.ም./, [Magazine of Forty Years of Gospel Ministry and of the Anniversary Celebration (July 1966–2006).] (Addis Ababa: Addis Ababa Full Gospel Believers' Church, 2006); ETHIOPIAN GENNET CHURCH, የ50ኛው ዓመት የወርቅ ኢዮቤልዩ በዓል, [The Golden Anniversary of Fifty Years.] (Addis Ababa, 2001).

137 See KYÖSTI ROININEN, "A Condensed History of the Finnish Mission in Ethiopia" (Unpublished manuscript, private collection, 2001).

138 EEVA HILPINEN, ed., *Lähetystyön monet kasvot: Suomen vapaa ulkolähetys 70 vuotta. = Manifold missions. Finnish Free Foreign Mission 70 years.* (Vantaa: Suomen vapaa ulkolähetys, 1997), 56–59. The text is presented in Finnish and English.

139 ASTA TILLANDER, *Näkymättömän lähettiläs: Anna-Liisa Mattsonin elämä*, [The Invisible Messenger. The Life of Anna-Liisa Mattsson.] (Vantaa: Aika Oy, 1996). See also AINO ROININEN, *Koskettakaa Lastani: Sairaanhoitajan kokemuksia Etiopiassa*, [Touch My Child! From the Ex-

undertaken a number of studies of their foreign missions, collecting archive material, conducting interviews, and publishing a Swedish book series. As part of this series, Gunilla Nyberg Oskarsson has produced a meticulous account of the Swedish mission endeavors to Ethiopia, spanning from 1959 to 1980.[140] There are also a couple of Swedish missionary biographies, as well as an extensive article on missions in the two volume publication on the occasion of the centennial of the Swedish Pentecostal movement which includes the Ethiopian missions.[141]

A lot of historical material can also be found in the many unpublished theses archived in Ethiopian seminaries, which have not yet been sufficiently explored by previous publications.[142] At the Lutheran Mekane Yesus Seminary, the largest group of B.Th. theses pertains to the Pentecostal and Charismatic movements. Though of different depth and quality, many of them provide valuable perspectives on the Charismatic movement within the ECMY,[143] other Pentecostal churches,[144], or cer-

periences of a Nurse in Ethiopia.] (Vantaa: RV-Kirjat, 1988); VEIKKO MANNINEN, *Mannisentie: Toimittanut Maja Hurri*, [Manninen's Way. Edited by Maja Hurri] (Vantaa: Aika Oy, 1995); HEIKKI KUMPULAINEN, *Puskatimpurin Päiväkirja*, [Diary of a Bush Carpenter.] (Vantaa: Aika Oy, 1997).

140   NYBERG OSKARSSON, *Svensk Pingstmission i Ethiopien (1959–1980)*

141   See TAGE JOHANSSON, *Med Gud i vardagen och bland medicinmän*, [With God Every Day and Among Medicine Men.] (Avesta: STC, 1996); RUTH RAMSTRAND, *Guds lilla piga far dit pepparn växer*, [God's Little Maid Goes Where the Pepper Grows.] (Huskvarna, 2002); JAN-ÅKE ALVARSSON, "Från kaffeplantage till tv-studio: Några huvuddrag i svensk pingstmission," [From Coffee Plantation to TV studio: Some Main Features in the Swedish Pentecostal Mission.], in *Pingströrelsen*, ed. CLAES WAERN, vol. 2, *Händelser och utveckling under 1900-talet*. [*The Pentecostal Movement*, part 2, *Events and Developments in the 1900s*.] (Övebrö: Libris förlag, 2007), 135–186.

142   Digital photographs of all relevant theses at the respective seminaries were acquired during research trips in 2003 to 2005. Theses made available to the seminary libraries after March 2005 unfortunately could not be considered by this study.

143   DAWIT OLIKA, "Parallelisms Between Charismatic Prophecy in EECMY and Qallu Institution of Oromo Traditional Religion" (B.Th. thesis, Mekane Yesus Seminary, 2002); DEMEKE BOTAMO, "The Reasons of Split and the Call for Unification in Evangelical Believers of Hosanna Town" (B.Th. thesis, Mekane Yesus Seminary, 2002); DURESSA MABESHA TAKA, "Charismatic Movement and Its Effects in the Aira District of the EECMY" (B.Th. thesis, Mekane Yesus Seminary, 2002); FANUEL ABERA, "The Introduction of Evangelical Christianity and the Effects of Charismatic Renewal in Gore Bethel Mekane Yesus Congregation" (B.Th. thesis, Mekane Yesus Seminary, 1999); MENGESHA AGA, "Evangelism and Charismatic Movement in Ghimbi District Western Synod EECMY 1914–1999" (B.Th. thesis, Mekane Yesus Seminary, 2000); MINTESINOT BIRRU, "The Impact of Charismatic Movement and Its Result Among Evangelicals in Gedeo Area" (B.Th. thesis, Mekane Yesus Seminary, 2002); THOMAS DEBELA, "The Effect of Charismatic Renewal upon Church Growth in the Central Synod" (B.Th. thesis, Mekane Yesus Seminary, 1999); TILAHUN TADESSE, "Gulele Bethel Evangelical Church Mekane Yesus at Present: Does it Need Revival?" (B.Th. thesis, Mekane Yesus Seminary, 1999); TILAYE KEBEDE, "Lamp on the Mountain: History of the Entoto Evangelical Church Mekane Yesus 1962–1974" (B.Th. thesis, Mekane Yesus Seminary, 1995).

144   ASHEBIR KETEMA, "The History of Ethiopian Guenet Church: From 1974–1992" (B.Th. thesis, Mekane Yesus Seminary, 1993); SELESHI KEBEDE, "The History of the Guenet Church"; LALISSA DANIEL GAMECHIS, "The Teaching of the Apostolic Movement and the Danger Behind" (B.Th. thesis, Mekane Yesus Seminary, 2001); MUSSIE ALAZAR, "Amanual-Mahiber: Foundation and Growth" (B.Th. thesis, Mekane Yesus Seminary, 2000).

tain issues connected with Pentecostal and Charismatic growth.[145] The Mennonite
Meserete Kristos College also holds a number of B.A. theses of similar relevance to the
study of the history of Pentecostal and Charismatic movements in Ethiopia.[146] Finally the Ethiopian Graduate School of Theology, which is a joint venture of Ethiopian
Protestant churches and the only Protestant facility granting a Master of Theology,
holds a number of Master theses by Charismatics and Pentecostals alike, offering
their perspective on the Ethiopian revival, which usually includes an abstract of its
history.[147] There are no institutions in Ethiopia with PhD programs in theology

---

145   DANIEL FITE, "The Challenges of Denominational Conflicts in the Context of Ethiopian Evan-
      gelical Churches"; DANIEL TESSO NEDJO, "The Growth and Impact of Evangelical Christianity
      in Bodji District 1941–2000" (B.Th. thesis, Mekane Yesus Seminary, 2001); DURESSA MABESHA
      TAKA, "Charismatic Movement and Its Effects in the Aira District of the EECMY"; GALLO AY-
      LATE, "The Konso District in the South West Synod: A Case Study on the Conflict of 1990 up
      to February 2000" (B.Th. thesis, Mekane Yesus Seminary, 2000); GETANEH BEFEKADU, "The
      Missiological Strategies in the Growth of Evangelical Christianity in Sadi-Dalle Wabera Pres-
      bytery of WWBS" (B.Th. thesis, Mekane Yesus Seminary, 2001); GUDINA TOLA, "Prophecy
      in the New Testament And Its Effects in the Central Synod's Congregations" (B.Th. thesis,
      Mekane Yesus Seminary, 2001); "The Introduction and the Growth of Evangelical Christian-
      ity in Lalo Qille Presbytery of Western Welega Bethel Synod" (B.Th. thesis, Mekane Yesus
      Seminary, 2000); JETO HORDOFA, "'Troubled But Not Destroyed': The Effects of the Persecu-
      tion of 1978–1991 (1970–1983 E.C.) on the Congregations of Western Wollega Bethel Synod"
      (B.Th. thesis, Mekane Yesus Seminary, 1999); MIESA YACHIS, "Charismatic Movement and Re-
      lated Problems in South Ethiopia Synod of EECMY" (B.Th. thesis, Mekane Yesus Seminary,
      1993); MIHIRETU DUGUMA, "Church Growth With Special Reference to Dale Leka Presbytery
      in WWBS" (B.Th. thesis, Mekane Yesus Seminary, 2001); REGATU OLANA, "Establishment
      and Growth of Evangelical Christianity in Anfillo Presbytery of WWBS (1936–1998)" (B.Th.
      thesis, Mekane Yesus Seminary, 1999).
146   See AMANUEL SEGEBO, "The History of God's Work in the Life of Gambella Meserete Kris-
      tos Church 1989–2002" (B.A. thesis, Meserete Kristos College, 2002); ASSEFA GELETA AYANA,
      "The History of Degem Meserete Kristos Region (1969–2002)" (B.A. thesis, Meserete Kris-
      tos College, 2002); ELIAS DALELO, "The Secret for the Rapid Growth of Hossana Meserete
      Kristos Church" (B.A. thesis, Meserete Kristos College, 2002); GIRMA HAILE, "The Brief His-
      tory of Dire Dawa Meserete Kristos Church" (B.A. thesis, Meserete Kristos College, 2002);
      LEBETA GOSHU KUMSA, "History of Meserete Kristos Church in Wellega (1966–2002)" (B.A.
      thesis, Meserete Kristos College, 2002); TESHOME SORI, "Insights for an Effective Evangelism
      in Nekemte Meserete Kristos Church and Its Surroundings" (B.A. thesis, Meserete Kristos Col-
      lege, 2002); ABERA ERTIRO, "The History of the Meserete Kristos Church at Nazareth: From
      1951–2003" (B.A. thesis, Meserete Kristos College, 2003); TEFERA MEKETA, "The History of
      South Addis Ababa Meserete Kristos Church and Its Growth" (B.A. thesis, Meserete Kristos
      College, 2003); GIRMA SORMOLO, "Penetration Between the Two Dominant Horns: The Histori-
      cal Birth, Growth and Expansion of Harar Meserete Kristos Church in the Midst of Muslim and
      Traditional Orthodox Belief" (B.A. thesis, Meserete Kristos College, 2004); ATRSAW GEREMEW
      BELAY, "The History of Bahir Dar Meserete Kristos Church" (B.A. thesis, Meserete Kristos
      College, 2004); ALEMU SAMUEL, "History of the Meserete Kristos Church Growth at Metahara
      Since 1967" (B.A. thesis, Meserete Kristos College, 2004); YONAS SEIFU, "The Background, the
      Progression and the Contemporary Nature of Music in the Ethiopian Evangelical Churches"
      (B.A. thesis, Meserete Kristos College, 2004); DAMENE DEGU, "The History of Evangelical
      Christianity in Arsi Sire" (B.A. thesis, Meserete Kristos College, 2004); GETAHUN BOGALE,
      "The History of Yayu Meserete Kristos Church and Its Growth" (B.A. thesis, Meserete Kristos
      College, 2004).
147   See esp. TEKA OBSA FOGI, "The Charismatic Movement in the EECMY: Some Doctrinal
      and Practical Issues; An Explorative and Evaluative Case Study; The Case of the EECMY
      Congregations in Nekemte" (M.Th. thesis, Ethiopian Graduate School of Theology, 2000);
      BULUTSE FUTUWI, "An Introduction to the Theology and Growth of Independent Churches

or religious studies and there have only been few dissertations about to Ethiopian Pentecostalism at universities worldwide.[148]

As this scope of theses illustrates, the bulk of recent research in Pentecostal and Charismatic movements was conducted at the mainline Protestant seminaries in Ethiopia, especially since the Pentecostal seminaries did not require a larger thesis.[149] Likewise a number of histories by mainline Protestants about their respective denominations treat Pentecostal Christianity in Ethiopia as well. In histories of the MKC this pertains mostly to the Nazaret revival and its effects on the church.[150] Other histories mention Pentecostal churches and the Charismatic movement where necessary, in order to create a more comprehensive account, for example Eide's history of *Revolution & Religion in Ethiopia*, or Launhardt's presentation of *Evangelicals in Addis Ababa*.[151]

Scholarship about Ethiopian Pentecostalism thus has significantly increased, but the overall source archive is still rather fragmented. Most accounts either are lim-

---

in Ethiopia With Special Reference to Rhema Faith Church: A Critical Approach" (M.Th. thesis, Ethiopian Graduate School of Theology, 2002); ABDISSA BENTI LEYE, "The Origin and Growth of the Ethiopian Misgana Evangelical Church 1983–2000" (M.Th. thesis, Ethiopian Graduate School of Theology, 2002); TSADIKU ABDO, "Where Does Mulu Wongel Stand in its Trinitarian Concept: East or West? A Critical Approach to Ethiopian Mulu Wongel Church's Theology of Trinity" (M.Th. thesis, Ethiopian Graduate School of Theology, 2003); ESCKINDER TADDESSE WOLDEGEBRIAL, "An Introduction to the Biblical and Historical Pattern of Church Government: With a Special Reference to Its Application in the Ethiopian Full Gospel Believers Church; A Critical Approach" (M.Th. thesis, Ethiopian Graduate School of Theology, 2003); YOHANNES SHERAB, "The Rapid Growth of "Jesus Only" Movement: Some of the Contributory Factors for its Growth in South West Ethiopia" (M.Th. thesis, Ethiopian Graduate School of Theology, 2005).

148 TIBEBE ESHETE, "Growing Through the Storms," published as TIBEBE ESHETE, *The Evangelical Movement in Ethiopia*. Outside of this detailed work, there are only three more theses at the Fuller Theological Seminary, and a psychological study of Spirit possession in Ethiopia, see HAILE WOLDE MICHAEL, "A Comparative Study of Leadership Development Methods with Reference to the Ethiopian Full Gospel Church" (Ph.D. thesis, Fuller Theological Seminary, 1993); ALEMAYEHU MEKONNEN, "Effects of Culture Change on Leadership in the Pentecostal/Charismatic Churches in Addis Ababa, Ethiopia" (Ph.D. thesis, Fuller Theological Seminary, School of World Mission, 1995); BARBARA SINGLETON, "A Clinical Phenomenology of Spirit Possession Beliefs and Practices in the Evangelical Churches of Addis Ababa, Ethiopia" (Ph.D. thesis, The Professional School of Psychology, 1996). An older DMiss thesis at Fuller Theological Seminary only briefly mentioned the FGBC, see SEPPO S. VÄISÄNEN, "The Challenge of Marxism to Evangelical Christianity with Special Reference to Ethiopia" (D.Miss. thesis, School of World Mission, Fuller Theological Seminary, 1981), 192–193.

149 The Ethiopian Full Gospel Theological College offers a B.A. in Theology but did, as of 2005, not require any thesis work, the same is true of the Addis Ababa Bible College, funded by the American Assemblies of God. The Bible College of the Addis Ababa Full Gospel Believers' Church and the Pentecostal Theological College belonging to the Hiwot Berhan Church (HBC) do not offer degrees on the bachelor level.

150 See HEGE, *Beyond Our Prayers*, 147–160; TILAHUN HAILE, "የወንጌል ሥርጭት ታሪክ በኢትዮጵያ በአጭሩ የተጻፈ," [A Short History of the Spread of the Gospel in Ethiopia.] (Unpublished manuscript, Evangelical Theological College, Addis Ababa, 2000), 87–100.

151 See EIDE, *Revolution and Religion in Ethiopia*; LAUNHARDT, *Evangelicals in Addis Ababa (1919–1991)*, 156–160. Another instance is ESKIL FORSLUND, *The Word of God in Ethiopian Tongues: Rhetorical Features in the Preaching of the Ethiopian Evangelical Church Mekane Yesus*, Studia missionalia Upsaliensia; 58 (Uppsala: Swedish Institute for Mission Research, 1993), 160–165.

ited to a particular church or weave the story of Pentecostal and Charismatic into
their treatment of a different research topic. However, recently a couple of histories
from different backgrounds have sought to present a more comprehensive picture of
Ethiopian Pentecostalism, which spans multiple churches and contexts. One is an
Amharic revival history presented by the FGBC pastor Bekele Woldekidan.[152] The
main interest of his book is to trace out the nature, history and future of *Revival in
Ethiopia*, as the book is titled. Though Bekele's historical account about the emergence of the FGBC is hardly different from that of his church, the broad interest
of his book has caused him to consider sources not cited before and to broaden his
narrative to include other churches and beginnings, in order to provide a comprehensive revival history. The other general history of Ethiopian Pentecostalism is part
of Tibebe Eshete's account of Ethiopian Protestantism, titled *The Evangelical Movement in Ethiopia: Resistance and Resilience.*[153] Tibebe's publication differs from
Bekele's writings in a number of ways. His primary research interest is to elucidate
the historical, social, and cultural factors for the rise of Ethiopian Pentecostalism, and
unlike Bekele he does not have a preference for the FGBC historical narrative, but
opts to leave matters open when his sources do not agree. However, he too is interested in situating the story of Ethiopia's Pentecostals in a larger narrative, identifying
it as one of the key factors to Protestant growth, since a certain "national strain" of
Pentecostalism renewed Protestant churches and drew out a "latent dimension" of
their spirituality.[154]

Therefore, the historiography of Ethiopian Pentecostalism is now starting to transcend its denominational origins and is being recognized as a valid research topic of
its own. As different histories begin to engage with one another about the origin of
the Pentecostal movement in Ethiopia, the factors determining its growth, and its
overall impact, they also contribute to the reification and establishment of this field
of interest.

1.4 Historical Narratives: Writing a History of Ethiopian Pentecostalism

As the overview of available sources in their historical, institutional, and political
contexts has shown, the history of Ethiopian Pentecostalism is told by many voices
in many stories and with multiple goals. In the course of less than twenty years,
Ethiopian Pentecostals had to adjust to the political upheavals of a country, which
transitioned from the Imperial government of Haile Selassie and its Orthodox state
church to a pluralist democracy, by way of a popular revolution abolishing old religious
alliances and the socialist military dictatorship of Mengistu Haile Mariam oppressing
many churches. The multiple accounts of Ethiopian Pentecostalism are articulated

---

152 BEKELE WOLDEKIDAN, ሪቫይቫል: ኢትዮጵያ እና የመጨረሻው መጨረሻ, [Revival. Ethiopia and the Final
     End] (Addis Ababa: Addis Ababa Full Gospel Believers' Church, 2002).
153 TIBEBE ESHETE, *The Evangelical Movement in Ethiopia.* This is a slightly revised and abridged
     version of his PhD thesis, TIBEBE ESHETE, "Growing Through the Storms"
154 See TIBEBE ESHETE, *The Evangelical Movement in Ethiopia,* 309, 314f.

within these political contexts and are informed by them as much as by the stories the seek to convey. Moreover, the political backgrounds of different sources overlap with their institutional setting, which in turn introduce another plethora of perspectives into historical accounts. This not only pertains to Pentecostal missions and churches, since the historiography of Ethiopian Pentecostalism has long been taken up by other Protestants as well. Finally, the many stories collected in written histories, newspaper reports, jubilee magazines, and oral accounts have been recited, reshaped, refuted, and realigned continuously, resulting in a sizeable pool of narratives, which needs to be delimited, sorted, and controlled by any history of Pentecostal and Charismatic movements in Ethiopia.

How can this rich source archive be traversed and analyzed in an academic history of Ethiopian Pentecostalism? Following methods of classical historiography, such an account might attempt to bracket all elements identified as fictional, it would aim to identify and bracket the context of its sources, and seek to sidestep the political thrust of its informants, in order to carve out a skeleton of facts, recover a chronology of actual events, and, perhaps, qualify the nature of the historical connections implicated therein. However, this not only significantly depletes the narrative abundance of the source archive and tends to leave a number of gaps to be filled by the best guesses of the researcher, it also comes with a significant theoretical challenge. For whereas historians in the past have mostly argued about the philosophical premises beneath their readings of history, the realism of the historiographical operation has altogether been challenged by the linguistic and cultural turns in two fundamental ways.[155] First, the notion of facts outside of their linguistic representation has forcefully been called into question from a number of vantage points, ranging from feminist theory to postcolonial studies and poststructuralist philosophy. Secondly, the linguistic representation of history has itself been scrutinized and subjected to literary analysis, most famously by Hayden White's *Metahistory*.[156]

Historians have thus been reassigned their place *within* the political, cultural, and linguistic representations of the world they had thought to transcend, because as Philip Sarasin notes, it is a "remarkable self-misunderstanding to presume that the inevitable selection of sources from an archive, the factual limitations of every possible research perspective, and the ineluctable interpretative activity in constructing dependencies would not fundamentally impair the 'truth' of historiographic accounts — but that the assertion that all reality is linguistically constructed would throw historians into the mirror cabinet of mere poetry."[157]

Indeed, if linguistic representation is found at the root of what has been called "historic facts" as well as underlying each history proper, then the analysis of these narrative forms of representation becomes an equally important part of historiography as is the search for material artifacts supporting said facts. Moreover, as Hayden

---

155   See PHILIPP SARASIN, *Geschichtswissenschaft und Diskursanalyse*, Suhrkamp-Taschenbuch Wissenschaft; 1639 (Frankfurt am Main: Suhrkamp, 2003), 23–25.
156   HAYDEN WHITE, *Metahistory: The Historical Imagination in Nineteenth-Century Europe* (Baltimore, MD: John Hopkins University Press, 1973). See chapter 6, p. 248ff. for White and three other philosophies of history that have centrally motivated the analyses proposed in this thesis.
157   SARASIN, *Geschichtswissenschaft und Diskursanalyse*, 55.

White observed, material artifacts and narrative representations are two sides of the
same coin:

> Recent theories of discourse, however, dissolve the distinction between realistic
> and fictional discourses based on the presumption of an ontological difference
> between their respective referents, real and imaginary, in favor of stressing
> their common aspect as semiological apparatuses that produce meanings by
> the systematic substitution of signified (conceptual contents) for the extra-
> discursive entities that serve as their referents. In these semiological theories of
> discourse, narrative is revealed to be a particularly effective system of discursive
> meaning production by which individuals can be taught to live a distinctively
> "imaginary relation to their real conditions of existence," that is to say, an
> unreal, but meaningful relation to the social formations in which they are
> indentured to live out their lives and realize their destinies as social subjects.[158]

In other words: material evidence and its narrative representation are inseparable
in the historical discourse, because fact and story derive their meaning from one
another. Certain historical events, like the presence of a specific minister, the prayer
meeting of some students, or the forced shut-down of a church may be seen as extra-
discursive entities, i.e. "real events" outside of their historiographical representation,
but their historical meaning is constituted by the fact that they function as referents
to a number of revival stories, which articulate theological ideas, denominational
identities, and historical plots. Historical analysis therefore must scrutinize both
sides of such stories in order to produce a full account. It thus remains important to
carefully document and date all of these "factual" events, but the relevance of such
an undertaking lies in the many "fictional" revival accounts about them.

Therefore, contrary to the fears of a "mirror cabinet of mere poetry," historiography after the linguistic turn does not mean to ignore, downplay or eclectically eclipse
what has been labeled "historic facts." Quite conversely such an endeavor depends on
meticulous research, since it will always attempt to throw the full complexity of the
historical entanglement at the narratives produced about the same, in order to read
and interpret them as what they are: meaningful stories about the past. Historiography of Ethiopian Pentecostalism thus becomes a literary, political, and historical
analysis of what has been said of this past, but it is also aimed at recovering the un-
said, the marginalized, even to hint at the impossibilities, the limits of the Pentecostal
historical discourse. This is also where the critical impulse of such a reading lies: it is
in the hope that by exposing the structure and the limits of a present discourse, the
field will be opened up for the articulation of new narratives.

Writing such a history that not only scrutinizes historical "facts" and "events" but
that seeks to analyze the plurality of their narrative representation is what this present
study aspires to. In so doing, four central topoi of Ethiopian Pentecostal historiography will be revisited. Two important questions of origin will be treated in chapters
two and three, namely, how histories relate the Ethiopian Pentecostal movement to
its missionary antecedent, and how they incorporate and combine different revival

---

158 HAYDEN WHITE, ed., *The Content of the Form: Narrative Discourse and Historical Represen-
     tation* (Baltimore, MD: Johns Hopkins University Press, 1987), x.

movements and groups to form a coherent story of Pentecostal beginnings. Chapter four analyzes the accounts about the political repression that Pentecostals suffered in the last years of Haile Selassie's reign, and studies the representation of persecution and politics. Finally, chapter five pertains to the Derg time, and looks at how histories represent the relatively opaque underground movement and how they relate persecution to the emergence of the Charismatic movement. The conclusion returns to the theoretic questions about historiography that were raised in this introduction, and lays out four methodological propositions for incorporating the complementarity of realistic and fictional discourses in the writing of history.

2 Relating to Missionary Beginnings: The Finnish and Swedish Pentecostal Missions in Ethiopia

The emergence of Pentecostalism in Ethiopia is closely connected to Finnish and Swedish Pentecostal missionaries, who came to the country in the 1950s. Both groups of missionaries were engaged in a wide range of developmental and evangelistic activities, both were quite fragmented in their organizational setup since they came from a congregationalist background, and each of them ultimately spawned an Ethiopian Pentecostal church. Though these missions were aware of each other's work and supported one another on occasion, their relationship grew increasingly competitive when a strong independent Pentecostal movement arose in Ethiopia, attracting many followers and contesting the presence of foreign missions. As a result of this constellation, the written and oral histories of Ethiopian Pentecostalism are permeated with differing accounts about the foreign missions, often critically engaging with one another's assessment of the mission enterprise.

The following analysis of mission histories will focus on the first two decades of Pentecostal missionary presence, since this is where the narrative engagement with the missions culminates. The primary interest will be to understand the representational strategies behind the historical accounts, in order to elucidate central dynamics in the historical debate about Pentecostal missions in Ethiopia. The analysis will begin by looking at the basic narrative schemes which drive different accounts about the missions and which seek to define the missionary contribution to the origins of Ethiopian Pentecostalism.

2.1 Defining the Missionary Contribution

When looking at the different accounts about the missions and their impact, three basic narratives emerge. The first and earliest is connected with histories that highlight the independent Pentecostal movement. Here, the missions are given a preliminary role at best, and the starting point of Pentecostalism is characterized more or less as a mission-independent event. This historical representation is countered by later missionary accounts, which seek to establish a central and lasting impact of the missions, especially with regard to the initial reception of Pentecostal spirituality in Ethiopia. Finally, churches that came out of the Finnish or the Swedish Pentecostal missions tend to oscillate between the two former narrative schemes. On the one hand they claim the missionary heritage and assert its importance, since it marks their own historical legacy and influence. On the other hand they also follow the historical idea of early missionary independence in order to reflect their own processes of emancipation from the missions.

In recent years, this basic historical debate about the contribution of the Finnish and Swedish Pentecostal missions has been complemented by fragmented stories about other Pentecostal missionaries or itinerant evangelists, some of which even preceded the arrival of the Northern Europeans. However, as the analysis will show, these other missionary contributions have not fundamentally altered the debate, but rather tend to be marginalized in the few historical accounts where they do find mention.

2.1.1   Highlighting Mission Independence

The earliest written account about Ethiopian Pentecostalism, Tormod Engelsviken's *Documentary Report*, is perhaps the most remarkable example for historical accounts marginalizing the missionary impact in favor of an independent Ethiopian movement. In the preface of his report, Engelsviken defined his aims as follows:

> This book is also a report on mission. The main characters are, however, not missionaries from the West, but Ethiopian students and other ordinary people [...] It is therefore also a report on how the Gospel can spread without foreign personnel, foreign money, big institutions, ambitious development programs and advanced theological education.[1]

With these words, Engelsviken introduces the central theme of his mission narrative: mission independence. His "report on mission" is to demonstrate how "Ethiopian students and other ordinary people" became the main agents of Pentecostalism in Ethiopia, and not "missionaries from the West." This basic assumption shapes Engelsviken's account of the Finnish and Swedish mission endeavors, their input in the emergence of Ethiopian Pentecostalism as well as their relationship to the national Pentecostal movement. Engelsviken summarizes his mission narrative as follows:

> The ground was prepared by the ministry of the missionaries, the reading of evangelical literature and by personal preparation in Bible study and prayer. As expectations increased, only a spark was needed to set the young people aflame for Christ. This spark was not a missionary or guest speaker from the West, but an African evangelist from neighbouring Kenya.[2]

This summary lends itself to a number of observations: First, there seems to be an actual story of revival to tell, with its own build-up ("the ground was prepared") and climax ("spark"). Secondly, an identifiable historic event is assumed to have initiated the revival. Third, since the missionaries had no direct involvement in this initial event, their ministry was merely part of preparatory groundwork, next to "evangelical literature" and personal "Bible study and prayer". Finally, there is an implicit statement of missionary ineffectiveness, which is based on a certain notion of African identity and authenticity, since the key event is explicitly stated to have been linked to an "African" minister from "neighbouring" Kenya, and not to a "missionary or

---

1   ENGELSVIKEN, "Molo Wongel," 7.
2   Ibid., 25.

guest speaker from the West." This mission-independent revivalist was Chacha Omahe, who plays an important role in many histories of Ethiopian Pentecostalism.[3]
Engelsviken characterizes Chacha's ministry as a turning point, in which the "gifts
of the Spirit [. . .] became an experienced reality for the nucleus of those who were
destined to become the human instruments for the revival God was going to send."[4]
The conclusion to the story is emphatically presented thereafter:

> It was not the white missionaries who had conveyed this experience, but one
> of Africa's own black sons.[5]

Following Chacha's ministry, Engelsviken immediately turns to the break with the
missionaries at the Finnish mission station in Addis Ababa, which he presents as a
consequence of Chacha's ministry. Here the story of the missionary beginnings of
Ethiopian Pentecostalism has reached its goal. The missions had been one of many
instruments to prepare revival, but in the end they were unable to convey the central
Pentecostal experience to their Ethiopian followers. This was left to "one of Africa's
own black sons," who in turn helped to bring about the only conceivable consequence
to this story: missionary emancipation.

This master narrative is in keeping with the sources Engelsviken quotes, who for
the most part came from the Full Gospel Believers' Church (FGBC), which was de-
liberately founded as a mission-independent church, partially by former congregants
of the Finnish mission. These sources often depict their time with the missions as a
pre-Pentecostal crisis experience of yearning and waiting,[6] or as setting the stage for
a Pentecostal harvest.[7] They also emphasize the role of literature[8] and independent
prayer. In these accounts, missionaries are not portrayed as actively involved; they
merely initiate a first contact with international Pentecostal publications and tracts[9],
and even delay the revival by telling the Ethiopians to wait for the Spirit.[10] This characterization of the missionaries and their ministry permeates Engelsviken's account
and foreshadows their later displacement by an independent Pentecostal movement:

> The Finnish missionaries who led the mission followed a cautious course. Many
> of the young students who listened to the preaching of the missionaries and
> served as interpreters would later become leaders in the independent Ethiopian

---

3 See section 2.4, 69ff.
4 ENGELSVIKEN, "Molo Wongel," 28–29.
5 Ibid., 29.
6 Ibid., 20.
7 E.g. ibid., 21: "[. . .] we were ready for harvest. Many of us were completely ripe."
8 Ibid., 22–23, 24. The Pentecostal literature consumed by the youths is still often mentioned in
   interviews and mainly consisted of magazines like *The Full Gospel Business Men's Voice*, *Herald
   of His Coming*, *Voice of Healing*, or writings by T.L. Osborn, Oral Roberts, Morris Cerullo, and
   A. A. Allen.
9 E.g. e.g. ibid., 22–23: "In the beginning the missionaries themselves provided us with tracts and
   magazines, but we read in them where we could write in order to get them ourselves! In this way
   we established contact with Christian leaders [. . .]"
10 Ibid., 20.

Pentecostal movement, but at this point in time the leadership lay firmly in the hands of two female Finnish missionaries.[11]

The same narrative scheme can be found in other early histories, deriving partly from Engelsviken, but also from similar oral sources.[12] A number of later histories also follow this trajectory. Alemayehu Mekonnen, for example, concludes that "like Paul in Ephesus (Acts 19:2)," the missions "had prepared young Ethiopians to seek and pray for the gifts of the Holy Spirit."[13] Teka Obsa, narrating the history of the charismatic movement in the Evangelical Church Mekane Yesus (ECMY), sketches the missionaries' involvement in the beginnings of the Pentecostal movement as follows: "The work of the missionaries was the first positive influence on the incipient Pentecostal movement, but there arose a disagreement between the young Ethiopians and the Finnish missionaries."[14] This example from the ECMY also illustrates that the narrative scheme of mission independence was absorbed by different denominational backgrounds beyond the FGBC.

Following their narrative interest of relating the missions' contributions only to the beginnings of an independent Ethiopian movement, most of these histories merely mention those mission efforts which had direct connections with the later independent group, namely, the Finnish mission station in the Addis Ababa Merkato area, and the work of the Swedish Philadelphia Church Mission (SPCM) in Awasa. Other places and initiatives by the Northern European missionaries[15] are either left out completely or only mentioned in brief and often inaccurately.[16] The narratives also seem largely uninformed of the complex structures of the European mission initiatives resulting from their congregationalist background. Rather, the mission organizations often appear as uniform and monolithic institutions.[17]

---

11 ENGELSVIKEN, "Molo Wongel," 20. The explicit mention of the missionaries' gender also alludes to one of the arguments in the later conflict, see section 2.5, 79.

12 E.g. YOSIEF KIDANEWOLD, "The History of the Pentecostal Movement in Addis Abeba" relies on Engelsviken and oral informants. TAYE ABDISSA, "The Pentecostal Development and the Rise of Charismatic Movement in Ethiopia" merely references an interview as source of his account on missions.

13 ALEMAYEHU MEKONNEN, "Effects of Culture Change on Leadership in the Pentecostal/Charismatic Churches in Addis Ababa, Ethiopia," 128.

14 TEKA OBSA FOGI, "The Charismatic Movement in the EECMY," 71. The author explicitly relies on ENGELSVIKEN, "Molo Wongel" and TAYE ABDISSA, "The Pentecostal Development and the Rise of Charismatic Movement in Ethiopia," and his work is in turn reflected by the Gubae Egziabiher Church (GEC) scholar Bulutse Futuwi, see BULUTSE FUTUWI, "An Introduction to the Theology and Growth of Independent Churches in Ethiopia With Special Reference to Rhema Faith Church," 56–58.

15 See section 2.2, 52ff., and section 2.3, 59ff., for details on the different places and initiatives in which the Finnish and Swedish missionaries worked.

16 BEKELE WOLDEKIDAN, ልደታ, 64–69 is the most detailed and accurate of the mission accounts following the independent narrative scheme. Yet, even here, the stories are focused on the Merkato chapel and the Awasa station, seemingly oblivious to the impact of other mission initiatives and later developments.

17 Cf. e.g. BULUTSE FUTUWI, "An Introduction to the Theology and Growth of Independent Churches in Ethiopia With Special Reference to Rhema Faith Church," 57.

2.1.2   Asserting the Missionary Contribution

Histories by Pentecostal missionaries or writers from mission backgrounds present quite a different outlook. As is to be expected, they cover a wider range of activities, map out the missionary history in detail, and to some extent reveal political differences within their organizations. More importantly, they also engage in the debate about the origins of early Pentecostalism, explicitly or implicitly claiming a central role for missionaries in contrast to their marginalization in other sources. For them, it is absolutely clear that Pentecostalism began with the arrival of the missions, as is exemplified by the following summary statement by a Finnish missionary:

> It was 1951 when the first Finnish missionaries came here. They were Anna-Liisa and Sanfrid Mattsson, our pioneers. And that was the beginning of the Pentecostal movement in Ethiopia.[18]

The most extensive history of the Finnish mission endeavors can be found in an unpublished manuscript, compiled by the missionary Kyösti Roininen.[19], who spent over three decades in Ethiopia. Roininen argues for a central and initial contribution of his Finnish mission. Even though he notes that the mission had only few converts, he firmly roots the Ethiopian revival here:

> Still the undeniable fact is that the work done by the Finnish Mission in the nineteen fifties opened the doors to one of the biggest outpourings of the Spirit and was the beginning to the revivals that in the coming decades touched millions of Ethiopians.[20]

After this opening statement, the *Condensed History* narrates the missionary beginnings in different parts of the country, and subsequently places the first Pentecostal experience squarely within the Finnish mission in Addis Ababa:

> The determined gospel work at Addis Abeba Marcato area brought good results. The first believer was baptized in the Holy Spirit during the Bible-week in 1962. The printing of parts of the new Bible translation and the special permit to distribute them, opened doors to spreading of the Gospel, not only in meetings, but also in schools, and among the army and police units.[21]

The interesting composition of this paragraph hints at the importance of this first Spirit baptism experience in the author's narrative. Instead of recording a number of converts as the consequence of "determined gospel work", one single occurrence of Holy Spirit baptism is mentioned as the first "result", even before the undoubtedly broader achievement of scripture distribution in schools, among the army, and the police forces. Thus it appears as if not so much "results" of "gospel work" are meant to be presented here, but a significant break-through: the first Pentecostal experience in Ethiopia. The author then turns to the emerging student movement:

---

18 Interview no. 104.
19 ROININEN, "A Condensed History of the Finnish Mission in Ethiopia."
20 Ibid., 2
21 Ibid., 5.

In the middle of this decade of growth an unexpected "expansion" took place; something that was at that time seen by some as being divisionary. Some students at the Addis Ababa University were filled with the Holy Spirit, and began a new independent work. This new movement took hold of large crowds of University and College students. The result of this move was the beginning of the Full Gospel Churches of Ethiopia.[22]

Roininen carefully positions the independent student movement in his narrative here. Not only is it subsequent in a temporal sense (middle of the decade as opposed to 1962); moreover, it certainly does not stand out as a novelty. A "decade of growth" had already begun when the student movement emerged, which, in apparent irony, is called "an unexpected 'expansion'." The author evidently does not want to acknowledge these developments as division, only "some" misunderstood it as such "at that time." His transdenominational outlook certainly articulates the author's openness to the movement, but it is also necessary to identify this "new independent work" as part of the same endeavor the missionaries were laboring in, especially since it affected their flock:

> Of the six original elders in this new church, three were from the Finnish Mission: Melese Wogu, Kebede Wolde Mariam and Fantahun Gebru. "The influence by the brothers that came from the Mission was a balancing factor in the beginning of the FGC [=FGBC]. They had for many years been under the sound teaching ministry of the missionaries, and were also themselves preachers": says Tormod Engelsviken, a professor of the Norwegian Mission [...] He has made a scientific study of the birth of FGC and has also written the history of this great Pentecostal Church Movement. The work in Addis Center was revived, and in the late sixties new national leaders were in charge of the work.[23]

Before conceding the significance of the Ethiopian exodus for the Addis Ababa mission station (the work had to be "revived"), Roininen first focuses on the missionaries' influence, tracing their work directly to the establishment of the FGBC. This assertion of missionary impact is even safeguarded by quoting Engelsviken as an academic authority.[24] Thus, the narrative presented here is a story of continuity from the missions to the independent movement. While the work of the missionaries cannot be presented as the only influence on the Ethiopian church, the Finnish mission

---

22 ROININEN, "A Condensed History of the Finnish Mission in Ethiopia," 5.
23 Ibid. It is unclear why only six elders are mentioned here, most sources report seven. See below, section 3.4.4, 132.
24 The source of this quotation is not indicated. Also the phrase "the brothers that came from the Mission" seems somewhat ambiguous in Engelsviken's statement (which mission?). There is a similar statement in ENGELSVIKEN, "Molo Wongel," 50, yet, at the same time the author limits any notion of continuity there: "It was the people from the Finnish Mission who were the 'oldest' as Christians and in virtue of their experience and knowledge had most influence during this time. They were also the ones who most vigorously fought for an independent, organized Ethiopian church body. The conflict with the missionaries may form part of the background for this."

is portrayed as the place of significant initial breakthroughs, and is even connected to the formation of the FGBC.[25]

On behalf of the Swedish Pentecostal missions, a similar narrative can be found in Ruth Ramstrand's account of her life as missionary in Liberia and Ethiopia.[26] Karl and Ruth Ramstrand were the leading Swedish missionaries in Ethiopia during the early years, and therefore sought to define their own contribution to the Pentecostal movement. In her memoirs, Ruth Ramstrand narrated the following unexpected outpouring of the Spirit in 1962, in a chapter titled "A Spiritual Breakthrough in the Summer Bible School:"

> We had asked the colleagues Birgit Olsson and Bernt Einarsson to take care of the prayer meeting together with our older children and to collect the students who wanted to participate. This had developed into a "dry" prayer meeting. No great pace or intensity. [...] Then the Holy Spirit suddenly fell over all, as we read it had done at the first Pentecost in Jerusalem, during the time of the first Christians. All who participated in the meeting fell to the ground. Many experienced a baptism in the Spirit and spoke in other languages. One of the Ethiopians brought forth a message in Swedish! And our Kristina, who then was eleven years old, brought forth a message in English. Five of the students were baptized in the Spirit and all were wrestled to the ground. Some wept, others rejoiced and all prayed and praised the Lord loudly.[27]

Hearing the noise, Ramstrands joined the meeting and identified the outpouring as identical with experiences in Sweden. For Ethiopia it thus marks the beginning of the Pentecostal experience:

> This was something that we knew in Sweden. Jubilation and praise, crying and confession of sins to one another. Something completely new in Ethiopia. A little dry prayer meeting with mostly children and youths, but God, the Lord and Creator of the universe, let his Spirit fall upon them. It was wonderful for us to have experienced this here in Ethiopia, here from the beginning on.[28]

It is evident that the event is represented as the initial outpouring of the Holy Spirit in Ethiopia, and as such it would compete with the impact of Chacha Omahe in Awasa: it occurred one year earlier and stands in direct contact to the missionaries. It is noticeable that Ruth Ramstrand does not mention Chacha Omahe at all in her book, but this might be explained by the fact that she left Ethiopia together with her husband in the beginning of 1963.[29] Her husband, Karl Ramstrand, however, returned

---

25 Cf. also ROININEN, *Koskettakaa Lastani*, 189–190 which states that the Ethiopian Pentecostal movement grew from the Merkato church.

26 RAMSTRAND, *Guds lilla piga far dit pepparn växer.*

27 Ibid., 187, also mentioned in interview no. 81. The story was also published in a magazine for the 40th anniversary of Hiwot Berhan Church (HBC), from where it was incorporated by BEKELE WOLDEKIDAN, ሕይወት, 83. However, since Bekele follows Engelsviken's independency paradigm, he subordinates this experience to the ministry of the Kenyan evangelist Chacha Omahe, both chronologically and in importance.

28 RAMSTRAND, *Guds lilla piga far dit pepparn växer*, 187.

29 See ibid., 202–212, where she narrates the long journey home to Sweden via car and boat.

to Ethiopia for one more working period and not only met Chacha in 1964,[30] but likely was familiar with the stories of his impact in 1963. Even so, he downplayed the importance of Chacha in his memoirs,[31] and the event of initial Spirit outpouring in this book was again the prayer meeting of 1962.[32] When Karl Ramstrand wrote about this incident closer to the time, he celebrated it as an instance of God's divine and unexpected intervention, but did not characterize it as the long awaited breakthrough leading to new opportunities.[33] It arguably became such a defining moment only later on, when the history of Ethiopian Pentecostalism was written, and competing narratives, such as Chacha's ministry, had emerged.

This marginalization of Chacha is strangely mirrored in the Kenyan evangelist's own account about the events, in which he in turn completely fails to mention the missionary contacts which brought him to Ethiopia, nor the role that the Swedish mission played for the movement. In his curriculum vitae from 1970, Chacha noted:

> Back in 1963 the Lord spoke to me about Ethiopia and in August of the same year I went to that country to teach the Bible in which venture the Lord blessed his Word mightily, about 165 received the Holy Spirit and spoke in tongues. This number included City and country believers. To follow up my Mission I went back to Ethiopia in 1964 and 1966 to superintend my new converts and as a result Spirit filled believers are now everywhere in Ethiopia sowing the Seed which is the word of God.[34]

At this point in time Chacha had already broken his relations with the missionaries for whom he had worked in Kenya, and had formed his own organization. Therefore he was probably not inclined to mention the instrumental role of Swedish missionaries in bringing him to Ethiopia. However, it is noticeable that his remarks do not reflect the mission-independence paradigm later so prevalent in Engelsviken's account. Rather, Chacha is the protagonist in a classic missionary tale: the Lord called him, he obeyed and God "mightily blessed" his work, the results being carefully quantified. Moreover, the Ethiopians are characterized as Chacha's "converts" who need his "supervision," and their role in bringing the end result ("Spirit filled believers are now everywhere in Ethiopia") is undefined.

2.1.3 Claiming the Missions' Legacy for Ethiopian Churches

This narrative dynamic of missionary influence versus mission independence is also evident in the ambiguous stance of histories from the two Pentecostal churches that the

---

30 Cf. e.g. KARL RAMSTRAND, Letter to supporting congregations, 30 August 1964, Karl Ramstrand Collection, Pingstarkiv Kaggeholm, Ekerö.

31 For example, Ramstrand introduced Chacha here with the characterization of Mattson-Boze, who said that "he is not a great teacher, but he can set people lose," see RAMSTRAND, *Det heliga äventyret*, 133.

32 EVY NORRMAN, "Transcript of Interview with Karl Ramstrand, conducted 27 September, 1989 by Jonny Bkörnler," Etiopien Interviews, Pingstarkiv Kaggeholm, Ekerö, 1989, 8; RAMSTRAND, *Det heliga äventyret*, 125. An influence by the Kenyan revivalist is not mentioned in either source.

33 KARL RAMSTRAND, "ETIOPIEN – ett mognande skördefält," [Ethiopia – A Ripe Harvest Field.], *Evangelii Härold* 45 (1962): 6–7.

34 CHACHA OMAHE, "Life and Experience in the Lord's Ministry": *From 1946–1970, July*, private collection, Mukiria Chacha, 1970.

missions initiated, namely, the Gennet Church (GC) and the Hiwot Berhan Church (HBC). Both churches claim their missionary heritage by noting its historic primacy and tracing its influence to the independent Pentecostal movement, most notably the FGBC. Yet at the same time they also seem to be interested in asserting their own mission independence and telling their story of mission emancipation.

One case in point is Seleshi Kebede's history of the Gennet Church.[35] The author notes that the Pentecostal revival "came to Ethiopia through Finnish missionaries in 1951"[36] and he is familiar with many details of the mission work. In describing the missionaries' input, there are no notions of them withholding or suppressing the Holy Spirit, instead the author asserts that the GC received their Pentecostal doctrine through the Finnish mission.[37] However, in the section titled "First Pentecostal Experience"[38] the author quotes a testimony by one informant in which the reception of the Holy Spirit is portrayed as anything but a smooth process. It is characterized as the result of a one or two year long struggle of intense longing for the "power of the Holy Spirit"[39], ending with the preliminary conclusion "that this gift is meant only for the missionaries."[40] Later, a certain believer encountered Spirit baptism, but whereas this may have taught the Ethiopians "that the gift is meant for us too,"[41] an actual breakthrough in experience is attributed to Chacha's ministry, much like in histories from the independent movement. When subsequently narrating the separation of believers from the Finnish mission and the formation of the FGBC, Seleshi's account is again reminiscent of the missionary reports, as he asserts that "those who split from the Finnish Mission were the first prominent leaders in Mulu Wengel [FGBC] church"[42]. Finally, the author's ambiguous stance on the Finnish mission heritage is again reflected in the last chapter, where he articulates his gratitude to the missionaries' for their commitment to Ethiopia and the doctrinal foundations laid by them, but notes at the same time that they were hindering national leadership and did not contribute enough to leadership training.[43]

Another instance of such an ambiguous narrative may be found in the magazine celebrating the GC's 50th anniversary, which is an interesting collage of historical excerpts, documents and interviews.[44] There are short histories narrating the mission beginnings and their achievements in different regions[45] as well as a portrait of the Finnish missionary Sanfrid Mattsson,[46] saturated with appreciation for this Pentecostal pioneer. However, there also is an interview with one of the early church leaders presenting in detail different Ethiopian groups that had broken off from the

---

35 SELESHI KEBEDE, "The History of the Guenet Church."
36 Ibid., 1.
37 See ibid., 4, 22–23.
38 Ibid., 4.
39 Ibid.
40 Ibid., 5.
41 Ibid.
42 Ibid., 8.
43 Ibid., 22–24.
44 ETHIOPIAN GENNET CHURCH, የ50ኛው ዓመት የወርቅ ኢዮቤልዩ በዓል.
45 Ibid., 15–17.
46 Ibid., 21–22.

Finnish mission.[47] In addition, the magazine provides the reader with an Amharic translation of the above-mentioned testimony, which details the long struggle for the Holy Spirit finally to be released under Chacha's ministry,[48] and places this story under the title "The first Pentecostal movement."[49]

Oral interviews from the HBC, the church which resulted from the Swedish mission work, show a similar ambivalence, even though the relationship between the Swedish missionaries and the Ethiopians was generally smoother and more amicable. Reminiscent of Swedish missionary reports, Ethiopian sources from the first church in Awasa emphasize that people from all over Ethiopia came to the SPCM summer Bible schools conducted there and received their initial Spirit baptism.[50] This outlook will also result in claims on the independent Pentecostal movement, for example in statements like: "In 1960 Ethiopian calendar, .. Mulu Wongel [=FGBC] split from us."[51] However, the same informant also contended that Pentecostal instruction about tongues and prophecies began with the Kenyan revivalist Chacha Omahe, and not with the missionaries, who, in his view, mainly taught about salvation and were opposed to loud and intense practices. Moreover, strong assertions of mission independence can be found in statements by HBC leaders:

> Now this is a fully independent indigenous church. If I come to this history, it is a long history. There was a time that we divorced. Especially when the communism came they left us you know, and we remained alone just under this persecution. So in fact when communism was over they tried to come again and then we said no. If you are coming we can do a partnership, but two organizations just recognizing one another.[52]

2.1.4 Marginalized Foreign Missions

As is evident from the sources cited so far, the debate about the missionary contribution to Ethiopian Pentecostalism centers on defining the role of the Finnish and Swedish missions. There also were a number of other Pentecostal missionaries, which however, are rarely mentioned, even though, some predate the arrival of the Northern European missions. The earliest Pentecostal mission endeavor is linked to three female American missionaries by the name of Bertha Dommermuth, Ruth Shippey and Ellen French who worked in Ethiopia from 1934 to 1938. All three had studied at the Elim Bible Institute in Lima, New York, and at least Dommermuth and Shippey had been ordained by Elim as "Ministers of the Gospel of Jesus Christ"[53]. Though the

---

47 ETHIOPIAN GENNET CHURCH, የ50ኛው ዓመት የወርች ኢ.የቤ.ልዩ በዓል, 18–20.
48 Cf. SELESHI KEBEDE, "The History of the Guenet Church," 4–5.
49 ETHIOPIAN GENNET CHURCH, የ50ኛው ዓመት የወርች ኢ.የቤ.ልዩ በዓል, 33.
50 E.g. interviews no. 12; 119.
51 Interview no. 12.
52 Interview no. 27.
53 RICE, *Sister Bertha, Sister Ruth*, 96-97. Tibebe Eshete (TIBEBE ESHETE, *The Evangelical Movement in Ethiopia*, 149) mistakenly states that they were from the Assemblies of God, New York. However, only French came from Avoca, New York state, and her denominational affiliation is not provided in any of the sources about her. Dommermuth and Shippey, on the other hand, came from Avoca, Pennsylvania (not New York). They were affiliated with an independent Pentecostal fellowship.

three missionaries had originally hoped to set up a mission station in interior Ethiopia, they only managed to establish a work in Addis Ababa, initially ministering to the Armenian and Greek communities, and later engaging in school work among Ethiopians and foreigners. After the Italian invasion in 1936 they stayed on for two more years, despite very difficult conditions for their work.[54] During this time they were asked by Swedish Lutheran missionaries and their Ethiopian coworkers to look after their Addis Ababa Entoto compound when the Swedish missionaries were forced to leave the country.[55] It was during this stay at the Entoto compound that the three missionaries were most successful, gathering young people affiliated with the Swedish Lutheran Mission and its school in Pentecostal prayer meetings.[56] After this work again was limited by political interference, the three women finally left Ethiopia in 1938, and no more long-term mission endeavors to Ethiopia have been undertaken by Elim missionaries since.[57]

The impact of this early Pentecostal mission enterprise by all appearances was rather limited, and there is no historical connection to the later Pentecostal groups. Even contemporaneous American Pentecostal sources outside Elim seem to be unaware of this mission. Though there are some articles in Pentecostal periodicals about the war between Ethiopia and Italy, none of them mention a Pentecostal mission there.[58] Later on, the Finnish missionaries Sanfrid and Anna-Liisa Mattsson evidently came across a mention of their work, but their knowledge was very vague. They merely mentioned the missionaries in two letters in order to illustrate the small scope of Pentecostal missions so far.[59] Apparently the three Elim missionaries them-

---

54 Their premises had been confiscated by the Italians, one of their followers killed, and the missionaries themselves were regarded with suspicion by other missions and the Italian occupants, RICE, *Sister Bertha, Sister Ruth*, 164–191.

55 Ibid., 178–180. Among their acquaintances also were Qes Badima and Emmanuel Gebre Selassie who later became instrumental in the formation of the ECMY, cf. e.g. LAUNHARDT, *Evangelicals in Addis Ababa (1919–1991)*, 142–145. Emmanuel Gebre Selassie was also in contact with the later Finnish and Swedish Pentecostal missionaries, RAMSTRAND, *Det heliga äventyret*, 109–110.

56 BERTHA DOMMERMUTH, ELLEN FRENCH, and RUTH SHIPPEY, "Revival in Ethiopia," *Elim Pentecostal Herald* 7 (51 1937): 10–11; RICE, *Sister Bertha, Sister Ruth*, 186–187.

57 This was confirmed in e-mail correspondence with Paul Johansson, chancellor of the Elim Bible Institute, PAUL JOHANSSON, E-mail to author, 10 October 2006. Hollenweger mentions the Elim Missionary Assemblies as being present in Ethiopia with four churches, and specifies Kenneth Oglesby as contact, see WALTER J. HOLLENWEGER, *Handbuch der Pfingstbewegung*, 10 vols. (Genf: Univ. Diss., 1965), II. Hauptteil, p. 12 . However, though Elim was informed about Oglesby's work (cf. e.g. IVAN Q. SPENCER, "Ethiopia," *Elim Pentecostal Herald* 7 (4 1956): 15), he did not work for Elim but rather as a free-lance missionary, occasionally collaborating with the SPCM. Since Oglesby did not have any churches of his own it is unclear what Hollenweger refers to here.

58 See e.g. STANLEY HOWARD FRODSHAM, "The Editor's Notebook," *The Pentecostal Evangel*, 1124 1935, 4, 9; HARRY J. STEIL, "Ethiopia versus Italy," *The Pentecostal Evangel*, 1120 1935, 1,17–18; HAROLD STREET, "The Lid is Off: The Truth About Ethiopia," *The Latter Rain Evangel* 29 (6 1938). Ironically, one of the articles in the Pentecostal Latter Rain Evangel (ibid.) is by a missionary from the Sudan Interior Mission (SIM), which the Elim missionaries called "a thorn in our flesh", because of the organization's opposition against their work, RICE, *Sister Bertha, Sister Ruth*, 186.

59 On two occasions "3 American sisters" are mentioned in correspondence, who stayed for "two years" during the Italian occupation, SANFRID MATTSSON, Circular letter, 25 June 1962, Sanfrid and Anna-Liisa Mattsson Collection, Fida Archives, Helsinki; ANNA-LIISA MATTSSON, Letter to Tapani Kärnä, 10 May 1964, Correspondence Others, Fida Archives, Helsinki.

selves had concluded that they had not left behind any established work,[60] and during a return visit in 1969 they found many of their most important followers pursuing different paths.[61] However, it is peculiar that the account about their trip does not mention the emerging Pentecostal movement in Ethiopia at all, even though they note that their airport escort included two Swedish Pentecostal missionaries[62] and that "[a]lmost every day was taken up with ministry, lunches, and speaking engagements."[63] It is unclear whether they simply were not aware of its existence,[64] or did not attribute it much significance. However, by all appearances they did not establish lasting contacts with the emerging Pentecostal movement, nor are there any manifest interests to trace their contribution to this revival.

So far, the only source which has taken up the story of the three Elim missionaries, is Tibebe Eshete's recent historical account. Tibebe first became aware of this early Pentecostal initiative during a visit at the Elim Bible Institute,[65] and based his report on oral information by representatives of the institute, the archive material found there,[66] and the biography of Bertha Dommermuth and Ruth Shippey by the Pentecostal writer Marie Rice. Since Tibebe is interested in providing a comprehensive chronology of Ethiopian Pentecostalism, his discovery of this early mission endeavor comes as a noteworthy achievement, but it has no consequence to his narrative of origin, since he notes that the missionaries' work "has not been a source of the Pentecostal movement"[67] and that the information about the Elim missions even "came as a surprise for the Ethiopian Pentecostals who instituted the movement."[68]

Another early Pentecostal minister working early in Ethiopia was the missionary Kenneth Oglesby. He had originally been an SIM missionary in northwestern Ethiopia, where he even had provided shelter to emperor Haile Selassie on one occasion, when the latter fled to Addis Ababa after his defeat by the Italian invaders in 1936.[69] When

---

60 See RICE, *Sister Bertha, Sister Ruth*, 191.

61 See ibid., 238–243.

62 See ibid., 238.It is unclear who the missionaries were. The SPCM correspondence does not mention their visit.

63 Ibid., 238, 240. Since this book was based on interviews with two of the missionaries, such additional information might well have gotten lost.

64 This is what Tibebe Eshete concludes, see TIBEBE ESHETE, *The Evangelical Movement in Ethiopia*, 151n20. However, given their contacts with Pentecostal missionaries and their multiple ministry engagements, this does not seem very likely.

65 See TIBEBE ESHETE, "Growing Through the Storms," 47. The current chancellor of the Elim Bible Institute, Paul Johansson, was a missionary to Kenya with personal connections to Chacha Omahe, which is probably what led Tibebe to him, cf. ibid., 291, 369 note 51. Johansson likely alerted him to the early Elim initiative, like he did in correspondence with this author as well, see PAUL JOHANSSON, E-mail to author, 25 July 2006.

66 See DOMMERMUTH, FRENCH, and SHIPPEY, "Revival in Ethiopia"; ELLEN FRENCH, "Field Report from Addis Ababa, Ethiopia," *Elim Pentecostal Herald* 8 (57 1938): 8–9; ELLEN FRENCH, "Field Report from Addis Ababa, Ethiopia," *Elim Pentecostal Herald* 8 (59 1938): 8.

67 TIBEBE ESHETE, "Growing Through the Storms," 279, cf. TIBEBE ESHETE, *The Evangelical Movement in Ethiopia*, 151.

68 TIBEBE ESHETE, "Growing Through the Storms," 47.

69 See COTTERELL, *Born at Midnight*, 92; RAMSTRAND, *Det heliga äventyret*, 107–108. BEKELE WOLDEKIDAN, ሪጅቫል, 132 apparently misread Ramstrand here and places the episode during the emperor's return from exile in 1941, being followed in this by TIBEBE ESHETE, *The Evangelical Movement in Ethiopia*, 154.

Oglesby turned Pentecostal, the SIM barred him from reentry after a sabbatical. However, on account of his former service to Haile Selassie, he managed to activate connections to the reinstated emperor, and returned to Ethiopia with a permit in 1956.[70] Working more or less as a free-lance missionary, he later also cooperated with the Swedish Pentecostal mission.[71]

With the exception of sources relating to Swedish and Finnish missionaries,[72] Oglesby was only remembered by two recent histories of Ethiopian Pentecostalism. Bekele Woldekidan devoted a section to him, however, not under his chapter about the beginnings of the Pentecostal movement in Ethiopia, but in a later part of the book, where he reviews the relationship of Haile Selassie with Pentecostal Christians in order to show that the Emperor had had enough encounters with Pentecostals to know that he should not ostracize the movement.[73] The second history mentioning Oglesby again is Tibebe, who included him under "External Influences"[74] while noting that "we do not know much about his role and legacy."[75]

Three visiting Pentecostals should also be mentioned here. In 1952 Jane Collins Daoud led a successful evangelism and healing campaign in the Addis Ababa stadium for two months, which received considerable public attention.[76] Apparently there even were official police records of healing testimonies given during this campaign,[77] and her campaign probably had a considerable impact at the time, lending her the popular title "St. Mary of the Stadium."[78]

Daoud's position in the histories of Ethiopian Pentecostalism, however, is the same as Oglesby's. She is mentioned by Bekele to demonstrate the Emperor's contact with Pentecostalism,[79] and Tibebe included her, "not because the visit [...] had any bearing on the rise of the Pentecostal movement in Ethiopia," but because it "publicly stressed a crucial element of the Pentecostal movement: the healing service, which later constituted a pivotal component of the activities of the Ethiopian Pentecostals."[80]

---

70 Ibid.; SPENCER, "Ethiopia."
71 RAMSTRAND, *Det heliga äventyret*, 107–109.
72 Ibid.; BEKELE WOLDEKIDAN, ረብሻ, 131–132; RAMSTRAND, *Guds lilla piga far dit pepparn växer*, 147–148; TILLANDER, *Näkymättömän lähettiläs*, 265–266.
73 See BEKELE WOLDEKIDAN, ረብሻ, 131–132.
74 See TIBEBE ESHETE, *The Evangelical Movement in Ethiopia*, 149–154.
75 See ibid., 154.
76 JANE COLLINS DAOUD, *Miracles and Mission and World-Wide Evangelism* (Dallas, TX, 1953), 72–105; see also BEKELE WOLDEKIDAN, ረብሻ, 132–134; TIBEBE ESHETE, *The Evangelical Movement in Ethiopia*, 152.
77 DAOUD, *Miracles and Mission and World-Wide Evangelism*, 78–105; BEKELE WOLDEKIDAN, ረብሻ, illustrations following p. 150.
78 Ibid., 133–134. Just prior to her Ethiopia campaign she had married the evangelist Mounir Aziz Daoud in Lebanon, who is rarely mentioned in connection with their ministry in Ethiopia, and in these early days rather seems to have stood on the sidelines of their joint ministry, cf. DAOUD, *Miracles and Mission and World-Wide Evangelism*, 72–105. On the Daoud's joint ministry, see also JAMES ALLAN HEWETT, "Daoud, Mounir Aziz," in *Dictionary of Pentecostal and Charismatic Movements*, 6th ed., ed. PATRICK H. ALEXANDER, STANLEY M. BURGESS, and GARY B. McGEE (Grand Rapids, MI: Zondervan, 1998), 237.
79 BEKELE WOLDEKIDAN, ረብሻ, 133–134.
80 TIBEBE ESHETE, *The Evangelical Movement in Ethiopia*, 152.

The two other Pentecostal visiting evangelists are only mentioned by Bekele. One of them was Brian Williams, whose visit to Ethiopia is only narrated briefly, in order to note that Haile Selassie had another encounter with a Pentecostal during Williams' "crusade" from February 26 to March 24, 1965.[81] Williams also ministered at the Finnish mission in Addis Ababa and other places, and Bekele notes that "people accepted the Lord, they were set free from bondage by evil spirits, they were healed from disease, and one brother who had come from the town of Harar was baptized in the Holy Spirit and spoke in tongues." The mention of the "brother from Harar" is peculiar, since this story pertains to the prominent revival movement there, which Bekele also extensively discusses in a different chapter, focused on the arrival of Pentecostalism in Ethiopia.[82] Yet, Bekele does not connect these two narratives at any point, and concludes his story about Brian Williams by again mentioning that the royal family frequently contacted the Pentecostal evangelist so that he might pray over them.

A later itinerant Pentecostal evangelist mentioned by Bekele was Ruth Heflin, who visited Ethiopia on three occasions, twice in 1967 and again in 1971.[83] She had come in contact with the Finnish missionaries Sanfrid and Anna-Liisa Mattsson and also ministered at their house in 1967.[84] The primary purpose of her trips seems to have been to deliver prophetic messages to emperor Haile Selassie in person, which she managed to do on two occasions.[85] However, she later also claimed a lasting impact on the Ethiopian revival:

> Even to this day, many of those who were baptized in the Spirit during those months of revival are leaders in the Lord's work in many places. One of them was Beta Mengistu, who is now considered by the Ethiopian church (which is scattered all over the world) to be the apostle of the church. [...] He, along with others of those young people who were products of those meetings, lead the church forward.[86]

Like Oglesby and Williams, Bekele only took up Heflin's visit in order to show that Haile Selassie received messages from God through Pentecostals. Yet he did not connect her ministry to the Ethiopian Pentecostal movement. Though he extensively

---

81 See BEKELE WOLDEKIDAN, ረብደሳ, 134. Cf. also Williams' diary entry about the Ethiopia visit, BRIAN DAVID WILLIAMS, "The Amazing Ethiopia Crusade: Diary Entry" (1965), http://web.ukonline.co.uk/brian.david.williams/diary/1964.html (accessed July 7, 2007).

82 See BEKELE WOLDEKIDAN, ረብደሳ, 84–87. With regard to the Harar revival and the alleged Brian Williams connection, see below, 104.

83 RUTH W. HEFLIN, *Harvest Glory: I ask for the Nations* (Hagerstown, MD: McDougal Publishing, 1999), 114–119, 126–131, 178–179, 411.

84 Ibid., 128; BEKELE WOLDEKIDAN, ረብደሳ, 135–136. Her ministry is also mentioned in interviews no. 5; 116. Apparently she had also come in contact with Swedish Pentecostal missionaries, RAMSTRAND, *Guds lilla piga far dit pepparn växer*, 216–217.

85 In this context Heflin reveals her royalist inclinations, in statements like "In the presence of a king there is a great sense of majesty and awe", which is continued by a reference to the prostration before the heavenly king in Rev. 1,17–18, RUTH W. HEFLIN, *Glory: Experiencing the Atmosphere of Heaven* (Hagerstown, MD: McDougal Publishing, 1990), 104.

86 HEFLIN, *Harvest Glory*, 131. This assertion does not match up with other sources about Betta Mengistu's Spirit baptism, including his own account, according to which he would already have been baptized in the Spirit in 1965. Cf. below, 93.

used Heflin's account, for example by taking up her estimation that "more than five hundred university students were filled with the Holy Spirit"[87], he did not engage with or even mention the above-quoted contention of her impact on the inception of Ethiopian Pentecostalism.

In general, therefore, it is evident that missionaries and evangelists outside the Finnish and Swedish mission endeavors only hold a marginal position in the historical archive about Ethiopian Pentecostalism. Most accounts do not seem to be aware of the early Elim missionaries and Oglesby's work in the country, neither do they consider it necessary to mention Pentecostal traveling evangelists as a source of outside influence. The two recent sources introducing these narratives to the historiography of Ethiopian Pentecostalism are no exception. Bekele does not connect their stories to the revival in Ethiopia itself, but only to the Imperial government, in order to show that Haile Selassie knew Pentecostalism well and had the power to stop persecution, but instead had chosen to ignore God's messages sent to him by these Pentecostal envoys. Thus, these stories are not connected to Bekele's mission narrative, but to his later report about the persecution of Pentecostals and ultimately, in his view, the spiritual cause to the revolution. Tibebe Eshete on the other hand, took up some of these stories because they complement his interest to provide a comprehensive account of "external influences" to Ethiopian Pentecostalism. However, they are not important for his narrative, since only the Finnish and Swedish Pentecostal missions "had a palpable influence upon the development of the Pentecostal movement in Ethiopia."[88]

The evaluation of the Swedish and Finnish influence, in turn, is subject to certain narrative schemes, which define the missionary contribution to the origins of Ethiopian Pentecostalism. The earliest and strongest narrative scheme is that of mission independence, which originated with the national Pentecostal movement in alliance with a Western missionary, who connected it to the mission-critical impulses of his time. The resulting story assigns only a preparatory role to the European missionaries who are otherwise unable to actually spark the revival. This view, in turn, has been contested strongly by missionary accounts and the histories they inform, which clearly demarcate their influence in the emergence of Ethiopian Pentecostalism. The missionaries' legacy, however, has only been reluctantly claimed by the churches resulting from their work. While they adopt the missionary heritage in order to assert their historical primacy in contrast to the FGBC's narrative, they nevertheless illustrate the strength of the independence narrative by providing their own accounts of mission emancipation.

The main differences in these histories converge around three specific issues: the nature and extent of the missionaries' work, their contribution to the beginning of the Pentecostal revival in Ethiopia, and their relationship to the independent movement. These three issues will therefore be examined in the remainder of the chapter, which details the Finnish and Swedish Pentecostal mission work, analyzes the stories told about the Kenyan revivalist Chacha Omahe, and finally studies accounts of the first separation of believers from the Finnish mission.

---

87 Ibid., 128; cf. BEKELE WOLDEKIDAN, ረፒዛናa, 136.
88 TIBEBE ESHETE, *The Evangelical Movement in Ethiopia*, 153.

2.2   The Finnish Pentecostal Mission

2.2.1   The Establishment of a Free Mission

The Finnish Pentecostal mission initiatives in Ethiopia began with the arrival of Anna-Liisa and Sanfrid Mattsson on September 23, 1951.[89] Sanfrid Mattsson was a member of the Swedish minority in Finland,[90] and joined the Pentecostal movement in 1912.[91] He is often characterized as a humble, friendly, and personable man, who was especially skilled in business, whereas his significantly younger wife Anna-Liisa is portrayed as a brilliant polyglot and energetic leader.[92] In 1937 they founded their mission organization Scripture Publishers To Every Creature (SPTEC), which was strictly based on the principles of faith missions, having been inspired by the work and writings of Hudson Taylor.[93] This understanding of mission not only influenced their earlier initiatives in Finland, but significantly shaped their work and organization in Ethiopia as well.

This meant first and foremost that Mattssons were careful to protect the independence of their work and organization, which often left them in opposition to forces calling for a more central coordination of the Finnish Pentecostal mission efforts. Due to the strong emphasis on congregationalism in the Finnish Pentecostal movement, any attempts to centrally coordinate or administrate mission efforts had always been discussed controversially, since they were seen as a threat to the autonomy of local congregations. In Mattssons' time the main issue in this regard was the reestablishment of the Finnish Free Foreign Mission (FFFM) and related attempts at creating central policies for the coordination and financing of foreign missions.[94] Mattssons

---

89 ROININEN, "A Condensed History of the Finnish Mission in Ethiopia," 1.
90 Sanfrid Mattsson was not much of a linguist and admits in correspondence that writing in good Finnish is difficult for him, see SANFRID MATTSSON, Letter to Tapani Kärnä, 27 April 1963, Sanfrid and Anna-Liisa Mattsson Collection, Fida Archives, Helsinki.
91 ANNA-LIISA MATTSSON and SANFRID MATTSSON, Letter to Tapani Kärnä, 19 November 1962, Sanfrid and Anna-Liisa Mattsson Collection, Fida Archives, Helsinki.
92 E.g. TILLANDER, Näkymättömän lähettiläs, 257; also interview no. 102. This constellation is still reflected by Ethiopian sources, e.g. in ETHIOPIAN GENNET CHURCH, የ5ዐ⁷ው ዓመት የወርቅ ኢየቤልዩ በዓል, 22, quoting Sanfrid's solomonic answer to the question of headship in his household: "It is true, I am the head, I am the chief of the house. My wife on the other hand is the neck, the neck is what turns the head."
93 For Taylor's influence on their understanding of mission, cf. TILLANDER, Näkymättömän lähettiläs, 123–126.
94 The FFFM was founded in 1927 and approved as a serving body by some congregations. However, due to opposition by some local churches against all central activities, it was suspended in 1929 and not reactivated until 1950. Cf. K. B. WESTMAN et al., Nordisk Missionshistoria, [Scandinavian Mission History.] (Stockholm: Missionsförbundets Förlag, 1949), 261–262; LAURI K. AHONEN, "Finland," in The New International Dictionary of Pentecostal and Charismatic Movements, ed. STANLEY M. BURGESS and EDUARD M. van der MAAS (Grand Rapids, MI: Zondervan, 2002), 104; VELI-MATTI KÄRKKÄINEN, "'From the Ends of the Earth' – The Expansion of Finnish Pentecostal Missions from 1927–1997," The Journal of the European Pentecostal Research Association 20 (2000): 125–126; VELI-MATTI KÄRKKÄINEN, "The Pentecostal Movement in Finland," The Journal of the European Pentecostal Research Association 23 (2003): 120. Kärkkäinen mentions 1928 as the founding year, but the festschrift for the 70th anniversary of the FFFM dates its beginnings to 1927, albeit without mentioning the years of suspended activities, see HILPINEN, Lähetystyön monet kasvot, 13.

regretted the reactivation of the "old bone"[95] FFFM, and while they were not completely against such helper organizations, they strongly opposed any centralization in the areas of finances and sending out of missionaries, fearing that this would only paralyze the mission movement.[96]

This competitive constellation of two organizations and mission principles accompanied the first decades of the Finnish mission work in Ethiopia. Mattssons' SPTEC was the only registered Finnish Pentecostal mission organization in Ethiopia and thus served as the public and legal face for all Finnish Pentecostal mission initiatives. However, Mattssons did not have the resources nor the intention to financially support other missionaries, since they strictly applied faith mission principles to their work, even refusing regular support for their own personal needs.[97] Thus, other missionaries working with SPTEC in Ethiopia were sent out and financed by their home churches, and this support was most often channeled through the FFFM.[98] The missionaries also had the ultimate responsibility for their respective stations, independently organizing the work, reporting to donors and mission offices in Finland, and securing the means for their projects.[99] The work was of course coordinated through correspon-

95 ANNA-LIISA MATTSSON and SANFRID MATTSSON, Letter to Yrjö Nurmi, Tapani Kärnä, Kunnas, Otto Koivukangas, Oiva Uusitupa and Arvo Hankkio, 7 September 1963, Sanfrid and Anna-Liisa Mattsson Collection, Fida Archives, Helsinki.

96 This is taken up in several of their letters, see esp. MATTSSON and MATTSSON, Letter to Tapani Kärnä, November 19, 1962; and MATTSSON and MATTSSON, Letter to Yrjö Nurmi, Tapani Kärnä, Kunnas, Otto Koivukangas, Oiva Uusitupa and Arvo Hankkio, September 7, 1963. They often voice their opposition to a certain paragraph 36, which apparently dictated that the financing of missionaries should only come from the local church they were sent from, while the FFFM would assist with the conversion and transfer of funds. This would, of course, significantly reduce fundraising options for independent faith mission organizations like SPTEC, cf. PAULI RUNOLINNA, E-mail to author, 7 December 2006; MATTSSON and MATTSSON, Letter to Yrjö Nurmi, Tapani Kärnä, Kunnas, Otto Koivukangas, Oiva Uusitupa and Arvo Hankkio, September 7, 1963. The matter was further complicated by the fact that Mattssons retained their mission home in Larsmo, Finland, which served in missionary education, and did not yield to demands to give up control over it. In SANFRID MATTSSON, Letter to Tapani Kärnä, 26 April 1963, Sanfrid and Anna-Liisa Mattsson Collection, Fida Archives, Helsinki Sanfrid lamented that the (then former) FFFM director Odin Finell had tried to take the economic control over Larsmo out of their hands several times.

97 In their correspondence both often point to a "written agreement" with the Lord from 1936, in which they consent to not rely on human support, but on God alone, e.g. MATTSSON and MATTSSON, Letter to Tapani Kärnä, November 19, 1962; MATTSSON, Letter to Tapani Kärnä, April 26, 1963; ANNA-LIISA MATTSSON and SANFRID MATTSSON, Letter to Tapani Kärnä, 29 July 1963, Sanfrid and Anna-Liisa Mattsson Collection, Fida Archives, Helsinki; cf. also TILLANDER, Näkymättömän lähettiläs, 146–149. Accepting any large or continuous amounts for their personal need was seen by them as violating this agreement, ANNA-LIISA MATTSSON and SANFRID MATTSSON, Letter to Tapani Kärnä, 27 December 1967, Sanfrid and Anna-Liisa Mattsson Collection, Fida Archives, Helsinki. The founding document of SPTEC also reveals strict faith mission principles: formalized fund raising and incurring debts were explicitly forbidden, TEUVO AURA and URHO MIETTINEN, Letter of Approval by the Ministry of Justice to the foundation of Scripture Publishers to Every Creature, 19 April 1951, Later Correspondence, Fida Archives, Helsinki, §6.

98 Interview no. 78.

99 Mattssons explicitly mention that the stations were their manager's responsibility, with the exception of Merkato, which the Mattssons had helped to establish, ANNA-LIISA MATTSSON and SANFRID MATTSSON, Letter to Tapani Kärnä, 6 May 1968, Sanfrid and Anna-Liisa Mattsson Collection, Fida Archives, Helsinki.

dence and missionary meetings, and there are examples of missionaries supporting one another.[100] Yet, there was no central cash flow to the different projects, and only a limited distribution of other resources to the individual stations.[101] Despite this decentralized organization, Mattssons retained the central leadership, since they were the only legal representatives of the Finnish Pentecostal work in Ethiopia, a role they defended for a long time. They were finally forced out of their position in a difficult political process in the beginning of the 1970s, eventually resulting in an official transferral of all SPTEC property in Ethiopia to the FFFM in 1978.[102] The decentralized organization and the leadership conflicts illustrate that the Finnish Pentecostal mission in Ethiopia was by no means a uniform entity. This quality also impacted its later engagement with the emerging Ethiopian Pentecostal church, since there were considerable differences of opinion among the missionaries about how to respond to these developments.

---

100   For example when the missionaries Rawson and Marja Muffett, who came to Merkato in 1967, could not secure enough support from their churches in England, Mattssons planned to support them with food produce from their farm in Wolmera, ANNA-LIISA MATTSSON and SANFRID MATTSSON, Letter to Tapani Kärnä, 4 November 1967, Sanfrid and Anna-Liisa Mattsson Collection, Fida Archives, Helsinki.

101   Even the scriptures for distribution, bought and imported by Mattssons, were largely resold to the other missionaries, see ANNA-LIISA MATTSSON and SANFRID MATTSSON, Letter to Tapani Kärnä, 8 March 1968, Sanfrid and Anna-Liisa Mattsson Collection, Fida Archives, Helsinki.

102   Already in 1968, Mattssons allude to an attempt to establish another Finnish Pentecostal mission organization next to theirs, MATTSSON and MATTSSON, Letter to Tapani Kärnä, May 6, 1968. The disagreements finally came to a head in 1972/73. There was growing discontent among the missionaries regarding the structure of the SPTEC. The FFFM attempted to register a station as theirs, and the manager of the SPTEC mission home in Larsmo effectively bypassed Mattssons in direct negotiations in Finland, see TILLANDER, Näkymättömän lähettiläs, 337–341. At the same time the Ethiopian Ministry of Education demanded a replacement for Mattssons for a number of reasons, while the two missionaries involved the royal family in order to secure continuation of their work permits, interview no. 78; cf. also MANNINEN, Mannisentie, 136–138. In August 1972, Mattssons stepped down in a meeting with representatives from the SPTEC and the FFFM and a new leader for the mission was chosen, who for a number of reasons never actually filled the position, ROININEN, "A Condensed History of the Finnish Mission in Ethiopia," 8. In 1973 a new leader was installed without Mattssons' consent, and they were forced to leave Wolmera in the same year, TILLANDER, Näkymättömän lähettiläs, 337–341. After Sanfrid Mattsson's death in 1976, an agreement between the SPTEC and the FFFM was signed in 1978, transferring all property to the FFFM, including the right to operate under SPTEC's name, SCRIPTURE PUBLISHERS TO EVERY CREATURE, "Document of Transferral of all Property to the Free Finnish Foreign Mission from March, 1978," Later Correspondence, Fida Archives, Helsinki, 1978; VILHO KIVIKANGAS, Letter to Åke Hällzon, n.d. Later Correspondence, Fida Archives, Helsinki. It was not until after the fall of the military government in 1992 that the name of the registration was changed, due in part to the increasing development funds by the Finnish government, which were channeled through FFFM, interview no. 69. After the Mattssons' removal from the mission leadership, Anna-Liisa founded the Bethlehem Children's Home, which also caused some irritations in subsequent years, especially with regard to mission property in Awasa, cf. KYÖSTI ROININEN, Letter to Tapani Kärnä, 26 September 1984, Later Correspondence, Fida Archives, Helsinki; KYÖSTI ROININEN, Letter to Veikko Manninen, n.d. Later Correspondence, Fida Archives, Helsinki). It finally was taken over by the FFFM in 1991, three years after Anna-Liisa's death, ROININEN, "A Condensed History of the Finnish Mission in Ethiopia," 8–9.

2.2.2 The Scope of Finnish Pentecostal Missions

Most mission-related histories about the Finnish Pentecostal mission in Ethiopia do not refer to its organizational and mission-political diversity, but rather present it as a more or less uniform entity, engaged in a considerable scope of mission and development work.[103] The first SPTEC project was a vocational school (farming, carpentry, handicrafts), started by Mattssons after protracted negotiations in 1955 in the town of Wolmera, approximately 35 km west of Addis Ababa. Later, an orphanage for boys was added to the station. In 1956 spiritual meetings were begun in Addis Ababa by Helvi Halme in a provisional building behind the house she rented in the Merkato area. This meeting became one of the early centers of the Pentecostal movement in Ethiopia and was moved to a larger facility in 1975. New SPTEC headquarters were opened in 1967 by Mattssons near the Addis Ababa University, which also included a scripture distribution center and a reading room.

In Holeta, a small town near Wolmera, the Finnish Canadian missionaries Helmi and Aulis Tuomi established a school, an orphanage for girls and a clinic between 1962 to 1964. In the Kefa province the work commenced in 1964 with the opening of a school and a clinic in Tcheqorsa, as well as a clinic in Shebe. The latter was expanded to a mission center in 1967, including a church and a library. When Tuomis moved the girls' orphanage from Holeta to Awasa in 1966, the Finnish mission work began in the Sidama province, initially in close cooperation with the Swedish Pentecostal missionaries there. In 1971 a youth center was opened in Asmara, which was expanded to include a school in 1977. The missionaries conducted evangelistic outreach at all of the work places and in the neighboring villages and towns. Some missionaries worked as itinerant evangelists. Mattssons were very engaged in scripture distribution work and traveled widely as a result of their many contacts. At times, the Finnish missionaries were involved in children's radio programs, and they set up Bible seminars in different places, as well as Bible correspondence courses. In addition, they were involved in human aid, such as the distribution of clothes, shoes and food. By 1978, when all Finnish missionaries were expelled by the Derg, forty-one missionaries had been working in the different projects.[104]

The not unproblematic combination of spiritual ministry with development work was not without critics. In one of their letters Mattssons comment:

> It is tiring that the friends in Finland do not understand that the work here at first is open for clinics and schools, and then, when we distribute clothes, a little soap, milk powder and in Wolmera beans and other kinds of food, these many hearts are opened.[105]

Thus, caring for human needs was emphasized as a means for spiritual outreach, contrary to the early Finnish Pentecostal tendency to focus strictly on evangelistic

---

103   The following overview of Finnish Pentecostal mission initiatives is based on ibid.; and SELESHI
      KEBEDE, "The History of the Guenet Church."
104   HILPINEN, *Lähetystyön monet kasvot*, 58.
105   ANNA-LIISA MATTSSON and SANFRID MATTSSON, Letter to Veikko Manninen and Tapani Kärnä,
      7 August 1968, Sanfrid and Anna-Liisa Mattsson Collection, Fida Archives, Helsinki.

work.[106] Moreover, development and human aid undoubtedly were a political necessity, especially when the mission worked in so-called "Ethiopian Church areas" according to the Missions' Decree of 1944. Though the legal position of missions had been improved by these regulations, negotiations with authorities on national and local levels could still be difficult and unsuccessful when there were no sufficient political contacts. Part of SPTEC's successes in Ethiopia thus can be attributed to the imperial contacts Mattssons had acquired. They had come to meet Emperor Haile Selassie in England, where he had resided in exile during the Italian occupation of Ethiopia.[107] This apparently opened the door for the approval of their first project by the Ministry of Education in 1953.[108] Mattssons kept in contact with the imperial family throughout their time in Ethiopia, being received by the emperor at audiences for his birthday and Christmas,[109] befriending his eldest daughter,[110] and even being invited to use the emperor's summer residence for a short vacation.[111] Their good relations to the head of state was a card Mattssons frequently used and knew how to play, for example in order to successfully secure special permissions for scripture distribution in schools, the army, the royal guard, and prisons. These privileges corresponded with a warm allegiance toward the emperor, as their 1967 Christmas newsletter suggests:

> The nation of Ethiopia is developing rapidly under the able leadership of His Imperial Majesty Haile Selassie and His capable government.[112]

---

106   One missionary, for example, mentions that he was sent out by his church under the strict mandate of only preaching the gospel, interview no. 69.

107   The Mattssons had stayed in England from 1936 to 1937, apparently in order to become familiar with the Wesleyan missionary Lettie Cowman and her mission school in Swansea, intending to gain ideas for their own work. During their stay they learned of the Ethiopian emperor and his exile in England, which aroused their interest. Through a missionary acquaintance they finally managed to attain an audience with Haile Selassie in London on 11 September, 1936, and met him again one year later in Bath. For more details about these meetings see TILLANDER, *Näkymättömän lähettiläs*, 135–137, 149-150, 152–154.

108   ROININEN, "A Condensed History of the Finnish Mission in Ethiopia," 1.

109   MATTSSON and MATTSSON, Letter to Tapani Kärnä, November 4, 1967; ANNA-LIISA MATTSSON and SANFRID MATTSSON, Circular letter, 7 January 1968, Sanfrid and Anna-Liisa Mattsson Collection, Fida Archives, Helsinki.

110   Princess Tenagnework was a loyal follower of the Orthodox church. However, her personal piety of prayer and reading the Bible opened up venues for spiritual fellowship with Mattssons, MATTSSON and MATTSSON, Letter to Tapani Kärnä, March 8, 1968; also mentioned in interview no. 71.

111   TILLANDER, *Näkymättömän lähettiläs*, 325–331.

112   ANNA-LIISA MATTSSON and SANFRID MATTSSON, Christmas Newsletter 1967, n.d., Sanfrid and Anna-Liisa Mattsson Collection, Fida Archives, Helsinki. It is unclear whether Mattssons were politically inclined toward the emperor or merely looked to him as a result of a somewhat theocratic understanding of society and mission. In their correspondence Mattssons frequently point to their mission endeavors among different government officials inside and outside Ethiopia. Anna-Liisa took this up as a special ministry in the years after Sanfrid's death. She brought Bibles to different embassies, sent them to diverse presidents for Christmas, visited the former Sha's wife Farah Diba (Farah Pahlavi) in exile on Contadora, attempted to deliver a Bible to Tito in Yugoslavia and eventually died in Moscow on an unsuccessful quest to personally present a Bible to Mr. Gorbachev, having ignored warnings about her failing health, cf. TILLANDER, *Näkymättömän lähettiläs*, 342–406.

In later years, as the power of the emperor was fading, their orientation toward the royal family may occasionally have hindered an effective assessment of the situation.[113] Moreover, it probably dampened their relationship to the independent Pentecostal movement, which was unable to secure religious freedom under Haile Selassie's government, and was led by university students, who were educated in an intellectual environment marked by intense discussions of political reforms.

Understanding the diversity and scope of the Finnish Pentecostal mission work in Ethiopia also is essential for an adequate assessment of the often-encountered allegations that the missionaries "hid the teaching of the Holy Spirit,"[114] or did not propagate Pentecostal doctrine clearly enough. Considering the degree of independence of SPTEC's missionary work in Ethiopia, such generalizations are of course impossible to affirm or negate altogether. However, a number of observations with regard to the Finnish mission endeavors may elucidate the background of such allegations.

First of all, it is important to consider the Finnish Pentecostal background of the missionaries. Its strong emphasis on congregational autonomy had led the Finnish movement to a refusal of laying down doctrinal statements. Even in central Pentecostal debates, such as the question of tongues as the initial physical evidence of Spirit baptism, there were no theological declarations, though there appeared to be an affirmative consensus in practice.[115] Their contempt of doctrinal statements of course has not saved the Finnish Pentecostal movement from divisions. Mattssons frequently alluded to these conflicts in their correspondence and voiced their concern that they may weaken the Pentecostal vigor in these last hours. They often called for a laying down of doctrinal and practical conflicts in the name of brotherly love and humility.[116] The refusal to define Pentecostal doctrines in combination with Mattssons' concern not to let theological issues triumph over brotherly love may have been contributing to the misperceptions regarding their Pentecostal identity.

Secondly, it is evident that the mission's financial and human resources were considerably stretched in different development projects, which in turn were social, strategic, and political necessities. However, this not only diverted the missions attention from purely spiritual matters, it also turned the mission into a political and developmental agent with all attached responsibilities and difficulties.[117] The resulting political considerations are occasionally discussed in the Ethiopian sources, naming

---

113   A former missionary recalled demands by the Ministry of Education for other negotiating partners, because the Mattssons would rather hint at their imperial contacts than deal with matters at hand. Furthermore, ibid., 356 narrates how during the beginnings of the revolution Mattssons feared for their security because of their strong relations to the emperor's family, yet they still turned to the royal family for protection.

114   Interview no. 123.

115   KÄRKKÄINEN, "The Pentecostal Movement in Finland," 110; LAURI K. AHONEN, *Missions Growth: A Case Study on Finnish Free Foreign Mission* (Waynesboro, GA: Gabriel Resources, 1984), 37–38.

116   E.g. MATTSSON, Letter to Tapani Kärnä, April 27, 1963. Of course, Mattssons had their own positions on which they would strongly insist.

117   An Ethiopian fellow worker at Wolmera laments, for example, that people only came to the mission station for the "benefits", ETHIOPIAN GENNET CHURCH, የ5ዐኛው ዓመት የወርቅ ኢዩቤልዩ በዓል, 28–29.

fear of political consequences as reason for the missionaries' reluctance toward fanning the flames of a potentially uncontrollable Pentecostal revival.[118]

More importantly though, there seems to be a fundamental incompatibility between the Mattsson's agenda as faith missionaries and the trajectory of Pentecostal revival histories.[119] What essentially drove Mattssons' work was a strong desire to call people to salvation, the belief that scripture distribution was the main key to this work, and an ever-present sense of the urgency of their work, "before the anti-Christ fully lays hands on all."[120] An outpouring of the Holy Spirit was seen as a very important means for prospering the work, but apparently not as a goal in and of itself. In a letter from 1962 Mattssons wrote:

> We believe that a true outpouring of the Spirit from above is the only means that the Lord can bring his work to blessing and we pray for that.[121]

Mattssons apparently saw spiritual revivals to be entirely in God's sovereign hands, but this was not something to be brought about by propagating Pentecostal doctrines or experiences. Rather, a Spirit outpouring needs to be awaited prayerfully, as another letter indicates:

> I emphasize that the Spirit outpouring and revival is most important in our own lives and the mission. Pray on our behalf, so that we can take time for prayer and quiet time before the word of God. In Jesus name and blood, Amen.[122]

Overall, it appears that Mattssons' story is more or less one of end-time salvation for the lost, potentially assisted by an outpouring of the Holy Spirit. Though they undoubtedly saw themselves as Pentecostals, brought Pentecostal teaching and materials, and rejoiced in Spirit baptisms of believers, Pentecostal doctrines and practices were not seen as goals by themselves, but were measured by what they would contribute to an exhaustive spread of the gospel.

This may help to explain the striking contrast between the many accounts depicting Holy Spirit experiences in Ethiopia and Mattssons' correspondence, in which Spirit baptisms are only mentioned briefly and infrequently.[123] Occurrences celebrated by others as key events in the Pentecostal revival are at all even mentioned here, e.g. Chacha Omahe's ministry, or the previously cited Spirit baptism of one

---

118   E.g. BEKELE WOLDEKIDAN, ८ॻ.ঢ়ॻॕ, 79–80.

119   Since the faith mission principles laid down by Mattssons were at times heavily debated, this observation does not extend to all of SPTEC's work. Yet, Mattssons' central role should not be underestimated here, especially since they set the course for the entire enterprise and were heavily involved in the Merkato station, which often functioned as the main stage in the Finnish-Ethiopian Pentecostal identity debate because of the conflicts encountered there.

120   MATTSSON and MATTSSON, Letter to Tapani Kärnä, March 8, 1968.

121   SANFRID MATTSSON, Letter to Tapani Kärnä, Mr: Manninen, Mr. Kunnas, 26 June 1962, Sanfrid and Anna-Liisa Mattsson Collection, Fida Archives, Helsinki.

122   ANNA-LIISA MATTSSON and SANFRID MATTSSON, Letter to Otto Koivukangas, 28 August 1968, Sanfrid and Anna-Liisa Mattsson Collection, Fida Archives, Helsinki. The words in these sentences are all capitalized, reflecting their importance.

123   Spirit baptism is only mentioned four times in Mattssons' correspondence over the period of six years, most of the time in factual statements without attached narratives.

believer in the Finnish mission.[124] It is not until 1966/67 that incidents of baptism in the Holy Spirit were mentioned more frequently by Mattssons and are attributed with more significance because of a new quantitative dimension.[125] In earlier times, when the Swedish Pentecostal missionaries were already writing enthusiastic reports about revival,[126] Mattssons still noted that they were waiting for an end-time outpouring of the Holy Spirit.[127] Certain events at Merkato and elsewhere obviously did not have the same significance to them.

It is of course not of interest here to decide which representation of the events is "correct" or historically more accurate, if this were possible to ascertain at all. Rather, the differences noted here illustrate the scope of interpretation regarding the history of Ethiopian Pentecostalism. Occurrences later incorporated in revival narratives as key events, obviously did not necessitate this understanding to all Pentecostal observers. These interpretative differences may have been contemporary to the actual events, or they may have evolved later as a result of secondary narratives producing full revival accounts. However, they help to understand the apparent difficulties in integrating the Mattssons' and SPTEC's legacy into the historical constructions of Ethiopian Pentecostal identity.

2.3 The Swedish Pentecostal Mission

The work of the Swedish Pentecostal missionaries is often reduced to their summer Bible school in Awasa, which was undoubtedly the most valued part of the Swedish mission enterprise in Ethiopian Pentecostal histories. However, much like the Finnish Pentecostal mission, the Swedish initiatives were quite diverse, including considerable human aid and development projects. They were also subject to substantial internal fragmentation in the beginning, due to the congregationalist structure of the Swedish Pentecostal movement. Swedish Pentecostal congregationalism of course did not simply consist of a more or less precarious power-balance of autonomous congregations, but rather opened up the way for the charismatic, loosely-structured, but nonetheless central leadership of Lewi Pethrus.[128] Pethrus' power was not only conditioned by

---

124   See above, 41.
125   E.g. in 1967: "The Lord has been good with us in the last times. Many have been blessed in different stations and many have been baptized in the Holy Spirit." ANNA-LIISA MATTSSON and SANFRID MATTSSON, Letter to Tapani Kärnä, 17 June 1967, Sanfrid and Anna-Liisa Mattsson Collection, Fida Archives, Helsinki.
126   E.g. GÖSTA LINDAHL, "Seger i Etiopien," [Victory in Ethiopia], *Evangelii Härold* (41 1964): 8–9, 23.
127   ANNA-LIISA MATTSSON and SANFRID MATTSSON, Letter to brothers Manninen, Kärnä, Venäläinen, 5 August 1964, Sanfrid and Anna-Liisa Mattsson Collection, Fida Archives, Helsinki.
128   For an introduction to the organization of the Swedish Pentecostal movement, see NILS-OLOV NILSSON, "The Swedish Pentecostal Movement 1913–2000: The Tension Between Radical Congregationalism, Restorationism, and Denominationalism" (Ph.D. thesis, Columbia Theological Seminary, 2001), esp. 126–159; BERTIL CARLSSON, *Organizations and Decision Procedures within the Swedish Pentecostal Movements* (Mariefred, 1974), esp. 22–32; DAVID D. BUNDY, "Pethrus, Petrus Lewi," in *The New International Dictionary of Pentecostal and Charismatic Movements*, ed. STANLEY M. BURGESS and EDUARD M. van der MAAS (Grand Rapids, MI: Zondervan, 2002), 986–987. A novelistic treatment of important political constellations in the

his charismatic and energetic style of leadership, or the historical importance of his Stockholm Philadelphia Church, but was also maintained through central print media and organizational structures.[129] The most important print media to be mentioned here are the weekly *Evangelii Härold* (Herald of the Gospel) and the daily newspaper *Dagen*, both of which were also used as political instruments in the Swedish prelude to Ethiopian missions.[130] Another central institution was the mission board of the Philadelphia Church in Stockholm, led by the Mission Secretary. Like in Finland, an attempt was made at establishing a central mission organization in the Swedish Free Mission (SFM), which eventually also failed, resulting in the dissolution of the SFM with the incorporation of its name and property rights into Pethrus' Stockholm Philadelphia Church from which it had grown.[131] This new SFM was understood merely as a service provided by one independent congregation to another, but it nevertheless remained customary for the Stockholm Philadelphia Church to send out the first missionaries into a new mission field, to make significant financial contributions, and to be consulted about new initiatives.[132] Moreover, almost all missionaries worked with recommendations from the SFM, since an authorization by a central Swedish organization was often necessary for visa issues and other formalities.[133]

---

formation of the Swedish Pentecostal movement was produced by Per Olov Enquist, see PER OLOV ENQUIST, *Lewis Reise* (München: Hanser, 2003). The article on Sweden in the "New International Dictionary" seems to marginalize Pethrus' role and power as well as the Swedish conflicts about leadership, cf. LAURI AHONEN and JAN-ENDY JOHANNESSON, "Sweden," in *The New International Dictionary of Pentecostal and Charismatic Movements*, ed. STANLEY M. BURGESS and EDUARD M. van der MAAS (Grand Rapids, MI: Zondervan, 2002), 255–257.

129 These central organizations grew in importance for Pethrus' leadership after he resigned from his pastoral position in the Philadelphia Church in Stockholm in 1958, cf. ALF LINDBERG, "The Swedish Pentecostal Movement: Some Ideological Features," *EPTA Bulletin* VI (2 1987): 40–46.

130 On the importance of the *Evangelii Härold* for missions, see DAVID D. BUNDY, *Visions of Apostolic Mission: Scandinavian Pentecostal Mission to 1935*, Acta Universitatis Upsaliensis; 45 (Uppsala: Uppsala Universiteit, 2009), 388–398.

131 The SFM was established in 1924, but already lost its role as a central mission agency for Swedish Pentecostalism in the so-called "Franklin dispute" of 1929. One of the main issues herein had been the freedom of local congregations' missions against the centralization efforts of the SFM and its policies. However, the dispute also had to do with the establishment of strong relations between the SFM and the Free Bible Institute, as well as the fusion of two Pentecostal churches in Stockholm's south involving one of the SFM leaders. Pethrus viewed these organizational connections as a threat to the centrality of his Philadelphia church and played the card of congregational freedom in order to attain the dissolution of the SFM. See DAVID D. BUNDY, "Swedish Pentecostal Mission Theory and Practice to 1930: Foundational Values in Discussion," *Mission Studies* 14 (1997); BUNDY, *Visions of Apostolic Mission*, 452–475; ALF LINDBERG, *Väckelse, Frikyrklighet, Pingströrelse: Väckelse och frikyrka från 1800-talets mitt till nutid*, [Revival, Free Church Movement, Pentecostal Movement: Revival and Free Churches from the Middle of the 1800s to Today.] (Ekerö: Kaggeholms folkhögskola, 1985), 184–212; CARLSSON, *Organizations and Decision Procedures within the Swedish Pentecostal Movements*, 63–75; NILSSON, "The Swedish Pentecostal Movement 1913–2000," 140–146; JOEL HALLDORF, *Lewis Brev: Urval ur Lewi Pethrus korrespondens*, [Lewis Letters. Selection from Lewi Pethrus' Correspondence.] (Örebro: Libris, 2007), 86–92; ENQUIST, *Lewis Reise*, 320–373.

132 See NYBERG OSKARSSON, *Svensk Pingstmission i Ethiopien (1959–1980)*, 222–223.

133 CARLSSON, *Organizations and Decision Procedures within the Swedish Pentecostal Movements*, 74–75; NYBERG OSKARSSON, *Svensk Pingstmission i Ethiopien (1959–1980)*, 222.

2.3.1 Fragmented Beginnings

Due to a number of incidents, four Swedish Pentecostal mission organizations emerged in Ethiopia right from the start. Unlike the Finnish Pentecostals, who had a central organization in SPTEC, it took until 1973 to unite the Swedish mission endeavors. The first Swedish Pentecostal missionary to pursue his interest in Ethiopia was Elof Höglund. Having previously worked in Liberia from 1939 to 1949, he decided in 1950 not to return there, but claimed that he had to follow a divine calling to Ethiopia, which he had received a long time ago.[134] In 1954, Höglund and his family relocated to Valla. They became members of the Philadelphia Church there and managed to interest the congregation in their planned mission work in Ethiopia. After a first exploratory visit to Ethiopia in 1956, Höglund drew up a plan for opening an "industrial mission work, including a Technical School for young Ethiopians, mainly carpentry and woodwork; also an agricultural training farm for modern farming; and Bible training and teaching."[135] A second exploratory visit followed, in which Höglund was accompanied by Karl Ramstrand and Arvid Malmvärn. Ramstrand had previously worked together with Höglund in Liberia, where he had also married the missionary Ruth Andersson.[136] After the missionary couple had returned to Sweden in 1954, they became interested in Höglund's new mission initiative to Ethiopia.[137] Arvid and Kärstin Malmvärn had also been interested in missions to Ethiopia for a long time.[138] They belonged to the "Kristen Gemenskap", a church which resulted out of a split from the Free Church in Stockholm-Östermalm in 1952.[139] Both churches had at times been ostracized by the mainstream Pentecostals,[140] which was significant for the further developments.

---

134   Höglund reported that while he was attending a preparatory language course in the Stockholm Philadelphia church as mission candidate for Liberia, he felt called to pray for Ethiopia in a vision in 1936, see ELOF HÖGLUND, "Etiopien-Missionen," In: Full Gospel Mission, special issue (Jönköping, 1969), 2. Like with the Mattssons, it seems to have been the emperor's fate that sparked his interest, since Haile Selassie then had just left Ethiopia in his flight from the Italian invasion. Höglund's divinely received interpretation of these events was that God wanted to "humble" the Ethiopian emperor and people "in order for them to receive the gospel and salvation." He claims to have seen a map of Ethiopia, on which God had pointed to a place southwest of Addis Ababa.

135   See NYBERG OSKARSSON, Svensk Pingstmission i Ethiopien (1959–1980), 25 for a facsimile of the original application letter.

136   Cf. RAMSTRAND, Det heliga äventyret, 41–100; RAMSTRAND, Guds lilla piga far dit pepparn växer, 23–137.

137   Cf. RAMSTRAND, Det heliga äventyret, 103–104; RAMSTRAND, Guds lilla piga far dit pepparn växer, 139–141.

138   They also report to have received their calling to Ethiopia in the 1930s, see NYBERG OSKARSSON, Svensk Pingstmission i Ethiopien (1959–1980), 32. Kärstin Malmvärn apparently even sought Lewi Pethrus' advice about her calling, who discouraged her from pursuing this vision, interview no. 35.

139   Ibid. The split had to do with the Latter Rain Movement, see NILSSON, "The Swedish Pentecostal Movement 1913–2000," 177; HALLDORF, Lewis Brev, 285–286; CITYKYRKAN, "City Pingstförsamling – kort historik," [The City Pentecostal Church – A Short History.] (2007), http://www.cks.se/forsamling/historik_1.htm (accessed February 3, 2007).

140   NILSSON, "The Swedish Pentecostal Movement 1913–2000," 172–181, 185–186; ARNE BJÖRKMAN, "Väckelse i motvind," [Revival in Headwind.], Midnattsropet! (2 1998): 1, http://www.maranata.se/MR/98/2-98/motvind.html (accessed February 3, 2007).

Höglund's plans for Pentecostal mission work in Ethiopia faced a strong opposition right from the start, most notably by Lewi Pethrus himself and the Philadelphia Church mission board secretary Samuel Nyström.[141] A conglomerate of arguments was brought forth against the endeavor, in which four main points prevail: First, the Swedish Lutherans had already established a thriving work in Ethiopia.[142] Secondly, there were doubts about Höglund's integrity and his ability to cooperate with others. Third, the manner in which the Ethiopia initiative was handled violated the existing structures and processes for new mission initiatives. Fourth and finally, by including Malmvärns from the "Kristen Gemenskap", the Ethiopia mission friends had associated themselves with "separatist movements" in the Swedish Pentecostal church.[143] When the conflict began with the denial by the Evangelii Härold to publish information about the new mission initiative, the driving factor behind the opposition seems to have been the doubts about Höglund. However, the dispute quickly led to matters of church structure and congregational freedom when the Valla congregation refused to accept Lewi Pethrus' and Samuel Nyström's assessment of Höglund.[144] Though the accusations against Höglund were plausibly refuted by Valla, he appears to have remained the primary obstacle in finding a way out of the impasse. Relations smoothened somewhat in 1958 when Valla indicated their flexibility in who was to lead the Ethiopia mission, offering to put Ramstrand in leadership over Höglund. This, however, was perceived by Höglund as an unnecessary sacrifice of his person,[145]

---

141 Cf. NYBERG OSKARSSON, *Svensk Pingstmission i Ethiopien (1959–1980)*, 24–32. The draft by the Valla pastor Bertil Lindstedt (BERTIL LINDSTEDT, "Historik över Etiopienmissionen under Åren 1955–1968," [History of the Ethiopia Mission in the Years 1955–1968], Valla Collection, Pingstarkiv Kaggeholm, Ekerö, 1968) is a detailed and helpful reference to these conflicts.

142 The argument had more weight to it, because of the work of the Lutheran Bible-True Friends, who, like Pentecostals, had rejected much of liberal Bible exegesis, cf. LAUNHARDT, *Evangelicals in Addis Ababa (1919–1991)*, 41–45.

143 Cf. GUNNAR ERIKSSON, "Protokoll fört vid sammanträde med den av Filadelfiaförsamlingen, Valla och Lewi Pethrus utsedda kommittén, bestående av bröderna Arvid Bramwall, Herbert Gustavsson, William Jansson och Gunnar Jogensjö, vars uppgift var att undersöka förhållandena angående Etiopienmissionen," [Minutes taken at the meeting of the committee appointed by the Philadelphia congregation, Valla and Lewi Pethrus, consisting of the brothers Arvid Bramwall, Herbert Gustavsson, William Jansson and Gunnar Jogensjö, whose task it was to investigate the matters regarding the Ethiopia mission], Valla Collection, Pingstarkiv Kaggeholm, Ekerö, 1958, point 8.

144 The more the Valla elders and pastor questioned Pethrus' and Nyström's estimation of Höglund and his plans, the more the Stockholm leadership associated them with Höglund's independent spirit, who was willing to ignore established procedures and demarcated boundaries in pursuit of his perceived calling. Finally, the fierce debate culminated in 1957 in an editorial by Lewi Pethrus in the Dagen, titled "Pull yourselves away from them," in which Pethrus lashed out against "impossible and unclear" mission initiatives which were not in agreement with the Pentecostal movement and were associated with those who before had "worked in the direction of splitting the Pentecostal revival", concluding with Rom 16:17 to "move away from them", see LEWI PETHRUS, "Drager eder ifrån dem," [Pull Yourselves Away from Them.], *Dagen*, November 18, 1957, 2. This implicit, but clear attack against the Valla initiative had an ironic twist in the fact that the Valla pastor, Bertil Lindstedt, acted as the editor for the Finland edition of the Dagen at the time, LINDSTEDT, "Historik över Etiopienmissionen under Åren 1955–1968," 4. Moreover, Valla's replies to the accusations were neither published in the Dagen nor in the Evangelii Härold.

145 HÖGLUND, "Etiopien-Missionen," 4.

which now led to conflicts between him and the congregation, culminating in the revocation of his power of attorney at the end of 1958, and ultimately in his exclusion from the Valla congregation in 1959.[146] Ramstrand now was made leader over the Ethiopia mission endeavor, which before he had refused out of consideration for Höglund.[147] This transition of power of attorney was not without difficulties, since the mission rights had already been granted by the Ethiopian government on 1 July, 1958. Consequently, both parties fought to retain these rights.[148]

Höglund collected his supporters in an independent organization, the Swedish Industrial Mission (SWIM), and began his work in Ethiopia in 1959 in the southwestern town of Jima.[149] In the same year, Ramstrand and his family moved to Ethiopia, in order to investigate possible locations for what would become the Swedish Philadelphia Church Mission (SPCM). Originally Ramstrand had hoped to go to a remote area that had not been touched by missions yet, and therefore applied to open a vocational school in Masslo. However, the Ethiopian government denied the application, expressing their interest in such a school in the newly founded town of Awasa in the Sidama region, which Ramstrand reluctantly obeyed.[150] The Sidama region

---

146 The trigger for these last conflicts apparently was Höglund's cooperation with different congregations outside the main Pentecostal movement. The Valla congregation, wanting to lay low politically after the conflicts, tried to no avail to convince Höglund to respect these boundaries, LINDSTEDT, "Historik över Etiopienmissionen under Åren 1955–1968," 6–8.

147 See ibid., 6, 8. Ramstrand apparently had tried to maintain a peaceful relationship with Höglund, whom he considered a "trailblazer" for missions, but also a "bulldozer", see NORRMAN, "Transcript of Interview with Karl Ramstrand, conducted 27 September, 1989 by Jonny Bkörnler," 7–8; RAMSTRAND, *Det heliga äventyret*, 99. However, the conflicts and differences between the two are visible in contemporary sources. Ramstrand, for example, called Pethrus polemic editorial "prophetic" in light of the splitting developments in Ethiopia, and mentions that he himself has not set foot to Jima more than once since Höglund began his work there, see KARL RAMSTRAND, Letter to brother Mårastam, 1 October 1966, Tage Johansson Collection, Pingstarkiv Kaggeholm, Ekerö; cf. also RAMSTRAND, *Det heliga äventyret*, 111, 142. Höglund also harshly criticized the work of the SPCM in Ethiopia, even to the point of bemoaning the costs for Ramstrand's large family in Addis Ababa, while they were still looking for a place for their work, see HÖGLUND, "Etiopien-Missionen," 5.

148 LINDSTEDT, "Historik över Etiopienmissionen under Åren 1955–1968," 6, 8 After the Valla congregation learned of Höglund's departure for Ethiopia in 1959, they immediately sent out a telegram to the Ethiopian authorities about the transfer of leadership. Höglund in turn spent much of 1959 fighting to secure the mission rights over his competitors, cf. FINN ARNE IMSEN, *Verksamhetsberättelse avgiven vid Sällskapet Svensk Industriell Missions årsmöte hos Greta och Filip Alpsten, Tallkrogen, fredagena, den 18 mars 1960*, [Activity Report Given at the Swedish Industrial Mission Society yearly meeting at [the residence of] Greta and Filip Alpsten, Tallkrogen, Friday, 18 March, 1960], SWIM Collection, Pingstarkiv Kaggeholm, Ekerö, 1960.

149 The decision to start in Jima came from a meeting with Indian Pentecostals whom Höglund had met in Ethiopia. They suggested this place to Höglund, who was immediately satisfied, when he identified it on a map as the place which God had shown him in his vision decades earlier, HÖGLUND, "Etiopien-Missionen," 3. The mission rights were granted to SWIM on 17 June, 1960, cf. ANNA OLOFSEN, EINAR ALFREDSSON, and FILIP ALPSTEN, "Årsberättelse avgiven vid Svensk Industriell Mission i Etiopien årsmöte is Stockholm den 26 maj 1961," [Yearly report given at the Swedish Industrial Mission in Ethiopia yearly meeting in Stockholm on 26 May, 1961], SWIM Collection, Pingstarkiv Kaggeholm, Ekerö, 1961.

150 Ruth Ramstrand describes this lengthy negotiation process with the authorities as a "spiritual battle", not with the authorities, but rather between Karl Ramstrand and the Lord, who

had already seen years of missionary presence with the Sudan Interior Mission (SIM) and the Norwegian Lutheran Mission and was declared an open area in 1961.[151] This established missionary presence was the primary reason for Ramstrand's reluctance to go to Awasa,[152] and his assessment of the situation was later confirmed by the fact that the mission in the beginning mainly attracted converts from these missions.[153]

Meanwhile Höglund's relations to the SWIM committee grew tense as well, ultimately again resulting in the revocation of his power of attorney on behalf of the SWIM in 1962.[154] Frans Larsson from the Philadelphia Church in Jönköping henceforth acted as representative for the SWIM, while Höglund finally settled on the outskirts of Jima, founding the third Swedish Pentecostal mission organization in Ethiopia, the Full Gospel Mission (FGM).[155]

The fourth Swedish initiative to be mentioned here, was the so-called Addis Hiwot (Amharic: New Life) project, which was started by Arvid and Kärstin Malmvärn. In pursuit of their calling to Ethiopia, Arvid Malmvärn had participated in the joint investigative journey with Höglund and Ramstrand in 1957. During this trip he had become acquainted with the Finnish missionaries Sanfrid and Anna-Liisa Mattsson, and since he was a farmer, they asked him to look after the farm in Wolmera during their leave in 1959. Malmvärns thus became the first Swedish Pentecostal missionaries to Ethiopia, when they set out to oversee Mattsson's farm in January 1959.[156] In 1961 they moved to Addis Ababa and, along with helping out in different initiatives, they pursued the establishment of their own work.[157] Supported by the Ethiopian government and Save the Children (Sweden) they finally started a rehabilitation farm

---

had to break the missionary's will in order to lead the mission to the place he had prepared, RAMSTRAND, *Guds lilla piga far dit pepparn växer*, 150–153.

151   TOLO, *Sidama and Ethiopian*, 223. Local opposition against the SIM had been strong in certain sub-districts before the Sidama region was declared an "open region", ibid., 206–223.

152   RAMSTRAND, *Guds lilla piga far dit pepparn växer*, 150.

153   NYBERG OSKARSSON, *Svensk Pingstmission i Ethiopien (1959–1980)*, 49–51.

154   A letter by a lawyer who was entrusted with the matter because of Höglund's apparent failure to cooperate with this transition, states reasons for the break-up. Problems in Höglund's management and his failure to report are criticized there, but the primary reason seems to have been the alleged misappropriation of financial resources allotted to lease land for Höglund's personal expenses, ERIK T. BENDZ, Letter to Elof Höglund, 12 October 1962, Filadelfiaförsamlingen Jönköping Collection, Religiösa organisationer, Jönköpings läns folkrörelsearkiv, Jönköping.

155   NYBERG OSKARSSON, *Svensk Pingstmission i Ethiopien (1959–1980)*, 36. Höglund later called this new initiative a "free mission, a faith mission with the whole Bible as role model" (HÖGLUND, "Etiopien-Missionen," 5), perhaps indicating less formalized structures in this new enterprise.

156   See NYBERG OSKARSSON, *Svensk Pingstmission i Ethiopien (1959–1980)*, 33–34. Mattssons had declined a request by Höglund to work together officially, ANNA-LIISA MATTSSON and SANFRID MATTSSON, Letter to Otto Koivukangas, Veikko Manninen, and Tapani Kärnä, 24 August 1968, Sanfrid and Anna-Liisa Mattsson Collection, Fida Archives, Helsinki, but gave considerable initial support to the Swedes, cf. e.g. LINDSTEDT, "Historik över Etiopienmissionen under Åren 1955–1968," 4, 8. The Philadelphia Church mission board director Samuel Nyström objected to this support in reference to criticisms of Mattsson's independent work by Finnish Pentecostal leaders, SAMUEL NYSTRÖM, Letter to Bertil Lindstedt, 3 June 1955, Valla Collection, Pingstarkiv Kaggeholm, Ekerö. When Ramstrands came to Ethiopia, they were received by Malmvärns at the Wolmera farm, which also served as their first abode, cf. RAMSTRAND, *Guds lilla piga far dit pepparn växer*, 144–145.

157   NYBERG OSKARSSON, *Svensk Pingstmission i Ethiopien (1959–1980)*, 70–71.

for lepers in Tibele, in the Great Rift Valley, offering medical treatment for people affected by Hansen's Disease while giving them the opportunity to work on the farm and learn a trade.[158] When Malmvärns returned to Sweden in 1971, more than 1,000 people with leprosy had been treated at Addis Hiwot and its later branch Tesfa Hiwot (Amharic: Hope of Life). The work was taken over by Save the Children (Sweden) on January 1, 1971 and finally was turned over to the Ethiopian government in 1975.[159]

Thus, the Swedish Pentecostal mission work was quite fragmented in the beginning, but unlike the Finnish mission efforts, this was neither intended in order to guarantee organizational freedom, nor was there a central entity speaking for all these Swedish initiatives. This began to change at the end of the 1960s, in a process which involved the consolidation of responsibilities in Sweden as well. In 1966 discussions arose in Sweden about unifying the first three missions, largely initiated and furthered by the Philadelphia Church in Jönköping.[160] Ramstrand initially opposed the idea of unifying the SWIM and the SPCM,[161] so that the Philadelphia Church in Jönköping only took over the responsibility for the SWIM in 1967 and sent out Tage and Birgitta Johansson to oversee the work.[162] After Karl Ramstrand had moved back to Sweden in 1969, it was decided that Tage Johansson should succeed him as representative of the SPCM, and at the same time it was suggested by Valla that the Jönköping church should now take over the responsibilities as the "contact congregation" for the SPCM as well.[163] After lengthy negotiations between Tage Johansson,

---

158 Though Malmvärns were sent out by the "Kristen Gemenskap" in Stockholm and their work was also connected to the Valla Ethiopia committee, these Swedish Pentecostal churches were not prepared to take the financial risks attached to this work. Therefore Arvid Malmvärn initially registered the enterprise under his own name, and it was not until much later that the SPCM took over the responsibility for the work, ibid., 71–72; interview no. 35.

159 Ibid., 79.

160 The congregation in Jönköping had not been directly involved in mission work, which is why this engagement was somewhat questioned. Though the missionaries Frans and Rosa Larsson, who worked in Jima with Höglund, were members in this church, they were supported by the SWIM foundation. Tage Johansson indicates that there was a strong interest on behalf of Jönköping's pastors to solve the situation in Ethiopia, but also that the SWIM was looking for ways to reunite with the other Pentecostal mission initiatives, especially after the Swedish International Development Cooperation Agency (SIDA) had offered financial support, cf. JOHANSSON, *Med Gud i vardagen och bland medicinmän*, 67–69.

161 See NYBERG OSKARSSON, *Svensk Pingstmission i Etiopien (1959–1980)*, 36–38. In a lengthy letter from 1966, Ramstrand states several reasons for his reluctance: the conflict between the SWIM and Höglund, whom he did not want to affront; that the SPCM was already over-engaged and would thin out its capacity by integrating Jima; that the original vision was only one place for a venture like Awasa; and that, in his opinion, the Lord had closed the door to Jima, see KARL RAMSTRAND, Letter to Tage Johansson, 26 September 1966, Karl Ramstrand Collection, Pingstarkiv Kaggeholm, Ekerö.

162 Tage also had an explicit mandate to "heal the split", to which he dedicated his work, interview no. 14.

163 See NYBERG OSKARSSON, *Svensk Pingstmission i Etiopien (1959–1980)*, 38; JOHANSSON, *Med Gud i vardagen och bland medicinmän*, 83. In 1969 Ramstrand apparently was not opposed to the unification of the SWIM and the SPCM anymore, but was the one who suggested this solution.

the Jönköping pastor Bo Hörnberg, and Elof Höglund,[164] the latter agreed to transfer the FGM to the Jönköping church in 1974, resulting in the unification of the three remaining Swedish initiatives under the responsibility of the Jönköping Philadelphia church.[165] The SPCM subsequently established its administrative center in Addis Ababa, the work being centrally directed from there.

2.3.2 The Scope of Swedish Pentecostal Missions

Altogether, Swedish Pentecostal missionaries were working in nine different locations before the Ethiopian revolution, all of which were in the southern half of the country, with the exception of Addis Ababa.[166] Like the Finnish mission, all of the initiatives were a combination of developmental and spiritual work. There were vocational schools in Awasa, Jima, and Ziway, which not only offered industrial skills to young Ethiopians, but also enabled the mission to participate in the local economy, and served as a source for skilled labor and income.[167] Other educational benefits like elementary schools, literacy programs, evening schools and handicraft schools for women were offered in Awasa, Tibele (Addis Hiwot), Wendo, Kibish, Ziway, Worancha, and Jima. The SPCM operated a health clinic in Wendo, and health services, such as vaccination, ambulant medical treatment, and health education were offered by all the mission stations in places without established public health care facilities. Moreover, the mission engaged in relief programs during the famine of 1972/3 and in water development projects. For financing these operations the missionaries also received help from various aid organizations outside the Pentecostal fold, including considerable development funds by the Swedish government.[168]

The spiritual work of the Swedish mission was largely affected by the location of its first center in Awasa. Although the SPCM was the first foreign mission within the new town,[169] the area around Awasa was home to established communities of Protestant

---

164   Höglund initially rejected the idea, because in his view Awasa was "not a New Testament mission", because of its industrial engagements, ELOF HÖGLUND, Letter to Bo Hörnberg, 29 April 1968, Tage Johansson Collection, Pingstarkiv Kaggeholm, Ekerö.

165   See ELOF HÖGLUND, Letter to the Ministry of Education, 5 February 1974, Valla Collection, Pingstarkiv Kaggeholm, Ekerö. Johansson called it a "holy hour" when he announced the unification of the missions to the Ministry of Education, JOHANSSON, *Med Gud i vardagen och bland medicinmän*, 67.

166   These were: Awasa, Jima, Tibele, Wendo, Worancha, Addis Ababa, Kibish, Masslo, and Ziway. For detailed accounts of the different projects, see NYBERG OSKARSSON, *Svensk Pingstmission i Ethiopien (1959–1980)*.

167   In connection to a controversy with the Ethiopian authorities, who demanded income taxes on the vocational school's sales, Ramstrand mentions that the income for the Ethiopian year 1961 (9/1/1968–8/31/1968) had been about 38,000 Ethiopian Birr (appr. 15,300 US$ then), see KARL RAMSTRAND, Letter to Bernt Einarsson, 19 November 1969, Karl Ramstrand Collection, Pingstarkiv Kaggeholm, Ekerö.

168   These were most of all Save the Children (Sweden), SIDA, Svenska Journalen, Erikshjälpen, and Christian Relief Development Association (CRDA). The Swedish government funds granted by SIDA were channelled through Stiftelsen Svenska Pingstmissionen U-landshjälp (PMU), the development agency of the Swedish Pentecostal movement. Ethiopia apparently was the first country in which Swedish Pentecostals received Swedish government development funds, NYBERG OSKARSSON, *Svensk Pingstmission i Ethiopien (1959–1980)*, 241.

169   Ramstrands were glad to point out that they had arrived before the Catholic church, and that if other Protestant missions were to settle in Awasa, the SPCM would "step on their toes", see

Christians. Ramstrand was aware of the potential of this constant influx of Protestant Christians to the new city. He encouraged his following, which primarily consisted of young men, to participate in ministry and he was open to their input. Moreover, he sought to avoid direct confrontation with the Orthodox church and the authorities by abstaining from baptizing new believers himself.[170] Though the missionaries taught adult baptism by immersion and participated as preachers at baptismal services, they left it to the Ethiopian believers to perform the actual baptismal act.[171] In fact, the first baptisms of Pentecostal believers in the Awasa congregation were most probably performed by Ethiopians with an SIM background.[172] This delegating of risks to the Ethiopian believers may seem questionable, but it also implied a significant transferal of ecclesial authority to the native Christians, and thus probably was attractive for both sides. The position of the Swedish Pentecostals was also strengthened by the comity agreements between Norwegian Lutheran Mission and the SIM, which had divided the region around Awasa between the two missions.[173] As a result, Christian groups seeking an alternative to their assigned mission could only join the SPCM, since the other two missions would not agree to work outside their assigned areas. Though heavily criticized for this, the SPCM gladly took on this role. Believing his own theology to be superior, Ramstrand decided to "go forth in love, but to follow

---

KARL RAMSTRAND and RUTH RAMSTRAND, Circular to supporting congregations and friends, 28 January 1961, Karl Ramstrand Collection, Pingstarkiv Kaggeholm, Ekerö.

170 NYBERG OSKARSSON, *Svensk Pingstmission i Ethiopien (1959–1980)*, 51. The problem was, of course, that many converts had been Orthodox, so that baptism would be an illegal act of conversion. A story of SIM missionaries who were expelled from Ethiopia for baptizing, was used to illustrate the danger of baptism, cf. TAGE JOHANSSON and OWE WALLBERG, Letter to Willis Säve, Arne Pettersson, and the Philadelphia Church in Stockholm, 27 November 1969, Tage Johansson Collection, Pingstarkiv Kaggeholm, Ekerö.

171 Ibid.

172 NYBERG OSKARSSON, *Svensk Pingstmission i Ethiopien (1959–1980)*, 51 even states that it was SIM evangelists who baptized, but does not indicate her sources here. This would of course be significant since the SIM was strictly dispensational at the time. However, at least former Ethiopian SIM members seem plausible as baptizers, since in 1962 Ramstrand mentions "believing and baptized brothers from the large revival areas west of us", who participated in the Swedish mission after having moved to Awasa. In the same letter he reports that in 1961, 52 people had been baptized "in connection to our work, but through the native brothers", KARL RAMSTRAND, Excerpt of a letter from March 13, 1962, quoted in the yearly mission report from 1961/1962, Etiopien Rapporta, Pingstarkiv Kaggeholm, Ekerö.

173 These comity agreements on mission areas were the result of considerable tensions between the earlier SIM and the Norwegian Lutheran Mission in Kambata/Hadiya, Sidama and Gamu Gofa from 1949–1953. The difficulties mainly revolved around different policies in the payment of evangelists, and the engagement in elementary education. The SIM strongly demanded that the evangelists be supported by the local churches, whereas the Norwegian Lutherans simply employed and paid local evangelists, some of whom had previously worked for SIM, cf. STAFFAN GRENSTEDT, *Ambaricho and Shonkolla: From Local Independent Church to the Evangelical Mainstream in Ethiopia. The Origins of the Mekane Yesus Church in Kambata Hadiya*, Studia Missionalia Svecana; 82 (Uppsala: The Swedish Institute of Missionary Research, 2000), 86–88; TOLO, *Sidama and Ethiopian*, 156, 174; COTTERELL, *Born at Midnight*, 136–137. Furthermore the SIM had been reluctant to involve themselves deeply in elementary education without direct connection to evangelistic work, further increasing the attractivity of the Norwegian mission, which imposed no such relation between school work and evangelism, TOLO, *Sidama and Ethiopian*, 157–160. See also FARGHER, *The Origins of the New Churches Movement in Southern Ethiopia, 1927–1944*, 294–297.

God's Word", since "the Word must of course go before friendship and the opinion of men."[174]

This competitive dynamic helped to open up new branches of work, for example, when Christians from Worancha approached the SPCM for support in teaching and health care.[175] Moreover, the influx of Protestant Christians gave the mission ample opportunities for recruiting native evangelists and furthering their work through them.[176] Considerable networks of Christian communities were established by these traveling Ethiopian evangelists and teachers, supported by missionary visits to the villages, and linked at conferences in Awasa. When discussions arose concerning whether or not the village congregations were somehow subordinate to the mission, it became clear that there was no room for formalizing or legalizing these operative relationships with the SPCM, since its work permit was limited to Awasa.[177] However, the mission and the church in Awasa continued to play a central role through their financial support and their theological authority, for example in arranging special Bible courses for evangelists. Ethiopian ministers from Awasa also supported the work in other Swedish Pentecostal mission stations.[178] The same arrangement was later employed in Wendo and Worancha. Missionaries and Ethiopian evangelists would visit Christian groups in the surrounding villages, conferences and Bible courses were offered to their representatives and evangelists, while organizational commitments remained unclear.[179]

In places where the Swedish Pentecostal missions were less successful in their spiritual work, cooperation with Ethiopian Pentecostals was even more important. The SWIM in Jima had not managed to establish a congregation until 1968 and apparently was less successful in gaining converts or securing resources for mission work

---

174 See KARL RAMSTRAND, Circular to supporting friends, 26 December 1961, Karl Ramstrand Collection, Pingstarkiv Kaggeholm, Ekerö. Whereas the Pentecostals had more in common with the SIM in their shared emphasis of adult baptism, the SIM was strictly dispensational at the time, strongly renouncing Pentecostal theology and experience. However, the importance of these theological differences probably should not be overemphasized with regard to the Ethiopian Christians. While for some of the Lutherans, the baptism issue may have been a reason to seek a mission alternative, for many, the SPCM may just have been the closest evangelical mission, or simply another opportunity to find support for their congregations and villages.

175 NYBERG OSKARSSON, *Svensk Pingstmission i Ethiopien (1959–1980)*, 101–105.

176 Ibid., 49–52 narrates this influx of, at first, primarily young men, among them a Christian by the name of Kemere, who was an important leader for the mission in the early years. His son Philipos later was one of the first students initiating Pentecostal meetings at the Addis Ababa University, see section 3.3, 118. Of the three first elders in Awasa, two previously had been with the SIM, and one had merely been in contact with SIM missionaries, but was converted at the SPCM, see ibid., 58f; also mentioned in interviews no. 119; 12; 100.

177 See ibid., 59. Leaving the boundaries of their assigned area also posed a legal risk for the missionaries, cf. ibid., 60–61, but due to local opposition the work certainly was not without risks for the native evangelists.

178 An example here is Chinia Enjaja, who originally was one of the first elders in Awasa, then worked as a pastor at Addis Hiwot in Tibele and later as an evangelist in Ziway, after the SPCM had started their vocational school there, ibid., 82, 211.

179 Ibid., 90–94, 110–115. The missionaries only had limited success in convincing the village groups to adopt a church structure like their own, e.g. electing spiritual elders for the church who were not necessarily identical with the community (*maḥəbär*) elders, cf. ibid., 111–112.

in the surrounding Kefa province. When one of the elders of the independent Pentecostal group in Addis Ababa (FGBC) came to the mission and informed them of his
calling to work in Jima, he was accepted by the missionaries and paid as pastor of the
Jima congregation.[180] This almost entailed the closure of the mission church in 1973,
since the authorities associated it with the independent FGBC, which did not have a
permission to operate.[181] In Addis Ababa the contact with the FGBC had initially
developed because of university students who had been at the Awasa conferences, but
a close organizational cooperation never materialized.[182] Consequently, the SPCM
started its own congregation in 1974.[183]

Next to administrating or facilitating Sunday services and training evangelists,
the missions engaged in other spiritual activities, such as evening Bible studies, youth
programs, Sunday school, youth choirs, women's meetings, etc. However, probably
the most successful engagement of all, was the Bible conference or Bible school, held in
Awasa for several weeks each summer. It was begun in 1962 with over 400 Christians,
mostly from Awasa and the surrounding areas. The conference teachers came from
the Awasa mission staff.[184] This annual meeting grew quickly and developed into
a very successful yearly gathering. The conference was advertised through written
invitations and personal recommendation and many reported to have received their
Spirit baptism there, referring to the meeting as their "garage"[185], a place for spiritual
maintenance and "repairs". Soon the Awasa conference hosted youths from all over
the country, serving as a hub for the early Pentecostal movement. The missionaries
often invited foreign guests as ministers at this conference, the most important one of
whom, at least in Ethiopian narratives, was the Kenyan evangelist Chacha Omahe.

2.4   A "Kenyan Match": Chacha Omahe

The central role often attributed to the evangelist Chacha Omahe[186] is visible in
many accounts, which depict him as the one who initiated the Pentecostal revival in

---

180   Ibid., 131–140.
181   Ibid., 141–142.
182   Cf. below, 145ff.
183   NYBERG OSKARSSON, *Svensk Pingstmission i Ethiopien (1959–1980)*, 150–151.
184   Ruth Ramstrand suggested that the idea of these meetings came from the Ethiopian evangelist
      Kemere, who was working with them, see RAMSTRAND, *Guds lilla piga far dit pepparn växer*,
      177.
185   This was a term frequently encountered with informants in Awasa.
186   Starting with Engelsviken (ENGELSVIKEN, "Molo Wongel," 25–29), the Kenyan is most often
      called Omahe Chacha. Contemporary sources as well as Chacha's own curriculum vitae, how-
      ever, give his name as Chacha Omahe, or simply Chacha, HARALD JOHANSSON, "Pingsteld
      över Etiopien," [Pentecostal Fire Over Ethiopia.], *Evangelii Härold* (48 1963): cf. e.g. JOSEPH
      MATTSSON-BOZE, "Mighty Outpouring of the Holy Ghost in Ethiopia: 100 Students in the
      Bible-School Baptized in the Holy Spirit!" *Herald of Faith* 31 (12 1963): 12; RAMSTRAND, Let-
      ter to supporting congregations, August 30, 1964; *Herald of Faith*, "Glorious Outpouring of the
      Holy Spirit in Ethiopia," 3 1964, 14; KARL RAMSTRAND, Letter to supporters, 22 August 1965,
      Karl Ramstrand Collection, Pingstarkiv Kaggeholm, Ekerö; *Herald of Faith*, "A Pentecostal
      Revival at the University in Addis Ababa," 10 1966, 13; CHACHA OMAHE, "Life and Experience
      in the Lord's Ministry."

Ethiopia. In early missionary correspondence he was listed as "one of the tools God used to ignite the fire,"[187] Engelsviken saw in him a much awaited spark,[188] and in similar terminology, the Pentecostal pastor Bekele Woldekidan called him a "Kenyan match."[189] Informants contended that Chacha's work "will never be forgotten in the history of [...] the emergence of the Pentecostal Churches in Ethiopia,"[190] since he was the one who "just released the Holy Spirit,"[191] and his visits were like an Ethiopian Pentecost:

> That was actually, maybe uh, like in the Acts, in Acts chapter 2 — just a manifestation of the power of the Holy Spirit.[192]

Most narratives mention only one visit by Chacha to Awasa and Addis Ababa, where the evangelist spoke at the summer conference and at the Merkato Finnish mission. Though some histories mention that there already were a few Spirit-baptized Ethiopians before Chacha came, all accounts agree that Spirit baptism with the initial evidence of speaking in tongues was experienced in an unprecedented intensity and frequency during these visits. In the words of an eyewitness in Awasa:

> The fire descended. We shouted, we cried, we forgot the place we were in. We spoke in tongues. Life didn't seem like life.[193]

2.4.1 Historical Context

Despite this veneration for Chacha and the emphasis on his impact, most sources are not well informed about the Kenyan and his background. One informant characterizes him as uneducated, with merely a 4th grade education.[194] Another holds that he was brought to Sweden for Pentecostal theological training and pastored a congregation called Jordan Church.[195] The majority of sources, however, do not provide any information about Chacha's educational nor his denominational background. This uncertainty about the evangelist's biography and role in Kenya is noteworthy, since he had a certain standing in Kenya.

Chacha Omahe hailed from the Kuria people, an ethnic group residing in Northern Tanzania and south-Western Kenya. He was born in the Mara region of Tanzania and moved to Kenya in the early 1930s.[196] Chacha's father died before he was born, and he lost is mother at a young age as well. He attended a primary school sponsored by Elim

---

187 KARL RAMSTRAND, Letter to supporting congregations, 26 October 1965, Karl Ramstrand Collection, Pingstarkiv Kaggeholm, Ekerö.
188 ENGELSVIKEN, "Molo Wongel," 25.
189 BEKELE WOLDEKIDAN, ረኀዴነት, 78; see also TIBEBE ESHETE, *The Evangelical Movement in Ethiopia*, 159 quoting one of the early leaders with the same metaphor.
190 BULUTSE FUTUWI, "An Introduction to the Theology and Growth of Independent Churches in Ethiopia With Special Reference to Rhema Faith Church," 58.
191 Interview no. 111.
192 Interview no. 123.
193 Interview no. 12.
194 Interview no. 91; see also SELESHI KEBEDE, "The History of the Guenet Church," 5.
195 Interview no. 119.
196 Much of the information about Chacha gathered here was gained through personal e-mail correspondence and a telephone interview with his son, Mukiria Chacha, who also made some of Chacha's personal documents available to the author.

missionaries (Lima, New York). However, he was only allowed to attend until grade four, since his older brother and his wife needed his help on their farm.[197] In 1946 Chacha returned to the Elim mission and began serving as an evangelist. From 1952 to 1954 he attended a Theological Study Course with the Elim Missionary Assemblies in Bukira, and began to study Greek and the New Testament through correspondence courses.[198] He was ordained as a pastor with the Elim Missionary Assemblies in 1961, and after a few months of studies in creative writing, journalism, and language in Zambia, he came to Nairobi as a pastor in 1962. The Elim Missionary Assemblies had then just founded Pentecostal Evangelistic Fellowship of Africa (PEFA), and Chacha became an overseer for its Central and Eastern districts, and in 1964 he was appointed as Regional Chairman for Nairobi.[199] He also became instrumental in starting the PEFA mission among the Maasai.[200] However, in 1969 Chacha broke away from PEFA, following a dispute with the mission's leadership. During one of his visits to Ethiopia he had met a Swedish missionary by the name of Bengt Sundh, who was interested in setting up a mission station in Kenya. Chacha invited him to Kuria, for which PEFA wanted him to apologize, because Sundh did not belong to their organization. Chacha did not concede and was asked to leave the mission. A number of Kenyan pastors left PEFA with him and together they established the International Fellowship for Christ in 1972. Throughout his life, Chacha pursued his interest in languages and Bible translations through a number of courses, and began to translate the New Testament into the Kuria language, which was completed by the time of his death in 1990. Chacha's contacts with the SPCM in Ethiopia had come through the Swedish-American evangelist Joseph Mattsson-Boze, for whom he had also worked as a translator.[201] Mattsson-Boze, who called him "one of our leading

---

197 The Swedish missionary Mattsson-Boze also mentioned his poor background, cf. JOSEPH MATTSSON-BOZE, "Africa: Report from the Training Center for Young Nationals in Ethiopia," *Herald of Faith* 34 (10 1966): 13; MATTSSON-BOZE, "Mighty Outpouring of the Holy Ghost in Ethiopia."

198 See CHACHA OMAHE, "Life and Experience in the Lord's Ministry."

199 Cf. ibid.; JOHANSSON, E-mail to author, October 10, 2006. On Pentecostalism in Kenya and the PEFA, see RONALD PAUL WESTBURY, "The Nature and Status of Ministry Practices of the Pentecostal Evangelistic Fellowship of Africa" (Ph.D. thesis, Asbury Theological Seminary, 2002), 22–36; DAVID J. GARRARD, "Kenya," in *The New International Dictionary of Pentecostal and Charismatic Movements*, ed. STANLEY M. BURGESS and EDUARD M. van der MAAS (Grand Rapids, MI: Zondervan, 2002), 150–155. Cf. also WILLIAM B. ANDERSON, *The Church in East Africa 1840–1974* (Dodoma: Central Tanganyika Press, 1981), 168–170 on the impact of T. L. Osborn's evangelistic campaign in 1957. The work in Kenya, at the time was fairly small however. The Nairobi district, for example, apparently only consisted of one church at the time, see WESTBURY, "The Nature and Status of Ministry Practices of the Pentecostal Evangelistic Fellowship of Africa," 36.

200 See EVA S. BUTLER, *In the Shadow of Kilimanjaro: Pioneering the Pentecostal Testimony Among the Maasai People* (Salisbury Center, NY: Pinecrest Publications, 2002). Eva Butler was the daughter of the Elim-founder Ivan Spencer and was a missionary in Kenya from 1953 to 1989. She had a good relationship with Chacha, and mentioned his contributions in many places of her book, which also includes pictures of him.

201 Joseph Mattsson-Boze was a Swedish Pentecostal who emigrated to the USA in 1933 to pastor a Scandinavian Pentecostal church in Chicago. After he resigned from the pastorate in 1958, he became an itinerant evangelist spending a significant amount of time in East Africa, especially in Kenya. Mattsson-Boze was involved in the Latter Rain movement and edited the Pentecostal

brethren and a seasoned teacher of the Word of God,"[202] recommended Chacha to the
SPCM missionaries for their yearly Bible school in Awasa when he could not accept
their invitation to the 1963 conference himself.[203]

Not only is Chacha's background largely unknown in Ethiopia, even the frequency
and dating of his visits to Ethiopia are debated. Most histories rely on Engelsviken's
"Documentary Report" and therefore follow his dating of Chacha's first (and only
mentioned) visit to the year of 1963.[204] However, some eyewitnesses in Awasa place
this visit two years later.[205] This discrepancy in dating Chacha's ministry is discussed
extensively by Bekele Woldekidan,[206] who concludes indefinitely, hoping for further
evidence in the future.[207] Such evidence can be found in contemporary Pentecostal
journals and correspondence. A report by Harald Johansson in the *Evangelii Härold*
from 1963 mentions Chacha as one of two teachers (next to the local missionary Gösta
Lindahl) at the Awasa conference, which began on September 15, 1963.[208] The events
described here align with the eyewitness reports, the main discrepancy remains in the
dating.[209] Furthermore, Ramstrand reported that Chacha wasn't able to attend the
summer conference in 1965, even noting the disappointment of the attending students,
which indicates that the popularity Chacha already had attained.[210]

Following the reports in the *Evangelii Härold*, the *Herald of Faith* and other missionary correspondence from Awasa, two more visits by Chacha Omahe to the summer

periodical *Herald of Faith* from 1943-1970, see JOSEPH COLLETTI, "Mattson-Boze, Joseph D.,"
in *The New International Dictionary of Pentecostal and Charismatic Movements*, ed. STANLEY
M. BURGESS and EDUARD M. van der MAAS (Grand Rapids, MI: Zondervan, 2002), 867. For
the controversies around the Latter Rain movement in the Swedish Pentecostal movement and
Mattsson-Boze's involvement, see HALLDORF, *Lewis Brev*, 244–287.
202 MATTSSON-BOZE, "Mighty Outpouring of the Holy Ghost in Ethiopia."
203 Ibid.; JOHANSSON, "Pingsteld över Etiopien."
204 ENGELSVIKEN, "Molo Wongel," 25.
205 Interviews no. 119; 12; 100. One of the informants recited especially detailed memories, dating
many events exactly to the day. According to him the first believers during Chacha's initial
visit were baptized in the Holy Spirit on 21 ነሐሴ (*näḥase*) 1957, i.e., 27 August, 1965. (Bekele
apparently was told exactly the same date, cf. BEKELE WOLDEKIDAN, ८‌ዘ‌ይ‌ዛ‌ለ, 81.) Even the
weekday specified (Friday) corresponds to the date in 1965. The proposed dates in all oral
histories about Chacha encountered by this researcher range from 1961 to 1965. TIBEBE ES-
HETE, *The Evangelical Movement in Ethiopia*, 158 also mentions 1965 as the year of Chacha's
visit, citing an Elim Missionary News Report. However, this document refers to the summer
conference of 1964, since it dates to February 1965, i.e., before the 1965 summer conference,
see ELIM BIBLE INSTITUTE, "Missionary News Report: Ethiopia," *Elim Bible Institute Bulletin*
(February 1965).
206 BEKELE WOLDEKIDAN, ८‌ዘ‌ይ‌ዛ‌ለ, 80–84, 90–91.
207 Ibid., 91.
208 JOHANSSON, "Pingsteld över Etiopien." Cf. also Mattson-Boze's reports about this conference,
where he not only mentioned Chacha's ministry, but also called the Spirit outpouring in Awasa
"a direct outflow" from his "Africa Project", because of the impact his protégé had, MATTSSON-
BOZE, "Mighty Outpouring of the Holy Ghost in Ethiopia."
209 The report about the 1963 conference in *Herald of Faith*, "Glorious Outpouring of the Holy
Spirit in Ethiopia" also lines up with the oral informants, including an initial dispute about
Chacha's teachings, which even runs through some testimonies presented here.
210 RAMSTRAND, Letter to supporters, August 22, 1965; RAMSTRAND, *Det heliga äventyret*, 137–138.

conferences can be confirmed: in 1964[211] and 1966[212]. Chacha also mentioned these three visits to Ethiopia in his curriculum vitae of 1970.[213] Yosief Kidanewold indicates in a list that Chacha also came in 1967,[214] but the conference report by the SPCM only named Ramstrand and Mattsson-Boze as teachers.[215]

On his journey back from the 1963 Awasa conference Chacha visited the Finnish mission station at Merkato, were he preached and prayed for the baptism in the Holy Spirit.[216] After this meeting the mission did not invite him for a second time, but during one of his later visits, he preached at a meeting of Ethiopian Pentecostals.[217] He is also reported to have initiated spiritual revival in Holeta, another branch of the Finnish mission work.[218] In 1964 Chacha was also invited to speak at the leper settlement Addis Hiwot in Tibele.[219]

2.4.2 Representations of Chacha's Visits

The rather scant historical information in most histories of Ethiopian Pentecostalism is complemented by a plethora of narratives about the actual events during the Kenyan's visit, in which Chacha's prominence is emphasized or refuted, depending on

---

211 LINDAHL, "Seger i Etiopien"; RAMSTRAND, Letter to supporting congregations, August 30, 1964.
212 ROLAND NELSSON, "Gamla tiders väckelse bland universitetsstuderande," [Old-time Revival Among University Students.], *Evangelii Härold* (42 1966): 7; MATTSSON-BOZE, "Africa"; cf. NYBERG OSKARSSON, *Svensk Pingstmission i Ethiopien (1959–1980)*, 262. See also BEKELE WOLDEKIDAN, ረጰያ፟ስ, illustrations following p. 113, for a facsimile of a training course certificate from 1966 with Chacha's signature.
213 See CHACHA OMAHE, "Life and Experience in the Lord's Ministry."
214 YOSIEF KIDANEWOLD, "The History of the Pentecostal Movement in Addis Abeba," 65.
215 OWE WALLBERG, "Hälsning från bibelskolan i Awasa," [Greetings from the Bible School in Awasa.], *Evangelii Härold* (45 1967): 5. Mattsson-Boze's report also does not mention Chacha, see JOSEPH MATTSSON-BOZE, "Ethiopia: In Audience with the Emperor: Great Miracles," *Herald of Faith* 35 (10 1967): 7–8.
216 For a contemporary account of Chacha's preaching at the Finnish mission chapel, cf. *Herald of Faith*, "Glorious Outpouring of the Holy Spirit in Ethiopia," last testimony on p. 26. Some sources argue that Chacha was invited to the Finnish mission by the initiative of Ethiopians who had heard about the Awasa meetings, see TAYE ABDISSA, "The Pentecostal Development and the Rise of Charismatic Movement in Ethiopia," 18; also mentioned in interview no. 91. The duration of Chacha's visit at the Merkato Finnish mission is usually specified as one or two weeks, cf. e.g. SELESHI KEBEDE, "The History of the Guenet Church," 5; ENGELSVIKEN, "Molo Wongel," 26.
217 This probably was during the 1966 visit, where he is mentioned to have preached at the Hallelujah School, an elementary school initiative by an Ethiopian Pentecostal, interview no. 29; and at the premises rented by Pentecostal university students, interview no. 87. Mattsson-Boze also visited Addis Ababa in 1966, where he spoke at the Finnish mission, but without Chacha even though they had worked together in Awasa that year. There is a picture of this visit, showing only Mattson-Boze, Anna-Liisa and Sanfrid Mattsson, as well as Karl Ramstrand, see MATTSSON-BOZE, "Africa," 13. Chacha was not permitted to come to the mission, see below, 75.
218 SELESHI KEBEDE, "The History of the Guenet Church," 13. No date is provided here, and Chacha's influence is portrayed in a typical manner: "The charismatic experience was not known widely in the church but after Mr. Chacha prayed for some Christian leaders in Holetta, the ministry of the Holy Spirit spread in the whole church."
219 NYBERG OSKARSSON, *Svensk Pingstmission i Ethiopien (1959–1980)*, 82; ARVID MALMVÄRN, Letter to Arvid Sköldeberg, 17 September 1964, Addis Hiwot Botter Collection, Pingstarkiv Kaggeholm, Ekerö; also mentioned in interview no. 35.

the narrative scheme underlying the respective account. In this way the stories also serve as evaluations of the missionary contribution to the Pentecostal revival, and exhibit the competitive constellation between the independent movement, the Nordic missions, and the churches they spawned.

One area for such observations is the narrative representation of conflicts surrounding Chacha's visits. All accounts attribute a dynamic and simple style of preaching to the Kenyan evangelist, combined with a straightforward and determined attitude. After he had taught in Awasa for a few days during his first visit, a conflict apparently broke out among the Ethiopian participants with regard to Chacha's personal integrity and the credibility of his teaching about the Holy Spirit. One Swedish observer saw mainly Ethiopian "friends from other missions"[220] behind this conflict, who had been taught against baptism in the Spirit and the initial evidence of speaking in tongues. His report goes on to narrate the missionaries' attempt to reconcile the youths with the Kenyan evangelist by asserting the biblical nature of his teaching. Once the doubting youths were persuaded to resume their participation, the problem was solved, because a large portion of the group experienced Spirit baptism and asked Chacha for forgiveness. Chacha also told a similar story soon after the events, but the decisive breakthrough was not initiated by the help of the Swedish missionaries, but through his own prayers, endurance, and continued encouragement.[221]

Ethiopian informants who were eyewitnesses of the meeting with Chacha essentially tell the same story, but with a different take on the role of the missions.[222] While they point to their own background in the then dispensationalist SIM and their earlier conviction of having received the Holy Spirit with water baptism, they also assert that they had been exposed to Pentecostal teaching before Chacha's arrival. However something was still missing in the missionaries' teaching and practice in order for them to actually encounter the experience: the missionaries only taught basic salvation, they did not teach about the sign of speaking in tongues, they were opposed to shouting, or they simply did not practice it enough and thus failed to reap the fruits of their teaching. Consequently, the conflict about Chacha is not so much an issue of theology, but one of experience. When the hitherto unknown experience of tongues occurred in their midst, it was first associated with "Satanic" languages, and the Kenyan evangelist was likened to a "witch doctor", because he let his hair grow long and because there was shouting and groaning under his ministry. In these accounts, it therefore seems that when the missionaries help to reconcile the difference between their Ethiopian students and Chacha, they were not so much countering a dispensationalist doctrine, but rather had to make up for their failure to relay certain spiritual experiences before.

Stories of conflicts during Chacha's visit in the Finnish mission in Addis Ababa are also prevalent, but this time the roles are reversed: the missionaries oppose the

---

220   JOHANSSON, "Pingsteld över Etiopien."
221   See CHACHA OMAHE, "The Holy Ghost Revival in Ethiopia," private collection, Mukiria Chacha, 1963. This report of about two paragraphs came with six pages of testimonies of students in Awasa and Addis Ababa receiving the Holy Spirit. It was published with slight changes in Mattsson-Boze's paper *Herald of Faith* in March 1964, see *Herald of Faith*, "Glorious Outpouring of the Holy Spirit in Ethiopia."
222   Interviews no. 12; 119; 100. Cf. also BEKELE WOLDEKIDAN, ልደታዊ, 80–81.

Kenyan evangelist and most Ethiopians readily accept his teaching. Again, the main point of contention was Chacha's teaching about tongues, as one missionary narrates:

> Chacha was teaching there [*pauses*] just opposite to the Bible. He had been emphasizing that they started to speak in tongues and they were filled with Holy Ghost. And he had said even in the meeting that "Brothers here is a nail. Put Amharic into this nail, hang it there, don't use it. And you start to speak in tongues." And Hanna, sister Hanna rose up there, and — uh yah — she had a straight way in that meeting. She corrected Mister Chacha, and she said: "Please, you are now putting the things, the chariot in front of the horse. So the Bible says that they were filled with Holy Ghost, and because of that they started to speak in tongues." But the teaching of Chacha was that you just forget Amharic and you start to speak in tongues. And this makes a certain kind of speaking in tongues that finally leaves the Christian empty-hearted. And he does not receive power. The main sign is also that when you receive the Holy Ghost you would be filled with power.[223]

This second-hand report[224] starts with a strong assertion, namely, that Chacha's teaching was false, "just opposite to the Bible". This may seem like a surprisingly harsh statement, since at first glance the main issue is simply one of procedure: how does a Spirit-filled believer start to speak in tongues? Is there a way to prepare oneself, i.e., by laying down one's own language? Or should one simply wait for divine impartation? However, the strict separation and subsequence between filling in the Holy Spirit and speaking in tongues, which the informant argues for, indicates that there is more at stake than mere procedure. This is evident in the following statements. First, there seems to be a human capacity to imitate tongues, which is not of the Holy Spirit and leaves "the Christian empty-hearted." Secondly, simply speaking in tongues therefore can not be a clear evidence of Spirit baptism, there must be a different "main sign", the reception of "power."[225] Interestingly, the Finnish Pentecostal missionaries are characterized in this account by a position very similar to the questions brought forth by the Ethiopians in the Awasa conflict: the genuineness of tongues under Chacha's ministry is doubted in combination with some reservations toward a strict interpretation of the "initial evidence" doctrine. However, a general consensus is not mentioned here, the narration of events simply concludes with "sister Hanna's" answer, hinting at an unresolved conflict. This is also evident in later correspondence between Chacha and the missionaries. In 1966, when Chacha was

---

223 Interview no. 69.

224 Although this missionary was in Ethiopia during the time of Chacha's first visit, he was stationed in a different part of the country and never met the Kenyan preacher. His narrative is based on the story as told by the missionaries Helvi Halme and Hanna Ihalainen.

225 This is of course parallels the rather intricate debates surrounding the doctrine of "initial evidence" in the Pentecostal movement as a whole, where the occasionally experienced delay in the reception of tongues served to weaken the "initial evidence" postulate. Cf. e.g. GARY B. MCGEE, "Early Pentecostal Hermeneutics: Tongues as Evidence in the Book of Acts," in *Initial Evidence: Historical and Biblical Perspectives on the Pentecostal Doctrine of Spirit Baptism*, ed. GARY B. MCGEE (Peabody, MA: Hendrickson Publishers, 1991), 107–110 or more in detail CECIL M. JR. ROBECK, "An Emerging Magisterium? The Case of the Assemblies of God," *Pneuma* 25 (2 2003): 164–215.

planning another visit to Addis Ababa, he apparently asked the Helvi Halme and Hanna Ihalainen for forgiveness regarding earlier conflicts and for a chance to preach at the Addis Ababa Mekato mission again. Helvi Halme's answer[226] was unequivocal: While she signaled her forgiveness, her attitude toward his ministry was without compromise. She noted that Chacha's reports about what happened in Addis Ababa or Holeta were "not the same with reality," and more importantly that their fundamental disagreement about and Spirit baptism could not be worked out. Therefore, Chacha would not be received at the Merkato mission nor by any other Finnish mission.

The Finnish argumentation seems to be directly opposite to the Ethiopian representations of the story, like in the following report quoted by Engelsviken:

> Omahe Chacha came to Addis Ababa after the Bible Conference in Awassa was over. He found us praying when he came, but we did not know how to receive the Holy Spirit. Then he said: "You young people, you do not need to call down the Holy Spirit from heaven. The Holy Spirit is here. Cleanse your hearts from sin by the blood of Jesus Christ and you will be filled with the Holy Spirit." It was so simple that anyone of us could understand it. He did not exaggerate but kept everything down to earth. About fourty young people knelt down and were filled with the Holy Spirit during the two weeks he was there. Before Omahe Chacha came none of us was filled with the Spirit, except a young dresser from Wollega. But it seemed strange to us. He fell down on the floor on his forehead and shouted as if he was going to die. Most of us were scared of this. It was like being possessed by an evil spirit. We did not like his behavior, but the missionaries told us that he was filled with the Holy Spirit. When the Kenyan came, he was of great help to us. He was a Bible teacher and had a special gift to help people commit themselves to the Lord. He said: "The Holy Spirit came on the Day of Pentecost. He has helped you receive the Lord. He is with you and will give you his gifts. Believe in God and you will be filled with the Holy Spirit. Open up your hearts! You don't have to run here and there or jump up and down." Those who were filled with the Spirit spoke in tongues and some received a word of prophecy or an interpretation of tongues.[227]

The main problem is once again how to genuinely receive the Holy Spirit, but unlike the previously quoted missionary account, it is not Chacha's, but the missionaries' ministry that is under suspicion. They not only failed to freely administer the Spirit of God, but the one case of Spirit baptism resulting from their work is seriously questionable. The missionaries are also strangely absent from this account: the youths are praying alone, and there is no mention of the missionaries' presence (or objections) during Chacha's ministry. Furthermore, the description of Chacha's teaching serves as an outline of what was missing so far and thus can be read as a criticism to the missionaries' theology. To the Kenyan evangelist the Holy Spirit was not some far removed reality that sovereignly breaks into the life of the believer, but a

---

226   See HELVI HALME, *Letter to Chacha Omahe* (Private collection, Mukiria Chacha, 1966). This
       letter was relayed by Mukiria Chacha's son, his father had kept it among his files.
227   ENGELSVIKEN, "Molo Wongel," 26f.

present and immediate reality. His message was simple, practical and helpful, he was a Bible teacher. Moreover, his ministry was successful. In just two weeks of ministry the symbolic number of forty believers receive a genuine experience of the baptism in the Spirit, with the accompanying sign of tongues, prophecy and interpretation.

There are also less enthusiastic Ethiopian reports about the events in Addis Ababa. One informant, for example, agreed with the missionaries' criticism of Chacha's "shallow teaching"[228] and accepted the Spirit baptism of the Wolmera youth as sincere. However, other than the missionary quoted above, this observer did not conclude that a simple and perhaps questionable theology cannot lead to sincere experiences of Spirit baptism. Though the informant himself was not challenged by Chacha's teaching, and eventually had to find his own pathway to Spirit baptism, he still concluded regarding Chacha: "God honored his simple faith and [he] became an instrument for the expansion of His Kingdom in Ethiopia."[229]

2.4.3 Projections of Mission Independence

It is evident that the Chacha Omahe narratives are part of the wider debate on missionary contribution to the Ethiopian Pentecostal movement, and as such they are subject to the underlying narrative schemes, which are situated in denominational histories. In the strong independent master narrative, told most prominently by the FGBC, Chacha takes on a number of functions. First of all, Chacha's successes are used to outline deficiencies of the foreign Pentecostal missionary enterprise which in turn constitute the necessity of Ethiopian emancipation. This is not necessarily articulated in harsh criticism as seen above, but can also be packed in a more or less sympathetic analysis of the reasons for the missionaries' "fear" to fully allow Pentecostal experiences.[230] Racial differences may also be used to contrast the Kenyan revivalist with the missionaries. Nyberg Oskarsson quotes a missionary who noted that "a colored brother can of course take up problems that we Whites cannot take up"[231] and Engelsviken sees some "psychological effect" in the fact that Chacha was "African as the Ethiopians", which according to the Ethiopian informant quoted here, helped the natives to see that baptism in the Spirit was not "invented by white people".[232] Even though some followed Engelsviken in this,[233] a common racial or

---

228 SELESHI KEBEDE, "The History of the Guenet Church," 5.

229 Ibid., 6

230 E.g. BEKELE WOLDEKIDAN, ረጅመጉዞ, 79–80. Bekele carefully considers different reasons for the missionaries' reservation, but the overall verdict is clear nevertheless: "Even though the two mission organizations were Pentecostal, until this time they hadn't passed out the Pentecostal experience to the Ethiopians."

231 NYBERG OSKARSSON, Svensk Pingstmission i Ethiopien (1959–1980), 262.

232 ENGELSVIKEN, "Molo Wongel," 26.

233 E.g. YOSIEF KIDANEWOLD, "The History of the Pentecostal Movement in Addis Abeba," 4; TEKA OBSA FOGI, "The Charismatic Movement in the EECMY," 72.

"African" identity does not seem to be central in the Ethiopian accounts.[234] Chacha is even criticized for introducing racial categories.[235]

Secondly, later conflicts between the missionaries and the Ethiopian Pentecostal movement are projected back to the person of Chacha and compacted in story form here. An especially clear example can be found in the reports of Chacha's clashes with the Finnish missionaries at Merkato. Reportedly, there had been a number of instances where he had expressed his own disrespect of female leadership. During a particularly turbulent exorcism the Kenyan evangelist was apparently criticized by the missionaries together with an assertion of their own responsibility for the visitors and the overall program.[236] He is reported to have defied this intervention and furthermore rebuked the female missionaries. This is quoted in different ways: simply as "Keep quiet lady," spiritually packaged as "Woman keep quiet, for there was no keeping quiet while walking on the devil's territories," or more blatantly chauvinist as "Be quiet! This is the work of God and you must not interfere. I speak to you as a I speak to my wife!"[237] Though different in intensity, a matter of spiritual discernment and leadership authority is transformed into a gender issue and perpetuated as such in these narratives. It thus becomes an anticipatory exemplification of the later rejection of female authority, which Ethiopians gave as one of the reasons for their emancipation from the Finnish mission.[238]

Third, in contrasting Chacha's work with the missionaries' ministry and in foreshadowing subsequent conflicts in these stories, the Kenyan revivalist becomes the spiritual father of the Ethiopian Pentecostal movement. In his hybrid configuration as an African yet foreign evangelist, associated with the missionaries but only visiting, he is the ideal figure for this projection, allowing histories to trace the origins of the Ethiopian Pentecostal movement to its world-wide missionary roots, while asserting its mission independence. Consequently, Chacha Omahe is given firm grounding in the Pentecostal movement,[239] and the importance of his contributions is often pre-

---

234 One Swedish observer even maintained that the race argument had a very different connotation: the proud Ethiopians, regarding their darker southern neighbors as inferior, thought that if those "black Kenyans can receive the Holy Spirit and speak in tongues, why shall we not," interview no. 115.

235 One informant recounted a statement by Chacha from the pulpit that made him "very uncomfortable": "I praise the Lord for not being anyone, because I am not a white man," interview no. 91.

236 It is likely that exorcism was an essential part of Chacha's ministry, given their central role in the Kenyan revival of the late 1950s and early 1960s, cf. ANDERSON, *The Church in East Africa 1840–1974*, 168–170.

237 Cf. interview no. 91; TIBEBE ESHETE, *The Evangelical Movement in Ethiopia*, 158; ENGELSVIKEN, "Molo Wongel," 30.

238 See e.g. ibid., 29. Chacha's son, however, indicated that his father had no issues with female missionaries or a leading role for women in the church. He even had a female pastor in the church he founded in Kenya. MUKIRIA CHACHA, E-mail to author, 23 February 2010; MUKIRIA CHACHA, E-mail to author, 8 March 2010.

239 His position is occasionally overestimated to this end. He is characterized as "one of the leaders of the Pentecostals in Kenya" (TEKA OBSA FOGI, "The Charismatic Movement in the EECMY," 72), or even as "the famous leader in the East African Pentecostal movement in Kenya" (TAYE ABDISSA, "The Pentecostal Development and the Rise of Charismatic Movement in Ethiopia," 18). These designations may be reflections of Chacha's work as district overseer for the PEFA,

sented as an undisputed historical fact.[240] Yet, at the same time Chacha has a clearly delimited role: he was a match in the hand of God, used to light the spiritual fire among the already prepared Ethiopian believers. Although he was connected to the missions, he is not seen as their representative, and he did not have a permanent presence in Ethiopia. These limitations of Chacha's work can be used to assert Ethiopian independence:

> Although the instrumentality of Chacha Omahe should not be underestimated, the continuity of the Movement after his departure, is evidence that an independent Ethiopian Pentecostal Movement has been going on.[241]

These functions of the Chacha narratives help to understand the emphasis placed on the Kenyan evangelist in independent accounts and the implicit or explicit denial of his influence in mission histories.[242] Chacha Omahe's hybrid configuration as a non-European visiting missionary makes him the ideal character for providing an otherwise independent Pentecostal movement with mission-related (and thus orthodox) roots, while at the same time voicing mission criticism and anticipating the decrease of missionary influence.

2.5   Leaving the Finnish Mission

The narratives analyzed so far have revealed a rather implicit critical engagement with the missionary presence in the overall assessments of its input, or in contrasting the missions' deficiencies with Chacha Omahe's ministry. A more explicit engagement with the missions can be found in stories about Ethiopian Pentecostals breaking away from the missions.

The most often encountered separation narrative is the exodus of Ethiopian believers from the Finnish mission station in the Addis Ababa Merkato area. Other instances of conflicts and splits are also reported, but they generally do not assume the same paradigmatic role in historical accounts as this first Merkato split.[243] The centrality of the Finnish mission separation narrative is arguably due to the fact that

---

but the sources do not seem to be informed about any details, nor about the fact that Chacha's organization was only one of multiple Pentecostal denominations in Kenya.

240   See e.g. TIBEBE ESHETE, *The Evangelical Movement in Ethiopia*, 158, noting that "[m]ost of the informants are unanimous concerning the contribution of the Kenyan preacher," or BEKELE WOLDEKIDAN, ረድኤት, 80, contending that he has not "encountered either missionary or Ethiopian who was or is trying to deny that the person used by God for the ground-breaking ministry among the two mission organizations, in Awasa or at Merkato, was Chacha Omahe."

241   YOSIEF KIDANEWOLD, "The History of the Pentecostal Movement in Addis Abeba," 5. See also ENGELSVIKEN, "Molo Wongel," 28; TEKA OBSA FOGI, "The Charismatic Movement in the EECMY," 72.

242   No mention of Chacha is made in Finnish missionary correspondence or historical accounts. In interviews Chacha was only mentioned when asked about, the importance often attributed to him was more or less explicitly denied, interviews no. 69; 104. Swedish mission sources acknowledge his ministry, but most often do not emphasize his input or provide detailed narratives about his ministry.

243   See below, 145ff. for another example, i.e., the power struggle and separation between SPCM missionaries and the FGBC nucleus only a few years later.

three of the early leaders of the independent movement came out of the Finnish mission in this separation process,[244] and the event therefore became the main narrative for mission emancipation in the independent Pentecostal accounts. In addition, the sufficient complexity of the actual events have led to an array of representations and interpretations, articulating denominational identities and theological convictions, as well as the underlying narrative schemes of Ethiopian Pentecostal history.

2.5.1 Identifying the Separation Event

In Engelsviken's fairly extensive description of the "Break with the Missionaries,"[245] it is peculiar that he does not provide a date nor even a year when narrating this split from the Finnish mission.[246] The placement of the story in Engelsviken's report and his explicit reference to the mission-critical impetus of Chacha[247] would indicate some time after the Kenyan's first visit, and perhaps before the foundation of the independent student movement, since the latter is narrated subsequently. Other sources more explicitly place the event "soon after" Chacha's departure,[248] in 1964,[249] or in 1966.[250] What is the reason for this failure to provide a conclusive chronological determination for the event?

Chronological discrepancies and uncertainties are of course not unusual in mainly oral histories. However this issue is better understood when investigating what the different accounts qualify as the actual "separation event." One of the eyewitnesses quoted by Engelsviken, for example, specifically mentions a chronologically identifiable event, namely, when the students "decided to leave the mission, all of us at one time"[251] and rented their own premises in the Merkato area. However, the same narrative also reveals that this was merely the conclusion to protracted negotiations with the missionaries, thus characterizing the separation more as a process. This finds support in reminiscences by one of the participants in this separation, who recounts that the Ethiopians had already been conducting their own meetings prior to leaving the mission. They called their group "Hallelujah Fellowship", and only moved their home fellowship into rented premises after they had announced their departure from the Finnish mission chapel.[252] According to this informant, their fellowship was established together with Pentecostal students from Harar, who had come to Addis

---

244 i.e., Kebede Woldemariam, Melese Wogu, and Fantahun Gebre, see e.g. BEKELE WOLDEKIDAN, ራዕይና, 103.
245 See ENGELSVIKEN, "Molo Wongel," 29–33.
246 This is also encountered in other sources, such as YOSIEF KIDANEWOLD, "The History of the Pentecostal Movement in Addis Abeba," 12; ROININEN, "A Condensed History of the Finnish Mission in Ethiopia," 5; ETHIOPIAN GENNET CHURCH, የ50ኛው ዓመት የወርቅ ኢዮቤልዩ በዓል, 15.
247 ENGELSVIKEN, "Molo Wongel," 30.
248 TAYE ABDISSA, "The Pentecostal Development and the Rise of Charismatic Movement in Ethiopia," 19. Chacha's visit is dated to 1963 here.
249 NYBERG OSKARSSON, Svensk Pingstmission i Ethiopien (1959–1980), 263. The author does not indicate her source for this date.
250 SELESHI KEBEDE, "The History of the Guenet Church," 6; TIBEBE ESHETE, The Evangelical Movement in Ethiopia, 160.
251 ENGELSVIKEN, "Molo Wongel," 30–31. This is in turn referenced by YOSIEF KIDANEWOLD, "The History of the Pentecostal Movement in Addis Abeba," 12–13,17.
252 Interview no. 91.

Ababa as teachers, which would date the establishment of the "Hallelujah Fellowship" to the beginning of the school year 1966/67, i.e., earliest by September 1966.[253] In light of this fairly late dating, the mention of Chacha Omahe's influence in different separation accounts needs to be reevaluated. It is unlikely that his first visit in Addis Ababa in 1963 is directly connected to the split at the Finnish mission, at least not as directly as Engelsviken and other accounts claim.[254]

Mission sources, on the other hand, identify a different occasion altogether as the "actual separation", both in secondary historical accounts as well as in contemporary letters. It is not until the beginning of 1967 that the first mention of the conflicts is found in the correspondence by the Finnish missionaries, with scattered echoes following until September 1968.[255] In a letter from February 1967, Mattssons mention considerable problems at Merkato, noting that a big group had left Merkato when "some brothers were fishing in our fishing grounds."[256] A later reference to the events at Merkato is a bit more explicit:

> Our neighbors have been divided into four different lines in the work, but they try to reach an arrangement in the work. We were empty without a translator when they arranged the work in a different way, which we did not have anything to do with, and this happened without our knowledge.[257]

This obvious allusion to the division of the Swedes, coupled with the allegation of their involvement in the Merkato developments, reveals another dynamic in this emancipation process, namely, the competitive constellation between the Swedish and Finnish Pentecostal mission. A letter later in 1968 accused the Swedish missionaries directly, naming their desire for broader influence as the source of the problem.[258] The historical background for these allegations is the Swedish involvement in the ordination of elders for the university student movement. Three of these elders had previously separated from the Merkato Finnish mission, one of whom was Kebede Woldemariam, who used to work as a translator at Merkato.[259] Ramstrand's account of the events is compatible to the Finnish accusations, tracing the split in the Finnish mission church essentially to his teaching on church organization, and defending the SPCM's supportive actions with the necessity to stay involved in the independent revival movement.[260] This was, of course, a serious rupture in the relationship between

---

253 See also ibid., 17; interview no. 47.
254 See ENGELSVIKEN, "Molo Wongel," 30; TAYE ABDISSA, "The Pentecostal Development and the Rise of Charismatic Movement in Ethiopia," 19; TEKA OBSA FOGI, "The Charismatic Movement in the EECMY," 76; TIBEBE ESHETE, *The Evangelical Movement in Ethiopia*, 159. A number of these sources use Chacha's 1963 visit as chronological reference for the split.
255 This makes a split very soon after Chacha's visit even more unlikely.
256 SANFRID MATTSSON, Letter to brother Heinikainen, 17 February 1967, Sanfrid and Anna-Liisa Mattsson Collection, Fida Archives, Helsinki.
257 MATTSSON and MATTSSON, Letter to Tapani Kärnä, May 6, 1968.
258 MATTSSON and MATTSSON, Letter to Otto Koivukangas, Veikko Manninen, and Tapani Kärnä, August 24, 1968. Cf. also SANFRID MATTSSON, Letter to Tapani Kärnä, 24 June 1968, Sanfrid and Anna-Liisa Mattsson Collection, Fida Archives, Helsinki.
259 Interview no. 19.
260 Ramstrand apparently also sought active involvement in discussions with the mission leaders on behalf of the Ethiopian believers, KARL RAMSTRAND, Letter to Arne Petterson, 26 March 1968,

the two missions, which was even noticed in Finland and Sweden, leading to an investigation in 1968 by the leading representative of the Swedish-speaking Pentecostal churches in Finland and veteran missionary to Brazil, pastor Lars-Eric Bergsten.[261] It is important to note here that none of the primary or secondary mission sources narrate an earlier separation of Ethiopians, or refer to the independent Merkato meetings.[262] To them, the mission emancipation apparently first became manifest with the Swedish-assisted ordination of former Finnish mission aides as elders of the independent movement. It remains unclear whether the omission of the earlier Ethiopian exodus from Merkato in these missionary sources is due to their narrative focus, a lack of awareness, or doubts about the significance of the earlier Ethiopian initiatives.

Just as the actual separation "event" is contested in the histories of Ethiopian Pentecostalism, the subsequent relationship between the Finnish mission and independent Pentecostals is also represented in many different ways. Engelsviken, for example, who first established the tension between missionaries and Ethiopian Pentecostals in a number of ways, adopted a much more conciliatory tone after narrating the break. He contends that "the good relationship" between the mission and the independent group "was soon reestablished," that "some of the men and women among the Finnish missionaries were of rare spiritual quality," and that the "Finnish Mission is still regarded as the mission congregation with the closest ties to the Pentecostal Church in Ethiopia."[263] In oral histories, the picture is less harmonic and depends on the background of the informant. Those who emphasize the mission independence of Ethiopian Pentecostalism do not tend to follow Engelsviken's picture of a harmonic relationship after the split, but assert that the Ethiopian believers did not want to associate with missionaries anymore, and that they never went to the Finnish mission meetings again.[264] Informants coming from the mission background, on the other hand, point to more fluctuation between the groups. For example, one informant who was associated with the Finnish mission-founded GC told of his conversion among the later nucleus of the FGBC, but mentioned that he used to worship at the Merkato Finnish mission as well.[265] Another participant in the early split, who later did not stay in the FGBC, noted that the independent group remained separate from the mission but that he had asked the missionaries for forgiveness "for the way" the split was conducted.[266]

Finnish mission sources, on the other hand, on occasion even emphasize the support they gave to the independent movement at this time and later, for example by hosting training courses or providing office space when the FGBC was under political

Karl Ramstrand Collection, Pingstarkiv Kaggeholm, Ekerö. See also RAMSTRAND, *Det heliga äventyret*, 144–145, where he mentions that the accusation of "fishing in other waters" was brought against the Swedish.

261 RAMSTRAND, Letter to Arne Petterson, March 26, 1968. About Bergsten, cf. KÄRKKÄINEN, "The Pentecostal Movement in Finland," 125.

262 The only exception here is NYBERG OSKARSSON, *Svensk Pingstmission i Ethiopien (1959–1980)*, 262, apparently based on Engelsviken.

263 ENGELSVIKEN, "Molo Wongel," 32.

264 E.g. interviews no. 116; 87.

265 Interview no. 5.

266 Interview no. 91.

pressure.[267] However, at the same time, it appears that instances of such cooperation were much disputed among the Finnish Pentecostal missionaries. For example, the decision by one Finnish missionary to enroll FGBC evangelists in a Bible course based on the recommendation of their own elders, was opposed by other mission leaders, who had, according to this informant, resolved to isolate the independent Christians in the hope of their remorseful return.[268] Furthermore, some of the Finnish missionaries regarded the independent movement as dangerous for their mission because they had come into conflict with the Ethiopian authorities.[269] Even false allegations of sexual immorality at night-time prayer meetings were repeated in two missionary letters.[270] Finally, when pastor Bergsten after his above-mentioned investigation of the split recommended to cooperate with the Swedes and the independent Pentecostals, the majority of Finnish missionaries were opposed to such a measure. After complaining to the Finnish headquarters, they were assured that they were free to follow their line of non-cooperation.[271]

These differences in representing both the actual separation event as well as the subsequent relationship between the Finnish mission and the independent Pente-costals suggest that the emancipation of Ethiopian Pentecostals from their missionary roots was a multifaceted and open process that required the constant renegotiation of a precarious relationship. The later historical representation, however, was shaped by the larger narrative trajectories about the role of missions and their interest to point to defining moments in discussing the relationship between the missions and Ethiopian Pentecostals.

---

267 ROININEN, "A Condensed History of the Finnish Mission in Ethiopia," 6, 9–10, 18; interview no. 104. The latter informant even stated that there was "a very near cooperation between Full Gospel Church and mission", especially during the Derg time. However, a letter from 1986 also seems to indicate limits in what the Ethiopians were willing to accept, noting that the "Full Gospels, who are free from the slavery of mission, have paid the fee for their partici-pants at earlier courses", HEIKKI PENTTINEN, Letter to Tapani Kärnä, 13 February 1968, Later Correspondence, Fida Archives, Helsinki.

268 Interview no. 69. Some time after the split, the missionaries in charge at Merkato mentioned in a letter that some believers had returned to the mission, but they also indicated that a full return would only be possible if "they humble themselves", cf. MARJA MUFFETT and RAW-SON MUFFETT, Letter to Tapani Kärnä, 23 May 1968, Correspondence Others, Fida Archives, Helsinki.

269 One missionary recounted that many independent believers "came back" to the Finnish mission after their places were closed by the authorities. Because of their large number and fearing similar political difficulties the students were "begged not to come" to the mission station anymore, interview no. 102.

270 See ibid.; MATTSSON and MATTSSON, Letter to Otto Koivukangas, Veikko Manninen, and Tapani Kärnä, August 24, 1968. In 1967 allegations of a pregnancy conceived at a spiritual meeting were brought forth against Pentecostals in Debre Zeit, based on a testimony which did not hold up in court, cf. ENGELSVIKEN, "Molo Wongel," 55; ETHIOPIAN GENNET CHURCH, የ50ኛው ጓመት የወርቅ ኢዮቤልዩ በዓል, 27–28. It is probably an echo of these accusations when Mattssons, less than a year later, hint at a pregnancy resulting from a Pentecostal meeting in a town "about 50 km" from Addis Ababa. (Debre Zeit is just under 50 km away from Addis Ababa).

271 See MATTSSON and MATTSSON, Letter to Otto Koivukangas, Veikko Manninen, and Tapani Kärnä, August 24, 1968; TAPANI KÄRNÄ, Letter to Rawson and Marja Muffet, 27 May 1968, Correspondence Others, Fida Archives, Helsinki.

2.5.2 Determining the Causes of the Split

In correspondence to this overdetermination of the separation event, the many accounts also provided multiple reasons for the separation. One frequently cited issue is the problem of Ethiopian participation in leadership and ministry, which may be coupled with allegations of missionary paternalism, or, in defense of the missionaries, with references to the immaturity of the new believers or simply their rejection of Whites.[272] Another set of arguments revolves around debates about organizational structures. The Ethiopians' desire to turn the mission into an actual church is reflected by their demands to elect elders and deacons, to regularly collect financial offerings, and to broaden the Merkato work by evangelization and the founding of local branches.[273] The demand for church organization is occasionally justified by the observation that the mission was not able to retain many new believers due to its lack of an established congregation.[274] In contemporary correspondence, however, Mattssons maintained that they did not regard church organization possible under the political circumstances, and that they mainly had other matters on their agenda.[275] Another issue extensively brought into discussion here is the "Pentecostality" of the Finnish mission. Some sources note a disappointment, or even anger[276] among Ethiopians, because the missionaries had "hid the teaching of the Holy Spirit,"[277] while others mention conflicts over the application and intensity of Pentecostal practices.[278]

Moreover, the stated reasons may be constructed and applied to the separation narrative in very different ways. This is especially evident with regard to one issue often encountered in these emancipation accounts: female leadership. A number

---

272 E.g. Tibebe Eshete, *The Evangelical Movement in Ethiopia*, 159; Teka Obsa Fogi, "The Charismatic Movement in the EECMY," 75; Engelsviken, "Molo Wongel," 32; Mattsson and Mattsson, Letter to Otto Koivukangas, Veikko Manninen, and Tapani Kärnä, August 24, 1968; Ramstrand, Letter to Arne Petterson, March 26, 1968; also interviews no. 112; 71. The allegation of immaturity may also be repeated self-critically by Ethiopians, Seleshi Kebede, "The History of the Guenet Church," 6, or be turned against missionaries as a description of their work. Taye Abdissa, "The Pentecostal Development and the Rise of Charismatic Movement in Ethiopia," 19.

273 Engelsviken, "Molo Wongel," 31; Yosief Kidanewold, "The History of the Pentecostal Movement in Addis Abeba," 12; Teka Obsa Fogi, "The Charismatic Movement in the EECMY," 75–76; Tibebe Eshete, *The Evangelical Movement in Ethiopia*, 159. Some apparently also requested to sing songs composed by Ethiopians instead of translated European ones, interview no. 71.

274 Ramstrand, Letter to Arne Petterson, March 26, 1968; interview no. 91.

275 In a letter from 1968 Mattssons recounted the legal obstacles to mission work and the difficulties they had despite their imperial connections, Mattsson and Mattsson, Letter to Otto Koivukangas, Veikko Manninen, and Tapani Kärnä, August 24, 1968. They indicated that the Swedish are only able to involve with the Ethiopian congregation, because they did not register their own work in Addis Ababa with the government, but are rather "hiding behind the backs" of the Finnish mission, who were then invited to answer to the authorities. Moreover, Mattssons letters from 1966 to 1968 show their agenda to have been the distribution of clothes and other donated goods as well as new scripture distribution plans, aimed at reaching more Ethiopians with the word of God before Christ's imminent return.

276 Taye Abdissa, "The Pentecostal Development and the Rise of Charismatic Movement in Ethiopia," 20.

277 Interview no. 123

278 E.g., Seleshi Kebede, "The History of the Guenet Church," 6; Tibebe Eshete, *The Evangelical Movement in Ethiopia*, 159f. interview no. 123.

of histories report that the authority of the two women Helvi Halme and Orvokki Vuorinen leading the work in Merkato was questioned on account of their gender. However, the argument is made in many different ways.

In one of his letters, the Swedish missionary Karl Ramstrand implicitly claimed authorship of the gender argument:

> So we began with our Bible school in Awasa, and there we taught of course about the biblical congregation, and, as we see it that congregations should be led by indigenous elders. We tried to teach in all God's council, and we could not neglect to read the Bible, where it is written that Paul could not admit women to appear as teachers. This, of course, made some of the brothers of the work in Addis wonder if it was right that the sisters up there should have the whole leadership, and they said that, since no congregation is organized, despite the fact that they received lots of people and the sick were healed, the crowd was scattered. They wanted to have a biblical congregation arranged.[279]

In the Swedish Pentecostal gender debate, Ramstrand was a strong opponent of female leadership and women in preaching or teaching ministry, which were in his opinion signs of worldly influences in the church.[280] However, while Ramstrand's position may not come as a surprise, the placement and role of the gender argument in his depiction of the events is peculiar. First of all, the short report about the Awasa conference is framed by the keyword "biblical congregation." Ramstrand begins his narrative with teaching about it "in all God's council" and ends with the Ethiopians' desire for appropriate congregational arrangements. Moreover, a properly organized congregation is the foundation for all Christian labor; without it, the fruit perishes. Summing up his theology as "congregations should be led by indigenous elders", he hints at the fact that this viewpoint differs from others ("as we see it"), which is most likely aimed at the Finnish mission. However, somewhat surprisingly, Ramstrand's narrative does not continue to qualify these differences, for example by elaborating on indigenous leadership or the selection of elders. Rather, teaching "in all God's council" and reading the Bible, raises the issue of female ministry.[281] The unexpected emergence of the gender issue corresponds to its quick disappearance from Ramstrand's

---

279 RAMSTRAND, Letter to Arne Petterson, March 26, 1968. This part of the letter describes the involvement of the Swedish Pentecostals in the Merkato split, as signified by the ordaining of elders among the university students. It was apparently prompted by Bergsten's investigative visit.

280 Cf. NILS-OLOV NILSSON, "The Debate on Women's Ministry in the Swedish Pentecostal Church Movement: Summary and Analysis," *Pneuma* 22 (1 2000): 65, fn. 20. It is interesting to note that Ramstrand presents this as an uncontested "biblical" view. His fellow minister Mattsson-Boze, who also was present at this 1966 Bible school (NELSSON, "Gamla tiders väckelse bland universitetsstuderande," 7.), had taken a different stand on women in ministry, at least in the initial years of the debate, NILSSON, "The Debate on Women's Ministry in the Swedish Pentecostal Church Movement," 63, fn. 12.

281 The only connection to the qualification of elders is in his usage of the gender-qualified term "äldstebröder" (elder-brothers). Though a number of Bible translations prefer the term "äldste" (e.g. the 1917 translation "Bibeln eller den Heliga Skrift"), the term "äldstebröder" was commonly used in the Swedish Pentecostal communication, cf. e.g. LINDSTEDT, "Historik över Etiopienmissionen under Åren 1955–1968," 4–5, 7.

reminiscences. Though he mentions the impact of his gender argument, it is already watered down by the recipients, because the Ethiopians are merely wondering if the "sisters up there should have the *whole* leadership". They do not demand a complete replacement of the women in leadership, nor their removal from the teaching ministry, but rather some kind of sharing or responsibilities. Ramstrand's account therefore returns to the problem of congregation organization and the detrimental effects of the lack thereof. The issue of female leadership is also not raised again in subsequent passages. Instead Ramstrand merely recounts his attempt to intervene by talking to the leaders at Merkato and his standoff with Mattsson, which revolved around the ordination of elders by Swedish missionaries, and he finally concludes: "If our Finnish friends had been willing to work together here, both with the brothers and with us, the situation, which has come forth, would never have arisen."[282] This somewhat awkward placement and apparently subordinate role of the gender issue in Ramstrand's report leads to the conclusion that despite his strong stand on the problem, the argument has no central function in his account of the Ethiopian emancipation.[283] Female ministry and leadership seem to be merely one of many indicators as to why there is not yet a properly organized "biblical congregation".

Engelsviken presents the gender problem in a different way:

> The mission there [in Addis Ababa] was served by female missionaries who in practice, although not in theory, acted as pastors for the congregation. This would be a highly unusual situation in a country like Ethiopia. Female priests would be unthinkable in the orthodox tradition, and the young Christians could not find any passage in the Scriptures where women acted as pastors or teachers. Although the leading female missionary called herself "Bible teacher", she took care of many of the functions that were ascribed to a pastor. She was the one who regularly preached during the Sunday morning services. The leading Ethiopian brethren worked as interpretors and aides but without real responsibility for the leadership of the congregation and without part in the preaching ministry.[284]

There are a number of tensions in this text that appear to reflect the divergence of Engelsviken's sources on the issue. He begins by deferring the issue to a matter of practice, which is probably meant to indicate a basic agreement about female pastorship between the Ethiopians and the missionaries "in theory". Consequently, the problem arises with the cultural insensitivity of such practice, which was "highly unusual" in Ethiopia and even "unthinkable in the orthodox tradition". It is here that the account resorts to a theological argument: "the young Christians could not find any passage in the Scriptures where women acted as pastors or teachers." However,

---

282 RAMSTRAND, Letter to Arne Petterson, March 26, 1968.
283 This is supported by his later book, in which Ramstrand attested an "exceptionally good work" to the Finnish, "especially on Merkato", and saw the selection of elders as cause for the break, RAMSTRAND, *Det heliga äventyret*, 144.
284 ENGELSVIKEN, "Molo Wongel," 29. Copies of this account in almost similar wording can be found in TEKA OBSA FOGI, "The Charismatic Movement in the EECMY," 75; and BULUTSE FUTUWI, "An Introduction to the Theology and Growth of Independent Churches in Ethiopia With Special Reference to Rhema Faith Church," 56.

the weight of this biblical argument is undermined in two ways. First, unlike Ramstrand, Engelsviken does not resort to Bible verses explicitly against female teaching ministry or related theological positions, but rather describes it as a practice not found in scripture, at least in the reading of the Ethiopians. This is the second limitation of the argument, since Engelsviken does not explicitly state that there are no such Bible references. Following these general observations, the narrative turns to a specific conflict, indicated by the changing focus from female missionaries in general to one person, namely, the "leading female missionary". Contrary to the apparently equal roles of pastors and teachers beforehand, the problem now seems to be that the missionary does not limit herself to the self-ascribed role as "Bible-teacher", but rather acts as a pastor. However, this is again narrated as an issue of practice, since she does not presume herself to actually be a pastor, but merely functions as one. Moreover, the account does not explicitly criticize her presumed pastoral role, but rather focuses on the problem of sharing pastoral responsibilities: congregational leadership and (Sunday morning) preaching. The subsequent passages of Engelsviken's account also focus on the question of adequate ministry participation and leadership struggles, while the gender issue is not raised again, with the exception of a short mention of Chacha's rude and chauvinistic attitude toward the female Merkato missionaries.[285] The gender argument thus seems to be used in a way similar to Ramstrand's narrative, i.e., to initially, albeit vaguely, question the organizational setup of the Finnish mission at Merkato before turning to the "real" issues, power sharing and ministry participation. However, the argument here is justified in an entirely different way. We are not provided with a theological discussion, aimed at identifying an unbiblical congregational arrangement, but rather with the implicit criticism of an insensitive cultural practice, which is not necessarily contrary to scripture, but also not well enough supported by it in order to alleviate cultural uneasiness.[286]

A third example, an oral Ethiopian account, should suffice to illustrate the scope in which the problem of female leadership is presented and constructed:

> The pastors were women. There were two women pastors. [*short pause*] These woman pastors- [*breaks off*] There were several reasons. They were afraid. They were afraid to bring these young men into the Pentecostal experience. [*short pause*] They have read about the Holy Spirit baptism, but nobody prayed for them to be baptized with the Holy Spirit. [*pause*] When they got this experience a certain Chacha Omahe from Kenya, he prayed for them the first time. He came to Awasa for a conference. He came to the conference, he prayed for some young men in Awasa. Some were baptized, the news was heard here. They called him over to the Merkato area. He came and prayed for the young boys here, and they were filled with the Holy Spirit. Then they say, how come, how come these sisters didn't tell us this, didn't bring us into this experience? [*short pause*] So that, that created some kind of, um, resentment. That's one.

---

285 ENGELSVIKEN, "Molo Wongel," 30.
286 The culture argument is also found without explicit reference to Engelsviken in TIBEBE ESHETE, *The Evangelical Movement in Ethiopia*, 160.

The other thing is, these boys, young boys, now filled with the Holy Spirit, they wanted to preach, they wanted to do all sorts of things. And the ladies had a heavy hand on them. They wanted to control the whole thing. And the boys were uncontrollable. [*pause*] They wanted to lead, and the boys, the boys wanted to lead actually. They wanted to preach, and they were not allowed to preach. They wanted to do many things, lots of things, and the women said: "No. You can't do this, you can't do that." And they didn't like this. They didn't like this. [*pause*] That was another reason. [*pause*]
The third reason perhaps was, um, [*pause*] the Ethiopian, the Ethiopian mentality. These boys came from the Orthodox church. Their origin is in the Orthodox church. And in the Orthodox church we, we don't have women ministers. Women didn't minister. I think that must have also contributed. They, I don't think they liked being under the authority of women.[287]

Before presenting his list of reasons for the Merkato split, the informant points twice to the fact that the pastors were women. However, this is not immediately explained or expounded as one might expect. Rather, the informant pauses and then continues with completely different reasons, namely, that the missionaries did not relate Spirit baptism experiences, and that they did not relinquish control. Yet the gender issue nevertheless runs through his entire narrative: "woman pastors" were afraid to bring "these young men into the Pentecostal experience"; the "young boys", having just been filled with the Spirit, wonder why "these sisters" have been hiding this experience from them; "these boys" want to be active in ministry, but "the ladies had a heavy hand on them"; the "boys were uncontrollable", and the "women said no". Instead of relying on contrasts like "missionaries/natives", "foreigners/Ethiopians", "leaders/followers", the conflict representation is entirely gender determined, though there undoubtedly were male teachers and missionaries as well as female believers. Therefore it does not come as a surprise that the third stated reason finally deals with the gender question in a more explicit fashion. Yet, there are no theological arguments to explain these difficulties as one might expect from the initial problem statement of "woman pastors". Moreover, though the informant states that there were no "woman ministers" in the Orthodox church, the problem apparently was not just one of female ministry, but female leadership as a whole, "being under the authority of women". It is interesting to note that an "Ethiopian mentality" and Orthodox "origin" are given as reasons, instead of Bible verses or theological positions, even though the informant works as a pastor for a Pentecostal church which to this day does not allow women to serve as pastors or elders, or even to minister to a mixed congregation, unless a man is presiding over the meeting. Furthermore, the frequent breaks and careful wording in the presentation of this third reason indicate that the informant has difficulties in finding satisfactory ways of expressing the problem, even though it runs through his entire narrative. This may have to do with a certain sensitivity for the interview situation, or his own difficulties with such views. At any rate, it is clear that the gender issue in this narrative differs in function and content from Ramstrand and Engelsviken. More than merely initially discrediting

---

287 Interview no. 112

the mission workers at Merkato, it functions as basic binary opposition underneath all other explanations of the conflict. At the same time, even though the option most likely exists in the informant's theological repertoire, there are no biblical references like the ones found in the other two accounts. The issue is displayed as merely cultural, or even as being due to Ethiopian Orthodox traditions.

In concluding these observations about the Finnish mission separation accounts, it appears that they too are subject to narrative schemes constructing and refuting different legacies in the history of the Ethiopian Pentecostal movement. Main actors, places, and issues are identified in accordance to these narrative trajectories, which qualify the nature of the split and the development of the relationship between missionaries and Ethiopians. Furthermore, a number of theological positions regarding church organization, mission, Pentecostal identity, contextuality, and even gender roles are woven into these accounts as reasons for the separation. This plethora of competing narratives arguably reflects the historical situation more than any single one of them, since even the earliest sources could not agree on the actual event of the split, its causes or significance.

Likewise, the analysis of the Chacha Omahe narratives has shown that different concepts of the missionary engagement permeate Ethiopian Pentecostal mission histories in their selection and articulation of historic material. For histories interested in articulating Ethiopian mission independence, Chacha thus became the "match" that lit the Pentecostal fire, while in missionary writings he is hardly mentioned at all.

This dichotomy of missionary versus Ethiopian Pentecostalism was introduced to the historical archive by the young national movement reflecting its missionary past, in alliance with the Norwegian Lutheran missionary Engelsviken, whose "report on mission" decidedly was not about "missionaries from the West." Missionary accounts explicitly or implicitly countered this tale of an Ethiopian Pentecostalism largely independent of their input, by tracing their own impact to the national movement. These very different historical trajectories have opened up the field for multiple nuances in relating the missionary input to the beginnings of Ethiopian Pentecostalism, illustrating the complexity of the Pentecostal mission encounter.

3   Discovering Origins: Ethiopian Revival Movements and the Foundation of a Pentecostal Church

Tormod Engelsviken's *Documentary Report* contains a surprising twist in its chapter about the Pentecostal missions. After having narrated Chacha's ministry and the separation of Ethiopian believers from the Finnish mission, which he calls a "starting point" for independent Pentecostalism,[1] Engelsviken asserts at the very end of the chapter:

> It was, however, not the group of young Christians who broke away from the Finnish Mission that was the real origin of the independent Ethiopian Pentecostal movement. That movement started in the fall of 1965 when some few young students at the Haile Selassie I University in Addis Ababa followed the call of God to commit themselves fully to his service. They should be the instruments for the great revival among the university students which later would give the movement its influence and peculiar character. They represent the beginning of what is called popularly in Ethiopia "Molo Wongel", and which is an abbreviated translation of the name of the church: "The Full Gospel Believers' Association."[2]

This idea of a "real origin," which is completely independent of missionary influence, is in keeping with Engelsviken's general narrative throughout the *Documentary Report*. The arrival of the European missionaries, their work in Ethiopia, the first Pentecostal awakening sparked by Chacha Omahe, and the break-away of Ethiopian Pentecostals from missionary influence are all narrated under the chapter title "Preparation." The heading "Revival" is reserved for the subsequent chapter, which focuses on the Addis Ababa student movement and their establishment of the first Ethiopian Pentecostal church. Furthermore, this "real origin" is thought to be completely independent of missionary influence, since it was not even started by the "group of young Christians who broke away from the Finnish Mission," but by divinely inspired students, who simply "followed the call of God to commit themselves fully to his service." Furthermore, this "real origin" represents the nucleus of the Full Gospel Believers' Church (FGBC), which thus is implicitly identified as the primary instance of Ethiopian Pentecostalism.

This notion of a "starting point" and a "real origin" also indicates that Engelsviken had to reconcile two distinct tales about the origin of independent Pentecostalism in Ethiopia: the break-away faction at the Merkato Finnish mission and that of the university students in Addis Ababa. However, there are not only two, but altogether four

---

1   See ENGELSVIKEN, "Molo Wongel," 29.
2   Ibid., 33.

revival groups which lay claim to the origin of Ethiopian Pentecostalism. In addition
to the group that broke from the Merkato Finnish mission and to the university students, there are reports of earlier revivals in the towns of Harar and Nazaret, whose
leaders later contributed to the formation of the FGBC. The story of the revival
movement in Harar usually begins with a number of dramatic conversions of students
at the Harar Teacher Training Institute (TTI).[3] From there it is reported to have
spread to the local high school and to other places in the country by way of various
teaching assignments that were part of the curriculum. After completing their studies
in the summer of 1966, three of the Harar leaders came to Addis Ababa, where they
teamed up with the group that had left the Finnish mission, and began an independent Pentecostal meeting at a different place in Merkato. This meeting later merged
with the university students, and the three Harar leaders and three members of the
Finnish mission group were among the first seven elders of the FGBC in 1967. In
Nazaret, high school students started a prayer and Bible study group called "yäsämay
bərhan,"[4] which quickly gathered momentum in the school year of 1964/1965 and featured enthusiastic prayers, exorcisms, prophecies, and, to some extent, speaking in
tongues. Members of this group came to Addis Ababa for further studies after their
graduation and got involved in the university student movement as well. Histories
of the Addis Ababa university student group, in turn, usually begin with a prayer
meeting in 1965 hosted by four students in their dormitory, which quickly drew large
crowds. The group soon rented its own premises and hosted national conferences that
became central to the formation of the FGBC.

Since large parts of these four revival movements joined in the formation of the
FGBC, the legacy of these different beginnings had to be incorporated into the history of this first Pentecostal church, producing a number of claims to the "real origin"
of Ethiopian Pentecostalism. This chapter about the early revival movements therefore begins by studying the politics of historical memory in a chronological review
of sources. Subsequently the narratives about the currently two most prominently
featured groups are analyzed, which are the Nazaret High School revival and the Addis Ababa University student movement. The chapter closes with the foundation of
the FGBC, exploring the identity politics articulated by the different groups in the
commemoration of this event.

---

3 TTIs were established to cope with the notorious shortage of teachers in Ethiopia. The TTI
   recruits usually had completed a ninth grade education and were then enrolled in a three year
   training program, cf. BEKELE WOLDEKIDAN, ራዕይሳል, 84; also mentioned in interview no. 39. The
   trainees could then go on to teach in the public schools, but a number of them also enrolled in
   the Addis Ababa University to continue their education.
4 This name was taken from a favorite song of the group, and means "sunshine of heaven". For the
   words of the song see ABERA ERTIRO, "The History of the Meserete Kristos Church at Nazareth,"
   17; or TILAHUN BEYENE, ". . .ቤት ክርስቲያኔን እሥራለሁ. . . ": የመሰረተ ክርስቶስ ቤት ክርስቲያን ታሪክ, [". . .I build
   My Church. . . ": The History of the Meserete Kristos Church.] (Addis Ababa: Meserete Kristos
   Church, 2002), 91.

3.1 A Genealogy of Revival Stories

There are different ways of relating the multiple revival stories to one another. The
earliest history by the FGBC from 1978, for example, presented a providential reading
of the multiple origins of Ethiopian Pentecostalism:

> Starting in 1963, in about the same time frame, youths who were living in
> different parts of the country began to exhibit a similar life change and practice,
> because God baptized them with the Holy Spirit he had brought down. It is
> unknown how this happened, since they were not connected by phone, letter,
> or any other way, and since they did not know one another. The situation is
> difficult to interpret and to explain, but a spiritual movement took root among
> the youths. In the church, in the homes, and sometimes on different fields
> young students, girls and boys, met praying, singing, and frequently studying
> the Bible.[5]

Engelsviken, on the other hand, as was already mentioned, suggested that while
there were many movements, there was a "real origin" in the Addis Ababa student
movement, which is thus identified as the root of the FGBC. The recent history
of Protestantism in Ethiopia provided by Tibebe Eshete in turn, provided more of a
teleological reading of history in understanding the different movements as tributaries
forming the larger stream of Ethiopian Pentecostalism.[6]

However, all of these histories tend to de-historicize the problem by adding an
interpretative layer of origin and historical destination while not considering the context and identity politics of their sources. Therefore the following remarks will seek
a different way of relating the revival stories to the formation of an institutionalized
Ethiopian Pentecostalism: a genealogy of said revival stories in their institutional
contexts.

3.1.1 Contemporaneous Missionary Correspondence

The earliest source for the different revival movements in Ethiopia is the correspondence by Swedish Philadelphia Church Mission (SPCM) missionaries and their publications in the Swedish Pentecostal weekly *Evangelii Härold*. Through their Awasa
summer conferences, their work in Addis Ababa and travels by Karl Ramstrand and
other missionaries, the Swedish Pentecostals were well connected to their Ethiopian
counterpart and tried to remain involved in their movement.

Reporting about the 1965 summer Bible conference, the SPCM missionary Karl
Ramstrand mentioned in a letter that out of 100 delegates, about ten had come from
Harar, where "revival had broken out" among the TTI students, and "many have
been saved and many were baptized in the Spirit."[7] The Harar group probably was
the largest group of delegates from outside Awasa at this conference. The Nazaret
movement is also briefly mentioned albeit less specifically. Finally the letter notes
that "brother Fantahun, an elementary school teacher from Addis" preached at the

---

5 Ethiopian Full Gospel Believers' Church, ሙሉ ወንጌል ቤተ ክርስቲያን ከለደት እስከ . . ., 2.
6 Cf. Tibebe Eshete, *The Evangelical Movement in Ethiopia*, 154–162.
7 See Ramstrand, Letter to supporters, August 22, 1965.

conference, who in turn was one of the youths worshiping at the Finnish mission.
The 1965 Awasa conference in Ramstrand's correspondence thus was an early hub,
connecting revivalists from Awasa, Nazaret, Harar, and Addis Ababa. Two months
later, Ramstrand mentioned that he had received many letters from the conference
participants, from Harar and elsewhere.[8] As an example of these contacts he translated and forwarded a letter written by the Harar teacher trainee Betta Mengistu,
in which Betta reports evangelistic advances in the north of Ethiopia. As part of
his teacher training curriculum Betta had been assigned to a internship in Segeneyti,
Eritrea, about 62 km southeast of Asmara. He told Ramstrand that he and a "sister
Alem" (Alem Bisrat) were preaching in the Orthodox church in Asmara, witnessed
to Orthodox youths, and spoke about the Holy Spirit in an unnamed faith (holiness)
mission. Their efforts led to seven Spirit-baptized believers, all high school students.[9]

In the beginning of 1966 three more letters by Harar teacher trainees were forwarded by Ramstrand and published in the Swedish Pentecostal periodical *Evangelii
Härold*.[10] They tell of the beginnings of the Harar revival, of mass conversions there,[11]
and the opportunity to preach at a local school auditorium to 400–500 youths. Furthermore a vision-impaired girl is reported to have been healed, as well as a man
who had been deaf-mute for 25 years.[12] The Harar youths also mention the spread
of their revival to Dire Dawa, Asmara, and Addis Ababa, even into the Lutheran
churches and the Ethiopian Orthodox Church (EOC). One of the letters was written
by Betta Mengistu and reports "the Lord is working in A. [Asmara]." A story in this
letter relates to a "brother from the University" in Addis Ababa, who had been in
Asmara witnessing about the Holy Spirit, but was not Spirit-baptized himself until
"we came to A. and met him." Now as a freshly Spirit-filled believer he "was preaching
gladly," and about to return to Addis Ababa to continue his studies. This unnamed
brother was Ogbazghi Sium, who ran a student prayer meeting in Addis Ababa. He
knew other youths in Addis Ababa who had been baptized with the Holy Spirit in
the Awasa summer conference of 1965 and was part of the early Pentecostal student
movement in the capital.[13]

Thus the Harar revivalists were prominently featured in the Swedish correspondence and publications, which is unlike the other movements. The Nazaret movement
is not mentioned in Ramstrand's correspondence apart from the above-cited short notice from 1965. There is also no report about Ethiopians leaving the Finnish mission

---

8 See RAMSTRAND, Letter to supporting congregations, October 26, 1965.
9 The first Spirit-baptized believers apparently were two boys from the holiness mission, who then
   witnessed to their friends.
10 *Evangelii Härold*, "Brev från infödda lärare i Etiopien," [Letters from Native Teachers in Ethiopia.], 7 1966, 10. The article contains three letters by G. (probably Getachew Mikre), A. A.
   (Assefa Alemu), and B. M. (Betta Mengistu).
11 "In one class 56 girls were saved and also many boys [...] in one grade 9 class of 19 girls, 18 were
   saved in one week. [...] I remember one Sunday morning on which more than 100 people gave
   their life to Christ.", ibid.
12 Two of the Harar leaders also recount in interviews the gradual healing of an insane beggar that
   they had befriended by sharing their school lunches with him, interviews no. 130; 47.
13 Ogbazghi Sium denied in personal correspondence that he received the Holy Spirit through Betta
   Mengistu, but insists that this happened two weeks before Betta arrived in Asmara and through
   the prayer of Alem Bisrat, OGBAZGHI SIUM, E-mail to author, April 16, 2008.

until after the formation of the FGBC, and the Addis Ababa University student movement is featured much less prominently than Harar. The first mention of the Addis
Ababa movement is in a letter by the missionary Allan Wedin from 1966. He first
gave an enthusiastic report about his trip to Harar and the revival there, and only
made a brief remark about the Addis Ababa group at the end:

> Here in Addis one such Christian group has rented a house and we will have
> meetings together. I try to help them as well as I can. They are mostly students
> from the University, so they do not have much money.[14]

In this sketchy portrait of humble beginnings, Wedin did not seem to be aware of
the previous university student prayer meeting in a student dormitory, which later
became the foundational myth in histories of the FGBC. In his subsequent correspondence Wedin wrote more about the establishment of an Ethiopian congregation
in Addis Ababa, but he did not suggest that the university students played a special role.[15] Instead he spoke of the "brothers," and the "congregation," and when
introducing the first seven elders of the congregation, he did not mention that one of
them, Philipos Kemere, came from the university student group. He linked him to his
origins in the SPCM instead: "His father is one of the leading brothers in Awasa."[16]

In the Swedish periodical *Evangelii Härold* there were occasional articles mentioning the university student involvement in the Addis Ababa revival, but only in rather
unspecific ways.[17] It was not until 1970, in a portrait of Philipos Kemere, that the
initial university student prayer meeting was treated in detail. Here, for the first time
in Swedish writings, the meeting is established as the nucleus of the Addis Ababa
Pentecostal movement, under the headline "So the Revival Began:"

> In a few years the revival has quickly spread among youths in Addis Ababa.
> The beginning was insignificant. Philipos and three other students, captured
> by love for Jesus and in confidence in God's promise, began to pray for revival
> among Ethiopia's youth. The meeting was held in the beginning in a little
> house, which they rented and where they themselves resided. They turned
> their beds into seats every evening and the room was filled with longing people.
> Three nights a week they held the meeting. Trusting in God, they rented a
> larger locality. Today they have activities in many places in Addis Ababa and
> the congregation experiences how God saves sinners even in the higher classes
> of society.[18]

---

14 ALLAN WEDIN, Circular letter, 7 May 1966, Allan Wedin Collection, Pingstarkiv Kaggeholm,
   Ekerö.
15 See ALLAN WEDIN, Circular letter, 26 September 1966, Allan Wedin Collection, Pingstarkiv
   Kaggeholm, Ekerö; ALLAN WEDIN, Circular letter, 1 January 1966, Allan Wedin Collection,
   Pingstarkiv Kaggeholm, Ekerö; ALLAN WEDIN, Letter to Samuel Halldorf, 20 January 1967,
   Allan Wedin Collection, Pingstarkiv Kaggeholm, Ekerö.
16 Ibid.
17 Cf. KARL RAMSTRAND and OLOF NILSSON, "Etiopien i Blickpunkten," [Ethiopia in the Limelight.],
   Evangelii Härold (28 1966): 9; NELSSON, "Gamla tiders väckelse bland universitetsstuderande."
18 MARGARETHA HELLSTRÖM, "Frälst ungdom i Etiopien," [Saved Youth in Ethiopia.], *Evangelii
   Härold* (3 1970): 11.

This was also the first time that the *Evangelii Härold* presented a coherent historical narrative of the Addis Ababa movement. However, while earlier correspondence
and reports had suggested a multiplicity of origins and actors, and prominently featured the Harar revival, this article followed the Addis Ababa University students'
account. Their story consisted of a fairly linear narrative, in which a congregation
with many subsidiaries emerges from the humble beginning of a student prayer group.
No mention is made of the other Ethiopian revival groups, which had contributed to
the emergence of the Addis Ababa church. This shift in the Swedish historical narrative was not without a political context. In the fall of 1969 the newly-founded FGBC
largely withdrew from the mission.[19] Due to his Awasa roots in the SPCM, Philipos
became the most important contact for the mission within the FGBC,[20] so that it
is no surprise that his story about the Addis Ababa student prayer movement now
guided the historical memory of the Swedish mission. The earlier Harar contacts like
Assefa Alemu and Betta Mengistu, who also were elders of the FGBC, probably kept
more of a distance from the missionaries during this time.

3.1.2   Early Histories

The early histories are especially important for this genealogy. They incorporated the
different stories in a larger historical narrative of Ethiopian Pentecostalism, thereby
revealing in their composition which groups were still influential at the time of their
writing.   As was shown above, the first written history of Ethiopian Pentecostalism,
Tormod Engelsviken's *Documentary Report*, considered the Addis Ababa University
student movement as the "real origin" of Ethiopian Pentecostalism. Engelsviken laid
this out as a linear development, beginning with a small student prayer meeting, which
first grew into a large group, then rented its own premises, next organized national
conferences, founded the first mission-independent Ethiopian Pentecostal church, and
finally applied for registration with the Ethiopian government.[21] Engelsviken did not
really connect this trajectory to the faction that broke away from the Finnish mission
nor to the SPCM, except for briefly noting that the eldership included individuals from
these backgrounds as well.[22] Furthermore, he suggested that the revival spread from
Addis Ababa to the rest of the country side rather than the other way around. Though
he admitted that "[i]n some places groups had already for some time been actively
praying and testifying," he also asserted that it was the student movement, which
started a "systematic work," and that the revival was "a spiritual movement which
fanned out from the University through man-to-man contacts and testimonies."[23]
Moreover, Engelsviken seems to have been unaware of the Harar movement of 1966

---

19 Cf. below, 149.
20 The article also claims that Philipos was the "first who was baptized in the Holy Spirit in the
    Sidama province, yes, perhaps even in the whole country," which is an entirely new idea in the
    Swedish correspondence. In 1969, Philipos had also written an article for the *Evangelii Härold*
    asking for support for the FGBC, see PHILIPOS KEMERE, "Seger och skördetider i Etiopien,"
    [Victory and Harvest Time in Ethiopia.], *Evangelii Härold* (33 1969): 10–11.
21 See ENGELSVIKEN, "Molo Wongel," 35–52.
22 See ibid., 50.
23 Ibid., 43.

and its spread to other towns, or the background of some of the FGBC elders in this revival.

He did, however, interview at least one leader from the Nazaret group who had not joined the FGBC.[24] Yet, his story is not part of the "Revival" chapter, but is included under the previous chapter "Preparation" alongside the Pentecostal missions. Here, Engelsviken quotes a testimony by his informant in order to "illustrate the strong sense of expectation and the fervent prayer that was dominant among many young Ethiopian Christians during the time immediately before the revival broke out."[25] The testimony sets out with the expectation that the Biblical events around Pentecost, narrated in Acts 2, could still happen today, and the informant notes that two youths in Nazaret and Harar "were praying with friends that this may happen."[26] However, the quote seems to break off prematurely. It ends by mentioning that the Nazaret youths discovered simultaneous prayer, but there is no narrative closure with regard to the Acts 2 expectation or any outcome in Nazaret and Harar. Instead Engelsviken concluded that still "a spark was needed to set the young people aflame for Christ," which is an allusion to the Chacha Omahe visit immediately following this section.[27] The group which broke away from the Finnish mission also did not attain a prominent role in Engelsviken's narrative, but instead he seemed to downplay their role. Though he noted that they were the "'oldest' as Christians and in virtue of their experiences and knowledge had most influence during this time,"[28] he did not consider them part of the "real origin" nor does he follow their story in any noteworthy detail.

Engelsviken thus apparently preferred a straight trajectory from the university student movement to the establishment of the FGBC even at the risk of under-representing the missions and other revival movements. This focus on the university student group can be explained by the fact that Engelsviken recruited most of his sources from the FGBC. At the time of his research, key leaders of the Nazaret, Harar and Addis Ababa Merkato groups were no longer part of the FGBC. The members of the Nazaret group had not been able to secure their influence in the formation of the FGBC and a number of them later joined the Meserete Kristos Church (MKC).[29] The Harar group, on the other hand, originally had wielded a considerable influence on the early FGBC, with three of their main leaders, Assefa Alemu, Betta Mengistu, and Zeleke Alemu being among the first seven elders of the church. However, by the early 1970s, all three of them were no longer in this position nor part of the FGBC. Betta Mengistu left Ethiopia in 1971 and completed two Master degrees and a PhD in Education in the USA and subsequently worked in Kenya.[30] Zeleke Alemu

---

24 See ENGELSVIKEN, "Molo Wongel," 24–25. Engelsviken did not mention names in his report, but the story points to Solomon Kebede. Solomon has been a key informant for other accounts, in which he clearly marked his participation in the Addis Ababa movement, see e.g. HEGE, *Beyond Our Prayers*, 147–160.
25 ENGELSVIKEN, "Molo Wongel," 24.
26 Ibid., 25.
27 Ibid.
28 Ibid., 50.
29 See below, 130ff. for details.
30 From 1979 to 2004 Betta worked for the International Bible Society in Nairobi. During this time he founded a church here, and only after the fall of Mengistu's regime in Ethiopia, he again engaged in ministry work in his home country, sponsored by the Assemblies of God (AG).

and Assefa Alemu retired from their leadership positions in the FGBC in 1971 and were hired by the SPCM.[31] Zeleke worked as a pastor in Awasa and in 1971 got the opportunity to commence further studies in Sweden at the University of Lund, and after a short time back in Ethiopia he finally emigrated to the USA via Sweden in the beginning of the 1980s.[32] Assefa Alemu worked for the SPCM in Jima for some months after leaving the eldership.[33] He returned to Addis Ababa in 1972 after the FGBC had been shut down by the government and ministered in the emerging home fellowships.[34] However, since he was one of the most important proponents of the so-called Deliverance doctrine,[35] he fell out with the FGBC over this issue in 1974 and emigrated to the USA soon thereafter.[36] The story of the group that had split from the Finnish mission at Merkato is similar. Like the Harar revivalists, they had three representatives among the first eldership of the FGBC. However, by the time of Engelsviken's research two of them were no longer part of the church, and a third may not have been inclined to hold up the legacy of the group.[37] Therefore, it is likely that the stories of Nazaret, Harar, and the Merkato group were not a significant part of the FGBC narrative archive anymore when Engelsviken began to study the history of the church.

After leaving the International Bible Society in 2004 he started his own organization, called Beza International, networking his different ministries in the USA, Kenya and Ethiopia, see BENJAMIN PIPER, "Mercy Center Addis Ababa: NGO or No?" (2004): 3–4, http://www.case-web.org/assets/cases/case_36.pdf (accessed June 18, 2007); BEZA INTERNATIONAL, "About Beza" (2007), http://www.bezainternational.org/page7/page7.html (accessed October 26, 2007).

31 Tage Johansson mentioned in 1971 that "three of the finest elders in Addis are no longer in the eldership," one of them being Assefa, see TAGE JOHANSSON, Letter to Bo Hörnberg, 2 December 1971, Tage Johansson Collection, Pingstarkiv Kaggeholm, Ekerö. A later letter mentions that Zeleke also was not among the elders, see TAGE JOHANSSON, Letter to Bo Hörnberg, 12 March 1972, Tage Johansson Collection, Pingstarkiv Kaggeholm, Ekerö.

32 See NYBERG OSKARSSON, Svensk Pingstmission i Ethiopien (1959–1980), 187; also mentioned in interview no. 130. After his return to Ethiopia, Zeleke did not resume active ministry, and again left Ethiopia for Sweden in the beginning of the 1980s. In 1984 he accepted a calling to pastor an Ethiopian church in Dallas, Texas, where he stayed until 1998, when he began a ministry among African immigrants for the Lutheran Missouri Synod. After working with multiple immigrant congregations, he founded Grace Ethiopian Church in 2005, which is still under his pastorate. See The Prince of Peace Communicator, "Birth of a Daughter Congregation, Grace Ethiopian Lutheran Church," 10 2005, 1, http://www.poplc.org/Communicator/2005/20050306.pdf (accessed October 26, 2007); also see interview no. 130.

33 NYBERG OSKARSSON, Svensk Pingstmission i Ethiopien (1959–1980), 134; JOHANSSON, Letter to Bo Hörnberg, March 12, 1972.

34 see TAGE JOHANSSON, Letter to Petrus Hammerberg, 24 January 1973, Tage Johansson Collection, Pingstarkiv Kaggeholm, Ekerö.

35 On the movement in Ethiopia, see below, 210. Tage Johansson voiced concerns regarding Assefa's deliverance ministry in 1972, see TAGE JOHANSSON, Letter to Bo Hörnberg, 1 May 1972, Tage Johansson Collection, Pingstarkiv Kaggeholm, Ekerö. Assefa's prominent role in the early Deliverance Movement was also mentioned by several informants, interviews no. 69; 87; 131.

36 In the USA he ministered to Ethiopian immigrants, earned his PhD in theology, and has worked as a pastor in the Ethiopian Christian Fellowship Church in the Kansas City metropolitan area since its foundation in 1987. See TIBEBE ESHETE, The Evangelical Movement in Ethiopia, 340f. ETHIOPIAN CHRISTIAN FELLOWSHIP CHURCH IN KANSAS, "Who we are" (2007), http://ecfck.com/Mission.aspx (accessed November 10, 2007).

37 See below, 106, for details.

This assumption is supported by Yosief Kidanewold's B.A. thesis about the Pentecostal movement from 1976.[38] Though Yosief's overall narrative, especially regarding the beginnings of Pentecostalism in Ethiopia, heavily relied on Engelsviken,[39] he provided a somewhat detailed account of the events at the Harar TTI, based on an interview with one of the Harar leaders in August 1976.[40] Following this account, Yosief not only narrates the beginnings of the Harar revival in detail, he also portrays the Harar group as "one of the significant factors in the spread of the Pentecostal movement all over the Ethiopian provinces."[41] Finally, Yosief directly links the Harar revivalists to the establishment of the Pentecostal movement in Addis Ababa:

> As we shall see in the next chapter, those who were pioneers in the Harar
> Pentecostal Movement also played a significant role in the organization of the
> Pentecostal Movement in Addis Ababa in collaboration with the Ethiopian
> Pentecostals from the Finnish Mission Church in Merkato and the University
> Students running the Chapel at Sidist Kilo.[42]

In this next chapter, titled "Growth",[43] Yosief's thesis at first closely follows Engelsviken, narrating the establishment of the University student movement and their first "national conference." However, he then departs once more from Engelsviken by noting that the youths who had split from the Merkato Finnish mission were joined by "active participants in the Harar Pentecostal movement and who later were elected as church elders."[44] Thus in contrast to Engelsviken, who had left the Merkato faction in order to turn to the "real origin" of the Ethiopian Pentecostal movement, Yosief Kidanewold established a second Addis Ababa center. Furthermore he gave the Finnish mission break-away and the Harar Pentecostals considerably more weight when listing the first elders of the FGBC:

> Three of the church elders were those who had been in the Finnish church at
> Merkato. Others were those who began the Harar Pentecostal Movement and
> had been transferred to Addis Ababa in 1966. The remaining one was from the
> University students.[45]

Yosief's Harar narrative was not taken up by later histories.[46] Instead the first FGBC history from 1978 confirms the observation that the Addis Ababa University student prayer group became the "real origin" for this church fairly early on. The

38 YOSIEF KIDANEWOLD, "The History of the Pentecostal Movement in Addis Abeba."
39 Most notably, he agrees with Engelsviken that the Finnish mission should not be considered as origin of the "independent Ethiopian Pentecostal Movement," which in turn "is better understood when we consider the beginning of the involvement of university students in Addis Ababa." See ibid., 5.
40 See ibid., 9–10. Yosief did not expose names in his report, which in 1976 would have been a security risk, but the details of the story told point to Zeleke Alemu.
41 Ibid., 10.
42 Ibid.
43 Ibid., 11–24.
44 Ibid., 17.
45 Ibid., 18.
46 The only exception to this are two lines in LAUNHARDT, *Evangelicals in Addis Ababa (1919–1991)*, 157.

document only briefly mentions spiritual movements in Nazaret and Harar, where "souls found salvation, miracles and wonders were seen and the fruits of the Spirit began to be revealed," but breaks off noting that "many pages would be necessary for writing what was done in all the places the spiritual revival spread to."[47] At the same time, the document provides a very detailed narrative of the university student movement, tracing its development from a section titled "The Conception of a Church – the Prayer of Four People" to the establishment of the FGBC under the headline "Young Elders in a Grown Up Church."[48] As a consequence, most sources, which depend on Engelsviken or written and oral accounts from the FGBC, seem to be unaware of the Harar group or its impact.[49]

In the first histories, therefore, the representations of the different revival groups seem to correlate with availability of informants. By the time these histories were written in the middle of the 1970s, the majority of leaders within the FGBC hailed from the Addis Ababa University student movement, since many leaders of the other revival groups had left the church for different reasons. This arguably led to the prominence of the university students' prayer meeting central in FGBC histories and Engelsviken's report. However, as Yosief Kidanewold's thesis shows, some of the original informants from the other revival groups could still be found within Ethiopia, and could significantly alter the overall narrative when interviewed.

In the following decades, the FGBC basically kept its narrative of the origin of mission-independent Ethiopian Pentecostalism, while two of the other revival groups were integrated by the histories of other denominations: The Nazaret *yäsämay bərhan* movement began to feature prominently in Mennonite histories, and the Addis Ababa Merkato faction was rediscovered by the Gennet Church (GC). The historical memory of the different revival movements thereby more or less consolidated into denominational trajectories, as the following sections will document.

3.1.3 Full Gospel Believers' Church Histories

The Full Gospel Believers' Church (FGBC) continued to establish the Addis Ababa University student group as its core origin, marginalizing other places of revival. A jubilee magazine from 1992, celebrating twenty-five years of the church, merely mentioned Harar and Nazaret as two of four places where "the revival in our country was first seen or began," without providing any further details.[50] While the magazine noted that it is "is difficult to say whether the revival in our country was first seen or began in Harar or Addis Ababa, Nazaret or Asmara or Awasa"[51] the text subsequently

---

47 ETHIOPIAN FULL GOSPEL BELIEVERS' CHURCH, ሙሉ ወንጌል ቤተ ክርስቲያን ከልደት እስከ ..., 3.

48 Ibid., 4–13.

49 Cf. e.g. TAYE ABDISSA, "The Pentecostal Development and the Rise of Charismatic Movement in Ethiopia," 16–26; YESHITELA MENGISTU, "The Story of the Meserete Krestos Church" (B.Th. thesis, Mekane Yesus Seminary, 1983); HAILE WOLDE MICHAEL, "A Comparative Study of Leadership Development Methods with Reference to the Ethiopian Full Gospel Church," 169–178; TEKA OBSA FOGI, "The Charismatic Movement in the EECMY"; BULUTSE FUTUWI, "An Introduction to the Theology and Growth of Independent Churches in Ethiopia With Special Reference to Rhema Faith Church," 56–62.

50 ETHIOPIAN FULL GOSPEL BELIEVER'S CHURCH, የኢትዮጵያ ሙሉ ወንጌል አማኞች ቤተ ክርስቲያን 25ኛ ዓመት በዓል, 9.

51 Ibid.

only traces the development of the university student meeting to the establishment of the FGBC.[52] The Finnish mission split is not brought up at all, and although there is mention of a Sunday afternoon program at Merkato, the writing makes it seem as if this was part of the university group's initiatives. Similarly, the fortieth anniversary magazine of the Addis Ababa FGBC from 2006 does not mention Harar, Nazaret, nor the Merkato group at all, but begins its story in 1965 with the first prayer meeting of students leading to the first national conference in July 1966, which is also the chronological reference point for the anniversary.[53]

In contrast to these omissions in jubilee magazines, the FGBC historian Bekele Woldekidan has taken up the Nazaret and Harar stories quite extensively in his book "Revival in Ethiopia."[54] However, the overall thrust of this history is in line with the other sources from his church since he established the university student meeting as the real origin of Ethiopian Pentecostalism while marginalizing the other early movements. Bekele portrays the Nazaret *yäsämay bərhan* movement as a proto-Pentecostal revival in a section titled "Can anything good come out of Nazaret?"[55] In his narrative, the students are depicted as more or less stumbling upon revival, learning through trial and error. For example, when a demon manifested itself in their midst, they reportedly first sought advice from their parents, testing traditional methods like holy water and sacrificing coffee grounds, before "the word of the Lord saying that 'in my name they will drive out demons' reached them for help and training."[56] Bekele concludes:

> Even though they did not understand the situation properly and at the time they could not call it baptism in the Holy Spirit or Pentecostal practice, new things began to be seen in the meetings the students led. For example, youths began to emerge among them who spoke in tongues, gave prophecies, saw visions. However, because of a lack of management arising from a lack of knowledge, there was a time in which these occurrences, [meant] to be a strong helper of the revival, also were a great obstacle to the revival.[57]

Similarly, Bekele's Harar section stops short of a full revival narrative. He mainly focuses on the conversion and Spirit baptism experiences of the three Harar leaders who later became elders in the FGBC: Zeleke Alemu, Assefa Alemu, and Betta Mengistu. He does not cite Yosief Kidanewold's account or the brief references to

52 ETHIOPIAN FULL GOSPEL BELIEVER'S CHURCH, የኢትዮጵያ ሙሉ ወንጌል አመኞች ቤተ ክርስቲያን 25ኛ ዓመት በዓል, 9–10.

53 ADDIS ABABA FULL GOSPEL BELIEVERS' CHURCH, የ40ኛ ዓመት የወንጌል አገልግሎትና የምስጋና በዓል መጽሔት /ሕምሌ 1958–1998 ዓ.ም./, 3–6.

54 See BEKELE WOLDEKIDAN, ሪቫይቫል, 74–78, 84–87.

55 See ibid., 74–78. Although Bekele is aware of Hege's extensive account of the movement (cf. ibid., 158) he does not reference his account here and provides quite a different narrative. It is also interesting to note that Bekele narrates the Nazaret events before telling about the arrival of Chacha Omahe, i.e., before the "Pentecostal match" lit the fire. However, since he doubts the late dating of Chacha's arrival, this would be an anachronism, cf. above, 72.

56 Ibid., 78.

57 Ibid. By "occurrences" turning into "obstacles" he probably means a false prophecy that severely damaged the group's reputation for a while, see below 113.

Harar in histories of the Nazaret *yäsämay bərhan* movement,[58] but seems to rely exclusively on Assefa, Betta, and Zeleke as informants.[59] After a short episode telling of Zeleke' and Assefa's attempt to minister among the youths at Nazaret, Bekele does not trace the path of the Harar movement further, but pursues a detail in their story for answering a question about the correct date for Chacha Omahe's first visit to Ethiopia.[60]

Moreover, Bekele groups and prioritizes the revival beginnings in another way by asserting that the "Azusa wind" first came to Ethiopia by way of Chacha's ministry in Awasa,[61] while Nazaret and Harar to him were examples of another "Pentecostal wind" that wasn't stirred up by the "Azusa wind."[62] This analogy seems to suggest a difference in standing between the Awasa conferences and the Nazaret/Harar movements, but the university student prayer meeting supersedes them all. In a section titled "All roads lead to Addis Ababa"[63] Bekele shows how three of the four students who established the university prayer meeting had encountered their Spirit baptism through the movements in Harar, Nazaret and Awasa. Since all three "winds" thus are united in the nucleus of the university student meeting, Bekele concludes that here lies the "real origin" of Ethiopian Pentecostalism:

> Like "312 Azusa Street" this house was the place chosen by God for the outbreak of the Pentecostal revival in Ethiopia.[64]

3.1.4 Mennonite Histories

The Nazaret *yäsämay bərhan* movement, which was only occasionally hinted to in the early sources and characterized as a proto-Pentecostal revival by Bekele, found a prominent place in histories with a Mennonite background, either from missionaries or their Ethiopian church, the MKC. The Nazaret group had early contacts with Mennonite missionaries, and after a conflict with the student movement in Addis Ababa in 1966 a significant part of the *yäsämay bərhan* group did not participate in the formation of the FGBC, but remained independent for a while and gradually merged with the Mennonite MKC from 1973 on.[65]

The first reference to the Nazaret movement in Mennonite histories can be found in a 1983 B.Th. thesis about the history of the MKC by Yeshitela Mengistu.[66] Quite con-

---

58 See below, 112.
59 See also Tibebe Eshete's account of the Harar revival, which likewise is exclusively based on interviews with these three leaders and focuses on their stories only, see TIBEBE ESHETE, *The Evangelical Movement in Ethiopia*, 154–156.
60 See above, 72, for Bekele's problem in dating Chacha's visit. Assefa Alemu received his Spirit baptism in early 1965 through Kebede Woldemariam from the Finnish mission, who, in turn, was reportedly Spirit-baptized under Chacha Omahe's ministry. This connection would make the dating of Chacha's initial visit to 1965 impossible.
61 See BEKELE WOLDEKIDAN, ረብያňለ, 59, 78.
62 See ibid., 59, 75, 84.
63 Ibid., 88–92.
64 Ibid., 90.
65 HEGE, *Beyond Our Prayers*, 156f.
66 YESHITELA MENGISTU, "The Story of the Meserete Krestos Church," 16f.

trary to Engelsviken's dismissal of the Nazaret revival as a proto-Pentecostal prayer group, it is given a prominent role in the formation of the FGBC here:

> When some of these students [from the Nazaret group] entered university, they took these unique experiences with them and opened the Mullu Wongel Church [FGBC] in Addis Ababa together with fellow students from other churches.[67]

Other accounts from an MKC background follow this assertion.[68] The most detailed and frequently referenced narration of the events in Nazaret is found in Nathan Hege's book about the Mennonite mission in Ethiopia and the emergence of the MKC from this mission.[69] Here the origin of the Addis Ababa University student movement is traced to the *yäsämay bərhan* movement by establishing a succession of Spirit baptisms:

> In the summer of 1965, a delegation of Semay Birhan youths attended a two-week conference at the Philadelphia Church Mission (Swedish Pentecostal) in Awassa. One evening during the conference, Birhane Abreha, a student from Addis Ababa University, joined a prayer meeting of the Semay Birhan group and was baptized by the power of the Spirit. He and Solomon [the leader of the Nazaret group] bonded in the Spirit. After returning to Addis Ababa, they prayed for Birhane's intimate friend and classmate, Teka Gebru, who also experienced the baptism of the Holy Spirit. These three started to witness and pray for university students, and the movement spread fast and wide among university students and later among high school students even outside Addis.[70]

Due to the ready availability of Hege's publication and the scarcity of other sources outside Ethiopia, some Western accounts are unaware of other influences on the early Pentecostal movement and therefore even produced the rather awkward assertion that the FGBC has grown "out of the influence of the Mennonite mission"[71] or that it is one of "two branches"[72] the Mennonites established.

---

67 Yeshitela Mengistu, "The Story of the Meserete Krestos Church," 17.
68 E.g. Negewo Boset, "Persecution and Church Expansion: The Growth of Opposition Between the Religious Authorities and Jesus as it was Experienced in the Primitive Church and Extends to the Present Church of Ethiopian Meserete Kristos" (B.Th. thesis, Evangelical Theological College, 1994), 103, quoting a statement by Yeshitela Mengistu (Yeshitela Mengistu, "The Story of the Meserete Krestos Church," 16) that "youth from that town [Nazaret] were instruments for the formation of Full Gospel."
69 See Hege, *Beyond Our Prayers*, 147–160. The MKC historian Tilahun Beyene closely follows Hege's account, which he in turn had helped to shape, cf. Tilahun Beyene, ". . . ቤተ ክርስቲያኑን እሥራሉ. . . ": የመሰረት ክርስቶስ ቤተ ክርስቲያን ታሪክ, 89–97; Hege, *Beyond Our Prayers*, 15.
70 Ibid., 151. The author goes on to assert that the "Semay Birhan chapel at Nazareth still remained a prominent center of prayer where many university students in the movement went on the weekends. This continued until the university students rented a large house for prayer and worship in Addis."
71 Neil Lettinga, "Ethiopian Protestantism: The "Pente" Churches in Ethiopia" (2000), http://www.bethel.edu/~letnie/AfricanChristianity/EthiopiaProtestantism.html (accessed February 10, 2009).
72 Joachim Persoon, "New Perspectives on Ethiopian and African Christianity: Communalities and Contrasts in Twentieth Century Religious Experience," *Exchange* 34 (4 2005): 312.

The Harar movement is occasionally mentioned by these accounts as well, but only in the context of a specific story, which links the *yäsämay bərhan* movement to the teaching about the Holy Spirit at the Finnish mission via the Harar revival.[73] The role of the Finnish mission in this story is marginal. A convert from this mission by the name of Getachew Mikre reportedly told the Harar TTI student Zeleke Alemu about the outpouring of the Holy Spirit at the mission, without having experienced Spirit baptism himself. Zeleke then reportedly shared this information with a Nazaret youth, both of whom then began to pray for baptism in the Holy Spirit, which they later encountered independently of one another. In this way, Harar and Nazaret are established as revival movements of equal precedence and standing, while linked to a center of established Pentecostalism, the Finnish mission. This endeavor to prominently situate the Nazaret movement in the early Pentecostal history can even be taken one step further as this informant from the MKC shows:

> The Finnish mission, it's appointed a Pentecostal mission. It was already there before we experienced this infilling of the Holy Spirit. But it was contained. There was no movement. Any experience happened within church building. There was no movement. Heywet Berhan, I mean Swedish Philadelphia [Mission], it was another Pentecostal mission. It happened in Awasa, it was contained. It didn't grow into a movement, or it didn't go out of the church. But the one in Nazaret, and also in Harar — these are simultaneous movements. The different characteristic in my opinion: those who went to teacher training they stayed only for two years. So they easily leave. The one [movement] in Nazaret, you have those living in Nazaret, also students from high school. So there was more retention capacity in there.[74]

By juxtaposing the Nazaret meetings against the "contained" mission endeavors, the informant claims a certain level of importance for the *yäsämay bərhan* group.[75] Nazaret was the place where the Ethiopian Pentecostal movement was actually born because of the uninhibited nature of this outpouring. The same argument can hardly be made with regard to Harar, which, as the informant admits, was a "simultaneous movement." Therefore the informant turns to the question of sustainability by pointing to Nazaret's "retention capacity."

There is another point of connection between Nazaret youths and the Harar movement. The Harar youth Zeleke Alemu experienced his conversion on November 15, 1963, following a Bible study held by a group of Protestant Christians at the Harar TTI, which was comprised mostly of teacher trainees who had received their secondary education at the Nazareth Bible Academy, run by the Mennonite mission.[76] However, Zeleke's conversion is narrated to have taken place outside the Bible study meeting, and the other Christian youths apparently did not accept his Spirit baptism expe-

---

73 For a full discussion of this story, see below, 112.
74 Interview no. 19.
75 Cf. also ETHIOPIAN GENNET CHURCH, የ5ዐኛው ዓመት የውርቅ ኢዮቤልዩ በዓል, 12 for a similar statement.
76 See BEKELE WOLDEKIDAN, ሪብያሳ, 85; also mentioned in interview no. 130. For an overview of the Nazareth Bible Academy cf. SHETLER, "The Nazareth Bible Academy in Retrospect." Initially, the school offered courses on teaching, which would help facilitate the transition to the teacher training institutions offered by the government, see ibid., 55.

rience and his allegedly exuberant expressions.[77] Zeleke then started his own small prayer group and joined up with others, like Assefa Alemu and Betta Mengistu who had been converted and Spirit-baptized.[78] This initial connection of Zeleke's conversion to Mennonite youths from Nazaret is not taken up in any of the Mennonite/MKC accounts.

3.1.5 Finnish Mission and GC Histories

Histories originating with the Finnish mission and with the church that came out of the mission, the Gennet Church (GC), are relevant to this chronological review of sources in two respects. On the one hand, the early Harar revival had some points of contact with the Finnish mission group, which leads to the question how these sources represent the Harar revival. On the other hand, the group that split from the mission's center in the Addis Ababa Merkato area was one of the influential contributors to the formation of the FGBC. Therefore, it is of interest to explore whether and how the legacy of this group is incorporated into the mission-related historical memory of early Pentecostalism.

As was mentioned above, the first point of contact between the Finnish mission and the Harar group was Getachew Mikre, who attended the Finnish Free Foreign Mission (FFFM) congregation at Merkato before continuing his education at the Harar TTI. Here, he reportedly told Zeleke Alemu about the Spirit baptisms that he had witnessed at the Finnish mission, though he had not yet encountered this experience himself.[79] Two of the later Harar leaders report an initial influence by Getachew in their conversions, bringing them together, and relaying Pentecostal literature. After the revival had begun, the contact to the Addis Ababa Merkato Finnish mission was deepened in March 1965, when the Harar group sent Assefa Alemu to Addis Ababa to see the evangelist Brian Williams, who was ministering there, in the hopes to invite him to Harar.[80] Though Assefa met Brian Williams, he did not succeed in inviting him to Harar, but more importantly, he met Kebede Woldemariam, who later became one of the youths who departed from the Finnish mission. Through Kebede, Assefa received baptism in the Holy Spirit and in water during this trip. After his return to Harar, Assefa first baptized Zeleke Alemu in water, before the two of them together baptized the remainder of the group.[81] The Addis Ababa connection was further intensified in a visit by Kebede Woldemariam to Harar.

Harar informants have mentioned these early contacts to the Addis Ababa Finnish mission in interviews, they do not give much weight to them. Instead, Getachew's

77 Cf. BEKELE WOLDEKIDAN, ሪቫይቫል, 84–85 with regard to Zeleke's initial enthusiasm. One informant reports that the group even invited an itinerant British minister, who insisted that speaking in tongues was demonic, interview no. 130.

78 For their stories, see YOSIEF KIDANEWOLD, "The History of the Pentecostal Movement in Addis Abeba," 9–10; TIBEBE ESHETE, *The Evangelical Movement in Ethiopia*, 155f. BEKELE WOLDEKIDAN, ሪቫይቫል, 84–87.

79 Interview no. 130. As was mentioned above, this exchange is also used by Nazaret revival narratives to situate both the Harar and the Nazaret revivals within the existing Pentecostal networks, see above, 102. See also HEGE, *Beyond Our Prayers*, 148f. TILAHUN BEYENE, "...ቤተ ክርስቲያኔን እሥራለሁ...": የመሰረተ ክርስቶስ ቤተ ክርስቲያን ታሪክ, 92; also interviews no. 19; 32.

80 Interview no. 39.

81 Interviews no. 39; 130.

input is given little weight in their historical narrative. There are no stories about his own conversion, his experiences at the Finnish mission, or his ministry at Harar. One informant even contended that he was "the last person" in Harar to be baptized in the Spirit.[82] Likewise, the role of Kebede Woldemariam seems to be contentious. While two Harar informants mentioned the water baptism of Assefa in Addis Ababa by Kebede and his later visit in Harar, a third stated that inviting Kebede to Harar was "not a good advice" and prefers not to link the Harar water baptisms to Addis Ababa at all, but instead tells how the Harar youths all baptized one another. This is probably what led Tibebe Eshete to contend in his history of Ethiopian Pentecostalism that Harar was a completely independent revival. He reports that the Harar leaders baptized themselves or each other in a small waterhole nearby, or even a barrel,[83] and concludes:

> Informants who participated in this early revival experience often reminisce with a grimace at the way they conducted these baptismal rites without an experienced and knowledgeable person to guide them.[84]

While it may not be surprising that the Harar revivalists are not interested in further exploring their connections to the Finnish mission, it is noteworthy that the sources from the Finnish mission and the GC do not attempt to do so either. Getachew's name was only mentioned once in an interview with an FFFM missionary. However, he did not mention that Getachew had attended the Finnish mission in Addis Ababa, but only used him to connect Nazaret and Harar.[85] The later contacts between Kebede Woldemariam and Harar are not mentioned as well, despite or perhaps because of the fact that they played into the later split from the Finnish mission. In the summer of 1966, when Assefa Alemu, Betta Mengistu, and Zeleke Alemu had graduated from the Harar TTI, another Finnish mission congregant, Fantahun Gebre, helped facilitate employment for them at the American Mission School in Addis Ababa, where he was working as well. The three Harar revivalists then established their small Pentecostal congregation in the Merkato area together with Kebede Woldemariam, Fantahun Gebre, and Melese Wogu from the Finnish mission, who informed the missionaries that they would no longer be attending.

While the Harar connections are not mentioned in sources from the Finnish mission or the GC, they occasionally use the eldership roles of Kebede, Fantahun, and Melese in the FGBC in order to connect the mission's legacy to the formation of the first independent Pentecostal church. In the first history of the GC, a 1990 B.Th. by Seleshi Kebede, the author first quotes Yeshitela Mengistu's assertion that members of the Nazaret *yäsämay bərhan* group "later opened the Mullu Wongel Church in Addis Ababa"[86] and then counters:

---

82 Interview no. 39.
83 TIBEBE ESHETE, *The Evangelical Movement in Ethiopia*, 155n38; also mentioned in interview no. 47. One informant recounts with amusement the difficulties of baptizing Assefa's wife in a barrel, who at the time was nine months pregnant, interview no. 130.
84 Ibid., 155.
85 Interview no. 69.
86 Quotation of YESHITELA MENGISTU, "The Story of the Meserete Krestos Church," 17 in SELESHI KEBEDE, "The History of the Guenet Church," 8.

Even if the above reports have their own truth, it is known that those who split from Finnish Mission were the first prominent leaders in Mulu Wengel church.[87]

However, Seleshi's history does not provide a detailed narrative about how the group that departed from the Finnish mission came to their position in the FGBC. He only briefly mentions that they rented their own premises in the Merkato area and then simply states that "the new church was later named Mulu Wengel (Full Gospel) Church," skipping the university student movement and the unification of the groups altogether.[88] His informant for this part was a man by the name of Mola Beri, who according to his own testimony at first worshiped with the Merkato group, but later became dissatisfied with "gossip" spread by them.[89] Mola apparently did not join the FGBC, but stayed behind and became part of the GC.[90]

Similarly, other sources from the GC do not trace the development of the Merkato group. For example, the GC jubilee magazine of 2001 simply quotes the first pastor of the church saying that the "formation of the Full Gospel Believers' Church in part was together with people who had left the Finnish mission chapel."[91] The FFFM missionary Kyösti Roininen also merely links his mission to the establishment of the FGBC without providing an historical narrative, but simply quoting Engelsviken's assertion of the importance of the elders who had come out of the Finnish mission.[92]

Therefore it appears that the FFFM or GC sources are primarily interested in demonstrating the impact of their former members in the FGBC, and are not inclined or well-informed enough to narrate the interim between the split and the ordination of elders in the FGBC in any detail. Details about the independent Merkato group can only be found in interviews with the ones who broke from the Finnish mission or the Harar revivalists who joined them around the same time.[93]

Moreover, the later merger of the Merkato group with the university student movement was a contested issue among the former. One of the FFFM converts, Kebede Woldemariam, studied at the Addis Ababa School of Fine Arts in close proximity to the meeting place of the university students and therefore joined them early on. Melese Wogu, who had left the Finnish mission together with Kebede, at first opposed this move as well as any notion of uniting the two groups in a common church, which reportedly led to an ongoing conflict between the two.[94] However, the two localities merged anyway and when the FGBC was formed, Melese and Kebede both were included among the first seven elders of the church. However, after a visit to Sweden's Pentecostal churches in 1971, Melese left the FGBC in disagreement with the

---

87 SELESHI KEBEDE, "The History of the Guenet Church," 8.
88 Ibid., 7.
89 See ETHIOPIAN GENNET CHURCH, የ５ዐኛው ዓመት የወርቅ ኢዮቤልዩ በዓል, 30–31.
90 See SELESHI KEBEDE, "The History of the Guenet Church," 6.
91 ETHIOPIAN GENNET CHURCH, የ５ዐኛው ዓመት የወርቅ ኢዮቤልዩ በዓል, 18.
92 See ROININEN, "A Condensed History of the Finnish Mission in Ethiopia," 5. Cf. above, 42, for the full quote and its context.
93 Interviews no. 91; 47; 130; 39.
94 Mentioned in interviews no. 91; 130. One of these informants maintained that there was "a real struggle" between the groups.

churches centralized denominational structure.[95] He emigrated to the USA in 1976. Since Kebede had left the Merkato group early on, he probably was not inclined to uphold their legacy in the history of the FGBC; moreover, he also emigrated to the USA before 1976. A third elder from the Merkato group, Fantahun Gebre also did not stay in leadership for very long.[96] Therefore, much like the Harar movement, the Addis Ababa Merkato group did not have anyone to inject their story into the first histories by the FGBC. The FFFM and the GC, on the other hand, were mainly interested in linking their work to the FGBC by way of the Merkato split, without providing too much detail about the interim.

Concluding this review of available sources about the early Pentecostal groups, it appears that only two of the movements have found a lasting place in historical memory, which is linked to their integration in denominational histories. The university student prayer meeting became the foundational event for the FGBC. The MKC in turn took up the *yäsämay bərhan* movement as part of its own history. The Harar revival and the group that split from the Finnish mission, on the other hand, did not attain a prominent place. Instead, they are only mentioned where needed to establish certain points in other revival histories. The Harar revival, though prominently featured in early missionary correspondence, in later histories is mostly cited for its connection with the Nazaret group and in stories about the FGBC elders from this group. The group that split from the Finnish mission is used by sources from the FFFM and the GC to trace the missionary legacy to the foundation of the FGBC, without any apparent interest in the detailed history of the group.

The different ways in which the stories about the early revival movements are arranged in the respective institutional contexts reveal a competitive constellation in the writing of histories about early Ethiopian Pentecostalism. It appears as if the two premises laid out in Engelsviken's *Documentary Report* serve as parameters for these later histories as well. They all endeavor to link up their stories to the formation of the FGBC as the institutional correlate of Ethiopian Pentecostalism, and hope to establish a certain movement as the "real origin" of Ethiopia's revival by making different claims of originality, primacy, and importance.

Moreover, the review of sources also suggests that the genealogy of present historical knowledge about the different revival groups is bound up with individual actors from these groups. In the MKC there were individuals from the *yäsämay bərhan* movement, who saw to it that their story would receive a prominent place in this church's revival memoirs. On the other hand, when representatives from the Harar revival movement and the Merkato group resigned from their positions and membership in the FGBC, their stories appear to have left this particular church with them. The legacy of these movements is now mostly connected to the biographies of their founders, most notably those who became and still are well-known ministers in

---

95 Interview no. 91. Melese was reportedly inspired by the congregationalism of Swedish Pentecostalism and disagreed with denominational structures. He probably did not leave the FGBC until 1972. A letter by Tage Johansson from December 1971 indicates that he was still part of the Addis Ababa congregation then, but Johansson also notes that Melese was "very friendly" after his return from Sweden, see JOHANSSON, Letter to Bo Hörnberg, December 2, 1971, cf. NYBERG OSKARSSON, *Svensk Pingstmission i Ethiopien (1959–1980)*, 275.

96 For the few details available about Fantahun, see below 210.

the worldwide Ethiopian Pentecostal community. Other important revivalists of the time, like the woman Alem Bisrat, generally do not receive such a treatment.

These dynamics in writing Ethiopian Pentecostal history are testimony to the fluidity and structural openness of the early revival groups, which in turn may indicate that the assumed revival group identities were secondary productions of the historical discourse. The process of producing such identities will be explored further with regard to the Nazaret *yäsämay bərhan* movement and the Addis Ababa University student group.

3.2   The Nazaret *yäsämay bərhan* Movement

The integration of the story of the Nazaret *yäsämay bərhan* movement into the history of the MKC comes with two narrative functions: on the one hand it serves as the historic explanation of the Charismatic outlook of this Mennonite denomination, and on the other hand it is used to mark the legacy of later MKC leaders in the formation of the Ethiopian Pentecostal movement. These two functions of the story confront the group with the task of historically establishing two identities, a Mennonite and a Pentecostal one. Both are fraught with difficulties, however. Though the *yäsämay bərhan* group had its roots with the Mennonite mission and in the end was absorbed by the church the mission had initiated, many sources inside and outside the MKC seek to avoid an association of this early revival movement with a foreign mission. The group's Pentecostal identity on the other hand has been put into question with regard to the movement's original encounter of Holy Spirit baptism, as the detailed exploration will show. This issues is also related to the question of chronological precedence and importance of the Nazaret movement in comparison to the Harar revival.

3.2.1   Orthodox and Mennonite Roots

The two recent histories by Bekele Woldekidan and Tibebe Eshete situated the roots of the Nazaret *yäsämay bərhan* movement within the Ethiopian Orthodox Church.[97] Bekele Woldekidan begins his report on Nazaret with "students from the Emperor Galawdeos school" who "by the means of their *haymanotä abbäw* spiritual fellowship began to hold spiritual meetings in a house, they called 'chapel.'"[98] Consequently, in Bekele's account, Orthodox students more or less by themselves stumble on the idea of Bible study, prayer meetings and eventually salvation and Spirit baptism, while retaining their Orthodox identity:

---

97 See BEKELE WOLDEKIDAN, ሬ፡ይ፡ሳ, 74–78; TIBEBE ESHETE, *The Evangelical Movement in Ethiopia*, 156f.

98 BEKELE WOLDEKIDAN, ሬ፡ይ፡ሳ, 76. The *haymanot abbäw* was an Orthodox student association founded in 1957, aimed at educating Ethiopian Christians about their faith, cf. HEYER, *Die Kirche Äthiopiens*, 341–343; ASFAW DAMTE, "Haymanotä abäw," in *Encyclopaedia Aethiopica*, ed. SIEGBERT UHLIG (Wiesbaden: Harrassowitz, 2005), 1075–1076. The association fell dormant under the Derg and its official reactivation failed after the military regime was ousted. It apparently was a mission-critical movement from its inception, cf. TIBEBE ESHETE, *The Evangelical Movement in Ethiopia*, 156n41.

How the students came into a situation like this, they do not know for sure. But they had not been thinking of it or planning it. Even though there are two or three, who know about the beginning, they had not planned it to be like this, they had not [even] dreamt of it. But all are sure that they did not change their faith, including Solomon Kebede, who then was the president of the school's *haymanotä abbäw* association. As they were learning and teaching at an Orthodox school, they even had the hope that all of the people of Nazaret would follow their Christian search.[99]

This tendency to portray the *yäsämay bərhan* group as a purely Orthodox revival movement is in keeping with other parts of Bekele's account about the Nazaret developments, who treats it as a proto-Pentecostal revival, as a "wind that was not roused by the Azusa wind," i.e. a revival without Protestant connections.[100] Furthermore, he likens the *yäsämay bərhan* movement to the much more recent *imanuel maḥəbär*, an Orthodox Charismatic renewal movement, which spread from Nazaret to different places in the country, and eventually broke away from the EOC to form the Emanuel United Church.[101]

Likewise, Tibebe Eshete also attributes an Orthodox origin and identity to the Nazaret movement. Although unlike Bekele, he finds it "quite possible that news of the Pentecostal faith might have come to the attention of some of the members of the [Nazaret] Bible study group and spurred the search process,"[102] he nevertheless contends that the contact to other Protestants, like the Mennonite mission, was a secondary development ensuing when the group was forced to find a meeting place outside of their school. Though they accepted financial assistance by the Mennonite mission for renting premises, Tibebe asserts that this did not taint their self-understanding as Orthodox:

> When members of the *Semay Berhan* decided to accept the offer, they did so with a firm position of maintaining their identity as Orthodox Christians who had experienced salvation and the actions of the Holy Spirit.[103]

Quite opposite to these accounts, histories from a Mennonite or MKC background point to an early and continuous involvement of their mission with the *yäsämay bərhan* student group. Here, the story of the Nazaret movement begins with a group of high school students, who approached the medical director of the local Mennonite hospital, Dr. Rohrer Eshleman, with a request for English lessons.[104] These linguistic lessons on the Gospel of John reportedly led to Bible discussions, and later to the participation

99   BEKELE WOLDEKIDAN, ሪኔዳና, 76–77.
100 Ibid., 75.
101 On the Emanuel United Church see MUSSIE ALAZAR, "Amanual-Mahiber"; SCHRÖDER, "Äthiopien."
102 TIBEBE ESHETE, *The Evangelical Movement in Ethiopia*, 156.
103 Ibid., 157 (italics Tibebe Eshete). Tibebe also notes here that this independence was not maintained, since "later events led to the forging of closer relations between the students and the Mennonites, the outcome of which was the the establishment of a semi-independent institution called, the *Meserete Kristos Church*."
104 E.g. YESHITELA MENGISTU, "The Story of the Meserete Krestos Church," 16; NEGEWO BOSET, "Persecution and Church Expansion," 101–102; HEGE, *Beyond Our Prayers*, 147–146; TILAHUN

of youths in public worship services on the Mennonite hospital grounds. The question of an Orthodox versus Protestant affiliation is not settled in these accounts. Especially the missionary sources seem to avoid explicit conversion narratives or terminology. Yeshitela Mengistu quotes Dr. Eshleman simply saying that "we learned the way of the Lord together."[105] Hege asserts that the missionaries "explained that becoming a born-again Christian did not necessarily mean they had to leave the Orthodox Church," and mentions that a number of students in the English class made a "faith commitment."[106] This hesitance probably reflects the situation the missionaries were in. Operating a hospital in an area that was closed to foreign mission always came with the danger of having the whole operation shut down if the mission was caught proselytizing. The Mennonite mission at first tried to evade this rule by baptizing its converts, but was severely reprimanded for this action and refrained from baptisms in the future.[107] Therefore a more explicit evangelical conversion terminology in describing Dr. Eshleman's Bible class only appears in later Ethiopian sources. The MKC historian Tilahun Beyene, for example, asserts that the students before were only church members "by name", whereas now were led by the missionaries to "true salvation", and finally "accepted the Lord Jesus as personal savior."[108]

Apparently the students soon decided to establish their own meeting place outside of the mission compound and the MKC. The earliest written source about the Nazaret movement, provides the following account:

> That group became active, and started to hold prayer meetings in their school. They did not want to worship in the mission church for reason of not being identified with foreign faith. Dr. Eshleman brought the matter to the church council and a house was rented for them outside the hospital compound. The Doctor made benches and other necessary things for them and Ethiopian advisors were assigned to them; and [they] were left to themselves. They will conduct their own worship service and some times invite guests. Slowly they started to increase in number and grow in a different way from that of the mission church.[109]

This passage illustrates the ambivalence of negotiating the relationship to the Mennonite mission and the MKC in historical narratives. The group does not want to be "identified with foreign faith," but seeks and finds a solution by way of the "mission church" nevertheless. The house is outside the "hospital compound" but rented by the missionaries. Though "advisors were assigned to them," they "were left to themselves." Despite the marked difference to the mission from the start, the group "slowly" grew "in a different way from that of the mission church." Altogether, Yeshitela's report does not suggest a relationship that is easily disentangled by dichotomies of Orthodox

BEYENE, "...ቤተ ክርስቲያንን እግራለሁ...": የመሰረተ ክርስቶስ ቤተ ክርስቲያን ታሪክ, 89–90; ABERA ERTIRO, "The History of the Meserete Kristos Church at Nazareth," 16.
105 YESHITELA MENGISTU, "The Story of the Meserete Krestos Church," 16.
106 HEGE, *Beyond Our Prayers*, 148.
107 See ibid., 128–131. Ethiopian converts, however, baptized each other nevertheless, but never in the presence of missionaries.
108 TILAHUN BEYENE, "...ቤተ ክርስቲያንን እግራለሁ...": የመሰረተ ክርስቶስ ቤተ ክርስቲያን ታሪክ, 90.
109 YESHITELA MENGISTU, "The Story of the Meserete Krestos Church," 16.

vs. Protestant or foreign vs. indigenous. Instead, Yeshitela marks the distance in a
different way:

> A new group took responsibility when the older were leaving after finishing high
> school. The gap to the mission church now widened and new practices started
> to be seen among them. Mass prayer and exorcism are good examples that
> were seen in their meetings. All this time the Nazareth congregation paid the
> house rent and continued to invite their elders to their own elders meetings.[110]

Thus, for Yeshitela it is not an Orthodox identity as proposed by Tibebe that
coincided with the widening of "the gap to the mission church," but new Charismatic
practices within the group. Yet at the same time, the "Nazareth congregation" (i.e.,
the "mission church") still financially supported the group and sought organizational
ties. Consequentially, the new experiences cannot fully separate the student group
from the MKC, but they do lend the young movement its own profile. Later Mennonite
sources follow the same dual pattern of affirming both the differences and the ties
between the *yäsämay bərhan* movement and the MKC. On the one hand, they highlight
the Charismatic identity of the group in opposition to the church, for example by
stating that "[l]ike the Jerusalem church the Ethiopian Meserete Kristos Church was
inactive before it received the power of the Holy Spirit …;"[111] that the *yäsämay
bərhan* movement "terrified the Mission Church because of their new worshiping and
prayer style;"[112] or that "MKC members began to wonder what would happen to
this movement unless someone gave mature leadership."[113] On the other hand, the
first Spirit baptism in the *yäsämay bərhan* group is presented as a milestone for the
Mennonite Church as well: "This was the first filling with the Holy Spirit in the
Meserete Kristos Church."[114] Furthermore, a number of sources tell of an MKC elder
who was assigned to the group as supervisor, but soon encountered Spirit baptism as
well and subsequently functioned as a mediator between the group and the church.[115]

Thus, while sources outside the MKC can easily afford to qualify the *yäsämay
bərhan* movement as an Orthodox renewal movement with accidental ties to Mennonite
Christianity in Ethiopia, histories from the MKC background have a more complex
history to integrate. In consequence, the Nazaret student movement is set apart from
the Mennonite mission and the MKC by its very contribution to the church after its
(re)integration, i.e., the youth's Pentecostal experiences and outlook. This identity is
more suitable for articulating the group's difference to the church and the possibility of
its later integration, rather than dwelling on a supposed Orthodox identity or mission
independence. Placing the emphasis on mission independence would not have set
it apart clearly enough from the MKC, which had just emerged from the Mennonite

---

110   Ibid., 16–17.
111   NEGEWO BOSET, "Persecution and Church Expansion," 100. This is the introduction to the
      yäsämay bərhan narrative told to show "how the Holy Spirit power revived Meserete Kristos
      Church" (ibid., 101).
112   ABERA ERTIRO, "The History of the Meserete Kristos Church at Nazareth," 17.
113   HEGE, *Beyond Our Prayers*, 153.
114   TILAHUN BEYENE, "…ቤተ ክርስቲያኔን እሠራለሁ…": የመሰረት ክርስቶስ ቤተ ክርስቲያን ታሪክ, 92.
115   Cf. NEGEWO BOSET, "Persecution and Church Expansion," 103; HEGE, *Beyond Our Prayers*,
      153–154; ABERA ERTIRO, "The History of the Meserete Kristos Church at Nazareth," 17.

mission in a process of nationalization, including debates about the role of missions.[116]
Insisting on an Orthodox identity, on the other hand, would not have plausibly allowed
the group to join the Mennonite church. Thus, the Pentecostal outlook of the group
serves as the defining identity marker of difference to what would be the movement's
mother church later on.

3.2.2   Finding a Pentecostal Identity

The presumed Pentecostal identity not only kept the Nazaret student movement distinct from Mennonites in MKC histories, it is also of central importance for asserting
the group's legacy with regard to the beginnings of Ethiopian Pentecostalism. This
function requires a story of Holy Spirit baptism, which is clearly recognizable as such
and can be woven into the early history of Pentecostalism in Ethiopia, preferably in
a prominent position. Nathan Hege's account of the Nazaret revival is an illustrative
example of how these two requirements are met in historical narratives about the
yäsämay bərhan movement:

> The annual Christian Life Conference of Meserete Kristos Church (MKC) met
> at the Nazareth Bible Academy in 1964. At the meeting, Solomon Kebede (by
> 1997, chairman of the church) met his friend Zeleke Alemu, who already had
> come to a saving knowledge of Christ. While discussing about life and growth
> in Jesus, Zeleke, who had some contact with Getachew Mikre in the Finnish
> Pentecostal Mission in Addis Ababa, told Solomon that God still baptizes be-
> lievers with the Holy Spirit just as on the Day of Pentecost (Acts 2). Both
> resolved to earnestly pray that they would receive this baptism and become
> servants of the Lord. Zeleke left for Harar, a city 250 miles to the east, where
> he was a student at the Teachers' Training Institute (TTI). Later, at about
> the same time, both received the baptism, Solomon in Nazareth and Zeleke in
> Harar.[117]

The structure of this passage invokes a typical Pentecostal trajectory of Spirit
baptism. The protagonists "already had come to a saving knowledge of Christ," but
apparently were still looking for more in their "life and growth in Jesus." When
they hear the story of a present-day outpouring of the Holy Spirit "just as on the
Day of Pentecost (Acts 2)," they "earnestly" seek this experience for themselves and
subsequently are rewarded with an unmediated encounter of the Holy Spirit in their
respective locations. Secondly, the Nazaret story is integrated into the beginnings
of Ethiopian Pentecostalism. The news of present-day Pentecost originates with the
Finnish mission, and thus is rooted in the global Pentecostal movement. At the same

---

116   The nationalization of the Mennonite mission churches was a longer process, from 1959 to 1964,
       cf. HEGE, *Beyond Our Prayers*, 128–146. The protracted discussions on whether the name
       should include "Mennonite" indicates that this was also an identity debate, cf. YESHITELA
       MENGISTU, "The Story of the Meserete Krestos Church," 12; HEGE, *Beyond Our Prayers*, 136.
       For a list of the names proposed, see TILAHUN BEYENE, ". . . ቤተ ክርስቲያኑን እያራለሁ. . . ": የመሠረተ
       ክርስቶስ ቤት ክርስቲያን ታሪክ, 81.
117   HEGE, *Beyond Our Prayers*, 148–149. Cf. also NEGEWO BOSET, "Persecution and Church
       Expansion," 102; TEKA OBSA FOGI, "The Charismatic Movement in the EECMY," 73; TILAHUN
       BEYENE, ". . . ቤተ ክርስቲያኑን እያራለሁ. . . ": የመሠረተ ክርስቶስ ቤት ክርስቲያን ታሪክ, 92 for similar accounts.

time, no missionaries are reported to have "brought" this revival to them, it was only the news about it that spread. Furthermore, the story not only relates the Nazaret group to the Harar revival, it also establishes them as coequal.

However, the details of the story to some extent do not match the overall narrative thrust. Most notably, the actual Spirit baptism experience lacks specificity. Whereas the meeting of the two youths is dated and located exactly and is provided with sufficient detail about an underlying event, the dual reception of the "baptism" is stated in a summary without pointers to specific incidents. This peculiar absence of a specific Spirit baptism narrative suggests difficulties in locating a definitive event as the starting point of the charismatic career of the Nazaret group. Instead, the meeting between Solomon and Zeleke serves as a historic anchor for the Nazaret revival, providing an initial event while assuring the Pentecostal nature of these beginnings. Secondly, the relationship to Harar in terms of importance or temporal precedence remains unresolved, since the protagonists from both locations encountered "Spirit baptism" at "about the same time."

One story in particular sheds light on the probably fairly inchoate nature of the Nazaret revival experiences, and the integration of the related reports into a story of Pentecost. The story is told by a number of sources and comprises several issues of Pentecostal theology and practice, such as prophecy, demon possession, discernment, and speaking in tongues. Furthermore, since the underlying event apparently was a serious disruption to the youth fellowship in Nazaret, it is difficult to integrate into a Pentecostal history of growth and progress.

Although the story is told in different versions, its main content is usually the same: one or two female participants of the group,[118] uttered a prophetic message about the imminent return of Jesus Christ, accompanied by the speaking of tongues. This message excited the assembled students, who spread it to their school. However, after a short time the "leaders discovered that the girl had a deceiving spirit"[119] and thus concluded that the prophecy was false. Since the prophecy had caused quite some turmoil, including the closure of the local high school for one day, the leaders of the *yäsämay bərhan* movement were temporarily suspended. In addition, a significant number of participants left the group over this incident.

There are different strategies of integrating the reports of this rather embarrassing incident into histories of the *yäsämay bərhan* movement. Histories from outside the MKC occasionally take it to mark the end of an independent Nazaret student movement, for example by asserting that the "movement was quenched" or that it was assimilated by the MKC as a result.[120] Others prefer not to mention the incident at all, mostly following the more or less typical trajectory of success and growth,[121]

---

118   HEGE, *Beyond Our Prayers*, 150 and TILAHUN BEYENE, ". . . ቤት ክርስቲያኗን እሥራለሁ. . . ": የመሠረተ
       ክርስቶስ ቤተ ክርስቲያን ታሪክ, 93 only mention one youth, whereas other sources mention two women
       prophesying, cf. ABERA ERTIRO, "The History of the Meserete Kristos Church at Nazareth,"
       20; also interviews no. 19; 92; 39. All informants explicitly note the female gender.
119   HEGE, *Beyond Our Prayers*, 150.
120   Interview no. 112; TIBEBE ESHETE, *The Evangelical Movement in Ethiopia*, 157.
121   YESHITELA MENGISTU, "The Story of the Meserete Krestos Church," 16f–17; TEKA OBSA FOGI,
       "The Charismatic Movement in the EECMY," 73–74.

or only to merely hint at it without telling the story.[122] The Mennonite historian
Nathan Hege, on the other hand, pursued a more offensive strategy. In his book, the
disruptive event is evaluated as a valid learning experience, helping the movement to
mature in its Pentecostal identity:

> The remnant participating in the Semay Birhan group continued and gradually
> picked up momentum, both in vitality and in numbers meeting at the chapel in
> Nazaret. [. . .] The group had genuine experiences of speaking in tongues and
> exercising other gifts. However, now they tested every experience with scrutiny
> and discernment to guard against another deception of the evil one.[123]

In additions to these different strategies of integrating the story into a Nazaret
revival account, the representations of the events also were shaped by later theological debates in Ethiopian Pentecostalism, especially with regard to recurring spirit
possessions, discernment of spirits, and the nature of tongues.

Though all sources agree that the false prophecy was caused by demonic influence,
there is no accord with regard to the cause of the possession, its proper discernment,
or treatment. Only one history suggests that the discerning of the messages was
indeed possible, because of false statements they contained.[124] All other accounts
seem less optimistic about the possibility of rational discernment. Here the prophecy
is vaguely reported to have been about "future events", or more specifically about the
imminent return of Christ and the end of the world.[125] Thus the listeners are faced
with the classic dilemma of prophecies about future events: only the later fulfillment
of the prophecy will reveal whether it was true and its warnings were to be heeded.
Moreover, since the prophetess is discovered to "not have been driven by the Holy
Spirit, but to be held captive by a false spirit,"[126] this is not so much an issue of
scrutinizing the message, but one of discerning the spirit behind it. Furthermore,
according to some accounts the prophetess had actually been delivered from an evil
spirit beforehand, which added further complexity to the matter:

> There was one who was originally demon-possessed, but who was delivered, but
> was re-possessed by the demon. And this lady, this girl, spoke in tongues.[127]

Thus, the story becomes one of possession, deliverance, and re-possession. The
notion of re-possession or of Christians being inflicted by demons must be explained,
since it is theologically problematic on account of the conflicts with the Deliverance

---

122 E.g. NEGEWO BOSET, "Persecution and Church Expansion," 102: "Of course we passed through
     various testings, persecution, and deceiving spirits". Cf. also BEKELE WOLDEKIDAN, ሪፃይፃል, 78,
     quoted above, 100.
123 HEGE, *Beyond Our Prayers*, 150. Cf. also TILAHUN BEYENE, ". . . ቤተ ክርስቲያኗን እሥራለሁ. . . ":
     የመሰረተ ክርስቶስ ቤተ ክርስቲያን ታሪክ, 93 for a similar statement.
124 Cf. ABERA ERTIRO, "The History of the Meserete Kristos Church at Nazareth," 20. According
     to Abera the prophetess stated that Jesus shall come back soon, "for they are making animals
     suffer". This seemed wrong to Abera, as "Jesus' primary concern was not for the suffering of
     animals but perishing sinners.". A second prophetess claims that she is the returned Christ.
125 HEGE, *Beyond Our Prayers*, 150; also interviews no. 92; 19.
126 TILAHUN BEYENE, ". . . ቤተ ክርስቲያኗን እሥራለሁ. . . ": የመሰረተ ክርስቶስ ቤተ ክርስቲያን ታሪክ, 93.
127 Interview no. 19.

movement. Therefore, when asked to relate the story more in detail, the informant makes some important modifications:

> She was demon-possessed, we prayed for her, [*pause*] and she was relieved for some time. But she didn't care to come to our prayer and things like that.[128]

Here the person is not mentioned to have been "delivered", but rather, she was merely "relieved for some time", which renders the exorcism more or less incomplete. The informant also points to the person's failure to integrate into the group and follow its spiritual activities, apparently questioning the sincerity and genuineness of her faith.

Other informants solve the problem of re-possession by pointing to the inefficacy of the group's exorcist practices:

> Now the demon cry, we don't know how to cast out in the name of Jesus at that time. With our Orthodox background, we know how they cast out demon: in the name of Saint Gabriel and Michael. We just pray on the water — they pray in the Orthodox, when they pour the water — they cry, and like that. We have that [experience], we use it here. But we were so cheated. The demon was just trying to cheat us, deceive us like that, but afterwards we got really, ... when we read the New Testament how the demon [are] cast out, and so we corrected that kind of thing.[129]

Quite contrary to the statements above, the exorcism did not fail because it was incomplete or not sustained by personal faithfulness. Rather the means of deliverance were altogether wrong, since the Orthodox rites are considered ineffective. The story thus becomes a testimony to the group's lack of experience, but also to its pioneering achievements when things were corrected later on.

A more important problem with this story, however, is that the woman reportedly appeared just like the others, or in Hege's words she "pretended to be filled by the Holy Spirit [...] and spoke in tongues."[130] This ambiguity of a spiritual gift so central to Pentecostal experience is of course problematic. Consequentially, one informant who was in a leading position narrates his difficulties in accepting his own first glossolalic utterances, because of the "false tongues" just weeks before:

> When I started to speak in tongues, uh, what, did I say, what's happening with me? It was spontaneous. And I wanted to check, whether it is of the same spirit, or a different one. So I stopped it, because I was the only one, you know. I stopped it and I checked my life. But in my life I see that I had hid [from] sin, I wanted to give my life to the Lord even up today. I wanted to testify,

128 Interview no. 19.

129 Interview no. 92. Cf. also Bekele Woldekidan, ሪቫይቫል, 77–78 narrating similar attempts at exorcisms. Hege, *Beyond Our Prayers*, 150; Tilahun Beyene, "...ቤተ ክርስቲያኔን እሥራለሁ...": የመሰረተ ክርስቶስ ቤተ ክርስቲያን ታሪክ, 93; and Abera Ertiro, "The History of the Meserete Kristos Church at Nazareth," 20 agree that the group only mistakingly assumed that the woman was delivered.

130 Hege, *Beyond Our Prayers*, 150.

and what is in me, is all full light. So I said: "It's no problem." But I didn't
continue, I stopped it.[131]

Like in many other testimonies, this account narrates the eruption of speaking in
tongues "spontaneously" during prayer, without intercession by fellow Pentecostals.
However, far from being an "initial evidence" of the baptism in the Holy Spirit, glossolalia here became a reason for initial concern, because of the previously experienced
ambiguity. Though the ensuing self-examination gives the informant enough reason to
believe that his case is different, he still is not confident enough to continue speaking
in tongues.

In what follows, the informant mentions how he subsequently suppressed his
tongues and that only after learning of glossolalia occurring in Harar, he allowed
himself to resume:

> Then I released myself with speaking in tongues. And others also started speak-
> ing in tongues. So the movement started there. Simultaneously in Harar.[132]

Encouraged by reports of similar experiences, glossolalia is freed from its stigma
and is integrated into the group. Incidentally, this is also where the informant marks
the starting point of the Nazaret movement, and furthermore, even though only the
previous Harar experience had made this "release" of tongues possible, he reaffirms
that the movement in Harar had started "simultaneously."

This recurring affirmation of the simultaneousness of the Harar and Nazaret out-
pourings in *yäsämay bərhan* accounts probably are motivated by stories from Harar
revivalists claiming just the opposite. One such account is presented in Bekele Woldekidan's history. Unlike the reports from Nazaret, Bekele's Harar narrative does not
mention the meeting between Zeleke and Solomon prior to their Spirit baptism.[133]
Instead, the first contact came when the Harar revivalists attempted to minister in
Nazaret during their Easter break in 1965:

> In that year, when the schools were closed for the Easter holiday, Zeleke and
> Assefa went from Harar to Nazaret for ministry. They wanted to witness to
> the Nazaret "*yäyämay bərhan*" youths about the baptism in the Holy Spirit
> and pray for them by laying on of hands. But the ones from Nazaret weren't
> willing. First, in those days a difficult confusion had come to them that was
> connected to a prophecy. After they had contracted difficulties and had been
> scattered, there were only very few left in number. Secondly, since Zeleke was
> one of Nazaret's children, the Nazaret youths had heard the rumor that he
> was speaking prophecies while scattering dust on his head. Zeleke and Assefa
> searched for members in their respective homes and spoke to them. When they
> found ones that gave permission, they laid their hands on them and prayed
> for them. Though their number is not known, there were many among the

---

131 Interview no. 19.
132 Interview no. 19.
133 Similarly one Harar informant, who rejected the idea that Solomon and Zeleke could have
     discussed the Holy Spirit the summer before, interview no. 130.

ones for whom they prayed, who were filled with the Holy Spirit and spoke in tongues.[134]

In this way, Bekele clearly establishes Harar's precedence over Nazaret. Though at first rejected, due to the Nazaret confusion and rumors about Zeleke, the two Harar youths finally succeed in bringing genuine Spirit baptism to Nazaret, which is evidenced by speaking in tongues. This 1965 Easter episode was also related in interviews with Harar informants, one of whom explicitly stated that this "was the time" the Nazaret youths "received the Holy Spirit."[135]

However, in the account of a Nazaret informant, the same visit and its outcome are portrayed quite differently:

> So, we prayed in Nazaret to be filled. Nobody came and prayed for us. Uh, I mean [before] I was baptized. But when the group from Harar came, they wanted to pray for us. But when they wanted to lay their hands on us, we didn't want them to lay their hands on us. Because since we had deceiving experiences. One of them wanted to pray for us, [*pause*] uh, his sister was the one who was possessed with demon. So we had our own question.
>
> So, when they came — we used benches in the chapel — when they came to lay their hands, we hid ourselves by going under the bench. [*laughs*] Uh, you understand. We didn't want them to lay their hands. Even then they said: "Say Halleluhalleluhalleluia, halleluhalleluia." It's a kind of formula. You know, halleluia. They said: "Repeat it, repeat it, fast, fast, fast, and then you will speak in tongues." We didn't like that also. That was the formula they used.[136]

The visit by the Harar Pentecostals thus serves to substantiate the independence of Nazaret from Harar mission endeavors, by using the previous "deceiving experiences" as a resource for healthy scepticism, even toward Harar. The fact that one of them was related to the "one who was possessed with demon",[137] is provided as initial reason for doubting their practices and legitimacy. However, this argument is not explored further, and does not seem to be strong enough for an open confrontation. Instead an evasive solution is sought by hiding "under the bench." Finally, a more substantial argument is provided for rejecting the Harar authority: the tongues they are trying to bring forth are not genuine, they are mere babble brought forth by a "formula."

In conclusion, it would appear that the stories surrounding the Nazaret revival are not easily integrated into a typical Pentecostal trajectory. Especially the reports about an early disruption of the group by a false prophecy inflict central Pentecostal practices with an undesirably ambiguity, and thereby put into question the experiences of the group. This in turn may be used by sources outside the *yäsämay bərhan*

---

134 BEKELE WOLDEKIDAN, ረቢያሜኣ, 87.
135 Interview no. 130; 39.
136 Interview no. 19.
137 This was also confirmed in other interviews, including Zeleke himself, interviews no. 87; 39; 130. Zeleke pointed out that his sister is now working in a prominent position in the Addis Ababa FGBC.

movement, in order to disregard Nazaret as a proto-Pentecostal phenomenon and subordinate it to the ministry of the more established revival group from Harar. Sources from the MKC and the *yäsämay bərhan* group, on the other hand, pursue a twofold strategy in asserting an early and unambiguous Pentecostal identity of the movement. First, while it may not be possible for them to point to a specific Spirit baptism narrative as the starting point of the movement, the meeting between Solomon and Zeleke and their common resolve to seek for themselves this experience serve to anchor the Nazaret movement both chronologically and theologically. The notion of Zeleke and Solomon embarking on a common quest also has the welcome side effect of establishing Nazaret and Harar as simultaneous movements, refuting any idea of a Harar precedence. Secondly, the embarrassing incident of a false prophecy, lack of discernment, and fake tongues, is dealt with head-on: far from discrediting the experience of the group and marking its end, it is established as its real beginning and became a source of a special spiritual competence, enabling the *yäsämay bərhan* group to discern and critique the experience and practices of other revival groups.

3.3   The Addis Ababa Student Movement

The centrality of the Addis Ababa Student prayer meetings in the Ethiopian Pentecostal histories corresponds to a relative quantity of available sources. As the foundational event in FGBC histories, it probably is the most consolidated story among the tales of mission-independent beginnings. The narrative usually consists of the same elements: the foundation of a private prayer meeting by students of the Haile Selassie University, a characterization of these founders, and the unexpected growth of the meetings, resulting in the move of the group to a larger facility, which not only required a financial leap of faith, but simultaneously turned the prayer meeting into a church-like operation, that later functioned as a platform for the unification of the different Pentecostal beginnings and the establishment of the first national Pentecostal church, the FGBC. In accordance with this trajectory, the stories seem to presume an invariable identity of the Addis Ababa student movement, despite the obvious transitions in leadership, locality, and meeting structures. Thus a small prayer meeting of a handful of students is established as the "beginning [of Ethiopian Pentecostalism] as an independent movement,"[138] as a "decisive event in the history of the Pentecostal movement,"[139] or as Ethiopia's "312 Azusa Street."[140]

3.3.1 Laying the Foundations

In September of 1965 four Addis Ababa university students, who had previously come in contact with the Pentecostal movement, began to live together in a rented house and commenced a prayer meeting there, which quickly attracted other students. In keeping with the foundational role attributed to these meetings, most histories charge this student initiative with an air of intentionality. Engelsviken, for example,

---

138 ENGELSVIKEN, "Molo Wongel," 35.
139 TIBEBE ESHETE, *The Evangelical Movement in Ethiopia*, 161.
140 BEKELE WOLDEKIDAN, ረዥያተሽ, 90.

contends that the students, who were invigorated by the 1965 Awasa conference, "took a decisive step of faith when they made up their minds to leave the University campus, where no religious meetings were allowed," and rented a house, which was to "serve both as dormitory and 'chapel'."[141] Another source suggests that when the students acquired their new place "[t]hey also dedicated this small room before God to make it the revival place for the Pentecostal movement."[142]

However, according to an informant who was one of the students renting the first "chapel", the primary motive was rather mundane.[143] In the aftermath of the failed coup d'état of 1960, which had seen significant support by the Addis Ababa students, the central university dormitory and boarding services had been discontinued, requiring students to secure their own living with a monthly allowance of 50 Ethiopian Birr provided by the university.[144] Therefore, some evangelical students decided to come together as tenants in order to find affordable housing near to the university campus. The abode they jointly rented for 25 Ethiopian Birr in the Arat Kilo area[145] by all appearances was anything but ideal. It is described as a small, primitive and dirty place with two bedrooms, which was not suitable for studies and only had the advantage of proximity to the university.[146] After a short while the students decided to hold a prayer meeting among themselves, skipping their lunches on the Orthodox fasting days Wednesday and Friday in order to come together for prayer at their house instead. The meeting became known to other evangelical students and grew as a result, which a number of sources describe as an evangelistic accomplishment of the students.[147] However, increased attendance was not an unlikely development, since evangelical student meetings were not a novelty in the city,[148] and the proximity of the student prayer meeting to the university campus was a clear advantage.

The legacy of this original prayer meeting place is furthered in the sources by the tribute paid to its founders. The most comprehensive introduction of the students was provided by Bekele Woldekidan:

---

141 ENGELSVIKEN, "Molo Wongel," 35.

142 TARIKU WOLDEMICHAEL and YONAS ASHAGARI, "The Establishment of Addis Ababa Mulu Wongel Believers' Church" (Unpublished manuscript, private collection, 1999), 2.

143 Interview no. 64.

144 See also TESHOME G. WAGAW, *The Development of Higher Education and Social Change: An Ethiopian Experience*, African Series; 2 (East Lansing, MI: Michigan State University Press, 1990), 209–210. This was thought to disperse student unrest by making it more difficult for students to centrally meet and plot political activities, but apparently it did not reach the desired effect.

145 The house always goes as the "Arat Kilo" chapel, although it actually was closer to "Amist Kilo", across the patriarch's residence, near St. Mary's, see map in ENGELSVIKEN, "Molo Wongel," 6; also ETHIOPIAN FULL GOSPEL BELIEVERS' CHURCH, ሙሉ ወንጌል ቤተ ክርስቲያን ከልደት እስከ . . ., 4.

146 See ibid.

147 Cf. e.g. ENGELSVIKEN, "Molo Wongel," 35; TAYE ABDISSA, "The Pentecostal Development and the Rise of Charismatic Movement in Ethiopia," 21; TEKA OBSA FOGI, "The Charismatic Movement in the EECMY," 77.

148 The Sudan Interior Mission (SIM) had already established a center for the university students where Christian fellowships congregated, among them the Ethiopian University Students' Christian Fellowship, which had been founded by Ogbazghi Sium, Weldeab Yishak, Fasil Nahum, Adnew Alemayehu and others, see OGBAZGHI SIUM, E-mail to author, April 16, 2008.

Ogbazghi was a convert from Asmara who had come into the gospel before. Philipos, being a child of the south, was a second-generation evangelical Christian. Teka and Berhane, who had accepted the Lord in June of 1964, were engineering college students in their second year. A new thing for the old and new Christians was revealed in their midst. This was the baptism in the Holy Spirit. Ogbazghi had gone to Asmara for vacation in the previous rainy season, was baptized in the Holy Spirit, and returned. The ones, who had witnessed to him about this new revelation and who had prayed for him to be baptized with the Holy Spirit, were the Harar Teacher Training Institute graduates Betta Mengistu and Alem Bisrat. Berhane had gone down to Awasa in the previous rainy season for the conference, got baptized in the Holy Spirit and returned. The ones praying for him were the Nazaret *yäsämay bərhan* youths. Philipos' father was at first a Kale Heywot Church [SIM] Christian and later an evangelist in the Awasa Swedish Philadelphia Church. He [Philipos] had been ministering in translating for the missionaries when he was in Awasa area. It is believed that he probably got acquainted with the Holy Spirit in this time in Awasa. Teka, not yet. But he wanted it very much.[149]

Introducing his four protagonists here, Bekele not only notes that they had received salvation, but also considers the precise circumstances of their Spirit baptisms, even when he has little or nothing to tell (Philipos, Teka). More than just providing the reader with historical information, the presentation of these backgrounds is important for Bekele's overall trajectory. Later on, youths from the Pentecostal missions, from Nazaret, from Harar and from the Addis Ababa University would merge in the formation of the FGBC, but by tracing out the different contexts in which the students received their Spirit baptism, Bekele shows that the university student group already was a merger of all revival movements at its core. This of course supports his notion that this little student dorm truly was Ethiopia's "312 Azusa Street."

However, the issue of identifying the original tenants of the student home is more complex when comparing all sources about the university student group. While a couple of sources name the same people as Bekele, i.e., Berhane Abreha, Ogbazghi Sium, Philipos Kemere, and Teka Gebru,[150] a number of others add a fifth person, Girma Tessema.[151] However, Girma himself noted in an interview that he did not live with the four students this early on, but only joined them as a tenant, when the

---

149 BEKELE WOLDEKIDAN, ረጀጽግ, 89
150 See e.g. TARIKU WOLDEMICHAEL and YONAS ASHAGARI, "The Establishment of Addis Ababa Mulu Wongel Believers' Church," 2; TIBEBE ESHETE, *The Evangelical Movement in Ethiopia*, 161.
151 See e.g. BULUTSE FUTUWI, "An Introduction to the Theology and Growth of Independent Churches in Ethiopia With Special Reference to Rhema Faith Church," 61; ESCKINDER TADDESSE WOLDEGEBRIAL, "An Introduction to the Biblical and Historical Pattern of Church Government," 72; TSADIKU ABDO, "Where Does Mulu Wongel Stand in its Trinitarian Concept: East or West? A Critical Approach to Ethiopian Mulu Wongel Church's Theology of Trinity," 74.

group moved to a bigger house.[152] Yosief Kidanewold, on the other hand mentioned only three students, though it is unclear who is excluded here, since he did not give any names.[153] Moreover, for Yosief, the Spirit baptisms of these students were not connected to any existing mission or group, but came as the result of Bible study and prayer, while the students were away from Addis Ababa in fulfilling their Ethiopian University Service requirement.[154] Ogbazghi Sium on the other hand denied that he was part of the four students renting this first abode.[155] Instead he named as fourth tenant another student by the name of Gaim Kibreab, who is not mentioned by any of the other histories. Ogbazghi notes that he had begun the Ethiopian University Students' Christian Fellowship together with others already in 1963 and that Teka Gebru and Berhane Abreha were converted in a Bible study he conducted. While the groups were different entities, there was overlap in attendance and Ogbazghi himself also ministered with Pentecostals. Since Ogbazghi later prominently disagreed with the decision of the Pentecostal students to form a national church, it is peculiar that FGBC sources include him here, whereas he himself denies this. Others still seem to be aware of his status as a relative outsider. In an interview, one of the original tenants first named Ogbazghi in his lineup of the original chapel founders, but then stated that "he did not want to live with us."[156]

3.3.2 Change and Continuity

These differences in establishing the original "founders" of the university student group indicate that this "origin" probably was rather fluent and not as deliberate and defined as later histories suggest. Furthermore, a number of transitions soon took place, which significantly altered the setup of the group. The rapid growth of the prayer meeting fundamentally changed its character and identity. Only a few months after its inception, the group moved to a bigger house, new preachers led the meetings, and soon it had grown into a student movement, which transcended the university campus, encompassed a few hundred Christians and saw the introduction of regular Sunday services. Moreover, there was a clear transition in leadership. Hardly any of the prayer group "founders" were in a leading position two years later, when their movement founded the FGBC. Ogbazghi, as already mentioned, did not agree with

---

152 Girma joined the group fairly early on and still today is a readily available informant in the FGBC on the early developments, which probably led these sources to mention him as one of the founders.

153 See YOSIEF KIDANEWOLD, "The History of the Pentecostal Movement in Addis Abeba," 6.

154 The Ethiopian University Service was established in 1964 and mandated all university students to provide community services in mostly rural areas for one full year before their fourth year of studies. Over two thirds of the students worked as teachers, and others provided technical, medical, political, or juridical assistance. The dispersal of students all over the country significantly accelerated the spread of leftist ideas, but, as several informants suggest, also assisted the proliferation of Pentecostal beliefs when the students spread their faith. For a comprehensive treatment of the Ethiopian University Service see TESHOME G. WAGAW, *The Development of Higher Education and Social Change*, 187–202; also BAHRU ZEWDE, *A History of Modern Ethiopia 1855–1991*, 222.

155 See OGBAZGHI SIUM, E-mail to author, April 16, 2008.

156 Interview no. 64. This informant also mentioned his brother as another person renting the house.

the decision to form a church. Berhane Abreha and Teka Gebru were not included in
the leadership of the new church. Girma Tessema, who is sometimes counted as one of
the prayer meeting founders, became a deacon of the FGBC, but he was not included
in the eldership. Only Philipos Kemere became one of the first seven elders, but a
number of sources attributed this to his background in the Swedish mission rather
than to his participation in renting the first house.[157] These obvious transitions in
character and leadership of the Addis Ababa movement are to be expected in such a
rapidly growing group, but it is problematic for narratives proposing that the "real
origin" of the FGBC lies in the small university student prayer meeting. Informants
from the Finnish mission and Harar backgrounds, therefore, point precisely to this
change in leadership in order to refute the idea that the FGBC had its origin with
the initiative of the Addis Ababa University students.[158]

Histories interested in tracing the beginning of the FGBC to the first small prayer
meeting therefore need to produce a narrative of continuity which incorporates the
different changes in a larger trajectory. They achieve this by highlighting certain transition points and marking them as the place of deliberate and paradigmatic structural
changes. The multifarious and arguably haphazard transformations in these first two
years are thus integrated into a teleological process of growth and development.

An instructive example for studying this narrative dynamic is the first move of
the prayer group to a larger facility. This move is often told in great detail, since
its function is to mark the transition from a loose fellowship to a larger church-like
movement, like in the following oral account quoted by Engelsviken:

> We knew that we could not receive all the people who wanted to come anymore,
> and we began to pray for a larger house. Then the Lord sent us one hundred
> Ethiopian dollars in an envelope. We never knew from whom. We understood
> that the Lord was trying to tell us that he had some place in mind for us. We
> sent two men to look for a house. They came back and said they had found it.
> We asked what the monthly rent would be. They said 250 dollars. That was
> exactly ten times the amount we were paying for the old house. "Let us have
> faith," said one of the two, "the Lord can do it." Before looking for the house
> we thought of getting a place where we could have many people come and hear
> the word of God. We had no plans for a church, and when we came and saw
> the house they had found, it almost exactly suited our purpose. It was in front
> of Nazareth School in Addis Ababa, and it belonged to an Ethiopian senator.

---

157   Cf. the composition of elders presented in BEKELE WOLDEKIDAN, ሪብያሳ, 103. See also HELL-
      STRÖM, "Frälst ungdom i Etiopien."
158   This view was expressed in interviews, where it was also noted that there were failed bids to
      install more of the original student meeting leaders in key positions, cf. interviews no. 91; 39.
      Perhaps in response to such criticisms other sources give external reasons for the exclusion of
      the "chapel founders" from the FGBC eldership. Tarike Woldemichael and Yonas Ashagari
      mention that Girma was simply not elected as elder because he was absent during the election
      while Teka "refused to be elected as a leaders since he identified himself that leadership was
      not his gift," see TARIKU WOLDEMICHAEL and YONAS ASHAGARI, "The Establishment of Addis
      Ababa Mulu Wongel Believers' Church," 12, 15 Likewise, TIBEBE ESHETE, The Evangelical
      Movement in Ethiopia, 170 argues that the university students were spared from leadership
      responsibilities in order to "allow them to have their primary focus on their studies."

The man was willing to rent us the house, but asked us to find somebody who would be a guarantor for the payments of the rent. None of us had the money, and it was quite difficult for us to find a man who would make the guarantee. Finally we asked one of our own Ethiopian professors at the University. He agreed to be the guarantor and we got the house. Several of us had raised the question: Will we be able to pay for the rent? The first month came, and we had the money. The second month came; we had the money. In fact, we never ran out of money. We always had what we needed. The only problem we faced in the new chapel was that it was too small. We counted four hundred people at some meetings and then our meetings lasted too long![159]

This story is framed by the growth in meeting attendance, which leads to the quest for new premises in the beginning and yet continues to be "the only problem" even in the larger house. Because of this growth, the group was faced with considerable financial and organizational responsibilities that neither they themselves were sure about nor that they were trusted with by their potential landlord. In detailing the process step by step, the transformation of their formerly timid expectations is depicted, with persistence and faith in God as the main keys. Furthermore, it is God himself who guides the transformation: after praying for a larger meeting place, the Lord "sent" a financial contribution, showing "that he had some place in mind for us," and doubts about the tremendous financial challenge are overcome by the trust that "the Lord can do it." In the end, God's promise does not fail. Month by month, sufficient provision is encountered.

Corresponding with the interest of establishing continuity, this move to a new facility and larger financial responsibilities may also be depicted as a simple quantitative increase, with the size of the congregation mirroring the group's investment:

And by and by that meeting grew, and later on, they came out from that. They used to pay twenty-five Birr rent, and they were forty then. And they came out and rented a bigger house at 250 Birr. And at the end of the year they became 400. So everything grew tenfold.[160]

Being a significant transition point, the move is also used to anchor changes in the structure and program of the student fellowship. Yosief Kidanewold notes:

According to one of the informants the house rent was paid from the offerings and contributions which the congregation used to make, particularly after every Sunday service. Thus the Movement continued in the second Chapel with a larger congregation. This time Sunday morning service, (9:00 to 12:00 A.M.) began for the first time in the history of the independent Ethiopian Pentecostal Movement.[161]

159 ENGELSVIKEN, "Molo Wongel," 39.
160 Interview no. 1
161 YOSIEF KIDANEWOLD, "The History of the Pentecostal Movement in Addis Abeba," 8. The notion that the group rather than individuals acted as tenants and/or paid the rent is probably not correct. Several sources indicate that only the living room was used as a meeting hall and individual tenants occupied the remaining bedrooms of the new house, see esp. ETHIOPIAN FULL GOSPEL BELIEVERS' CHURCH, ሙሉ ወንጌል ቤተ ክርስቲያን ከልደት እስከ ..., 8. The rent including

Along with these financial and organizational changes, this first move is also used to mark the maturation of the spiritual services of the group. One source notes that while before the students "were simply reading the Bible with no explanation and prayed", now there were sermons and "[s]peakers began to preach."[162] Engelsviken presented the earlier meetings as a "spontaneous and voluntary work that had emerged" and contends that "the meetings were better organized" in the new premises.[163] Likewise, despite the multiple stories of healing and exorcism during the first prayer meeting, healing services are only reported to have become institutional practice in the new building.[164] Next to the establishment of a Sunday service, the week's program now also included a regular prayer night on Fridays.[165]

In accordance with the paradigmatic role of the move, some informants do not fail to mention their own contributions to this first significant transition. One of the former students, for example, in presented his own input as decisive for the move in an interview statement:

> One day, I said this place is not enough, why not we rent a big house. And they asked me. About thirty of us, after we finished our prayer after our class, I said let's look now out for a house. And these people, since I used to pray a lot, whatever suggestion I give, they assume that it has come from the Lord. So they didn't ask, they said ok.[166]

Similarly, another informant pointed to the fact that he paid the first rent "from my pocket,"[167] while a third one narrated how he won his college professor to act as guarantor.[168] Even Swedish missionaries mentioned their material contributions to the new place.[169]

It is evident that this first move of the meeting locality became a central place for the historical articulation of the multiple transitions the community had undergone. Marking these as effects of a bold and deliberate search for more suitable premises, the whole transformation is turned into a deliberate and comprehensible process de-

---

utilities was divided between these ten tenants, resulting in a contribution of 30 Birr per month by each of them. These monthly dues are reported to have been a "heavy thought on each of them when the time for paying the rent came," which also indicates an individual responsibility. However, communal offerings assisting the tenants are also not unlikely, since it is noted that by God's provision they were all able to pay the rent each month.

162 Tariku Woldemichael and Yonas Ashagari, "The Establishment of Addis Ababa Mulu Wongel Believers' Church," 2, 5.

163 Engelsviken, "Molo Wongel," 37, 40.

164 Cf. e.g. ibid., 38, 40–41; Yosief Kidanewold, "The History of the Pentecostal Movement in Addis Abeba," 8.

165 Several sources mention this to be the source of later allegations of "immorality", cf. e.g. Engelsviken, "Molo Wongel," 41; Yosief Kidanewold, "The History of the Pentecostal Movement in Addis Abeba," 8; Tariku Woldemichael and Yonas Ashagari, "The Establishment of Addis Ababa Mulu Wongel Believers' Church," 6.

166 Interview no. 19

167 Cf. ibid., 5.

168 Interview no. 64.

169 Nyberg Oskarsson, *Svensk Pingstmission i Ethiopien (1959–1980)*, 264 refers to one missionary telling her how he and Karl Ramstrand donated benches, a platform, podium, and installed electric wiring.

lineating the steps of developing a small prayer meeting into a congregation. Even though the group changed its meeting place several times soon after,[170] the later moves are not depicted in such detail or assume the same centrality as this first and paradigmatic one. It is here that most histories lay the tracks to the formation of the Addis Ababa congregation before they continue to narrate the establishment of a national Pentecostal network.

It is apparent that the representations of the Addis Ababa student prayer meeting and its development were shaped by the claim that herein lies "the real origin" of the Ethiopian Pentecostal movement. The establishment of a simple prayer meeting is magnified by attributing it with the intention to found a church, naming and characterizing its founders and carefully tracing the individual changes in order to establish a historic continuity from a small private gathering to a large congregation and finally the foundation of the Full Gospel Believers' Church.

3.4 Forming an Ethiopian Pentecostal Church

In 1966 and 1967 the growth and networking of the different Ethiopian revival initiatives resulted in the formal establishment of an independent Pentecostal church. Most accounts about this process center on four key steps: a conference in Addis Ababa with representatives from different groups all over Ethiopia, the decision to found a church, the election of its name, and the ordination of elders for the Addis Ababa church.[171]

3.4.1 Securing a National Mandate

On August 4–8, 1966,[172] the university students hosted a conference at their rented premises, which encompassed Pentecostal youths from several Ethiopian cities. This meeting is often called the "first national conference", a phrase which was probably coined by Engelsviken in keeping with his narrative interest of asserting national independence.[173] Accordingly, a number of later writings emphasize the importance of this gathering,[174], presenting the event as "a watershed in the history of the Pente-

---

170 BEKELE WOLDEKIDAN, ራዕይና, 103 lists seven meeting places for the time from 1965 to 1978.

171 A fifth important step would be the application for registration as a national church, which will be considered in section 4.1, 138.

172 The Ethiopian date provided for the beginning of the four-day conference is ነሐሴ (näḥase) 28 , 1958, see BEKELE WOLDEKIDAN, ራዕይና, 98

173 See ENGELSVIKEN, "Molo Wongel," 44. Engelsviken's informants do not use the word "national", calling the event simply "conference" or "great meeting", cf. ibid., 45. Neither do the other early sources, see YOSIEF KIDANEWOLD, "The History of the Pentecostal Movement in Addis Abeba," 13–14 and TAYE ABDISSA, "The Pentecostal Development and the Rise of Charismatic Movement in Ethiopia," 24. The first Amharic source calls it the "first countrywide spiritual conference", using the term አገር አቀፍ (agär aqäf: lit. encompassing the country) instead of the word ብሔራዊ (bəherawi): national, pertaining to the nation.

174 Cf. e.g. TARIKU WOLDEMICHAEL and YONAS ASHAGARI, "The Establishment of Addis Ababa Mulu Wongel Believers' Church," 8; TEKA OBSA FOGI, "The Charismatic Movement in the EECMY," 78; BULUTSE FUTUWI, "An Introduction to the Theology and Growth of Independent Churches in Ethiopia With Special Reference to Rhema Faith Church," 60; BEKELE WOLDEKIDAN, ራዕይና, 97.

costal movement."[175] For these histories, the conference not only was the first formal Pentecostal gathering administered by Ethiopians, but also the site of important decisions leading to the unification of the different Pentecostal groups in one national organization.

However, contrary to this notion of a national conference, many written histories are rather unspecific about where the participants of the meeting had come from, relying on phrases like "from all the provinces where the movement had reached."[176] Engelsviken quotes an informant providing a list of cities: Harar, Nazaret, Jima, Mekele, Asmara, Awasa, Debre Zeit, "and many other places."[177] Another list published three years later adds Bahir Dar, Dire Dawa, Shashemene, Ambo, Debre Berhan, and Gondar.[178] It is not unlikely that the early network of Pentecostal students had indeed reached all of these places already. However, such lists nevertheless overstate the scope of this first Addis Ababa conference, since according to most sources there were only about one hundred participants, which was less than expected. Many reportedly were unable to attend due to the short-noticed invitation,[179] and most of the youths probably were from Addis Ababa and the nearby Nazaret.[180] Furthermore, the conference seems to have been organized rather spontaneously, with participants having to secure their own accommodations and the hosts setting up makeshift cooking arrangements.[181]

It may also be doubted whether there actually were participants from Awasa other than those who, like Philipos Kemere, were already studying in Addis Ababa. The Awasa conference still served as the major hub for the Pentecostal groups and was going to be conducted some weeks later, so that there was little incentive for Awasa Christians to travel up to Addis Ababa. Nevertheless, some histories suggest that the Awasa conference organized by missionaries was more or less replaced by an independent one in Addis Ababa. Engelsviken, for example, notes:

> The Bible Conferences in Awasa contained happy memories for many, and already in the summer of 1966 the leaders decided to call in a national conference in Addis Ababa. [...] This was a conference where the Ethiopians themselves had the full responsibility. Still missionaries participated in the deliberations, but the leadership itself was in Ethiopian hands.[182]

In similar fashion, Bekele Woldekidan contends that one of the most important results of the conference was that the task of spreading of the gospel was taken out of the missionaries hands and given to Ethiopians.[183] However, there are a number of

---

175   TIBEBE ESHETE, *The Evangelical Movement in Ethiopia*, 166.
176   TAYE ABDISSA, "The Pentecostal Development and the Rise of Charismatic Movement in Ethiopia," 24.
177   ENGELSVIKEN, "Molo Wongel," 45.
178   ETHIOPIAN FULL GOSPEL BELIEVERS' CHURCH, ሙሉ ወንጌል ቤተ ክርስቲያን ከልደት እስከ ..., 10. The list includes the towns listed by Engelsviken, with the exception of Asmara and Jima.
179   See BEKELE WOLDEKIDAN, ሪብይባል, 97–98.
180   This was stated by one of the observers, interview no. 87.
181   Cf. ETHIOPIAN FULL GOSPEL BELIEVERS' CHURCH, ሙሉ ወንጌል ቤተ ክርስቲያን ከልደት እስከ ..., 10. One eyewitness also mentioned that it was a "rushly organized conference", interview no. 64.
182   ENGELSVIKEN, "Molo Wongel," 44.
183   BEKELE WOLDEKIDAN, ሪብይባል, 98.

indications that the Awasa and Addis Ababa conferences were not in direct competition with one another and that the latter did not replace the former. First, the Awasa
conference did not suffer in attendance because of the event in Addis Ababa. In 1966
the missionaries hosted approximately 150 participants in Awasa, and although this
was less than the 200 Ramstrand had anticipated, it was still more than the 100,
who had attended the year before.[184] Secondly, there still was a close cooperation
and fellowship with the SPCM in Awasa. Just prior to the Addis Ababa conference,
students from the capital had collaborated with missionaries in Awasa by teaching at
the summer Bible course for Sidaminya speakers,[185] and after the Addis Ababa conference many youths from the capital reportedly came to the Awasa conference.[186]
Third, the Swedish missionaries and their Ethiopian coworkers in Awasa probably
were not even aware of the Addis Ababa conference, or if the were, they did not
attribute much significance to it.[187] Fourth and finally, the Addis Ababa conference
did not attain permanence like the one in Awasa. It was hosted again on a larger scale
in 1967 and 1969, but only in irregular intervals thereafter. The 1969 gathering was
even conducted at the premises of the Swedish Philadelphia Church Mission (SPCM)
in Addis Ababa, because the Ethiopian meeting places had been closed down by the
government. All of these indications make it unlikely that the hub of the Ethiopian
Pentecostal national network transitioned from the SPCM Bible conference in Awasa
to the university students in Addis Ababa by means of this "first national conference."

The results of the Addis Ababa conference are also difficult to assess. There are no
minutes or written agreements from the conference, but there are a number of quite
diverse reports about what was decided. Engelsviken records a number of agreements,
among them "the important decision [...] to organize the movement as an independent church," that this church should first be organized in Addis Ababa, the election
of four representatives to keep the contact between the groups and locations, and
the determination of a name for the movement.[188] The 1978 FGBC jubilee magazine
is even more explicit: six agreements are presented here, including a thirteen-point

---

184 See KARL RAMSTRAND, Letter to the Philadelphia Church in Gränna, 28 August 1966, Karl
     Ramstrand Collection, Pingstarkiv Kaggeholm, Ekerö; RAMSTRAND, Letter to supporters, Au-
     gust 22, 1965; RAMSTRAND, *Det heliga äventyret*, 139. It is also not unlikely that the 200
     participants anticipated in RAMSTRAND and NILSSON, "Etiopien i Blickpunkten" could not be
     accommodated due to financial restraints. In a letter four weeks prior to the conference, Ram-
     strand mentioned that while sifting and answering applications for the conference, still about
     100 applicants were in need of financial assistance in order to participate, KARL RAMSTRAND,
     Letter to the Philadelphia Church in Gränna, 1 August 1966, Karl Ramstrand Collection,
     Pingstarkiv Kaggeholm, Ekerö.
185 By 1966 the Awasa conference or Bible course had been divided into two, one earlier one for
     surrounding Sidama nationals, and the later and bigger one in Amharic, which congregated
     participants from all over Ethiopia. The earlier one ended on August 1, 1966, just four days
     prior to the Addis Ababa conference, and saw the preaching of students from Addis Ababa
     during the second of the two weeks, ibid.
186 One informant even mentioned that "most of us" went down to Awasa, interview no. 87.
187 For example, the 1966 Awasa conference report in the Evangelii Härold is titled "Old-time
     Revival Among University Students", but does not mention anything about the Addis Ababa
     meetings or the efforts to organize. In interviews conducted with early Ethiopian leaders at
     Awasa, there was also no mention of the Addis Ababa conferences. Rather, they seem to view
     Awasa as the early Ethiopian center, from which the FGBC later departed.
188 ENGELSVIKEN, "Molo Wongel," 45–48.

statement of faith.[189] The later FGBC historian Bekele Woldekidan, on the other hand, is less pronounced about the outcome of the conference. Of the results, which he contends "were clear for many," only one is mentioned, namely, the notion that the responsibility for evangelizing had been transferred from the missionaries to the Ethiopians. Yet, according to Bekele, it was still unclear how to transform this "theory" into reality.[190] An informant who attended the conference, in turn only recalled the resolution to form a "network connection" by paying ministry visits to one another.[191] Due to the diversity of these reports, it is impossible to affirm or negate any of these supposed conference decisions. However, the reports seem to follow the same dynamics as those of the first move of the university prayer group to a new building: They identify a certain event as a crucial transition point and explain a number of subsequent developments by reference to deliberate decisions surrounding this event. Four such decisions are of particular importance for most narratives: the agreement to form an organization, the determination of its name, the formal establishment of the Addis Ababa congregation, and the attempt to register with the government. By including these steps among the conference decisions, the organizational consolidation of the independent Pentecostal movement is safeguarded by a strong mandate representing the diversity of groups gathered there.

3.4.2 Becoming a Pentecostal Church

Despite this presumed majority mandate, sources note that the decision to form an organization caused some controversy, which led to the first split in the group. Engelsviken, for example, wrote the following about the agreement to form an "independent Ethiopian church":

> It took some time and some discussion to reach this agreement. Many, especially among the University students would rather that the movement should remain a free revival movement within the already established churches and missions in Ethiopia. They did not want to form their own denomination. There were also many who resented the label "Pentecostal". They would rather be called simply "Christian", and be able to work wherever the doors were open in order to win people for Christ and lead them to the experience of the Holy Spirit. Many of those who thought along these lines had heard about the East-Africa revival movement within the churches in Kenya, Uganda and Tanzania.[192]

In what follows, Engelsviken argues that this vision shared by "many" was "connected with considerable difficulties." His main argument is that there were already

---

189 See ETHIOPIAN FULL GOSPEL BELIEVERS' CHURCH, ሙሉ ወንጌል ቤተ ክርስቲያን ከልደት እስከ . . ., 10–11. The agreements mentioned here are: 1) to conduct a similar conference every year, 2) to propagate the gospel in the different places, 3) to make the power of the Holy Spirit known in the established churches, 4) to attempt to obtain an official permit for the meetings, 5) the name for the church, and 6) the statement of faith.

190 See BEKELE WOLDEKIDAN, ሪቫይቫል, 98.

191 Interview no. 64.

192 ENGELSVIKEN, "Molo Wongel," 45–46. Very similar also YOSIEF KIDANEWOLD, "The History of the Pentecostal Movement in Addis Abeba," 14–15.

church-like chapels in operation, and since, to his understanding, gatherings of more than five people were illegal, the movement was forced to register with the government, demanding some sort of organization. Yet, Engelsviken concludes that "[t]hose who favored organizing their own church carried the day."[193] There is no mention of continued opposition against the idea of registration or any splits in his account.

However, a number of later sources indicate that at least one prominent member left the group over this issue. Ogbazghi Sium, who some of these sources consider as one of the four "founders" of the Addis Ababa student prayer meeting and who was engaged in ministry among Lutherans and Orthodox, did not join the newly formed movement but remained in the Evangelical Church Mekane Yesus (ECMY) to which he belonged.[194] For Bekele's narrative the doubts about forming a new denomination thus became "Ogbazghi's question,"[195] which is presented as one of the first two decisive tests for the chapel. Bekele does not only consider this matter for historic reasons. Rather, he sees the same question being raised by members of the established churches and even Pentecostal believers today, which leads him to defend the existence of a Pentecostal church. Therefore Bekele's answer to the question does not just consider the circumstances of these early years, but he also points to the FGBC's later contributions to the Ethiopian Christian landscape in numerical growth and spiritual insight, which, he argues, could have never been achieved if the youths had been held back by Ogbazghi's objection.

In comparing Engelsviken's and Bekele's accounts, it is somewhat surprising that it is the Pentecostal historian who considers this ecumenical question more in depth and not the Lutheran missionary. Engelsviken may not have heard about Ogbazghi Sium during his research, but it is still noticeable that he does not reflect the prospects of a charismatic movement within the established churches. Perhaps he was disillusioned by the opposition to Pentecostalism he had seen during his service, or he was not inclined to such considerations since they might have interfered with his notion of a complete mission independence of Ethiopian Pentecostals. For Bekele, on the other hand, the mention of Ogbazghi is important, because it allows him to engage in a specific debate. He mentions that "Pentecostalism was taught to be a heresy in the evangelical churches" and contrasts the ECMY's deficits with the FGBC's achievements.[196] In similar fashion oral informants have pointed to the failed acceptance with the established churches as a reason for their decision to form a church.[197]

---

193   ENGELSVIKEN, "Molo Wongel," 46.
194   BEKELE WOLDEKIDAN, ረኅብናት, 100–102; TIBEBE ESHETE, *The Evangelical Movement in Ethiopia*, 171; also interview no. 87.
195   "Ogbazghi's question" is the phrase which governs Bekele's entire discussion of the problem, cf. BEKELE WOLDEKIDAN, ረኅብናት, 100–102.
196   Ibid., 101–102. In a hardly concealed criticism of organized church development, Bekele points out the benefits of the FGBC "church establishment model" to first preach the gospel and then found a church: "When the gospel is not preached and sinners are not saved, can the church be considered planted? When the kingdom of God is not enlarged, can it be said the church has grown up?"
197   Interviews no. 87; 20.

3.4.3 Names and Claims

The election of a name for the Addis Ababa Pentecostal movement is presented as a
fairly smooth process in early histories. Engelsviken simply noted:

> After some discussion one [they] agreed on the name "The Old Time Full
> Gospel Believers' Association", a name which was much too long for daily use
> and therefore most often was abbreviated to "the Full Gospel Church", or even
> shorter in Amharic "Molo Wongel".[198]

Similarly, the FGBC jubilee magazine from 1978 mentioned that at the conference of 1966, the group chose the name ጥንታዊት የእግዚአብሔር ቤተ ክርስቲያን (ṭəntawit
yäʾəgziʾabiher betä krəstiyan), Ancient Church of God), which was also used for the
first application for registration.[199] Since this name was not well accepted, another
one was chosen and made official at the third Addis Ababa conference in 1969: የሙሉ
ወንጌል አማኞች ማህበር (yämulu wängel ʾamañoč mahəbär, Full Gospel Believers' Fellowship).[200] It is not indicated here why the first name did not find acceptance with
many, nor that there was much argument over the issue, rendering it a mere formal-
ity.

However, in the later Meserete Kristos Church (MKC) histories, the naming of the
church was turned into a somewhat scandalous issue, which is cited as a reason for
members of the yäsämay bərhan group to depart from the newly formed organization:

> Two names were proposed for their fellowship: Semay Birhan (Heavenly Sun-
> shine) and Tintawit Yegziabiher Mehaber (God's Old-Time Association). Ke-
> bede Woldemariam from the Finnish Mission group chaired the meeting. Tin-
> tawit Yegziabiher Mehaber was chosen, but the government refused to grant
> its registration, because "Old Time" could refer to the Orthodox Church. The
> committee preparing the application, assuming that the Semay Birhan group
> was not satisfied with the new name, did not include Nazareth when listing
> the places where they had churches. Because of this, a significant number of
> the Semay Birhan group remained separate, thinking that perhaps it was by
> God's direction that Nazareth was not included. In 1967, the Old Time group
> again proposed two names: Mulu Wengel (Full Gospel) and Semay Birhan.
> The name Mulu Wengel was chosen by majority vote; this action marked the
> official beginning of the Mulu Wengel Church.[201]

Hege's account suggests that in the newly formed Pentecostal church, the old
revival group identities played a large role. The name of the Nazaret movement was
one of the ones suggested, but the meeting chair was from the "Finnish mission."[202]

---

198 ENGELSVIKEN, "Molo Wongel," 46; cf. also YOSIEF KIDANEWOLD, "The History of the Pente-
      costal Movement in Addis Abeba," 15, following Engelsviken's account.
199 ETHIOPIAN FULL GOSPEL BELIEVERS' CHURCH, ሙሉ ወንጌል ቤተ ክርስቲያን ከአደት እስከ ..., 11, 15.
200 Ibid., 15.
201 HEGE, Beyond Our Prayers, 151–152.
202 The explicit mention of Kebede Woldemariam's name is most likely connected to allegations
      of manipulation brought against him. Tilahun Beyene hints at this in a somewhat awkwardly
      formulated sentence: "The chairman of the time said that Ancient Church of God was elected,"
      see TILAHUN BEYENE, ". . . ቤተ ክርስቲያኗን እሥራለሁ. . . ": የመሰረት ክርስቶስ ቤተ ክርስቲያን ታሪክ, 94. Bekele

The committee, which apparently did not include members of the Nazaret movement, then allegedly came to the conclusion that the *yäsämay bərhan* group did not want to be included in the application under the new name, which in turn led a core of this group to "remain" by themselves. This separation of group identities appears to be cemented when the name is again not chosen in the second round.

Contrary to this notion of a definite split because of the naming controversy, informants from the FGBC occasionally point to a later reason for the *yäsämay bərhan* group leaving the independent Pentecostal movement, as is illustrated by this account:

> But there is another story for that. It was the persecution. We were under persecution, we had no license, you know. No permit to gather. Whereas, you know, the Mennonite Church, the Mennonite mission, had a permit, and they were gathering there, you know. Um, and that place belonged to them. They were tolerant, you know this Mennonite mission, they were tolerant.
>
> So finally, when persecution persisted here in Addis and everywhere, the Finnish mission leaders — uh the Mennonite mission leaders, they approached these brothers in Nazaret. Not only in Nazaret, in Dire Dawa, and in Asebateferi. They told them why don't you — we will not oppose your doctrine about the Holy Spirit — they said you can be a part of us. You can join our church and be a member. You can do whatever you like. So when they they got this, they just joined them. I remember clearly, this was what happened. So many Christians, who were with us even at the beginning, they simply joined them.[203]

According to this informant, the group in Nazaret and other places accepted the offer of shelter by the MKC only because of the continuous "persecution." In this view they had been considered part of the FGBC movement up until then, breaking away because of political difficulties. A similar source even insisted that the Addis Ababa elders "informed" the Nazaret group to join the MKC in light of their circumstances, and that they should work to influence them.[204]

Therefore, it is evident once again that central steps to the formation of the FGBC are used to assert revival group identities. The parts of the *yäsämay bərhan* movement that joined the MKC use the naming controversy to point to the strength of their own revival and the failure of the FGBC to integrate their heritage. Informants from the FGBC, in turn, contend that their church embodied the identity of Ethiopian Pentecostalism, and that this original unity was only broken by the tempting offer of Mennonites to shelter some of their members during times of trouble.

Woldekidan explicitly mentions the allegations of manipulation while distancing himself from them. After noting that the name "Ancient Church of God" had been suggested by the chairman Kebede Woldemariam himself, he writes: "I have encountered Nazaret children saying that he exerted pressure in the election process so that the name he had brought to the election would be elected," see BEKELE WOLDEKIDAN, ረገይታ, 100.

203 Interview no. 87. The idea that it was actually the persecution, which drove youths to the MKC was also encountered in other interviews, e.g. interviews no. 91; 63.

204 Interview no. 63.

3.4.4 Missionaries and the Ordination of Ethiopian Elders

The ordination of elders for the Addis Ababa congregation is where most narratives about the foundation of the FGBC culminate, since this event marks the actual formation of a church out of the many revival movements. This merge is usually illustrated by naming the elders according to their background:

> Among the first seven elders, Zeleke Alemu, Assefa Alemu and Betta Mengistu were from Harar, as was seen before. At this time the three were teachers at the American Mission School in Addis Ababa. Kebede Woldemariam, Melese Wogu, and Fantahun Gebre were from the Merkato Finland mission, and Philipos Kemere was from the Awasa Philadelphia Church.[205]

Due to Philipos' involvement with the Addis Ababa University prayer group, he may also be identified as their candidate in a similar listing.[206]

There was no elder from the Nazaret group, although they were probably still involved with the joint fellowship at that point in time. This is indicated by the memories of Solomon Kebede, a leader of the *yäsämay bərhan* group, which suggest that he was familiar with the procedure of the election process:

> Seven brothers, who had been chosen to serve as church elders by seventeen brothers selected [for this task] a few days before, were presented to the assembly and gained recognition.[207]

However, the selection of elders came with an additional problem: who would ordain them? The only established Pentecostals at that point in time were missionaries, which of course led to a dilemma of legitimacy versus independence. If missionaries were asked to perform the ordination, the acceptance of their authority might inhibit the group's independence, but without an established power, the legitimacy of the new elders might be in question. The most likely candidates to perform the ordination of elders were the Swedish missionaries, since Karl Ramstrand had often taught and encouraged the Ethiopians to form their own church by electing elders, and relations with the SPCM were still smooth.

The way the elders were elected also likely betrays Swedish influence instead of a "traditional Ethiopian way of deciding in matters of leadership" as Engelsviken contends.[208] In the Swedish Pentecostal movement at the time, elders were either

---

205 BEKELE WOLDEKIDAN, ረብይbelieve, 103.
206 See YOSIEF KIDANEWOLD, "The History of the Pentecostal Movement in Addis Abeba," 18, quoted above, 98.
207 SOLOMON KEBEDE, "በዚህ ስም ከመታወቁ በፊት," [Before It Was Known by This Name.], in የኢትዮጵያ ሙሉ ወንጌል አመኞች ቤት ክርስቲያን 25ኛ ዓመት በዓል: ከ 1959–1984 [The 25th Anniversary of the Ethiopian Full Gospel Believer's Church: From 1959 to 1984], ed. ETHIOPIAN FULL GOSPEL BELIEVER'S CHURCH (Addis Ababa, 1992), 16. The fact that the leader of the Nazaret group knew about the election details is of course another indication against to the notion that the *yäsämay bərhan* youths split away right after the conflicts regarding the name. The naming conflict is also hinted at by the first sentence of these short reminiscences: "I remember the beginning of the church before it was known by this name."
208 ENGELSVIKEN, "Molo Wongel," 49–50. The author contrasts this process, which he sees in a close alignment with the biblical pattern provided in Acts 6:1–6, with a "'democratic election' in our Western meaning", which divides "the people in majorities and minorities."

appointed by those already in leadership, or elected by the church, based on the suggestion of a nominating committee.[209]

The Swedish sources about the ordination also help to determine the date of the event. Engelsviken as well as other sources following him date the election and ordination of elders to October 1966.[210] However, such an early date comes with considerable chronological difficulties. The Merkato congregation consisting of believers from the Finnish mission and the Harar revivalists had only just been established in September of 1966, and for a while the group resisted the idea of joining up with the university students.[211] Therefore it seems unlikely that elders could have been ordained in October, i.e., only one month after the Merkato group had even been established. The Swedish mission correspondence also offers a later date. Ramstrand mentioned that the elders were ordained by Swedish missionaries while he was on leave for Christmas 1966/67,[212] and a report by Allan Wedin about the event explicitly stated that the ordination ceremony was performed on January 1, 1967.[213] Wedin also noted in this letter, that the Swedish had planned to perform the ordination already in October of 1966, but that this was not possible at the time.

This delay in actually performing the ordination may hint at the controversy of bringing the groups together as well as some discussions about the role missionaries should play in this process. One informant focused on these issues in detail:

> And the next step is the elders. Who was going to ordain? And we were trying to avoid foreigners. We don't wanna be a missionary church. This should be an indigenous Ethiopian church. We don't want any foreigners [pause] to be involved in our movement.
>
> And [pause] what they said, was that you have to be ordained by an ordained person, and none of us Ethiopians are ordained. And that has created a big problem. And here at this time the Swedish missionaries were very, very eager to ordain ministers, I mean elders. This is just for politics, you know. And some of us didn't like it. Some of us said: "No, we can be [pause] we can do it ourselves." So we were having discussion after discussion. Finally they won, and well, let them, let them do it one time.
>
> So we asked them who are you going to ordain? They don't know me, they don't know the rest of my — first they know three people from us. I've never been in Awasa, never gone to Awasa. So they picked three people and we said no. [pause] We canceled that and we picked ourselves. We included those people that they have suggested, we didn't drop them, uh, we accepted them.

209 CARLSSON, *Organizations and Decision Procedures within the Swedish Pentecostal Movements*, 34–35. The authority of this committee is indicated here by the statement that it appoints "the ones who are going to be elected."

210 ENGELSVIKEN, "Molo Wongel," 49; YOSIEF KIDANEWOLD, "The History of the Pentecostal Movement in Addis Abeba," 17; ESCKINDER TADDESSE WOLDEGEBRIAL, "An Introduction to the Biblical and Historical Pattern of Church Government," 104. Other sources are less specific, only mentioning the year.

211 Cf. above, 106.

212 RAMSTRAND, Letter to Arne Petterson, March 26, 1968.

213 WEDIN, Letter to Samuel Halldorf, January 20, 1967. Cf. also NYBERG OSKARSSON, *Svensk Pingstmission i Ethiopien (1959–1980)*, 266–267.

And then seven people, seven of us were picked. And then we went to the congregation. And they asked one of them to pray for us. And they prayed for us. And immediately they wrote to Sweden and said that we have ordained elders. We don't know these people, they never taught us, we don't know them. These are the first times some of us have seen them, but they wanted to get the credit.[214]

In taking up the discussions about the involvement of the Swedish mission and who should be ordained as elders, the informant delivered an account which is very critical of the missions and in its structure resembles a temptation narrative. Originally, the group set out with the strong determination to "avoid foreigners" in order not to be identified as "missionary church". However, doubts about the legitimacy of an Ethiopian ordination created a problem with this intention, while the missionaries, the compromising power, were "very very eager" to be called for help. Though some members shied away from this obvious solution and tried to encourage the group to rely on their own authority, endless discussions finally led to a giving in: "let them do it one time." Even though the missionaries demonstrated their inability to assist in the task of selecting the appropriate people,[215] the attempt to cancel the foreign involvement failed. The congregation still asked for "one of them" to pray for the elders, which eventually led to the dreaded consequences: the missionaries immediately reported the event to their supporting congregations, trying to take the credit for the indigenous church.[216] Though this description is obviously driven by regrets about the event, it nevertheless reveals the fault lines and the complexity of this election and ordination of the first elders. While entirely new issues were being faced and individual interests had to be reconciled, there was no final authority on which the whole group could depend due to their diverse backgrounds.

However, unlike this account, the involvement of the Swedish missionaries in preparing and conducting the ordination of the first FGBC elders is either ignored or carefully masked in most histories. The 1978 FGBC jubilee magazine, for example, records that the first elders "accepted the responsibility after it was prayed for them by means of one elder", without providing further details about this ominous intercessor.[217] A number of written and oral accounts even prefer not to mention external involvement at all,[218] whereas others merely note that the idea of an elders'

---

214 Interview no. 91.
215 Ramstrand mentioned that the discussions about forming a congregation "drew out", perhaps referring to this negotiation process, see RAMSTRAND, Letter to Arne Petterson, March 26, 1968.
216 The letter by Allan Wedin (WEDIN, Letter to Samuel Halldorf, January 20, 1967) is an example for such a report, stating that "we ordained elders." However, the letter makes clear that this was by Ethiopian initiative and that the church remained an independent congregation. Moreover, the event did not receive any publicity among the Swedish Pentecostals, there is not even a mention of it in the *Evangelii Härold*.
217 ETHIOPIAN FULL GOSPEL BELIEVERS' CHURCH, ሙሉ ወንጌል ቤተ ክርስቲያን ከለደት እስከ . . ., 9.
218 YOSIEF KIDANEWOLD, "The History of the Pentecostal Movement in Addis Abeba"; ETHIOPIAN FULL GOSPEL BELIEVER'S CHURCH, የኢትዮጵያ ሙሉ ወንጌል አመኞች ቤተ ክርስቲያን 25ኛ ዓመት በዓል; SOLOMON KEBEDE, "በዚህ ሰም ከመታወቁ በፊት"; BEDRU HUSSEIN, "የወንጌል ሥርጭት ታሪክ በኢትዮጵያ: የቅርብ ዓመታት የወንጌል ሥርጭት ልምድ," [The History of Evangelization in Ethiopia: The Experience of Evangelization in Recent Years.], in የኢትዮጵያ ሙሉ ወንጌል አማኞች ቤተ ክርስቲያን: የወንጌል ስርጭት

election was based on consultations with the SPCM missionaries.[219] Even where the involvement of the Swedish missionaries in the ordination is explicitly mentioned, it is simultaneously guarded against. Tibebe Eshete states that, being invited to do so, the missionary Ramstrand laid his hands on the new elders and prayed for them, "while at the same time, the congregation made a corporate prayer to officiate as well as consummate the act of ordination," and thus by this double performance the Ethiopians "resolved the dilemma of a delicate subject that involved issues of legitimacy, doctrinal identification, and autonomy."[220] Bekele Woldekidan also states that Ramstrand performed the ordination, but immediately points to previous attempts by the missions to gain control over the movement, and that the elders resisted such moves.

The contention found here and elsewhere[221] that Ramstrand performed the ordination is noteworthy. Ramstrand was usually not shy of mentioning how he had taught and encouraged the Ethiopians with regard to the election of elders, but even he himself clearly stated that he was in Sweden at the time of the actual ordination took place.[222] The report by Allan Wedin also explicitly makes note of this:

> I had wanted that we should wait until Ramstrand comes from Sweden, but our brothers here in Addis did not want that. They said that now the Christians want that we should form a congregation and we don't want to wait. Brother Wallberg came up from Awasa, so he and I laid hands on our beloved brothers.[223]

For the Ethiopian memoirs, however, Ramstrand is the most fitting candidate. Not only was he the most prominent of the Swedish missionaries, he is also remembered as an advocate of Ethiopian independence.[224] Owe Wallberg on the other hand, who had come to assist Wedin in the ordination, did not have the lasting sympathies of the group. When he succeeded Ramstrand in Addis Ababa, he tried to reassert the mission's authority over the FGBC meetings, which were hosted at the SPCM compound at that point in time. This led to a break of communications between the FGBC and

---

ሰልት ለኢትዮጵያ ጽኝ ዓውድ ጥናት ፣ የጥቲት 13–15 ቀን 1985 ዓ.ም. *[The Ethiopian Full Gospel Believers' Church: Second Research Convention for the Evangelization Strategy for Ethiopia, 23–25 March, 1993]*, ed. ETHIOPIAN FULL GOSPEL BELIEVER'S CHURCH (Addis Ababa, 1993), 3–14; TARIKU WOLDEMICHAEL and YONAS ASHAGARI, "The Establishment of Addis Ababa Mulu Wongel Believers' Church"; BULUTSE FUTUWI, "An Introduction to the Theology and Growth of Independent Churches in Ethiopia With Special Reference to Rhema Faith Church"; GIRMA ZEWDE, ኢትዮጲስ: አንደኛው, [Ethiopis, vol. 1.], 3rd ed. (n.p., 2001); also interview no. 1.

219 ENGELSVIKEN, "Molo Wongel," 49; ESCKINDER TADDESSE WOLDEGEBRIAL, "An Introduction to the Biblical and Historical Pattern of Church Government," 75; also interview no. 87.

220 TIBEBE ESHETE, *The Evangelical Movement in Ethiopia*, 170.

221 See BEKELE WOLDEKIDAN, ሪዝይባል, 103; also interviews no. 69; 39.

222 RAMSTRAND, Letter to Arne Petterson, March 26, 1968.

223 WEDIN, Letter to Samuel Halldorf, January 20, 1967.

224 Contrary to this perception, Ramstrand probably desired to retain his influence over the movement precisely by helping to establish the church. In a letter justifying his help with the ordination of elders despite the obvious affront this would be to the Finnish, he noted that the Swedish mission could not take the risk to be left "outside of it all", and that now they had "in any case a possibility to influence the development," see RAMSTRAND, Letter to Arne Petterson, March 26, 1968.

the SPCM, at which point Ethiopians turned to Ramstrand for help.[225] Therefore, it is not surprising that most historical accounts prefer to link the ordination with Ramstrand rather than Wallberg.

Therefore, much like the other events leading up to the formation of the FGBC, the historical representation of the election and ordination of elders is used to articulate diverse claims and ideas about the true identity of this church. The FGBC historian Bekele Woldekidan has called his church the "firstborn child of the revival" and its "direct result."[226] This notion certainly is tangible in the many accounts about the formation of the FGBC, its "real origins", revival antecedents, and foundational events. These stories contain numerous claims of fatherhood to this "firstborn child of the revival," even by groups, which did not end up joining this particular denomination.

The multiplicity and divergence of these histories and their arguments point to the plurality of actors, movements, institutions, and interests, and thereby highlight the fluid networks underlying the genesis of the Ethiopian Pentecostal movement and the FGBC. As different narratives about this history were produced, they became subject to politics of inclusion and exclusion, articulated in claims of historical precedence, as well as personal and institutional interests. The dynamics of this process suggest that the identities of the early revival movements and the key events in the formation of the FGBC were not simply "found" in the past, but formed and created by the historical discourse of Ethiopian Pentecostals.

---

225   See section 4.1.3, 145.
226   BEKELE WOLDEKIDAN, ረዥበሃ, 99.

4 Defining the Politics of Persecution: Pentecostals in the Ethiopian Empire

In 1967 the leadership of the Full Gospel Believers' Church (FGBC) submitted an application for registration as a religious association, which explicitly invoked the provisions of the Civil Code of 1960 and the corresponding regulative decree of 1966.[1] However, at the time the legal recognition of indigenous religious associations outside of the Ethiopian Orthodox Church (EOC) was a very contentious issue, turning this application into a test case for the fairly young legislation on religious associations. Moreover, since the nucleus of the FGBC consisted of young Ethiopian intellectuals, and the government hierarchies were closely tied to the EOC, this application played into the general political dynamic of the last Haile Selassie years: the impulses of modernization, increasingly and forcefully articulated by university students and graduates, challenged the old hierarchies of the predominantly Orthodox ruling class.[2]

At the same time, the Pentecostal movement had grown and spread to an extent that it sporadically attracted public attention and concern. This is exemplified by a riot against Pentecostals in the town of Debre Zeit, approximately 25 km outside of Addis Ababa, which for the first time turned the attention of the press on this "unconventional religious youth group."[3] It was in the aftermath of this riot, that the FGBC application for registration was rejected by the authorities and the applicants were ordered to close their meeting places. At first, the Pentecostals complied with this order and regrouped in private house meetings. However, these mostly private home meetings slowly reemerged as semi-public gatherings after a few months. At first this development did not meet any government response, but the pressure on the Pentecostals began to increase again from 1971 on. In November of that year the Security Department of the Ministry of the Interior sent a letter to a number of executive offices, in order to remind them to enforce the ban of Pentecostal meetings. In April 1972 the Addis Ababa FGBC was ordered to close its meeting place, which they complied with for a few months. However, this time the renewed attempt at public resurfacing was met with a much stronger response: On August 27, 1972 the

---

1 Cf. above, 5ff., for the relevant legislation. For the full text of the application, see ENGELSVIKEN, "Molo Wongel," 51–52.

2 For a convincing treatment of this dynamic, its history, and continuation during the Derg, see HOLCOMB and IBSSA, *The Invention of Ethiopia*. See esp. p. 319–328 for the situation of young intellectuals during the later years of the Ethiopian Empire. See also the memoirs by Emmanuel Abraham, who belonged to the Evangelical Church Mekane Yesus (ECMY) and was the only non-Orthodox official in Haile Selassie's government, EMMANUEL ABRAHAM, *Reminiscences of My Life* (Oslo: Lunde forlag, 1995). He frequently mentions the negative impact that his church membership had on his career, in which he apparently only succeeded because he had already served Haile Selassie during the Emperor's exile in London and managed to retain his favor.

3 See *The Ethiopian Herald*, "Youth and Adults Clash in Debre-Zeit," September 21, 1967, 5.

police rounded up a gathering of 250 Pentecostals and subsequently pressed charges against them. Detainees who pled guilty to the charge of participating in an illegal gathering were fined up to 200 Ethiopian dollars, while the others were tried in court and sentenced to six months in prison, i.e., the maximum possible sentence by the Penal Code.[4] The Pentecostals appealed this sentence to the High Court but did not succeed in overturning the ruling. The final ruling of July 18, 1973 upheld the verdict of the lower court, but suspended the prison sentence in favor of a three-year probation. The probation was condition on the suspension of any further meeting activities. The news of the whole affair slowly bubbled up through the foreign press and attracted some international attention, which culminated in a *Newsweek* article and an investigation by the World Council of Churches (WCC). However, despite this international after play, Pentecostals were unsuccessful in gaining official recognition in Imperial Ethiopia and once again relied on house meetings until the Ethiopian revolution brought a short period of religious freedom.

The contemporaneous sources and later histories about these events constitute a complex archive of legal issues, political interpretations, and persecution narratives, which allow some insight into the negotiation of such complex processes and the histories produced about them. Moreover, as was argued in the introduction, the events surrounding the application for registration, the 1972 arrests, and their aftermath were of central importance to the first histories of Ethiopian Pentecostalism. They were not just recent encounters to be processed, but the site of important political articulations, since these first histories were written right after the Ethiopian revolution of 1974. The refutation of the movement's alleged illegality and harmfulness therefore became essential to improving the public image of the FGBC in politically turbulent times. In later histories, however, the political opposition of the FGBC under Haile-Selassie tended to be eclipsed by the more recent and more intense suppression of churches during the Derg time. Moreover, the Ethiopian People's Revolutionary Democratic Front (EPRDF)'s sustained policies of religious freedom did not necessitate a strong apologetic thrust of historical accounts. Therefore, the following analyses of persecution narratives about Imperial Ethiopia will center mostly on the early accounts of the events, which were produced up until 1978.

4.1   Setting the Stage: The Application for Registration

For the early histories, the events of 1967, i.e., the application for registration, the first riots against Pentecostals, and finally the rejection of the application, serve as a paradigmatic starting point for a larger story of persecution during the last Haile Selassie years. It is here that most histories introduce a fundamental antagonism between the state and the Pentecostal movement, determining the opposing factions, alluding to later conflicts, and establishing their interpretative paradigms, which subsequently govern the persecution narratives. Furthermore, the application for registration was a paradigmatic legal encounter between church and state playing into the

---

4   Cf. above, 6.

politics of the Derg time. Thus, precisely because of the failed registration request, the narratives must establish the legitimacy of the church here, in contrast to the perceived illegitimacy and injustice of political oppression against them. Both of these functions of the 1967 narrative—laying out the conflict of church and state, and establishing the legitimacy of the FGBC despite the refused government recognition—are met with different strategies by the early histories.

4.1.1 Persecution as Evidence of Systematic Injustice

The Pentecostal persecution experience under Haile Selassie is of central importance to the first written history of Ethiopian Pentecostalism, Engelsviken's *Documentary Report*. In reporting about the events of 1967, Engelsviken sets the course for the main purpose of his paper, namely, raising awareness of the repression of Pentecostals and the subsequent political and ecumenical deliberations. As he transitions his narrative from a chapter titled "Revival" (chapter 3) to one titled "Affliction" (chapter 4),[5] the application for registration functions as the link between the two. In the concluding section of the "Revival" chapter, Engelsviken establishes the significance of the application with the following introductory remarks:

> It may seem a little unwarranted that we spend some time pointing to the fact that the Molo Wongel Church applied for registration as a church, but in the light of successive events this is of great importance. As under all regimes bent on controlling the people, registrations are an effective tool to achieve this.[6]

By setting the application in "the light of the successive events" under a "regime bent on controlling the people," Engelsviken already implies a rather unpleasant outcome. His critical remarks against the registration of religious bodies also have to be seen in light of this assessment of the Imperial government, since the requirement and process as such were not dissimilar to many other Western countries, including Engelsviken's homeland of Norway.[7] Registration in the wrong hands, however, becomes an "effective tool" for "controlling the people", and the optimistic application for registration in Engelsviken's narrative becomes a sign of illegitimate government politics and practices.

After these introductory remarks, Engelsviken continues by noting Ethiopia's commitment to freedom of religion in the Constitution, and its affirmation of international treaties.[8] However, after quoting the application in full, he closes with a foreboding: "When the answer finally came, it was not what the young leaders of the church had

---

5   The full chapter titles are: "Revival 1965-1967. 'It was a revival created by the Holy Spirit'" and "Affliction 1967-1971. 'Stones will fall on your heads'," cf. ENGELSVIKEN, "Molo Wongel," 34, 53.
6   Ibid., 50.
7   Cf. *Act Relating to Religious Communities* (1969), http://www.legislationline.org/legislation. php?tid=2&lid=924 (accessed February 26, 2008). In a number of specifics, the Norwegian legislation about registration of religious bodies was not dissimilar to that of Ethiopia. Though registration of religious communities was not required like in Ethiopia, there were certain advantages to registration: it safeguarded the community's name, confirmed its legal standing as a religious body, and reduced red tape in the application for the yearly government grants.
8   Cf. ENGELSVIKEN, "Molo Wongel," 51.

expected."[9] Thus the stage is set for a conflict of church and state, the latter of which has already been qualified as a regime that does not adhere to the standards of human rights.

The following chapter, dealing with "Affliction", accordingly sets out with the riot in Debre Zeit of September 1967, which, according to Engelsviken, had "serious repercussions," since now "the eyes of the authorities were directed towards the Pentecostals with suspicion and fear for similar unrest in other places."[10] At this point, the author leaves his chronological trajectory and does not proceed with the rejection of the application and the closing of the Addis Ababa churches in the fall of 1967, but turns to later persecution experiences in Bahir Dar, Dire Dawa, and Dessie in 1968 and the following years.[11] By connecting these local riots and linking them with political intent, Engelsviken describes them as part of a systematic and national effort against Pentecostal believers:

> Usually the sufferings would be inflicted upon the Pentecostals by the people instigated and supported by orthodox local priests and/or the local police authorities. [...] Although the initiative was taken locally, this does not mean that the persecution was without encouragement from central orthodox and political authorities. On the contrary, we shall document that the local authorities acted under orders from the highest authority when they tried to fight the Pentecostal church with all available means. In order to fully understand this, we must first look at what happened with the application for registration which was submitted to the Government in April 1967 before any severe persecution had occurred anywhere in the country as far as Pentecostals were concerned.[12]

With the immediately following section "The Application Turned Down," Engelsviken has come full circle in linking the central refusal of registration with the local opposition. According to him, the FGBC was refused registration because of the riots in Debre Zeit and fear of similar unrest, although "[n]othing wrong had been found"[13] in the doctrine of the church, its morals or influence on members. Engelsviken criticizes this decision, because riots hardly are "a valid reason for denying the innocent party its constitutional right," since the intolerance of "some people" and the persecution they instigated "cannot in the least justify the Ethiopian government's clamping down on the *victims* of that persecution."[14] The refusal of registration in Addis Ababa then leads to new local difficulties as Engelsviken had already foreseen:

> The Security Department was not content with just denying the church registration and ordering it to discontinue all its activities. It wanted to make

---

9 ENGELSVIKEN, "Molo Wongel," 52.
10 Ibid., 56.
11 Cf. ibid., 56-61.
12 Ibid., 61.
13 Ibid., 62.
14 Ibid., 63, emphasis Engelsviken.

sure that the Pentecostals abided by the order and that the local authorities intervened if necessary.[15]

Thus the application for registration and its refusal are closely connected to early persecution experiences, which according to Engelsviken reveal an unjust alliance of Ethiopian Orthodox and political authorities. The role of the Orthodox church as instigator of local riots is important, since the Orthodox-Pentecostal tension is central for Engelsviken's account, which essentially frames the persecution experience as an ecumenical issue. Moreover, as the political powers were not willing to acknowledge basic human and constitutional rights, the Pentecostals were forced to circumvent the system and continue to assemble in secret. Consequently, when the churches slowly reemerged in public in 1968, this was only possible, because "the authorities seemed to be more occupied with student unrest at the University than the Pentecostal Christians."[16]

The account by Yosief Kidanewold[17] largely relies on Engelsviken, but places a stronger emphasis on legal arguments. Yosief sets out with the erroneous notion that the "Ethiopian Constitution required the registration of every mission and church within the country," and that there was a rule "that made illegal a meeting in which more than five people gathered without permission."[18] He concludes:

> Thus, to ensure the security of the congregation in Addis Abeba, the church elders wrote a letter of application to the Ministry of the Interior on April 1967.[19]

According to Yosief, the application for registration therefore was motivated simply by the legal parameters in place, not by a repressive government as such. Furthermore, Yosief notes that meetings before successful registration were legally backed by article 45 of the Constitution, guaranteeing freedom of assembly.[20] In contrast to Engelsviken, Yosief therefore does not set out to criticize the legal and political

---

15 Ibid., 64. The author goes on to quote an excerpt of the letter which argues that the Pentecostals are a subsidiary of foreign missions, and therefore have to produce a letter of permission in accordance with the regulations regarding missions. Engelsviken dated the letter to October 1, 1967, but a later government reference to the letter dates it to November 2, see SOLOMON KEDIR, Letter to Haile Giorgis Workeneh, Mayor of Addis Ababa, 10 November 1971, cf. facsimile of the letter in GIRMA ZEWDE, ኢትዮጵስ, 139–142.

16 ENGELSVIKEN, "Molo Wongel," 65.

17 YOSIEF KIDANEWOLD, "The History of the Pentecostal Movement in Addis Abeba," 19-24.

18 Ibid., 19, cf. also 15. He seems to rely on ENGELSVIKEN, "Molo Wongel," 46, 210 in these statements. However, the registration requirement for churches did not result from the Constitution, but rather from the Civil Code, which declared all religious bodies outside the EOC as associations and thereby required their registration. No legislation could be found to support the rather awkward five-person-rule, which would have been in stark contradiction to the freedom of assembly provided by the Constitution and would have deemed the majority of households as illegal gatherings. It may be a misunderstanding of art. 411 Civil Code, which requires that the memorandum of associations has to be signed by at least five founders, or it may have arisen from a rule of thumb employed by Pentecostals to keep their meetings safe and family-like, cf. also ibid., 210, quoting such a statement.

19 YOSIEF KIDANEWOLD, "The History of the Pentecostal Movement in Addis Abeba," 19.

20 With regard to associations this is difficult to sustain, since the regulations for the control of associations explicitly stated that "No association shall carry out any activities other than those

systems as such, but presumes its legitimacy and explores the lawfulness of the Pentecostal endeavors. While noting that the answer to the application was delayed for seven months, his narrative continues with the successful second FGBC conference in Addis Ababa in July of 1967, which went uninterrupted and saw a large number of converts.[21] Only after narrating this undisturbed activity by Pentecostals in Addis Ababa, he turns to the riot in Debre Zeit, and the one in Bahir Dar in 1968, for both of which he also notes significant Orthodox involvement.[22] Turning back to Addis Ababa in 1967 and the denial of registration, he once more establishes the legal parameters:

> Seven months had passed before the church elders received a reply to the application for recognition. If the law had been followed, the church ought to have been recognized, since there was a Legal Notice that "If no answer was received within sixty days of the submission of the application, permission could be regarded as granted."[23]

As was pointed out above,[24] this is an erroneous interpretation of the 1966 Legal Notice, but it illustrates Yosief's interest to treat the matter as a legal issue. In what follows, Yosief closely adheres to Engelsviken's account of the rejection of the application, the closure of the FGBC meeting places, and the letter by the chief of the Security Department to all provinces, warning of the Pentecostals. He then closes his legal argument with the following conclusion:

> The church elders, by now, understood that Article 40 and 45 were not put into practice as far as the Ethiopian Government was concerned.[25]

Yosief thus ends on a note similar to Engelsviken, i.e., that an unjust system prevented the Pentecostals from claiming their constitutional rights, but other than Engelsviken, the legal system itself or the demand of registration was not the indicator of an unjust regime. Rather, it was the failure to put the law into practice. Thus, whereas Engelsviken establishes the right of the FGBC to exist as a corporate body in contrast to the Ethiopian political and legal system, which he considers as flawed, Yosief essentially derives the legitimacy of the Pentecostal underground movement from the government's failure to adhere to its own law and procedures, which in turn are not called into question as such. For both, the Orthodox opposition is significant, at least in initiating riots and causing bad press for Pentecostals, with Engelsviken apparently detecting more of a systemic involvement, which is important for his goal of framing the Pentecostal persecution as an ecumenical issue.

---

necessary to effect the establishment thereof [...]," cf. TSAHAFE TAEZAZ AKLILU HABTE WOLD, "Legal Notice No," §4.
21 See YOSIEF KIDANEWOLD, "The History of the Pentecostal Movement in Addis Abeba," 19–20.
22 Ibid., 20-21. The only documented source here is ENGELSVIKEN, "Molo Wongel."
23 YOSIEF KIDANEWOLD, "The History of the Pentecostal Movement in Addis Abeba," 22. The quote is from ENGELSVIKEN, "Molo Wongel," 51.
24 See above, 6.
25 YOSIEF KIDANEWOLD, "The History of the Pentecostal Movement in Addis Abeba," 23. Art. 40 relates to freedom of religious practice, art. 45 to freedom of assembly.

4.1.2 Persecution as a Spiritual Opportunity

A very different account of the application process was provided by the FGBC itself in its earliest written history, made available on the occasion of the dedication of its first building in 1978. Its narrative is framed by a spiritual outlook on revival and growth, which is what ultimately justifies the decision to pursue legal registration:

> Since the spiritual revival spread very much in 1967, the lives of many people were changed for God's glory. In order to obtain a legal permit for this spreading and growing spiritual ministry, the elders of the church, who had taken the management responsibility for the Addis Ababa prayer house, submitted a proper application to the Ministry of Justice to be registered as a faith organization under the name "Full Gospel Believers' Fellowship", invoking the faith paragraph. The church elders, believing that a legal permit was necessary to freely spread the revival used by God in wonderful ways over all of Ethiopia, tried to get the permit completed as quickly as possible by repeatedly reminding the office considering the matter. The believers in Addis Ababa and outside of Addis Ababa were asked to come together in prayer, so that God would make this permit issue a success and that it would be finished quickly. Many prayed strongly for the requested permit issue and poured out their tears before the face of God.[26]

In contrast to Engelsviken and Yosief, the application was not primarily motivated by political or legislative demands, but most of all by the growth of the movement and its missionary commitment to the whole country. Though the legal parameters are briefly alluded to in noting that a "proper application ... invoking the faith paragraph" was handed in and that a "legal permit was necessary," the matter is essentially portrayed as a spiritual issue. Registration is believed to be the tool for spreading the movement over the whole country, and thus all believers join in prayer so that God would give their application speedy success. The emphasis on prayer as well as the careful wording that the elders were simply "believing" the permit to be necessary is noticeable in light of the outcome of the request.

Though the document notes the spread of the movement to Debre Zeit and Bahir Dar,[27] it does not tell the story of the riots in these places, but rather turns to the disappointing results of the application right away. Without reference to specifics, the Minister of the Interior informed the representatives pursuing the registration that though "no fault or lack" was found with the group, it was "impossible to give them the permission of assembly, even under the invoked faith paragraph."[28] The elders then were forced to wait for the church members at their respective chapels on Sunday morning in order to turn them back. The congregants in turn responded with disappointment:

> While the believers said: "Why? Do we not have freedom of religion?" "Has it not been said that faith is a private matter?", and while they asked questions

---

26 ETHIOPIAN FULL GOSPEL BELIEVERS' CHURCH, ሙሉ ወንጌል ቤተ ክርስቲያን ከልደት እስከ ..., 13.
27 See ibid., 6, 9.
28 Ibid., 13.

that could not be answered many times after this, they voiced their complaint to God, and returned to the places they had come from.[29]

These remarks provide an interesting example of a spiritual embedding of political government criticism. While freedom of religion and a statement by the emperor about religion as a private matter are invoked,[30] these politically critical questions are ones "that could not be answered." Instead, the complaint is not directed toward the legal system nor the executive ignoring legal provisions, but to God himself. He was the One the believers had asked for help, so to Him the believers complain. After having done so, there is nothing else to do, but to return home.

This return, however, is not portrayed as a defeat, but as a path to victory in the next section titled "Repairing the Wounds of Persecution."[31] What originally was intended as "comfort homes," turns into "prayer houses" or "home chapels", which then grew significantly and in some areas even moved to rented facilities to accommodate the influx of visitors. Now a deeper meaning of the refused registration is revealed:

> The closing of the big chapels was the cause for the spread of the gospel into every town and the work of God widening beyond expectation. God, in his wisdom, captured the maliciously brewed plan to close the prayer houses for good results, so that his name be praised in faithfulness.[32]

These are the closing remarks to the growth and spread narrative that had ushered in the narrative of the application for registration. While the elders had originally "believed" that an official registration was necessary for extending the movement "all over Ethiopia", God had foreseen that only with the closing of the "big chapels" there could be a "spread of the gospel into every town." Therefore, the initial irritation at the outcome of the registration request, despite all prayer efforts, is replaced by a rediscovery of God's faithfulness. Since God himself had turned around the malicious plans, all political and legal efforts, be it on the side of the Pentecostals or their opponents, were in effect rendered useless. Consequently, the slow re-emergence of the movement in public is legitimized as a necessary result of the successful gospel work:

> Since God's word, which cannot be restrained or bound, became stronger and spread, it became necessary to rent a house suitable to accommodate the work [...] As public worship meetings began and the house filled, it became regular practice to conduct the meetings in a tent on the compound.[33]

In contrast to Engelsviken's and Yosief's accounts, the spiritual outlook generated in this early FGBC history does not necessitate an explicit system critique as legit-

---

29 ETHIOPIAN FULL GOSPEL BELIEVERS' CHURCH, ሙሉ ወንጌል ቤተ ክርስቲያን ከለደተ እስከ . . ., 14.
30 According to TIBEBE ESHETE, *The Evangelical Movement in Ethiopia*, 31, there was an epi-thet attributed to the Ethiopian modernizing emperors that stated: "Faith is [a matter] of the individual, country is [a matter] of the country."
31 See ETHIOPIAN FULL GOSPEL BELIEVERS' CHURCH, ሙሉ ወንጌል ቤተ ክርስቲያን ከለደተ እስከ . . ., 14–16.
32 Ibid., 14.
33 Ibid., 15.

imization strategy. Furthermore, since the events are rooted in God's providence, a political analysis of the opposition is not necessary, neither the imperial government nor the EOC are named as enemies. In part, this restraint should be attributed to the situation the church was in when this history was written in 1978. Though the Ethiopian revolution had originally established freedom of religion and the FGBC had been granted some land on which they managed to erect their first building, the Addis Ababa church had already suffered repressions in 1976 and Pentecostals were hard pressed in other regions of the country. Furthermore, at the end of 1978, when the dedication of the building took place and this document was distributed, the Red Terror already was in full swing, highlighting the precariousness of politics, the effects of which were felt only eleven months later, when the new church was closed and confiscated and not returned until after the Derg had come to an end. In such an unstable political situation it was probably considered wise to refrain from explicit references to politics, which in turn highlights the robustness of this spiritual narrative of persecution under difficult circumstances.

4.1.3   Persecution as an Issue for Political Negotiations

In addition to the early histories produced about the 1967 events, there is another important source in the contemporaneous missionary correspondence by Swedish Philadelphia Church Mission (SPCM) missionaries. These letters open up a third perspective on the application in a number of ways. First, it is in the nature of internal and contemporaneous writings to display more of an open-ended process of ongoing political negotiations, rather than presenting a progression of a pre-configured antagonistic clash. Secondly, the Pentecostal missionaries had a genuine interest in avoiding and reducing conflicts between Pentecostals and the state, since their residence in Ethiopia largely depended on a good relationship to the government. The emphasis on negotiations in these letters and the absence of a persecution narrative point to this political interest. Thirdly, because of the mediation and shelter that the SPCM offered to the FGBC, this issue played into the dynamics of the occasionally strained relationship between the mission and its Ethiopian counterparts, which highlights the multifariousness of the political field navigated by the FGBC.

One important source from this time was the SPCM representative in Addis Ababa, Allan Wedin, who also knew the leaders of the FGBC well, not least because he had assisted in the ordination of the first seven elders of the church in January 1967.[34] However, in reviewing Wedin's correspondence from the first half of 1967, the surprising observation is that he appears to be uninformed about the application request submitted in April 1967.[35] Even later correspondence shows that he was unsure when exactly the registration bid was handed in.[36]

---

34 See above, 135ff.

35 Altogether, Swedish archives contain five relevant letters by Wedin that date to before the application was rejected in September 1967. Two of these were written after the application was submitted, the others would have coincided with its preparation. Though a number of them make references to the Ethiopian movement and its growth, the matter of its legal status is not raised in any of them.

36 In two letters from September 1967, Wedin mentioned that the application was submitted "almost a year ago" and "eight months ago," respectively, cf. ALLAN WEDIN, Letter to Sundsvall

It is not unlikely that after the ordination of the FGBC elders by the SPCM missionaries, the church kept the missionaries somewhat at bay to assert their independence. Furthermore, an incident from 1967, which Ramstrand reported in his memoirs, reveals that this relationship was strained at times.[37] Ramstrand recalls how a controversy surrounding a wedding ceremony in Awasa led to the FGBC distancing themselves from the SPCM and threatening to boycott the 1967 Awasa summer conference.[38] Ramstrand describes the argument he had with the leadership in Addis Ababa:

> We called together the brothers in Addis to hear what they had to say about the matter. I understood that this did not just pertain to the wedding. It looked as if they took this as a pretense not to come to us. Were the Finnish right when they said that these brothers were anti-white? I don't know, but a certain nationalism had seized them. We and our mission were not worth much.[39]

Ramstrand subsequently not only notes that the Bible conference that year was nevertheless attended by 150 participants including three translators from Addis Ababa, but he also triumphantly reports the Ethiopians' remorseful return, as a response to the closure of their meeting places in September, only weeks after the conference:

> The brothers in Addis tried in vain to get their congregation registered. The matter was constantly delayed. It was an illegal, underground work which they had to operate. Premises were closed and they were exposed to different harassments. The same people who five weeks before had boycotted us, now came to us, humble and friendly.[40]

This quite strong disruption in the relationship between missionaries and Ethiopians makes it likely that Wedin indeed did not learn about the application for registration until September 1967, i.e. immediately after the closing of the FGBC meeting places.[41] Wedin therefore saw the closures as directly related to the riot in Debre Zeit, and provided a detailed report about this riot, which apparently saw the mob

---

Congregation, 25 September 1967, Allan Wedin Collection, Pingstarkiv Kaggeholm, Ekerö; AL-
LAN WEDIN, Letter to Samuel Halldorf, 29 September 1967, Allan Wedin Collection, Pingstarkiv
Kaggeholm, Ekerö. However, even the later dating would conflict with the date on the cover letter
of the application as quoted by Engelsviken, April 24, 1967, ENGELSVIKEN, "Molo Wongel," 51.

37 RAMSTRAND, *Det heliga äventyret*, 149–150.
38 The wedding ceremony was performed by a Swedish missionary. The controversy surrounded the
bride, who previously had been pledged to a man outside the church and after her conversion
chose to marry a believer instead. The Ethiopian Pentecostals apparently feared to be associated
with breaking traditions and promises.
39 RAMSTRAND, *Det heliga äventyret*, 149–150.
40 Ibid., 153–154.
41 Cf. WEDIN, Letter to Sundsvall Congregation, September 25, 1967; WEDIN, Letter to Samuel
Halldorf, September 29, 1967; Wedin's correspondence also allows a precise dating of the Debre
Zeit incident to 17 September 1967. In the first letter from Monday, 25 September, he states that
the order to close all meeting places had come "on Saturday" in the wake of the Debre Zeit riots
the Sunday before, see WEDIN, Letter to Sundsvall Congregation, September 25, 1967. See also
The Ethiopian Herald, "Youth and Adults Clash in Debre-Zeit."

destroying the meeting place in Debre Zeit along with the burning of Bibles and (probably choir) garments. Contrary to later historical accounts, Wedin did not link the riot directly to Orthodox opposition, but to a local bar owner:

> Here in Debre Zeit a large number of young men from the Ethiopian air force had been saved. Since they had experienced salvation, they had no desire to go to the tavern and drink, and they even left the tavern women. But the owner of the tavern became angry, and when the court would not condemn them, he himself hired a crowd of loose folk, who were equipped with sticks, which were taken from a fence, with many nails, together with axes and pistols.[42]

According to Wedin, the incident received bad press, which led to the closing of the FGBC chapels only six days after the Debre Zeit incident.[43] Unfortunately Wedin does not cite what he read or where. The English article in the *Ethiopian Herald* was rather amicable.[44] It did not directly blame the youths for the clashes. Instead, they were presented as the result of disagreements between "parents" and their "children", in which the government authorities had to assume a conciliatory role. A court application by the "parents" was rejected "on grounds of freedom of religion," and when the clashes occur with allegedly over 6,000 people attacking Pentecostals, "[p]olice rushed to the trouble spot and prevented serious injuries on both sides."[45]

In contrast to later historical accounts, Wedin did not conclude that the closure of the chapels was the final ruling on the registration request. Instead, he reported that a "a high employee in the Security Department" told the elders: "You have been growing much too quickly, you must take it a little easier."[46] Wedin still noted in June 1968:

> Until now the congregation has not received a proper answer if they may open the chapel for public meetings.[47]

---

42 WEDIN, Letter to Samuel Halldorf, September 29, 1967. The mention of the court case probably is in reference to judicial proceedings regarding some accusations against the Pentecostals, told in a number of other sources. The most prominent story pertains to a prostitute who testified against the Pentecostals that one of them had raped her and she conceived, However, she was unable to sustain the accusation in court and allegedly had been bribed to make the accusation, cf. ENGELSVIKEN, "Molo Wongel," 55; ETHIOPIAN GENNET CHURCH, የ50ኛው ዓመት የወርቅ ኢዮቤልዩ በዓል, 27. ENGELSVIKEN, "Molo Wongel," 54–55 and YOSIEF KIDANEWOLD, "The History of the Pentecostal Movement in Addis Abeba," 20 also mention a rich bar owner or merchant, but state that there was a collaboration with Orthodox clergy. By conjoining the Debre Zeit incident with the Bahir Dar riot, which by all accounts was led by an Orthodox priest, the EOC opposition altogether receives a larger focus in these sources.

43 WEDIN, Letter to Sundsvall Congregation, September 25, 1967; WEDIN, Letter to Samuel Halldorf, September 29, 1967. This would date the order for the closure to September 23, not to October as ENGELSVIKEN, "Molo Wongel," 62 contends.

44 See *The Ethiopian Herald*, "Youth and Adults Clash in Debre-Zeit."

45 The notion that there were no injuries of course does not match up with the reports of involved Pentecostals, cf. e.g. TIBEBE ESHETE, *The Evangelical Movement in Ethiopia*, 178.

46 WEDIN, Letter to Samuel Halldorf, September 29, 1967.

47 ALLAN WEDIN, Letter to Sundsvall congregation, 25 June 1968, Allan Wedin Collection, Pingstarkiv Kaggeholm, Ekerö. Wedin also mentions that the church already met for prayer every day, except for Sunday.

The Swedish correspondence therefore suggests that neither the Ethiopian Pentecostals nor the missionaries were willing to let the case rest, but instead tried to appeal
directly to the emperor. While the FGBC elders apparently succeeded in handing a
petition to the emperor personally,[48] the Swedish missionaries tried to employ their
good connection to Haile Selassie's oldest daughter Princess Tenagnework and her
daughter Princess Sophia.[49] In December 1967 they managed to arrange an audience
with Princess Tenagnework, together with one of the FGBC elders,[50] and after about
a year, Wedin saw a measured success to their efforts:

> It is now almost a year ago that the authorities have closed the chapels, and
> we have since been in negotiations with the authorities. The elders in the
> congregation have worked hard in order to find a solution to the situation,
> but without success. A month ago I made contact with princess Sophia, from
> whom we rent the house in Addis Ababa, and put forward the question for Her
> Highness if she wanted to help us. She loved to do so and now we have received
> a proposal from the authorities that the congregation may receive the right to
> work in 11 provinces of the country. Ethiopia has 14 provinces so three are
> exempt. In these three the state church has much power, and there is nothing
> to do about this right now. The princess said to me that this could of course
> change after a short while, and I answered: I believe so too.[51]

Addis Ababa apparently was one of the areas closed by the agreement. Therefore
Wedin hoped to obtain meeting rights for the mission, which could then function as
an umbrella for the Ethiopian Pentecostals. The Ministry of Education, presiding
over mission matters, signaled a general willingness to concede such rights if the mission were to establish their meeting premises in conjunction with a school.[52] Wedin
and Ramstrand pursued this idea for some time,[53] but apparently there were some

---

48 Wedin narrated, how Ethiopian Pentecostals stopped the emperor's convoy in Debre Zeit to hand
    him a letter about the incident, see WEDIN, Letter to Samuel Halldorf, September 29, 1967.
49 The mission had a close relationship with princess Sophia, since they were renting property from
    her. Contacts with the princess on behalf of the Ethiopian congregations were mentioned in
    a number of letters, see WEDIN, Letter to Sundsvall Congregation, September 25, 1967; ALLAN
    WEDIN, Letter to Sundsvall Congregation, 26 December 1967, Allan Wedin Collection, Pingstarkiv
    Kaggeholm, Ekerö; ALLAN WEDIN, Letter to coworkers, 24 February 1967, Allan Wedin Collection,
    Pingstarkiv Kaggeholm, Ekerö; ALLAN WEDIN, Letter to Norris Leffler, 12 August 1968, Allan
    Wedin Collection, Pingstarkiv Kaggeholm, Ekerö.
50 See WEDIN, Letter to Sundsvall Congregation, December 26, 1967. According to Ramstrand, he,
    Wedin and Haile Woldemichael were received in this audience, RAMSTRAND, Det heliga äventyret,
    154.
51 WEDIN, Letter to Norris Leffler, August 12, 1968. See also WEDIN, Letter to Sundsvall congre-
    gation, June 25, 1968 mentioning the same arrangement. However, still in November of 1968
    Wedin mentions that the group had not received a written notice about this permit regarding the
    11 provinces that was promised to them, see ALLAN WEDIN, Letter to Norris Leffler, 24 Novem-
    ber 1968, Allan Wedin Collection, Pingstarkiv Kaggeholm, Ekerö.
52 See WEDIN, Letter to Norris Leffler, August 12, 1968.
53 He had planned that the mission would rent the land and establish a school, while the FGBC
    would build a chapel. This idea was greeted by the FGBC elders with enthusiasm according to
    Wedin, see ALLAN WEDIN, Letter to Norris Leffler, 11 September 1968, Allan Wedin Collection,
    Pingstarkiv Kaggeholm, Ekerö.

reservations with the mission board in Sweden.[54] In the meantime the Swedish missionary Arvid Malmvärn, who had established his own work in the leprosy farm Addis Hiwot and was independent from the SPCM, gave a house he owned near the Addis Ababa Old Airport to the Ethiopians in 1968, who used it as one of the places for their services.[55]

When Wedin returned to Sweden at the beginning of 1969 and subsequently embarked on a new mission initiative to Yemen,[56] and Ramstrand succeeded him in Addis Ababa for a short while before returning to Sweden himself. Ramstrand pursued a more underhanded strategy by simply accommodating the FGBC congregation in the mission headquarters, especially for baptisms and conferences, without seeking an official meeting permit.[57] The FGBC national conference of 1969, for example, was hosted in the Swedish mission compound, without English interpreters and under the responsibility of the Ethiopian church. This large and probably loud meeting[58] scheduled for two and a half weeks became the target of a mob attack, which brought it to the attention of the police and the secret service, and eventually left the SPCM in some legal difficulties, since it was unclear whether the mission had previously acquired assembly rights in Addis Ababa.[59]

Ramstrand was scheduled to retire and return to Sweden immediately after the conference, which left the aftermath and the legal dispute to his successor Owe Wallberg. Wallberg then decided to take a different stance toward the Ethiopian meetings at the compound, demanding that they should be conducted in English and Swedish, and that he should have the right to preach there as well. He probably intended to

---

54 See ALLAN WEDIN, Letter to Norris Leffler, 12 November 1968, Allan Wedin Collection, Pingstarkiv Kaggeholm, Ekerö; WEDIN, Letter to Norris Leffler, November 24, 1968. Cf. also NYBERG OSKARSSON, *Svensk Pingstmission i Ethiopien (1959–1980)*, 271–272.

55 RAMSTRAND, Letter to Bernt Einarsson, November 19, 1969; cf. also NYBERG OSKARSSON, *Svensk Pingstmission i Ethiopien (1959–1980)*, 272; interview no. 35. The house was not big enough to host all FGBC congregants and thus served as one of many "chapels" in Addis Ababa. However, in January 1970, the FGBC held its Ethiopian Christmas celebration there with an estimated 2,000 people, made possible by the addition of four tents, HAILE WOLDEMICHAEL, Letter to Karl Ramstrand, n.d., probably Jan/Feb 1970, Karl Ramstrand Collection, Pingstarkiv Kaggeholm, Ekerö.

56 See ALLAN WEDIN, Letter to Norris Leffler, 14 January 1969, Allan Wedin Collection, Pingstarkiv Kaggeholm, Ekerö.

57 See NYBERG OSKARSSON, *Svensk Pingstmission i Ethiopien (1959–1980)*, 273–273; KARL RAMSTRAND, Letter to Owe Wallberg, 22 November 1969, Karl Ramstrand Collection, Pingstarkiv Kaggeholm, Ekerö.

58 See RAMSTRAND, *Det heliga äventyret*, 164–169. Ramstrand notes here that between 1,000 and 2,000 participants came to the meetings, and that he was afraid that they had disturbed the minister for post and telegraph, whose house was behind the mission compound. However, since this minister was the ECMY member Emmanuel Abraham, this did not turn out to be a problem.

59 Ramstrand said that he believed that Höglund had secured the mission rights for Addis Ababa, but did not know how to obtain proof for that, due to the difficulties in the mission's formative years, see ibid., 167. Ramstrand's insistence on his "right to invite our friends to our private compound for meetings" was a rather weak line of defense, which he tried to sustain through personal contacts with high officials, see e.g. KARL RAMSTRAND, Letter to Owe Wallberg, 10 November 1969, Karl Ramstrand Collection, Pingstarkiv Kaggeholm, Ekerö.

relieve the pressures by the authorities with these measures,[60] but instead this led to a break between the FGBC and the Swedish missionaries. In the fall of 1969, the Ethiopian Pentecostals moved their services out of the Swedish mission compound and to rented premises.[61] An extensive correspondence ensued at the end of 1969 and beginning of 1970, in which the elders of the FGBC complained to Ramstrand about Wallberg, apparently in the hopes of reversing the missionary's appointment.[62] Ramstrand sided with the Ethiopians and tried to influence Wallberg, hoping that "perhaps the misunderstanding between the mission and the brothers can be worked out."[63] However, his suggestions were greeted with reluctance, and he reacted with disappointment about the development of the SPCM after his departure.[64]

Despite this serious disruption in the relationship between the FGBC and the SPCM, there were instances of cooperation in the following months and years.[65] The SPCM invited the Ethiopian Pentecostals to send representatives on a visit to Sweden for a preaching tour, aimed at raising funds for literature work. The FGBC accepted the invitation, and Haile Woldemichael and Melese Wogu traveled to Sweden in the summer of 1971. After the visit, the Ethiopians followed up on promised material support, asking for funds for a literature program, musical instruments, and other aid.[66] In answer to their request, a budget of about 25,000 Ethiopian Dollars was assigned to the FGBC literature work, of which they received ten percent right away, and a collection of instruments was taken up in Swedish churches.[67] Furthermore

---

60 See NYBERG OSKARSSON, *Svensk Pingstmission i Ethiopien (1959–1980)*, 149, 273–274; OWE WALLBERG, Letter to Karl Ramstrand, 22 October 1969, Owe Wallberg Collection, Pingstarkiv Kaggeholm, Ekerö.
61 See PHILIPOS KEMERE, Letter to Karl Ramstrand, 18 November 1969, Karl Ramstrand Collection, Pingstarkiv Kaggeholm, Ekerö; OWE WALLBERG, Letter to Sigvard Harknäs, 27 October 1969, Owe Wallberg Collection, Pingstarkiv Kaggeholm, Ekerö.
62 Philipos Kemere for example asked Ramstrand in a letter: "What is the attitude in Sweden towards the work here? Are they completely settled up believing that they have their right representatives? To be sincere, do you mention to them what our wishes are?" Kebede Woldemariam seconded in another letter: "It seems to me that it will be good if someone from Sweden is sent to Philadelphia Church in Ethiopia to take the office work and brother Wallberg is left only for prayer and gospel work." See PHILIPOS KEMERE, Letter to Karl Ramstrand, 14 January 1970, Karl Ramstrand Collection, Pingstarkiv Kaggeholm, Ekerö; KEBEDE WOLDEMARIAM, Letter to Karl Ramstrand, 16 February 1970, Karl Ramstrand Collection, Pingstarkiv Kaggeholm, Ekerö.
63 KARL RAMSTRAND, Letter to Owe Wallberg, 21 January 1970, Karl Ramstrand Collection, Pingstarkiv Kaggeholm, Ekerö.
64 Ramstrand voiced his dissent in dire projections of the future, envisioning the SPCM becoming a classical mission agency, while he and Malmvärns' "Addis Hiwot" organization would collaborate with the "free Pentecostal church" in Ethiopia, see KARL RAMSTRAND, Letter to Petrus Hammarberg, 31 December 1969, Karl Ramstrand Collection, Pingstarkiv Kaggeholm, Ekerö; KARL RAMSTRAND, Letter to Arvid Malmvärn, 1 April 1970, Karl Ramstrand Collection, Pingstarkiv Kaggeholm, Ekerö.
65 Cf. NYBERG OSKARSSON, *Svensk Pingstmission i Ethiopien (1959–1980)*, 274–275.
66 KEBEDE WOLDEMARIAM, Letter to Pastor Bo Hörnberg, 4 November 1971, Filadelfiaförsamlingen Jönköping Collection, Religiösa organisationer, Jönköpings läns folkrörelsearkiv, Jönköping.
67 BO HÖRNBERG, Letter to Kebede Woldemariam, n.d., probably Jan/Feb 1971, Filadelfiaförsamlingen Jönköping Collection, Religiösa organisationer, Jönköpings läns folkrörelsearkiv, Jönköping.

it was decided to support Ethiopian evangelists working in remote areas with funds administrated by the "indigenous congregations."[68]

Overall, the contemporaneous missionary correspondence of 1967 to 1970 therefore suggests much more of an open-ended process in negotiating the legality of the FGBC. In the letters to their supporters, the missionaries consistently conveyed the opinion that all the difficulties could be solved with proper negotiations or arrangements. This strategy was coupled with a reluctance to adopt a persecution narrative or to directly criticize the established system, setting it in contrast to the later historical productions, which in turn do not mention the informal contacts to the royal family or even the missionary involvement in this matter. The FGBC's voice, in turn, for the most part is not represented in the missionary correspondence, but their actions suggest that they accepted and at times sought the missionaries' help as one option among others. The Ethiopians were wary of losing their independence, which not only put limits on the missionaries' agency on their behalf, but also suggests that there was an ongoing negotiation of political strategies in the Pentecostal community.

The analysis of the historical archive about the application for registration and its rejection thus reveals three basic plots: a foundational system criticism embedded in a persecution narrative, an expression of spiritual resilience based on the notion of a sovereignly directed history, and the call for negotiations within the given political system. As the following parts will show, these perspectives do not only pertain to the application process of 1967, but also run through the historical representations of later conflicts with the Imperial government.

4.2   Identifying the Persecutor

Between the initial closure in 1967 and 1971, there are no reports of any substantial conflicts between the FGBC and the government, even though Pentecostal meetings slowly reemerged in public. However, political efforts to curb the spread of Pentecostalism were intensified again toward the end of 1971 and culminated in the mass arrest of Pentecostals in the summer of 1972. These arrests, the events leading up to them and their legal aftermath marked a new intensity in the confrontation between the Pentecostals and the government. The government circulated documents demanding the closure of the FGBC nationwide, it adopted a zero-tolerance policy on Pentecostal meetings, there were legal proceedings, and the verdict against the Pentecostals was upheld in the High Court. Furthermore, for the first time, the events found some resonance in the international press, and were brought before a number of ecumenical circles, including the WCC. The sources about Pentecostalism in Ethiopia reflect this new intensity in a flurry of narratives.

---

[68] RUNE SKOOG, "Protokol fört vid fältkonferens för Etiopien den 10/12–1971 i City Pingstkyrkan, Stockholm, med representanter från etiopienmissionerande församlingar," [Minutes of the Field Conference for Ethiopia on 10 December, 1971 in the City Pentecostal Church, Stockholm, with Representatives from the Congregations Conducting Missions in Ethiopia], Filadelfiaförsamlingen Jönköping Collection, Religiösa organisationer, Jönköpings läns folkrörelsearkiv, Jönköping, 1971. One informant recounts how the SPCM supported his work in setting up a Bible school for the FGBC in Jima, interview no. 92.

Endeavoring to lay out the causes for this intensification of political pressure on Pentecostals, historical accounts consistently cite two sources: a speech by the new patriarch of the EOC, given at his investiture on May 9, 1971,[69] and a government circular from the fall of 1971 calling for the closure of the FGBC meetings in Addis Ababa and elsewhere. These sources are not only taken as evidence of a systematic and prepared campaign, which culminated in the arrests of 1972, they also serve to identify and characterize the main actors presumed to be behind the persecution: the EOC and the Imperial government. This is important, because the identification of the persecutor influences important aspects of the persecution account.

4.2.1 The Election of the Patriarch

Engelsviken begins his narrative of the 1972 persecution with a colorful description of the investiture of Theophilos.[70] Having just arrived in Ethiopia two days before, the author evidently had vivid memories of the ceremony, which he summarizes as a "strange introduction to a country and a church where Patriarch and Emperor still ruled the masses together."[71] Accordingly, Engelsviken detects a looming problem in the coronation speech of the patriarch:

> The speech of the patriarch was designed to fit the occasion. By outsiders it was understood as a general declaration of faithfulness and loyalty to the church of which he now had become the formal head. Some Ethiopians, however, grasped the ominous significance of the speech. When the speech later was broadcast over Ethiopian radio and printed in the press, it became clear that Patriarch Theophilos, who was one of the vice-presidents of the All-African Conference of Churches and a spokesman for ecumenical understanding abroad, had announced in his inaugural speech a different attitude altogether within the borders of Ethiopia.[72]

The Norwegian missionary goes on to quote some excerpts from the speech:

> "As I am the Ethiopian Patriarch," said the newly crowned prince of the church, "I shall keep and make others keep the faith and doctrines of the Ethiopian Orthodox Church. Dear brothers, I assure you before the Almighty God that I shall keep the Orthodox Tewahido faith and doctrine [...] till the end of my life; and that I shall teach for the good of the believers with all the power and ability I have. In our age, I oppose and endeavour to eradicate any movement or teaching that is contrary or against the Orthodox Church. I shall make believers keep the rules and commandments that are contained in the faith, doctrine, and moral of the Ethiopian Orthodox Tewahido Church."[73]

---

69 Abuna Theophilos succeeded Abuna Basilios, who had died in 1970. Theophilos had already been acting patriarch during a longer time of Basilios' illness.
70 See the chapter titled "Persecution 1972-1973" in ENGELSVIKEN, "Molo Wongel," 142–213.
71 Ibid., 143.
72 Ibid., 142–143.
73 Ibid., 143. Ellipsis J.H.

Though Engelsviken notes that the speech was broadcast by radio and the press, he unfortunately does not specify his source here, which makes it difficult to verify the statements. The transcripts of the patriarch's words in the Amharic newspaper *Addis Zaman* and their English translation in the *Ethiopian Herald* of May 11, 1971 suggest a less forceful language. The closest comparable text to Engelsviken's quote that could be found in the *Ethiopian Herald* is the following excerpt from the statement of faith pronounced by Theophilos during the ceremony:

> As patriarch of Ethiopia, I shall by the grace of God maintain the Orthodox faith of our Church. In the presence of God, calling Whom to my witness, I make a solemn pledge before you, my brothers, that I will keep the faith till the end of my life and proclaim it for the guidance and salvation of others as long as there lies strength in me. I will exert all my ability for the discarding of every teaching and movement that may battle against the Orthodox Church in our times. I will abide by the Laws of the church that are in vogue and help the evolution of Laws and regulations which are required for the better maintenance of the Church's Orthodox faith, discipline, worship and morals.[74]

Though the differences between these texts are too great to attribute merely to translation differences, their similar setup and the overlap in certain phrases makes it likely that this statement of faith by Theophilos formed the base for the quote provided by Engelsviken. This assumption is supported by a 1973 *Newsweek* article titled "Persecuting the Sects", which quotes from the same passage in order to make the very point Engelsviken is trying to make, but uses a wording much closer to the original transcript.[75] Engelsviken's quotation thus would be a slightly radicalized interpretation of the patriarch's words and intentions: "maintaining" the faith is taken to mean "keep and make others keep," "exerting to discard" opposition movements is turned into "endeavour to eradicate," and the pledge to help with legislation for a "better maintenance" of the faith is interpreted as "making believers keep the rules and commandments" of the EOC. Such overstatements were not uncommon when the speech of the patriarch was reviewed by Pentecostals after the arrests of 1972. The Pentecostal *Logos Journal* even quoted the patriarch with the following words: "Today when I am taking this position in front of our King and the faithful orthodox believers, I swear to destroy any religious group which are unfit to the Orthodox Church."[76]

Engelsviken took the patriarch's words as evidence that "a church policy of confrontation had been drawn up by the top leader of the church,"[77] which however is less likely given the original tone of the statement. However, the evolution of the patriarch's words in Pentecostal memory indicates that Engelsviken was probably

---

74 *The Ethiopian Herald*, "Statement of Faith Made at Investiture," May 11, 1971, 1, 3, 7. The Amharic transcript in the *Addis Zaman* is identical in content, see *Addis Zaman*, "የፓትሪያርኩ በዓለ ሢመት ተከበረ," [Vestiture of the Patriarch Celebrated.], May 11, 1971, 7–8.

75 See *Newsweek. International Edition*, "Persecuting the Sects," January 15, 1973, 32. The quote reads: "to exert all my energy against every teaching and movement that may battle against the Ethiopian Church."

76 See *Logos Journal*, "Persecution in Ethiopia," May-June 1973, 12–16.

77 See ENGELSVIKEN, "Molo Wongel," 143.

correct when he noted that "[m]any evangelical Christians in Ethiopia, including the Pentecostals, understood the speech as a clear threat."[78] This is also supported by contemporaneous sources. Only ten days after Theophilos' coronation, Tage Johansson, who was the country representative of the SPCM at the time, voiced his concerns in a letter:

> Otherwise we feel good on the field even if it looks as if we are going to meet harsher times. There has been a new archbishop here, who is said to have openly declared his program against any associations, which are involved in mission. And in this the Pentecostals are the worst.[79]

This outlook in Johansson's correspondence signals a significant change in the expectations of the SPCM missionaries toward Theophilos, since in 1967 they apparently had sought to enlist his support for the FGBC application for registration, and reportedly left a personal meeting with him with an optimistic outlook.[80]

By the time the arrests had taken place in 1972, however, it already was a fairly common interpretation among Pentecostals to trace their difficulties to the new patriarch, thereby identifying the EOC as the actual persecutor instead of the Imperial government. An article in *Christianity Today*, which was published only three months after the Pentecostal meeting was rounded up, contained the following statement:

> Many Ethiopian Pentecostals believe the opposition has been inspired by the Ethiopian Orthodox Church, which claims about 40 per cent of the population. [...] And it is no secret that the Orthodox patriarch, Abuna Theophilos, views the movement as a threat; it is attracting large numbers of young people from Orthodoxy.[81]

Even the high-profile publication about the arrests in the international edition of *Newsweek* in January 1973 set out with the coronation of the patriarch and stated:

> Under Theowophlos's leadership, the hidebound Ethiopian Church has managed to enlist Emperor Haile Selassie's security apparatus in a campaign of terror against the 50,000 Ethiopians who have abandoned Orthodoxy and converted to the Full Gospel Church.[82]

The wide circulation of the *Newsweek* magazine prompted a preemptive response in the government newspaper *Ethiopian Herald*, which was printed two days before

---

78 See ENGELSVIKEN, "Molo Wongel," 143.
79 TAGE JOHANSSON, Letter to Bo Hörnberg, 19 May 1971, Tage Johansson Collection, Pingstarkiv Kaggeholm, Ekerö. Johansson obviously depended on secondary information ("is said to have"), but the information aligns with his general expectations regarding the patriarch. In a letter written on 23 April, ten days after the patriarch had been elected, he noted similar fears and mentioned that there was an increasing pressure to abstain from converting Orthodox Christians, see TAGE JOHANSSON, Letter to Bo Hörnberg, 23 April 1971, Tage Johansson Collection, Pingstarkiv Kaggeholm, Ekerö.
80 See TAGE JOHANSSON, "Angående förföljelsen i Etiopien," [Regarding Persecution in Ethiopia], Tage Johansson Collection, Pingstarkiv Kaggeholm, Ekerö, 1974.
81 DECOURCY H. RAYNER, "Persecution in Ethiopia," *Christianity Today*, 3 1972, 55.
82 *Newsweek. International Edition*, "Persecuting the Sects," 32.

the *Newsweek* issue came out.[83] The article strongly repudiates the notion that the inaugural speech of the patriarch "two years ago" had anything to do with the recent arrest of Pentecostals. Instead the government action is portrayed to have been driven by a simple security rationale:

> The writer [of the Newsweek article] tries to make out a case of the Orthodox Church versus the Pentecostalists, which is simply a malicious conjecture. He tries to conceal the fact that it is the duty of the police, according to the Constitution and the law of the land, to protect the peace of the people.[84]

The article then attempts to substantiate the notion that Pentecostals are threatening the "peace of the people" by citing previously circulated rumors of sexual orgies in Pentecostal meetings, by pointing to an alleged disrespect of the young Christians for elders and the country, and by suggesting that Pentecostals "despise the teachings of Orthodox Church, thus clearly violating the principle of freedom of practice of religion."[85] The argument is thus turned around: far from being a persecutor, the EOC is seen as under attack by Pentecostals and needs government protection. Furthermore, the article points out that the registration of the movement had been refused after "an investigation of the record of their activities," and that "[i]n the face such refusal and despite several warnings, the sect continued to operate." Consequently, according to the *Ethiopian Herald*, the government was mandated to act and to enforce its orders against the Pentecostal defiance of governmental authority.

While the argumentation of this text is discredited by the utilization of unsubstantiated rumors and the cynical notion that the arrest of Pentecostals was an act of protecting religious freedom, the political thrust of the article is of interest. Against the tendency to explain the opposition to Pentecostals as the campaign of another religious community, the government press article labors to inject the Imperial Court's reasoning and agency, in order to assert its authority and influence, which tends to be eclipsed in accounts focusing on the role of the patriarch.

4.2.2 The Government Circular

The second source that historical accounts often quote for setting up the 1972 persecution narrative is a circular letter, signed by Col. Solomon Kedir, "Minister Deta"[86] and "Chief Officer of Public Security" on November 10, 1971. It was sent to Dr. Hailegiorgis Worqneh, mayor of Addis Ababa, and distributed in copy to the 14 provinces of Ethiopia, the Imperial Government, the Ministry of Education, the EOC, the headquarters of the Addis Ababa police force, and, for reference, to the Minister of the

---

83 Since *Newsweek* was published on Mondays and the *Ethiopian Herald* appeared every day except Monday, it may have seemed opportune to reply beforehand in the widely circulated Saturday issue. This preemptive response makes it unlikely that the *Newsweek* article had "somehow slipped through the Ethiopian censorship" as ENGELSVIKEN, "Molo Wongel," 189 contends.

84 *The Ethiopian Herald*, "Newsweek's Report on Pentecostalists Unfounded," January 13, 1973, 2.

85 Ibid.

86 The label "Minister Deta" was a derivative of the French "ministre d'État", and in Ethiopia indicated a minister of lower rank. See JOSEPH TUBIANA, "Brave New Words: Linguistic Innovation in the Social and Economic Vocabulary of Amharic since 1960," *Journal of Semitic Studies* 30 (1 1985): 91–92.

Interior.[87] The letter sets out by reminding its recipients of the rejection of the Pentecostal application for registration in 1967, which forbade them to work without a permit. It calls for an executive enforcement of this meeting ban and that "steps should be taken against those working outside the order to bring them before the law." Much of the following text then is devoted to absurd allegations against Pentecostals: the Pentecostals are accused of sexually seducing "boys and young girls failing in school;" of sexual orgies in their meetings and the inevitable corruption of girls thus violated; of disrespect for cultural standards by letting their hair grow long, wearing "tight pants," standing in people's way, and insulting the elderly; of fraudulent practices in their services by conjuring up money or staging false miracles; of pressing people to become their followers by pointing to the imminent end of the world; and finally of disrespect for the national flag and other teachings corrupting society. As absurd as these accusations of immorality and lack of patriotism may seem, their centrality in the government letter suggests that the legal argument of banning Pentecostals rested on them. According to the "Legal Notice No. 321" of 1966, the registration of an association could only be denied if the application provided false or misleading information, if the association pursued "unlawful or immoral" purposes, or if it was a detriment to "national unity or interests."[88] The letter evidently implied the latter, since the author concluded his list of supposed atrocities with a clear verdict against Pentecostalism and Jehovah's Witnesses, whom he believed to be of equal character:

> Moreover, after so many illegal deeds performed by the adherents of the two faiths mentioned, with [only] some of many having been exposed above, how can we estimate that they are religious organizations? When these organizations which are known to be found all over the world, where they are not disturbed but also not accepted, are seen to have spread and be working in our country, how can we let this pass in ignorance? If the followers of these religions say: "In article 40 of the Constitution it says that the religious practices of all those living in the empire should be respected and are not forbidden to be exercised freely," then they only take the letter of the law to their defense. Though the law says this, it should not be forgotten that in the same paragraph there are strong words that read: "as long as there is not disturbance of the welfare of the people, or morality or political order."[89]

The remainder of the letter states that names of leaders, the meeting places, days and times in Addis Ababa have been recorded, so that action can be taken, and it calls on the government agencies and all Ethiopians "to keep the peoples' moral standard and unity, to keep the country's peace and purity, and to purge and forever eliminate this known public preaching and faith."

In analyzing the representation of this letter in the later persecution narratives, it is first of all noticeable that a number of sources insist that the letter was a "secret

---

87 A facsimile of the letter can be found in GIRMA ZEWDE, ኢትዮጵስ, 139–142.
88 Cf. above, 6.
89 SOLOMON KEDIR, Letter to Haile Giorgis Workeneh, Mayor of Addis Ababa, November 10, 1971, 3.

circular."[90] However, the letter itself shows no evidence of secrecy. There is no stamp of confidentiality on the Amharic facsimile,[91] nor do the wide circulation or the call to enlist further government and civil agencies support this notion. The document rather appears to have been a semi-public memorandum, as Tibebe Eshete indicates,[92] and thus Pentecostals obtained a copy fairly early on. However, the notion of secrecy is helpful to some accounts, since it may be used to indicate a larger conspiracy operation against the Pentecostals:

> The secret document seems to have been issued with the cooperation of the Orthodox leaders and the then Chief Security officers, Colonel Solomon Kedir, and probably other authorities as well.[93]

The idea of an active Orthodox participation in the drafting of the letter is a widely held notion that probably originated with the seal of the Mission Department of the patriarchate of the EOC on the first and the last page of the copy that the Pentecostals obtained. Some take this as evidence of merely a cooperation between church and state,[94] while others see the letter originating with the EOC who circulated it "by way of the Minister of the Interior,"[95] or even see the government agencies merely as recipients of the circular.[96] The *Logos Journal* later even took the letter as evidence of an executive power of the church:

> The police leader presented the pastor with a letter signed by the Ministry of Public Security and stamped with the Imperial Ethiopian Seal. By the order of the Patriarch of the Ethiopian Orthodox Church (the state church) all pentecostal believers who insisted on meeting to worship were to be arrested and punished.[97]

---

90 E.g. ENGELSVIKEN, "Molo Wongel," 144; YOSIEF KIDANEWOLD, "The History of the Pentecostal Movement in Addis Abeba," 46; ETHIOPIAN FULL GOSPEL BELIEVERS' CHURCH, ሙሉ ወንጌል ቤተ ክርስቲያን ከልደት እስከ ..., 17.

91 Girma Zewde's book, which provides the facsimile, is one of the few sources not contending that it was a secret document, see GIRMA ZEWDE, ኢትዮጲስ, 139–142.

92 TIBEBE ESHETE, *The Evangelical Movement in Ethiopia*, 179.

93 YOSIEF KIDANEWOLD, "The History of the Pentecostal Movement in Addis Abeba," 46. *Logos Journal*, "Persecution in Ethiopia" contended that "[w]hile officials have denied the existence of such letters, believers have smuggled several out of the country." In a similar notion ENGELSVIKEN, "Molo Wongel," 144 stated that the "secret circular ... was intercepted by people sympathetic to the cause of the Pentecostals." Later, an FGBC anniversary magazine concluded that the letter was written to "complete the conspiracy that the government was involved with and supported," see ETHIOPIAN FULL GOSPEL BELIEVER'S CHURCH, የኢትዮጵያ ሙሉ ወንጌል አማኞች ቤተ ክርስቲያን 25ኛ ዓመት በዓል, 11.

94 Girma Zewde, for example, contends that patriarch Theophilos already went to the emperor together with Solomon Kedir in September/October 1971 to reverse Haile Selassie's religious policy on religion, which was characterized by the phrase: "The country is the country's, faith is personal," see GIRMA ZEWDE, ኢትዮጲስ, 137. Bekele Woldekidan just notes that the letter was stamped by the both the Ministry of the Interior and the "secretariat of the patriarch of the Orthodox Church," see BEKELE WOLDEKIDAN, ሪ፰ይባል, 138

95 BEDRU HUSSEIN, "የወንጌል ሥርጭት ታሪክ በኢትዮጵያ: የቀርብ ዓመታት የወንጌል ሥርጭት ልምድ," 4.

96 TAYE ABDISSA, "The Pentecostal Development and the Rise of Charismatic Movement in Ethiopia," 28.

97 *Logos Journal*, "Persecution in Ethiopia," 12.

However, the letter itself mentions the EOC only as recipient of a copy and gives no indication of Orthodox participation in the drafting of its content. More importantly, a closer look at the facsimile makes it very likely that the EOC seal was secondary and not part of the original letter. The copy that the Pentecostals had obtained was part of an internal redistribution in the EOC, which is indicated by an added postscript on the facsimile. It notes that the letter originated with the "Security [Department] of the Ministry of the Interior of the Royal Ethiopian Empire" and was disseminated to the attending clergy of a national convention of priests, which was held from August 28 to September 1, 1972 in Addis Ababa, "in order to educate them, namely, that the peace of the country is to be guarded."[98] The seal of the EOC therefore was one of approval, and not of authorship. Furthermore, the date of this distribution among Orthodox priests, i.e., in the week after the arrests of Pentecostals took place in Addis Ababa, indicates that the dissemination was not part of a concerted effort preceding the government action, but rather a reaction to current events.

While the official Orthodox affirmation of false rumors against Pentecostals lends itself to severe criticism in the persecution accounts,[99] the tendency to interpret the seal as a sign of authorship is another example for the marginalization of the government's agency in the construction of the persecutor, portraying it as a puppet in the hands of the Pentecostals' theological opponent.

More importantly, the presentation of the content of the circular in most accounts ignores its legal rationale. All narratives focus on repudiating the rumorous allegations of immorality, which were given much room in the circular, and thus undermine its overall credibility and the substance of the government orders. However, the main legal argument of the government is eclipsed by this reception, because it ultimately did not rest on the accusations of immorality but on the charge of illegal assembly. Moreover, this rationality probably was straightforwardly concealed in the reception process. This is evident when comparing the Amharic facsimile of the letter to its full translation provided in Engelsviken's report,[100] which apparently was not produced

---

98 Cf. SOLOMON KEDIR, Letter to Haile Giorgis Workeneh, Mayor of Addis Ababa, November 10, 1971, cf. GIRMA ZEWDE, ኢትዮጲስ, 142. This post-script also dates the copy obtained by the Pentecostals to September 1972 earliest. Engelsviken also mentions the distribution of the letter at such a conference, but erroneously dates the gathering to the fall of 1971, i.e., presumably immediately after the letter was written in November. The date for the conference given in the facsimile, however, is 22–26 ነሐሴ (nähase) 1964, which translates to the date provided above. The report about the assembly in the Addis Zaman also confirms this dating, see Addis Zaman, "የኢትዮጵያ ስብከያን ጉባኤ ተናነት ተጀመረ," [Assembly of Ethiopia's Preachers Begun Yesterday.], August 29, 1972, 1, 7.

99 ENGELSVIKEN, "Molo Wongel," 149, for example, calls the Orthodox seal "[m]aybe the most disgusting aspect of the whole letter", since "[i]t meant that it [the EOC] put all its spiritual authority behind the lies."

100 See ibid., 145–148. Two formal discrepancies must discussed when comparing the facsimile to the English translation as provided here. First, the date given in the English copy is "November 8, 1971" whereas the date on the facsimile (30 ነሐሴ [nähase] 1964) would translate to 10 November. It is not unlikely that this is a simple conversion error from the Ethiopian to the Gregorian calendar, especially in light of the fact that the preceding Ethiopian year was a leap year, pushing all dates back by one day in the following year. The second discrepancy is in the reference number, where the facsimile reads "2337/3077" and Engelsviken notes "2337/3072", which is likely to be a simple misreading of the last digit. Otherwise, one would have to

by the Norwegian himself, but probably was part of the information Pentecostals relayed to the press.[101] The opening paragraph of the letter, which establishes the main point of the writing, reads as follows in this English version:

> On October 1, 1967 we have sent you a copy of a letter, No. M/1492/3077 concerning the different churches in the country, especially the Pentecostal Christians who are meeting in various houses and who go preaching and singing around the city. The same copy has been sent and given to all the governors in order to urge them to take the Pentecostal Christians to court if they gather for prayer.[102]

The absence of any justification or legal argument for the government order "to take the Pentecostal Christians to court" does not cast a good light on the reasoning of the Imperial authorities. However, this is due to an important omission by the translator of the letter, since the Amharic original is more explicative with regard to the government's legal arguments:

> Concerning the Pentecostals or the Ancient Full Gospel Belief adherents and other similar preachers, we recall that a letter was written to the honorable provincial rulers and deputies on 2 November 1967 under the reference number M/1492/3077, which was made known to the town hall via copy, [stating that] considering the ensuing damages to society, the meeting houses established in different places were closed and they should not work without a permit, and having revealed the matter at the time to the preacher founders on 23 September 1967, [the letter further stated] that proper control was to be exercised on them so that they could not spread similar preaching while going around in the towns, and that steps should be taken against those working outside the order to bring them before the law.[103]

The translation thus omitted decisive parts of the government's original rationale for banning Pentecostal meetings and following up on the order later on. The meeting places were to be closed "considering the ensuing damage to society" and a permit was withheld. The feared "damage to society" apparently is what the letter intends to substantiate by subsequently relying on slanderous rumors about the Pentecostals. Furthermore, the founders of the movement had been orally informed before the written order had gone out, so that any legal action taken against them would be on account of defiance of government orders. By omitting both points in the translation,

---

assume that Solomon Kedir wrote two letters to the same recipients with the same structure, arguments, and largely the same content within two days, which certainly is the less likely hypothesis.

101 Engelsviken himself does not indicate whether he was provided with the translation or had produced it himself. However, earlier excerpts in *Newsweek* and the *Logos Journal* concur verbatim with the full text that Engelsviken provides, indicating that all three had a common source. See *Newsweek. International Edition*, "Persecuting the Sects," 32, *Logos Journal*, "Persecution in Ethiopia," 14.

102 ENGELSVIKEN, "Molo Wongel," 148.

103 SOLOMON KEDIR, Letter to Haile Giorgis Workeneh, Mayor of Addis Ababa, November 10, 1971, 1, cf. GIRMA ZEWDE, ኢትዮጵስ, 139.

the government order and the follow-up letter become much more arbitrary, and lose whatever internal justification they may have had. The letter therefore is not only used in Pentecostal discourse to point to the EOC as the main instigator of persecution, it also serves to further discredit or conceal the rationality of the government. The document's strong reliance on acrid gossip about the Pentecostals of course lent it to such use.

Altogether, there seems to be a tendency in the persecution narrative to assign the central agency of persecution to the EOC, thus identifying the church, not the state as the main persecutor. By marginalizing the Imperial government's role in the process, by focusing on refuting only its more questionable arguments, and by eclipsing legal argument it brought forth, the government's authority is delegitimized. At the same time, much of the intentionality and agency in the persecution process is ascribed to the EOC, from the speech of the patriarch to the church's supposed instigative role in turning the Imperial authorities against the Pentecostals. This may have corresponded with experiences of conflict between Pentecostals and Orthodox Christians, be it clergy or otherwise. However, when taking a closer look at the primary sources cited by these persecution narratives as evidence, the EOC's alleged central role and the Imperial government's lack of legal rationality is more difficult to sustain.

4.3   Identifying the Persecuted

In 1971 and 1972 the Imperial government not only pressured the FGBC, but other religious groups as well. It also imposed sanctions on Jehovah's Witnesses, Oneness Pentecostals, and even the Pentecostal missions, demonstrating its unawareness of the differences between these groups and cutting across established denominational boundaries with its actions. Therefore, it is of interest to investigate whether and how these boundary lines are re-established in historical accounts along with the identity of the persecuted community.

4.3.1   Excluding Heterodox Movements

With regard to the delimitation of the persecuted community, another important ommission can be observed in the translation of the government letter discussed above. The Amharic original mentions Jehovah's Witnesses three times as one of the target groups for the governmental concerns and actions. In the beginning it asserts that earlier the Jehovah's Witnesses had been effectively banned, but now they were revived by Pentecostalism and in fact spread alongside Pentecostal preaching. The next reference is made to the Jehovah's Witnesses in the context of an alleged lack of patriotism on behalf of the Pentecostals.[104] Finally, toward the end, the letter informs that steps preparing action have been taken against "these two illegal faiths, i.e., Pentecostals and Jehovah's Witnesses." None of these statements became part of

---

104   Unfortunately the facsimile is too fragmented in this area (bottom of p. 2) for a clear translation.

the English translation as quoted by Engelsviken, which gives the English government letter an exclusively Pentecostal focus.

A similar tendency can be found with regard to the actual arrests on August 27, 1972, which were not limited to Pentecostals only, but included a comparable amount of Jehovah's Witnesses as well.[105] Engelsviken, for example, though mentioning the detention of Jehovah's Witnesses,[106] immediately excluded them from the community of the persecuted:

> The adherents of the Jehovah's Witnesses had, however, mighty and influential friends with money who soon bailed them out of prison, and it is not known that anything more happened to them.[107]

Similarly, an early report stated that the Pentecostals received a worse treatment than the Jehovah's Witnesses, which is even ascribed to the arrival of the latter: "Later some Jehovah's Witnesses were brought in, and the Pentecostals were moved to worse conditions."[108]

The fact that Pentecostals and Jehovah's Witnesses were considered as similar by the government points to another issue that is usually omitted from persecution narratives: the Jesus Only movement and its anti-trinitarian theology. Oneness Pentecostalism arrived in Ethiopia in 1968 by way of two missionaries from the United Pentecostal Church (UPC). They succeeded in recruiting the effective and outspoken former FGBC evangelist Teklemariam Gezahegne for the movement, who subsequently founded the Apostolic Church of Ethiopia (ACE), which he still leads to this day. The measurable success of Oneness Pentecostalism, especially in the southern part of the country, brought the movement to public attention, and the name "United Pentecostal" had the potential of confusing all of Ethiopian Pentecostalism with anti-trinitarian doctrine. This concern was raised several times by the SPCM missionary Tage Johansson as the political tension built up in 1971 and 1972.[109] Already in April of 1971 he noted that the Jehovah's Witnesses are against the trinity, too, and that their missionaries had been expelled. He goes on to assert that all other difficulties the mission is having will be a "child's play" if the government decides to move against the United Pentecostal Mission, since it might be confused with other Pentecostals.[110]

---

105 ENGELSVIKEN, "Molo Wongel," 155-156 mentions 270 Pentecostals to 250 Jehovah's Witnesses; YOSIEF KIDANEWOLD, "The History of the Pentecostal Movement in Addis Abeba," 47 reports 295 Pentecostals of 480 arrests made that day according to the newspapers.

106 ENGELSVIKEN, "Molo Wongel," 155-156.

107 Ibid., 156.

108 *Life of Faith*, "Evangelicals Imprisoned in Ethiopia," October 14, 1972, 1.

109 Cf. JOHANSSON, Letter to Bo Hörnberg, April 23, 1971; TAGE JOHANSSON, Letter to Bo Hörnberg, 4 May 1971, Tage Johansson Collection, Pingstarkiv Kaggeholm, Ekerö; TAGE JOHANSSON, Letter to Bo Hörnberg, undated, probably April/May, 1972, 1972, Tage Johansson Collection, Pingstarkiv Kaggeholm, Ekerö; JOHANSSON, Letter to Bo Hörnberg, May 1, 1972; TAGE JOHANSSON, Letter to Bo Hörnberg, 12 May 1972, Tage Johansson Collection, Pingstarkiv Kaggeholm, Ekerö; TAGE JOHANSSON, Letter to Bo Hörnberg, 8 July 1972, Tage Johansson Collection, Pingstarkiv Kaggeholm, Ekerö.

110 JOHANSSON, Letter to Bo Hörnberg, April 23, 1971. Only eleven days later, he supplemented a statement by a Norwegian (probably Lutheran) missionary that the work of this particular

Such a confusion of Oneness Pentecostals with the SPCM was not unlikely for two additional reasons. First, Teklemariam Gezahegne had previously published a book with the help of the SPCM, which was now seen as a liability.[111] Secondly, a Finnish missionary who had fallen out with the Finnish Free Foreign Mission (FFFM), wrote a letter to the Ministry of Education in April of 1972, in which he voiced his discontent with the development of the Pentecostal missions and the independent movement.[112] The letter apparently brought forth the misinformed accusation that Kyösti Roininen of the FFFM, the SPCM, and the Ethiopian Pentecostals had collaborated "in the absurd attempt to establish the large spiritual organization called 'United Pentecostal Church'."[113] Tage Johansson was alarmed by this letter, especially since he knew that the missionary had also been orally questioned by the Ministry of Education, in which he "presumably said significantly more."[114] Consequently, Johansson directed some efforts to controlling the damage. In April/May he wrote to the emperor to "let him understand that we believe in the trinity"[115] and handed a statement of faith to different government agencies. At the same time he hoped that princess Tenagnework, who was informed about the differences between the "Jesus Only" movement and the other Pentecostal groups, would inform her father accordingly.[116] In July 1972, he mentioned that the letter was taken up by the mission committee in the Ministry of the Interior,[117] and that he had sent a card to the Emperors birthday in the name of the SPCM, wishing him "the blessing of God the Father, God the Son, and God the Holy Ghost."[118]

The concern not to be confused with Oneness Pentecostals apparently was also shared by members of the FGBC. Johansson noted that when a delegation from this church was asked during an audience with the emperor whether they were Pentecostal,

---

evangelist who had gone over to the UPC "has caused the eyes of the authorities to be on us [the SPCM] in particular," JOHANSSON, Letter to Bo Hörnberg, May 4, 1971.

111   According to Johansson, the missionary who facilitated the publication did not know Amharic, which was unfortunate, since the book contained some extreme teaching, for example, "that those who are not Spirit-baptized will go to hell," see JOHANSSON, "Angående förföljelsen i Etiopien," 3.

112   This letter, which almost caused the eviction of the Finnish missionaries Anna-Liisa and Sanfrid Mattsson, is mentioned in TILLANDER, *Näkymättömän lähettiläs*, 337; MANNINEN, *Mannisentie*, 136–138; JOHANSSON, Letter to Bo Hörnberg, May 1, 1972; JOHANSSON, Letter to Bo Hörnberg, May 12, 1972; JOHANSSON, Letter to Bo Hörnberg, July 8, 1972. The name of the missionary is not mentioned anywhere, but Johansson quotes a passage from the letter, which would identify him as Lauri Lähdeaho to observers familiar with the Finnish mission in Ethiopia: "In 1948 [(i.e., 1956)] according to the Ethiopian calendar, I began work in the St. Paul hospital . . .", JOHANSSON, Letter to Bo Hörnberg, May 12, 1972; see also TAGE JOHANSSON, Letter to Bo Hörnberg, 20 December 1972, Tage Johansson Collection, Pingstarkiv Kaggeholm, Ekerö; JOHANSSON, "Angående förföljelsen i Etiopien," 4. Apparently Höglund was involved in these accusations as well.

113   Quoted by JOHANSSON, Letter to Bo Hörnberg, May 12, 1972.

114   Ibid.

115   JOHANSSON, Letter to Bo Hörnberg, undated, probably April/May, 1972,

116   JOHANSSON, Letter to Bo Hörnberg, May 1, 1972.

117   JOHANSSON, Letter to Bo Hörnberg, July 8, 1972.

118   Johansson had no illusions that the Emperor would read and muse about his greetings, but hoped that the Secret Service would get his trinitarian message, interview no. 14.

some answered with "no" in fear of being identified with the United Pentecostal Mission.[119]

In the spring of 1972, Johansson reported that "[n]ow the authorities have really taken on the United Pentecostal (Jesus Only)," because the police had struck and destroyed their meeting place in Awasa and Teklemariam Gezahegne had been arrested.[120] After these brief words about what by other accounts was an extensive and brutal mob attack, in which Teklemariam even lost his six-month-old son,[121] Johansson immediately turns to hearsay regarding plans of the government to take actions against the SPCM, to the shutting down of the FFFM meeting place by the authorities, the closing of different smaller Pentecostal groups, and the intention to close the FGBC as well.[122] Thus, for Johansson, the actions against the Jesus Only movement were linked to a general government campaign against Pentecostals and other religious minorities.

The experience of the Oneness Pentecostals is, however, not reflected in any of the later persecution accounts. This is testimony to the complete alienation of the Jesus Only movement in trinitarian Pentecostalism and the histories it produced. Most sources do not make any references to Oneness Pentecostals at all, and the ones that do, leave them out of the persecution narrative. Engelsviken, for example, devoted a whole section to the Jesus Only movement in his chapter titled "Doctrine."[123] Here he notes that the political authorities were not "able to distinguish between the different groups of 'Pentecostals',"[124] and that "the relationship between the authorities and the Molo Wongel Church steadily deteriorated under the confusion caused by the United Pentecostals."[125] However, his subsequent chapter titled "Persecution" makes no reference to the United Pentecostals or their persecution experience at all, nor does he refer to perceived anti-trinitarianism when noting that Jehovah's Witnesses were arrested at the same time as Pentecostals and that "the authorities at the time were unable to distinguish clearly between the two groups."[126]

Similarly the FGBC history from 1978 does not mention the Oneness group in its persecution account. It is only after the conclusion of the persecution narrative, that the paper turns to doctrinal difficulties within the movement and reports the foundation of two churches preaching a "foreign gospel" in a section titled "Which kind of Pentecostal."[127] While the document is aware of the confusion such splits

119 See JOHANSSON, "Angående förföljelsen i Etiopien," 3.
120 JOHANSSON, Letter to Bo Hörnberg, undated, probably April/May, 1972,
121 Cf. the ACE history by Freeman (FREEMAN, *Unseen hands*, 139–143), which in general is a rather hagiographic account of Teklemariam's life, but probably accurately reflects the overall brutality of the Awasa incident.
122 According to Johansson, the latter did not materialize, since the leaders could convince the authorities that they were not "Jehovah's Witnesses or Jesus Only," JOHANSSON, Letter to Bo Hörnberg, undated, probably April/May, 1972,
123 ENGELSVIKEN, "Molo Wongel," 127–130.
124 Ibid., 129.
125 Ibid., 130.
126 Ibid., 156.
127 See ETHIOPIAN FULL GOSPEL BELIEVERS' CHURCH, ሙሉ ወንጌል ቤተ ክርስቲያን ከልደት እስከ ..., 25. The two churches that are alluded to here were the Oneness ACE, and the Gospel Deliverance Church (GDC).

would cause in estimating the doctrinal soundness of the mainstream Pentecostals, it also asserts that there was a common understanding of the differences between the Pentecostal groups:

> Therefore, when the rumor was heard that a certain man was "Pente", a question not known to be asked before now began to be asked: "Which kind of Pentecostal?"[128]

4.3.2 Excluding Other Christian groups

Most histories not only exclude doctrinally conflicting groups like the Jehovah's Witnesses or Oneness Pentecostals from their account, but the same tendency can also be observed with regard to the Pentecostal missions, who also encountered political difficulties in 1972 and 1973. In April 1972, the Finnish mission meeting place in Merkato was closed by the authorities and remained so for several weeks.[129] The SPCM missionary Tage Johansson suspected that this had to do with unfulfilled promises of a clinic, but also suggested that the timing was related to the tougher stance toward Pentecostals adopted by the government:

> Now that action was taken against the Pentecostals, the authorities considered that they could close the meeting place in the city, since they still did not have the clinic. [130]

The FFFM representatives evidently appealed to the emperor,[131] and soon resumed public meetings. When the FGBC chapels were closed in the summer, many Pentecostals came to the still open Finnish mission, despite the earlier difficulties with the mission. One FFFM missionary remembers the uneasiness with this return of believers on account of the political difficulties:

> When they closed their chapels first – the government closed some of them — they all wanted to come back to our place. And we had about two three thousand just hanging around the building. And we begged them not to come, because of the persecution. And the Orthodox church and the police, they were all watching us.[132]

On Sunday, April 1, 1973, the Finnish mission in Merkato was closed again, and nine people were arrested, including the British missionary serving as pastor.[133] The

---

128 ETHIOPIAN FULL GOSPEL BELIEVERS' CHURCH, *ሙሉ ወንጌል ቤተ ክርስቲያን ከልደት እስከ* ..., 25–26.
129 ROININEN, "A Condensed History of the Finnish Mission in Ethiopia," 7.
130 JOHANSSON, Letter to Bo Hörnberg, May 1, 1972. Johansson also speculated that the Finnish never had a proper meeting permit in Addis Ababa. Another context for the action were the above-mentioned accusations by a Finnish missionary against the FFFM that they had collaborated with the Oneness Pentecostal missionaries, cf. JOHANSSON, Letter to Bo Hörnberg, May 12, 1972; JOHANSSON, Letter to Bo Hörnberg, July 8, 1972.
131 JOHANSSON, Letter to Bo Hörnberg, undated, probably April/May, 1972,
132 Interview no. 102.
133 See *Logos Journal*, "Further News from Ethiopia," July–August 1973, 41. According to this article the arrests took place shortly after midnight. The small number of detainees supports the notion that the arrest took place outside a meeting time. JOHANSSON, "Angående förföljelsen i Etiopien" reports eight arrests, the missionary and seven Ethiopians.

people were released on bail right away, but the congregation in Addis Ababa remained closed for over a year.[134]

These events generally are not integrated into the persecution narratives. The only such attempt was made by the *Logos Journal*, which in the July–August issue of 1973 printed a follow-up letter to their report of the 1972 mass arrest of FGBC Pentecostals, mentioning the closure of the FFFM and the temporary arrests.[135] However, when the same letter was quoted by Engelsviken two years later, it is more or less in a passing reference and the year-long closure of the mission is not mentioned.[136] Even the brief FFFM history provided by Kyösti Roininen also does not set the two closures of the mission in 1972 and 1973 in a general persecution narrative, but rather briefly mentions them under the headline "The Expanding Work in the Midst of Growing Resistance."[137] In the same way, the histories written from the background of the Gennet Church (GC), which grew out of the work of the FFFM, also do not make any reference to the closures,[138] but begin their own persecution narrative with the Ethiopian experiences after the revolution of 1974.[139]

For the SPCM a similar observation can be made. In the beginning of 1973, the SPCM station in Jima came under pressure from the authorities demanding its closure.[140] The reason for this was a perceived association with the FGBC, invoked by the fact that one missionary had submitted an FGBC statement of faith to the authorities as the mission's own.[141] Furthermore, the SPCM had closely collaborated with the FGBC in the work in Jima, and had employed Assefa Alemu, one of the first Addis Ababa FGBC elders, as pastor for the Jima congregation in 1971.[142] After lengthy negotiations with government authorities, Tage Johansson managed to prevent the looming closure and was urged to obtain additional paperwork from the authorities in Addis Ababa. However, these difficulties are not mentioned anywhere outside the Swedish writings and histories.

---

134 ROININEN, "A Condensed History of the Finnish Mission in Ethiopia," 7. The Swedish missionary Tage Johansson again linked the closure to a permit issue, arguing that the permit was for a school, which the Finnish did not have on their premises, cf. TAGE JOHANSSON, Letter to brother Martin, 17 April 1973, Tage Johansson Collection, Pingstarkiv Kaggeholm, Ekerö; JOHANSSON, "Angående förföljelsen i Etiopien," 5.

135 *Logos Journal*, "Further News from Ethiopia."

136 ENGELSVIKEN, "Molo Wongel," 195–196.

137 ROININEN, "A Condensed History of the Finnish Mission in Ethiopia," 7.

138 Cf. esp. SELESHI KEBEDE, "The History of the Guenet Church"; ETHIOPIAN GENNET CHURCH, የ5ዐኛው ዓመት የወርቅ ኢዮቤልዩ በዓል.

139 Cf. e.g. ASHEBIR KETEMA, "The History of Ethiopian Guenet Church," 3–5.

140 Relations to the government had been difficult in the two years prior as well, cf. NYBERG OSKARSSON, *Svensk Pingstmission i Etiopien (1959–1980)*, 140–142.

141 Cf. TAGE JOHANSSON, Letter to Bo Hörnberg, 5 February 1973, Tage Johansson Collection, Pingstarkiv Kaggeholm, Ekerö. In addition Höglund had given some unfavorable statements when questions by the police, and the Jesus Only issue apparently played a role in this, ibid.

142 See NYBERG OSKARSSON, *Svensk Pingstmission i Etiopien (1959–1980)*, 134. JOHANSSON, "Angående förföljelsen i Etiopien," 5 calls Assefa the "founding pastor". However, relations between the SPCM and Assefa were not always smooth as Tage Johansson's correspondence shows, e.g. JOHANSSON, Letter to Bo Hörnberg, May 1, 1972; TAGE JOHANSSON, Letter to Bo Hörnberg, 21 June 1972, Tage Johansson Collection, Pingstarkiv Kaggeholm, Ekerö; TAGE JOHANSSON, Letter to Bo Hörnberg, 27 August 1972, Tage Johansson Collection, Pingstarkiv Kaggeholm, Ekerö.

Furthermore, there are examples of political pressure and limitations placed on Christian groups outside the Pentecostal fold. For example, in response to the 1972 arrests of FGBC Pentecostals, the English Brethren mission stopped holding public meetings in Addis Ababa after consulting with the Ministry of Education, because the permit for their headquarters did not explicitly allow for an assembly.[143] Moreover, in 1973 a number of Baptist congregations were targeted in southern Ethiopia and saw the arrests of some of their evangelists when they became independent of the Sudan Interior Mission (SIM).[144] None of these were mentioned in press publications about the arrests of Ethiopian Pentecostals nor in later persecution histories.

4.3.3 Profiling the Persecuted

In addition to delimiting the community of persecuted to the FGBC, this church is also presented as championing the fight for religious freedom in a number of accounts. This helps to underscore the antagonism between persecutor and persecuted: the failures of the government to administer justice and freedom of religion is precisely what the Pentecostals are portrayed to be fighting for in their persecution narrative. For example, the FGBC church history of 1978 provides the following account about the Sunday in April 1972 following the order to close all chapels:

> Being anxious to worship God and to listen to the Holy Word, the believers were streaming to the prayer house on Sunday morning. The leaders of the church and the police sent to enforce the law were saying that there would be no meeting and tried to get the people to return. The musicians stowed away their musical instruments and choir robes in one sister's car and stood there. The women, who were among those standing surprised at the situation, cried. Others: "Why? What have we done? Do we not have freedom of religion? Doesn't our Constitution allow religious meetings? What crime have we performed that was outside government regulations and the law?" As they poured out their tears of distress, the believers returned to their neighborhoods. However, the Holy Spirit fire lit by God, was not easily quenched by human power or influence.[145]

Though the leaders cooperated with the order to close the chapels and with the police sent to the site, the Pentecostal community is characterized with remarkable unity in their disappointment and call for justice. There is a uniform response to the closure: the women cry, while the inquiry of "others" only has one theme, namely, the legal justifications for the closure. In this way, the Pentecostal community is not only constituted by the encountered opposition and their shared grief, it is also characterized by one common goal: to champion the plight for freedom of religion and justice, which is denied to them by the government entities. However, once the political grievances are stated, there is no report of open defiance or hidden resistance. Instead, the believers pour out "tears of distress" and return home. This is where the Pentecostals encounter another authority coming to their aid, namely,

---

143   JOHANSSON, "Angående förföljelsen i Etiopien," 5.
144   Ibid.
145   ETHIOPIAN FULL GOSPEL BELIEVERS' CHURCH, ሙሉ ወንጌል ቤተ ክርስቲያን ከልደት እስከ ..., 18.

"the Holy Spirit fire," which is "not easily quenched by human power or influence." Therefore, while the community of persecuted is united around its grief and frustration with legal injustice, it is sustained by the Holy Spirit and prompted to uphold its purpose. The same theme resonates through the rest of the persecution account in this publication. Strengthened by the authority of the Holy Spirit movement, the Pentecostal community becomes a prime example of the fight for justice and religious freedom in imperial Ethiopia.

Similarly, Yosief Kidanewold quotes two of his informants who reported their feelings and achievements after the arrests in August 1972:

> We realized that the government has been corrupted. The Constitution written on paper was not true in practice. Previously we were calling Ethiopia our motherland. But the persecution had led us to question this sincerity. The first three or four days we were treated badly. However, there was only one dead among us. We were questioning some of their orders which was surprising to some of the guards. This helped in improving some strict rules in the jail. The jail was a place of deterioration instead of being a rehabilitation center.[146]

Once again, the mention of disappointment over the "corrupt" government serves to define the community of the persecuted in contrast to the state. Whereas before, the Pentecostals saw Ethiopia as "our motherland," the sincerity of their belonging now was in question because of the opposition by the state, setting the Pentecostals apart from the land they lived in. Yet, precisely in this forced opposition to the state, the narrative assumes a strongly defiant tone, signified most of all by the remarkably cynical phrase "However, there was only one dead among us."[147] In their new position of exile and defiance, the community of the persecuted is able to challenge the authority it is confronted with, and thus becomes a champion of justice and rehabilitation in an unjust system.

The FGBC is thus identified and profiled as the real persecuted community, the true counterpart of the persecutor. Though a number of other groups were targeted alongside the FGBC, the singularity of this church is affirmed by excluding other groups from the persecution account and by characterizing them it as the champion of the fight for freedom of religion, mirroring the injustices inflicted upon Christian minorities by the Ethiopian Empire.

4.4 Managing Persecution Politics

The arrests of 1972 were surrounded by involved and complex politics, within the Pentecostal community itself as well as in its external relations. Pentecostals are reported to have negotiated with the Emperor and the EOC in the time leading up to the arrests of 1972, they apparently argued over political strategies, took different paths in the legal aftermath of the arrests, managed international press contacts, and

---

146   Yosief Kidanewold, "The History of the Pentecostal Movement in Addis Abeba," 48.
147   This probably refers to a young man who died in the dire prison conditions when medical care for a probably preexisting illness was refused to him, cf. Engelsviken, "Molo Wongel," 166.

were drawn into international ecumenical politics extending as far as the WCC in Geneva.

4.4.1 Audiences and Negotiations

In the months leading up to the arrests, members of the FGBC managed to secure an audience with Haile Selassie in Addis Ababa on at least two occasions.[148] The first audience took place in December 1971, and reportedly was sought by the Pentecostals in response to the slanderous rumors about them.[149] As a result, the matter was deferred to a commission for further investigation, which eventually led to an official order by the Security Department in April 1972, mandating the closure of all FGBC meeting places. In response to the order, the Pentecostals went before the Emperor one more time where they failed to reverse the decision, but apparently were told to refrain from meetings until a further study would be undertaken.[150]

Despite the obvious political failure of these audiences with Haile Selassie, the Emperor is attributed with a positive attitude toward the Pentecostals in most historical accounts, where he even may be characterized as having assumed "the role of protector of all Christians [in] Ethiopia."[151] Sources note that when receiving Pentecostals in his Court, "he listened sympathetically to their story and seemed irritated by the action of the state church leaders."[152] Similarly, Engelsviken stated that the Pentecostals were under the impression that Haile Selassie "was personally sympathetic to their case and wanted to help them."[153] The failure to negotiate an agreement is instead attributed to the Imperial Court and the EOC. The Emperor was not "properly informed"[154], his advisors "either prevented the Emperor from getting all the information he needed or interfered with the carrying out of his orders,"[155] and most of all "[l]ater it was discovered that all the bishops and the patriarch himself had threatened to resign their positions if the Emperor gave full freedom to the independent evangelical churches."[156] The head of state, after all, was "almost 80 years

---

148 There probably were other encounters with the Emperor in different regions, like the above-mentioned audience in Debre Zeit, and apparently one in Asela, mentioned in BEKELE WOLD-EKIDAN, ራ፡ይ፡ሳ, 138.
149 *Logos Journal*, "Persecution in Ethiopia," 14 dated the audience to December, 26 and 27. (The first day was probably when the appointment was secured.) Cf. also ENGELSVIKEN, "Molo Wongel," 151–153.
150 Cf. *Logos Journal*, "Persecution in Ethiopia," 15; ENGELSVIKEN, "Molo Wongel," 154; ETHIOPIAN FULL GOSPEL BELIEVERS' CHURCH, ሙሉ ወንጌል ቤተ ክርስቲያን ከልደት እስከ . . . ; BEKELE WOLD-EKIDAN, ራ፡ይ፡ሳ, 138. *Logos Journal*, "Persecution in Ethiopia," 15 mentions two audiences, one on 21 April and one with 15 believers on 26 April.
151 ENGELSVIKEN, "Molo Wongel," 151–152.
152 *Logos Journal*, "Persecution in Ethiopia," 15.
153 ENGELSVIKEN, "Molo Wongel," 152.
154 *Kristeligt Dagblad*, "Pinsekirken forfølges stadig i Ethiopien," [The Pentecostal Church is Steadily Persecuted in Ethiopia.], November 3, 1972.
155 ENGELSVIKEN, "Molo Wongel," 152.
156 *Logos Journal*, "Persecution in Ethiopia," 15. The same claim is made by ENGELSVIKEN, "Molo Wongel," 153.

old at this time, and many were of the opinion that he was not any longer able to effectively control the acts of his men and see to it that his will was obeyed."[157]

While the contrast between Haile Selassie's apparently mostly sympathetic ear for the Pentecostals and the subsequent harsh actions of the government, will easily have suggested such a reading to the Pentecostals, this interpretation also successfully deprives the Emperor and the meetings with him of any political significance. The stories thus affirm that the most central power of Ethiopia's government is devoid of a political agency and rationale, leading to the assumption of different agents behind the scenes.

However, in 1972 the Pentecostal Christians not only tried to find a political solution in audiences with the emperor, they even met with leaders of the EOC. The SPCM missionary Tage Johansson reported on June 21, 1972:

> To cross over to a somewhat different matter, I met Kebede these days. [...]
> I heard that they recently have had meetings with a couple of factions of the
> Orthodox (Coptic) Church. The first meeting was with representatives of a
> reform-friendly part within the Orthodox Church. They are said to have offered
> the Addis congregation to work and preach within their framework, but they
> should also make concessions and compromises. Among others, they should
> certainly not baptize. The other meeting was with the conservative wing in the
> church and they by and large apparently had the same suggestion and demand.
> We shall see how this all unravels.[158]

With their chapels closed, the Pentecostals apparently explored all their options, including negotiating an arrangement of spreading renewal within the EOC. For Tage Johansson this was an interesting development, since as an expatriate missionary he had no interests of the Pentecostal movement clashing with the established religious order, which might turn the political authorities against his mission as well. In the same letter he also mentioned that the Ethiopian Pentecostals were interested in publishing about the closure of their chapels in the foreign press, and that they have been contacted by a journalist in this regard. Johansson considered this a dangerous move as this may lose them whatever sympathy remained in the imperial family and the government agencies. Therefore, the Swedish missionary welcomed direct negotiations with the EOC, as this may help him to convince the Pentecostals not to pursue a confrontational strategy. Thus his report is open and generally positive. Even the demand to refrain from baptizing, which had been a central practice of the mission as well,[159] is not dismissed or even marked as an issue of concern. Rather, Johansson concludes on a cautious but positive note: "We shall see how this all unravels."

---

157 Ibid., 152. The exception to this general narrative dismissing Haile Selassie as a political agent can be found in the recent FGBC history by Bekele Woldekidan (BEKELE WOLDEKIDAN, ፈያጺä, 134–139), holding the Emperor accountable for the attempt "to stop God's visit" to the country.

158 JOHANSSON, Letter to Bo Hörnberg, June 21, 1972, 2.

159 Believers' baptism had been an important part of the SPCM's teaching about the Christian initiation. Furthermore, in order to minimize the legal risks for the expatriate missionaries, the mission relied on Ethiopians performing the act, cf. above, 67.

When Engelsviken took up reports of these meetings three years later, there is no such optimism in his narrative nor in the sources he quotes.[160] Furthermore, the story is not even put in the context of the 1972 persecution, but is already told immediately after the declination of the FGBC's bid for registration. The negotiations thus have no part in the main persecution narrative, but are part of the preparatory events. Though Engelsviken sets out on a positive note here by reporting that "[o]ne of the most important" meetings was the one with the "progressive" Abba Habte Mariam, Dean of the Trinity Cathedral, he makes it clear from the start that there were demands that could not be met:

> Leaders in the orthodox church extended serious invitations to cooperations to the Pentecostals. They offered them freedom to travel around with a letter from the orthodox church and preach in its churches. However, there were certain strings attached. First of all they had to pass through a course to receive instruction about the customs and teachings of the orthodox church. They also had to commit themselves to teach in accordance with the traditions of the orthodox church. When the Pentecostals presented the message they felt obliged to preach, it turned out that the orthodox church was not interested at all.[161]

Unlike Johansson's hopeful outlook, Engelsviken does not see a genuine offer in these consultations. Though the invitation was "serious", it came with "certain strings attached" and the hierarchy "was not interested at all" in the message of the Pentecostals.

The Norwegian missiologist then immediately turns to the more adverse negotiations, with Qes Solomon, "leader of the Department of Preaching and a close friend of the acting patriarch", who according to Engelsviken represented "the most important contact with the hierarchy of the orthodox church."[162] Qes Solomon reportedly informed the Pentecostals that he knew that his opposition "came from the flesh, and that God did not like it, but he had to do it anyway" in order to prevent his church from being "empty in ten years."[163] The EOC representatives then are further reported to have threatened and invited the Pentecostals at the same time without offering to discuss theological differences, while the Pentecostals refused to give in. Engelsviken seems to mistrust his sources here somewhat,[164] and therefore subsequently sets out to demonstrate himself that there were "[s]erious doctrinal convictions at stake" and not just "youthful arrogance or selfish dreams of independence from authority."[165]

For demonstrating these theological differences, Engelsviken relied on interviews he conducted with Pentecostals specifically about their relation to the EOC, which may indicate that he had to turn to sources outside the meeting narratives in or-

---

160   ENGELSVIKEN, "Molo Wongel," 73–79.
161   Ibid., 73.
162   Ibid.
163   Ibid., 74.
164   He notes that the conversation "took place some years ago and is retold according to memory by one party," see ibid.
165   Ibid.

der to find theological arguments. Moreover, after extensively invoking a number of disagreements about the role of saints, the authority of the patriarch, education of priests, the relevance of Orthodox liturgy, priestly hypocrisy, salvation, the institution of the "soulfather," and more,[166] Engelsviken did not conclude with the recommendation of theological dialog, but returns to the church politics of the day, by quoting "a very important person in the orthodox church" allegedly revealing a long-term strategy that by repeatedly falsely accusing the Pentecostals of wrongdoing, they "will finally be convicted."[167] As if the theological differences had not been enough, the very intention and capability of the EOC for dialog is questioned. The othering of the "real" persecutor thus is complete: meetings with the hierarchy failed because of a lack of seriousness, there were irreconcilable theological differences, and instead of dialog options, the Pentecostals were faced with a political opponent willing to employ even false accusations instead of honest theological engagement.

In all the sources about the 1972 persecution, there are only two more brief references to the dialog efforts between Pentecostals and the Orthodox hierarchy. Yosief Kidanewold used the failed meetings as an example to substantiate the following assertion:

> Although the doctrinal issues should not be underestimated, the charges of the Orthodox leaders have not been directly based on them. Since the beginning of the Pentecostal movement, the major concern of the Ethiopian Orthodox leaders has been to prevent Orthodox youth from abandoning their faith in favour of joining the Full Gospel Church. To this end, the Orthodox leaders have resorted to every possible means to defend the faith even at the expense of defaming the Pentecostal movement.[168]

The most recent mention of the talks was provided by Tibebe Eshete, who simply notes that the contact ended in "disappointment."[169] According to Tibebe's informant, the reasoning of the patriarch to request the Pentecostals to "abandon their faith" was not driven by theology, but by a market analogy: "[W]hy do you seek to open a kiosk (a small shop) when there is already a large mall?"[170]

In comparing Tage Johansson's contemporaneous missionary perspectives with subsequent historic accounts about these ecumenical contacts, it is evident that the later sources give them a more marginal role. While Johansson apparently had been informed about them by the FGBC leaders themselves and had enough reason for an optimistic outlook, later histories, already looking back on the failed dialogs and the arrests of Pentecostals, either prefer not to mention that such meetings once had been an option, or use them as an example of a theological gap impossible to

---

166 Cf. ibid., 74–78.
167 Ibid., 78.
168 Yosief Kidanewold, "The History of the Pentecostal Movement in Addis Abeba," 44–45. After these lines Yosief relayed a report about a "talk with one of the popular Orthodox leaders," who informed the FGBC delegation that "he understood that what the Pentecostalists were saying was Biblical and correct," but that he would also "keep on using false and fabricated rumours against the movement in order to ensure the survival of Orthodoxy."
169 Tibebe Eshete, *The Evangelical Movement in Ethiopia*, 180.
170 Ibid.

bridge. Furthermore, instead of mentioning demands and theological arguments by the EOC, later accounts seem mostly interested in discrediting the intentions of the Orthodox representatives, suspecting malicious political intentions of a church that felt threatened by Pentecostal growth.

4.4.2 Defense Strategies

After the official closure of Pentecostal meetings in April 1972, most accounts simply note that the FGBC had complied with the government order and had resorted to smaller house meetings. However, on Sunday, August 21, 1972 between 250 and 270 Pentecostals were arrested in one place. A "house meeting" of this size needs an explanation, yet only very few sources have addressed this discrepancy. Engelsviken notes, for example, that the believers "reckoned they were safe in a house belonging to a member of the imperial family," because the house they were meeting in belonged to one of Haile Selassie's grandchildren, Princess Sophia, and was rented by a third party.[171] Yet, even though Engelsviken was aware of the size of the meeting and the fact that it was not conducted in the home of one of the Pentecostal believers, he did not address the fact that this was not in keeping with the strategy of the church he recorded just one page before, i.e., to divide "the church in small groups which should continue to meet in the homes."[172]

However, there are a number of indications that the rounded up meeting was not simply a house meeting that had grown out of control, but a deliberate and controversial attempt to resume public worship. One of the leaders of the time pointed to such intentions in an interview:

> We told them that you should not be more than twenty or thirty. But some didn't listen to us. And in one place there were four hundred at one time. This was underground. Finally the government came to know about it, and they got the big truck and took all to prison, four hundred of them.[173]

Similarly, Tage Johansson asserted in a letter that the meeting was based on a deliberate decision to hold public meetings, and a controversial one at that. Already reporting about the rounded up meeting on the day of the arrests, he mentioned that the preceding Friday he had advised one of the elders against resuming meetings before they could have another audience with the emperor and that the FGBC elders had a heated discussion about the matter the next day, in which the proponents of conducting Sunday public services won the upper hand.[174] A few days later he reported that he heard that one of the elders had long planned to resume public meetings. Johansson immediately notes that "this is a grave matter" and that an-

---

171 ENGELSVIKEN, "Molo Wongel," 155. The site apparently was rented by a British Christian nurse who operated a kindergarten there. She allowed the FGBC to conduct their Sunday meetings on the premises, reportedly with the Princess' consent.
172 Ibid., 154.
173 Interview no. 91.
174 Cf. JOHANSSON, Letter to Bo Hörnberg, August 27, 1972. Writing on the evening of the arrests, Johansson does not yet seem to be aware of the scale of the police action or the severity of the incident. He only turns to the matter toward the end of his letter and simply notes that "Filippus and some [others] were detained by the police."

other elder was "absolutely against getting started."[175] Furthermore he recites the Ethiopian government's position that this was not a "Christian meeting," but an "assembly without permission." Only two days later he reiterated that there was no unity in the leadership of the congregation about starting "a meeting of this scale", that there was opposition against this move from within, that he himself had warned the Ethiopians, and that according to one of his contacts many Pentecostals were simply immature.[176]

While the controversial decision to resume large Sunday services apparently continued to be debated after the arrests, the detainees were met with a prosecution strategy which was not conducive to Pentecostal unity. After being held outside the police station for three days,[177] the group was hauled to the district court and presented with the charge of illegal assembly. The ones pleading guilty to the charge were immediately sentenced to a fine of 50 to 200 Ethiopian dollars, whereas the others at first were denied the right of bail and brought to jail, which, given the conditions of Ethiopian prisons, was a disturbing experience for the young students.[178] In the subsequent weeks they were tried in smaller subgroups and received a jail sentence of six months.[179] Most of the sentenced Pentecostals immediately appealed the ruling to the High Court, which led to their release on bail in the weeks to follow. By the beginning of January 1973, only two Pentecostals were left in prison, both of whom had decided not to pursue their case further but to simply serve the sentence.[180] The High Court's final verdict from July 18, 1973 upheld the ruling of the District Court, but suspended the sentence in favor of a probation period strictly forbidding the defendants to conduct further meetings or participate therein.[181]

These different trajectories that Pentecostals followed in the legal aftermath of the arrests are of course a challenge to the assumption of political uniformity within the persecuted community. While the two prisoners who had decided against the appeal and for serving their sentence, were not publicly visible and therefore could be

---

175   TAGE JOHANSSON, Letter to Bo Hörnberg, 2 September 1972, Tage Johansson Collection, Pingstarkiv Kaggeholm, Ekerö.

176   See TAGE JOHANSSON, Letter to Bo Hörnberg, 4 September 1972, Tage Johansson Collection, Pingstarkiv Kaggeholm, Ekerö.

177   ETHIOPIAN FULL GOSPEL BELIEVERS' CHURCH, ሙሉ ወንጌል ቤተ ክርስቲያን ከልደት እስከ ..., 20 speaks of even four days and nights.

178   Apparently many of them were released on bail before their final trial in October, cf. ENGELSVIKEN, "Molo Wongel," 192.

179   Comparing this ruling to the provisions of the Penal Code art. 476, cf. above, 6, it seems that the court considered the group refuting the charge as "ringleaders, organizers or commanders", thereby eligible to the maximum punishment of six months in prison, whereas the compliant ones were fined with less than the maximum possible fine.

180   See TAGE JOHANSSON, Letter to Bo Hörnberg, 10 January 1973, Tage Johansson Collection, Pingstarkiv Kaggeholm, Ekerö; JOHANSSON, Letter to Petrus Hammerberg, January 24, 1973.

181   Engelsviken states that the probation was three years, whereas FGBC sources indicate one to two years, cf. ENGELSVIKEN, "Molo Wongel," 208; ETHIOPIAN FULL GOSPEL BELIEVERS' CHURCH, ሙሉ ወንጌል ቤተ ክርስቲያን ከልደት እስከ ..., 23; ADDIS ABABA FULL GOSPEL BELIEVERS' CHURCH, የ40ኛ ዓመት የወንጌል አገልግሎትና የምስጋና በዓል መጽሐት /ሕምሌ 1958–1998 ዓ.ም./, 13. A further appeal was not possible in the Ethiopian legal system.

ignored by historical narratives,[182] the group pleading guilty and accepting the fine in the first hearing apparently was more of a challenge. Though by many accounts they were a minority, they also were the first ones to be released, and their guilty plea could suggest to observers that parts of the Pentecostal community recognized the illegitimacy of their meeting. Therefore, many sources chose to employ different strategies of neutralizing the "guilty" pleas. First of all, most accounts assert that it was only a small fraction of detainees who accepted the charge of meeting illegally.[183] Numbers are of course notoriously difficult to obtain in this regard. One article references a group trial of sixty-one Pentecostals, in which fifty defendants pleaded not guilty.[184] Yosief Kidanewold also insisted that "[v]ery few" pled guilty, though according to his numbers only 165 of originally 295 arrests remained in custody.[185] Another strategy to neutralize the "guilty" pleas is to reiterate why the only justifiable plea was "not guilty," and why a dissenting vote would be due to some sort of misunderstanding. For example, a letter written by FGBC leaders to the World Assembly of the United Bible Societies, which convened in Addis Ababa in September 1972, is quoted by Engelsviken with the following statements:

> Some who admitted they were "guilty" (though it was not clear to them or to anyone else of what they were guilty) were fined, some as much as $200, and released. But most claimed that they were not guilty, pointing out that in Ethiopia there was supposed to be freedom of worship and religion.[186]

Ignoring the actual legal matter at stake, i.e., the control of associations, the Pentecostals based their case on the constitutionally guaranteed right of freedom of religious practice. To plead guilty thus either meant to forfeit this right or to admit that the meetings were not of a religious nature, both of which are illegitimate options for the Pentecostal narrative. Therefore, another early account, after presenting essentially the same argument, simply concludes: "Hence committed Pentecostals did not feel it right to plead 'guilty'."[187]

With the legal proceedings for the remainder of the detainees still pending and increased efforts to alert the international public to the Ethiopian situation, it was important to protect the Pentecostal legal argument, especially against dissenting votes from within the persecuted community, even at the expense of their alienation.

---

182   Tage Johansson is the only source mentioning these two dissenting cases, see JOHANSSON, Letter to Bo Hörnberg, January 10, 1973; JOHANSSON, Letter to Petrus Hammerberg, January 24, 1973.

183   Cf. e.g. *Life of Faith*, "Evangelicals Imprisoned in Ethiopia"; *Kristeligt Dagblad*, "Pinsekirken forfølges stadig i Ethiopien"; RAYNER, "Persecution in Ethiopia"; ENGELSVIKEN, "Molo Wongel," 156.

184   *Kristeligt Dagblad*, "Pinsekirken forfølges stadig i Ethiopien" citing the government newspaper *Addis Zaman*, cf. *Addis Zaman*, "በሕግ የተከለከለ ማኅበር አቋቁመው ተሰበሰቡ የተባሉ 480 ሰዎች ተከሰሱ," [480 People Indicted, Said to Have Established and Assembled in an Association Forbidden by the Law.], September 1, 1972, 1.

185   See YOSIEF KIDANEWOLD, "The History of the Pentecostal Movement in Addis Abeba," 47. The fact that this would mean that not very few, but 130 of the detainees pled "guilty" is not reflected by the author.

186   ENGELSVIKEN, "Molo Wongel," 157–158.

187   *Life of Faith*, "Evangelicals Imprisoned in Ethiopia."

Four years later, however, with Haile Selassie's government abolished and the FGBC celebrating its joint building effort, the description of the same event is given in a significantly more conciliatory tone, paired with a more nuanced legal argument:

> After the defendants had been individually called by name on the base of these charges and asked about themselves, the question was brought before them: "Are you guilty or not?" Then they answered: "You have found me worshiping God, singing and praying on the basis of freedom of religion; but you have not found me establishing an association." Every once in a while some answered: "Yes, I am guilty." While the majority of the defendants revealed that they did not believe they were guilty, the few who believed in their "guilt" chose to plead "guilty" without having committed a crime, because they thought of their children abandoned at home, remembered that they had a large responsibility if harm would befall their land or kin, or some because they had attended prayer meeting for the first time and had been invited to hear the gospel of salvation.[188]

While these statements labor for a better understanding of those pleading guilty, the better option of course is still considered not to comply. Tage Johansson offered a very different perspective. In a letter written only eight days after the arrests, he noted:

> Some are free now, since they paid a fine. Others do not want to recognize that they were wrong in having an illegal meeting.[189]

Though it is unclear whether Johansson's internal comments only reflect his own sentiments or also those of his informants from within the movement, it is apparent that the only justifiable strategy for Johansson was one of compliance. He therefore developed a critical attitude toward the political strategy of the majority group and saw no merit in pursuing the issue legally. In an internal manuscript of 1974, titled "Regarding the Persecution in Ethiopia," he wrote:

> We again brought forth the desirability to seek for an audience with the Emperor during the fall, but some elders considered that they should fight through the different court authorities to the highest court. They did not understand if they did that, the emperor would still remain the last authority, and therefore they could just as well save many thousand dollars in attorney fees and go directly to him, so that he, who earlier had been their friend, would not get the impression that they ignore him and go to the foreign press.[190]

---

188 ETHIOPIAN FULL GOSPEL BELIEVERS' CHURCH, ሙሉ ወንጌል ቤተ ክርስቲያን ከለደት አስከ ..., 20.
189 JOHANSSON, Letter to Bo Hörnberg, September 4, 1972.
190 JOHANSSON, "Angående förföljelsen i Etiopien." The dating of the manuscript is uncertain. It mentions events from the fall of 1973 with some distance and therefore should be dated to at least 1974. At the same time, a much later date would not make sense, since the revolution would have canceled the significance of a document carefully considering the political constellations in imperial Ethiopia.

4.4.3 International Press Relations

The remarks by Johansson touch upon another critical political issue, namely, the publicity strategy of the Pentecostals. In addition to pressing the matter legally and seeking political and ecumenical contacts inside and outside of Ethiopia, a number of Pentecostals tried to enlist the help of international journalists. While later Pentecostal sources occasionally point to the articles published about their case, the activities involved in attracting such journalistic attention are usually not explored.[191] One of the first elders of the group, for example, after mentioning the widespread *Newsweek* article in an interview, immediately insisted that "when God moves, he attracts his own storytellers."[192]   Therefore, the initiatives taken by the Pentecostals are only visible in the sources presenting more of a political narrative, i.e., most importantly Engelsviken's "Documentary Report" and Tage Johansson's correspondence. The latter is especially helpful in elucidating the dynamics of Pentecostal politics in this regard, since the internal nature of his remarks and his critical attitude toward a more confrontational strategy led him to employ dissenting votes for his narrative.

As the main contact to Swedish Pentecostalism, Johansson apparently felt under pressure from two sides to facilitate press reports: from Ethiopian Pentecostals, who were seeking to recruit him in mobilizing the international press,[193] as well as from his Swedish supporters, who wanted to publish the case. Only eight days after the arrests he wrote to the Jönköping pastor in response to his question "What can we do?"[194] Johansson mentioned that he had discussed publishing in the foreign press with one of the FGBC elders, who had advised against this option. He further noted that this could have dire consequences for innocent people, and that judging from earlier articles in the *Dagen*, he does not trust the editorial staff to understand the risks their articles may entail while the benefit of "sensational articles" are unclear. Apparently Johansson succeeded in preventing a Swedish publication during the first months.[195] Johansson's fears about the repercussions of Swedish publications were confirmed in the following months when Höglund translated an article from another Swedish Christian newspaper, and sent it to the Ministry of Education claiming it

---

191   Cf. e.g. Ethiopian Full Gospel Believers' Church, ሙሉ ወንጌል ቤተ ክርስቲያን ከለደት እስከ ..., 23–24; Girma Zewde, ኢትዮጲስ, 136; Ethiopian Full Gospel Believer's Church, የኢትዮጵያ ሙሉ ወንጌል አመኞች ቤተ ክርስቲያን 25ኛ ዓመት በዓል, 12.

192   Interview no. 47.

193   In Johansson, "Angående förföljelsen i Etiopien" he notes that he told an elder that in order to help with press publications, he would first have to resign as mission representative in order not to disappoint his "friends" in the Ministry of Education, who had helped the mission at various times.

194   Johansson, Letter to Bo Hörnberg, September 4, 1972.

195   Engelsviken, "Molo Wongel" contends that the *Dagen* published the first article on the persecution on September 13, 1972, but while this particular issue contained a piece about the pilot Ragnar Ljungquist in Ethiopia, there is no mention of any persecution of Pentecostals. See *Dagen*, "Ragnar Ljungquist i Etiopien: Piloten börjar flygturen med att bedja till Gud," [Radnar Ljungquist in Ethiopia: The Pilot Begins the Flight by Praying to God.], September 13, 1972, 5. Ethiopia turns up in the newspaper every now and then in the following months, but the first article about the arrest of Ethiopian Pentecostals actually did not appear until December 6. See Lars Dunberg, "Kristna fängslade i Etiopien," [Christians Imprisoned in Ethiopia.], *Dagen*, December 6, 1972, 3.

had been published in the Pentecostal *Dagen*.[196] Johansson's opposition to foreign publication is also visible in the Swedish Pentecostal periodical *Evangelii Härold*. It is not until during the revolution of 1974 that the periodical makes mention of the 1972 arrests, in an article by Tage Johansson himself.[197]

However, the opposition of Ethiopian Pentecostals to international press publications, which Johansson occasionally cited, probably was not the majority view of Ethiopian Pentecostals. In October 1972, he wrily commented on the hopes placed in publicity and the efforts directed toward it from the beginning on:

> With regard to whether or not to publish in newspapers, I believe that some here almost have too much faith in that. If this had helped, the matter would be resolved by now, since journalists are said to have gotten hold of the matter already in the first week. There are plenty of journalists in Addis from what I have heard.[198]

If indeed journalists had learned of the affair in the first week, like Johansson claimed with regard to a Reuters journalist,[199] his estimation that the Pentecostal publication strategy was not met with much success at the beginning seems to be correct. The story was first picked up by a number of smaller Christian newspapers, and from there it bubbled up to the more influential press organs over time. The first article was printed in the Norwegian Christian daily *Vårt Land* on September 15, 1972.[200] This paper also printed several updates on the situation in the course of the next days and weeks, highlighting the interest and activities of the Norwegian Lutheran Church during this time.[201] On October 14, the British Holiness paper

---

196 See JOHANSSON, Letter to Bo Hörnberg, December 20, 1972. Apparently the Dagen prompted other Swedish newspaper articles about the persecution. According to Johansson, Höglund had received a clipping from the Christian daily, *Hemmets Vän*, by way of "a good soul", and promptly translated it and sent it to the Ministry of Education, claiming it had been published in the Pentecostal paper *Dagen*. Johansson apparently had good contacts in the Ministry, was informed about the document and managed to avert damage. The letter of December 20 also mentions the recent *Dagen* article: "...even if he passes on the article in the *Dagen*, we trust that we can clear this up with the Lord's help."

197 TAGE JOHANSSON, "Etiopien – problemfyllt land: Men väckelsetider väntas," [Ethiopia – a Country Full of Problems: But a Time of Revival is Expected.], *Evangelii Härold* (37 1974): 2–4, 22.

198 TAGE JOHANSSON, Letter to Bo Hörnberg, 6 October 1972, Tage Johansson Collection, Pingstarkiv Kaggeholm, Ekerö. Later Johansson noted that when he informed the elders that he was not a suitable person to forward material to the press, they told him that "all the material" had already been given to people who could do so.

199 JOHANSSON, "Angående förföljelsen i Etiopien," 4.

200 See *Vårt Land*, "Kristne forfølges i Etiopia," [Christians Persecuted in Ethiopia.], September 15, 1972, 1, 15.

201 See ibid.; *Vårt Land*, "Forfølgelsene i Etiopie: 'Spanningen har vært der lenge,"' [Persecution in Ethiopia: "Tensions had been there for a long time."], September 16, 1972, 1,15,23; *Vårt Land*, "Protest mot forfølgelse," [Protest Against Persecution.], September 18, 1972, 3; *Vårt Land*, "Må skaffe oss solide opplysninger om Etiopia: Biskop Lønning til Addis – undersøker om kristenforfølgelser," [Must Obtain Solid Information about Ethiopia for Ourselves. Bishop Lønning to Addis – Investigation of Persecution of Christians.], September 20, 1972, 1; *Vårt Land*, "'Forfølgelsen av de unge kristne ikke typisk for situasionen i Etiopia.'," ["Persecution of the Young Christians is not Typical for the Situation in Ethiopia."], September 22, 1972, 2; *Vårt Land*, "Biskop Lønning hjem fra Etiopia: Religionsforfølgelsene blir kanskje løst ved norsk

Life of Faith followed suit.[202] November saw a long article in the Danish *Kristeligt Dagblad*, a mention in the East African church organ *Target*, and most importantly in the American periodical *Christianity Today*.[203] However, as Engelsviken notes, "the news of the persecution in Ethiopia did not reach the world at large until January 1973"[204] when the international edition of the American *Newsweek* magazine reported about the arrests.[205] The international edition of *Newsweek* was not sold in the USA, but it was circulated worldwide including the streets of Addis Ababa, and therefore had the most visible impact in Ethiopia and prompted the above-mentioned reply in the *Ethiopian Herald*.[206] However, all this press attention came with no visible benefit for the Pentecostals, and the only journal to follow up on their case appears to have been the American Pentecostal periodical *Logos Journal*.[207]

Johansson's opposition to the Pentecostal publicity attempts were not just based in the dangers he feared for the mission and their obvious failure in generating the desired results. He considered it to be an integral part of a failed and controversial strategy of confrontation, which according to him was paired with personal interests and advantages:

> One of the elders, who, as I have found out, privately received 4,000 dollars from an Englishman who wanted to publish about the persecution, then said to me that "we absolutely do not need any intercession before the Emperor." He himself was not in danger, and he had received this large sum privately and could have thought of others. Many of the ones who had been in the meeting when the arrests happened, would certainly not have gone if they had known about the Emperor's answer during the unsuccessful audience. But the leaders probably believed that they could ignore this.[208]

---

initiativ," [Bishop Lønning Home from Ethiopia: Religious Persecution Can Perhaps be Solved through Norwegian Initiative.], October 6, 1972, 1, 19; *Vårt Land*, "Unge kristne dømmes i disse dager," [Young Christians are Judged These Days.], October 27, 1972, 1, 19. Cf. also ENGELSVIKEN, "Molo Wongel," 192, quoting the last article.

202 *Life of Faith*, "Evangelicals Imprisoned in Ethiopia."
203 *Kristeligt Dagblad*, "Pinsekirken forfølges stadig i Ethiopien"; *Target*, "Persecution in Ethiopia?" November 25, 1972, 12; RAYNER, "Persecution in Ethiopia."
204 ENGELSVIKEN, "Molo Wongel," 187.
205 The sources behind this article are unclear, but the many inaccuracies it contains suggest that the information took a complex route. The *Christianity Today* article as the most likely source is too dissimilar to have been used by *Newsweek*.
206 Cf. above, 154. Though Johansson notes that the rumors spread about the Pentecostals in the reply in the *Ethiopian Herald* were not worse than what was spread in the press before, it was the first time that the English edition carried a piece lashing out against Pentecostals, cf. TAGE JOHANSSON, Letter to Bo Hörnberg, 24 January 1973, Tage Johansson Collection, Pingstarkiv Kaggeholm, Ekerö.
207 See *Logos Journal*, "Persecution in Ethiopia"; *Logos Journal*, "Further News from Ethiopia." According to Engelsviken the Ethiopian Pentecostals had written a number of letters to the editor of *Logos Journal*, Dan Malachuk, see ENGELSVIKEN, "Molo Wongel," 194–196. The contact most likely came by way of Mattsson-Boze who had handed over his *Herald of Faith* to Malachuk's Logos International in 1971, see ROBERTS LIARDON, *The Azusa Street Revival: When the Fire Fell – An In Depth Look at the People, Teachings, and Lessons* (Shippensburg, PA: Destiny Image, 2006), 215.
208 JOHANSSON, "Angående förföljelsen i Etiopien," 4.

While Johansson's accusations of personal advantages at the expense of others are impossible to verify, it is interesting that despite his strong criticism and even such harsh allegations, he later on participated in veiling Pentecostal politics and disunity in the production of persecution histories. In 1974 Tormod Engelsviken approached Johansson for some information regarding the SPCM and the independent Pentecostal movement while he was working on his *Documentary Report* in the USA.[209] Engelsviken asked a number of specific questions, among others dealing with the persecution of 1972, and inquired if there were any points in need of correction on behalf of the Ethiopian Pentecostals.[210] Johansson's reply is in stark contrast to his internal remarks. He answered that "the leadership of Full Gospel in Addis had, according to my opinion, very fine teachers," and that they instructed everybody to behave wisely, which later was not heeded by "one or another group which absolutely did not belong to Full Gospel."[211] Even his most important misgiving in the internal document, i.e. the refusal to seek justification with the Emperor, is glossed over in this letter:

> When the persecution came, I and some Finnish missionaries offered to seek an audience with the emperor, but this did not take place. Different viewpoints about different matters can of course be brought forth, but I will not go into that.[212]

This striking difference between Johansson's letter to Engelsviken and his internal remarks must of course be understood in the context of the persecution situation itself. His reluctance to disclose internal difficulties to an outside observer, reveals Johansson's concern about the Pentecostals' security when he wrote these lines only two years after the event and in the midst of the Ethiopian revolution.[213] This points to an important external factor leading to veiling of political intentions and conflicts in the creation of persecution stories.

4.4.4 Ecumenical Deliberations

One final and instructive example for the management of politics in the persecution discourse can be found in the ecumenical aftermath of the arrests, which extended all the way to the WCC.[214] Already in the beginning of September, ecumenical contacts

---

209 The two missionaries apparently had not met during Engelsviken's stay in Ethiopia. Engelsviken had sent his request to the Philadelphia Church mission secretary in Stockholm, who forwarded it to Tage Johansson, see TAGE JOHANSSON, Letter to Tormod Engelsviken, 6 July 1974, Tage Johansson Collection, Pingstarkiv Kaggeholm, Ekerö.
210 See TORMOD ENGELSVIKEN, Letter to Tage Johansson, 13 July 1974, Tage Johansson Collection, Pingstarkiv Kaggeholm, Ekerö.
211 TAGE JOHANSSON, Letter to Tormod Engelsviken, 8 September 1974, Tage Johansson Collection, Pingstarkiv Kaggeholm, Ekerö.
212 Ibid.
213 These concerns are clearly stated in his request for the letter to "be kept totally private and not be deposited anywhere else but in your file," see ibid. In his earlier and first answer to Engelsviken he also requested to see the manuscript before publication, see JOHANSSON, Letter to Tormod Engelsviken, July 6, 1974.
214 The following statements are based on the extensive account provided by ENGELSVIKEN, "Molo Wongel," 169–184; 200–207; 211-213, supported by further research in the somewhat fragmented Geneva archives of the WCC. Most of the documents cited below could be obtained

were initiated with Norwegian Lutherans. Engelsviken notes that this happened at
the consent of the Ethiopian Pentecostals:

> The line of action that ultimately was decided upon by the Pentecostals them-
> selves and by missionaries who wanted to assist them in their struggle, was to
> appeal to Christians outside Ethiopia ...[215]

From September 25 to 29, 1972, the first World Assembly of the United Bible
Society (UBS) was hosted in Addis Ababa, which was a highly public affair. It was
opened with a speech by Emperor Haile Selassie and with a benediction by the EOC
patriarch Theophilos. Among the 170 delegates were high-ranking representatives of
the EOC, and the meeting received considerable attention in the government newspaper *Ethiopian Herald* in six articles from September 14–30, four of which were on the
front page.[216] The two Norwegian representatives to the assembly, the general secretary of the Norwegian Bible Society, Rev. Birger Mathisen, and Lutheran bishop Dr.
Per Lønning, were charged by the Norwegian bishops to investigate the situation of
the Ethiopian Pentecostals while in Addis Ababa.[217] They established contact with
the FGBC, visited one of their underground meetings,[218] and discussed the matter
with the Minister of Agriculture, who also was the chairman of the Bible Society
of Ethiopia at the time.[219] The Norwegian activities at the UBS assembly raised
public awareness for the Pentecostals, which was an undesirable development for the
Ethiopian government and Orthodox clergy and according to Engelsviken resulted in
considerable tension at the assembly.[220]

The Norwegian delegates, together with Dr. Laton Holmgren, the general secretary
of the American Bible Society, brought up the possibility of taking the matter to the
WCC, which according to Engelsviken originated with the Ethiopian Pentecostals
themselves. He quotes a written statement read at the closing session of the UBS
council:

---

from the archives and are quoted directly, unless the corresponding note explicitly states
"referenced/quoted by Engelsviken."

215   ENGELSVIKEN, "Molo Wongel," 172.
216   Cf. *The Ethiopian Herald*, "United Bible Societies World Assembly Here," September 14,
1972, 1, 2; *The Ethiopian Herald*, "World Assembly of United Bible Societies to be Held Here
Soon," September 19, 1972, 1, 8; *The Ethiopian Herald*, "U.B.S: Assembly Opens Tomorrow,"
September 24, 1972, 3, 10; *The Ethiopian Herald*, "His Majesty Opens First UBS Assembly,"
September 26, 1972, 1, 7; *The Ethiopian Herald*, "Let the Word Speak," September 27, 1972,
2; *The Ethiopian Herald*, "1st World Assembly of United Bible Societies Ends at Africa Hall,"
September 30, 1972, 1, 2.
217   See also *Vårt Land*, "Må skaffe oss solide opplysninger om Etiopia"; *Vårt Land*, "Biskop Lønning hjem fra Etiopia: Religionsforfølgelsene blir kanskje løst ved norsk initiativ."
218   The contact between the groups probably was facilitated by Knut Sigurd Aasebø and Ogbazghi
Sium, who also attended the UBS assembly, see *The Ethiopian Herald*, "United Bible Societies
World Assembly Here"; OGBAZGHI SIUM, E-mail to author, 15 July 2008.
219   Cf. ENGELSVIKEN, "Molo Wongel," 176–179; also JOHANSSON, Letter to Bo Hörnberg, October 6, 1972; JOHANSSON, "Angående förföljelsen i Etiopien." During their discussion the two
Norwegians apparently also threatened the Minister with the consequences of negative publicity.
220   Cf. ENGELSVIKEN, "Molo Wongel," 178.

Moreover we have received word from some of our Pentecostal friends who have expressed their deep gratitude for our interventions on their behalf and who urge us to continue our efforts after returning home by giving their plight suitable publicity, asking Bishop Lønning and Mr. Mathisen to report the situation in full to the World Council of Churches, which seems to be the appropriate body to take the necessary steps.[221]

Around the same time, the Ethiopian Pentecostals wrote a letter to Canon Burgess Carr, the general secretary of the All Africa Conference of Churches (AACC) on September 27, while the UBS meeting was still going on. However, this letter never received an answer.[222]

Upon the return of the Norwegian representatives, the Council on Foreign Relations of the Church of Norway requested the Assembly of Bishops "to take an initiative with the World Council of Churches."[223] On November 9, the Assembly wrote a letter to the newly inaugurated general secretary of the WCC, Dr. Philip Potter,[224], requesting him to contact the EOC in order to "clear away misunderstandings."[225] At the same time, there were initiatives by the American Bible Society to alert the WCC.[226] Furthermore, the Norwegian initiative found full support in Denmark, articulated by Johannes Langhoff, bishop of the Copenhagen diocese and member of the Central Committee of the WCC, who on November 17 notified Dr. Potter of his endorsement for the Norwegian appellation to the WCC.[227] In Denmark and Norway the political initiatives were accompanied by WCC critical articles in Christian newspapers.[228]

The WCC moved quickly to investigate the matter. On November 26, the Executive Secretary of the WCC Commission of the Churches on International Affairs, Eduardo Bodipo-Malumba, who apparently was entrusted with studying the case, went to Ethiopia to undertake an investigation, together with Kodwo Esuman Ankrah,

---

221 Ibid., 179. Johansson notes that the idea was raised first during the UBS assembly and met with approval by Pentecostals, see JOHANSSON, Letter to Bo Hörnberg, October 6, 1972.

222 Quoted in part by ENGELSVIKEN, "Molo Wongel," 172–174. When asked to comment on Engelsviken's report about the unanswered letter, the WCC also could not find any evidence that a reply had been sent, see NINAN KOSHY, Letter to Philip Potter, 17 September 1975, Ethiopia Correspondence, WCC Archives, Geneva.

223 See resolution quoted by ENGELSVIKEN, "Molo Wongel," 181.

224 Dr. Potter began his service as general secretary on Nov. 1, 1972.

225 See quotes of the letter in ENGELSVIKEN, "Molo Wongel," 182. Unfortunately the letter could not be located in the WCC archives, but the acknowledgment letter by Philip Potter of Nov. 14 to Bishop Kaare Støylen, confirms the receipt and date of the letter.

226 In an internal memo, Potter noted on Nov. 17: "It would seem that the various Bible Societies, following the UBS meeting in Addis Ababa, are making a concerted attack through us. I have to see the U.S. Bible Society man on his request next week." See PHILIP POTTER, Memo to Leopoldo Niilus, 17 November 1972, Philip Potter Correspondence, WCC Archives, Geneva.

227 See JOHANNES LANGHOFF, Letter to Philip Potter, 16 November 1972, Philip Potter Correspondence, WCC Archives, Geneva.

228 The *Kristeligt Dagblad*, for example, implicitly accused the WCC of hypocrisy in that it spoke out against apartheid where it would not have to risk confronting one of its member churches, but in the case of Ethiopia the council has chosen to remain silent because of the membership of the EOC, see *Kristeligt Dagblad*, "Pinsekirken forfølges stadig i Ethiopien." WCC criticism can also be found in *Vårt Land*, "Må skaffe oss solide opplysninger om Etiopia."

African Secretary of the WCC Commission on Inter-Church Aid, Refugee and World Service.[229] According to Engelsviken, they did not meet with Pentecostals during this trip, but most of all contacted the EOC and Lutheran organizations.[230]

After some further study,[231] a first preliminary report was drafted by Bodipo-Malumba.[232] It is testimony to the difficulties of adequately assessing the situation with a limited understanding of Pentecostalism as a whole and the situation in Ethiopia in particular. While unable to "affirm that the difficulties certain Pentecostals and similar groups are encountering in Ethiopia can be described and denounced as 'persecution of Christians'," Bodipo-Malumba calls for "tact, discretion and full understanding in order to be able to help both the authorities in Ethiopia and the Pentecostal leaders with acceptable advice." Apparently trying to make sense of the situation with a mission-critical paradigm, he arrived at the misconception that there "exists a traditional nucleus of Pentecostal churches in Ethiopia, which has been able to operate with less difficulties than other denominations in Ethiopia," and that the difficulties had been caused by a certain sector of Pentecostals "brought about by outside missionaries." He notes the confusion of Pentecostals with Jehovah's Witnesses in the eyes of the authorities, but apparently is under the false impression that this was due to a Pentecostal embrace of the political stance of the Jehovah's Witnesses. Furthermore he states that the "concept of 'religious liberty'" is "more narrowly construed in Ethiopia" than in Western countries, contends that there is a "conscious search for 'martyrdom' by some Pentecostals," and suggests that the matter should be dealt with first an foremost within the AACC. Bodipo-Malumba concludes:

> What I am driving at is certainly not an attitude of 'laissez faire, laissez passer' but rather a call to churches and missions, both in Ethiopia as well as outside, to sit together in a Christian spirit to discuss the circumstances that have led up to certain unfortunate developments. Thus, these could perhaps not only be overcome, but avoided in [the] future and missionaries might help one another to deeper understanding.[233]

After this rather inconclusive report, the WCC continued to work on the matter in preparation of the Ethiopian patriarch's visit to Geneva on June 12–14, 1973.

---

229   Cf. EDUARDO BODIPO-MALUMBA, Letter to Canon Burgess Carr, 22 November 1972, Philip Potter Correspondence, WCC Archives, Geneva; WORLD COUNCIL OF CHURCHES, "The Situation of Members of the Pentecostal Movements in Ethiopia," Correspondence Member Churches: EOC, WCC Archives, Geneva, 1973.

230   Cf. ENGELSVIKEN, "Molo Wongel," 200. While Engelsviken's criticism of not hearing "the case presented by those most deeply involved in it" seems justified, the WCC apparently saw the Lutheran World Federation and its branches as a place for neutral information, cf. POTTER, Memo to Leopoldo Niilus, November 17, 1972.

231   E.g. in Dec. 1972 Bodipo-Malumba reported about a meeting with an Ethiopia missionary, see EDUARDO BODIPO-MALUMBA, Letter to Leopoldo Niilus and Philip Potter, 12 December 1972, Correspondence Member Churches: EOC, WCC Archives, Geneva.

232   See EDUARDO BODIPO-MALUMBA, Memo to Philip Potter: Pentecostals and others in Ethiopia, 10 January 1973, Philip Potter Correspondence, WCC Archives, Geneva. It is quoted verbatim in ENGELSVIKEN, "Molo Wongel," 200–202.

233   BODIPO-MALUMBA, Memo to Philip Potter: Pentecostals and others in Ethiopia, January 10, 1973, 2.

Patriarch Theophilos was to stop by after a three-week tour of the USA and a number of consultations were planned on ecumenism and interreligious dialogue, as well as development and education programs in Ethiopia. As the case of the Pentecostals in Ethiopia unfolded, the patriarch's visit was apparently thought to be the right opportunity for some diplomacy on the matter. A thirty minute private conversation between Philip Potter and Theophilos had been scheduled to take place during a coffee break on June 13, and when the program was sent to the Ethiopian ambassador, he was notified beforehand that "[i]n his discussion with the Patriarch the General Secretary of the World Council of Churches will raise the question of the situation of Pentecostals in Ethiopia."[234]

Meanwhile Eduardo Bodipo-Malumba had continued his investigations and prepared a report about "The Situation of Members of the Pentecostal Movements in Ethiopia," which was distributed to those involved in the visit of the patriarch.[235] This report is considerably better informed than the previous one. Here, the Pentecostal groups are distinguished correctly, there is significantly more information about the events leading up to the arrests, and the legal and political parameters for churches in Ethiopia are, for the most part, laid out adequately. Bodipo-Malumba ends with a clear vote:

> 4a. The present difficulties can be viewed in the context of the history of the missionary involvement in Africa and in the light of the way in which European and American expatriates have too often shown utter disregard for African traditions and, in the present case, genuine African Christian traditions. We feel however that it should rather be considered in the light of the true religious revival which is now manifesting itself all over the world and which in each geographical situation becomes an authentic local movement.
>
> 4b. We feel therefore that in a Christian State due attention should be given to such forms of Christian witness both by the official Church and by the government. It is in this light that we would plead for the granting of a right of association for the indigenous Pentecostal groups.
>
> 4c. At the same time we would plead that, in a Christian State, if men and women are arrested for having broken the law because of their belief and ways of worship, they should be given every opportunity to have their rights protected and to be treated humanely. We feel that in this respect the State Church has a very important role to play as part of its fundamental commitment to Christ.[236]

---

234 CLÉMENT BARBEY, Letter to the Ambassador of Ethiopia, 1 June 1973, Philip Potter Correspondence, WCC Archives, Geneva.

235 See WORLD COUNCIL OF CHURCHES, "The Situation of Members of the Pentecostal Movements in Ethiopia." Bodipo-Malumba is not mentioned as the author in the paper, but Philip Potter thanked him in a private note for the "excellent job" done on it, see PHILIP POTTER, Note to Eduardo Bodipo-Malumba, 10 June 1973, Correspondence Member Churches: EOC, WCC Archives, Geneva.

236 WORLD COUNCIL OF CHURCHES, "The Situation of Members of the Pentecostal Movements in Ethiopia," 3–4.

There is no information about the content or the results of the private discussion between Dr. Potter and Abuna Theophilos regarding the detained Pentecostals. The press release about the patriarch's visit, issued on June 14, 1973, only hints at the issue in expressing the hope "that, in the spirit of religious liberty and of ecumenical cooperation and goodwill, it will be possible for all Christians to reach out in witness and service to all the people in Ethiopia," as well as in the mention of the private conversation between the general secretary of the WCC and the EOC patriarch, in which they "also spoke about ways of improving church relations within Ethiopia, bearing in mind that the Ethiopian Orthodox Church comprises the vast majority of the country's Christians."[237] The careful wording of these passages illustrates the difficulties of the WCC to raise the matter with one of its founding members, and the limits of such an intervention. The fact that the press release is "the closest the WCC came to an official reaction to the persecution in Ethiopia" as Engelsviken correctly observed,[238] therefore seems to be grounded in the political complexities of ecumenical dialog.

Engelsviken was not only well informed about the deliberations in Geneva,[239] he was also actively involved in trying to secure international allies for the Ethiopian Pentecostals. Therefore, Engelsviken profoundly criticized the lack of a clear official reaction by the WCC in his *Documentary Report*, which had not only framed the persecution narrative largely as an ecumenical problem between Orthodox and Pentecostal Christians, but also devoted a significant portion to the involvement of the WCC. Interweaving the deliberations of church politics with the situation of Pentecostals in Ethiopia, Engelsviken clearly marked his disappointment with the ecumenical structures and their failure to impact the problem:

> While the Patriarch and the leaders in Geneva exchanged pleasantries — and hopefully some hard talk — the trial of the Ethiopian Pentecostals entered its final phase. After almost eleven months of agony, after having been forced to wander in and out of prison, after having spent days and weeks in courts, and thousands of dollars on defense lawyers and legal bickering, after a time of fear and hope, the verdict was pronounced by the High Court on July 18, 1973. The sentence from the Addis Ababa District Court was upheld. [240]

Since Engelsviken was hoping to publish his *Documentary Report* he sent relevant excerpts of it to Dr. Philip Potter for comments, noting that: "[i]t has not been my aim to attack the WCC, but I found the reports I received about its activity during the persecution to be a kind that forced me to some rather negative conclusions, especially the report from Eduardo Bodipo-Malumba, whose name I do not mention

---

237 WORLD COUNCIL OF CHURCHES, "Press Release: Ethiopian Patriarch Visits World Council of Churches," Correspondence Member Churches: EOC, WCC Archives, Geneva, June 14, 1973, 2.

238 ENGELSVIKEN, "Molo Wongel," 206.

239 In a letter to the WCC Engelsviken indicated that he received substantial internal material by way of the involved Norwegian bishops Dr. Per Lønning and Dr. Kaare Støylen, as well as Rev. Birger Mathisen, cf. ENGELSVIKEN, Letter to Philip Potter, September 2, 1975.

240 See e.g. ENGELSVIKEN, "Molo Wongel," 207.

in the report."[241] The involved WCC staff members felt unjustly accused and were especially exasperated to find the January memo by Bodipo-Malumba quoted in full, although it was marked as confidential and ranked as only a preliminary document.[242] Accordingly, the answer to Engelsviken included the more nuanced June report and suggested he publish this one instead of the January memo though "this will obviously mean that you have to revise substantially the section on the WCC."[243]

Engelsviken's publication plans did not materialize, therefore it is unclear what impact this information would have had on his narrative. However, the *Documentary Report* did not end on a negative note anyway. Quite conversely, Engelsviken drew his own conclusions about the overall positive impact of the political pressures on ecumenical circles. Citing internal sources about the WCC Central Committee meeting in Geneva in August 1973,[244] he made note of two developments. First, the Norwegian bishop and Central Committee member Kaare Støylen was informed that in a meeting with Philip Potter and others, "highranking leaders in the orthodox church in Ethiopia had admitted to wrong doing in the treatment of the Pentecostal groups," and that this would not be repeated in the future.[245] Secondly, Engelsviken contends that in another meeting between Støylen and another Central Committee member, the EOC bishop Samuel used "*verbatim* quotations from this author's paper on the Pentecostals."[246] Though the paper reportedly was only quoted in its critical aspects, Engelsviken portrays this unexpected reception of his manuscript as an instance of ecumenical learning, since it indicated that "the church had in our opinion taken a big step towards a relevant evaluation of the Pentecostal movement and away from violent confrontation." Furthermore, the Ethiopian bishop informed his counterpart about the establishment of a committee "to continue to investigate the life and doctrine of the Pentecostal groups," which according to Engelsviken "is possibly also merely a reference" to his paper containing a "similar proposal."[247] This "paper" was Engelsviken's report to the ECMY General Assembly in January 1973, which was not received as intended there, but instead, all of the recommendations contained in it were turned down. Therefore, while the ecumenical gap between the ECMY and the Pentecostals could not be overcome at the time, Engelsviken now saw this "possible reference" as an indication of his labors bearing fruit in the most unlikely place and enthusiastically concluded his narrative:

---

241   ENGELSVIKEN, Letter to Philip Potter, September 2, 1975.

242   In an internal letter by Ninan Koshy to Philip Potter, he even accused Engelsviken of having selected the January memo, because "the author has obviously found this particular one convenient to support his case," see KOSHY, Letter to Philip Potter, September 17, 1975. However, it may also be the case that Engelsviken simply had not received the more accurate and balanced June report before.

243   PHILIP POTTER, Letter (draft) to Tormod Engelsviken, 17 September 1975, Ethiopia Correspondence, WCC Archives, Geneva. Other comments made pertained to Engelsviken's surprise at the WCC's decision to conduct its own investigation, and the nature of the WCC's intervention not via public statements but direct dialog.

244   The Central Committee member Bishop Støylen gave a report to Engelsviken in a letter.

245   ENGELSVIKEN, "Molo Wongel," 211.

246   Ibid., 213. Emphasis Engelsviken.

247   Ibid.

If the Ethiopian Orthodox Church on its part has taken up the recommendation and has decided to go ahead with its own investigation, it is an encouraging sign that the church takes seriously a Christian movement which has come to Ethiopia to stay![248]

Considering the centrality of ecumenical deliberations to Engelsviken's account, it is striking that almost all of the Ethiopian Pentecostal sources which depend on Engelsviken make no reference to the involvement of the WCC and other ecumenical bodies at all. The only exception is the FGBC history of 1992, which, however, even though it explicitly cited Engelsviken, did not follow his main intent.[249] Despite the document's own portrayal of persecution as an ecumenical problem,[250] it offers no comments and criticism, nor even hopes and expectations in connection with the ecumenical deliberations after the arrests. Rather, the account simply mentions the fact that the AACC and the WCC had been informed, lists the church's supporters in Norway, Denmark and the USA along with their contributions, and then concludes:

> This affection seen in churches from different parts of the world demonstrates the unity of the church, which is the body of Christ, and is a sign of [its] nature of love and brotherhood.[251]

This difference between Engelsviken's focus on the WCC affair and its omission in Pentecostal accounts, who otherwise noticeably rely on Engelsviken's narrative trajectory, points to what was suggested at the beginning of this chapter. Different political perspectives and narrative trajectories about persecution as a whole inform the persecution histories. Systemic criticism, as voiced by Engelsviken, calls for a response on behalf of political actors, and by framing the matter as a decidedly ecumenical issue, Engelsviken's *Documentary Report* focused on a political stage on which he himself could also play a role.

Ethiopian Pentecostal accounts, on the other hand, developed a historical narrative of a suffering but defiant underground movement, sustained by the Spirit of God. Though the FGBC leaders apparently tested other political paths as well, like the one suggested by their Norwegian allies, a story of spiritual resilience in the face of political oppression arguably lended more agency to a hard-pressed minority movement. Overtly political activities, like enlisting the foreign press or initiating ecumenical deliberations, not only are irrelevant to such a narrative, they even tend to threaten its very core.

When the Swedish missionary Tage Johansson mentioned the idea of taking the case to the WCC he in turn asked if "the hopes of the indigenous brothers" to succeed

---

248 ENGELSVIKEN, "Molo Wongel," 213. This sentence can be viewed as concluding statement to Engelsviken's report, since this part is only followed by a small chapter on the Ethiopian revolution (pp. 214–225), which more or less functions as an after play, signaling the uncertain future and keeping the issue alive.

249 See ETHIOPIAN FULL GOSPEL BELIEVER'S CHURCH, የኢትዮጵያ ሙሉ ወንጌል አመኞች ቤተ ክርስቲያን 25ኛ ዓመት በዓል, 13.

250 In connection with the circular letter of Nov. 1972, the document comments: "That people in faith organizations collaborated in destroying other Christians and associated with the government is a sad event." See ibid., 12.

251 Ibid., 13.

in this way "aren't premature."[252] He feared that this would only lead to "false blame" being placed on the Emperor and his family, which would be a "utterly wrong," since "they have been warm friends to the work." Johansson reiterated that the only way forward for Pentecostals is to represent their case before the Emperor, which is of course the instrument that a Pentecostal missionary like he himself had learned to play and where he could be of help.

The incompatibility of these different perspectives has resulted in a number of tales endeavoring to define this first encounter of Ethiopian Pentecostals and the state. A number of sources represent the events of 1967–1973 as the first instance of persecution of Ethiopian Pentecostals. As the analysis has shown, the underlying narratives strongly rely on a fundamental antagonism between persecutor and persecuted. This is why it is necessary to determine the actual persecutor, in most cases the EOC, and to strongly delimit the persecuted community as well as any political contacts between the antagonists. Such persecution narratives may be framed in different ways, either as systemic conflict between freedom and repression or as the story of God's supreme intervention against worldly resistance. The reward of this fairly extensive project is a stringent moral narrative, but this may not always match up with the outlook of contemporaneous sources by fellow Pentecostals, especially when their interest is not in furthering the persecution narrative but in highlighting the remaining political possibilities.

---

252   See JOHANSSON, Letter to Bo Hörnberg, October 6, 1972.

5 Accounting for the Underground: Persecution and the Proliferation of Pentecostalism During the Derg

Although the Ethiopian revolution of 1974 had originally promised freedom of religion, its Marxist turn increasingly brought pressure on many churches. The Ethiopian Orthodox Church (EOC) was targeted first and forcefully aligned to the new power center, whereas the Protestant churches, Pentecostal and mainline, soon were subject to political oppression and marginalization, which lasted throughout the Derg time. With most of their churches closed, key leaders arrested, tortured and even killed, many congregations and even whole denominations resorted to house meetings and secret cell structures until the revolutionary government was ousted in 1991 and religious groups were again allowed to operate freely.

A second development that ran parallel to the struggle of the Protestant churches is the growth of Charismatic movements within the largest mainline Protestant churches. While Charismatic movements had already entered these churches before the Ethiopian revolution, their proponents did not yet hold any considerable influence within their respective denominations, nor were they recognized by the Pentecostal movement, which instead was striving to establish itself as an independent entity. However, between 1974 and 1991, the Charismatic movement in the mainline churches gained considerable momentum, and it had become a visible force in a number of denominations by the time Mengistu was chased from power. Although the growth of the Charismatic movements continued unabated in the following years and perhaps even accelerated, the persecution under the Derg often serves as primary referent for explaining this growth.

Both of these developments, the ubiquitous persecution of Protestant churches and the growth of the Charismatic movement, are central factors for the historical archive about the Derg, which spans more than a decade and a half. On the one hand, the oppressiveness of the military government prevented the production of written material, especially among the fairly de-institutionalized Pentecostal groups. On the other hand, the story of persecution now became one that was shared by many churches, which in turn broadens the scope of sources to be considered. Since a number of accounts link the persecution experience in the mainline Protestant churches to the Charismatic movement, they are of additional relevance for the following analyses.

In order to analyze the historical narratives about this time, it is necessary to begin with an overview of the most important developments that took place in the EOC, the mainline Protestant churches, and the Pentecostal churches during the difficult and turbulent Derg era. Especially for the Pentecostal churches such a historical synopsis has not yet been provided in sufficient detail, which necessitates a more elaborate account in order to anchor the subsequent analyses. At the same time this overview will not just highlight the political complexity of churches navigating an oppressive regime, but also expose the fragmented and limited nature of the historical source archive about Pentecostals during this time.

5.1   Ethiopia's Churches During the Derg

5.1.1   The Ethiopian Orthodox Church

At the onset of the revolution, the EOC hierarchy took a remarkably ambivalent stance. Whereas in the Bodyguard Coup of 1960, Patriarch Abuna Basilios' public excommunication of the insurgents had been instrumental in suppressing the uprising, his successor Abuna Theophilos at first remained silent when the revolution began early in 1974. His church did not speak out until August when it responded to the new draft of the Constitution, stating that it "deeply deplores and opposes the spirit and letter of some of the provisions contained in the Draft Constitution of Ethiopia . . . i.e., the proposed separation of Church and State and the disestablishment of the Orthodox Church."[1] However, less than a month later, the patriarch signaled his full support for the revolution when in his broadcast on Ethiopian New Year's Day, he did not offer the traditional and constitutionally demanded eulogy for the Emperor and his family, but instead "blessed the revolutionaries and defined the emerging political forces as a 'holy movement'."[2] Haile Selassie was deposed the next day.[3]

Despite its continued public support for the revolution,[4] the EOC was dramatically affected by the reforms of the following months. As the former state church, it lost much of its influence and constitutional privileges. Furthermore, its economic base was severely curtailed by the land reforms of 1975.[5] Land had been a major source of income for the EOC and in the traditionally Orthodox areas of northern

---

1   Quoted in SCHOLLER and BRIETZKE, *Ethiopia: Revolution, Law and Politics*, 128. See also CALVIN E. SHENK, "Church and State in Ethiopia: From Monarchy to Marxism," *Mission Studies* 11 (2 1994): 208.

2   HAILE MARIAM LAREBO, "The Orthodox Church and the State in the Ethiopian Revolution, 1974–84," 150. See also SHENK, "Church and State in Ethiopia," 219.

3   This shift of allegiance by the patriarch was only one of many factors leading to the deposition, since the Derg had systematically isolated the Emperor by that time, at last with an intense campaign of vilification, beginning at the end of August, see e.g. TEFERRA HAILE-SELASSIE, *The Ethiopian Revolution 1974–1991*, 126–127. However, the fact that he church did not wield its substantial popular power in defense of the Emperor, but supported the revolution is not featured prominently enough by most histories of the revolution.

4   Still in January 1975 Theophilos wrote to the general secretary of the World Council of Churches (WCC): "We believe that Ethiopia will be stronger and more united because of this progressive change. The political philosophy of the new era is essentially the philosophy of the Church. The Church has been teaching basic equality among men of all races and religions, self-reliance for the masses of the Ethiopian people and social and economic justice for all. [. . .] We are inclined to think that the position of the Ethiopian Orthodox Church and the situation in Ethiopia in general have been misrepresented to our colleagues in Geneva," see ABUNA THEOPHILOS, Letter to Philip Potter, 20 January 1975, Correspondence Member Churches: EOC, WCC Archives, Geneva.

5   For the land reforms and their implementation see esp. OTTAWAY and OTTAWAY, *Ethiopia*, 66-81; HARBESON, *The Ethiopian Transformation*, 130–144; HALLIDAY and MOLYNEUX, *The Ethiopian Revolution*, 104–112.

Ethiopia land leases served as a major recruitment base for priests.[6] With the nationalization of all rural and urban lands on March 4, 1975 and July 26, 1975 respectively,
the church lost its urban territory as well as its sharecropping income in the south,
and while the land use remained with the priest-farmers in the north, the obligation
to commit a son to priesthood was lifted. The government provided the church with
a meager annual budget to compensate for the loss, which also brought the church
further under state control.[7] Moreover, Patriarch Abuna Theophilos could not win
the lasting approval of the Derg. On February 18, 1976 he was deposed and arrested
on charges of fraud, nepotism and misdemeanor. He was murdered in prison roughly
two years later, and his death was not confirmed until after the Derg was ousted in
1991. The deposition of Theophilos and the subsequent election of the monk Melaku
Wolde-Mikael as Patriarch Tekle-Haimanot invoked the protest of the Coptic Church
of Egypt, which did not recognize the new patriarch, arguing that the forceful replacement of a living patriarch was an illegitimate and uncanonical procedure. A
number of Orthodox sister churches and the Roman Catholic Church, on the other
hand, approved of the new patriarch. Since the EOC was a founding member of the
World Council of Churches (WCC) and there had been excellent relations to Theophilos, the Council began its own investigations of the matter and received reports from
other churches.[8] In the end, the WCC did not adopt a clear position, since it was
torn between the Coptic Church's protests, assurances by the EOC that everything
was in accordance with canon law, and the opinion of other Orthodox churches. It
never officially recognized the election of Tekle-Haimanot nor congratulated him, but
continued its communication with the EOC and the patriarch nevertheless. At the
same time, the Council expressed its concern about the situation in a number of
press statements and sent diplomatic letters to the Ethiopian government and other
politicians pleading for the release of the arrested patriarch and bishops.[9]

---

6   Land was leased to priest-farmers who in turn had to commit one of their sons to priesthood.
    In the south, land owned by the EOC was farmed out on a sharecropping basis. It is estimated
    that the EOC owned five percent of all land or twenty percent of all cultivated land, see SHENK,
    "Church and State in Ethiopia," 210.
7   See ibid., 210–212; GIULIA BONACCI, "Ethiopia 1974–1991: Religious Policy of the State and Its
    Consequences on the Orthodox Church," in *Ethiopian Studies at the End of the Second Millenium:
    Proceedings of the XIVth International Conference of Ethiopian Studies November 6–11, 2000,
    Addis Ababa*, ed. BAYE YIMAM et al. (Addis Ababa: Institute of Ethiopian Studies, Addis Ababa
    University, 2000), 597; HAILE MARIAM LAREBO, "The Orthodox Church and the State in the
    Ethiopian Revolution, 1974–84," 151.
8   See e.g. KOFI APPIAH-KUBI, "Report on the Pastoral Visit to the Ethiopian Orthodox Church,
    14th–21st July, 1976," Correspondence Member Churches: EOC, WCC Archives, Geneva, 1976;
    H.R. WEBER, "Impressions from a Stay in Addis Ababa, 30th Sept*": to 12th Oct. 1976*, Ethiopia
    Correspondence, WCC Archives, Geneva, 1976; PAULOS MAR GREGORIOS, "Report on a Visit
    to Ethiopia, October 27–31, 1976," Correspondence Member Churches: EOC, WCC Archives,
    Geneva, 1976.
9   See e.g. PHILIP POTTER, Letter to the Chairman of the Provisional Administrative Council of
    Ethiopia, 10 January 1977, Ethiopia Correspondence, WCC Archives, Geneva; PHILIP POTTER,
    Letter to Lieutenant-Colonel Mengistu Haile-Mariam, Chairman of the Provisional Administra-
    tive Council of Ethiopia, 27 May 1977, Ethiopia Correspondence, WCC Archives, Geneva; PHILIP
    POTTER, Letter to Lieutenant-Colonel Mengistu Haile-Mariam, Chairman of the Provisional Ad-
    ministrative Council of Ethiopia, 13 May 1977, Ethiopia Correspondence, WCC Archives, Geneva;
    WORLD COUNCIL OF CHURCHES, "WCC Alarmed and Saddened by Situation in Ethiopia," *World*

After the deposition of Theophilos, the Derg increasingly sought to co-opt the EOC as a nationalistic rallying base, since it was caught up in the Ogaden war and opposed by several regional liberation movements.[10] The new hierarchy largely cooperated with the Derg, while dissenting clergy were held in prison or driven into exile.[11] In 1978 Patriarch Tekle-Haimanot dismissed nine of the fourteen bishops of the Holy Synod under the pretext of new retirement regulations. Furthermore, he began to appear alongside Mengistu Haile Mariam at parades or in public imagery and clearly stated his support for the revolution.[12] There are reports that especially in later years he proved to be more insubordinate than the Derg had hoped,[13] but matters never came to a head, and when the patriarch died in 1988, he received a state funeral, which was an unprecedented honor for an Ethiopian patriarch.

Tekle-Haimanot's successor, Abuna Merkorios showed greater political conformity still and was elected as a member of the national parliament, the Shengo. As a result of this political co-optation, the EOC once again was subject to a sudden political realignment within months after the Derg was ousted and the Ethiopian People's Revolutionary Democratic Front (EPRDF) had risen to power. Abuna Merkorios abdicated in August of 1991, and in October the general manager of the church was replaced by the transitional government, despite its general policy of non-interference in religious affairs. The Holy Synod elected Abuna Paulos as the new patriarch, who was crowned on July 12, 1992, one day after the burial of the remains of his former

---

Council of Churches Communication (8 1977). An especially interesting letter in this regard was sent to Fidel Castro by the general secretary of the WCC and attempted to utilize the apparently good relations with Castro for enlisting him to intervene with Mengistu Haile Mariam on behalf of the detained Orthodox clergy.

10 See HAILE MARIAM LAREBO, "The Orthodox Church and the State in the Ethiopian Revolution, 1974–84," 152–153; JÖRG HAUSTEIN, "Navigating Political Revolutions: Ethiopia's Churches During and After the Mengistu Regime," in *Falling Walls: The Year 1989/90 as a Turning Point in the History of World Christianity*, ed. KLAUS KOSCHORKE, Studien zur Außereuropäischen Christentumsgeschichte (Asien, Afrika, Lateinamerika); 15 (Wiesbaden: Harrassowitz, 2009), 117–136. The co-optation of the church did not mean that there was no anti-religious rhetoric or occasional violent opposition on the local level, see SHENK, "Church and State in Ethiopia," 212; BONACCI, "Ethiopia 1974–1991," 601–602.

11 E.g. the present patriarch and protege of Abuna Theophilos, Abuna Paulos, spent seven years in the Derg prison before he was allowed to study abroad. Abuna Matthias was a prominent bishop who fled to England and became a vocal critic of the Derg's treatment of the EOC.

12 In 1979 Tekle-Haimanot wrote to the general secretary of the WCC: "The members of the Holy Synod are constantly meeting to discuss questions pertaining to their responsibility, the role of the Ethiopian Orthodox Church in Socialist Ethiopia, the Development and Inter-Church Aid Commission and other issues very helpful in the building of the new society," see ABUNA TEKLE-HAIMANOT, Letter to Philip Potter, 13 March 1979, Correspondence Member Churches: EOC, WCC Archives, Geneva.

13 Tekle-Haimanot reportedly canceled public appearances with Mengistu and entered a fast in protest of the napalm and cluster bombings of Eritrea and Tigre, see "Abuna Takla Haymanot," *Wikipedia. The Free Encyclopedia* (2008), http://en.wikipedia.org/wiki/Abuna_Takla_Haymanot (accessed September 2, 2008); MARKUS LESINSKI, "Gefangen in der Geschichte? Die Äthiopische Orthodoxe Kirche," in *Mit wachsender Begeisterung: Evangelische Christen in Äthiopien*, ed. HENNING UZAR (Hermannsburg: Missionshandlung Hermannsburg, 1998), 97. Unfortunately these reports are not documented further. Heyer still saw Tekle-Haimanot as politically conforming and interpreted this stance as patient monastic suffering, HEYER, "Die Orthodoxe Kirche Äthiopiens im zehnten Revolutionsjahr," 217

patron, Patriarch Theophilos.[14] This change in the patriarchate once again caused major controversy, especially when Abuna Merkorios went into exile and claimed that he had not abdicated freely, but was forced out of office.[15] He was supported by a number of expatriate bishops, most notably in the USA, who protested against the election of Paulos while Merkorios was still alive and finally declared their administrational independence as the "Ethiopian Orthodox Church in the Western Hemisphere" with its headquarters in New York.[16] While Paulos quickly found recognition as the new patriarch, and even the relations with Cairo were finally mended in 2007,[17] the split in the expatriate EOC in North America and Europe continues to the present. In July 2007, Merkorios anointed thirteen bishops for North America together with Archbishops of the exile synod, which led to the mutual excommunication of the two EOC factions, furthering the split.

5.1.2 Mainline Protestant Churches

The mainline Protestant Churches in Ethiopia were significantly stronger in the southern and western periphery than in the traditional political centers of Addis Ababa and northern Ethiopia. On account of their juxtaposition to the traditional establishment they often, willingly or unwillingly, became an ally for the revolutionary movement. Therefore, they were targeted later than the EOC, but as the Derg consolidated its hold on Orthodox Christianity and increasingly discovered that it would have to rule Ethiopia from the old center rather than from the periphery, they were subject to a more systematic and brutal repression than the EOC, and a path of coexistence or cooperation between state and Protestant churches did not emerge until the end of the 1980s.

The Lutheran Evangelical Church Mekane Yesus (ECMY) had strong personal ties to the Imperial government in its president Emmanuel Abraham,[18] who served in Haile Selassie's government. Its core constituency, however, consisted of the politically underrepresented Oromo. This fact together with the church's strong focus on development also lent the ECMY an Empire-critical voice on occasion, which was

---

14 See OTTO FRIEDRICH AUGUST MEINARDUS, *Two Thousand Years of Coptic Christianity* (Cairo: American University in Cairo Press, 2002), 234.

15 See ABUNA MERKORIOS, "To all Clergy and Followers of the Ethiopian Orthodox Church Residing Both Inside and Outside the Country," Correspondence Member Churches: EOC, WCC Archives, Geneva, October 20, 1992.

16 See ABUNA MELKE SEDEK, "Unprecedented Crisis Facing the Ethiopian Church," Correspondence Member Churches: EOC, WCC Archives, Geneva, August 12, 1992; ABUNA YESEHAQ, "Resolution by the Archdiocese of the Ethiopian Orthodox Church in the Western Hemisphere from September 21, 1992," Correspondence Member Churches: EOC, WCC Archives, Geneva, September 21, 1992; ARCHDIOCESE OF THE ETHIOPIAN ORTHODOX CHURCH IN THE WESTERN HEMISPHERE, Circular from November 29, 1992, 29 November 1992, Correspondence Member Churches: EOC, WCC Archives, Geneva. The letters are also very critical of Paulos' conduct while he was in exile in the USA, indicating that the split had some roots already in the time of the Derg.

17 Cf. WCC MEDIA, "WCC News: Coptic & Ethiopian Orthodox Churches Reconcile" (2007), http://www.wfn.org/2007/07/msg00139.html (accessed July 19, 2007).

18 Emmanuel Abraham, president of the church from 1963–1985, had been in the service of the Emperor since 1939 and had assumed different ministerial positions in Haile Selassie's government, see EMMANUEL ABRAHAM, *Reminiscences of My Life*, 29–228.

personified in the church's general secretary Gudina Tumsa.[19] At the onset of the revolution, Emmanuel Abraham was detained on account of his former role in the Imperial court. At the same time, the ECMY general secretary Gudina Tumsa engaged positively with the revolution, calling for reforms and offering the church's overall affirmative, though not necessarily uncritical, political input.[20] The ECMY cooperated in turning over its development projects to the government, its leaders, most notably Gudina Tumsa, cast their visions of a more just Ethiopia, and the church played a decisive role in coordinating an ecumenical forum of churches in Ethiopia, the Council for the Cooperation of Churches in Ethiopia (CCCE). However, as the revolution developed into a military dictatorship, latest in the Red Terror of 1977, it became increasingly clear that the political ambitions of the church were interpreted as a political challenge by the Derg, as the new leaders strove to assert their own control over the peripheries.[21] Whereas before the church had freely turned over its development projects, now the Derg shut down and confiscated central facilities of the church, i.e., the Radio Voice of the Gospel, the Mass Media Programme building and the Evangelical College in Debre Zeit. The ideological differences between the ECMY and the Derg also increasingly became clear, leading to more confrontations, like at the interreligious seminar convened by the Derg in March 1978. After having been arrested and detained for a few weeks on two occasions in 1978 and 1979, the general secretary of the church, Gudina Tumsa, was abducted by secret police on July 28, 1979 and murdered the same night, which was not confirmed until after the

---

19 Cf. EIDE, *Revolution and Religion in Ethiopia*, 59–60. In 1973 Gudina Tumsa called for a land-reform and even refused to include the Emperor in the General Prayer as the liturgy and the constitution demanded, which was quite a scandalous issue at the time, see PAUL E. HOFFMAN, "Gudina Tumsa's Legacy: His Spirituality and Leadership," in *The Life and Ministry of Rev. Gudina Tumsa: General Secretary of the Ethiopian Evangelical Church Mekane Yesus (EECMY); Report Volume & Lectures of the Missiological Seminar Sponsored by the Gudina Tumsa Foundation at Mekane Yesus Seminary, Makanissa, April 18-21, 2001*, ed. PAUL E. HOFFMAN (Addis Ababa: Gudina Tumsa Foundation, 2003), 19–21; SÆVERÅS, AUD, *Der lange Schatten der Macht: Augenzeugenbericht. Die Geschichte von Tsehay Tolessa und Gudina Tumsa, dem ermordeten Generalsekretär der Mekane-Yesus-Kirche in Äthiopien* (Gießen: Brunnen Verlag, 1993), 57.

20 Like all members of the former administration, Emmanuel Abraham was detained for some months. Though he was one of only few who survived the mass assassination of former ministers in November 1974, his ties to the former government and his imprisonment probably weakened his political influence in the church. See HAUSTEIN, "Navigating Political Revolutions"; cf. also PAUL E. HOFFMAN, ed., *The Life and Ministry of Rev. Gudina Tumsa: General Secretary of the Ethiopian Evangelical Church Mekane Yesus (EECMY); Report Volume & Lectures of the Missiological Seminar Sponsored by the Gudina Tumsa Foundation at Mekane Yesus Seminary, Makanissa, April 18-21, 20001* (Addis Ababa: Gudina Tumsa Foundation, 2003); PAUL E. HOFFMAN, ed., *Witness and Discipleship: Leadership of the Church in Multi-Ethnic Ethiopia in a Time of Revolution; The Essential Writings of Gudina Tumsa, General Secretary of the Ethiopian Evangelical Church Mekane Yesus (1929–1979)* (Addis Ababa: Gudina Tumsa Foundation, 2003); GEBREMEDHIN, "The Ethiopian Evangelical Church Mekane Yesus under Marxist Dictatorship," 94–96.

21 See GERD DECKE, "The Role of Gudina Tumsa in a Critical Dialogue between Marxism/Socialism and Christianity," in *The Life and Ministry of Rev. Gudina Tumsa: General Secretary of the Ethiopian Evangelical Church Mekane Yesus (EECMY); Report Volume & Lectures of the Missiological Seminar Sponsored by the Gudina Tumsa Foundation at Mekane Yesus Seminary, Makanissa, April 18-21, 2001*, ed. PAUL E. HOFFMAN (Addis Ababa: Gudina Tumsa Foundation, 2003), 101–128; HAUSTEIN, "Navigating Political Revolutions."

Derg was ousted.[22] Gudina's wife, Tsehay Tolessa was imprisoned without trial for ten years and subject to severe torture.[23] In 1981 the ECMY main office building was confiscated, and the political repression continued in the different synods of the church with a large number of churches closed, property taken over, clergy imprisoned and church members harassed.[24]

In the wake of these events, a heated dispute arose about the church's political strategy, between the ECMY, seeking for a more cooperative strategy to avoid further repressions, and some of its mission partners calling for continued political engagement with the Derg.[25] From the middle of the 1980s onward the relationship between the ECMY and Mengistu's government de-escalated, which was partly due to the human aid channeled by the church, and partly an effect of the ECMY seeking to collaborate where possible. The ECMY quietly assisted in the controversial resettlement campaigns, followed the invitation to participate in the drafting of the new Constitution, and its president, Francis Stephanos, was elected to the parliament (Shengo).[26] By 1989 about 350 congregations had been reopened.[27]

The Sudan Interior Mission (SIM)-affiliated churches, the largest Protestant community in Ethiopia then and now, were in a more precarious position than the Lutherans at the onset of the revolution for a number of reasons. First, the establishment of the national church, known as Kale Heywet Church (KHC), was still in process. Though the SIM-related churches had already formed the informal Fellowship of Evangelical Believers in 1956,[28] the decision to found a formal body of

---

22 See EIDE, *Revolution and Religion in Ethiopia*, 175–179. There is an extensive amount of literature commemorating Gudina's life and ministry, see e.g. SÆVERÅS, AUD, *Der lange Schatten der Macht*; ØYVIND M. EIDE, "Gudina Tumsa: The Voice of an Ethiopian Prophet," *Svensk Missionstidskrift* 89 (3 2001): 291–321; TORMOD ENGELSVIKEN, "Gudina Tumsa, the Ethiopian Evangelical Church Mekane Yesus, and the Charismatic Movement" (Unpublished manuscript, private collection, 2003); HOFFMAN, *The Life and Ministry of Rev. Gudina Tumsa*; HOFFMAN, *Witness and Discipleship*; LAUNHARDT, *Evangelicals in Addis Ababa (1919–1991)*, 239–267; GEBREMEDHIN, "The Ethiopian Evangelical Church Mekane Yesus under Marxist Dictatorship."

23 See SÆVERÅS, AUD, *Der lange Schatten der Macht*.

24 Eide's estimates of churches closed vary from 540 to 700 of altogether 2,500 parishes, cf. EIDE, *Revolution and Religion in Ethiopia*, 250; EIDE, "Gudina Tumsa," 316.

25 In 1982 the ECMY asked the Berliner Missionswerk to refrain from mentioning its name in connection with its regime-critical publications. Perceiving itself as true heir of Gudina Tumsa's political legacy the mission denied this request, and the relations between the ECMY and the Berliner Missionswerk were suspended, while the latter drew heavy criticism from another German mission partner, the Evangelical Lutheran Mission from Hermannsburg. See HAUSTEIN, "Navigating Political Revolutions"; DECKE, "The Role of Gudina Tumsa in a Critical Dialogue between Marxism/Socialism and Christianity," 117; HOFFMAN, "Gudina Tumsa's Legacy," 34; EIDE, *Revolution and Religion in Ethiopia*, 212. A similar dispute also arose between two Norwegian mission partners, see ibid., 213–214, GEMECHU OLANA, *A Church under Challenge: The Socio-Economic and Political Involvement of the Ethiopian Evangelical Church Mekane Yesus (EECMY)* (Berlin: dissertation.de, 2006), 99–106.

26 See EIDE, *Revolution and Religion in Ethiopia*, 241–245.

27 See ibid., 245.

28 See JOHN CUMBERS, *Count It All Joy: Testimonies from a Persecuted Church as Told to John Cumbers* (Kearney, NE: Morris Publishing, 1995), 20; ALBERT E. BRANT, *In the Wake of Martyrs: A Modern Saga in Ancient Ethiopia* (Langley: Omega Publications, 1992), 238. The Fellowship of Evangelical Believers was legally recognized in 1964 and while it was intended as an umbrella organization for all Protestants regardless of their baptismal practice, it only saw the participation

SIM-related churches, with its own name, constitution, headquarters, and general secretary, was not adopted until February 15, 1971.[29] It took another three years until the head office and the first general secretary were actually able to commence their work, throwing the first central government of the KHC right into the turmoil of the revolution.[30]

Secondly, the relationship between the KHC and the SIM quickly grew complicated and agitated, and remained the same throughout the Derg time. On the one hand, the SIM was under enormous political pressure from the start, since despite its Canadian roots it was perceived as a US-American mission and linked by socialist propaganda to "American imperialism" and the CIA. The SIM soon was emersed in constant quarrels with the mandatory labor union,[31] and within the first years, many of the key SIM projects had been taken over by the government while the mission's staff in the country was reduced from over 400 to 37.[32] On the other hand, the KHC leaders were offended by instances of missionary paternalism and felt that the SIM was abandoning its work too quickly, and that it should have turned over its development projects to the church instead of to the government.[33]

Third, the revolution had taken root inside the church at its outset, especially in the southern areas where the KHC was a strong but perhaps unintentional advocate of modernization.[34] The KHC historian Getachew Bellete has provided interesting

---

of churches related to the SIM and the Baptist General Conference Mission. GETACHEW BELLETE, ኡሎሄ እና ሃሌሉያ: የኢትዮጵያ ቃል ሕይወት ቤት ክርስቲያን ታሪክ, ቅጽ ሦስት, (ከ1966–1992 ዓ.ም.), [Sighs and Hallelujahs. The History of the Kale Heywet Church in Ethiopia, vol. 3, 1974–2000] (Addis Ababa: Ethiopian Kale Heywet Church, 2000), 67 dates the establishment of the Fellowship to 1963.

29 See FARGHER, *The Origins of the New Churches Movement in Southern Ethiopia, 1927–1944*, 301; CUMBERS, *Count It All Joy*, 20. The desire for this formation and subsequent independence apparently came from the churches themselves, and met some resistance from the more congregational missionaries.

30 Ethiopians attributed much of this delay to lack of missionary cooperation, see GETACHEW BELLETE, ኡሎሄ እና ሃሌሉያ: የኢትዮጵያ ቃል ሕይወት ቤት ክርስቲያን ታሪክ, ቅጽ ሦስት, (ከ1966–1992 ዓ.ም.), 71–72. The KHC could not find recognition under the revolutionary government, therefore it officially stayed under the already accredited Fellowship of Evangelical Believers, see CUMBERS, *Count It All Joy*, 24.

31 Quarrels with the union are a constant part of the SIM director's memoirs, cf. JOHN CUMBERS, *Living With the Red Terror: Missionary Experiences in Communist Ethiopia* (Kearney, NE: Morris Publishing, 1996). The SIM had about 1,300 employees by the time the revolution began, see ibid., 287.

32 See ibid., 4, 75. For slightly different figures (333–41), see GETACHEW BELLETE, ኡሎሄ እና ሃሌሉያ: የኢትዮጵያ ቃል ሕይወት ቤት ክርስቲያን ታሪክ, ቅጽ ሦስት, (ከ1966–1992 ዓ.ም.), 104. At times, the SIM considered pulling out of Ethiopia completely, which never materialized, see e.g. CUMBERS, *Living With the Red Terror*, 187; FARGHER, *The Origins of the New Churches Movement in Southern Ethiopia, 1927–1944*, 306.

33 See CUMBERS, *Living With the Red Terror*, 277–279; CUMBERS, *Count It All Joy*, 247–251 for a missionary's take. The KHC historian Getachew Bellete provided a complimentary account of the grievances, including the accusations by the government, see GETACHEW BELLETE, ኡሎሄ እና ሃሌሉያ: የኢትዮጵያ ቃል ሕይወት ቤት ክርስቲያን ታሪክ, ቅጽ ሦስት, (ከ1966–1992 ዓ.ም.), 104–111. The relationship between the church and its mission partner continue to be difficult to the present, see FARGHER, *The Origins of the New Churches Movement in Southern Ethiopia, 1927–1944*, 306, 308, 309–310.

34 As Donald Donham (DONHAM, *Marxist Modern*, 94–97, 117–121) has pointed out, the SIM's North American anti-modernism actually had the opposite effect in rural Ethiopia: the missionary emphasis on reading, on breaking with traditional customs, and even the implicit opposition of

examples of the revolution arriving at the grassroot level with the help of the church:[35] Some churches at first rejoiced over the land, which abolished the oppressive tenure system, and they believed that socialism was compatible with Christianity. Therefore a number of KHC members and leaders participated in administration of the land reform, and the churches welcomed and logistically supported the student campaigners, who had been sent to organize the revolution at the local level. However, political strife soon ensued. The student campaigners increasingly took over the political discourse as well as church property in some instances,[36] and the land reform caused quarrels inside the church, since some church members and leaders helped to drive out former land owners. In this process, a number of former Christians also became revolutionaries and turned against the church.[37]

With its own structure still very young and the abrupt dissembling of its former missionary support, the KHC was hit hard by the increasing pressure on Protestant Christianity at the beginning of the 1980s. There are numerous reports of suppression, arrests, torture, and even murder of KHC members, evangelists, or leaders.[38] By 1984/5 the church had suffered the closure of around 1,500 of its almost 2,400 congregations, most of which were in southern rural settings.[39] From the middle of the 1980s onward, the political pressure was lifted somewhat. Since the state increasingly attempted to tap into the SIM development resources , it even issued permits as "spiritual workers" to missionaries.[40] Furthermore, a number of churches were reopened in the late 1980s, either with permission by the government or in an act of civil disobedience that was tolerated by the local authorities.[41]

The Mennonite Meserete Kristos Church (MKC), on the other hand, had managed to avoid closures the longest, despite serious harassment especially in their denominational center in Nazaret.[42] The church had adapted as much as possible to the

---

the Protestant Christians to the Orthodox Amhara settler class had a modernizing implication. Donham contends that "[t]his was the 'pre-revolution' in Maale upon which the revolution of 1975 came to depend. It was partly on this basis that the revolutionary state penetrated ever deeper into local society in the 1980s. [...] None of this would have been possible without the local, Christian-educated vanguard." (p. 120)

35 See GETACHEW BELLETE, ኤሎሄ እና ሃሌሉያ: የኢትዮጵያ ቃለ ሕይወት ቤተ ክርስቲያን ታሪክ, ቅጽ ሦስት, (ከ1966–1992 ዓ.ም.), 79–96.
36 The campaigners would increasingly use the church buildings for their own meetings, limiting the congregations' access to them.
37 See also the detailed ethnographic account of similar processes in Maale provided by DONHAM, Marxist Modern, 151–162.
38 See the detailed regional report in GETACHEW BELLETE, ኤሎሄ እና ሃሌሉያ: የኢትዮጵያ ቃለ ሕይወት ቤተ ክርስቲያን ታሪክ, ቅጽ ሦስት, (ከ1966–1992 ዓ.ም.), 179–282, also including a detailed list of closed churches. Cumbers also has collected and sorted such reports by region, see CUMBERS, Count It All Joy.
39 See GETACHEW BELLETE, ኤሎሄ እና ሃሌሉያ: የኢትዮጵያ ቃለ ሕይወት ቤተ ክርስቲያን ታሪክ, ቅጽ ሦስት, (ከ1966–1992 ዓ.ም.), 281; for comparable numbers (1,700 out of 2,791), see also EIDE, Revolution and Religion in Ethiopia, 270. For an ethnographic local account of church closure in Maale, see DONHAM, Marxist Modern, 162–164.
40 See FARGHER, The Origins of the New Churches Movement in Southern Ethiopia, 1927–1944, 308–309.
41 See e.g. CUMBERS, Count It All Joy, 60, 63. Approximately 700 churches remained closed throughout the Derg regime, EIDE, Revolution and Religion in Ethiopia, 170.
42 See HEGE, Beyond Our Prayers, 172–181.

revolution by complying with the requirement of teaching Marxism in their Bible
Academy, by moving Sunday services to the afternoon so that believers could attend
the obligatory Kebele meetings, and by educating its members about church life under a socialist regime.[43] However, in 1982, when the MKC already believed it had
"weathered the storm,"[44] the entire denomination was shut down, including all its
parishes, and saw the confiscation of its schools and property.[45] Six of the church
leaders were imprisoned for four years. The church regrouped in house fellowships[46]
and was not reopened until after the Derg had fallen from power. Other small Protestant churches were affected by closure as well, like the Emmaniel Baptist Church and
the Southern Baptist Church.[47]

5.1.3   The Full Gospel Believers' Church

After the arrests and legal proceedings of 1972/73, the Full Gospel Believers' Church
(FGBC) had remained underground for the last two years of the Imperial government,
but it swiftly reacted to the changing political circumstances at the onset of the revolution. In August of 1974, the Addis Ababa leaders convened a national meeting in the
ECMY Youth Hostel, in order to reestablish their national network.[48] The meeting
was attended by 44 representatives from different regions and saw the establishment
of an "Ethiopian Full Gospel Believers' Church Coordinating Committee" consisting
of seven members.[49] Possibly as early as September 1974, latest by January 1975,
the FGBC resumed public meetings in Addis Ababa.[50] This bold step apparently
came at the heels of negotiations with the new authorities, the outcome of which is
not entirely clear. It is interesting to note that while the later histories insist that an

---

43 See ibid., 161–171.

44 Ibid., 27.

45 See ibid., 17–29. Eide's notion that the congregation in Wonji was not shut down, (EIDE, *Revolu-
    tion and Religion in Ethiopia*, 171) does not agree with the MKC church historians who explicitely
    mention the closure of this place as well, cf. HEGE, *Beyond Our Prayers*, 28; TILAHUN BEYENE,
    ". . . ቤተ ክርስቲያኔን እሥራለሁ. . . ": የመሰረተ ክርስቶስ ቤተ ክርስቲያን ታሪክ, 133.

46 These house fellowships could be quite extensive. For example, for Dire Dawa, Girma Haile
    provides a list of 51 individuals, who had offered their house to study groups, prayer, or other
    meetings. For the organization and content of the house meetings, see GIRMA HAILE, "The
    Brief History of Dire Dawa Meserete Kristos Church," 15; also PETER DULA, "Reading Yoder
    in Ethiopia: The Spirit of God and the Politics of Men, 1974–1991" (Unpublished manuscript,
    private collection, 2002), 21–24.

47 EIDE, *Revolution and Religion in Ethiopia*, 172.

48 It is unclear to what degree the meeting actually was an answer to the onset of the revolution.
    While Engelsviken (ENGELSVIKEN, "Molo Wongel," 223) contends that the meeting intended "to
    discuss the future of the church in light of the recent political developments," the FGBC history
    from 1978 notes that the church had grown substantially and notes as the main agenda "to consult
    how they could watch over and care for the church's ministry and life in the strong winds of the
    persecution coming against it," cf. ETHIOPIAN FULL GOSPEL BELIEVERS' CHURCH, ሙሉ ወንጌል ቤተ
    ክርስቲያን ካልደት እስከ . . ., 28.

49 See ibid.

50 Ibid., 32 notes that in መስከረም (*mäskäräm*) 1967 (Ethiopian calendar) "the usual Full Gospel Church
    ministry was resumed in public." Engelsviken, on the other hand, and with him Yosief Kidanewold
    date this to January 1975, see ENGELSVIKEN, "Molo Wongel," 224; YOSIEF KIDANEWOLD, "The
    History of the Pentecostal Movement in Addis Abeba," 49. Since mäskäräm is the first month
    of the Ethiopian calendar, it is also possible that this discrepancy is due to a simple conversion
    error one way or another.

official permission was granted,[51] the earlier sources, which undoubtedly had more reason to celebrate such an achievement, at best only hinted at a contact with the authorities.[52] This period of public meetings and structural consolidation lasted until May of 1976, when the church was evicted from their rented premises on account of a local riot and subsequently found no support with the executive or judicial authorities in the district.[53] In the same year, however, the church was granted a piece of land by the city authorities, and in January 1977 the FGBC embarked on a building project after an apparently lively debate about the risks of such an undertaking in Ethiopia's present instability.[54] Due to a number of practical difficulties, the project took almost two years and was completed in October 1978, when the FGBC dedicated its first church building. However, after only eleven months, the church was closed and its property confiscated on Sunday, September 9, 1979.[55] The church was reorganized and remained in underground house fellowships until the end of the Derg.

There are not many records regarding the political oppression of the FGBC outside of Addis Ababa. Moreover, it is difficult to establish how far the young church had penetrated Ethiopia beyond its early centers and university towns. Since the FGBC was still in the middle of establishing its national structure at the outset of the revolution, there are no lists of preaching places or congregations at that time. Pentecostal preachers had reached many remote places during student campaigns under Haile Selassie and the Derg, but the measure and longevity of their evangelistic achievements is largely unknown.[56] However, the sporadic information available about locations outside of Addis Ababa indicates that the closure of the church in the capital came

---

51 See Ethiopian Full Gospel Believer's Church, የኢትዮጵያ ሙሉ ወንጌል አመኞች ቤተ ክርስቲያን 25ኛ ዓመት በዓል, 11; Addis Ababa Full Gospel Believers' Church, የ40ኛ ዓመት የወንጌል አገልግሎትና የምስጋና በዓል መጽሔት /ሐምሌ 1958–1998 ዓ.ም./, 14. The FGBC 40-year anniversary video even displays a document as proof, which unfortunately is too blurry to read, see Addis Ababa Full Gospel Believers' Church, የ40 አመት የወንጌል አገልግሎት (ሐምሌ 1958–1998 ዓ.ም.) ዶክመንተሪ ቪ.ሲ.ዲ., [Documentary VCD of Forty Years of Gospel Ministry (July 1966–2006).] (Addis Ababa, 2006), min. 16:30. The document appears to hold official government stamps and the revolutionary signature "ኢትዮጵያ ትቅደም" (ityopya təqdäm), "Ethiopia First!").

52 Engelsviken knows of no such agreement, and Yosief Kidanewold cites an informant that a revokable permission was granted for three months and later extended indefinitely, see Engelsviken, "Molo Wongel," 224; Yosief Kidanewold, "The History of the Pentecostal Movement in Addis Abeba," 49. Most importantly the church's own historians noted that the movement's leaders had announced their plans in detail to a number of authorities, and since their letter found no opposition, they simply proceeded with establishing public meetings, see Ethiopian Full Gospel Believers' Church, ሙሉ ወንጌል ቤተ ክርስቲያን ከልደት እስከ . . ., 31–32.

53 See Yosief Kidanewold, "The History of the Pentecostal Movement in Addis Abeba," 49; Taye Abdissa, "The Pentecostal Development and the Rise of Charismatic Movement in Ethiopia," 30; esp. Ethiopian Full Gospel Believers' Church, ሙሉ ወንጌል ቤተ ክርስቲያን ከልደት እስከ . . ., 33-35; Ethiopian Full Gospel Believer's Church, የኢትዮጵያ ሙሉ ወንጌል አመኞች ቤተ ክርስቲያን 25ኛ ዓመት በዓል, 11; Addis Ababa Full Gospel Believers' Church, የ40ኛ ዓመት የወንጌል አገልግሎትና የምስጋና በዓል መጽሔት /ሐምሌ 1958–1998 ዓ.ም./, 14. Some of these sources hold that the riot was instigated by the local Kebele authorities.

54 See Ethiopian Full Gospel Believers' Church, ሙሉ ወንጌል ቤተ ክርስቲያን ከልደት እስከ . . ., 35–36.

55 See Addis Ababa Full Gospel Believers' Church, የ40ኛ ዓመት የወንጌል አገልግሎትና የምስጋና በዓል መጽሔት /ሐምሌ 1958–1998 ዓ.ም./, 14.

56 In the town of Gimbi, West Welega province, for example, there had been a small FGBC house fellowship in the 1970s, which was discontinued after some years due to its leaders moving to other areas. It was reestablished in 1985 and turned into a church in 1992, after the end of the

fairly late, if not last. In Bahir Dar, the FGBC group had obtained an official permit at the beginning of the revolution, but after only 18 months they encountered local opposition by the Derg in cooperation with the EOC, which led to the closure of the church and the revocation of their license.[57] In June 1978 Pentecostal youths were imprisoned in western Welega for refusing to shout revolutionary slogans.[58] In the southern town of Yirga Alem, a local Pentecostal fellowship joined the FGBC in 1974 and subsequently rented a premise from the Kebele as its meeting place.[59] After intermittent periods of closure, members and leaders of this church were arrested in April of 1979 and the church continued as an underground fellowship.[60] Among them was the well-known singer and evangelist Tesfaye Gabbiso, who was held in prison for seven years without trial and was subject to beatings, torture and mistreatment. His case was widely reported, making him perhaps the most prominent Pentecostal victim of the Derg.[61]

Though the extent of political repression varied between regions, it appears that all of the local FGBC congregations remained closed throughout the Derg.[62] The churches regrouped in small home groups, and despite the limits of such underground structures, the FGBC managed to expand during the Derg. Its membership grew significantly and it reached new regions, especially toward the end of the Derg time when repressions became less severe. These expansions apparently were not centrally administered, but mostly resulted from FGBC members moving or local fellowships branching out to other towns. In the southern towns of Awasa, Dilla and Sire, for example, the local FGBC congregations were established as house fellowships between 1985 and 1989.[63], and in the central eastern town of Metahara an FGBC fellowship was

---

Derg. See MENGESHA AGA, "Evangelism and Charismatic Movement in Ghimbi District Western Synod EECMY 1914–1999," 8–9.

57 Interview no. 63. The dates provided by the informant here are flawed and do not correspond to the rest of the biography provided. However, the context of the remarks indicates that the closure happened while the Derg was still struggling with different political movements, so probably at the beginning of the Red Terror, i.e., 1977/8. See also TSEGA ENDALEW, "Protestant Mission Activities and Persecutions in Bahər Dar, 1968–1994: A Chronicle," in *Ethiopia and the Missions: Historical and Anthropological Insights*, ed. VERENA BÖLL, ANDREU MARTÍNEZ D' ALÒS-MONER, and EVGENIA SOKOLINSKAIA (Münster: Lit, 2005), 214–216.

58 JETO HORDOFA, "'Troubled But Not Destroyed'," 31–32. Some of these youths also belonged to the ECMY.

59 Interview no. 76.

60 See *Keston News Service*, "Tesfaye Gabiso"; interview no. 76.

61 See ibid.; CUMBERS, *Count It All Joy*, 66–67; LILA W. BALISKI, "Theology in Song: Ethiopia's Tesfaye Gabbiso," *Missiology* 25 (4 1997): 449–450; TIBEBE ESHETE, *The Evangelical Movement in Ethiopia*, 246f. VERNON CHARTER, "Contested Symbols: Music, Revolution, and Renewal in Ethiopian Protestant Churches," *EthnoDoxology* 3 (3 2006): 9–10, http://instructor.prairie. edu/charterv/Documents/Theology%20of%20Worship/Charter%20-%20Contested%20Symbols. pdf (accessed December 12, 2008). Others, like Teshome Worku and Haile Bekele were arrested alongside with Tesfaye and suffered a similar fate, see BEKELE WOLDEKIDAN, ረገደታ, 142.

62 Interview no. 1.

63 Cf. MINTESINOT BIRRU, "The Impact of Charismatic Movement and Its Result Among Evangelicals in Gedeo Area," 10–11; DAMENE DEGU, "The History of Evangelical Christianity in Arsi Sire," 9–10; also interview no. 76. In Sire the establishment resulted from church members moving to the town, whereas the Awasa church was a branch of the underground Yirga Alem fellowship.

established in 1987.[64] The possibilities for growing such house fellowships varied with the local conditions, since security concerns were high when the political pressure was strong. One prominent member of the FGBC, for example, reported in an interview, that he became a member of the church in Yirga Alem while it was closed for a time in 1976.[65] He was invited to one of their local house fellowships after attending a Sunday service at the ECMY, and subsequently remained with the group and received his water baptism there. Quite the opposite story was told by a Charismatic member of the MKC who after moving to Bahir Dar in 1985 was not accepted by the local FGBC fellowship out of security concerns. He remained without any church affiliation until his own denomination established a small fellowship in 1987.[66]

When the EPRDF took over, the FGBC congregations soon reemerged, now discovering their significant rise in membership. In Addis Ababa, for example, the confiscated building was returned within months after the EPRDF had entered the capital and the church held its first public worship service on December 29, 1991 with an estimated 15,000 worshipers.[67] The FGBC now for the first time was officially registered as a religious association and was free to operate anywhere in the country, though in some regions it took a few years until religious equality was realized in practice.[68]

5.1.4 The Finnish Mission and the Gennet Church

With regard to the Finnish Free Foreign Mission (FFFM) and the church that grew from it, the Gennet Church (GC), a somewhat more comprehensive and detailed account can be given, based on two unpublished sources, the "Condensed History" by the FFFM missionary Kyösti Roininen and the Bachelor thesis of the GC pastor Ashebir Ketema.[69] At the time of the revolution, the Finnish Mission was working in four regions of Ethiopia: Shewa (Addis Ababa, Holeta, Wolmera), Kefa (Shebe, Chekorsa), Sidama (Awasa), and Eritrea (Asmara). Especially in Sidama the mission had been successful in establishing local churches. There were eleven churches in this region when the revolution began, prompting the FFFM to organize a fellowship of Sidama churches for mutual encouragement.[70] With the exception of Asmara,

---

64 See ALEMU SAMUEL, "History of the Meserete Kristos Church Growth at Metahara Since 1967," 28.
65 Interview no. 112.
66 Interview no. 7.
67 ADDIS ABABA FULL GOSPEL BELIEVERS' CHURCH, የ40ኛ ዓመት የወንጌል አገልግሎትና የምስጋና በዓል መጽሐፍ /ሕምስ 1958–1998 ዓ.ም./, 15.
68 In Bahir Dar, for example, riots and clashes, reportedly prompted by the EOC, amounted to a strong opposition against the Pentecostals. The FGBC was not licensed locally until 1993/4, and after an escalation during a 1994 conference, violence decreased, mostly due to the political protection Pentecostals now enjoy. See TSEGA ENDALEW, "Protestant Mission Activities and Persecutions in Bahər Dar, 1968–1994," 216–218; also interviews no. 125; 63.
69 See ASHEBIR KETEMA, "The History of Ethiopian Guenet Church"; ROININEN, "A Condensed History of the Finnish Mission in Ethiopia." Both sources, though lacking in detail and political analysis, provide a regionally sorted historical overview of the FFFM and the GC during the Derg.
70 See ASHEBIR KETEMA, "The History of Ethiopian Guenet Church," 20. ROININEN, "A Condensed History of the Finnish Mission in Ethiopia," 4 notes that when the GC was established in 1978, the majority of churches came from the Sidama area.

neither the missionaries nor the church encountered significant political difficulties until 1978.[71]

Perhaps the most significant development of these initial years was the establishment of an independent Ethiopian congregation in Addis Ababa. After its temporary closure in 1973, the congregation at the FFFM Merkato work center had increased significantly in the final year of Haile Selassie's reign, since it was the only Pentecostal church in town that remained open.[72] However, soon after the revolution, the FFFM congregation once again suffered a major split and was left with only a few members.[73] In 1976, the Finnish Mission set out to reestablish its church work at Merkato by appointing elders and hiring two Ethiopians for full-time work, Hiruy Tsige and Anberber Gebru.[74] They apparently managed to form a thriving congregation, and on April 15, 1977, Hiruy Tsige wrote a letter to the representative of the FFFM, Kyösti Roininen, informing the mission of the desire of the church to independently pay all of its expenses beginning May 1, and to become a local church under the name "Sefere Gennet Church."[75] Roininen's reply was favorable, stating that it had been "our prayer and wish that, one day, this Church would be able to stand by itself as a National Church."[76]

In 1978, the political pressure on the FFFM increased significantly, first in Wolmera and Holeta. After the mission had received permission for a new Health Center and while it was waiting to be given the tenancy of land, the Derg established a new garrison of 100,000 soldiers at Wolmera, and declared the Wolmera and Holeta as military areas, forbidding the presence of foreigners. The mission was forced to turn over their projects to the government, the church building of the Holeta congregation was taken over and some Christians were imprisoned.[77] In Kefa, pressure also increased at the beginning of 1978, when a number of mission stations, including the FFFM were searched through by the local security police for alleged anti-communist activi-

---

71 The Asmara work had only begun in 1971 with the intention of building a school, a library, and a youth center. Due to the difficult situation in Eritrea, the FFFM missionaries left again in 1974, having established only the youth center, which was the nucleus of the church they left behind. After two years, the church was closed in December 1976, resulting from "an armed incident at the church between the security police and the guerilla-organization," ibid., 7. The FFFM managed to renew its agreement with the government and a school was opened in March 1977, run by nationals, which continued to operate even when the FFFM was expelled from other parts of the country, see ibid., 13.
72 Ibid., 8 reports a church membership of 300 and Sunday attendance of 1,000 for this time.
73 See ETHIOPIAN GENNET CHURCH, የ50ኛው ዓመት የወርቅ ኢዮቤልዩ በዓል, 19; ROININEN, "A Condensed History of the Finnish Mission in Ethiopia," 9; also mentioned in interview no. 5. The background of this split is not elicited in any of the sources, but it is not difficult to imagine that at a time when the propagation of freedom of religion came with many opportunities to establish churches and abolished the need for a missionary umbrella, the Ethiopian believers would be less likely to tolerate any grievances with the missionaries in charge.
74 See ibid., 12. Despite a later fall-out with the FFFM and the GC, Hiruy Tsige is a prominent figure of the GC history, whereas Anberber Gebru is not mentioned, see ETHIOPIAN GENNET CHURCH, የ50ኛው ዓመት የወርቅ ኢዮቤልዩ በዓል.
75 "Sefere Gennet" ("Area of Paradise") was the name of the area in which the congregation was located.
76 For facsimiles of both letters see ETHIOPIAN GENNET CHURCH, የ50ኛው ዓመት የወርቅ ኢዮቤልዩ በዓል, 20.
77 See ROININEN, "A Condensed History of the Finnish Mission in Ethiopia," 10; ASHEBIR KETEMA, "The History of Ethiopian Guenet Church," 11–12.

ties. Just two months after the inauguration of the Shebe Health Center, the FFFM
was informed on May 26, 1978 that all their missionaries must leave Kefa within 24
hours.[78] The church buildings in Shebe and Chekorsa were taken over by the farmer's
association, and since most members subsequently left the church, the congregations
nearly collapsed.[79] Two days after the expulsion from Kefa, the FFFM missionaries
in Ethiopia gathered and agreed to draw down their work. For a short time three
missionaries remained at Awasa and two in Addis Ababa to oversee the transition of
the work. The Awasa orphanage was closed and the children living there either were
transferred to the Adventist boarding school or returned to close relatives.[80] In Addis
Ababa, a meeting was held in June, to which twenty church leaders were invited in
order to form a fellowship of the Finnish Mission Churches. The assembled ministers
resolved to establish a Home Missions Fund in connection to the already independent Sefere Gennet Church and to use the name Gennet Church in all localities (e.g.
Holeta Gennet Church) as well as for the national structure (i.e., Ethiopian Gennet
Church). In addition, a committee consisting of eleven men was chosen to coordinate
the national work.[81] The Addis Ababa pastor Hiruy Tsige was named as representative of the FFFM in Ethiopia, and on July 18, 1978 the last Finnish missionaries left
Ethiopia.[82]

In the following year, Hiruy Tsige faced strong headwinds as representative of the
mission. He had to administrate the closure of a number of FFFM projects while
others had to be turned over to the Derg. Moreover, he had to deal with certain
accusations by labor unions against the mission, and was even imprisoned over this
dispute for some time.[83] At the same time there apparently was growing discontent
with his management and leadership from the side of the FFFM and the Ethiopian
church. In July/August of 1979, Kyösti Roininen made another trip to Ethiopia in
order to sort out these difficulties.[84] A meeting was held on July 28, 1979 with the
elders of the Addis Ababa church, representatives of the GC and Kyösti Roininen.
In this meeting Hiruy Tsige was confirmed as "the fully authorized representative
taking care of the affairs with the Ethiopian government," but at the same time his
authority was reigned in by the appointment of an assistant in charge of "keeping the
connection with the churches in the provinces," and an accountant who would be able
to access the FFFM bank account.[85]

---

78 See ROININEN, "A Condensed History of the Finnish Mission in Ethiopia," 10–11. The FFFM
   projects in Shebe and Chekorsa were nationalized. See also ASHEBIR KETEMA, "The History of
   Ethiopian Guenet Church," 15. All other missions, including the Swedish Philadelphia Church
   Mission (SPCM) had already been expelled earlier in 1978, cf. NYBERG OSKARSSON, *Svensk
   Pingstmission i Ethiopien (1959–1980)*, 143, 257.
79 See ASHEBIR KETEMA, "The History of Ethiopian Guenet Church," 15–16. The congregation in
   Shebe reportedly was left with 7 members, in Chekorsa with 2. At the end of the 1980s both
   churches grew again.
80 See ROININEN, "A Condensed History of the Finnish Mission in Ethiopia," 12.
81 See ibid., 13; SELESHI KEBEDE, "The History of the Guenet Church," 23; ASHEBIR KETEMA, "The
   History of Ethiopian Guenet Church," 29.
82 ROININEN, "A Condensed History of the Finnish Mission in Ethiopia," 13.
83 Interview no. 5; see also ibid.
84 Roininen already had returned to Ethiopia for a four-month trip in January, see ibid.
85 See HIRUY TSIGE and BERHANU KEBEDE, "Minutes of the Meeting of the Elders of Sefere Guennet
   Church and of the Representatives of Guennet Churches Associated with the Finnish Mission Held

Only one month after this meeting, the Addis Ababa church at Merkato was occupied by militia during the Sunday service and shut down.[86] A large number of believers were detained for questioning, and Hiruy Tsige, his assistant as mission representative, and the Addis Ababa assistant pastor were held in prison for seven months.[87] Just prior to the Addis Ababa closure, the congregations in Holeta and Wolmera were also closed, their buildings confiscated alongside the mission property, and in Holeta there were some arrests.[88] Both congregations saw a significant decrease in membership, and the remnant continued in small home fellowships. Intermittent attacks on the remaining leadership brought instability to the churches and in 1988 both were placed under Addis Ababa Gennet Church administration. In Sidama, the expulsion of the missionaries had the opposite effect: the churches continued to function and grew in number. All except one remained open throughout the Derg.[89] In Asmara, the church was able to continue under the umbrella of a school.[90]

The imprisoned church leaders in Addis Ababa were released in March 1980, and in July the FFFM representative Kyösti Roininen returned to Addis Ababa, in order "to determine the prospects of continuing the work of the Mission."[91] His return led to a fallout between him and Hiruy over alleged mismanagement of mission property.[92] Since a number of the GC elders did not side with Hiruy in this matter, he resigned from the church and subsequently joined a house fellowship, which grew into the Harvest Church of God (HCG) under his leadership.

Meanwhile the Finnish missionaries had been successful in reestablishing their presence in the country.[93] In 1981, the Ministry of Education agreed to a new school

---

on Saturday 28th of July 1979 in Sefere Guennet Church, Addis Ababa," Later Correspondence, Fida Archives, Helsinki, 1979. It was also decided to channel the evangelism aid through the Addis Ababa church account for administrative reasons, and that the church should negotiate the raise of the Merkato rent directly with the authorities.

86 See ROININEN, "A Condensed History of the Finnish Mission in Ethiopia," 13; ASHEBIR KETEMA, "The History of Ethiopian Guenet Church," 3; also interview no. 5. Ashebir dates the closure to 1980, see also SCHRÖDER, "Äthiopien"; ETHIOPIAN GENNET CHURCH, የ5ዐኛው ዓመት የወርቅ ኢየቤልዩ በዓል, 17. However, in an official letter to the Minister of Public Works & Housing, Roininen dates the occupation of the premises to August 1979, see KYÖSTI ROININEN, Letter to the Minister of Public Works & Housing, 5 December 1980, Later Correspondence, Fida Archives, Helsinki. Furthermore, the date provided by Ashebir, August 20, 1980, was a Wednesday. If August is substituted by the Ethiopian equivalent, the month of ነሐሴ (näḥase), the 20th would have been a Sunday in 1979 (Eth. cal. 1971), but not in 1980 (1972).

87 The number of arrests was estimated at 350, see ASHEBIR KETEMA, "The History of Ethiopian Guenet Church," 3.

88 See ibid., 7–12. Ashebir once again dates these closures to June of 1980, but Roininen mentions that Holeta was closed before Addis Ababa, therefore most likely in June 1979, see ROININEN, "A Condensed History of the Finnish Mission in Ethiopia," 13.

89 ASHEBIR KETEMA, "The History of Ethiopian Guenet Church," 21–22. Apparently even new church buildings were erected in the region, see HEIKKI PENTTINEN, "Report about trip to Ethiopia from May 25 - July 21, 1981," Later Correspondence, Fida Archives, Helsinki, 1981.

90 See ibid.

91 ROININEN, "A Condensed History of the Finnish Mission in Ethiopia," 14.

92 See SCHRÖDER, "Äthiopien"; also interviews no. 5; 69.

93 There also were some diplomatic efforts to reclaim the confiscated property. Representatives of the FFFM met the Ethiopian Commissioner of Relief and Rehabilitation during his visit to Finland in 1981 and handed him a detailed list of all confiscated property, totaling to 1.1 mill. Eth. Birr, see UNTO KUNNAS, VEIKKO MANNINEN, and KYÖSTI ROININEN, Letter to Mr: Ato Shimeles

project in Asmara and the orphanage in Wolmera was returned to the FFFM.[94] In January 1982 an agreement with the Ministry of Health was signed for the construction of a health center in Holeta.[95] While the premises in Addis Ababa were not returned, the FFFM succeeded in acquiring a lease of another sizeable property, which was not only used as mission headquarters, but also for the underground GC. Furthermore it hosted the archives of the FGBC and was used for joint Bible courses of the GC, FGBC, and MKC.[96] The FFFM collaborated with the SPCM in a relief program during the drought in Welo, and after a number of attempts to reenter the Kefa province, the mission signed an agreement for the development of Health Services in the Shebe area and was able to reclaim the clinic and the church in Shebe in 1989. By the end of the Derg, the FFFM had over 25 missionaries stationed in the country.[97] While the missionaries were not invited to underground GC church services in Addis Ababa for security reasons, their relative freedom to travel in the country helped them to inter-connect the rural churches and to provide practical help, for example, by secretly distributing Bibles or corrugated iron sheets for church roofs.[98]

The GC in Addis Ababa set up an elaborate underground network and engaged in supporting the establishment of new congregations in rural areas, which also helped to strengthen the Addis Ababa church's position. In the Shewa region, new congregations were founded in Acheber, Oger, Terhogne, and Nazaret between 1987 and 1989.[99] These churches received ministry support from the Addis Ababa Gennet Church and were placed under their care. In the Kefa region, an underground home fellowship was established in Jima in the 1980s, which served Protestants from other churches as well, and subsequently branched out to the west and southwest of Jima.[100] A first congregation in northern Ethiopia emerged out of an FGBC fellowship in Kombolcha, Welo, when a number of GC members moved there and set up an underground fellowship with support by ministers from Addis Ababa. The most significant growth of GC churches occurred in Sidama, where in 1988 forty churches were recorded, and 120 in 1992. Because of the strength of the Sidama churches, and since they had established a local fellowship before the national structure was founded, their local governing

Adugna, Commissioner of Relief and Rehabilitation, 26 May 1981, Later Correspondence, Fida Archives, Helsinki.

94   See ROININEN, "A Condensed History of the Finnish Mission in Ethiopia," 15–16. The building had never been officially confiscated, PENTTINEN, "Report about trip to Ethiopia from May 25 - July 21, 1981." In Asmara, the school was not completed until 1989, due to the ongoing war in Eritrea.

95   See KYÖSTI ROININEN and WEGAYEHU SAHLU, Letter of Understanding Between the Finnish Mission and the Ministry of Health Concerning the Construction and Operation of Holeta Health Center, 15 January 1982, Later Correspondence, Fida Archives, Helsinki. Due to a disagreement between the Ministry of Health and the National Development and Planning Commission, the work was not begun until 1984. Roininen claims that Mengistu Haile Mariam himself decided the issue in favor of the mission, see ROININEN, "A Condensed History of the Finnish Mission in Ethiopia," 16.

96   See ibid., 15, 17–18.

97   Cf. ibid., 16–17.

98   ibid., 189; also interview no. 104.

99   See ASHEBIR KETEMA, "The History of Ethiopian Guenet Church," 13, 26–28.

100   See ibid., 16–19.

body ran somewhat parallel to the GC in Addis Ababa.[101] In 1987, the Sidama Gennet Church suffered a split when a number of local congregations bypassed the Sidama fellowship, received direct support from the FFFM, and subsequently refused to sign a new constitution, which also aimed to regulate such matters.[102] This split was not reconciled until 1992. Meanwhile, the Addis Ababa Gennet Church made use of the growing political vacuum in the capital and began to meet in larger groups, while also formalizing the church's national structure.[103] In 1988 a constitution was drafted and put into effect in 1989.[104]

After the Derg fell from power, the confiscated property was returned to the Addis Ababa church. In numerous places in the country new Gennet congregations were established from previous underground fellowships or personal contacts.

5.1.5 The Swedish Mission and the Hiwot Berhan Church

The SPCM was in a position similar to the FFFM at the onset of the revolution. Outside of the headquarters in Addis Ababa, the mission had projects in the southwest (Jima, Karo/Kibish in the Omo valley), south (Awasa, Wendo Genet, Worancha, Yirga Alem, Ziway) and southeast of Ethiopia (the leprosy rehabilitation farms Addis Hiwot and Tesfa Hiwot, Masslo).[105] From 1972 to 74 the Swedish Pentecostals also began engaging in relief work with a resettlement site in northern Kefa (Botter) as well as food distribution and health services in southernmost Bale (Dolo Bay, Somali Border).[106] Moreover, the SPCM had just become the only representative of all Swedish Pentecostal initiatives in Ethiopia with the takeover of Swedish Industrial Mission (SWIM) in February of 1974.

A number of the mission projects had sparked local Pentecostal congregations, some of which were governed by Ethiopian elders (Awasa, Wendo Genet), an Ethiopian pastor (Jima, Addis Hiwot), or an evangelist in collaboration with Swedish missionaries (Worancha). After the collaboration with the FGBC failed in Addis Ababa, an SPCM congregation was established there in May 1974 and led by an Ethiopian pastor. However, all of these congregations financially depended on the SPCM for

---

101 See ibid., 23–24. However, their representatives were part of the Ethiopian GC.

102 Ibid., 21–22; ROININEN, "A Condensed History of the Finnish Mission in Ethiopia," 18–19. The Sidama Fellowship tried to complain about this matter to the FFFM in Finland in 1987, see SIDAMO GENET CONGREGATION COMMITTEE, Letter to Tapani Kärnä, 25 April 1987, Later Correspondence, Fida Archives, Helsinki; DOCTOR DEBISO, Letter to Finnish missionaries, 5 August 1987, Fida International, Fida Archives, Helsinki. The strong emphasis on congregationalism in the Finnish Pentecostal movement of course left some missionaries reluctant to let central governing bodies control their relationships with individual churches.

103 See ASHEBIR KETEMA, "The History of Ethiopian Guenet Church," 4. Other open churches apparently hosted these congregations.

104 Ibid., 4, 29.

105 Cf. section 2.3, 59, for more details NYBERG OSKARSSON, *Svensk Pingstmission i Ethiopien (1959–1980)*. Though Addis Hiwot and Tesfa Hiwot were taken over by Rädda Barnen/Save the Children Sweden in 1970/1, the Swedish Pentecostal missionaries continued to collaborate in development and spiritual work.

106 See ibid., 214–220.

their staff and other assets, and their real estate belonged to the mission.[107] The
work of the SPCM itself was led solely by Swedish missionaries, with occasional but
not institutionalized participation of Ethiopian nationals during the yearly field conferences.[108] Toward the end of his last term in Ethiopia in 1969, Karl Ramstrand
had put forward a five-year-plan of turning over the mission work to Ethiopians,
which would have only had two mission representatives working in Ethiopia in 1974.
However, Ramstrand's plan was not taken up in any serious manner, neither by the
Ethiopian SPCM field conference, nor in Sweden.[109] The main concern voiced against
turning over the mission property was the impossibility of establishing an officially
registered Ethiopian church in Imperial Ethiopia.

The Ethiopian revolution at first appeared to abolish this restriction, and the
SPCM invited representatives of its congregations to the yearly mission meeting in
Awasa in July 1975. The representatives agreed to form their own association under
the Ethiopian name of Hiwot Berhan Church (HBC).[110] The church began to use
this name in its official correspondence, but the application for registration was not
received favorably.[111] Consequentially, the HBC was no legal entity and could not
take over property from the mission. When such transfers were made, they needed to
go to individuals or to a foundation. In Awasa, for example, the piece of the property
containing the church building and a smaller workshop was handed over to a group
of elders in 1977, who stood as its owners.[112]

Despite this limitation, the work of the HBC and the SPCM continued without
major political resistance in the first few years of the Derg. In Addis Ababa the
new SPCM headquarters were established alongside the Ethiopian congregation. The
mission hosted large conferences in 1975 and 1977, the latter of which also served the
FGBC, since it had been evicted from their rented property in 1976.[113] In Jima a

---

107   The only exception was the church in Wendo Genet, which had been turned over in 1973 to
       a foundation established by the elders of the church there, see NYBERG OSKARSSON, *Svensk
       Pingstmission i Ethiopien (1959–1980)*, 97.
108   See ibid., 230–231.
109   See ibid., 230. Ramstrand voiced his disappointment about this development by complain-
       ing about "those who are interested in running a conventional mission" in a letter to Arvid
       Malmvärn at the end of 1969, noting that his contributions will now go to the FGBC in-
       stead, see KARL RAMSTRAND, Letter to Arvid Malmvärn, 15 December 1969, Karl Ramstrand
       Collection, Pingstarkiv Kaggeholm, Ekerö.
110   The name means Light of Life Church and was chosen in reference to John 8:12. See NYBERG
       OSKARSSON, *Svensk Pingstmission i Ethiopien (1959–1980)*, 153, 231; also interviews no. 100;
       103; 12.
111   Though it was already decided in 1975 to apply for registration, the application was not
       prepared until 1977, and reportedly not handed in until 1978, see MEKRU BEKELE, Letter to
       Tage Johansson, 1 August 1977, Tage Johansson Collection, Pingstarkiv Kaggeholm, Ekerö;
       NYBERG OSKARSSON, *Svensk Pingstmission i Ethiopien (1959–1980)*, 153, 231. These delays
       may have been caused by political difficulties between the Awasa church and the Addis Ababa
       representatives. The application request was never answered, but the church was informed in
       November 1979 that the application was "lost" at a point in time when the Addis Ababa HBC
       congregation had been shut down by the authorities.
112   See ibid., 201.
113   Ibid., 150–151. The 1977 conference went for nine days and reportedly had a peak attendance
       of around 2,000 participants, from all over Ethiopia, including the northern regions, see MEKRU
       BEKELE, Letter to Tage Johansson, August 1, 1977.

three-month Bible school was established in 1976,[114] and in Worancha a new church and Bible school building were erected in 1975, with open air meetings being held as late as 1979.[115] However, here as in Wendo Genet and Masslo, the Ogaden war and its repercussions caused serious disruptions to the work in 1977 and 1978, and in the case of Masslo the missionaries left altogether.[116] Likewise in Kibish the SPCM missionaries were evacuated because of guerilla warfare in the region.[117] In Addis Ababa there was an armed breach at the SPCM compound during the Red Terror in the fall of 1977, which ended peacefully, however, and without loss of property to the mission.[118]

The more systematic and direct political opposition against the SPCM and HBC began in 1978 in the Kefa province. In February, there was a large police meeting in Jima, at which one of the government leaders spoke out against foreign missions, and in March the mission station there was searched through by local officials. On April 8, 1978 the SPCM mission compound in Jima was taken by force and the missionaries were given 24 hours to leave the province.[119] The congregation in Jima was reorganized in home fellowships, and stayed underground until the end of the Derg. In Addis Ababa the HBC was closed one year later when in May 1979 the Sunday morning service was disrupted and many of the visitors arrested and held for a short time. In the fall, the Bible school was closed as well. The congregation continued in house meetings. The SPCM compound remained open, though there was an attempt to raise the rent to an exorbitant level, which was successfully thwarted by the mission.[120] The churches on the leprosy rehabilitation farms Addis Hiwot and Tesfa Hiwot were closed in 1981 and the congregation transitioned to smaller home meetings.[121] In Awasa, sporadic arrests had occurred in 1978/9, but the popular summer conferences were still held in 1979 and 1980.[122] Toward the end of 1979, the SPCM was asked by the government to upgrade their vocational school into a technical gymnasium for 150 students.[123] Though the mission at first was reluctant, it eventually complied with the request and the new school began its work in the fall of 1980.[124] However, on August 15, 1983, the school was taken over by the government

---

114 NYBERG OSKARSSON, *Svensk Pingstmission i Ethiopien (1959–1980)*, 138, 142.

115 Ibid., 107–109,112.

116 See ibid., 96, 122–123, 210.

117 See ibid., 181–182; also interview no. 115. The SPCM evacuated the missionaries against their own estimation that they were safe in the area. In 1980 relief work was begun again in the area.

118 See ibid., 153.

119 Ibid., 143. This expulsion happened after the SIM's eviction, but before the FFFM's.

120 See ibid., 153–154.

121 See ibid., 86.

122 See ibid., 192–193, 198.

123 This was part of a larger initiative of the Ministry of Education to improve secondary education, since the same request was also brought forward to the ECMY and the Adventist mission with regard to their vocational schools, see OSVALD HINDENES, "Anteckningar förda vid samråd på Utbildningsministeriet den 12 november 1979," [Notes taken at a consultation with the Ministry of Education on November 12, 1979], Filadelfiaförsamlingen Jönköping Collection, Religiösa organisationer, Jönköpings läns folkrörelsearkiv, Jönköping, November 12, 1972.

124 See BO HÖRNBERG and TAGE JOHANSSON, Letter to The Provisional Military Government of Socialist Ethiopia, The Ministry of Education and Fine Arts, 6 December 1979, Filadelfi-

and the adjacent church was closed and subsequently turned into a store.[125] The church in Awasa was reorganized into about forty fellowships.[126]

The work of the SPCM continued on a smaller scale, and focused mainly on relief and development in collaboration with the Relief and Rehabilitation Commission. Furthermore, the SPCM assisted the HBC by employing evangelists under their umbrella, for example as "management advisors."[127] The intensity of the political repressions against the church varied from region to region and over time. In Wendo Genet, Worancha, and Ziway the churches continued throughout the Derg without closure, though in Ziway all active church members had been put in jail for two months in 1983.[128] In Awasa, the home fellowships managed to come together for larger one-day-meetings in HBC or GC churches in the surrounding villages, and they would also baptize new believers in the Awasa lake at night or in rural places.[129] In other places, such as Bahir Dar, new churches were established in the underground.[130]

The time of political repression was accompanied by difficulties inside the HBC. Right from the establishment of the church, there had been a power struggle between the old center of the church in Awasa and the new denominational center in Addis Ababa. Almost half of the members of the new executive committee came from Awasa, and though these were the founding elders of the church there and of the denomination as a whole, their opponents saw this as an excessive representation of one local church. This dispute finally led to the excommunication of these key Awasa figures on behalf of the Addis Ababa denominational government, which in turn resulted in the Awasa church splitting away with a number of branches. In the following years there were two HBC churches in Ethiopia, even within the town of Awasa itself. Negotiations regarding the split were begun in 1984, and the two denominations were reunified and drafted a new constitution before the end of the Derg.[131] However, the centrality and importance of the Awasa church in relation to the denomination as a whole remained an issue inside the HBC, especially since Addis Ababa did not have a strong congregation.[132]

After the Derg fell, the reunified church registered with the government in December of 1991.[133] The confiscated buildings in Addis Ababa, Awasa, Addis Hiwot and

---

aförsamlingen Jönköping Collection, Religiösa organisationer, Jönköpings läns folkrörelsearkiv, Jönköping; NYBERG OSKARSSON, *Svensk Pingstmission i Ethiopien (1959–1980)*, 197–197.

125 See ibid., 202–203; also interviews no. 12; 34. Some members were put in jail for some months, where beatings also occurred.

126 Interviews no. 12; 34.

127 Interview no. 125.

128 See RAMSTRAND, *Det heliga äventyret*, 189; NYBERG OSKARSSON, *Svensk Pingstmission i Ethiopien (1959–1980)*, 212–213. In Ziway the church continued to meet publicly, but moved its baptisms to a lake further away.

129 Interview no. 34.

130 In 1984, the HBC accepted a Pentecostal home fellowship in Bahir Dar, begun by one of their members in 1974, mentioned in interview no. 57.

131 Interview no. 125. Ibid., 202 briefly hints at this split.

132 Interview no. 34. The Awasa church holds the privilege to bypass the regional leadership and participate in the national leadership directly, which is debated now and then.

133 Interview no. 125.

Tesfa Hiwot were returned to the HBC and a number of new churches were built in the following years.[134]

5.1.6 Other Pentecostal Groups

When the revolution began in 1974, the original flurry of independent Pentecostal groups, chapels, and ministries had consolidated somewhat, due not least to the political pressure during the last years of Haile Selassie's reign. Most Pentecostals outside the FGBC joined either the Finnish or Swedish Pentecostal mission churches or the MKC.

The only other independent Pentecostal church was the Apostolic Church of Ethiopia (ACE), which belongs to Oneness Pentecostalism and therefore denies the doctrine of the trinity, as was mentioned above. At the time of the revolution, the church was not in a good condition, since it had been heavily targeted by the political repressions against Pentecostalism under Haile Selassie.[135] As was already mentioned, the Awasa church had been destroyed in 1972 in a brutal mob attack, and the congregation apparently frayed. Awasa had been an important center for the denomination as a whole, since a large part of its following was in the south. The leading evangelist in the area, Teklemariam Gezahegne, who later took over the leadership of the whole denomination, could not continue this work in Awasa and was forced to relocate to Addis Ababa, where he apparently did not immediately connect with the existing church structure. Furthermore, in April of 1972, the church was banned nationally, and the United Pentecostal Church (UPC) missionaries, who had begun the work in Ethiopia and led the administrative work, were expelled.[136] The repressions against the church, the expulsion of the missionaries and Teklemariam's relocation to Addis Ababa, upset the power balance within the church, leading to internal conflicts that ended with a split in May 1975 and Teklemariam assuming control of the ACE.[137]

With the Ethiopian revolution, the political pressure on the church was lifted. Public services were resumed in 1974, and the ACE registered some growth again in 1975.[138] In August 1976, Teklemariam applied for a land grant in Addis Ababa, which was approved. With the help of the American UPC and (mostly labor) contributions by the Ethiopian members, the ACE managed to construct a church building, which was dedicated four years later, August 30, 1980.[139] This was at a time when other Pentecostal churches, like the FGBC had already been closed and confiscated. A land grant was also received in Chole, and most notably in Awasa, where a new building was completed in 1977.[140] The ACE was never shut down throughout the Derg and despite

---

134 The Awasa church was re-opened two months after the Derg was ousted, see interview no. 34.
135 See FREEMAN, *Unseen hands*, 139–152; also JOHANSSON, Letter to Bo Hörnberg, undated, probably April/May, 1972,
136 See FREEMAN, *Unseen hands*, 144–146.
137 See ibid., 153–162.
138 See ibid., 164.
139 Ibid., 190–192; SCHRÖDER, "Äthiopien," section Ethiopian Apostolic Church, p. 1; also interview no. 108.
140 FREEMAN, *Unseen hands*, 169, 180–182.

incidents of local opposition, no closure of local congregations has been reported.[141] Especially in the 1980s, the ACE managed to grow significantly and spread, especially in the west and most significantly the south of Ethiopia, also by taking over Lutheran churches.[142] The ACE at present is one of the major Pentecostal churches of Ethiopia, although it is largely ostracized and isolated in Ethiopia's Christian community.

Another early split in the FGBC occurred in 1974 over the Christian Deliverance doctrine. Casting out of demons had been a strong feature of the Pentecostal movement from the start, but a doctrinal dispute erupted over the possibility of demon possession among born-again Christians when publications and audio recordings of Derek Prince began to circulate in Ethiopia in the early 1970s. This issue had a peculiar twist in that one of the first elders and leaders of the FGBC, Fantahun Gebre, suffered from epileptic seizures, which those of the Deliverance faction, among them another FGBC elder, attributed to demon possession.[143] A final attempt to reconcile the theological differences on this issue failed in 1974 and led to the excommunication of the deliverance leaders, who subsequently began the Gospel Deliverance Church (GDC).[144] The issue continued to stir the FGBC; however, since some of the proponents of Christian Deliverance ministry had remained inside the FGBC, most prominently the evangelist Yemaneberhan Endale. He was excommunicated in August 1976, joined the GDC one year later, and became the leading figure of this church in 1978.[145] At this time the church consisted only of the Addis Ababa congregation, though reportedly there also was a larger following in Welega. In the same year, the church was shut down by the government and saw the arrest of some key leaders. This

---

141   Freeman, who gives ample room to incidents of opposition and imprisonment (see e.g. FREEMAN, *Unseen hands*, 180–182, 201–205), certainly would have found church closures worth reporting. Trinitarian Pentecostals also point to the fact that while they were underground, the ACE operated throughout the Derg, interview no. 64.

142   This is reported by sources from within and outside of the Jesus Only Movement, see ibid., 200–201, 208–210; TSADIKU ABDO, "Where Does Mulu Wongel Stand in its Trinitarian Concept: East or West? A Critical Approach to Ethiopian Mulu Wongel Church's Theology of Trinity," 64; ENGELSVIKEN, "Gudina Tumsa, the Ethiopian Evangelical Church Mekane Yesus, and the Charismatic Movement," 10. For a detailed report of such a take-over, see YOHANNES SHERAB, "The Rapid Growth of "Jesus Only" Movement," 72–78.

143   The story of Fantahun Gebre is somewhat mysterious in the Ethiopian sources. While Deliverance sources still entertain the idea of demon possession, others tell that he was ministering in Bahir Dar when the riot of 1968 occurred, and was severely beaten on the head, causing blood clots resulting in epilepsy. Furthermore, while he is mentioned as one of the ones who first split from the Finnish Mission in Addis Ababa, as lively preacher at the 1965 Awasa conference, and as one of the first FGBC elders, nothing is told of his later role and life later on, other than that he passed away, or "probably died." Cf. RAMSTRAND, Letter to supporters, August 22, 1965; ETHIOPIAN FULL GOSPEL BELIEVER'S CHURCH, የኢትዮጵያ ሙሉ ወንጌል አመኞች ቤተ ክርስቲያን 25ኛ ዓመት በዓል, 14; also interviews no. 53; 69; 130; 18. The allegation of a demon possession causing the epilepsy and ultimately his death later was brought forward especially forcefully by the ACE pastor Teklemariam Gezahegne, see FREEMAN, *Then Came the Glory*, 62.

144   SCHRÖDER, "Äthiopien," Ethiopian Gospel Deliverance Church, p. 1 dates this to 1973, but two oral sources with intimate knowledge of the conflict mention 1974 as date, interviews no. 53; 64. Both sides of the conflict recall an 11 hour meeting, at which the theological differences were resolved, but which in the end failed nevertheless, since neither group wanted to apologize to the other.

145   See ibid., section Ethiopian Gospel Deliverance Church, p. 1; BERHANU NEGA, "Life Story of Yemaneberhan Endale" (Unpublished paper, Addis Ababa, 2001), 15; also interview no. 53.

almost brought the church to an end, since many congregants sought refuge in the established churches and a split occurred within the remaining body over the doctrine of Full Salvation.[146] The remainder of the GDC managed to survive by congregating in a couple of Addis Ababa mainline churches, but since their doctrine was ostracized by most Protestant churches, they often had a difficult stand. After the Derg fell, the church reemerged and was able to reestablish itself and grow, especially since it increasingly found acceptance within the Protestant community, which culminated in the GDC joining the Evangelical Churches' Fellowship of Ethiopia (ECFE) in 2000.

5.2   Pentecostal Accounts of the Derg

As the overview of available sources in the introduction has shown, there are hardly any sources by Pentecostals which were produced during the Derg. With few exceptions, their story was virtually drowned out by information about the EOC and mainline Protestant churches. The influence and involvement of missions in the Ethiopian Pentecostal churches significantly decreased as well, and whatever information missionaries did have, they were reluctant to share in their correspondence. The overview of Pentecostals during the Derg in this chapter has also demonstrated the effects of this scarcity of sources, in that only a fragmented account could be produced, largely based on information gathered from oral interviews, a few written memoirs, and an occasional mention of local churches in seminary theses with a different topic.

The historical narratives about Pentecostalism during the Derg often compensate for this lack of information by telling a larger story of the significance of persecution for their church. In these stories, the Derg time appears as a monolithic historical totality marked by persecution, which in turn effects two historical overextensions. On the one hand, the initial years of the revolution, in which the position of the Pentecostals was all but clear, are interpreted in light of the later persecution experiences. On the other hand, the persecution narrative is central for interpreting church history after the Derg as well, even though the political context had changed considerably.

5.2.1   Sent by God to Bring Revival

The recent and influential Amharic church history by the FGBC pastor Bekele Woldekidan titled *Revival in Ethiopia*[147] is an instructive example of Ethiopian Pentecostals recapturing their history during the Ethiopian revolution in larger retrospective narratives. Though the book does not produce much detail about the Derg time, it wrestles extensively with what this period means for the Ethiopian church as a whole. In the beginning of his narrative, Bekele introduces the 1974 revolution with the following words:

> His [Haile Selassie's] government tried to stop God's visitation, using the police force and judicial institutions. God in turn, used his own army and stopped

---

146   Interview no. 53. According to the Full-Salvation doctrine, salvation is intended to penetrate the whole body, freeing it from sickness and ultimately death, and this state must be worked out by fasting, prayer and faith.

147   See Bekele Woldekidan, ሪቫይቫል.

that government. Right at the end of the 18th month after the Addis Ababa Full Gospel Church was closed by force, on February 27, 1974, the Ministerial Council collapsed. Right at the beginning of the 22nd month, on June 21, the military council [Derg] was founded. Right in the 36th month (that is exactly three years), on August 27, 1975, the death of the king was announced to Ethiopia and the world. Are these things by accident? I don't think so. The all powerful God was working what he had announced before.[148]

At first glance Bekele's assessment of the revolution as an act planned and carried out by God with "his own army" may seem like an echo of an early enthusiasm about the revolution, which could also be found in the Pentecostal community. However, a closer look reveals that this is not the case. The quote is part of a lengthy chapter titled "Do not Denounce Prophecy," which Bekele calls the central chapter in his book.[149] Here the author sets out by mentioning prophecies about the coming demise of the Ethiopian empire and puts them through a number of tests to affirm their accuracy and validity. Bekele then continues by establishing the Emperor's spiritual responsibility for the country and for what happened to Pentecostals during his reign,[150] followed by a number of encounters Haile Selassie has had with Protestant and Pentecostal missionaries and evangelists, including the Pentecostal traveling minister Ruth Ward Heflin. Finally he contrasts Ruth Heflin's messages to the emperor with the persecution of Pentecostals in 1972. It is here that he reaches the above-quoted conclusions about the Ethiopian revolution as an act of divine judgment responding to Haile Selassie's defiance of "God's visitation." Thus, the setting of the quote makes clear that the point is not to praise the revolution, but to place it in the context of a sovereignly directed, meaningful history.

Furthermore, even though Bekele contends that the revolution was an act of God, the following sections also show that he does not even see the initial revolution as a positive development. Though he briefly mentions the abolishment of the "intensely hated and feared feudalist land tenure", the housing reform, the student mobilization, and the reorganization of society in different local associations, he does not praise them as beneficial accomplishments, but notes that now "all the work accomplished under the old order was insulted," and that the new rulers "bragged that one day an earthly paradise would be installed on earth."[151] Most notably, the one significant reform to church politics which Bekele does not mention here is the abolishment of the constitutional link between the state and the EOC. This is left to a later chapter where the notes that while the Derg had removed Orthodox Christianity as state religion in theory, only the later EPRDF was "to show this in practice."[152]

---

148   BEKELE WOLDEKIDAN, ሪቫይቫል, 139. Girma Zewde shows a similar affinity to ascribe a special significance to the calendar, see GIRMA ZEWDE, ኢትዮጲስ, 175–188. Contending that the month of የካቲት (*yäkatit*), roughly February) had long been "the month of bloodshed and massacres" he lists out events that happened in February from the 15th century on, providing an especially detailed list for the Derg time, which of course had begun with a revolution in just this month.
149   See BEKELE WOLDEKIDAN, ሪቫይቫል, 115–150.
150   Bekele notes that Haile Selassie was the "first spiritual power" of the land and that he had the power to stop the persecution of Pentecostals, see ibid., 123–124.
151   See ibid., 140.
152   See ibid., 119.

Thus Bekele makes it very clear that God's judgment on Haile Selassie did not usher in a new and better era, but was the beginning of a time of total upheaval, which according to Bekele continues to the present.[153] Yet, despite all the unrest, Bekele still asserts that everything that happened was in God's will and plan.

In the following chapter, titled "Some of the Results of the Revolution" he discusses the unintended effects of the Derg rule in preparing Ethiopia for revival.[154] Insisting that Ethiopia was asleep spiritually, he sees the "sleeping animal rising"[155] in a number of ways. People were driven out of their country and into the unsettling diaspora abroad, where they were "guests for the country" and "without family nearby."[156] The ones remaining in Ethiopia were stripped of all their assurances, and with the politicization of religion they could not even find peace there. However, with all these unsettling effects, Bekele also sees a strengthening of the Ethiopian churches. Missionaries were forced to release their fellowships into independence sooner than they had intended. The underground church provided much better pastoral care and encouraged ecumenism as well as lay ministry, all in all establishing a vibrant community of believers that had passed many trials. Furthermore, Ethiopian evangelical churches were opened everywhere around the world, leading to an awakening among the exiled Ethiopians.[157] As these exiled Pentecostals continue to grow roots in their countries of residence, Bekele sees a tremendous potential for evangelization, resting to a large part on the second generation.[158] Finally, Bekele even calls the EOC and the Protestant churches in Ethiopia to a renewed spirit of ecumenism, which takes the past experiences into account. Pointing to the loss of the EOC privilege of state religion and to the common ground in the Apostolic Confession, the Nicene Creed, and the Athanasian Creed he invites the EOC and Protestant churches alike to join together in a new spirit of unity, tolerance, and honest confessions of past offenses against one another.

Toward the end of this chapter, Bekele realizes that his juxtaposition of the violent totality of the Derg regime with such positive effects of reviving Ethiopians inevitably leads to the question of theodicy. He faces this question head-on at the end of the chapter, in a section titled "Does God Side with the Wicked?":

> Reading this chapter, some believers or unbelievers may come up with some questions in their mind. In all these upheavals, was it really God who struck Ethiopia for 26 years without mercy? The one who sent hunger and war, Red and White Terror claiming millions of lives, was the "good" God? The one who sent a stirring into every house, causing many to flee from their land and

---

153 See esp. ibid., 147. See also the comparison of the of Haile Selassie's and the Derg's performance, ibid., 145–146.

154 See ibid., 151–166.

155 See ibid., 152.

156 See ibid., 154.

157 Bekele even likened this diaspora to the scattering of the first church. So far, hardly any work has been done on Pentecostals in the Ethiopian exile communities. For the situation in Germany, cf. HAUSTEIN, "Pfingstbewegung und Identität im Kontext äthiopischer Migranten in Deutschland."

158 See BEKELE WOLDEKIDAN, ረቫይቫ, 161–163.

the shake-up of many lives, is the God we call "our God"? The one bringing the confusion created in the churches, was the God who "loves us"?[159]

Bekele throws three answers at this problem, which are not necessarily compatible.[160] First, he notes that there are also other influences in the world, evil ones like Satan and natural phenomena. Since God is not the only one to whom bad events can be ascribed, a careful study of causes and effects is necessary. Secondly, Bekele notes that while God does not side with the wicked, he knows their plans, warns his people beforehand, and may turn evil plans into good results. Finally, God may let painful things happen on earth if they are conducive to his plan of salvation, since he is more concerned about people's heavenly life than their short earthly one. This, in the end, sums up the intent of the chapter: as a result of the violent decades of the past, the stage is now prepared for revival, more so than it was before the revolution.

This story line of Bekele's history, with its providential motif and related tropes, can be found in many other Pentecostal accounts, be it in oral interviews, written summaries or seminary theses. With Bekele this persecution narrative flows into an all-encompassing story of divine judgment and redemption, which as such mirrors and reverts the totality of the Derg's oppressive power. While much of the suppression suffered by the Derg is left unspoken or de-historicized, it is precisely this somewhat hidden and iconified totality of persecution which drives an overarching master narrative that integrates the Derg's brutal realities into a meaningful tale about the revolution that also speaks the final word on Haile Selassie's reign as well as on the church today.

The following observations will attempt to probe this master narrative not at its iconified center, but at its fringes, i.e., how it relates to the revolution of 1974 and to the present time of relative religious freedom.

5.2.2 Ethiopian Socialism and Pentecostal Christianity

The first years of the Derg were of remarkable ambiguity for Ethiopia's Pentecostal churches, entailing new opportunities as well as insecurities. The government-declared policy of religious equality for the first time gave legal grounds to mission-independent Pentecostal churches, and brought them out of their relative obscurity in which they had remained for the last years of Haile Selassie's governance. At the same time, the Pentecostal missionary organizations were under pressure to relinquish control, both in turning their development projects over to the government as well as attempting to set up independent churches to weather what may come. The declaration of Ethiopian Socialism was received with mixed emotions, but was also taken up as a theological challenge to work for the common good by some churches and individuals inside and outside the Pentecostal fold. Even the Red Terror with all its tremendous atrocities, violence and instability, had an air of ambivalence to it, since it targeted the far-left wings of the revolution, and in effect diminished Pentecostalism's most passionate

---

159   BEKELE WOLDEKIDAN, ረብሻ, 168.
160   Cf. ibid., 168–170.

enemies.[161] Finally, it was at the height of the Red Terror that the FGBC had finally completed its first church building in Addis Ababa.

This initial ambiguity, however, contradicts the Pentecostal retrospective histories, which tend to read the 1974 revolution in light of the later oppressive power of the Derg. In contrast, the early sources clearly reveal a hopeful anxiety and political aspirations, which is marginalized in later accounts.

The primary reason for celebration is of course the promise of freedom of religion in post-revolutionary Ethiopia. For Engelsviken, who had left Ethiopia while Pentecostals were still imprisoned, this was the perfect ending of his report. Though he did conclude with some words of caution about the uncertainty of the future developments, his overall assessment was fairly enthusiastic. He notes that after "radical change in the political system of Ethiopia" the new rulers had established "complete religious freedom" as well as a "total separation of church and state", which would mean that the EOC would lose its "rights and privileges that were denied to other churches."[162] Engelsviken notes:

> This means that less than a year after the sentencing of the Pentecostals, the Orthodox Church had lost both its own privileged political status and its staunchest supporters within the Ethiopian government![163]

One year later Yosief Kidanewold celebrated the abolishment of Orthodox state religion with similarly enthusiastic words:

> For the first time since the fourth century A.D. of the Axumite period, the Ethiopian Orthodox church lost its old close ties with the Ethiopian government, which declared itself secular. This has meant that in Socialist Ethiopia all religious organizations are to be treated equally.[164]

In 1978, the FGBC jubilee magazine noted that the new government had declared a basic policy of freedom of religion that it upheld in various decrees and that the situation thus had improved in comparison to the "situation of persecution and destitution under the previous government."[165]

The last two references are more remarkable than Engelsviken's statements, since both works had been written after the public riot against the FGBC meeting place in Addis Ababa in 1976, which had led to its closure and revealed a considerable lack of support from local Kebele authorities for the Pentecostals. Though Yosief Kidanewold notes that "[f]or the time being, the Mulu Wongel church appears to be closed," he has a positive general outlook: "We shall look forward eagerly, expecting what the outcome of the future event would bring . . . ."[166] Likewise, the FGBC jubilee magazine, published on the occasion of the dedication of the church's first building, not only reviews the closure of its chapel in 1976, but seizes the opportunity to

---

161   See below, 217.
162   See ENGELSVIKEN, "Molo Wongel," 223–225.
163   Ibid., 223.
164   YOSIEF KIDANEWOLD, "The History of the Pentecostal Movement in Addis Abeba," 48–49.
165   ETHIOPIAN FULL GOSPEL BELIEVERS' CHURCH, ሙሉ ወንጌል ቤተ ክርስቲያን ከልደት እስከ . . ., 30.
166   YOSIEF KIDANEWOLD, "The History of the Pentecostal Movement in Addis Abeba," 50.

forcefully reiterate its belief in the government's policy of freedom of religion, calling
on the revolutionary powers to live up to their promise:

> In a time of revolution and new establishment, believed to take care that all
> Ethiopians would obtain their legal identity, rights and human dignity, how
> can anarchical Kebele dictatorship be understood? In a revolutionary time,
> while the backwardness of banditry is erased from every wilderness and every
> bush and is put under control, the illegal deeds committed in one Kebele in
> the middle of the city can be a banditry hidden from the central government
> or the people's security department, which has the responsibility? Or is there
> some different internal guideline, unknown to us, that the Full Gospel Church
> is not included in the decree issuing religious freedom in Ethiopia and the rule
> of complete equality between religions? How long will there be enemies of the
> gospel, who without specific information accuse this church, which has dwelt
> for several years in many different places clearly advancing the gospel ministry,
> with their fabricated allegation, saying at a time and hour of their choosing
> "we have discovered them to be illegal meetings working to damage country
> and kin in the name of religion," and who thereby contradict the freedom of
> religion and deceive society? Who will listen to this question?[167]

These critical remarks, published on the occasion of a milestone of religious freedom—namely, the inauguration of the first FGBC building, erected on land leased
to the church by the revolutionary authorities—of course signal the disappointment
of the Pentecostals regarding previous failures of the local authorities to keep the
revolutionary promise of religious equality, but more importantly they also clearly
indicate that this promise was still taken seriously and that the Pentecostals were not
shy of engaging in the politics of the day in order to secure that promise.

Later sources, however, tend to interpret the initial years of the revolution from
their subsequent persecution experiences, and therefore do not attribute much weight
to the early experience of religious freedom. It has already been mentioned that
Bekele Woldekidan asserts that while the Derg may have decreed freedom of religion,
the EPRDF was the first to actually "show this in practice."[168] When other sources
mention the initial positive effects of the regime change, like the acquisition of a
temporary meeting permit or the land donated by government authorities for the first
FGBC building, these are not explained by reference to an initial policy of freedom of
religion, but rather they appear as somewhat peculiar turns in an overall narrative of
persecution.[169] Likewise, a number of oral accounts mentioning the initial religious
freedom immediately followed up with a phrase signaling the shortlived nature of
these improvements, like in the following two excerpts:

> At that time, you know, the Derg government was just starting, uh, running the
> country. And, you know, at the beginning there was a freedom for Christians

---

167   ETHIOPIAN FULL GOSPEL BELIEVERS' CHURCH, ሙሉ ወንጌል ቤተ ክርስቲያን ከልደት እስከ . . ., 34.
168   BEKELE WOLDEKIDAN, ሪቫይቫል, 119.
169   Cf. ETHIOPIAN FULL GOSPEL BELIEVER'S CHURCH, የኢትዮጵያ ሙሉ ወንጌል አመኞች ቤተ ክርስቲያን 25ኛ
      ዓመት በዓል, 10–11; GIRMA ZEWDE, ኢትዮጲስ, 135; ADDIS ABABA FULL GOSPEL BELIEVERS' CHURCH,
      የ40ኛ ዓመት የወንጌል አገልግሎትና የምስጋና በዓል መጽሔት /ሕምሌ 1958–1998 ዓ.ም./, 14.

all over — as the Derg started ruling the country at the beginning. Not more than two or three, two or one years. Just not more than this.[170]

The Derg gave us this place. [INTERVIEWER: The Derg?] Yuh, in the Derg time we got this place. So the first worship is started in 71, 1971 in Ethiopian calendar. For only ten months we were waiting after ten months, and they closed.[171]

Other informants recall warning their fellow Pentecostals not to place too much trust in the promises of religious freedom, or mention their sense of urgency to prepare the church for harder times sure to come under a communist government.[172] One eyewitness, when asked if some Pentecostal Christians felt relieved since the revolution ended the Imperial ban of their church, answered with a clear "no" and turned to narrating "the most important story" how communist and Pentecostal students had already fought ideological battles at the Haile Selassie University.[173]

It is of course not surprising that retrospective histories about the Derg will tend to marginalize the initial signs of freedom and the hopes the church placed in them in light of the later persecution experience. However, another effect of this marginalization is that any trace of initial agreement with the revolution among the Pentecostals is either purged from the accounts or relegated to the fringes of the movement. Quite conversely, Yosief Kidanewold asserted in 1976 that "many Pentecostals are concerned both to defend their faith and to support socialist goals."[174] He goes on to quote in length from a translated Chinese book, allegedly widely circulated in Pentecostal circles, whose author argues for a separation of socialism and materialism, allowing an integration of Christianity and socialism:

Christianity is not materialism, for Christianity and materialism are fundamentally opposed. However, there is no conflict between the true spirit of Christianity and Socialism. Not only is there no conflict, but we believe that Christian faith reaches that which socialism has not attained and is an absolutely essential condition if socialism is to succeed. Indeed, all the idealistic principles of socialism are incorporated in Christian belief, since the birth and development of socialism has been directly or indirectly the result of the influence of Christianity.[175]

Yosief concludes his quotation from this source by stating that "[t]he above is quoted to illustrate what the position of the Pentecostal Christians [...] might look

---

170 Interview no. 63. With regard to the first FGBC public meetings and the last, the correct time span would be closer to four and a half years.
171 Interview no. 111.
172 Interviews no. 20; 5.
173 Interview no. 87. According to the informant, these students were part of the Ethiopian People's Revolutionary Party (EPRP) and would have destroyed many Pentecostals if it hadn't been for their demise in the Red Terror.
174 YOSIEF KIDANEWOLD, "The History of the Pentecostal Movement in Addis Abeba," 52.
175 Wu Yung Chuan, quoted by ibid., 53. Unfortunately, the original source could not be found. The full reference provided by Yosief reads: "Wu Yung Chuan, Questions Concerning Faith. (Liu Yih Ling, Trans., Evangelical Church Mekane Yesus Youth Office [N.P.], [N.D.], pp. 1-2."

like in their attempt to reconcile their faith with socialism."[176] It is unlikely that
Yosief's quote and conclusion were simply an act of pandering to the revolutionary
powers, since the idea that Christianity is the ultimate root of socialism and is needed
to prosper the same, would be significantly more offensive to a socialist regime than
simply arguing for a fundamental compatibility.

Most later sources generally make no reference to such ideas, and where they
do come up, they are marginalized as much as possible. Tibebe Eshete, for example, mentions that some members of the FGBC "even wrote articles enthusiastically
praising the change in the system of government," and adds somewhat mysteriously
in a note that though the articles could not be found, the authors had been identified
and confirmed their writings, but does not mention their names, motives, or present
stance on the issue.[177] Similarly, he contends that "[t]here were even some gestures
by some Pentecostal intellectuals to cooperate with the government by professionally
identifying themselves with concerns of the revolution," but again instead of providing names and details, the endnote after the sentence simply states that they were
"derided by the Pentecostals themselves and were blamed of conflating Marcos with
Marcs, (mixing up Marx with the Biblical Apostle Mark)."[178] It is only in the appendix of his book that Tibebe Eshete provides more specific information. Profiling
one of his informants for the above-quoted statements, Dr. Nigussie Tefera, who at
one point even was an elder of the FGBC, Tibebe notes that Nigussie "is one of the few
Pentecostal Christians who was willing to hold a sensitive position during the period
of the Derg for which he suffered partial ostracism from his Christian friends."[179]

Nigussie Teffera was also mentioned in an interview for the present book as an
example of Christians who went over to the new government in order "to receive
high positions in the communist administration."[180] However, though the informant
admitted that there was "plenty of that", he also contended that the "communist
administration" only took a "certain kind of unrooted Christians" and that "mostly"
the experience of the church was one of persecution.

Positive references to the Derg's initial policy of freedom of religion only appear at
the fringes of the Pentecostal discourse, namely, in two heterodox Pentecostal groups,
Oneness Pentecostalism and the Deliverance Movement. These are not simply positive
statements about the establishment of religious equality, but they are juxtaposed to
the alleged persecution by other Pentecostals, from which these two movements were
spared as a consequence of the new government. One informant from the ACE contends that the "trinitarians" united with the Orthodox "pope" against their church,
and then concludes "but the Derg came, .. and saved us."[181] The informant from the
GDC tells of strong opposition by Pentecostal missionaries against the new teaching,
including a circular sent by a certain SPCM missionary. He goes on to narrate how

---

176 Though Yosief Kidanewold gives no information about the nature of his involvement with the
     FGBC, the access to information he had as well as some of his statements suggest that he was
     at least sympathetic to if not a follower of the Pentecostal movement.
177 See TIBEBE ESHETE, *The Evangelical Movement in Ethiopia*, 264n34.
178 See ibid., 264n235.
179 See ibid., 352.
180 Interview no. 78.
181 Interview no. 108.

he confronted the missionary, and by citing the Derg's policy of religious equality and threatening to show the letter to government authorities, he pressured the missionary to recall the circular.[182]

The marginalization of the initial hopes and political aspirations that some Pentecostals had in the first years of the Derg, arguably is an effect of the later Pentecostal persecution narrative. The initial liberating effects of the revolution, the ambiguity of the first years, and any hint of Pentecostal collaboration threaten the totality of the persecution narrative and thus are leveled in retrospective accounts commemorating the oppression suffered by Pentecostal Christians in Ethiopia.

5.2.3 The Legacy of Persecution

The assumption of government power by the EPRDF clearly marked a new era for Ethiopian Pentecostals and other churches alike, since the new government not only had a stated policy of religious equality, but was prepared to enforce it in all regions. About ten months after the fall of the Derg, the Office of the Prime Minister wrote a letter to the Orthodox, Muslim, Catholic, and Protestant communities affirming religious equality and stating that any strife or religious discrimination would not be tolerated.[183] Pentecostal meetings and public conferences were now entitled to police protection, new burial sites were granted to Protestants, and in some of the northern and strongly Orthodox provinces, all religious communities were entitled to free land tenure for building churches.

In the occasionally tense multi-religious environment of Ethiopia, these transitions did not come without conflict. Especially in traditionally monoreligious areas, conversion was met with social ostracization, the refusal of burial places, destruction of property, and physical attacks, some even causing the loss of life. Girma Zewde provides a list of such incidents, including a newspaper article about an especially grim mob killing of an 18-year old youth, accused of having been a "Pente."[184] It is interesting to note, that Girma does not label these events as persecution, but merely as "troubles"[185] standing in the way of the government's attempt to establish religious equality. This is more than a mere terminological difference, since Girma's account is based on the premise that a new era of religious plurality has begun. He sets out with introducing the EPRDF's new religious policies, then points to the different religious clashes, and concludes with a call for unity and tolerance.

Most other Pentecostal accounts, however, tend to continue the persecution narrative, including the providential link between persecution and revival. This tendency can be observed, for example, in a recent FGBC video about the history of the church, which includes a report about a riot at the end of a Pentecostal "crusade" in Mekele in 2002. After narrating the end of the Derg and the reopening of the Addis Ababa church in 1992, the video continues with a long passage recounting the church's evangelistic advances with images from numerous services and public conferences: people dancing, responding to altar calls, receiving exorcisms, giving testimonies, and

---

182   Interview no. 53.
183   See facsimile provided by Girma Zewde, ኢትዮጵስ, 163–164.
184   See ibid., 162–173.
185   The word used here is ችግር (čəgər), trouble, issue, problem, complication), see ibid., 165.

demonstrating the healing they had encountered.[186] After this visual summary of the church's evangelistic power, the narrator injects that the gospel will not advance without effort, but that there is a price to pay. The video then turns to the incident in Mekele and reports that on the last day of a "crusade" the people of the area were mobilized against the Pentecostals, calling for their destruction and successfully disrupting the conference. This is accompanied by images of the stirred masses, a man with a gun calling the preacher off the stage, people running away from gun fire, and finally a bleeding young man smiling as his wounds are being treated.[187] At this point the narrator concludes: "God, however, turned this whole situation into something good." This is explained by the next passage featuring the pastor of the Addis Ababa church, Merid Lema, who contends that the people did not know what they were doing, but God turned the situation in favor of the churches, because after a short while, the churches were given land by the government in Mekele, first the FGBC, then all the others. Merid articulates the conclusion to the story: "That persecution brought this blessing."[188]

However, what is missing in this persecution narrative about the Mekele mob attack is that, unlike earlier days, the Pentecostals were now in a privileged position. As other reports indicate, the police forces were fighting on behalf of the Pentecostals and even killed two of the attackers who had laid their hands on police weapons and had threatened to fire into the Pentecostal crowd.[189] The protection that the Pentecostals enjoyed during this incident puts a strain on the persecution narrative, but the contrast becomes stark when the same pictures of the Mekele incident are used in the introductory sequence of the movie. Here they are underscored with a mournful sound track and framed with persecution imagery: The pictures are introduced by a Derg letter titled "Religion is the Enemy of the Revolution,"[190] and followed by an image of the bleeding Christ on the cross.

Another example of the tendency to interpret mob attacks against as part of a larger story of persecution can be found in a report by Addise Amado.[191] In what aims to be a "systematic survey"[192] of persecution, the reported instances are sorted into

---

186   ADDIS ABABA FULL GOSPEL BELIEVERS' CHURCH, የ40 ዓመት የወንጌል አገልግሎት (ሕምሌ 1958–1998 ዓ.ም.) ዶኩመንተሪ ቪሲዲ, [min. 28:29–36:08. This includes images of large conferences with Tolosa Gudina, Reinhard Bonnke, and Benny Hinn.

187   Ibid., min. 36:09–36:37.

188   Ibid., min. 37:27–37:29. The word used here is ስደት (sädät), lit. exile, flight from oppression), which is the Amharic term generally used to describe the political oppression under Haile Selassie and the Derg and is usually translated by informants with "persecution."

189   See U.S. DEPARTMENT OF STATE, BUREAU OF DEMOCRACY, HUMAN RIGHTS AND LABOR, "Ethiopia: International Religious Freedom Report 2003" (2003), http://www.state.gov/g/drl/rls/irf/2003/23705.htm (accessed January 10, 2009); ADDISE AMADO, Persecution in Ethiopia: Situation Analysis: Theological, Sociological, Economical and Political Interpretations and Implications (Addis Ababa: Voice of Martyrs Ethiopia, 2003), 68.

190   ADDIS ABABA FULL GOSPEL BELIEVERS' CHURCH, የ40 ዓመት የወንጌል አገልግሎት (ሕምሌ 1958–1998 ዓ.ም.) ዶኩመንተሪ ቪሲዲ, min. 01:18–01:50. The letter displayed in the sequence is given as a full facsimile in GIRMA ZEWDE, ኢትዮጲስ, 154–159. It originally was taken as proof of the systemic and ideological campaign of the Derg against religion, but its authenticity has since been heavily debated, cf. EIDE, Revolution and Religion in Ethiopia, 163.

191   See ADDISE AMADO, Persecution in Ethiopia: Situation Analysis.

192   Ibid., 1.

different types of oppression but taken out of their political and historical contexts.
Thus incidents from the reign of emperor Menelik, the Derg and the EPRDF are
placed side by side. In a number of places it is also unclear whether the report
uses the Ethiopian or European calendar, thereby making it difficult to judge under
which regime said events occurred.[193] The post-Derg mob attacks and discrimination
against Pentecostals thus become part of a larger persecution narrative, as the report
sets out to prove its hypothesis that "Ethiopian Orthodoxies persecute the Protestants
more seriously than the Muslims and often jointly."[194] Since the report was written for
the organization Voice of Martyrs Ethiopia, it may be suspected that the continued
persecution narrative is connected to an orchestrated global demand for stories of
Christian martyrdom.

The continued reading of opposition against Pentecostals and other Protestants
as persecution is not the only way that the persecution narrative influences the Pentecostal interpretation of present developments. Another, perhaps more forceful application of the persecution narrative is not one of comparison, but one of contrast
as the following passage by Bekele Woldekidan illustrates, in which he compares the
revolution by the Derg to the one brought by the EPRDF:

> In the previous revolution the trouble the churches encountered came from
> the outside, while they were healthy inside. In this revolution, however, the
> problems the churches have come from the inside, while from the outside they
> have been healthy so far. So far I have not heard [such news] from the Catholic
> Church, but the Orthodox Church, the Church of the Seventh Day Adventists
> and many of the Evangelical Churches have been unsettled by the revolution.
> With this [problem] inside, strife has entered many of them.[195]

This outlook is complemented by a later passage in Bekele's book, in a section
titled "God's Judgment is First on God's Family."[196] The author contends that while
the freedom came with much opportunity to spread the gospel, there are two great
threats hanging over the church like the sword of Damocles: people's lives deviate
from the standard of the Bible and many are not able to manage the responsibilities
that come with freedom. Revival will come when God's house is filled with holiness
again.

Similarly Girma Zewde laments that while the Evangelical Churches' Fellowship
of Ethiopia was established during the tough time of the Derg, it is now that it
needs strengthening for "[i]t is clear that if there is quarrel and animosity among one
another, God cannot work."[197]

---

193   Cf. e.g. ibid., 76–79, where an incident from Arba Minch is reported and dated to May 1989.
       However, a number of details in the story make it unlikely for the events to have happened
       before the Derg fell, thus the appropriate dating is most likely May 1997.
194   Ibid., 3.
195   BEKELE WOLDEKIDAN, ፈሪ ይሆናል, 147.
196   See ibid., 167.
197   GIRMA ZEWDE, እትዮጵስ, 150. For the establishment, structure and challenges of the ECFE,
       see DANIEL FITE, "The Challenges of Denominational Conflicts in the Context of Ethiopian
       Evangelical Churches," 17–30.

One Pentecostal pastor recounts the church growth during the persecution in an interview and then continues:

> So the persecution period, uh, we can say it was, uh, really a good time for the churches. It's benefited from the persecution. You know, uh, there was a real discipleship program. Everybody is, uh, you know, committed himself to Christ. But now, you know, with the freedom, there are a lot of problems and challenges. We prefer, we prefer really the persecution time.[198]

Contrasting the church during the Derg's persecution with its present state in times of relative freedom is a frequently encountered trope in historical narratives by Ethiopian Pentecostals. This can be applied to a number of areas. Informants comment on a loss of personal holiness, from people "living in sin" to movies and television increasingly appealing to Pentecostal Christians.[199] Others see a decrease in the quality of church attendance: people neglect small groups, instead of expecting suffering and martyrdom they come to the church for blessings and "a good wife", and even spiritual gifts like prophecy are now causing many problems.[200] A third cause of lament are the often difficult church politics coming with the issues of "sheep stealing", church splits, and a general weakening of the ecumenical relationship between Protestant churches.[201]

While personal ethics and the spiritual orientation of believers are a matter of concern within the churches, the problem of church politics has become a highly public affair. Many churches have suffered significant splits in recent years that ended up in Ethiopian courts, among them the three classic Pentecostal churches, the FGBC, the GC, and the HBC.

In the FGBC the conflict began with a draft for a new church constitution and basically centered on the issue of congregationalism versus denominationalism.[202] The Addis Ababa church, which had always been an informal center for the whole FGBC, argued for a congregational structure and wanted the Ethiopian head office to be understood as merely coordinating a fellowship of independent churches. The head office and a number of other churches countered that this would play to the advantage of the very strong Addis Ababa church, and that a denominational structure was needed in order to attain transparency in decision making, church structure and finances.[203] A further issue that reportedly played into this was that the Addis Ababa church was

---

198   Interview no. 95
199   E.g. interviews no. 63; 29.
200   Interview no. 95; 18; 3.
201   E.g. interview no. 87; see also quotes provided above.
202   See ESCKINDER TADDESSE WOLDEGEBRIAL, "An Introduction to the Biblical and Historical Pattern of Church Government," 80–81; and ADDIS ABABA FULL GOSPEL BELIEVERS' CHURCH, የ40ኛ ዓመት የወንጌል አገልግሎትና የምስጋና በዓል መጽሐት /ሕምሌ 1958–1998 ዓ.ም./, 16–18 for a view of the conflict from either side. See also BULUTSE FUTUWI, "An Introduction to the Theology and Growth of Independent Churches in Ethiopia With Special Reference to Rhema Faith Church," 69–70.
203   Apparently the constitution draft at one point also contained a clause limiting the size of a local congregation to 1,000 members and mandating the branching of churches larger than that, interview no. 131. This of course was a direct affront to the "mother church" in Addis Ababa which is significantly larger than that.

led by lay elders, whereas a number of the rural congregations were founded and led by full-time evangelists or pastors.[204] The conflict remained unresolved from 1993 until 1995, when the Addis Ababa church withdrew from the Ethiopian fellowship, and subsequently was brought to court by the Ethiopian fellowship over the use of its name and property.[205] Negotiations between both parties were resumed from 2000 to 2002, which led to a publicly celebrated reconciliation on September 7, 2002 and to the Ethiopian head office withdrawing the court cases it had initiated. However, in the following years no agreement could be reached on a new constitution, and the forty-year jubilee magazine published by the Addis Ababa church in 2006 still expected the two parties to go on separately until "God will solve ... the problem in his own way."[206]

In the GC a conglomerate of churches broke away from the central denomination in the Sidama region. One of the reasons was the issue of cooperating with mission partners like the FFFM, with the local churches seeking direct contact and the denominational head office attempting to channel all contacts and funds through Addis Ababa.[207] This of course corresponds to the strong congregationalist background of the Finnish Pentecostal movement and has caused difficulties within the FFFM itself. The group that split away was estimated at about 20,000 believers and has also been taken to court over the use of the name Gennet.[208]

In the HBC there has always been a precarious balance between the factual center in Awasa and the denominational head office in Addis Ababa. When some churches in rural areas south of Awasa wanted to establish their own regional head office, the Addis Ababa head office did not allow them to do so.[209] In response, these churches attempted to register as South Heywet Birhan, for which they were taken to court by the central office. The southern churches were not allowed to continue under the same name and subsequently registered as Yekal Birhan Church.[210]

The Pentecostal churches are not the only ones with this dynamic. Both of the largest denominations of the country, the KHC and the ECMY, have seen major splits

---

204 See ESCKINDER TADDESSE WOLDEGEBRIAL, "An Introduction to the Biblical and Historical Pattern of Church Government," 77–78; BULUTSE FUTUWI, "An Introduction to the Theology and Growth of Independent Churches in Ethiopia With Special Reference to Rhema Faith Church," 69–70.

205 The exact charges remain unclear, but it appears that the use of the name was one of the major issues. The Ethiopian government does not allow for two different entities to be registered by the same name on the federal level. For a time, the Addis Ababa church apparently managed to bypass this regulation by registering with the Addis Ababa municipality only as a regional entity, though it has some congregations elsewhere.

206 ADDIS ABABA FULL GOSPEL BELIEVERS' CHURCH, የ40ኛ ዓመት የወንጌል አገልግሎትና የምስጋና በዓል መጽሐት /ሐምሌ 1958–1998 ዓ.ም./, 18.

207 Local ethnic identities may play into this as well.

208 Interview no. 78. The informant indicates that the courts decided the matter in favor of the Sidama faction.

209 It is probable that the Awasa church was not in favor of such an undertaking, and perhaps influenced the decision in Addis Ababa in their favor.

210 Interview no. 34. Negotiations between the factions were still taking place by the help of SPCM missionaries in 2005, but it is unclear whether the conflict was resolved.

as well.[211] Next to fraying of the Pentecostal confessional landscape at the expense of the classical churches, these denominational splits and court cases are a source of much embarrassment in the Ethiopian Pentecostal discourse and are seen as a sign of the weakening of the church in the times of freedom.

However, the underlying assumption that the politically challenged Pentecostal churches in the underground were not fraught with similar political strains is difficult to sustain. As a few sources indicate, similar problems, even occasionally involving the same actors, were already present during the Derg. The times of religious freedom thus would have altered church politics less fundamentally than the persecution narratives claim, but rather brought them out into the public arena and provided new ways for their legal escalation.

For the FGBC one such source is Esckinder Taddesse's M.Th. thesis about church government in the FGBC.[212] Esckinder describes power struggles between the lay leaders in Addis Ababa and full time ministers during the Derg time, leading to disciplinary actions against the full timers in 1980, with the result that "strong charismatic leaders were discouraged." He furthermore contends that the Addis Ababa church, despite its own shortcomings, exerted all its power to force its lay leadership model on churches in the countryside that were following a different pattern. The author cites a number of examples where according to him lay leadership did not have good results, and then notes how lay leadership was forced on others nevertheless:

> In contrast to this, in the churches in south and southeast Ethiopia (Sidama and Bale), full time ministers not ecclesiastically ordained as pastors but who were ministers with a call from God continued to having the upper hand until they were forced to appoint lay elders by the Central Committee from Addis Ababa in 1984.[213]

One example of these full-time ministers mentioned in the thesis is Tsadiku Abdo, who was elected as general secretary of the FGBC in 2003 and strongly defended the case of the Ethiopian church against the Addis Ababa leadership. In this way, a direct line can be drawn to the later church split.

An account of political trouble within the GC during the Derg time has been provided in Kyösti Roininen "Condensed History."[214] He reported that within the Sidama Gennet Churches a "split-up took place 17.7.1987, when the proposed constitution for the Sidama Guenet Churches was introduced." The regional church was

---

211 These will not be explored further here. For the KHC split, which began in the Derg time, see MESFIN WOLDEAMANUEL, "A Surge for Independency: An Evaluation of the Nature and Development of Independent Churches in Ethiopia with Special Focus on the Hywet Kal Church" (M.Th. thesis, Ethiopian Graduate School of Theology, 2001). The politically and ethnically highly charged split in the ECMY has so far only been treated in writing in a seminary thesis, see MITIKU TESFA FUFA, "The Challenge of Language for the EECMY" (B.Th. thesis, Mekane Yesus Seminary, 1999).

212 See ESCKINDER TADDESSE WOLDEGEBRIAL, "An Introduction to the Biblical and Historical Pattern of Church Government." The thesis clearly defends the side of the Ethiopian FGBC, for which the author also works. It argues against a prominence of lay leadership and is dedicated "to the General Assembly of the Ethiopian Full Gospel Believers' Church."

213 Ibid., 78.

214 See ROININEN, "A Condensed History of the Finnish Mission in Ethiopia," 18–19.

divided between those who signed the constitution and those who did not. This split was reconciled after six years. Roininen's own congregationalist preference appears when he notes that during the time of the split the churches which had signed the constitution grew twofold, whereas the ones who had refused to sign grew seven-fold. His paper states no explicit reasons for the separation,[215] whereas an Ethiopian source squarely blames the missionaries for "giving a good salary, motor cycle and used clothes to those who followed them."[216] According to this paper, the churches then split away from the church fellowship and were able to grow more than the others through foreign assistance. While it is unclear whether foreign assistance was the main issue, or just one of many reasons as Roininen suggests, it is clear that the same dynamic played into this conflict that reemerged in the later split, i.e., direct contact with missionary agencies versus central administration.

With regard to the HBC, one leadership figure of this church reported in an interview that right from the establishment of the national structure in 1977, there had been some discontent regarding the influence that the Awasa church elders held.[217] This was coupled with a generational struggle within the denomination itself and eventually led to the excommunication of several Awasa elders. The church in Awasa did not accept this decision and finally split away from the Ethiopian church. The churches continued on separate paths for several years until reconciliation attempts bore fruit some time toward the end of the Derg regime.

These few and fairly sketchy sources only allow glimpses into the importance of church politics during the Derg time, which remain more or less concealed in the persecution accounts. These histories are primarily interested in upholding the image of an oppressed but internally untroubled church as a powerful counter-example to the present. The separation of church politics and persecution is even upheld in the above-cited sources regarding disputes and splits during the Derg. None of them connect the oppressive hand of the Derg on the churches to the politics within; moreover, the political accounts may even pass over the persecution encountered altogether. Esckinder Taddesse's thesis is a case in point. The word "persecution" only appears in an awkwardly distanced reference at the beginning of the relevant chapter,[218] but there is no mention of concrete instances in the remainder of the thesis. The author makes no allusions to church closures, underground organization of the church, or any arrests of leaders. Even when he names the full-time minister Teshome Worku as a counter-example to lay ministry, there is no reference to the seven years he spent in prison alongside Tesfaye Gabbiso and Haile Bekele, the three of whom arguably

---

215 Roininen only states that "[e]ven now one can find many reasons for what happened," see ibid., 18.

216 Ashebir Ketema, "The History of Ethiopian Guenet Church," 21.

217 Interview no. 125.

218 See Esckinder Taddesse Woldegebrial, "An Introduction to the Biblical and Historical Pattern of Church Government," 71: "As referred to in the unpublished historical notes of the literature department of the EFGBC, from its very inception the church has gone through severe persecution provoked by both political and ecclesiastical authorities." With the ubiquity of persecution stories in other accounts, it seems odd that Esckinder feels compelled to mention "unpublished historic notes" as evidence of persecution. Moreover, he provides no persecution narratives throughout the text.

were the most prominent victims of the Derg. Persecution and church politics thus remained mutually exclusive narratives.

Therefore, the Pentecostal persecution master narrative extends to the present church in a number of ways. Current riots are read as extrapolations of the same persecution story, despite the political changes that now play in favor of the Pentecostal churches. Moreover, even the present times and expressions of religious freedom cannot be celebrated as such, but are compared to a somewhat nostalgic notion of the purity of the persecuted body of Christ, while cases of local opposition under quite different circumstances are read in much the same way as the previous systematic repressions by the Derg. It is in these overextensions of the persecution narrative that it reveals its opaque center. The persecuted church is elevated above the concrete historical circumstances of the day and becomes the iconic antithesis to the political brutalities of the Derg as well as to the perceived moral corruption and power struggles of the present day.

5.3   Persecution and the Charismatic Movement

As was shown in the historical overview above, Pentecostals were not the only ones who suffered political oppression after the Ethiopian revolution but Protestants were targeted altogether. Moreover, most contemporaneous accounts of the Derg came from a mainline Protestant background, which not only meant that their respective churches in Ethiopia received a wider treatment, but also that much of the material about Pentecostals during this time comes from these sources. The Pentecostal persecution story thus is situated in a larger historical archive of similar content, with a number of non-Pentecostal sources not only informing about Pentecostalism during the Derg, but also making competing claims with regard to the meaning of persecution and the legacy of the churches' experience. Furthermore, many histories explicitly link the persecution experience with the Charismatic movements, which further strengthens interdenominational entanglement of church histories about the Derg time.

5.3.1   Sharing the Story of Persecution

Despite the far-reaching co-optation of the EOC during the Derg and the disruptions this has caused in the hierarchy of the church, Ethiopian Orthodox histories tend to write a history of continuity cast in persecution terms despite the church's alliance with the revolutionary rulers. For example, a recent history, published by the general secretariat of the patriarch affirms all patriarchs of the past and does not mention any disruptions or changes of political allegiance. Instead, the Derg years are cast in a persecution narrative, mentioning the suffering of Abuna Theophilos and Abuna Paulos before concluding:

> Like it is written: "Can a mother forget her children? Though a mother may not have pity on the ones born from her womb and forget them, I will never forget you, o Zion, says God." (Is. 49:14–15) God did not leave the Ethiopian

Orthodox Tewahedo Church to perish in the trials. In all the times of hardship, he did not forget her. Having passed all the times of trial, and having weighed everything carefully, she found that it happened in order to serve the Lord and the people.[219]

However, in contemporaneous and retrospective accounts of Protestant origin the status of the EOC is a contested one, as they often reveal a certain hesitance to count the EOC among the persecuted. The magazine *Christianity Today* is a case in point. In 1976 it reported in a somewhat triumphal manner that the new government broke down the "fear of the all-powerful Ethiopian Orthodox Church, which used to persecute evangelicals and imprison evangelists virtually at its will."[220] With the removal of the patriarch, its former "power [...] was dealt a final blow." Three years later an article titled "The Campaign to Root Out 'Alien' Religion in Ethiopia" noted that "only Islam and the Ethiopian Orthodox Church, whose leadership is conformist, qualify" as traditional religions, therefore clearly setting them apart from the persecuted community.[221] In 1985 this narrative was beginning to change, i.e. nine years after the Derg had violently aligned the church's hierarchy. An article under the headline "Ethiopia Continues to Impose Restrictions on the Church"[222] at first noted that the EOC was enjoying a state of "tenuous freedom," but also mentioned that the church's "influence has been reduced" and that "[f]ew Orthodox churches have been closed." However, it is clear that the present afflictions of the EOC were not seen as equivalent to those of the Protestants. Instead the EOC and the Catholic Church were included in an expected future community of persecuted Christians, since the magazine quoted some observers estimating that they "may soon face some of the same pressures experienced by the Protestant churches."[223]

Øyvind Eide, in his study titled *Revolution & Religion in Ethiopia* at first clearly excludes the EOC from the community of the persecuted for the time after 1979:

> With the consecration of 13 new bishops on 21 January 1979 the conflict between the government and the EOC subsided and the two were set on a course of cooperation. From now on the EOC was a vehicle of the regime. Its role was one of unconditional loyalty to the state and its policies. When the regime applied its harsh measures against denominational groups, labeled as foreign, the EOC supported it, as it had the previous regime. The patriarch, for example, denied in public that the government was pursuing a policy of persecution.[224]

---

219 GENERAL SECRETARIATE OF THE PATRIARCHATE OF THE ETHIOPIAN ORTHODOX TEWAHEDO CHURCH, የኢትዮጵያ ቤተ ክርስቲያን ትናንትናና ዛሬ, [The Church of Ethiopia Yesterday and Today.] (Addis Ababa: Commercial Printing Press, 1997), 18.

220 HAROLD W. FULLER, "Revolutionary Response in Ethiopia," *Christianity Today*, 23 1976, 33–34.

221 *Christianity Today*, "The Campaign to Root Out 'Alien' Religion in Ethiopia."

222 MUMPER, "Ethiopia Continues to Impose Restrictions on the Churches."

223 Like the EOC, the Catholic Church had been included by the 1983 provisional party's (COPWE) congress, see JAMES A. CURRY and RICHARD B. RILEY, "Notes on Church-State Affairs," *Journal of Church and State* 26 (1984): 149.

224 EIDE, *Revolution and Religion in Ethiopia*, 166.

However, Eide then continues with a report by the EOC Bishop Matthias of Jerusalem, who resigned his see in 1982 and went into exile in England. Eide recites the bishop's information about the different ways the EOC had been harassed and quotes the following statement from Abuna Matthias, without reconciling the difference to his own political judgment: "Although they have not succeeded, the junta has tried to recruit the Ethiopian Orthodox Church as an ally ... "[225]

Like Eide, the Mennonite missionary Nathan Hege included the EOC among the persecutors when he cited reviewers of his manuscript with the statement that the book should "not be preoccupied with the faults of either the Marxist government or the Orthodox Church, although evangelicals have suffered at the hands of both."[226] Tibebe Eshete, to the contrary, remarks that the relationship between the Orthodox church and the state was one of "ambiguity", with the Derg attempting to co-opt the church in a "love-hate relationship" and the church consciously cooperating in "the form of 'social gospel' as opposed to assuming the more demanding task of being a 'prophetic' voice."[227]

The Protestant view of the EOC during the Derg therefore seems to be somewhat inconsistent. Whether it is included in the community of persecuted Christians or considered to be an instrument of the Mengistu apparatus, apparently depends on how the Derg's co-optation measures are judged, how the church's role therein is defined, which part of the church's experience is in focus, and whether or not it is presented as a persecutor of Protestants. This ambiguity arguably reflects the complexities of the EOC's relation to the Derg as well as past and present ecumenical tensions between Orthodox and Protestant Christians.

As opposed to this uncertainty regarding the EOC, mainline Protestants and Pentecostals generally do not contest each other's persecution experience. Mainline Protestant sources usually include the oppression of Pentecostals in their persecution accounts, albeit only marginally in many cases. Sometimes they may even absorb Pentecostal experiences as their own. The seven-year imprisonment of the FGBC pastors Tesfaye Gabbiso and Teshome Worku, for example, was cited by Cumbers and by Tibebe as part of the KHC persecution narrative, as if both had belonged to this church.[228]

This general recognition among Protestants of one another's persecution experience, however, is connected to a narrative of competition between Pentecostals and mainline Protestants regarding their underground performance and legacy. For example, the FGBC pastor Bekele Woldekidan wrote:

> The revolution closed many evangelical churches in the city and the countryside, so that they could not meet in public anymore. It is possible to say

---

225   EIDE, *Revolution and Religion in Ethiopia*, 167. Cf. also ABUNA MATTHIAS, "Statement by Abune Matthias, Archbishop of the Ethiopian Orthodox Church," Correspondence Member Churches: EOC, WCC Archives, Geneva, 1982.

226   HEGE, *Beyond Our Prayers*, 242.

227   TIBEBE ESHETE, *The Evangelical Movement in Ethiopia*, 211.

228   See CUMBERS, *Count It All Joy*, 66–67; cf. also TIBEBE ESHETE, *The Evangelical Movement in Ethiopia*, 246. Tesfaye had a background in the KHC, but had been working with the FGBC for a long time before his arrest.

that the only church that wasn't unaccustomed to this situation was the Full Gospel Believers' Church, which until that time had already adapted to a life of persecution for about ten years. For all the others, the situation was very frustrating in the beginning.[229]

Quite to the contrary, a historian from the KHC strongly objected in an interview to the notion that the FGBC was more experienced with regard to persecution. Insisting that it was not only them but that "all evangelical churches were faced by the same experience," he continued:

> I don't agree with Mulu Wongel people for two reason. One, about the Holy Spirit. They are not agents for Holy Spirit. It was the Lord himself. Two, they are always try to associate themselves with the, I mean try to associate themselves with persecution, as if they [were the] ones who, I mean, experience suffering, persecution. No, it was the Lord's day. Every church was under persecution, not only Mulu Wongel.[230]

Eide, on the other hand, connected the oppression suffered by the ECMY to a theological argument against Charismatics, in order to highlight the persecution legacy of the Lutheran church:

> The experience of persecution left its mark on the theology of the EECMY, a *teologia crucis* (theology of the cross) in the tradition of genuine Lutheran theology. These may prove most valuable for the church when faced with the extremes of *teologia gloria* (theology of glory) of the Charismatic movements.[231]

Unlike their ambiguous stand toward the EOC, Pentecostals and mainline Protestants therefore do not contest one another's experience of oppression per se, but occasionally appear to engage in a competitive argument with regard to who actually "owns" the persecution narrative.

5.3.2   Who is a "Pente"?

Sources often underscore this commonality of the Protestant persecution experience by referring to a factor which links persecution to the spread of the Charismatic movement: During the Derg the derogatory label "Pente," originally invented for the Pentecostals only, was increasingly applied to all Protestant mainline churches and their followers in political campaigns against them.[232] This application of the term to all Protestants has outlived the Derg and today can be observed everywhere in Ethiopia, even as a self-designation. The prominence of the term is illustrated by the

---

229   BEKELE WOLDEKIDAN, ረዥጵቫኅ, 159.
230   Interview no. 107.
231   EIDE, *Revolution and Religion in Ethiopia*, 229, emphases Eide. Other sources suggest, however, Pentecostals have also cast their experiences in a theology of the cross, see BALISKI, "Theology in Song," esp. p. 453.
232   Cf. e.g. BAKKE, *Christian Ministry*, 253; BEKELE WOLDEKIDAN, ረዥጵቫኅ, 105–109; CUMBERS, *Count It All Joy*, 21–22; DONHAM, *Marxist Modern*, 144–146; TIBEBE ESHETE, *The Evangelical Movement in Ethiopia*, 146.

fact that the English Wikipedia article about Protestant churches in Ethiopia is titled "P'ent'ay," without any discussion about the appropriateness of the term.[233]

Most sources about this phenomenon are fairly recent, therefore the precise historical genesis of the term and of its overextension is not entirely clear. The first Pentecostal missions did not use the word "Pentecostal" as part of their names, and by all appearances the term did not arrive in Ethiopia's public discourse until about a decade later. A number of sources indicate that the label "Pente" began to be applied to the FGBC in the aftermath of the riots in Debre Zeit in September 1967.[234] It certainly was not present before, since the newspaper articles about this incident use neither the words "Pente" nor "Pentecostal" to address this movement, rather calling it an "unconventional religious youth group" instead.[235] However, the terms seem to have been introduced soon thereafter. In April of 1971, the Swedish missionary Tage Johansson reported that "during the last three and a half years there were warnings against Pentecostals in the radio here and in the newspaper of Ministry of Information."[236] The first legal entity to carry the name "Pentecostal" was the United Pentecostal Mission, which belonged to the UPC and arrived in Ethiopia in 1968. The fact that it was Oneness Pentecostals who introduced the legal name, caused additional worries for missionaries like Johansson. He saw the danger of his mission being linked to non-trinitarian teaching: "The Russellians [Jehova's Witnesses] have this too, of course, and they have been expelled some years ago."[237] This was not an unsubstantiated worry, since the circular letter by the Security Department in November of 1971 simultaneously targeted Pentecostals and Jehova's Witnesses, as was mentioned above.[238] The letter is also the first written evidence of the government linking the term "Pentecostal" to the FGBC, since it begins with the words: "Concerning the Pentecost or the Ancient Full Gospel Belief adherents and other similar preachers ... "[239] When the Amharic Newspaper *Addis Zaman* reported about the mass arrests of 1972, the front page article calls the group a "forbidden association" in the headline and introduces them in the text as "adherents of a faith called Pentecost."[240] The international reaction to the arrests probably brought the term "Pentecostal" to wider usage in Ethiopia as well. The 1973 reply of the *Ethiopian*

---

233   See "P'ent'ay," *Wikipedia. The Free Encyclopedia* (2009), http://en.wikipedia.org/wiki/P%27ent%27ay (accessed January 14, 2009), cf. also the discussion page of the article.

234   See ETHIOPIAN FULL GOSPEL BELIEVERS' CHURCH, ሙሉ ወንጌል ቤተ ክርስቲያን ከልደት እስከ ..., 12–13; TIBEBE ESHETE, *The Evangelical Movement in Ethiopia*, 146; also interview no. 64.

235   See *The Ethiopian Herald*, "Youth and Adults Clash in Debre-Zeit." See also TIBEBE ESHETE, "Growing Through the Storms," 270–271, who makes the same observation regarding the report in the Amharic newspaper *Addis Zaman*.

236   JOHANSSON, Letter to Bo Hörnberg, April 23, 1971.

237   ibid.; see also JOHANSSON, Letter to Bo Hörnberg, May 4, 1971. See also above, 161, for more information on this link.

238   See above, 160.

239   See SOLOMON KEDIR, Letter to Haile Giorgis Workeneh, Mayor of Addis Ababa, November 10, 1971, cf. GIRMA ZEWDE, ኢትዮጵስ, 139–142; see also section 4.2.2, 155. The use of the term ጸንጠቆስጡ (*panṭāqosṭe*, Pentecost) and the additional explanations of course indicate that the term Pentecostal was all but a standard label at the time.

240   *Addis Zaman*, "በሕግ የተከለከለ ማኅበር አጃቄመው ተሰበሰቡ የተባሉ 480 ሰዎች ተከሰሱ።"

Herald to the *Newsweek* article about the arrests is titled: "Newsweek's Report on Pentecostalists Unfounded."[241]

The first written evidence of the abbreviated label "Pente" is in the FGBC history from 1978. The paper makes it clear that the label had been in use for quite some time and that the church does not find the use of this "insulting name" acceptable. Its adherents would rather be called "born-again Christians", their faith and practices do not resemble Pentecostals in other countries, and moreover, Pentecostal experiences are a hope given to all the churches and are not a new faith.[242] However, by that time the label was apparently widely used already and applied to people from other churches as well:

> Without exception, all who hasten to witness to those not knowing Jesus Christ's salvation, who frequent prayer in all of their spare time, who make God's word, the Bible, the guideline for private life, in general all people of faith or who are zealous for God are attacked by members of their churches with the label "Pente" which was made up by today's society; but we would like to recall that "Pente" or "Pentecost" is not the church's public name.[243]

Other sources from the same time also note the overextension of the term "Pente" to all Protestants. In 1979, *Christianity Today* argued against the notion by the Austrian Evangelical Press Service that only Pentecostals were targeted by the government, by stating that "all Protestant churches and groupings are classed as Pentecostals and contemptuously called 'Penties' in the current campaign."[244] Two years later an article in a different magazine suggests a political connection of this overextension:

> A "Pentecostal" in government terminology is any evangelical Christian who will not shout the slogan "Above everything the revolution" and engage in ritual cursing of political enemies.[245]

In later retrospective accounts the label "Pente" is presented as part of a violent discursive practice of alienation and political persecution of Christians which accompanied the societal upheaval of the Red Terror. These reports also indicate that the term was increasingly used as a political instrument against Protestant Christians everywhere, even though accuser and accused may not always have known what it meant. The anthropologist Donald Donham recalled, for example, how KHC Christians in Maale at first accepted peasant association offices and worked in collaboration with the new rulers, until a new district administrator came. He closed and confis-

---

241 See *Newsweek. International Edition*, "Persecuting the Sects."
242 See ETHIOPIAN FULL GOSPEL BELIEVERS' CHURCH, ሙሉ ወንጌል ቤተ ክርስቲያን ከልደት እስከ ..., 12–13. See also pp. II–III: "The church has refused to use the identifier 'Pentecost' as its own name, because like God's word says, the Holy Spirit in-filling and the Holy Spirit gifts are something that can be accepted by all who have believed in Jesus Christ and found forgiveness of sin, and because they aren't a sign distinguishing the church from other churches, and because Pentecost is a blessing many churches have experienced and will be able to experience, ."
243 Ibid., II–III.
244 *Christianity Today*, "The Campaign to Root Out 'Alien' Religion in Ethiopia."
245 BROWN, "Religion and Revolution in Ethiopia," 52.

cated the church and its property, announcing that "whatever local Christians called themselves, they were really pente," thereby introducing the term to the local political discourse.[246] Cumbers has also collected a number of stories in which the "Pente" accusation plays a major role.[247] Others report of general threats against "Pentes" by government officials.[248] The mainline churches also had to answer to the charge of being or harboring "Pente," which put the Charismatic movement in their midst in a precarious position and contributed to the politicization of Charismatic Christianity.[249]

5.3.3 Persecution and Denominational Boundaries

The connection between persecution and the spread of the Charismatic movement, which is signified by the term "Pente," is also a basic historical assumption in many accounts about the Derg time. One Pentecostal informant connected persecution to the spread of the Charismatic movement in the following way:

> The Derg, the Derg, the persecution under the Derg regime contributed a lot to make the churches Charismatic. Because they came together, the persecution brought the underground, they all met together. They all met together. Then there was the Ethiopian Evangelical Students also, what we call the EVASU, what we call the EVASU was there. Then there was the Evangelical Christians, Christian Civil Servants. Government workers, company workers, they also formed an association. There were several movements. All these brought the believers together from different denominations. They came — the Mekane Yesus, the Kale Heywet, the rest — all of them came together underground. So they shared their experiences, they used to pray together, they studied the Bible together. And all Ethiopian churches became Charismatic. The Mekane Yesus became Charismatic, the Kale Heywet became Charismatic.[250]

In this account, the primary catalyst for the spread of the Charismatic movement is the persecution-induced removal of denominational boundary lines, indicated by the concept of an "underground" space for Christians where "they all met together." Though the informant mentions some interdenominational forums,[251] their ultimate function is not to encourage ecumenical dialog, but to bring believers together "in the underground." Furthermore, the presumed co-mingling of different churches in the underground appears to be a sufficient enough explanation for the advancement of Pentecostal practices. There is no reference to "a mighty outpouring of the Holy Spirit" or the like, but rather the persecuted Christians simply share their experiences,

---

246 DONHAM, *Marxist Modern*, 164, see also p. 144.
247 See e.g. CUMBERS, *Count It All Joy*, 68–69, 73–75, 84, 87, 121–123, 140, 157, 205–206.
248 See TIBEBE ESHETE, *The Evangelical Movement in Ethiopia*, 265.
249 For examples, see below, section 5.3.5, 239.
250 Interview no. 112.
251 Only one of these, the Ethiopian Evangelical Students' Association (EVASU), actually was formed before the Derg came to power, in 1972. The Evangelical Christian Workers' Association was established around 1980. See BEKELE WOLDEKIDAN, ሪቢፅቷል, 107. It is interesting that two inherently ecumenical forums that Pentecostals participate(d) in are not mentioned here: ECFE and its predecessor the CCCE.

pray and read the Bible together, and in consequence "all Ethiopian churches became Charismatic." This explanation therefore seems to presumes an inherent superiority of Pentecostal or Charismatic spirituality, because once all denominational barriers were abolished, this type of Christianity is seen to have spread without further reason.

This is not an uncommon historical explanation, especially among Pentecostals. However, it is difficult to reconcile with a number of detailed narratives about the underground structure of most churches. Many informants reported a tight security control in different places: the size of the groups was strictly limited, people were instructed to come to the meeting one by one in order to not arouse suspicion, cell groups did not know of each others' existence, and a chain communication system prevented the betrayal of leaders. New believers were first instructed individually before they were accepted into a group, and when someone did not show up two or three times, the meeting would be moved to another place or time.[252] The intensity of these security measures of course depended on the strength of the political apparatus and its control methods in a certain area or time, but where security was high, it was difficult if not impossible to organize interdenominational groups or incorporate unknown members from other churches. In Awasa, for example, all HBC informants concurred that their house programs were strictly limited to members of their own denomination and that they would not allow outsiders to come in.[253] Similarly in Bahir Dar, the FGBC house fellowships did not accept believers from other denominations on account of security concerns.[254] There are occasional reports of church members mingling in the home fellowships,[255] but overall the frequency and intensity with which the security precautions of house churches are narrated stand in contrast to the general notion of a blending of Protestants in the underground.

Instead of referring to a common "underground", the same idea about the spread of the Charismatic movement can also be presented by stating that Pentecostals simply joined the existing churches, as in the following account by Tibebe Eshete:

> Being the early victims of the heavy handed treatment of the *Derg*, the Pentecostals were one of the first to go underground, as they had done in the past. During the initial stage of their responses, some opted to join other evangelical churches that were still operating openly. In so doing, they became instrumental in the spread of the Pentecostal experience in the new churches in which they chose to be a part.[256]

Though Tibebe mentions "going underground," he does not seek to establish this as an explanation for the rise of the Charismatic movement, but contends that there was an "initial stage," in which Pentecostals joined some of the churches which were still open. Once again the Pentecostal mission is endowed with a sense of superior-

---

252   Interviews no. 95; 63; 37; 126; 34; 84; 131.
253   Interviews no. 126; 100; 34.
254   Interview no. 7.
255   One informant, for example, notes that while the denominations generally remained separate in the underground, the FGBC groups in Bale accepted members from the ECMY and KHC, when those failed to establish cell groups, interview no. 131. Others report prison as one of the places of interdenominational exchange, interview no. 76.
256   Tibebe Eshete, *The Evangelical Movement in Ethiopia*, 266 (emphasis in the original).

ity, Pentecostals were the active partner in overcoming denominational boundaries ("opted to join", "chose to be a part"), and there is no explanation about what actually happened and helped them to spread their faith once they entered a mainline church.

Even informants who are critical of the notion of Pentecostals being instrumental in the spread of the Holy Spirit, have employed the same historic idea in their narratives. When asked whether there may be a tendency in FGBC histories to claim the emergence of the Holy Spirit movement in Ethiopia as their own fruit, a Charismatic respondent affirmed the premise of the question and framed his response with own critical remarks of a deep-seated "pride" within the FGBC and their assertion of being the "first ones". However, the FGBC's basic historical assumption of persecution leading to Charismatic proliferation is not only repeated by this informant, it is even elevated to a biblical level in an interesting parallelism with the spread of the first church:

> Well, the tendency is there. Even though I don't say a hundred percent that's sure, uh true. There is pride in Mulu Wongel. Mulu Wongel would be like apostles, the first century apostles — just to stay together. But the persecution came and dispersed us to the denominational churches. That is how it penetrated into Lutherans, into Mennonite, Meserete Kristos, Kale Heywet and so on. But this kind of attitude, that we are the first one, that is deep down within them. I think you can find it.[257]

However, when probing this theory of Pentecostal proliferation with more specific narratives, a wide spectrum of interaction between Pentecostals and mainline churches appears. While there are some reports of such an influence of Pentecostals,[258] there are also accounts of their outright rejection. In Awasa, HBC members reported that they did not visit the local ECMY congregation, and if they tried, they were sent away.[259] When attending the local KHC in the same town, they were expected to attend quietly and conform to the church culture of their host.[260] In other areas, Pentecostals may have been allowed to use the buildings of the remaining mainline congregations, but this did not necessarily entail an influence on the host. For example, one thesis describing the history of the Charismatic movement in the Gedeo area in southern Ethiopia mentions that the FGBC was allowed to utilize ECMY or KHC chapels in the area for conferences. However when actually detailing the emergence of the Charismatic movement in both churches, the thesis does not mention any influence by the FGBC, but rather points to a number of developments inside these churches.[261] For Addis Ababa, one informant stated that the influence and effect

---

257   Interview no. 68.
258   E.g. interview no. 106. The informant reports that the local ECMY congregation in Debre Zeit hosted members from different denominations and that the Pentecostal believers had a significant impact.
259   Interview no. 34; 126.
260   Interview no. 100. One informant stated that the KHC only became Charismatic after the fall of the Derg, interview no. 126.
261   See MINTESINOT BIRRU, "The Impact of Charismatic Movement and Its Result Among Evangelicals in Gedeo Area," 11, 16–22. With regard to the ECMY there had actually been a central

Pentecostal and Charismatic groups had on ECMY congregations varied from place to place. While some churches, like at Arat Kilo or Kasanches, had "people who had a Charismatic background and Charismatic leanings" attending, there was no "charismatic presence in the congregation."[262] At the same time, a Pentecostal informant reported hostile receptions by the mainline Protestant churches in Addis Ababa, since they feared being targeted by the government on account of their presence.[263]

Other churches may have already been impacted by the Charismatic movement before the Pentecostal churches were closed. This can be said, for example, of three ECMY congregations in Addis Ababa: the Bethel church in Gulele, the Kolfe ECMY, and the Entoto ECMY. Furthermore the Addis Ababa Bole MKC had seen an incursion of Pentecostals and Charismatic worship as early as 1973,[264] and five years later the church became known for a healing revival, which is commonly credited to its Charismatic pastor, Daniel Makonnen.[265] Yet some sources still contend that before the closure of Pentecostal churches in Addis Ababa only "a few old people and a few members" went there, and that the church was not revived until after it was closed.[266]

5.3.4 Early Charismatic Origins

The idea that the persecution of Pentecostals led to their proliferation in mainline Protestant churches did not originate in histories about the Derg, but apparently had been in use before. As early as 1977 Taye Abdissa made the following observations regarding the consequences of the political oppression against the Pentecostals in the last Haile Selassie years:

> When the Pentecostal Christians in Addis Ababa were persecuted in 1972, as I pointed out above, they scattered to different denominations in the city and began to teach about the fulness of the Holy Spirit for the individuals within the church in secret. Many young people from each denomination received the fulness of the Holy Spirit and as the result the revival began.[267]

---

decision not to rent out churches, but to only welcome Pentecostals in the existing services, interview no. 122.

262 Interview no. 77.
263 Interview no. 64.
264 This was in connection to a group that had broken away from the Finnish Mission in 1971 and had established three independent chapels by the name of Zion. After their chapels were closed in 1973, they joined the MKC congregation in Bole for some time, see HEGE, *Beyond Our Prayers*, 159. In Nazareth the Mennonite Mission of course had been in contact with the Pentecostal revival as early as the 1960s, see section 3.2, 108.
265 Daniel Makonnen had been a member of the Zion group, and had never joined the FGBC. After studying in England from 1974 to 1976, he became the pastor of the Bole MKC congregation in 1977 and began his popular healing meetings probably as early as 1978, see EYOB DEMISSIE, "Pastor Daniel Makonnen (Ethiopian Church History)" (Major Paper, Ethiopian Theological College, 2003), 9–10; HEGE, *Beyond Our Prayers*, 170, 198–199; TEFERA MEKETA, "The History of South Addis Ababa Meserete Kristos Church and Its Growth," 59; TESFAYE TADESSE, "The Importance of Healing Ministry for Church Growth" (B.Th. thesis, Mekane Yesus Seminary, 2000), 18; DULA, "Reading Yoder in Ethiopia," 18.
266 Interview no. 1; 7.
267 TAYE ABDISSA, "The Pentecostal Development and the Rise of Charismatic Movement in Ethiopia," 30–31.

This paragraph functions as bridge between the two points of interest of Taye's thesis titled *The Pentecostal Development and the Rise of Charismatic Movement in Ethiopia.* After having narrated the beginnings of Ethiopian Pentecostalism and its difficulties in the last years of Imperial Ethiopia, Taye now turns to the Charismatic movement in general, and firmly links it to the persecution of Pentecostals in 1972. Though Taye notes that the Charismatic movement met strong resistance in the established churches, including ECMY, he concludes that despite this opposition there is no church "that has not been touched by this revival," and that "[e]ven the established and well organized churches which have a fixed liturgy and doctrine have many revivalists among them and the revival is also spreading and growing in their churches, e.g. Orthodox, Mekane Yesus."[268]

The subsequent chapter, "The Revivals Within ECMY" focuses on three centers of the early Charismatic revival in this church: Gore and Metu (in Ilubabor), the Mekane Yesus Seminary (Addis Ababa), and Bodji (Welega).[269] However, Taye's detailed historical narrative about the Charismatic movement in these centers does not match up with his general assertion of a Pentecostal spread to the mainline churches by way of persecution.

For Gore, the "Outpouring of the Holy Spirit"[270] is dated to the beginning of 1970, i.e., two and a half years before the political oppression against Pentecostals began in 1972.[271] Furthermore, Taye does not at all connect this Spirit outpouring to the existing Pentecostal movement in Ethiopia, but asserts that "[i]t was after the study of the book of Acts that Endalcachew and his friends were filled by the Holy Spirit."[272] The only human assistance mentioned here was offered by Iteffa Gobena, who had previously encountered the baptism in the Holy Spirit.[273] The source of Iteffa's experience is not recorded, and no links to existing Pentecostalism are made.[274] From Gore, the Charismatic movement spread to the nearby town of Metu within two years. In this context Taye mentions an FGBC evangelist, who had worked for the ECMY in both towns, but he does not provide any specific information about him, nor does he connect him in any way to the beginnings of the revival.[275]

---

268 TAYE ABDISSA, "The Pentecostal Development and the Rise of Charismatic Movement in Ethiopia," 31.
269 A fourth and very important center is only mentioned in passing: Nekemte (Welega). See below, 237.
270 TAYE ABDISSA, "The Pentecostal Development and the Rise of Charismatic Movement in Ethiopia," 36.
271 See ibid., 37f. The date given is "Feb. 13, 1962 E.C. on Friday night", with "February" denoting the Ethiopian month of የካቲት (*yäkatit*), which translates to Friday, February 20, 1970.
272 Ibid., 36.
273 Iteffa Gobena later served as President of the ECMY from 2001–2009.
274 Much later, TEKA OBSA FOGI, "The Charismatic Movement in the EECMY," 92 reported that Iteffa was prayed over by a fellow Christian, Tibebu Kumalo, and two teachers from the Harar Teacher Training Institute. He notes that "Kes Iteffa believes that the persons who prayed for him can be categorized as belonging to the Pentecostal denomination." In Iteffa's own testimony, his role in initiating the 1970 revival night is also reported, but his own experience of baptism in the Holy Spirit is not even alluded to, see ITEFFA GOBENA MOLTE, "Autobiography" (2008), http://www.ethiopianetwork.org/GobenaBio.html (accessed November 28, 2008).
275 Cf. TAYE ABDISSA, "The Pentecostal Development and the Rise of Charismatic Movement in Ethiopia," 44.

With regard to the Charismatic revival in the Addis Ababa Mekane Yesus Seminary, it could be expected that Taye is better equipped to make his case for the influence of persecuted Pentecostals in the inception of the charismatic movement, since this revival dates to after the arrests of 1972, it happened in the same city, and Taye was part of it himself. However, concurrent with later sources about the events at the seminary, Taye does not map out such an influence, but attributes the seminary revival to two students from Nekemte, Tesfaye Dinagde and Tolosa Gudina.[276] In Nekemte, however, the Charismatic movement had already begun as early as 1971 and soon aroused conflict between the revived youth and the leadership of the church. This resulted in a temporary exclusion of the Charismatic youth from the church until the conflict was reconciled by the general secretary of the ECMY, Gudina Tumsa in 1973.[277] The leaders of the movement were then sent to the seminary,[278] and when Tesfaye Dinagde quit the seminary, reportedly frustrated by continued opposition, Gudina Tumsa sought him out and made him the youth leader in this Synod.[279]

Taye does not detail these events in Nekemte, nor does he mention how Tesfaye Dinagde and Tolosa Gudina received the Holy Spirit. Other sources are also sketchy with regard to Tesfaye Dinagde Spirit baptism,[280] but Tolosa Gudina by all appearances was well connected to the Pentecostal nucleus in Ethiopia. He had been part of the *yäsämay bərhan* movement when he was a High School Student in Debre Zeit,[281] and had received the baptism in the Spirit there.[282] Furthermore, he apparently had good connections to the FGBC, since he arranged for its leaders, like Merid Lema, to speak at the seminary.[283]

Taye probably was informed about Tolosa's links to the Pentecostal movement since he had joined the seminary revival group in January 1974 and personally knew the involved students.[284] Therefore, it is noticeable that he does not take the op-

---

276   Tesfaye Dinagde changed his name to Waqtola Dinagde, and is now pastor of an Oromo church in Washington D.C. Tolosa Gudina now pastors a church in Atlanta and is a well-known traveling evangelist, who hosts annual revival meetings in the Addis Ababa stadium.

277   See Teka Obsa Fogi, "The Charismatic Movement in the EECMY," 86–89; also interviews no. 82; 122; Thomas Debela, "The Effect of Charismatic Renewal upon Church Growth in the Central Synod," 15–16. Before his appointment as general secretary Gudina had been pastor in Nekemte. Regarding his openness to the Charismatic movement, see Engelsviken, "Gudina Tumsa, the Ethiopian Evangelical Church Mekane Yesus, and the Charismatic Movement," 11–12; Hoffman, "Gudina Tumsa's Legacy," 17.

278   This also included Belina Sarka, who became a well-known healer and evangelist within the church.

279   Teka Obsa Fogi, "The Charismatic Movement in the EECMY," 88; also interview no. 82.

280   An unnamed evangelist is mentioned, by whom Tesfaye was prompted to pray fervently and received "fire in his mouth," reviving him to preach and teach. Later he reportedly connected with Pentecostals in Addis Ababa, interview no. 82. See also ibid., 86–87. A Pentecostal informant was encountered during research, who was a Harar Teacher Training Institute (TTI) graduate and claimed that he and a friend initiated the Charismatic movement in Nekemte through a house prayer meeting they led during a two month stay in Nekemte in 1967, interview no. 92.

281   Students from Nazaret had come to Debre Zeit and initiated a group there.

282   Teka Obsa Fogi, "The Charismatic Movement in the EECMY," 86; also interview no. 68.

283   Interview no. 82.

284   See Taye Abdissa, "The Pentecostal Development and the Rise of Charismatic Movement in Ethiopia," 47. His and Tolosa Gudina's B.Th. theses were the first Mekane Yesus Seminary

portunity in his thesis to point to this connection between the early Pentecostal movement and the Charismatic revival in the ECMY. Instead, the Pentecostals are only introduced to the story of the seminary revival when it was already well on its way:

> As the revival began to grow and started to plant its root deeply into the seminary compound, many young people from the Finnish Mission in Markato area, from the Mullu-Wongel or Full Gospel Believers, from Bole area and a few Christians from the National University began to come to participate in the prayer group meeting in 1974 when they heard about the revival.[285]

In his narrative about the third early center of the ECMY Charismatic movement, the revival in Bodji, Taye Abdissa points to his own influence. He was assigned to the Bila district for ministry during the summer vacation of 1975 and was introduced to a group in Bodji initiated by Ashenafi Desta. Ashenafi reportedly was there on his national service duty and "gave them the first testimony about the Holy Spirit."[286] As an Addis Ababa University student and a Charismatic, he would either have been connected to the ECMY youth center, in which many of the FGBC youths participated, or to one of the Pentecostal underground meetings. However, Taye makes no reference to Ashenafi's background, and reports that the actual Spirit outpouring occurred later in December of 1975, when he returned there with a group led by Belina Sarka.[287] A Pentecostal influence is not recorded anywhere, and Taye concludes:

> When I was assigned for summer vacation in 1975, in Bodji District, I got a chance for witness and teach the great work of God about the fulness and work of the Holy Spirit in some congregations. Today the revival spread to more than 15 congregations in Bodji and is moving to the other districts of ECMY of Western Synod.[288]

In conclusion, Taye Abdissa's treatment of the Charismatic movement in the ECMY puts the discussion of Pentecostal proliferation during the Derg into perspective in a number of ways. First of all, the content of the thesis, as well as its early date of origin (1977), are evidence of the emergence of the Charismatic movement well before the systematic persecution of Pentecostals by the Derg. Some stories even indicate a time predating the political suppression of the FGBC under Haile Selassie's government in 1972. The Charismatic movement may not have been a wide-spread phenomenon yet, but it had reached some important centers (Nekemte, the Addis Ababa Mekane Yesus Seminary). Furthermore, its front leaders, who today are well-

---

theses concerning the Charismatic movement, see also TOLESA GUDINA, "The Spiritual Gifts on I: Cor. 12: 8–10" (B.Th. thesis, Mekane Yesus Seminary, 1977).

285 TAYE ABDISSA, "The Pentecostal Development and the Rise of Charismatic Movement in Ethiopia," 48.

286 Ibid., 52.

287 DANIEL TESSO NEDJO, "The Growth and Impact of Evangelical Christianity in Bodji District 1941–2000," 28 dates this to 1977 and reports a different preliminary story, with two high school teachers from Addis Ababa whose denominational background is not identified.

288 TAYE ABDISSA, "The Pentecostal Development and the Rise of Charismatic Movement in Ethiopia," 57.

known ministers, such as Tolosa Gudina, Belina Sarka, Tesfaye Dinagde, were already part of the movement early on and had found some significant support, not only in the seminary, but also by the general secretary of the church, Gudina Tumsa.[289] Furthermore, a WCC document of 1974 also indicates that these developments were already visible to outside observers by the time the revolution began:

> The persecution of Pentecostal communities seems to be ended silently. The Ethiopian Orthodox Church is still very critical and highly concerned because it feels threatened, probably with justification. Recently there have been signs of Pentecostal influence in the ECMY as well. They seem to be active particularly among students. In addition, the wider charismatic movement seems to be taking hold in Ethiopia as well.[290]

Moreover, Taye's thesis documents that the general historic notion of Pentecostal persecution leading to its proliferation in mainline churches had already been invented before the persecution of Pentecostals by the Derg and had been applied to the story of the 1972 arrests.[291] However, just as in the later accounts, this general historic trajectory of explaining the emergence of the Charismatic movement by the entrance of repressed Pentecostals into the mainline churches was not sustained with the detailed information given. Instead, the Pentecostal influence is marginalized even where it could be linked to the early Charismatics, and Pentecostals are only portrayed as later participants in the mainline church revival.

5.3.5 Persecution from Within

Taye's thesis not only reveals that the idea of persecution leading to a Charismatic proliferation existed fairly early on, it is also the earliest document where the connection is made the other way around: being a Charismatic may lead to persecution in one's own church. The handwritten document reveals the following interesting correction of words:

> Some of the churches, such as Meserete Kiristos and ~~xxx~~ Birhane Wongel in Kera welcomed the movement and ~~almost all~~ some of the members received the fullness of the Holy Spirit and showed a dynamic growth whereas the other denominations such as the Orthodox churches, the Evangelical Church Mekane Yesus ~~persecuted~~ opposed the revivalists within their churches. In spite of the ~~persecution~~ opposition, today there is not any church that has not been touched by this revival. Even the established and well organized churches which have a fixed liturgy and doctrine have many revivalists among them and the revival

---

289   Though Gudina by all accounts was not a Charismatic, he evidently saw the benefits of this movement to his church and thus was prepared to give it room, see BAKKE, *Christian Ministry*, 253, note 80; ENGELSVIKEN, "Gudina Tumsa, the Ethiopian Evangelical Church Mekane Yesus, and the Charismatic Movement," 13–14.

290   KONRAD RAISER, "Report on Visit to Ethiopia: October 13–20, 1974," Ethiopia Correspondence, WCC Archives, Geneva, 1974, 4.

291   Later theses at the seminary adopted Taye's general narrative, e.g. MENGESHA AGA, "Evangelism and Charismatic Movement in Ghimbi District Western Synod EECMY 1914–1999," 22.

is also spreading ~~in~~ and growing in their churches, e.g. Orthodox, Mekane Yesus.[292]

The editing of the paragraph apparently was intended to tone down some of the assertions. Only "some" instead of "almost all" members are reported to have received the "Fullness of the Holy Spirit," and what before was called a "persecution" is reduced to "opposition." While Taye or an anonymous editor evidently were hesitant to use accuse the ECMY of "persecuting" the Charismatic movement, later histories do not refrain from such language when describing the political difficulties that the revival groups encountered inside the mainline churches during the Derg.

For example, in his B.Th. thesis about the Charismatic movement in the Gimbi district of the ECMY Western Synod, Mengesha Aga tells the following story:

> In Nejo a man called Obbo Temesgen Geleta welcomed the movement and they had meetings at his house. He was Nejo district secretary. But the church leaders betrayed the movement and persecuted the youth. The persecution was [from] both sides [in] that it was external and internal that [with?] the church leaders on one hand and the Derg government on the other hand. Therefore, the charismatic movement [was] carried out by the revived people [in the] underground until 1992.[293]

This quote clearly establishes a parallelism between the Derg's oppression of the churches and the resistance to revival groups in the ECMY by applying the term "persecution" to both. According to Mengesha, the betrayal of the Charismatic movement was only another side of the same persecution experience, it was "internal" as opposed to "external," the movement was confronted with "the church leaders on one hand and the Derg government on the other hand." The church leadership thus is counted among the persecutors.

However, there is a notable absence of specifics in this quote. First of all, the temporal setting is unclear. Immediately preceding the quote, a Charismatic conference in 1984 is mentioned for Nejo, but there is no clear reference as to how this conference relates to the establishment of the home fellowship. Secondly, it is unclear how the fact that the ECMY "Nejo district secretary" welcomed the Charismatic movement into his house relates to the statement that the "church leaders betrayed" the Charismatic youth. Did Temesgen Geleta, who clearly was in a leadership position himself, turn against the movement in his house or was there some sort of conflict between him and the rest of the district leadership? Thirdly, there are no details as to how the church leadership "betrayed" and "persecuted" the Charismatic movement.

The fourth and most important ommission, however, is the lack of any indication regarding the overall difficult political situation of the ECMY at the time. The whole Western Synod had been much affected by government oppression and saw the closure

---

292 TAYE ABDISSA, "The Pentecostal Development and the Rise of Charismatic Movement in Ethiopia," 31. This quote is the direct continuation of the quote above, see 235. "xxx" denotes an unreadable text under the correction marks. The corrected words are written above the crossed out text, and it is not clear if they are in Taye's handwriting or not.
293 MENGESHA AGA, "Evangelism and Charismatic Movement in Ghimbi District Western Synod EECMY 1914–1999," 23. This information is based on an oral interview, see note 38.

of 94 percent of its churches between 1981 and 1984.[294] The Nejo district was no exception. Eide reported that in October 1981 thirty-five Nejo district workers were arrested and kept in jail for three months, the Nejo superintendent even until May 1982.[295] The congregation in the town of Nejo was closed at the latest by February 1984, and in the whole district only one of eighty-one churches remained open.[296]

The contrast between Eide's account and Mengesha's statement illustrates that the political complexities resulting from the Derg's oppression of "Pentes" can easily result in two conflicting persecution accounts within one church. The pressure on local ECMY leadership as well as the infamous "Pente" attribution likely would have pitted the leadership against the Charismatic movement in their midst, especially if there was any preexisting conflict with the group or if their actions resulted in political danger for the church. The withdrawal of the church leadership's support in such an oppressive environment, on the other hand, likely would have had dire consequences. Thus, the church that sees itself as persecuted becomes the persecutor in the eyes of the Charismatic movement, and the situation itself remains a highly political charged topic even in later church histories.

Another example of such an "internal persecution" narrative is the B.Th. thesis by Jeto Hordofa, subtitled *The Effects of the persecution of 1978–1991 (1970-1983 E.C.) on the Congregations of Western Wollega Bethel Synod*. The main part of the thesis is a long chapter detailing the political repressions of the church under the Derg. This chapter sets out with a section titled "The Official Persecution,"[297] in which the author describes the political setting of the persecution,[298] continued by a detailed account of the different sufferings the synod as a whole endured: numerous mass arrests, the denial of justice, violence and mistreatment in prison, as well as the political targeting of individual church leaders and the youth.[299] This is followed by a section reflecting the "Outcome of the Persecution," in which the author considers the economic loss to the church through the confiscation and destruction of church buildings, and the loss in membership, because a number of people turned away from the church and even collaborated with the Derg authorities. Despite these political difficulties, the section "The Official Persecution" concludes with the following remarks:

> The persecution helped the evangelical Christians to exercise the true life in Jesus Christ, by their genuine fellowship. A real genuine love and fellowship was created among the believers. A time of coming to a more close relationship with God. The believers became strong in their faith during these years more than ever. Though strong warnings were given to believers never to worship

---

294 See EIDE, *Revolution and Religion in Ethiopia*, 185–194. See also Mengesha Aga's own account of these political difficulties, which is largely based on Eide, MENGESHA AGA, "Evangelism and Charismatic Movement in Ghimbi District Western Synod EECMY 1914–1999," 17–19.

295 EIDE, *Revolution and Religion in Ethiopia*, 189.

296 Cf. ibid., 188–190.

297 JETO HORDOFA, "'Troubled But Not Destroyed'," 18–30.

298 As in a number of sources, the main source of political repression is seen with the regional governor of Welega, Niguse Fanta, who apparently was very outspoken in his contempt for evangelical Christians. Cf. EIDE, *Revolution and Religion in Ethiopia*, 193–194.

299 See JETO HORDOFA, "'Troubled But Not Destroyed'," 21–25.

and many programmes were planned on Sundays to trap Christians, but they kept worshiping in private houses. The Almighty God gave them power to stand firm in this time of hardship, to testify His Great name.[300]

This assertion of harmony and deeper commitments is contrasted by the next section, titled "Persecution within Persecution."[301] Here, the author first makes the following general statement:

The pastors and leaders did not want to have the active and devoted religious youth close to them. So the youth suffered double persecution (from inside and outside).[302]

Jeto soon continues with more specific information:

Later on, some pastors and elders continued to persecute the youth as 'pentes'. The pro-charismatic people, who were much interested and involved in [the] Charismatic movement, even those who just had interest in worship or [were] active for worship, were regarded as pentes and were persecuted by the church. From outside, the church is persecuted as 'mette haymanot' and anti revolution. The church on the other hand persecuted the youth as 'pentes'. Later on the group of persecuted 'pentes' ended as FG [Full Gospel] believers.[303]

Finally, he concludes the section with the following sentences:

The youth say that the persecution from the elders was much worse than that of the Marxist cadires [cadres]. Persecution within persecution.[304]

These statements clearly are part of a different persecution narrative that is contrary to the general conclusion quoted above. Instead of an intensified faith and a unified body of Christ, they portray a deeply divided church, the leadership of which is attempting to alienate those of Charismatic persuasion.

This contrast can be explained by Jeto Hordofa's sources. The section regarding "The Official Persecution" relied on sources from the church leadership, pastors, elders and the Synod president,[305] whereas the part about the "Persecution within [the] Persecution" cites two informants, a male youth leader of a regional presbytery and a female youth, both of whom had been affected directly by political repression.

These two informants seem to have contributed one main historical event each to the "internal persecution" narrative, both probably dating to 1978, i.e., the beginning of the government oppression against the Protestant churches.[306] The first story tells

---

300   JETO HORDOFA, "'Troubled But Not Destroyed'," 29–30.
301   See ibid., 30–33.
302   Ibid., 31.
303   Ibid., 32–33. "mette haymanot" (መጤ ሃይማኖት /mäṭe haymanot) means "newcomer's religion" or "alien faith."
304   Ibid., 33.
305   Cf. ibid., 49 for a characterization of the informants. The Rev. Ula Fituma was not just an "administrative position" as stated here, but the West Welega Bethel Synod president, see EIDE, *Revolution and Religion in Ethiopia*, 194.
306   One event is directly dated to 1978, the other one indirectly in the characterization of informants, see JETO HORDOFA, "'Troubled But Not Destroyed'," 32, 49.

of a Marxist leaning youth from the church challenging the presbytery youth leader by the name of Dawit in front of the presbytery pastor on account of his "pente" activities, reportedly asking the pastor: "How can pente exist within Bethel?"[307] The presbytery pastor then allegedly "got angry and denounced Dawit and excommunicated him," which led to the elders withdrawing their support from the Charismatic youth.[308] However, Dawit and the pastor seem to have reconciled shortly thereafter, since the youth leader was re-admitted to communion and reinstated in his former position by the presbytery pastor.[309] The political motivation of the latter remains unclear in the short account, but it appears that there was a struggle between Charismatic and Marxist youths for influence in the church. The Marxist faction probably had more political weight, since the church at the time would have been negotiating the treacherous political waters of the Red Terror. The second event is connected to an arrest of a number of youths who refused to shout socialist slogans.[310] When they were arrested and mistreated, the church leadership as well as some of their parents reportedly did not speak out on their behalf, nor looked after them in prison.

Outside of these two main stories a vague reference is made to another arrest, in which the youth were told by the authorities that the church evangelists had provided them with a list of names. Furthermore, the Charismatics apparently did not find support for additional Bible study meetings within the church, and reportedly turned to the underground meetings organized by the emerging FGBC. This last observation points to another interest of Jeto Hordofa's "persecution within [the] persecution" narrative which appears at several places in the text, namely, to explain the emergence and success of the FGBC by reference to the failure of the ECMY to "feed the youth."[311] Jeta Hordofa concludes:

> The church by persecuting her own people founded another church which became a challenge to her.[312]

A third example of the "internal persecution" narrative is the B.Th. thesis by Mintesinot Birru pertaining to the Charismatic movement in the KHC and the ECMY in the Gedeo area.[313] Unlike the other two examples, this account is not motivated by personal involvement in the Charismatic movement, but apparently was a research assignment sparked by the interest in the history of a new church in the region,

---

307 Ibid., 30.

308 Ibid., 31.

309 The pastor reportedly later even encouraged the youth leader to stand fast even to the point of martyrdom, see ibid.

310 For a similar case, see EIDE, *Revolution and Religion in Ethiopia*, 247. The source reference made here to YOSIEF KIDANEWOLD, "The History of the Pentecostal Movement in Addis Abeba," 20 does not match up with the version of the manuscript held by this author. It would be somewhat surprising to find Yosief referring to an act of public opposition, since he is trying to make a case for the compatibility of Pentecostalism with the revolution.

311 JETO HORDOFA, "'Troubled But Not Destroyed'," 31.

312 Ibid., 33. The idea that in the end the ECMY is actually responsible for the foundation of the FGBC can also be read as a stab at triumphalist Pentecostal historiography.

313 See MINTESINOT BIRRU, "The Impact of Charismatic Movement and Its Result Among Evangelicals in Gedeo Area." The Gedeo area is located in the southern Ethiopia, in the Sidama region and is administered from the town of Dila.

the Calvary Holiness International Church (CHIC). The historical research about this church and the Charismatic movements preceding it are mostly based on oral interviews, which are almost exclusively from the CHIC itself.[314] This church traces its origins to four Charismatic groups within the KHC and the ECMY. The first of these groups emerged in 1977 in a local KHC congregation in Dila, the regional capital. Members of the main choir had heard about baptism in the Spirit and about different revival meetings in the area. After they had established a spiritual meeting on the KHC compound, "they found someone" who came and taught "secretly" about such things, "[b]ecause at the time the leaders did not like to hear and know about new revivals and baptism of the Holy Spirit."[315] The choir members are said to have received "tongue speaking and prophecy," and their experience reportedly was at the "root of the other meetings or Charismatic Movements in the area."[316] A similar development took place in the town of Chichu, where in 1981 a KHC "choir had been filled with the power and the gift of the Holy Spirit within three months," after its leader had read Pentecostal books and had found Charismatic contacts during a trip to Addis Ababa.[317] Under the influence of the leaders from the Chichu movement, a choir in Sakicha, this one belonging to an ECMY congregation, turned charismatic in 1983.[318] A leader from Sakicha, in turn, is reported to have brought about the Charismatic movement to a KHC choir in Gola in 1987.

When narrating the emergence of these meetings, the thesis mentions that three of the four groups encountered difficulties in their respective churches. These difficulties are fleshed out with some more detail in the subsequent section "Persecution."[319] In keeping with the idea that the Charismatic movements suffered "internal and external persecution,"[320] the section is divided into two parts, first "Persecution from Church Leaders" and secondly "Persecution from Local Officials." The first part begins with the following statement:

> When we see these four meetings in different places and time, we see all of them persecuted by the church leaders. Only Dilla-Koffe meeting was not persecuted by the church leaders like the rest of the meeting members. The Dilla-Koffe meeting or movement was stopped by the government persecution and their being scattered because of their job and marriage.[321]

It is important for this thesis to make a firm case regarding "internal persecution", because its main aim is to show that an uncompromising stance against Charismatics may simply lead to the undesirable result of new church establishments, like the

---

314   Cf. MINTESINOT BIRRU, "The Impact of Charismatic Movement and Its Result Among Evangelicals in Gedeo Area," 50.

315   Ibid., 16.

316   Ibid.

317   See ibid., 17–18.

318   Sakicha is out of the Gedeo area and further south, but is mentioned here due to its connections with Chichu and Gola.

319   See MINTESINOT BIRRU, "The Impact of Charismatic Movement and Its Result Among Evangelicals in Gedeo Area," 22–27.

320   Ibid., 24.

321   Ibid., 22.

CHIC.[322] Therefore the quote sets out with a strong assertion: "all of them" were "persecuted by the church leaders." The next two sentences contradict this notions somewhat: the Dila meeting was not "persecuted by the church leaders like the rest," it actually only was stopped by government action in combination with a membership fluctuation.

For the other meetings, the "internal persecution" experience is narrated in different levels of detail. In Chichu, the opposition by the church in combination with government repression led to the disappearance of the meetings. In Sakicha, the elders reportedly revealed "the places where the movement members were" to local authorities, who seized them and sent them to military service.[323] The most detailed stories are reported from Gola, where parents allegedly took harsh disciplinary action against their children,[324] but in the end the whole congregation was still divided between supporters and opponents of the movement.

The following section titled "Persecution from the Local Officials" reveals that the Derg only plays a secondary role for the overall persecution narrative. Instead of majoring on government actions, the role of the church in persecution is again highlighted here: in Sakicha it was "parents, church leaders and local officials" who persecuted the Charismatics, and in Gola the thesis states that "[t]he local officials of the government were making the way for the GAKHC [Gedeo Area KHC] church leaders to persecute the Goola Charismatic Movement members."[325]

It is peculiar that no reference is made here nor elsewhere in the thesis to the fairly strong repression of the Gedeo KHC during the Derg. In this area, 141 of 150 congregations had been closed before 1985,[326] and later on the SIM missionary John Cumbers collected a number of testimonies remembering the oppression suffered by the church, including a two-year imprisonment of church leaders.[327] One of these imprisoned church leaders, the general secretary of the Gedeo KHC, Balcha Bore, was interviewed by Mintesinot Birru for his thesis.[328] Since he was one of Cumbers' principal informants as well, it is unlikely that he would not have injected his persecution story into the interview, but there is no indication of his experiences in Mintesinot's thesis. Cumbers, on the other hand, makes no reference at all to the Charismatic movement or even any sort of disturbance within the KHC.

---

322   See, for example, the concluding remarks on p. 47: "I think most of the leaders understand that they should take care for the youngsters in any situation, so that they may not flee out from the church starting a new denomination in the area. Because these rejected Charismatics established new denomination in the area, this could be good teaching for come conservative church leaders."

323   See MINTESINOT BIRRU, "The Impact of Charismatic Movement and Its Result Among Evangelicals in Gedeo Area," 22.

324   See ibid., 22–23. Some parents are said to have tied their children up at home for the meeting times, others disowned their children altogether. Shaving of women's hair, forced marriages and sending young men to military service are reported here as well.

325   Ibid., 24.

326   See GETACHEW BELLETE, ኢሎጌ እና ሃሉጌ፡ የኢትዮጵያ ቃለ ሕይወት ቤተ ክርስቲያን ታሪክ, ቅጽ ሦስት, (ከ1966–1992 ዓ.ም.), 281.

327   See CUMBERS, *Living With the Red Terror*, 48–60.

328   See MINTESINOT BIRRU, "The Impact of Charismatic Movement and Its Result Among Evangelicals in Gedeo Area," 50.

The SIM missionary Brian Fargher, who had served in the neighboring district of Yrga Chefe for some time,[329] seems to counter the allegations of an "internal persecution" more directly. In a frequently cited essay, he dated the entrance of the Charismatic movement into the KHC very early,[330] and contended that "enthusiasts" within the church welcomed the confrontation with the government. According to Fargher, the "vast majority of Christians" had difficulties with "this new teaching", and while the Charismatics "often became unnecessarily loud," they found it hard to admit their own wrongdoing.[331] Fargher concludes with a tongue-in-cheek remark:

> Rejection by the majority was interpreted by the minority as a sure sign that they were indeed part of the selected group who had to suffer persecution for their faith.[332]

The "internal persecution" narrative of a number of seminary theses[333] therefore has not gone unchallenged. However, Fargher's paper does not deny the connection between the Charismatic movement and the government's actions, but simply assigns the blame to the revival groups themselves instead of to the church. Thus his ironic remarks are primarily targeted at the supposed moral authority of a "selected group" which was suffering "for their faith."

A quote from an ECMY thesis shows that such claims to moral authority may indeed be connected to the "internal persecution" narratives:

> Dietrich Bonhoeffer who died a martyr during Nazism, criticized his church in the following way. "We Lutherans have gathered like eagles round the carcase of cheap grace, and there we have drunk of the poison which has killed the life of following Christ. [...] We justified the world and condemned as heretics those who tried to follow Christ." Rev. James told me that some leaders of EECMY have persecuted charismatics. They even gave them to the Communist regime to be imprisoned and the leaders opposed the release of the charismatic[s] from the prison. In one Synod the leaders said to the authorities of a jail, "Do not release these people, if you release them they will trouble us." This is what, as Bonhoeffer said, justifying the world and condemning those who tried to

---

329 See CUMBERS, *Count It All Joy*, 247. The dating of this period is not given here, but the context would point to the time of the closure of different churches in the area, i.e., a significant time for these events.

330 He states that "[f]rom 1960–1975 the renewal movement shifted out of the churches, into the homes and then back into the churches again," sees "harmony achieved" by the end of the 1970s at the latest, and asserts that by the 1980s the movement "had become institutionalized and could hardly any longer be called a separate movement," see FARGHER, "The Charismatic Movement in Ethiopia 1960–1980," 351, 353–355.

331 Ibid., 349.

332 Ibid.

333 For further examples see e.g. DANIEL TESSO NEDJO, "The Growth and Impact of Evangelical Christianity in Bodji District 1941–2000," 17; ASFAW ATAMO, "Misunderstandings and Proposed Solutions Regarding Spiritual Gifts — with Special Emphasis on South Central Synod" (B.Th. thesis, Mekane Yesus Seminary, 1999), 5.

follow Christ, means. What right have these EECMY leaders to criticize the charismatics today if their hands become dirty in such a horrible works?[334]

This assertion of a present moral authority resonates with a theme that was observed in the Pentecostal persecution accounts described above. Just as in the Pentecostal narratives, these Charismatics have integrated the oppressive reality of the Derg on the churches as a whole into an overarching, meaningful account of judgment and redemption. The violent discursive practice of ostracizing Christians with the label "Pente" forms the base of their narrative about the Charismatic movement and its struggle within the established churches. This link between Charismatics and persecution not only defines the legacy of the movement, but also comes with certain claims to its legitimate role in the present church.

Altogether, therefore, there seem to be two ways of making the link between persecution and the rise of the Charismatic movement. One is to explain the emergence of Charismatics as a secondary consequence of persecution. The assumed leveling of interdenominational barriers in commonly endured political oppression thereby functions as a primary catalyst for the proliferation of Pentecostal experiences. This corresponds well to a Pentecostal master narrative of spread via persecution and is connected to an ecumenical assumption for the present church that by lowering denominational barriers the Spirit will move in Pentecostal fashion.

The Charismatics themselves, on the other hand, seem to prefer a different narrative. While on a general level they occasionally affirm the notion of persecution leading to Pentecostal proliferation, their more detailed accounts actually tend to hide the historical connections to Pentecostals. Instead they link their movement to persecution in the opposite way: being a Charismatic invites persecution by the church and the state. This story line not only subsumes all church conflict regarding the Charismatic movement under a persecution narrative, it also lends a strong moral authority to the Charismatic groups.

Therefore, Pentecostal and Charismatic histories about Christianity during the Derg are interested in their present application as they produce their accounts in retrospect. They reflect and subvert the endured political oppression (while historically de-contextualizing it) by placing it in larger and meaningful narratives of judgment and redemption, Pentecostal proliferation, or Charismatic endurance.

---

334 ASSEFA MEKONNEN, "A Clean Hearth for the Fire to Blaze: Evaluating Charismatic Movement in EECMY by Lutheran Theological Tradition" (B.Th. thesis, Mekane Yesus Seminary, 1997), 22–23. Bonnhoeffer quote abbreviated by J.H.

6   Conclusion: Writing Religious History

In his *Entdeckung der Religionsgeschichte* Hans G. Kippenberg set out with Hayden White's dictum that "there can be no 'proper history' which is not at the same time 'philosophy of history'."[1] This became the guiding proposition for Kippenberg's study of the emergence of History of Religions as a discipline in the age of modernity, in which he demonstrates that all histories of religion are saturated with philosophical premises informing their narrative, which in turn have to be analyzed historically in order to produce a coherent account about the formation of Religious Studies.

What Kippenberg has laid out for the historical study of religions in general, the present book has aspired to with regard to the history of a specific religious movement. The history of Ethiopian Pentecostalism, so it was proposed, cannot be limited to presenting events, sources and chronologies, but must take into account the many tales produced about about the past in order to map out the larger historical discourse. The study therefore began with Hayden White's proposition that realistic and fictional discourses are complementary sides of the same meaning-producing apparatus, which also meant that writing the history of Ethiopian Pentecostalism entailed retelling and analyzing the many stories about the past, instead of simply contrasting them with the available material evidence.

The methods applied and the resulting observations in this study resonate with a number of recent theory debates about historiography, which are influenced by poststructuralist and postcolonial philosophies. Some of these will now be outlined in brief as a way of concluding the findings of this study.

6.1   Narrativity: Storyboards of Pentecostal History

It is with good reason that Kippenberg prominently references Hayden White in his introduction, since White's *Metahistory* of 1973 has "triggered a lasting shock" in historiography.[2] In his treatment of 19th-century historians[3] and philosophers[4] Hayden White showed that "proper history and speculative philosophy of history are distinguishable only in emphasis, not in their respective contents."[5] Moreover, he also proposed a formalist approach in his analysis of historical and philosophical works

---

1   See Hans G. Kippenberg, *Die Entdeckung der Religionsgeschichte: Religionswissenschaft und Moderne* (München: C. H. Beck, 1997), 13; cf. White, *Metahistory*, xi.
2   Sarasin, *Geschichtswissenschaft und Diskursanalyse*, 259.
3   Michelet, Ranke, Tocqueville, Burckhardt.
4   Hegel, Marx, Nietzsche, Croce.
5   White, *Metahistory*, 427.

in order to uncover underlying modes of historiography and speculative philosophy, which are "in reality *formalizations* of poetic insights that analytically precede them."[6]

White laid out a two-dimensional structure for categorizing historiographies, which consists of three types of historical explanation, each with four possible modes.[7] The first way of historical explanation is "by emplotment," for which White proposes the four literary plots of Romance, Tragedy, Comedy, or Satire. The second level is explanation by argument, "seeking to explicate 'the point of it all' " by way of a Formist, Organicist, Mechanistic, or Contextualist approach. Finally, histories must seek some sort of ideological implication for the present, for which White suggests the possible world views of Anarchy, Conservatism, Radicalism, and Liberalism. Based on this structure, he asserts that any historian has to develop an explanatory strategy of selecting and combining the different modes of emplotment, argument, and ideological implication.[8] According to White, this is a "poetic act which precedes the formal analysis of the field," in which "the historian both creates his object of analysis and predetermines the conceptual strategies he will use to explain it."[9] Historical conceptions are thus grounded in linguistic theory, and White maintains that there are four principal styles of combining explanatory strategies, which are linked to the four principal tropes of poetic language: Metaphor, Metonomy, Synecdoche, and Irony.

This decidedly structuralist scheme of explaining 19th-century historiography is difficult to apply directly to the study of Ethiopian Pentecostalism for a number of reasons,[10] but Hayden White's mode of analysis—that is studying histories as literary works by querying their plots, arguments, and ideological implications—is useful for mapping out the many stories told about the movement.

For example, Engelsviken's account of the origins of Pentecostalism in Ethiopia, was essentially shown to be laid out in a plot of missionary emancipation, driven by his argument of the superiority of African independency over foreign missions. The missions' role therefore was merely preparatory: The actual starting point of revival was assigned to "one of Africa's own black sons," a clear and definite break with the missionary heritage is narrated right after this starting point, and the "real origin" of Pentecostalism cannot even be traced to the group with former missionary roots, but is placed with a completely mission-independent initiative. The ideological implication of Engelsviken's plot and argument is of course the inadequacy of Western

---

6 Ibid., xii, White's italics.

7 Cf. ibid., 7–29.

8 See ibid., 29–31. White sees "elective affinities" between the different modes of emplotment, argument, and ideological implication based on structural homologies between them, but maintains that these are not necessary combinations, since "the dialectical tension which characterizes the work of every master historian" comes from the inconsonance of decidedly working outside these affinities.

9 Ibid., 31.

10 White analyzes classical histories, whereas the present study was based on a fragmented archive of oral reports, contemporaneous sources, and historical accounts. Moreover the basic linguistic and rhetorical structures he proposes would need to be contrasted with Ethiopian literature and modes of history. Finally, White's goal of presenting "objective histories" as works of literature is not the problem of the present study, which rather sought for ways of incorporating the undoubtedly literary features of Ethiopian Pentecostal historiography into a Western academic account of its history.

missions and institutions in the African context, which are also evident in the failure of the Lutheran mission church and the World Council of Churches (WCC) to come to the Pentecostals' aid in their political oppression.

The persecution account brought forth by the Full Gospel Believers' Church (FGBC) in 1978, in turn, was plotted as a providentially directed revival, in which compliance with the worldly requirement of registration was not met with the desired results. However, by looking to God in prayer instead of arguing with the government, the church grew in spite or even because of the opposition it encountered. The argument is, of course, that God has planned to grow his church and will not be restrained by any opposition, which in turn has a powerful ideological implication in light of the Ethiopian revolution: defiance of politics and trust in God will sustain the church no matter what may come.

Bekele Woldekidan, in a similar vein, made the argument that God has been preparing Ethiopia for revival by way of the Derg. His plot therefore is a story of God actively preparing his church for revival through intervening in worldy politics. When Haile Selassie "tried to stop God's visitation," his government was abolished, and God now utilized an oppressive military dictatorship to scatter his people to the mainline churches and to all the corners of the earth, while creating a spiritual hunger in Ethiopia. After the regime had served its purpose, it was sovereignly brought down as well, and the stage was set for an unprecedented revival to take place. The ideological implication of Bekele's narrative is a warning to the church in the present time of freedom: Pentecostals themselves are in danger of standing in the way of God's revival because of moral compromise and the replacement of Christian brotherhood with church politics. Now the Pentecostal church may either repent and continue to be revived, or invite God's judgment.

These different plots are not more or less accurate ways of telling the "real" history of Ethiopian Pentecostalism. Rather, they make history real, because, as Hayden White has remarked in an important later essay, the reality of events is determined by the possibility of their inclusion in historical narratives:

> These events are real not because they occurred but because, first, they were remembered and, second, they are capable of finding a place in a chronologically ordered sequence. In order, however, for an account of them to be considered a historical account, it is not enough that they be recorded in the order of their original occurrence. It is the fact that they can be recorded otherwise, in an order of narrative, that makes them, at one and the same time, questionable as to their authenticity and susceptible to being considered as tokens of reality. In order to qualify as historical, an event must be susceptible to at least two narrations of its occurrence. Unless at least two versions of the same set of events can be imagined, there is no reason for the historian to take upon himself the authority of giving the true account of what really happened. The authority of the historical narrative is the authority of reality itself; the historical account

endows this reality with form and thereby makes it desirable by the imposition upon its processes of the formal coherency that only stories possess.[11]

The historical narrative, according to White, "displays to us a formal coherency to which we ourselves aspire,"[12] and this desire for a coherent account and an applicable conclusion is what ultimately constitutes the discursive importance of history. History delivers a temporary closure to our world, in which "reality wears the mask of a meaning, the completeness and fullness of which we can only imagine, never experience."[13] White sums up his point:

> Insofar as historical stories can be completed, can be given narrative closure, can be shown to have had a plot all along, they give to reality the odor of the ideal. This is why the plot of historical narrative is always an embarrassment and has to be presented as "found" in the events rather than put there by narrative techniques.[14]

6.2   Discourse: Empty Signifiers in Pentecostal Historiography

White's remarks about the need for narrative closure may help to depart from the structuralist affinities in his earlier *Metahistory*, since through them historiography can be connected to the politics of articulation, thereby relating narrativity to specific historical and institutional contexts.

Ernesto Laclau's and Chantal Mouffe's complex and nuanced theory of discourse, provides philosophical route for this endeavor, since they connect semiotics and politics. Laclau's and Mouffe's understanding of discourse, which is rooted in post-structuralist and post-Marxist debates, fundamentally rests on the established semiotic insight that "language (and by extension, all signifying systems) is a system of differences, that linguistic identities—values—are purely relational."[15] This relational interdependence of signifiers also means that "the *totality* of language is involved in each single act of signification,"[16] which in turn presupposes its closure, because if "the meaning of a term was purely relational and determined only by its opposition to all the others" then there needs to be a limitation to these relations by way of a closed system, since "only within it is it possible to fix in such a manner the meaning

---

11 HAYDEN WHITE, "The Value of Narrativity in the Representation of Reality," in *The Content of the Form: Narrative Discourse and Historical Representation* (Baltimore, MD: John Hopkins University Press, 1987), 20.

12 WHITE, *The Content of the Form*, 21.

13 WHITE, "The Value of Narrativity in the Representation of Reality," 21.

14 Ibid.

15 See ERNESTO LACLAU, "Why do Empty Signifiers Matter to Politics?" In *The Lesser Evil and The Greater Good: The Theory and Politics of Social Diversity*, ed. JEFFREY WEEKS (London: Rivers Oram Press, 1994), 168. Ferdinand de Saussure is of course explicitly invoked here. See also JACOB TORFING, *New Theories of Discourse: Laclau, Mouffe and Žižek* (Oxford: Blackwell, 2005), 87.

16 See LACLAU, "Why do Empty Signifiers Matter to Politics?" 168, emphasis Laclau.

of every element."[17] This idea of systemic closure is not to reinvoke structuralism, because the limits of a system are not absolute, but historical and precarious. Moreover, the limits already hint at the possibility of something outside of it, and thereby signify the system's arbitrary and contingent character:

> Thus, we are left with the paradoxical situation that what constitutes the condition of possibility of a signifying system—its limits—is also what constitutes its condition of impossibility—a blockage of the continuous expansion of the process of signification.[18]

Laclau and Mouffe insist that not only language but any "discursive totality," like society or history, "never exists in the form of a simply *given and delimited* positivity," instead "the relational logic will be incomplete and pierced by contingency."[19] However, while closure is impossible in this positive or ontological sense, it is also necessary, because without this "ficticious fixing of meaning there would be no meaning at all."[20] Therefore "[a]ny discourse is constituted as an attempt to dominate the field of discursivity, to arrest the flow of differences, to construct a centre."[21]

This center is constructed as a subverted reference to the antagonistic limits of the system. If discourse is a system of differences, its constitutive outside cannot be represented by a mere relation of opposition or contradiction, since these are differential relations themselves and would only collapse the constitutive limits of the system into an extended flow of differences. Therefore, the constitutive outside of a discourse can only be conceptualized as "radical negativity," as the antagonistic subversion of the conceptual system as such.[22] This subversive negativity beyond the system limits, in turn, can only be represented within the discourse as a subversion of its differential fixation of meaning: by collapsing differences within the system into a chain of equivalences, a discourse suggests a fundamental sameness with respect to the outside antagonist. Thus, "a formation manages *to signify itself* (that is, to constitute itself as such) only by transforming the limits into frontiers, by constituting a chain of equivalences which constructs what is beyond the limits as that which it *is not*."[23] This chain of equivalences, which Laclau calls an "empty signifier,"[24] is established in a

---

17 See ERNESTO LACLAU and CHANTAL MOUFFE, *Hegemony and Socialist Strategy: Towards a Radical Democratic Politics*, 2nd ed. (London: Verso, 2001), 113
18 LACLAU, "Why do Empty Signifiers Matter to Politics?" 168.
19 LACLAU and MOUFFE, *Hegemony and Socialist Strategy*, 110–111, emphasis Laclau/Mouffe.
20 See ERNESTO LACLAU, "The Death and Resurrection of the Theory of Ideology," *Journal of Political Ideologies* 1 (3 1996): 205.
21 LACLAU and MOUFFE, *Hegemony and Socialist Strategy*, 112.
22 The role of antagonism has changed in Laclau and Mouffe's theory. Whereas in *Hegemony and Socialist Strategy* it was assumed to be "responsible of the impossibility of society," i.e., the fundamental dislocation of anything social, in response to criticism it was later seen as "a discursive response to the dislocation of the social order," see TORFING, *New Theories of Discourse*, 128–129.
23 LACLAU and MOUFFE, *Hegemony and Socialist Strategy*, 143–144, emphases Laclau/Mouffe. The example given by Laclau and Mouffe is the construction of the colonized versus the colonizer, where a variety of differences in dress, language, skin color and customs are all taken to mean the same fundamental antagonism, constructing the colonizer as the anti-colonized, see ibid., 127–128.
24 LACLAU, "Why do Empty Signifiers Matter to Politics?"

hegemonic operation, temporarily halting the flow of differences and thus establishing a discursive identity. The popular articulation of this discursive identity is what constitutes a group, or "the people" in Laclau's terms.[25] All differences between members of the group and their demands are leveled by the overarching antagonism of the empty signifier, which also stands for the legitimacy of "the people" versus the establishment.

Laclau's and Mouffe's theory is intended to explain political revolutions rather than religious developments, but their propositions resonate with a number of observations made Ethiopian Pentecostal historical discourse. The most instructive example for the dynamics of the empty signifier in Ethiopian Pentecostalism can be found in the narratives of persecution, especially in the accounts about the 1972 arrests of Pentecostals. This story of persecution driven by a fundamental antagonism between persecutor and persecuted. Pentecostal accounts centrally relied on othering the persecutor, not in a negotiable relation of difference or opposition, but as an outside antagonist, situated beyond the limits of coherent legal, political, and ecumenical communication. Haile Selassie's government was portrayed as either having established a wretched legal system or being unwilling to adhere to its own laws, while the central political power of the Emperor himself was hollowed out by the contention that he was not well informed or by characterizing him as sympathetic but unable to help. With regard to the Ethiopian Orthodox Church (EOC), on the other hand, a number of theological differences were noted but at the same time dismissed as irrelevant, because the church and its patriarch are portrayed as political antagonists denying Pentecostals their right to existence in Ethiopia. This pure negativity of the persecutor is represented—in a process of subversion—by the unified Pentecostal community, in which all differences are collapsed into a chain of equivalences, which is marked by the common plight for freedom of religion, just laws, fair prosecution, and the spirit of Christian brotherhood. The marginalization of negotiation attempts with Imperial authorities, the exclusion of certain groups from the community of the persecuted, the selective translation of documents, as well as the enlisting of international allies and the foreign press show that this is a hegemonic operation, endeavoring to arrest the flow of political and ecumenical differences by the empty signifier of the persecuted community. This argument of course can be made both ways. The government circular of 1971 or the 1973 article in the *Ethiopian Herald* are testimony to a similar attempt by the Imperial government to portray Ethiopian Pentecostals as the pure negativity of Ethiopian society, subverting all its values and traditions.

A similar observation could be made with regard to the Derg time and the Charismatic movements inside the mainline Protestant churches. The "internal persecution" narrative asserting that the church itself betrayed the revived Christians to the government sets up a powerful antagonism by othering the church as an ally to the Derg. This narrative is no longer able to account for the political oppression that the mainline churches themselves suffered alongside the Charismatic movements, since this would reabsorb them into the persecution discourse. The moral aspirations con-

---

25 Cf. ERNESTO LACLAU, *On Populist Reason* (London: Verso, 2005), esp. pp. 67–171.

nected to these narratives, as well as their refutation by mainline church accounts, show that defining the persecution experience is a hegemonic endeavor.

Perhaps even the search for the "real origin" of Ethiopian Pentecostalism can be understood in such a way. The flow of different early revival movements and their connections is delimited by the equivalential chain of signifiers for Pentecostal revival, assuming that all groups are essentially seeking and making the same experience: the first outpouring of the Holy Spirit. The antagonists of this revival story are all elements threatening the notion of God's direct and unadulterated Spirit outpouring, such as hesitant missionaries, false prophecies, heterodox movements, or quarrels in the church. The different ways of telling this story consolidate the empty signifier of the "real origin" of Pentecostal revival, since the narrators compete over which original event can take its place. The fact that only the revival stories that were adopted by certain institutions found a lasting place in the historical discourse once more hints at the political hegemony linked to defining the empty signifier of "real origin" and thereby to the real identity of Ethiopian Pentecostalism.

All of this shows that the political is not an accidental or undesirable by-product of historiography but an essential and unavoidable feature, because meaningful historical narratives rely on hegemonic operations of collapsing differences in order to signify an antagonist outside: they produce historical meaning by limiting the flow of articulations. Moreover, if this is the case, the question of defining Pentecostalism or determining who is part of the Pentecostal/Charismatic community in a given context can only be answered adequately if histories follow these hegemonic politics and elucidate how Pentecostal identities are constructed and articulated as meaningful delimitations in a given temporal or spatial context.[26]

6.3   Genealogy: Descent and Emergence of the Pentecostal Movement

If historical meaning is produced in narratives within specific institutional and political contexts over the course of time, the history of this meaning production, i.e., the history of historiography, is an important field of study. This is of course an established point in historical research methodology. Scholars explore the genesis of present historical knowledge or a certain source archive by following chains of reference, searching for veiled, hidden, or forgotten sources, and, if possible, recovering the "original" version of a given story.

However, as Michel de Certeau has pointed out, the practice of *writing* history then takes on the form of a chronology and thus reverses the direction of historical inquiry. In writing, historians establish as the beginning of their narrative that which actually

---

26 See MICHAEL BERGUNDER, "Constructing Indian Pentecostalism: On Issues of Methodology and Representation," in *Asian and Pentecostal: The Charismatic Face of Christianity in Asia*, ed. ALLAN ANDERSON and EDMOND TANG, Asian Journal of Pentecostal Studies Series; 3 (London: Regnum Books, 2005), 177–213; MICHAEL BERGUNDER, *The South Indian Pentecostal Movement in the Twentieth Century*, Studies in the History of Christian Missions (Grand Rapids, MI: Eerdmans, 2008), 1–20.

was their "point of arrival" or "vanishing point" during research.[27] Furthermore, since the historical text must have an end, its point of departure actually becomes its destination, its final closure: a certain historical constellation from which a scholar began her research thus becomes the finale of her text. This "scriptural inversion" comes with a two-fold coercion: to propose an origin in the past and to speak into the present by way of instruction. The written history thus is a mirror writing that obfuscates historical practice, which, by contrast, originates in the present and speaks its findings into the past.

Against such invented origins and an implicit finality of historical writings, Michel Foucault has proposed a "wirkliche Historie" or an " 'effective' history" in his important essay *Nietzsche, Genealogy, History*.[28] In this treatise, Foucault is interested in Nietzsche's concept of genealogy as something "rejecting the meta-historical deployment of ideal significations and indefinite teleologies" and one that "opposes itself to the search for 'origins.' "[29] He sees three reasons for Nietzsche's rejection of origin: The first is a refusal of metaphysics coming with the search for essence. Foucault assents:

> What is found at the historical beginning of things is not the inviolable identity of their origin; it is the dissension of other things. It is disparity.[30]

Secondly, "[h]istory also teaches how to laugh at the solemnities of the origin," because "the origin always precedes the Fall."[31] Finally, there is the "false recognition" that the origin is "the site of truth." However, "behind the always recent, avaricious, and measured truth, it [history] posits the ancient proliferation of errors."[32]

Foucault explains the Nietzsche's rejection of *Ursprung* or origin by way of two similar, but different concepts, *Herkunft* and *Entstehung*, descent and emergence. In analyzing a *Herkunft* or descent, the genealogy "does not pretend to go back in time to restore an unbroken continuity that operates beyond the dispersion of forgotten things." Instead,

> [...] to follow the complex course of descent is to maintain passing events in their proper dispersion; it is to identify the accidents, the minute deviations—or

---

27 See MICHEL DE CERTEAU, *The Writing of History* (New York: Columbia University Press, 1988), 86–99.

28 See MICHEL FOUCAULT, "Nietzsche, Genealogy, History," in *Language, Counter-Memory, Practice*, ed. DONALD F. BOUCHARD (Ithaca, NY: Cornell University Press, 1977), 139–164. This essay was written in 1969/70, i.e., immediately after the publication of the *Archaeology of Knowledge* (1969) and is important for understanding Foucault's objectives therein as well as his subsequent turn to the question of power. Cf. PHILIPP SARASIN, *Michel Foucault zur Einführung* (Hamburg: Junius Verlag, 2005), 118–121. See also the editor's note as well as note 14, p. 142 in Foucault's essay.

29 FOUCAULT, "Nietzsche, Genealogy, History," 140. He notes that this is only one of two uses of *Ursprung* in Nietzsches work, where one is less reflected and used synonymously with other words denoting origin, whereas the other is used in a sense critical of ontology, which is where Nietzsche "is truly a genealogist."

30 Ibid., 142. This notion of disparity is connected to a "wide range of key terms, found in *The Archaeology of Knowledge*," see editor's note 14.

31 Ibid., 143.

32 Ibid.

conversely, the complete reversals—the errors, the false appraisals, and the faulty calculations that gave birth to those things that continue to exist and have value for us.[33]

Likewise, the *Entstehung* or emergence should not be viewed as "the final term of an historical development," but the genealogy must seek "to reestablish the various systems of subjection: not the anticipatory power of meaning, but the hazardous play of dominations."[34] Thus, descent recovers the disparity of the beginnings, and emergence disperses the notion of finality by historicizing development in the struggle of concrete forces.

If conducted in this way, history becomes an ally of the genealogy by way of their common opposition to the notion of origin:

> The genealogist needs history to dispel the chimeras of origin, [...] History is the concrete body of a development, with its moments of intensity, its lapses, its extended periods of feverish agitation, its fainting spells; and only a metaphysician would seek its soul in the distant ideality of origin.[35]

Moreover, Foucault insists that Nietzsche identified genealogy as "wirkliche Historie," because his criticism of history was only directed against history mastered by "a suprahistorical perspective," which "metaphysics can bend [...] to its own purpose"[36] "Wirkliche Historie" or "'effective' history," on the other hand, "differs from traditional history in being without constants," it "introduces discontinuity into our very being," it is profoundly interested in the singular, keeps the noble at a distance, and affirms "knowledge as perspective."[37]

Thus Foucault elevates the genealogy as the standard of historiography, fundamentally opposing the inversion of historical writing detected by de Certeau. Instead of traveling forward through time to trace what emerged out of supposed origins, historical research and writing are an archaeological operation, departing from the present, rediscovering fragmented layers and exposing the contingency of what has come to be.

This is why it was necessary in this study of Ethiopian Pentecostalism to laboriously trace, contrast, and link the available sources, departing from present historical knowledge and often arriving at disparate representations of an event, or perhaps an "empty" event, a palimpsest erased and overwritten again and again by later histories establishing origins. Chacha Omahe's ministry in Ethiopia can be seen as an example of this. The frequency, dating, and duration of his visits are uncertain in the Ethiopian Pentecostal discourse, nothing specific is known about the background of this Kenyan revivalist, and the stories about him conglomerate around his narrative function: the first experience of Holy Spirit baptism and conflict with the Pentecostal missionaries. Latest in Engelsviken's history, Chacha was endowed with the weight of origin with regard to Ethiopian Spirit baptism. As a visiting Kenyan with roots

---

33 FOUCAULT, "Nietzsche, Genealogy, History," 152.
34 Ibid., 148.
35 Ibid., 144–143.
36 Ibid., 152.
37 See ibid., 153–156.

in the global Pentecostal movement, he was the ideal figure for Engelsviken's narrative of African independency, and this is the role he kept in all sources about him, whether affirming his input or denying it. Similar examples of such empty events of original importance would be the break with the Addis Ababa Finnish mission, the inception of the first student prayer meeting in a private dorm and the first national conference of Ethiopian Pentecostals hosted by the students in Addis Ababa. They all were subject to a number of inscriptions by later sources, elevating them above the vicissitudes of history and the peculiarities contained therein.

Likewise, the exploration of the *descent* of the FGBC has arrived at an entangled disparity of different revival movements and missionary beginnings, the instabilities and fissures of which extended to the formation of this church and into its first years. However, with the *emergence* of Pentecostal and Charismatic denominations, the histories of Ethiopian Pentecostalism were disciplined and subjected to the "play of dominations," signified by the search for "real origins," the establishment of founding myths, the marginalization of certain stories, and different claims of originality and influence.

Finally, the structure and genesis of the corpus of sources also reveals the fragility and contingency of historical knowledge. The Derg's repressive power disrupted the production of histories about Ethiopian Pentecostalism, which in turn gave Engelsviken's unpublished manuscript a singular influence. Due to the unstable environment of the revolution, Tage Johansson refrained from voicing his irritation with the Ethiopian Pentecostal politics in his correspondence with Engelsviken, effectively removing his dissent from the historical archive. Probably as a side effect of tracing Chacha to a contact at the Elim Bible Institute, Tibebe Eshete became aware of the early Pentecostal mission initiative by three Elim missionaries, and inserted their story and its sources into the historical archive. In looking at its *Herkunft* and *Entstehung* the source archive about Ethiopian Pentecostalism thus reveals the same "original" fragmented disparity as the history it seeks to describe, and it points to a similar contingency due to the "play of dominations" in acquiring sources.

6.4   Context: A Never-Ending Story of Pentecostal History

By focusing on narrativity, discourse, and genealogy this study of Ethiopian Pentecostalism has attempted to remain true to White's proposition that realistic and fictional discourses are two inseparable aspects of historical meaning production. Like more traditional forms of history, the analyses were profoundly interested in the material aspect of the past by scrutinizing documents, calculating dates, drawing up chronologies, and investigating inconsistencies. At the same time, though, they were not intimidated by the ostensible positivity of events, but confronted the accounts of "what really happened" with their modes of representation by exposing narrative plots, analyzing the politics of the historical discourse, and exposing the contingency of historical knowledge by tracing its chronology.

However, what is the epistemological position of such a historiography, what is the context from which it speaks, and whom does it address? Is it a meta-history, a secondary treatment of historic representation that has been liberated from the burden of telling history itself? Or to the contrary, is it a part of that which it seeks to describe, subject to the same dynamics of narrativity, discursive hegemony, and historical contingency?

The present treatment of Ethiopian Pentecostalism and its theoretic reflection would of course point to the second conclusion, because the analyses proposed above are closely entangled with the discourse they describe. On the one hand, the research was deeply indebted to its informants, depending on the stories they told, on the political delimitations they drew, on the sources they held back or released, and on what they enhanced or what they forgot. With each new history of Ethiopian Pentecostalism, with each jubilee magazine, or with each additional informant, the narrative archive changes, requiring to adapt the analysis. On the other hand, since the description of the discourse of Ethiopian Pentecostal history is also a way of engaging with it, this history aspires to being referenced in turn. If this aspiration is met, the analyses will, to whatever degree, impact what can be said thenceforth. Highlighting contrasts between revival stories, proposing a historical emptiness of key events, presenting critical translation lapses, or disclosing Tage Johansson's allegations of political imprudence thus are articulations *within* the discourse of Ethiopian Pentecostal history, and whether they are taken up in an apologetic or accommodating manner, the field for subsequent analyses will have been altered .

In this way "the" history of Ethiopian Pentecostalism will continuously be deferred, its "real story" transformed, permuted, and ultimately postponed. This is the dynamic of the *différance* as described by Derrida:[38] just as the incessant *differing* of signifiers *defers* signification, the telling of histories continuously postpones historical meaning. History as such is no more possible than the deferred presence of the sign.[39]

The irreducible spatial and temporal referentiality of differentiation has caused Derrida to caution against a discourse analysis that assumes or appears to assume an exterior position, a supra-historical view of history.[40] In *Structure, Sign, and Play in the Discourse of the Human Sciences* he contends that all "destructive discourses [...] are trapped in a sort of circle:"

> This circle is unique. It describes the form of the relationship between the history of metaphysics and the destruction of the history of metaphysics. *There is no sense* in doing without the concepts of metaphysics in order to attack metaphysics. We have no language—no syntax and no lexicon—which is alien

---

38 See JACQUES DERRIDA, "Différance," in *Margins of Philosophy* (Chicago, IL: University of Chicago Press, 1982), esp. pp.7–12.

39 Cf. Derrida's deconstruction of a deferred presence that the sign substitutes, ibid., 20: "For the economic character of *différance* in no way implies that the deferred presence can always be found again, that we have here only an investment that provisionally and calculatedly delays the perception of its profit or the profit of its perception. [...] If the displaced presentation remains definitely and implacably postponed, it is not that a certain present remains absent or hidden. Rather, *différance* maintains our relationship with that which we necessarily misconstrue, and which exceeds the alternative of presence and absence."

40 This is also what was at the root of the intermittent but ongoing dispute between Derrida and Foucault, see ANTONIO CAMPILLO, "Foucault and Derrida: The History of a Debate on History," *Angelaki: Journal of the Theoretical Humanities* 5 (2 2000): 113–135.

to this history; we cannot utter a single destructive proposition which has not already slipped into the form, the logic, and the implicit postulations of precisely what it seeks to contest.[41]

By extension, Derrida contends that the "structural discourse on myths—*mythological discourse*—must itself be *mythomorphic*. It must have the form of that of which it speaks."[42] This is, Derrida seems to implicate, the fundamental self-misunderstanding of Lévi-Strauss: though he presumed to follow the epistemological discourse of the engineer in studying the structures of myth, he actually took on the role of the mythopoetical *bricoleur*. By piecemealing and reassembling myths he created the myth of mythology.[43] Moreover, the *bricolage* is the only way science can critically engage with myth, whereas the engineer, "who would supposedly be the absolute origin of his own discourse and would supposedly construct it 'out of nothing,' 'out of the whole cloth,'" is "a myth produced by the *bricoleur*."[44]

Furthermore, it is not only this semiological and structural referentiality of texts that should alert historians to the dangers of presuming that their position is exterior to the historical discourse. Derrida establishes a second and related referentiality in his reframing of semiology as grammatology. In *Signature Event Context* he contends that all writing supposes a dual absence: that of the addressee and that of the author. Writing not only implies the physical absence of an addressee, it also must "remain legible despite the absolute disappearance of every determined addressee in general for it to function as writing, that is, for it to remain legible."[45] Secondly, "[t]o write is to produce a mark that will constitute a kind of machine that is in turn productive, that my future disappearance in principle will not prevent from functioning and from yielding, and yielding itself to, reading and rewriting."[46] This legibility and iterability of the written sign, independent of a specific author's or recipient's presence, "carries with it a force of breaking with its context, that is, the set of presences which organize the moment of its inscription."[47] Derrida demonstrates that these traits of the written sign, the "mark," can be extended to all signification and concludes:

> Every sign, linguistic or nonlinguistic, spoken or written [...], as a small or large unity, can be *cited*, put between quotation marks; thereby it can break with every given context, and engender infinitely new contexts in an absolutely nonsaturable fashion. This does not suppose that the mark is valid outside its context, but on the contrary that there are only contexts without any center of absolute anchoring.[48]

---

41 JACQUES DERRIDA, "Structure, Sign, and Play in the Discourse of the Human Sciences," in *Writing and Difference* (London: Routledge, 1978), 280.

42 See ibid., 286.

43 See ibid., 282–288.

44 Ibid., 285.

45 JACQUES DERRIDA, "Signature Event Context," in *Margins of Philosophy* (Chicago, IL: University of Chicago Press, 1982), 315.

46 Ibid., 316.

47 Ibid., 317. According to Derrida "[t]his force of breaking is not an accidental predicate, but the very structure of the written," ibid.

48 Ibid., 320, emphasis Derrida.

Moreover, every mark thus recontextualized is in itself an instance of recontextualization,[49] as Derrida elaborates in his critique of Austin's philosophy of the performative and in his consideration of the signature. Contrary to Austin's notion that the success of a performative statement is determined by its conformance to an "ordinary" context, Derrida contends that said success can only be established on the grounds of performatives being "identifiable as *conforming* to an iterable model," their ability to be understood as a citation of another instance of the same performance.[50] Likewise, the signature, though it stands for an original presence of its author at the moment and place of its signing, is only valid as a citation of previous signatures like it: "In order to function, that is, in order to be legible, a signature must have a repeatable, iterable, imitable form; it must be able to detach itself from the present and singular intention of its production."[51]

Thus, an analysis of historical sources not only presupposes and effects their recontextualization, the cited sources themselves are citations, reiterations, and recontextualizations of their antecedents. This "play of differences supposes, in effect, syntheses and referrals which forbid at any moment, or in any sense, that a simple element be *present* in and of itself, referring only to itself."[52] Therefore, what the *différance* had implied for the study of Ethiopian Pentecostal history in general must be applied to the individual sources as well: their meaning is deferred in a play of presence and absence, as they cite and reiterate stories of the outpouring of the Holy Spirit in manifold contexts.

There is no reason then to claim an exterior position from which "the" meaning of historical utterances about Ethiopian Pentecostalism would become identifiable and transparent to these analyses. Instead their treatment is a way to participate in the reiteration, recontextualization, and deferring of history.

However, just as this present study of Ethiopian Pentecostalism is denied an ontological or epistemological privilege by the premises of *différance*, it also comes with the hope that by rewriting the story of Pentecostal and Charismatic movements in Ethiopia in an account focusing on narrative representations, discourse politics, and the genealogy of knowledge, a foundational ethos of the academic endeavor has been followed: to cite and extend the play of differences, rendering possible new citations, readings and articulations about Ethiopian Pentecostalism, to which this study now submits.

---

49 Cf. CAMPILLO, "Foucault and Derrida," 123: "It follows that there is no primary or originary actuality (either on the side of the author or on the side of the context) to which the ultimate sense of a discourse could be referred, and in virtue of which sense could be definitely determined, 'confined' or closed."

50 See DERRIDA, "Signature Event Context," 321–327, quote on p. 326.

51 Ibid., 328.

52 JACQUES DERRIDA, "Semiology and Grammatology: Interview with Julia Kristeva," in *positions*, rev. ed. (London: Continuum, 2002), 26.

Bibliography

ABDISSA BENTI LEYE. "The Origin and Growth of the Ethiopian Misgana Evangelical Church 1983–2000." M.Th. thesis, Ethiopian Graduate School of Theology, 2002.

ABERA ERTIRO. "The History of the Meserete Kristos Church at Nazareth: From 1951–2003." B.A. thesis, Meserete Kristos College, 2003.

"Abuna Takla Haymanot." *Wikipedia. The Free Encyclopedia* (2008). http://en.wikipedia.org/wiki/Abuna_Takla_Haymanot (accessed September 2, 2008).

Act Relating to Religious Communities. 1969. http://www.legislationline.org/legislation.php?tid=2&lid=924 (accessed February 26, 2008).

ADDIS ABABA FULL GOSPEL BELIEVERS' CHURCH. የ40 ዓመት የወንጌል አገልግሎት (ሐምሌ 1958–1998 ዓ.ም.) ዶክመንተሪ ቪሲዲ. [Documentary VCD of Forty Years of Gospel Ministry (July 1966–2006).] Addis Ababa, 2006.

—. የ40ኛ ዓመት የወንጌል አገልግሎትና የምስጋና በዓል መጽሐት /ሐምሌ 1958–1998 ዓ.ም./. [Magazine of Forty Years of Gospel Ministry and of the Anniversary Celebration (July 1966–2006).] Addis Ababa: Addis Ababa Full Gospel Believers' Church, 2006.

Addis Zaman. "የፓትሪያርክ በዓል ሢመት ተከበረ." [Vestiture of the Patriarch Celebrated.] May 11, 1971, 1,3, 5, 7–8.

—. "የኢትዮጵያ ሰባክያን ጉባኤ ተናንት ተጀመረ." [Assembly of Ethiopia's Preachers Begun Yesterday.] August 29, 1972, 1, 7.

—. "በሕግ የተከለከለ ማኅበር አቋቁመው ተሰበሰቡ የተባሉ 480 ሰዎች ተከሰሱ." [480 People Indicted, Said to Have Established and Assembled in an Association Forbidden by the Law.] September 1, 1972, 1.

ADDISE AMADO. *Persecution in Ethiopia: Situation Analysis: Theological, Sociological, Economical and Political Interpretations and Implications.* Addis Ababa: Voice of Martyrs Ethiopia, 2003.

AHONEN, LAURI K. *Missions Growth: A Case Study on Finnish Free Foreign Mission.* Waynesboro, GA: Gabriel Resources, 1984.

—. "Finland." In *The New International Dictionary of Pentecostal and Charismatic Movements*, edited by STANLEY M. BURGESS and EDUARD M. van der MAAS, 103–105. Grand Rapids, MI: Zondervan, 2002.

AHONEN, LAURI, and JAN-ENDY JOHANNESSON. "Sweden." In *The New International Dictionary of Pentecostal and Charismatic Movements*, edited by STANLEY M. BURGESS and EDUARD M. van der MAAS, 255–257. Grand Rapids, MI: Zondervan, 2002.

ALEMAYEHU MEKONNEN. "Effects of Culture Change on Leadership in the Pentecostal/Charismatic Churches in Addis Ababa, Ethiopia." Ph.D. thesis, Fuller Theological Seminary, School of World Mission, 1995.

ALEMU SAMUEL. "History of the Meserete Kristos Church Growth at Metahara Since 1967."
   B.A. thesis, Meserete Kristos College, 2004.

ALEMU SHETTA. "Reflection Paper to 23rd Meeting of the Committee of Mutual Christian
   Responsibility, January 21–24, 2002." Unpublished manuscript, private collection, 2002.

ALVARSSON, JAN-ÅKE. "Från kaffeplantage till tv-studio: Några huvuddrag i svensk pingstmission." [From Coffee Plantation to TV studio: Some Main Features in the Swedish
   Pentecostal Mission.] In *Pingströrelsen*, edited by CLAES WAERN, 135–186. Vol. 2, *Händelser och utveckling under 1900-talet.* [*The Pentecostal Movement*, part 2, *Events and
   Developments in the 1900s.*] Övebrö: Libris förlag, 2007.

AMANUEL SEGEBO. "The History of God's Work in the Life of Gambella Meserete Kristos
   Church 1989–2002." B.A. thesis, Meserete Kristos College, 2002.

ANDARGACHEW TIRUNEH. *The Ethiopian Revolution 1974–1987: A Transformation from an
   Aristocratic to a Totalitarian Autocracy.* Cambridge: Cambridge University Press, 1993.

ANDERSON, WILLIAM B. *The Church in East Africa 1840–1974.* Dodoma: Central Tanganyika Press, 1981.

ARÉN, GUSTAV. *Evangelical Pioneers in Ethiopia: Origins of the Evangelical Church Mekane
   Yesus.* Studia Missionalia Upsaliensia; 32. Stockholm: EFS Förlaget, 1978.

—. *Envoys of the Gospel: In the Steps of the Evangelical Pioneers, 1898–1936.* Studia Missionalia Upsaliensia; 75. Stockholm: EFS Förlaget, 1999.

ASFAW ATAMO. "Misunderstandings and Proposed Solutions Regarding Spiritual Gifts —
   with Special Emphasis on South Central Synod." B.Th. thesis, Mekane Yesus Seminary,
   1999.

ASFAW DAMTE. "Haymanotä abäw." In *Encyclopaedia Aethiopica*, edited by SIEGBERT UH-
   LIG, 1075–1076. Wiesbaden: Harrassowitz, 2005.

ASHEBIR KETEMA. "The History of Ethiopian Guenet Church: From 1974–1992." B.Th.
   thesis, Mekane Yesus Seminary, 1993.

ASSEFA GELETA AYANA. "The History of Degem Meserete Kristos Region (1969–2002)." B.A.
   thesis, Meserete Kristos College, 2002.

ASSEFA MEKONNEN. "A Clean Hearth for the Fire to Blaze: Evaluating Charismatic Movement in EECMY by Lutheran Theological Tradition." B.Th. thesis, Mekane Yesus Seminary, 1997.

ATRSAW GEREMEW BELAY. "The History of Bahir Dar Meserete Kristos Church." B.A.
   thesis, Meserete Kristos College, 2004.

AYMRO WONDMAGEGNEHU and JOACHIM MOTOVU. *The Ethiopian Orthodox Church.* Addis
   Ababa: Ethiopian Orthodox Mission, 1970.

BAHRU ZEWDE. *A History of Modern Ethiopia 1855–1991.* 2nd ed. Addis Ababa: Addis
   Ababa University Press, 2001.

—. *Pioneers of Change in Ethiopia: The Reformist Intellectuals of the Early Twentieth
   Century.* Oxford: James Currey, 2002.

BAKKE, JOHNNY. *Christian Ministry: Patterns and Functions Within the Ethiopian Evangelical Church Mekane Yesus.* Studia Missionalia Upsaliensia; 44. Oslo: Solum-Forlag, 1987.

BALISKI, LILA W. "Theology in Song: Ethiopia's Tesfaye Gabbiso." *Missiology* 25 (4 1997): 447–456.

BALISKI, PAUL. "Case Studies from the Bible and from History of Non-Biblical Charismatic Practices Which Have Been Divisive in the Body of Christ." In *The Biblical Use of the Gifts of the Holy Spirit: Seminar Convened at Ethiopia Graduate School of Theology, Addis Ababa, 30 October 2004*, 14–19. Addis Ababa: Unpublished collection, Ethiopian Graduate School of Theology, 2004.

BARRETT, DAVID B., GEORGE THOMAS KURIAN, and TODD M. JOHNSON. *World Christian Encyclopedia: A Comparative Survey of Churches and Religions in the Modern World.* 2nd ed. Oxford: Oxford University Press, 2001.

BAUEROCHSE, ERNST. "Die Arbeit in Äthiopien." In *Vision: Gemeinde weltweit: 150 Jahre Hermannsburger Mission und Ev.-luth. Missionswerk in Niedersachsen*, edited by ERNST-AUGUST LÜDEMANN, 585–709. Hermannsburg: Verlag der Missionsbuchhandlung, 2000.

BEDRU HUSSEIN. "የወንጌል ሥርጭት ታሪክ በኢትዮጵያ: የቅርብ ዓመታት የወንጌል ሥርጭት ልምድ." [The History of Evangelization in Ethiopia: The Experience of Evangelization in Recent Years.] In የኢትዮጵያ ሙሉ ወንጌል አማኞች ቤተ ክርስቲያን: የወንጌል ስርጭት ስልት ለኢትዮጵያ ፪ኛ ዓውድ ጥናት ፣ የካቲት *13–15 ቀን 1985 ዓ.ም. [The Ethiopian Full Gospel Believers' Church: Second Research Convention for the Evangelization Strategy for Ethiopia, 23–25 March, 1993]*, edited by ETHIOPIAN FULL GOSPEL BELIEVER'S CHURCH, 3–14. Addis Ababa, 1993.

BEKELE WOLDEKIDAN. ሪቫይቫል: ኢትዮጵያ እና የመጨረሻው መጨረሻ. [Revival. Ethiopia and the Final End]. Addis Ababa: Addis Ababa Full Gospel Believers' Church, 2002.

BERGUNDER, MICHAEL. "Constructing Indian Pentecostalism: On Issues of Methodology and Representation." In *Asian and Pentecostal: The Charismatic Face of Christianity in Asia*, edited by ALLAN ANDERSON and EDMOND TANG, 177–213. Asian Journal of Pentecostal Studies Series; 3. London: Regnum Books, 2005.

—. *The South Indian Pentecostal Movement in the Twentieth Century.* Studies in the History of Christian Missions. Grand Rapids, MI: Eerdmans, 2008.

BERHANU NEGA. "Life Story of Yemaneberhan Endale." Unpublished paper, Addis Ababa, 2001.

BEST, BRUCE. "Ethiopia: Growing Church Under Attack in Political Struggle." *One World* (74 1982): 5–6.

BEZA INTERNATIONAL. "About Beza" (2007). http://www.bezainternational.org/page7/page7.html (accessed October 26, 2007).

BJÖRKMAN, ARNE. "Väckelse i motvind." [Revival in Headwind.] *Midnattsropet!* (2 1998). http://www.maranata.se/MR/98/2-98/motvind.html (accessed February 3, 2007).

BONACCI, GIULIA. "Ethiopia 1974–1991: Religious Policy of the State and Its Consequences on the Orthodox Church." In *Ethiopian Studies at the End of the Second Millenium: Proceedings of the XIVth International Conference of Ethiopian Studies November 6–11, 2000, Addis Ababa*, edited by BAYE YIMAM et al., 593–605. Addis Ababa: Institute of Ethiopian Studies, Addis Ababa University, 2000.

BRANT, ALBERT E. *In the Wake of Martyrs: A Modern Saga in Ancient Ethiopia.* Langley: Omega Publications, 1992.

BROWN, JOHN. "Religion and Revolution in Ethiopia." *Religion in Communist Lands* 9 (1–2 1981): 50–55.

BULUTSE FUTUWI. "An Introduction to the Theology and Growth of Independent Churches in Ethiopia With Special Reference to Rhema Faith Church: A Critical Approach." M.Th. thesis, Ethiopian Graduate School of Theology, 2002.

BUNDY, DAVID D. "Swedish Pentecostal Mission Theory and Practice to 1930: Foundational Values in Discussion." *Mission Studies* 14 (1997).

—. "Pethrus, Petrus Lewi." In *The New International Dictionary of Pentecostal and Charismatic Movements*, edited by STANLEY M. BURGESS and EDUARD M. van der MAAS, 986–987. Grand Rapids, MI: Zondervan, 2002.

—. *Visions of Apostolic Mission: Scandinavian Pentecostal Mission to 1935.* Acta Universitatis Upsaliensis; 45. Uppsala: Uppsala Universiteit, 2009.

BUTLER, EVA S. *In the Shadow of Kilimanjaro: Pioneering the Pentecostal Testimony Among the Maasai People.* Salisbury Center, NY: Pinecrest Publications, 2002.

CAMPILLO, ANTONIO. "Foucault and Derrida: The History of a Debate on History." *Angelaki: Journal of the Theoretical Humanities* 5 (2 2000): 113–135.

CARLSSON, BERTIL. *Organizations and Decision Procedures within the Swedish Pentecostal Movements.* Mariefred, 1974.

CENTRAL STATISTICAL AGENCY and ORC MACRO. *Ethiopia Demographic and Health Survey 2005.* Addis Ababa: Central Statistical Agency, 2006.

CERTEAU, MICHEL DE. *The Writing of History.* New York: Columbia University Press, 1988.

CHARTER, VERNON. "Contested Symbols: Music, Revolution, and Renewal in Ethiopian Protestant Churches." *EthnoDoxology* 3 (3 2006). http://instructor.prairie.edu/charterv/Documents/Theology%20of%20Worship/Charter%20-%20Contested%20Symbols.pdf (accessed December 12, 2008).

CHERNETSOV, SEVIR. "Ethiopian Orthodox (Täwaḥǝdo) Church: History from the Second Half of the 19th Century to 1959." In *Encyclopaedia Aethiopica*, vol. 2, edited by SIEGBERT UHLIG, 421–424. Wiesbaden: Harrassowitz, 2005.

Christianity Today. "Ethiopian Casualties." April 15, 1977, 57–58.

—. "The Campaign to Root Out 'Alien' Religion in Ethiopia." September 7, 1979, 64.

—. "The Protestant Church is Thriving in an Otherwise Dismal Ethiopia." November 7, 1980, 94.

—. "Mission Agency Launches $8.2 Million Famine Relief Project in Southern Ethiopia." March 1, 1985, 43.

—. "New Growth for Ethiopian Church." October 6, 1989, 51.

CITYKYRKAN. "City Pingstförsamling – kort historik." [The City Pentecostal Church – A Short History.] (2007). http://www.cks.se/forsamling/historik_1.htm (accessed February 3, 2007).

CLAPHAM, CHRISTOPHER. *Transformation and Continuity in Revolutionary Ethiopia*. Cambridge: Cambridge University Press, 1988.

CLARKE, J. CALVITT. "Seeking a Model for Modernization: Ethiopia's Japanizers." *Selected Annual Proceedings of the Florida Conference of Historians* 11 (2004): 35–51.

COLLETTI, JOSEPH. "Mattson-Boze, Joseph D." In *The New International Dictionary of Pentecostal and Charismatic Movements*, edited by STANLEY M. BURGESS and EDUARD M. van der MAAS, 867. Grand Rapids, MI: Zondervan, 2002.

The Constitution of Ethiopia: Established in the Reign of His Majesty Haile Selassie I, July 16, 1931. 1931. http://www.worldstatesmen.org/Ethiopia_1931.txt (accessed February 20, 2008).

CORAZZA, MARTA TORCINI. "State and Religion in the Constitution and Politics of Ethiopia." *European Journal for Church and State Research* 9 (2002): 351–395.

COSTEA, PETER. "Church-State Relations in the Marxist-Leninist Regimes of the Third World." *Journal of Church and State* 32 (1990): 281–308.

COTTERELL, F. PETER. *Born at Midnight*. Chicago, IL: Moody Bible Institut, 1973.

CRUMMEY, DONALD. *Priests and Politicians: Protestant and Catholic Missions in Orthodox Ethiopia, 1830–1868*. Oxford: Clarendon Press, 1972.

—. "The Politics of Modernization: Protestant and Catholic Missionaries in Modern Ethiopia." In *The Missionary Factor in Ethiopia: Papers from a Symposium on the Impact of European Missions on Ethiopian Society, Lund University, August 1996*, edited by GETATCHEW HAILE, AASULV LANDE, and SAMUEL RUBENSON, 85–99. Studien zur interkulturellen Geschichte des Christentums; 110. Frankfurt am Main: Lang, 1998.

CUMBERS, JOHN. *Count It All Joy: Testimonies from a Persecuted Church as Told to John Cumbers*. Kearney, NE: Morris Publishing, 1995.

—. *Living With the Red Terror: Missionary Experiences in Communist Ethiopia*. Kearney, NE: Morris Publishing, 1996.

CURRY, JAMES A., and RICHARD B. RILEY. "Notes on Church-State Affairs." *Journal of Church and State* 26 (1984): 147–170.

Dagen. "Ragnar Ljungquist i Etiopien: Piloten börjar flygturen med att bedja till Gud." [Radnar Ljungquist in Ethiopia: The Pilot Begins the Flight by Praying to God.] September 13, 1972, 5.

DAMENE DEGU. "The History of Evangelical Christianity in Arsi Sire." B.A. thesis, Meserete Kristos College, 2004.

DANIEL FITE. "The Challenges of Denominational Conflicts in the Context of Ethiopian Evangelical Churches." B.Th. thesis, Mekane Yesus Seminary, 2001.

DANIEL TESSO NEDJO. "The Growth and Impact of Evangelical Christianity in Bodji District 1941–2000." B.Th. thesis, Mekane Yesus Seminary, 2001.

DAOUD, JANE COLLINS. *Miracles and Mission and World-Wide Evangelism*. Dallas, TX, 1953.

DAWIT OLIKA. "Parallelisms Between Charismatic Prophecy in EECMY and Qallu Institution of Oromo Traditional Religion." B.Th. thesis, Mekane Yesus Seminary, 2002.

DAWIT WOLDE GIORGIS. *Red Tears: War, Famine and Revolution in Ethiopia*. Trenton, NJ: Red Sea Press, 1989.

DECKE, GERD. "The Role of Gudina Tumsa in a Critical Dialogue between Marxism/Socialism and Christianity." In *The Life and Ministry of Rev. Gudina Tumsa: General Secretary of the Ethiopian Evangelical Church Mekane Yesus (EECMY); Report Volume & Lectures of the Missiological Seminar Sponsored by the Gudina Tumsa Foundation at Mekane Yesus Seminary, Makanissa, April 18-21, 2001*, edited by PAUL E. HOFFMAN, 101–128. Addis Ababa: Gudina Tumsa Foundation, 2003.

DEMEKE BOTAMO. "The Reasons of Split and the Call for Unification in Evangelical Believers of Hosanna Town." B.Th. thesis, Mekane Yesus Seminary, 2002.

DERRIDA, JACQUES. "Structure, Sign, and Play in the Discourse of the Human Sciences." In *Writing and Difference*, 278–294. London: Routledge, 1978.

—. "Différance." In *Margins of Philosophy*, 1–27. Chicago, IL: University of Chicago Press, 1982.

—. "Signature Event Context." In *Margins of Philosophy*, 307–330. Chicago, IL: University of Chicago Press, 1982.

—. "Semiology and Grammatology: Interview with Julia Kristeva." In *positions*, rev. ed., 15–36. London: Continuum, 2002.

DOMIANUS, HERMANN. "Die eigene Stimme klingt am schönsten: Das Phänomen des geistlichen Aufbruchs in Äthiopien." In *Mit wachsender Begeisterung: Evangelische Christen in Äthiopien*, edited by HENNING UZAR, 61–72. Hermannsburg: Missionshandlung Hermannsburg, 1998.

—. "Essay zum TEE-Lehrbuch: The Charismatic Movement within the Ethiopian Evangelical Church Mekane Yesus; A Theological Foundation for an African Lutheran Church between Tradition and Revival." Unpublished manuscript, private collection, 2005.

DOMMERMUTH, BERTHA, ELLEN FRENCH, and RUTH SHIPPEY. "Revival in Ethiopia." *Elim Pentecostal Herald* 7 (51 1937): 10–11.

DONHAM, DONALD L. *Marxist Modern: An Ethnographic History of the Ethiopian Revolution*. Berkely, CA: University of California Press, 1999.

DOULOS, MIKAEL. "Christians in Marxist Ethiopia." *Religion in Communist Lands* Summer 1986 (1986): 134–147.

DULA, PETER. "Reading Yoder in Ethiopia: The Spirit of God and the Politics of Men, 1974–1991." Unpublished manuscript, private collection, 2002.

DUNBERG, LARS. "Kristna fängslade i Etiopien." [Christians Imprisoned in Ethiopia.] *Dagen*, December 6, 1972, 3.

DURESSA MABESHA TAKA. "Charismatic Movement and Its Effects in the Aira District of the EECMY." B.Th. thesis, Mekane Yesus Seminary, 2002.

EIDE, ØYVIND M. *Revolution and Religion in Ethiopia: Growth and Persecution of the Mekane Yesus Church, 1974–85*. 2nd ed. Oxford: Currey, 2000.

—. "Gudina Tumsa: The Voice of an Ethiopian Prophet." *Svensk Missionstidskrift* 89 (3 2001): 291–321.

ELIAS DALELO. "The Secret for the Rapid Growth of Hossana Meserete Kristos Church."
B.A. thesis, Meserete Kristos College, 2002.

ELIM BIBLE INSTITUTE. "Missionary News Report: Ethiopia." *Elim Bible Institute Bulletin*
(February 1965).

EMMANUEL ABRAHAM. *Reminiscences of My Life*. Oslo: Lunde forlag, 1995.

EMMINGHAUS, CHRISTOPH. *Äthiopiens ethnoregionaler Föderalismus: Modell der Konfliktbewältigung für afrikanische Staaten?* Hamburg: Lit, 1997.

ENGELSVIKEN, TORMOD. "Molo Wongel: A Documentary Report on the Life and History of the Independent Pentecostal Movement in Ethiopia 1960–1975." Unpublished
Manuscript, The Free Faculty of Theology, Oslo, 1975.

—. "Gudina Tumsa, the Ethiopian Evangelical Church Mekane Yesus, and the Charismatic
Movement." Unpublished manuscript, private collection, 2003.

ENQUIST, PER OLOV. *Lewis Reise*. München: Hanser, 2003.

ESCKINDER TADDESSE WOLDEGEBRIAL. "An Introduction to the Biblical and Historical Pat-
tern of Church Government: With a Special Reference to Its Application in the Ethiopian
Full Gospel Believers Church; A Critical Approach." M.Th. thesis, Ethiopian Graduate
School of Theology, 2003.

ETHIOPIAN CHRISTIAN FELLOWSHIP CHURCH IN KANSAS. "Who we are" (2007). http://
ecfck.com/Mission.aspx (accessed November 10, 2007).

ETHIOPIAN EVANGELICAL CHURCH MEKANE YESUS. ይቅዳሴና የአምልኮ ሥነ ሥርዓት መጽሐፍ. [Book
of Liturgy and Worship.] 3rd ed. Addis Ababa, 2008.

—. "EECMY Synods" (2009). http://www.eecmy.org/synods.htm (accessed March 2, 2009).

ETHIOPIAN FULL GOSPEL BELIEVERS' CHURCH. ሙሉ ወንጌል ቤተ ክርስቲያን ከልደት እስከ ... መቸስ
ሰው ጌታ ኢየሱስን ፈልጎ ሲመጣ ተመለስ አይባል*!!* [The Full Gospel Church from Birth Until ...
Well, it is Impossible to Turn Back the People When They Come Wanting Jesus!!] Addis
Ababa, 1978.

ETHIOPIAN FULL GOSPEL BELIEVER'S CHURCH. የኢትዮጵያ ሙሉ ወንጌል አመኞች ቤተ ክርስቲያን 25ኛ
ዓመት በዓል*: ከ1959–1984.* [The 25th Anniversary of the Ethiopian Full Gospel Believer's
Church: From 1959 to 1984.] Addis Ababa, 1992.

ETHIOPIAN GENNET CHURCH. የ50ኛው ዓመት የወርቅ ኢዮቤልዩ በዓል. [The Golden Anniversary of
Fifty Years.] Addis Ababa, 2001.

ETHIOPIAN KALE HEYWET CHURCH. የአመነት አቋም. [Doctrinal Statement.] 3rd ed. Addis
Ababa, 2004.

—. "Mission" (2009). http://www.ekhc.org.et/Mission.htm (accessed March 2, 2009).

EVANGELICAL CHURCHES FELLOWSHIP OF ETHIOPIA. "Introduction to ECFE" (2009). http:
//www.ecfethiopia.org/introduction.htm (accessed March 3, 2009).

EVANGELICAL LUTHERAN MISSION IN LOWER SAXONY. "Annual Report 2008/2009" (2009).
http://www.elm-mission.net/fileadmin/uploads/I_Finanzen/jahrbuch_elm_2008-
laender-1.pdf (accessed March 4, 2009).

Evangelii Härold. "Brev från infödda lärare i Etiopien." [Letters from Native Teachers in
Ethiopia.] 7 1966, 10.

EYOB DEMISSIE. "Pastor Daniel Makonnen (Ethiopian Church History)." Major Paper, Ethiopian Theological College, 2003.

FANUEL ABERA. "The Introduction of Evangelical Christianity and the Effects of Charismatic Renewal in Gore Bethel Mekane Yesus Congregation." B.Th. thesis, Mekane Yesus Seminary, 1999.

FARGHER, BRIAN. "The Charismatic Movement in Ethiopia 1960–1980." *Evangelical Review of Theology* 12 (1988): 345–358.

—. *The Origins of the New Churches Movement in Southern Ethiopia, 1927–1944*. Studies of Religion in Africa; 16. Leiden: Brill, 1996.

FEDERAL DEMOCRATIC REPUBLIC OF ETHIOPIA, OFFICE OF THE POPULATION AND HOUSING CENSUS COMMISSION, CENTRAL STATISTICAL AUTHORITY. *The 1994 Population and Housing Census of Ethiopia: Results at Country Level*, vol. 2, *Statistical Report*. Addis Ababa, 1998.

FEDERAL DEMOCRATIC REPUBLIC OF ETHIOPIA, POPULATION CENSUS COMMISSION. *Summary and Statistical Report of the 2007 Population and Housing Census: Population Size by Sex and Age*. Addis Ababa, 2008. http://www.csa.gov.et/pdf/Cen2007_primineray.pdf (accessed February 27, 2009).

FORSLUND, ESKIL. *The Word of God in Ethiopian Tongues: Rhetorical Features in the Preaching of the Ethiopian Evangelical Church Mekane Yesus*. Studia missionalia Upsaliensia; 58. Uppsala: Swedish Institute for Mission Research, 1993.

FOUCAULT, MICHEL. "Nietzsche, Genealogy, History." In *Language, Counter-Memory, Practice*, edited by DONALD F. BOUCHARD, 139–164. Ithaca, NY: Cornell University Press, 1977.

FREEMAN, NONA. *Unseen hands: The Story of Revival in Ethiopia*. Hazelwood, MO: World Aflame Press, 1987.

—. *Then Came the Glory*. Minden, LA: Nona Freeman, 1994.

FRENCH, ELLEN. "Field Report from Addis Ababa, Ethiopia." *Elim Pentecostal Herald* 8 (57 1938): 8–9.

—. "Field Report from Addis Ababa, Ethiopia." *Elim Pentecostal Herald* 8 (59 1938): 8.

FRODSHAM, STANLEY HOWARD. "The Editor's Notebook." *The Pentecostal Evangel*, 1124 1935, 4, 9.

FULLER, HAROLD W. "Revolutionary Response in Ethiopia." *Christianity Today*, 23 1976, 33–34.

GALLO AYLATE. "The Konso District in the South West Synod: A Case Study on the Conflict of 1990 up to February 2000." B.Th. thesis, Mekane Yesus Seminary, 2000.

GARRARD, DAVID J. "Kenya." In *The New International Dictionary of Pentecostal and Charismatic Movements*, edited by STANLEY M. BURGESS and EDUARD M. van der MAAS, 150–155. Grand Rapids, MI: Zondervan, 2002.

GEBREMEDHIN, EZRA. "The Ethiopian Evangelical Church Mekane Yesus under Marxist Dictatorship." In *Changing Relations Between Churches in Europe and Africa: The Internationalization of Christianity and Politics in the 20th Century*, edited by KATHARINA KUNTER and JENS HOLGER SCHJØRRING, 89–108. Studien zur außereuropäischen Christentumsgeschichte; 11. Wiesbaden: Harrassowitz Verlag, 2008.

GEERTZ, CLIFFORD. *Works and Lives: The Anthropologist as Author*. Standford, CA: Stanford University Press, 1988.

GEMECHU OLANA. *A Church under Challenge: The Socio-Economic and Political Involvement of the Ethiopian Evangelical Church Mekane Yesus (EECMY)*. Berlin: dissertation.de, 2006.

GENERAL SECRETARIATE OF THE PATRIARCHATE OF THE ETHIOPIAN ORTHODOX TEWAHEDO CHURCH. የኢትዮጵያ ቤተ ክርስቲያን ትናንትና ዛሬ. [The Church of Ethiopia Yesterday and Today.] Addis Ababa: Commercial Printing Press, 1997.

GETACHEW BELLETE. ኤሎጼ እና ሃሌሉያ: የኢትዮጵያ ቃለ ሕይወት ቤተ ክርስቲያን ታሪክ, ቅጽ ሦስት, (ከ1966–1992 ዓ.ም.) [Sighs and Hallelujahs. The History of the Kale Heywet Church in Ethiopia, vol. 3, 1974–2000]. Addis Ababa: Ethiopian Kale Heywet Church, 2000.

GETAHUN BOGALE. "The History of Yayu Meserete Kristos Church and Its Growth." B.A. thesis, Meserete Kristos College, 2004.

GETANEH BEFEKADU. "The Missiological Strategies in the Growth of Evangelical Christianity in Sadi-Dalle Wabera Presbytery of WWBS." B.Th. thesis, Mekane Yesus Seminary, 2001.

GIRMA HAILE. "The Brief History of Dire Dawa Meserete Kristos Church." B.A. thesis, Meserete Kristos College, 2002.

GIRMA SORMOLO. "Penetration Between the Two Dominant Horns: The Historical Birth, Growth and Expansion of Harar Meserete Kristos Church in the Midst of Muslim and Traditional Orthodox Belief." B.A. thesis, Meserete Kristos College, 2004.

GIRMA ZEWDE. ኢትዮጲስ: አንደኛው. [Ethiopis, vol. 1.] 3rd ed. n.p., 2001.

GRENSTEDT, STAFFAN. *Ambaricho and Shonkolla: From Local Independent Church to the Evangelical Mainstream in Ethiopia. The Origins of the Mekane Yesus Church in Kambata Hadiya*. Studia Missionalia Svecana; 82. Uppsala: The Swedish Institute of Missionary Research, 2000.

GUDINA TOLA. "Prophecy in the New Testament And Its Effects in the Central Synod's Congregations." B.Th. thesis, Mekane Yesus Seminary, 2001.

GUDINA TUMSA. "The Role of a Christian in a Given Society." In *Witness and Discipleship: Leadership of the Church in Multi-Ethnic Ethiopia in a Time of Revolution; The Essential Writings of Gudina Tumsa, General Secretary of the Ethiopian Evangelical Church Mekane Yesus (1929–1979)*, edited by PAUL E. HOFFMAN, 1–12. Addis Ababa: Gudina Tumsa Foundation, 2003.

HAILE MARIAM LAREBO. "The Orthodox Church and the State in the Ethiopian Revolution, 1974–84." *Religion in Communist Lands* 14 (2 1986): 148–159.

HAILE MARIAM LAREBO. "The Ethiopian Orthodox Church." In *Eastern Christianity and Politics in the Twentieth Century*, edited by SABRINA PETRA RAMET, 375–399. Christianity Under Stress; 1. Durham: Duke University Press, 1988.

HAILE SELASSIE I. "Proclamation Promulgating the Revised Constitution of the Empire of Ethiopia." *Negarit Gazeta*, 2 1955, 3–19.

HAILE WOLDE MICHAEL. "A Comparative Study of Leadership Development Methods with Reference to the Ethiopian Full Gospel Church." Ph.D. thesis, Fuller Theological Seminary, 1993.

HALLDORF, JOEL. *Lewis Brev: Urval ur Lewi Pethrus korrespondens.* [Lewis Letters. Selection from Lewi Pethrus' Correspondence.] Örebrö: Libris, 2007.

HALLIDAY, FRED, and MAXINE MOLYNEUX. *The Ethiopian Revolution.* London: Verso Editions, 1981.

HALME, HELVI. *Letter to Chacha Omahe.* Private collection, Mukiria Chacha, 1966.

HARBESON, JOHN W. *The Ethiopian Transformation: The Quest for the Post-Imperial State.* Boulder, CO: Westview Press, 1988.

HAUSTEIN, JÖRG. "Pfingstbewegung und Identität im Kontext äthiopischer Migranten in Deutschland." In *Migration und Identität: Pfingstlich-charismatische Migrationsgemeinden in Deutschland*, edited by MICHAEL BERGUNDER and JÖRG HAUSTEIN, 107–126. Beihefte der Zeitschrift für Mission; 8. Frankfurt am Main: Lembeck, 2006.

—. "Navigating Political Revolutions: Ethiopia's Churches During and After the Mengistu Regime." In *Falling Walls: The Year 1989/90 as a Turning Point in the History of World Christianity*, edited by KLAUS KOSCHORKE, 117–136. Studien zur Außereuropäischen Christentumsgeschichte (Asien, Afrika, Lateinamerika); 15. Wiesbaden: Harrassowitz, 2009.

—. "Pentecostal and Charismatic Churches in Ethiopia" (2009). http://www.glopent.net/ Members/jhaustein/ethiopia/pentecostal-charismatic-churches-in-ethiopia (accessed February 28, 2009).

HEFLIN, RUTH W. *Glory: Experiencing the Atmosphere of Heaven.* Hagerstown, MD: McDougal Publishing, 1990.

—. *Harvest Glory: I ask for the Nations.* Hagerstown, MD: McDougal Publishing, 1999.

HEGE, NATHAN B. *Beyond Our Prayers: Anabaptist Church Growth in Ethiopia, 1948–1998.* Scottsdale, PA: Herald Press, 1998.

HELLSTRÖM, MARGARETHA. "Frälst ungdom i Etiopien." [Saved Youth in Ethiopia.] *Evangelii Härold* (3 1970): 10–11, 24.

HENZE, PAUL. *Layers of Time: A History of Ethiopia.* London: Hurst and Company, 2001.

Herald of Faith. "Glorious Outpouring of the Holy Spirit in Ethiopia." 3 1964, 14–16, 26.

—. "A Pentecostal Revival at the University in Addis Ababa." 10 1966, 15.

HEWETT, JAMES ALLAN. "Daoud, Mounir Aziz." In *Dictionary of Pentecostal and Charismatic Movements*, 6th ed., edited by PATRICK H. ALEXANDER, STANLEY M. BURGESS, and GARY B. MCGEE, 237. Grand Rapids, MI: Zondervan, 1998.

HEYER, FRIEDRICH. *Die Kirche Äthiopiens: Eine Bestandsaufnahme.* Theologische Bibliothek Töpelmann; 22. Berlin: De Gruyter, 1971.

—. "Die Orthodoxe Kirche Äthiopiens im zehnten Revolutionsjahr." *Ökumenische Rundschau* 34 (2 1985): 216–221.

—. "Chancen für das orthodoxe Äthiopien?" *Ökumenische Rundschau* 37 (3 1988): 342–345.

HILPINEN, EEVA, ed. *Lähetystyön monet kasvot: Suomen vapaa ulkolähetys 70 vuotta. = Manifold missions. Finnish Free Foreign Mission 70 years.* Vantaa: Suomen vapaa ulkolähetys, 1997.

HOFFMAN, PAUL E. "Gudina Tumsa's Legacy: His Spirituality and Leadership." In *The Life and Ministry of Rev. Gudina Tumsa: General Secretary of the Ethiopian Evangelical Church Mekane Yesus (EECMY); Report Volume & Lectures of the Missiological Seminar Sponsored by the Gudina Tumsa Foundation at Mekane Yesus Seminary, Makanissa, April 18-21, 2001,* edited by PAUL E. HOFFMAN, 13–36. Addis Ababa: Gudina Tumsa Foundation, 2003.

—, ed. *The Life and Ministry of Rev. Gudina Tumsa: General Secretary of the Ethiopian Evangelical Church Mekane Yesus (EECMY); Report Volume & Lectures of the Missiological Seminar Sponsored by the Gudina Tumsa Foundation at Mekane Yesus Seminary, Makanissa, April 18-21, 20001.* Addis Ababa: Gudina Tumsa Foundation, 2003.

—, ed. *Witness and Discipleship: Leadership of the Church in Multi-Ethnic Ethiopia in a Time of Revolution; The Essential Writings of Gudina Tumsa, General Secretary of the Ethiopian Evangelical Church Mekane Yesus (1929–1979).* Addis Ababa: Gudina Tumsa Foundation, 2003.

HOLCOMB, BONNIE K., and SISAI IBSSA. *The Invention of Ethiopia.* Trenton, NJ: Red Sea Press, 1990.

HOLLENWEGER, WALTER J. *Handbuch der Pfingstbewegung.* 10 vols. Genf: Univ. Diss., 1965.

HÖGLUND, ELOF. "Etiopien-Missionen." In: Full Gospel Mission, special issue. Jönköping, 1969.

ITEFFA GOBENA MOLTE. "Autobiography" (2008). http://www.ethiopianetwork.org/GobenaBio.html (accessed November 28, 2008).

JETO HORDOFA. "'Troubled But Not Destroyed': The Effects of the Persecution of 1978–1991 (1970–1983 E.C.) on the Congregations of Western Wollega Bethel Synod." B.Th. thesis, Mekane Yesus Seminary, 1999.

JOHANSSON, HARALD. "Pingsteld över Etiopien." [Pentecostal Fire Over Ethiopia.] *Evangelii Härold* (48 1963): 4.

JOHANSSON, TAGE. "Etiopien – problemfyllt land: Men väckelsetider väntas." [Ethiopia – a Country Full of Problems: But a Time of Revival is Expected.] *Evangelii Härold* (37 1974): 2–4, 22.

—. *Med Gud i vardagen och bland medicinmän.* [With God Every Day and Among Medicine Men.] Avesta: STC, 1996.

KESTON COLLEGE STAFF. "Improvements in the Church Situation in Ethiopia?" *Religion in Communist Lands* 14 (1986): 328–329.

Keston News Service. "Tesfaye Gabiso." January 24, 1985, 22.

KIPPENBERG, HANS G. *Die Entdeckung der Religionsgeschichte: Religionswissenschaft und Moderne.* München: C. H. Beck, 1997.

Kristeligt Dagblad. "Pinsekirken forfølges stadig i Ethiopien." [The Pentecostal Church is Steadily Persecuted in Ethiopia.] November 3, 1972.

KUMPULAINEN, HEIKKI. *Puskatimpurin Päiväkirja.* [Diary of a Bush Carpenter.] Vantaa: Aika Oy, 1997.

KÄRKKÄINEN, VELI-MATTI. "'From the Ends of the Earth' – The Expansion of Finnish Pentecostal Missions from 1927–1997." *The Journal of the European Pentecostal Research Association* 20 (2000): 116–131.

—. "The Pentecostal Movement in Finland." *The Journal of the European Pentecostal Research Association* 23 (2003): 102–128.

LACLAU, ERNESTO. "Why do Empty Signifiers Matter to Politics?" In *The Lesser Evil and The Greater Good: The Theory and Politics of Social Diversity*, edited by JEFFREY WEEKS, 167–178. London: Rivers Oram Press, 1994.

—. "The Death and Resurrection of the Theory of Ideology." *Journal of Political Ideologies* 1 (3 1996): 201–221.

—. *On Populist Reason.* London: Verso, 2005.

LACLAU, ERNESTO, and CHANTAL MOUFFE. *Hegemony and Socialist Strategy: Towards a Radical Democratic Politics.* 2nd ed. London: Verso, 2001.

LALISSA DANIEL GAMECHIS. "The Teaching of the Apostolic Movement and the Danger Behind." B.Th. thesis, Mekane Yesus Seminary, 2001.

LAUNHARDT, JOHANNES. *Evangelicals in Addis Ababa (1919–1991): With Special Reference to the Ethiopian Evangelical Church Mekane Yesus and the Addis Ababa Synod.* Münster: Lit, 2004.

LEBETA GOSHU KUMSA. "History of Meserete Kristos Church in Wellega (1966–2002)." B.A. thesis, Meserete Kristos College, 2002.

LESINSKI, MARKUS. "Gefangen in der Geschichte? Die Äthiopische Orthodoxe Kirche." In *Mit wachsender Begeisterung: Evangelische Christen in Äthiopien*, edited by HENNING UZAR, 89–100. Hermannsburg: Missionshandlung Hermannsburg, 1998.

LETTINGA, NEIL. "Ethiopian Protestantism: The "Pente" Churches in Ethiopia" (2000). http://www.bethel.edu/~letnie/AfricanChristianity/EthiopiaProtestantism.html (accessed February 10, 2009).

LIARDON, ROBERTS. *The Azusa Street Revival: When the Fire Fell – An In Depth Look at the People, Teachings, and Lessons.* Shippensburg, PA: Destiny Image, 2006.

Life of Faith. "Evangelicals Imprisoned in Ethiopia." October 14, 1972, 1,12.

LINDAHL, GÖSTA. "Seger i Etiopien." [Victory in Ethiopia]. *Evangelii Härold* (41 1964): 8–9, 23.

LINDBERG, ALF. *Väckelse, Frikyrklighet, Pingströrelse: Väckelse och frikyrka från 1800-talets mitt till nutid.* [Revival, Free Church Movement, Pentecostal Movement: Revival and Free Churches from the Middle of the 1800s to Today.] Ekerö: Kaggeholms folkhögskola, 1985.

—. "The Swedish Pentecostal Movement: Some Ideological Features." *EPTA Bulletin* VI (2 1987): 40–46.

Logos Journal. "Persecution in Ethiopia." May-June 1973, 12–16.

—. "Further News from Ethiopia." July–August 1973, 41.

LUNDGREN, MANFRED. "När traditioner och relationer satts på prov." [When Traditions and Relationships are Put to the Test.] *Svensk Missionstidskrift* 17 (1983): 32–38.

MANNINEN, VEIKKO. *Mannisentie: Toimittanut Maja Hurri.* [Manninen's Way. Edited by Maja Hurri]. Vantaa: Aika Oy, 1995.

MARCUS, HAROLD G. *A History of Ethiopia.* Berkeley, CA: University of California Press, 1994.

MARWEDEL, WOLFGANG. "Mitmachen, aber mit kritischer Distanz: Evangelium und Sozialismus in Äthiopien." *Zeitschrift für Mission* 10 (4 1984): 198–204.

MATTSSON-BOZE, JOSEPH. "Mighty Outpouring of the Holy Ghost in Ethiopia: 100 Students in the Bible-School Baptized in the Holy Spirit!" *Herald of Faith* 31 (12 1963): 12.

—. "Africa: Report from the Training Center for Young Nationals in Ethiopia." *Herald of Faith* 34 (10 1966): 12–14.

—. "Ethiopia: In Audience with the Emperor: Great Miracles." *Herald of Faith* 35 (10 1967): 7–8.

McDONNELL, KILIAN. "Lutheran Church – Mekane Yesus, Ethiopia, 1976: The Work of the Holy Spirit." In *Presence, Power, Praise: Documents on the Charismatic Renewal*, vol. 2, *Continental, National, and Regional Documents Numbers 38 to 80, 1975–1979*, edited by KILIAN McDONNELL, 150–182. Collegeville, MN: The Liturgical Press, 1980.

McGEE, GARY B. "Early Pentecostal Hermeneutics: Tongues as Evidence in the Book of Acts." In *Initial Evidence: Historical and Biblical Perspectives on the Pentecostal Doctrine of Spirit Baptism*, edited by GARY B. McGEE, 96–118. Peabody, MA: Hendrickson Publishers, 1991.

MEINARDUS, OTTO FRIEDRICH AUGUST. *Two Thousand Years of Coptic Christianity.* Cairo: American University in Cairo Press, 2002.

MENGESHA AGA. "Evangelism and Charismatic Movement in Ghimbi District Western Synod EECMY 1914–1999." B.Th. thesis, Mekane Yesus Seminary, 2000.

MESERETE KRISTOS CHURCH, ed. መሠረተ እምነት. [Foundation of Faith]. Addis Ababa, 1995.

MESFIN WOLDEAMANUEL. "A Surge for Independency: An Evaluation of the Nature and Development of Independent Churches in Ethiopia with Special Focus on the Hywet Kal Church." M.Th. thesis, Ethiopian Graduate School of Theology, 2001.

MIESA YACHIS. "Charismatic Movement and Related Problems in South Ethiopia Synod of EECMY." B.Th. thesis, Mekane Yesus Seminary, 1993.

MIHIRETU DUGUMA. "Church Growth With Special Reference to Dale Leka Presbytery in WWBS." B.Th. thesis, Mekane Yesus Seminary, 2001.

MINTESINOT BIRRU. "The Impact of Charismatic Movement and Its Result Among Evangelicals in Gedeo Area." B.Th. thesis, Mekane Yesus Seminary, 2002.

MITIKU TESFA FUFA. "The Challenge of Language for the EECMY." B.Th. thesis, Mekane
Yesus Seminary, 1999.

MULATU WUBNEH and YOHANNIS ABATE. *Ethiopia: Transition and Development in the
Horn of Africa.* Boulder, CO: Westview Press, 1988.

MUMPER, SHARON E. "Ethiopia Continues to Impose Restrictions on the Churches." *Christianity Today,* 14 1985, 70–72.

MUSSIE ALAZAR. "Amanual-Mahiber: Foundation and Growth." B.Th. thesis, Mekane Yesus
Seminary, 2000.

NEGEWO BOSET. "Persecution and Church Expansion: The Growth of Opposition Between
the Religious Authorities and Jesus as it was Experienced in the Primitive Church and
Extends to the Present Church of Ethiopian Meserete Kristos." B.Th. thesis, Evangelical
Theological College, 1994.

NELSSON, ROLAND. "Gamla tiders väckelse bland universitetsstuderande." [Old-time Revival
Among University Students.] *Evangelii Härold* (42 1966): 7, 11.

Newsweek. International Edition. "Persecuting the Sects." January 15, 1973, 32.

NILSSON, NILS-OLOV. "The Debate on Women's Ministry in the Swedish Pentecostal Church
Movement: Summary and Analysis." *Pneuma* 22 (1 2000): 61–83.

—. "The Swedish Pentecostal Movement 1913–2000: The Tension Between Radical Congregationalism, Restorationism, and Denominationalism." Ph.D. thesis, Columbia Theological
Seminary, 2001.

NORDLANDER, AGNE. "Charismatic Movement and Lutheran Theology in the Ethiopian
Evangelical Church Mekane Yesus." In *Med Kristus til jordens ender: Festskrift til Tormod
Engelsviken,* edited by KJELL OLAV SANNES, 193–202. Trondheim: Tapir Akademisk
Forlag, 2008.

NYBERG OSKARSSON, GUNILLA. *Svensk Pingstmission i Ethiopien (1959–1980).* [The
Swedish Pentecostal Mission in Ethiopia]. Huddinge: MissionsInstitutet-PMU, 1997.

O'MAHONEY, KEVIN. *The Ebullient Phoenix: A History of the Vicariate of Abyssinia
1839–1916.* Rev. as one book. Addis Ababa: United Printers, 2002.

OTTAWAY, MARINA, and DAVID OTTAWAY. *Ethiopia: Empire in Revolution.* London: Holmes
& Meier Publishers, 1978.

"P'ent'ay." *Wikipedia. The Free Encyclopedia* (2009). http://en.wikipedia.org/wiki/P%
27ent%27ay (accessed January 14, 2009).

PERHAM, MARGERY. *The Government of Ethiopia.* London: Faber and Faber, 1948.

PERSOON, JOACHIM. "New Perspectives on Ethiopian and African Christianity: Communalities and Contrasts in Twentieth Century Religious Experience." *Exchange* 34 (4 2005):
306–336.

PETHRUS, LEWI. "Drager eder ifrån dem." [Pull Yourselves Away from Them.] *Dagen,* November 18, 1957, 2.

PHILIPOS KEMERE. "Seger och skördetider i Etiopien." [Victory and Harvest Time in Ethiopia.] *Evangelii Härold* (33 1969): 10–11.

PIPER, BENJAMIN. "Mercy Center Addis Ababa: NGO or No?" (2004). http://www.case-web.org/assets/cases/case_36.pdf (accessed June 18, 2007).

RAMSTRAND, KARL. "ETIOPIEN – ett mognande skördefält." [Ethiopia – A Ripe Harvest Field.] *Evangelii Härold* 45 (1962): 6–7.

—. *Det heliga äventyret.* [The Holy Adventure]. Stockholm: Den Kristna Bokringen, 1986.

RAMSTRAND, KARL, and OLOF NILSSON. "Etiopien i Blickpunkten." [Ethiopia in the Lime-light.] *Evangelii Härold* (28 1966): 9.

RAMSTRAND, RUTH. *Guds lilla piga far dit pepparn växer.* [God's Little Maid Goes Where the Pepper Grows.] Huskvarna, 2002.

RAYNER, DECOURCY H. "Persecution in Ethiopia." *Christianity Today*, 3 1972, 54–55.

REED, DAVID ARTHUR. "Oneness Pentecostalism." In *The New International Dictionary of Pentecostal and Charismatic Movements*, edited by STANLEY M. BURGESS and EDUARD M. van der MAAS, 936–944. Grand Rapids, MI: Zondervan, 2002.

REGATU OLANA. "Establishment and Growth of Evangelical Christianity in Anfillo Pres-bytery of WWBS (1936–1998)." B.Th. thesis, Mekane Yesus Seminary, 1999.

RICE, MARIE S. *Sister Bertha, Sister Ruth.* Nashville, TN: Jonathan Publishers, 1984.

ROBECK, CECIL M. JR. "An Emerging Magisterium? The Case of the Assemblies of God." *Pneuma* 25 (2 2003): 164–215.

ROININEN, AINO. *Koskettakaa Lastani: Sairaanhoitajan kokemuksia Etiopiassa.* [Touch My Child! From the Experiences of a Nurse in Ethiopia.] Vantaa: RV-Kirjat, 1988.

ROININEN, KYÖSTI. "A Condensed History of the Finnish Mission in Ethiopia." Unpublished manuscript, private collection, 2001.

RUBENSON, SVEN. "The Missionary Factor in Ethiopia: Consequences of a Colonial Con-text." In *The Missionary Factor in Ethiopia: Papers from a Symposium on the Impact of European Missions on Ethiopian Society, Lund University, August 1996*, edited by GETATCHEW HAILE, AASULV LANDE, and SAMUEL RUBENSON, 57–70. Studien zur in-terkulturellen Geschichte des Christentums; 110. Frankfurt am Main: Lang, 1998.

SÆVERÅS, OLAV. *On Church-Mission Relations in Ethiopia 1944–1969: With Special Refer-ence to the Evangelical Church Mekane Yesus and the Lutheran Missions.* Studia mis-sionalia Upsaliensia; 27. Uppsala: Lunde, 1974.

SÆVERÅS, AUD. *Der lange Schatten der Macht: Augenzeugenbericht. Die Geschichte von Tsehay Tolessa und Gudina Tumsa, dem ermordeten Generalsekretär der Mekane-Yesus-Kirche in Äthiopien.* Gießen: Brunnen Verlag, 1993.

SARASIN, PHILIPP. *Geschichtswissenschaft und Diskursanalyse.* Suhrkamp-Taschenbuch Wis-senschaft; 1639. Frankfurt am Main: Suhrkamp, 2003.

—. *Michel Foucault zur Einführung.* Hamburg: Junius Verlag, 2005.

SCHOLLER, HEINRICH, and PAUL BRIETZKE. *Ethiopia: Revolution, Law and Politics.* Afrika-Studien; 92. München: Weltforum Verlag, 1976.

SCHRÖDER, GÜNTER. "Äthiopien: Religiöse Gemeinschaften, Organisationen und Institutio-nen. Ein Überblick." Unpublished manuscript, private collection, 1997.

SCHWAB, PETER. *Ethiopia: Politics, Economics and Society*. London: Frances Pinter, 1985.

SELESHI KEBEDE. "The History of the Guenet Church." B.Th. thesis, Mekane Yesus Seminary, 1990.

SHENK, CALVIN E. "Church and State in Ethiopia: From Monarchy to Marxism." *Mission Studies* 11 (2 1994): 203–226.

SHETLER, JAN BENDER. "The Nazareth Bible Academy in Retrospect." Unpublished manuscript, private collection, 1984.

SINGLETON, BARBARA. "A Clinical Phenomenology of Spirit Possession Beliefs and Practices in the Evangelical Churches of Addis Ababa, Ethiopia." Ph.D. thesis, The Professional School of Psychology, 1996.

SOLOMON KEBEDE. "በዚህ ስም ከመታወቁ በፊት." [Before It Was Known by This Name.] In የኢትዮጵያ ሙሉ ወንጌል አመኞች ቤተ ክርስቲያን 25ኛ ዓመት በዓል፡ ከ1959–1984 *[The 25th Anniversary of the Ethiopian Full Gospel Believer's Church: From 1959 to 1984]*, edited by ETHIOPIAN FULL GOSPEL BELIEVER'S CHURCH, 16. Addis Ababa, 1992.

SPENCER, IVAN Q. "Ethiopia." *Elim Pentecostal Herald* 7 (4 1956): 15.

SPENCER, JOHN H. *Ethiopia at Bay: A Personal Account of the Haile Sellassie Years*. Algonac, MI: Reference Publications, 1984.

STEIL, HARRY J. "Ethiopia versus Italy." *The Pentecostal Evangel*, 1120 1935, 1,17–18.

STREET, HAROLD. "The Lid is Off: The Truth About Ethiopia." *The Latter Rain Evangel* 29 (6 1938).

Target. "Persecution in Ethiopia?" November 25, 1972, 12.

TARIKU WOLDEMICHAEL and YONAS ASHAGARI. "The Establishment of Addis Ababa Mulu Wongel Believers' Church." Unpublished manuscript, private collection, 1999.

TAYE ABDISSA. "The Pentecostal Development and the Rise of Charismatic Movement in Ethiopia." B.Th. thesis, Mekane Yesus Seminary, 1977.

TEFERA MEKETA. "The History of South Addis Ababa Meserete Kristos Church and Its Growth." B.A. thesis, Meserete Kristos College, 2003.

TEFERRA HAILE-SELASSIE. *The Ethiopian Revolution 1974–1991: From a Monarchical Autocracy to a Military Oligarchy*. London: Kegan Paul International, 1997.

TEKA OBSA FOGI. "The Charismatic Movement in the EECMY: Some Doctrinal and Practical Issues; An Explorative and Evaluative Case Study; The Case of the EECMY Congregations in Nekemte." M.Th. thesis, Ethiopian Graduate School of Theology, 2000.

TEKLEMARIAM GEZAHEGNE. *The Identity of Jesus Christ*. Hazelwood, MO: World Aflame Press, 1989.

TESFAYE TADESSE. "The Importance of Healing Ministry for Church Growth." B.Th. thesis, Mekane Yesus Seminary, 2000.

TESHOME G. WAGAW. *The Development of Higher Education and Social Change: An Ethiopian Experience*. African Series; 2. East Lansing, MI: Michigan State University Press, 1990.

TESHOME SORI. "Insights for an Effective Evangelism in Nekemte Meserete Kristos Church and Its Surroundings." B.A. thesis, Meserete Kristos College, 2002.

The Ethiopian Herald. "Youth and Adults Clash in Debre-Zeit." September 21, 1967, 5.

—. "Statement of Faith Made at Investiture." May 11, 1971, 1, 3, 7.

—. "Newsweek's Report on Pentecostalists Unfounded." January 13, 1973, 2.

—. "United Bible Societies World Assembly Here." September 14, 1972, 1, 2.

—. "World Assembly of United Bible Societies to be Held Here Soon." September 19, 1972, 1, 8.

—. "U.B.S: Assembly Opens Tomorrow." September 24, 1972, 3, 10.

—. "His Majesty Opens First UBS Assembly." September 26, 1972, 1, 7.

—. "Let the Word Speak." September 27, 1972, 2.

—. "1st World Assembly of United Bible Societies Ends at Africa Hall." September 30, 1972, 1, 2.

"The Introduction and the Growth of Evangelical Christianity in Lalo Qille Presbytery of Western Welega Bethel Synod." B.Th. thesis, Mekane Yesus Seminary, 2000.

The Prince of Peace Communicator. "Birth of a Daughter Congregation, Grace Ethiopian Lutheran Church." 10 2005, 1. http://www.poplc.org/Communicator/2005/20050306.pdf (accessed October 26, 2007).

THOMAS DEBELA. "The Effect of Charismatic Renewal upon Church Growth in the Central Synod." B.Th. thesis, Mekane Yesus Seminary, 1999.

TIBEBE ESHETE. "Growing Through the Storms: The History of the Evangelical Movement in Ethiopia, 1941–1991." Ph.D. thesis, Michigan State University, 2005.

—. *The Evangelical Movement in Ethiopia: Resistance and Resiliance*. Waco, TX: Baylor University Press, 2009.

TILAHUN BEYENE. "...ቤተ ክርስቲያኔን እሥራለሁ...": የመሰረተ ክርስቶስ ቤተ ክርስቲያን ታሪክ. ["...I build My Church..." : The History of the Meserete Kristos Church.] Addis Ababa: Meserete Kristos Church, 2002.

TILAHUN HAILE. "የወንጌል ሥርጭት ታሪክ በኢትዮጵያ በአጭሩ የተጻፈ." [A Short History of the Spread of the Gospel in Ethiopia.] Unpublished manuscript, Evangelical Theological College, Addis Ababa, 2000.

TILAHUN TADESSE. "Gulele Bethel Evangelical Church Mekane Yesus at Present: Does it Need Revival?" B.Th. thesis, Mekane Yesus Seminary, 1999.

TILAYE KEBEDE. "Lamp on the Mountain: History of the Entoto Evangelical Church Mekane Yesus 1962–1974." B.Th. thesis, Mekane Yesus Seminary, 1995.

TILLANDER, ASTA. *Näkymättömän lähettiläs: Anna-Liisa Mattsonin elämä*. [The Invisible Messenger. The Life of Anna-Liisa Mattsson.] Vantaa: Aika Oy, 1996.

TOLESA GUDINA. "The Spiritual Gifts on I: Cor. 12: 8–10." B.Th. thesis, Mekane Yesus Seminary, 1977.

TOLO, ARNE. *Sidama and Ethiopian: The Emergence of the Mekane Yesus Church in Sidama.* Studia Missionalia Upsaliensia; 69. Uppsala: Uppsala Universitet, 1998.

TORFING, JACOB. *New Theories of Discourse: Laclau, Mouffe and Žižek.* Oxford: Blackwell, 2005.

TRANSITIONAL GOVERNMENT OF ETHIOPIA, OFFICE OF THE POPULATION AND HOUSING CENSUS COMMISSION. *The 1984 Population and Housing Census of Ethiopia: Analytical Report at National Level.* Addis Ababa: Central Statistical Authority, 1991.

TSADIKU ABDO. "Where Does Mulu Wongel Stand in its Trinitarian Concept: East or West? A Critical Approach to Ethiopian Mulu Wongel Church's Theology of Trinity." M.Th. thesis, Ethiopian Graduate School of Theology, 2003.

TSAHAFE TAEZAZ AKLILU HABTE WOLD. "Civil Code of the Empire of Ethiopia." *Negarit Gazeta*, 2 1960.

—. "Legal Notice No: 321 of 1966. Regulations Issued Pursuant to the Control of Associations Provision of the Civil Code of 1960." *Negarit Gazeta* 26 (1 1966): 1–10.

TSEGA ENDALEW. "Protestant Mission Activities and Persecutions in Bahər Dar, 1968–1994: A Chronicle." In *Ethiopia and the Missions: Historical and Anthropological Insights*, edited by VERENA BÖLL, ANDREU MARTÍNEZ D' ALÒS-MONER, and EVGENIA SOKOLINSKAIA, 209–220. Münster: Lit, 2005.

TSHAFE TAEZAZ TAFFARA WORQ. "The Penal Code of Ethiopia 1957." *Negarit Gazeta* 16 (1 1957).

TUBIANA, JOSEPH. "Brave New Words: Linguistic Innovation in the Social and Economic Vocabulary of Amharic since 1960." *Journal of Semitic Studies* 30 (1 1985): 85–93.

TURTON, DAVID, ed. *Ethnic Federalism: The Ethiopian Experience in Comparative Perspective.* Oxford: James Currey, 2006.

U.S. DEPARTMENT OF STATE, BUREAU OF DEMOCRACY, HUMAN RIGHTS AND LABOR. "Ethiopia: International Religious Freedom Report 2003" (2003). http://www.state.gov/g/drl/rls/irf/2003/23705.htm (accessed January 10, 2009).

UHLIG, SIEGBERT, ed. *Encyclopaedia Aethiopica.* Vol. 1. Wiesbaden: Harrassowitz, 2003.

VÄISÄNEN, SEPPO S. "The Challenge of Marxism to Evangelical Christianity with Special Reference to Ethiopia." D.Miss. thesis, School of World Mission, Fuller Theological Seminary, 1981.

Vårt Land. "Kristne forfølges i Etiopia." [Christians Persecuted in Ethiopia.] September 15, 1972, 1, 15.

—. "Forfølgelsene i Etiopie: 'Spanningen har vært der lenge.'' [Persecution in Ethiopia: "Tensions had been there for a long time."] September 16, 1972, 1,15,23.

—. "Protest mot forfølgelse." [Protest Against Persecution.] September 18, 1972, 3.

—. "Må skaffe oss solide opplysninger om Etiopia: Biskop Lønning til Addis – undersøker om kristenforfølgelser." [Must Obtain Solid Information about Ethiopia for Ourselves. Bishop Lønning to Addis – Investigation of Persecution of Christians.] September 20, 1972, 1.

—. "'Forfølgelsen av de unge kristne ikke typisk for situasionen i Etiopia.'" ["Persecution of the Young Christians is not Typical for the Situation in Ethiopia."] September 22, 1972, 2.

—. "Biskop Lønning hjem fra Etiopia: Religionsforfølgelsene blir kanskje løst ved norsk initiativ." [Bishop Lønning Home from Ethiopia: Religious Persecution Can Perhaps be Solved through Norwegian Initiative.] October 6, 1972, 1, 19.

—. "Unge kristne dømmes i disse dager." [Young Christians are Judged These Days.] October 27, 1972, 1, 19.

WCC Media. "WCC News: Coptic & Ethiopian Orthodox Churches Reconcile" (2007). http://www.wfn.org/2007/07/msg00139.html (accessed July 19, 2007).

Wallberg, Owe. "Hälsning från bibelskolan i Awasa." [Greetings from the Bible School in Awasa.] *Evangelii Härold* (45 1967): 5.

Westbury, Ronald Paul. "The Nature and Status of Ministry Practices of the Pentecostal Evangelistic Fellowship of Africa." Ph.D. thesis, Asbury Theological Seminary, 2002.

Westman, K. B., et al. *Nordisk Missionshistoria.* [Scandinavian Mission History.] Stockholm: Missionsförbundets Förlag, 1949.

White, Hayden. *Metahistory: The Historical Imagination in Nineteenth-Century Europe.* Baltimore, MD: John Hopkins University Press, 1973.

—, ed. *The Content of the Form: Narrative Discourse and Historical Representation.* Baltimore, MD: Johns Hopkins University Press, 1987.

—. "The Value of Narrativity in the Representation of Reality." In *The Content of the Form: Narrative Discourse and Historical Representation,* 1–25. Baltimore, MD: John Hopkins University Press, 1987.

Williams, Brian David. "The Amazing Ethiopia Crusade: Diary Entry" (1965). http://web.ukonline.co.uk/brian.david.williams/diary/1964.html (accessed July 7, 2007).

Wondeye Ali. በመከራ ውስጥ ያበበች ቤተ ክርስቲያን፡ የኢትዮጵያ ቃለ ሕይወት ቤተ ክርስቲያን ታሪክ, ቅጽ አንድ, (ከ1920–1933). [A Church Blooming in Hardship: The History of the Ethiopian Kale Heywet Church, vol. 1, 1928–1941]. Addis Ababa: Ethiopian Kale Heywet Church, 1998.

World Council of Churches. "WCC Alarmed and Saddened by Situation in Ethiopia." *World Council of Churches Communication* (8 1977).

Yeshitela Mengistu. "The Story of the Meserete Krestos Church." B.Th. thesis, Mekane Yesus Seminary, 1983.

Yohannes Sherab. "The Rapid Growth of "Jesus Only" Movement: Some of the Contributory Factors for its Growth in South West Ethiopia." M.Th. thesis, Ethiopian Graduate School of Theology, 2005.

Yonas Seifu. "The Background, the Progression and the Contemporary Nature of Music in the Ethiopian Evangelical Churches." B.A. thesis, Meserete Kristos College, 2004.

Yosief Kidanewold. "The History of the Pentecostal Movement in Addis Abeba: 1963–1976." B.A. thesis, Addis Ababa University, History Department, 1976.

Archives and Collections

Fida Archives. Helsinki, Finland:

> Later Correspondence.
>
> Fida International.
>
> Correspondence Others.

Jönköpings läns folkrörelsearkiv. Jönköping, Sweden:

> Religiösa organisationer, Filadelfiaförsamlingen Jönköping Collection.

Pingstarkiv Kaggeholm. Ekerö, Sweden:

> Tage Johansson Collection
>
> Valla Collection

WCC Archive. Geneva, Switzerland:

> Correspondence Member Churches: EOC.
>
> Philip Potter Correspondence.
>
> Ethiopia Correspondence.

List of Informants

Abby Emishaw; pastor of the Barnabas Church of the 7000 Elected. Addis Ababa, Ethiopia, Jan 14, 2005.

Abdisa Mengesha; pastor of the Ethiopian Evangelical Church Mekane Yesus. Bahir Dar, Ethiopia, Mar 10, 2005.

Abera Teferi; evangelist of the Gospel for the Nations Church. Addis Ababa, Ethiopia, Jan 19, 2005. (together with Atkilt Alemu)

Abraham Getachew; teacher at the Bible Army Church. Addis Ababa, Ethiopia, Mar 29, 2004.

Alemayehu Abayne; minister of the Emanuel United Church. Addis Ababa, Ethiopia, Jan 21, 2005.

Alemayehu Mulugeta; pastor of the Ethiopian church in Stuttgart, Gnade Christliches Zentrum. Stuttgart, Germany, May 16, 2004.

Alemu Shetta; director of the Gospel Ministry Department of the Ethiopian Evangelical Church Mekane Yesus. Addis Ababa, Ethiopia, Mar 26, 2004.

Amsalu Wagsato; chairman of the elders at the Bahir Dar Ethiopian Kale Heywet Church. Bahir Dar, Ethiopia, Mar 08, 2005.

Ashebir Ketema; head of the Spiritual Department of the Ethiopian Gennet Church. Addis Ababa, Ethiopia, Sep 22, 2003 and Feb 26, 2004. (together with Teklu Wolde)

Assefa Alemu; pastor of the Ethiopian Christian Fellowship Church in Kansas City, Kansas, USA. Telephone interview, Jul 06, 2007.

Assefa Olkeba; evangelist and founder of Wonderful Gift International Ministry. Addis Ababa, Ethiopia, Jan 12, 2005.

Ateka Alamirew; member of the Ethiopian Full Gospel Believers' Church. Bahir Dar, Ethiopia, Mar 06, 2005 and Mar 09, 2005.

Atkilt Alemu; pastor of the Gospel for the Nations Church. Addis Ababa, Ethiopia, Jan 19, 2005. (together with Abera Teferi)

Awnetu Makonnen; Registration Office of the Ministry of Justice of Ethiopia. Addis Ababa, Ethiopia, Mar 22, 2004.

Ayalewu Tessema; pastor of the Addis Ababa and Surrounding Evangelical Church Mekane Yesus. Addis Ababa, Ethiopia, Mar 25, 2004.

Ayele Alemayehu; pastor and founder of the True Light Church. Addis Ababa, Ethiopia, Mar 23, 2004.

Bakke, Johnny; missionary with the Norwegian Lutheran Mission. Addis Ababa, Ethiopia, Jan 27, 2005.

Bedru Hussein Muktar; principal of the Meserete Kristos College (Meserete Kristos Church). Addis Ababa, Ethiopia, Sep 19, 2003.

Bekele Woldekidan; pastor of the Addis Ababa Full Gospel Believers' Church. Addis Ababa, Ethiopia, Sep 26, 2003.

Belina Sarka; founder and president of El-Shaddai Evangelical Outreach Ministry. Addis Ababa, Ethiopia, Mar 30, 2005.

Benyam Temesgen; pastor of the Evangelical Maranata Church. Awasa, Ethiopia, Feb 26, 2005.

Betta Mengistu; founder and chairman of Beza International Ministries. Telephone interview, Aug 02, 2007.

Chinia Enjaja; elder at the Awasa Ethiopian Heywet Birhan Church. Awasa, Ethiopia, Feb 14, 2005.

Daniel Gezahegne; director of the Swedish Philadelphia Church Mission. Addis Ababa, Ethiopia, Mar 18, 2004.

Daniel Makonnen; founder and president of the Gospel Light Church. Addis Ababa, Ethiopia, Mar 04, 2004.

Demissew Kasaye; Orthodox student at the Ethiopian Graduate School of Theology. Addis Ababa, Ethiopia, Sep 27, 2003.

Endale Gebeyehu; coordinator of the northern region of the Meserete Kristos Church. Bahir Dar, Ethiopia, Mar 16, 2005.

Endale Gebremeskel; principal of the Addis Ababa Bible College (Assemblies of God). Addis Ababa, Ethiopia, Sep 18, 2003.

Ermias Tadese; evangelist of the Ethiopian Gennet Church. Bahir Dar, Ethiopia, Mar 15, 2005.

Ermias Zenebe; pastor of the New Covenant Baptist Church. Addis Ababa, Ethiopia, Jan 28, 2005.

Esckinder Tadesse; principal of the Ethiopian Full Gospel College. Addis Ababa, Ethiopia, Mar 24, 2005.

Eshetu Gurmu; founder of the Ethiopian Evangelical Church in Frankfurt. Frankfurt, Germany, May 14, 2004. (together with Getu Tadese)

Eshetu Worike; pastor of the Rhema Gospel Church. Addis Ababa, Ethiopia, Feb 26, 2004.

Fällsten, Gert; former missionary with the Swedish Philadelphia Church Mission. Telephone interview, Sep 12, 2006.

Fekadu Ayele; national overseer of the Ethiopian Living Word Evangelical Church of God of Prophecy. Addis Ababa, Ethiopia, Jan 28, 2005.

Fekadu Demissie; principal of the Addis Ababa Full Gospel Bible College. Addis Ababa, Ethiopia, Jan 28, 2005.

Fekede Tefera; Addis Ababa and Surrounding Evangelical Church Mekane Yesus. Addis Ababa, Ethiopia, Mar 31, 2004.

Firew Bekele; pastor of the Gospel Light Church. Awasa, Ethiopia, Feb 23, 2005.

Firey Lemma; pastor of the Christian Temple Church. Addis Ababa, Ethiopia, Feb 01, 2005.

Gashaw Oryion; member of the Meserete Kristos Church. Bahir Dar, Ethiopia, Mar 19, 2005.

Gebeyu Lera; member of the Ethiopian Heywet Birhan Church. Awasa, Ethiopia, Feb 16, 2005.

Gelagay Emeru; evangelist of the Meserete Kristos Church. Bahir Dar, Ethiopia, Mar 07, 2005.

Gennet Tefari; evangelist of the Evangelical Maranata Church. Addis Ababa, Ethiopia, Jan 27, 2005.

Getachew Belete; head of the Communication and Literature Department of the Ethiopian Kale Heywet Church. Addis Ababa, Ethiopia, Mar 11, 2004.

Getahun Nesibu Teseme; pastor of the Ethiopian Evangelical Praise Church. Addis Ababa, Ethiopia, Feb 03, 2005.

Getenet Bekele; pastor of the Emanuel United Church. Awasa, Ethiopia, Feb 21, 2005.

Getu Ayaley; senior pastor of the Ethiopian Heywet Birhan Church. Awasa, Ethiopia, Feb 07, 2005.

Getu Tadese; elder of the Ethiopian Evangelical Church in Frankfurt. Frankfurt, Germany, May 14, 2004. (together with Eshetu Gurmu)

Girma Tessema; member of the Addis Ababa Full Gospel Believers' Church. Addis Ababa, Ethiopia, Feb 02, 2005.

Girma Worku; chairman of the elders at the Bahir Dar Emaniel Baptist Church. Bahir Dar, Ethiopia, Mar 14, 2005.

Girmachew Birhan; evangelist of the Ethiopian Heywet Birhan Church. Bahir Dar, Ethiopia, Mar 03, 2005. (together with Nurhuse Alemu, and Samuel Bishaw)

Gotzen, Gerald; former missionary to Ethiopia. telephone interview, Sep 12, 2006.

Haile Gebriel; bishop of the Ethiopian Orthodox Church. Addis Ababa, Ethiopia, Mar 15, 2004.

Hargestam, Karl; evangelist of the Joshua Campaign International and Swedish representative of the Swedish Philadelphia Church Mission. Addis Ababa, Ethiopia, Mar 12, 2004 and Mar 15, 2004.

Hiruy Tsige; overseer of the Harvest Church of God. Addis Ababa, Ethiopia, Mar 20, 2004.

Israel Eltamo; teacher at the Awasa Ethiopian Heywet Birhan Church. Awasa, Ethiopia, Feb 14, 2005.

Johansson, Birgitta; former missionary of the Swedish Philadelphia Church Mission. Jönköping, Sweden, Aug 12, 2004. (together with Tage Johansson)

Johansson, Tage; former missionary of the Swedish Philadelphia Church Mission. Jönköping, Sweden, Aug 12, 2004. (together with Birgitta Johansson)

Kassa Agefari; pastoral secretary of the Meserete Kristos Church. Addis Ababa, Ethiopia, Mar 30, 2004.

Kebede Degu; founder of Zion The Holy Spirit Ministries. Addis Ababa, Ethiopia, Sep 23, 2003.

Kindeya Hailu; senior pastor of the Evangelical Maranata Church. Addis Ababa, Ethiopia, Jan 18, 2005. (together with Mekbib Desta)

Kinfe-Gebriel Matthewos; pastor of the Penial International Church. Addis Ababa, Ethiopia, Mar 26, 2004.

Lemma Degefa; head of the Evangelism Department of the Evangelical Churches' Fellowship of Ethiopia. Addis Ababa, Ethiopia, Mar 23, 2005.

Leul Hailu Gebre; pastor of the Reformed Presbyterian Church. Addis Ababa, Ethiopia, Jan 25, 2005.

Lisanekristos Matewos; Catholic priest. Addis Ababa, Ethiopia, Jan 24, 2005.

Malmvärn, Seth; Swedish missionary, son of Arvid and Kärstin Malmvärn. Addis Ababa, Ethiopia, Jan 19, 2005.

Mamusha Fenta; principal of the Pentecostal Theological College (Ethiopian Heywet Birhan Church). Addis Ababa, Ethiopia, Sep 23, 2003.

Mebrate Melese; evangelist of the Meserete Kristos Church. Awasa, Ethiopia, Feb 10, 2005.

Mekbib Desta; pastor of the Evangelical Maranata Church. Addis Ababa, Ethiopia, Jan 18, 2005. (together with Kindeya Hailu)

Mekuria Mulugeta; founder and owner of Heywet Tesfa Radio. Addis Ababa, Ethiopia, Mar 25, 2005.

Melese Wogu; executive director of the Ethiopian Outreach Ministry. Addis Ababa, Ethiopia, Mar 30, 2005.

Mengistu Jemebere; pastor of the Addis Ababa Full Gospel Believers' Church. Addis Ababa, Ethiopia, Mar 29, 2005.

Merid Lemma; senior pastor of the Addis Ababa Full Gospel Believers' Church. Addis Ababa, Ethiopia, Apr 01, 2004.

Mersha Hailu; pastor of the Rhema Faith church. Awasa, Ethiopia, Feb 23, 2005.

Mesfin Tariku; member of the Ethiopian Evangelical Church Mekane Yesus. Awasa, Ethiopia, Feb 12, 2005. (together with Misrak Muluwork)

Mezgebu Tsemru; pastor of the Emanuel United Church. Addis Ababa, Ethiopia, Mar 28, 2005.

Mikael Wendimu; pastor of the Annointing Word of God International Church. Addis Ababa, Ethiopia, Mar 19, 2004.

Mileon Fasika; pastor of the Lutheran Church in Ethiopia. Addis Ababa, Ethiopia, Feb 02, 2005.

Milkias Borena; elder at the Awasa Ethiopian Heywet Birhan Church. Awasa, Ethiopia, Feb 14, 2005.

Minas Biruk; Ethiopian Full Gospel Believers' Church head office. Addis Ababa, Ethiopia, Sep 30, 2003.

Misrak Muluwork; member of the Ethiopian Evangelical Church Mekane Yesus. Awasa, Ethiopia, Feb 12, 2005. (together with Mesfin Tariku)

Muffett, Marja; former missionary with Fida International (formerly Free Finnish Foreign Mission). Telephone interview, Oct 06, 2006. (together with Rawson Muffett)

Muffett, Rawson; former missionary with Fida International (formerly Free Finnish Foreign Mission). Telephone interview, Oct 06, 2006. (together with Marja Muffett)

Mukiria Chacha; son of Chacha Omahe, resident in Nairobi, Kenya. Telephone interview, Dec 23, 2010.

Mulugeta Ashagere; denominational leader of the Ethiopian Christian Brethren Church. Addis Ababa, Ethiopia, Feb 01, 2005.

Mulugeta Tadesse; pastor of the Emenet Christ Church. Addis Ababa, Ethiopia, Jan 21, 2005.

Muluwork Mekuria; director of Youth With a Mission in Ethiopia. Addis Ababa, Ethiopia, Feb 28, 2004.

Negatu Arregaw; pastor of the Bible Baptist Fellowship. Addis Ababa, Ethiopia, Jan 18, 2005.

Nurhuse Alemu; evangelist of the Ethiopian Heywet Birhan Church. Bahir Dar, Ethiopia, Mar 03, 2005. (together with Girmachew Birhan, and Samuel Bishaw)

Penttinen, Heikki; missionary with Fida International (formerly Free Finnish Foreign Mission). Addis Ababa, Ethiopia, Mar 18, 2004.

Possner, Martin; missionary with the Evangelical Lutheran Mission/German Hermannsburg Mission. Addis Ababa, Ethiopia, Sep 11, 2003.

Ramstrand, Ruth; former missionary with the Swedish Philadelphia Church Mission. Telephone interview, Sep 12, 2006.

Roininen, Aino; missionary of Fida International (formerly Free Finnish Foreign Mission) in Ethiopia. Iisalmi, Finland, Aug 02, 2004. (together with Kyösti Roininen)

Roininen, Kyösti; missionary and former representative of Fida International (formerly Free Finnish Foreign Mission) in Ethiopia. Iisalmi, Finland, Aug 02, 2004 (together with Aino Roininen), and telephone interview, Feb 23, 2007.

Runolinna, Pauli; missionary of Fida International (formerly Free Finnish Foreign Mission). Helsinki, Finland, Aug 04, 2004.

Rutten, Brian; missionary with the Pentecostal Assemblies of God Canada. Addis Ababa, Ethiopia, Sep 12, 2003. (together with Valerie Rutten)

Rutten, Valerie; missionary with the Pentecostal Assemblies of God Canada. Addis Ababa, Ethiopia, Sep 12, 2003. (together with Brian Rutten)

Samuel Bishaw; evangelist of the Ethiopian Heywet Birhan Church. Bahir Dar, Ethiopia, Mar 03, 2005. (together with Girmachew Birhan, and Nurhuse Alemu)

Sara Kororesa; evangelist of the Ethiopian Evangelical Church Mekane Yesus. Awasa, Ethiopia, Feb 11, 2005.

Seleshi Kebede; associate general secretary of the of the Evangelical Churches' Fellowship of Ethiopia, pastor of the Ethiopian Gennet Church. Addis Ababa, Ethiopia, Sep 19, 2003.

Sewalem Tsegaye; pastor of the Emmanuel Light and Life Church. Bahir Dar, Ethiopia, Mar 10, 2005.

Simeon Mocha; evangelism director at the Southern Synod of the Ethiopian Evangelical Church Mekane Yesus. Awasa, Ethiopia, Feb 25, 2005.

Sisay Chaka; evangelist of the Ethiopian Gennet Church. Awasa, Ethiopia, Feb 10, 2005.

Solomon Kebede; regional director of the International Bible Society in Ethiopia. Addis Ababa, Ethiopia, Oct 01, 2003.

Solomon Melaku; senior pastor at the Awasa Winner's Temple. Awasa, Ethiopia, Feb 22, 2005.

Tadele Geremew; pastor of the Assemblies of God. Bahir Dar, Ethiopia, Mar 09, 2005.

Tadesse Eshete; pastor of the Source of Life Evangelical Church. Addis Ababa, Ethiopia, Jan 11, 2005.

Tariku Mitiku; priest of the Catholic Church of Ethiopia. Addis Ababa, Ethiopia, Mar 27, 2005.

Tariso Onchire; coordinator of the Awasa Evangelical Churches' Fellowship. Awasa, Ethiopia, Feb 25, 2005.

Tasgara Hirpo; former pastor of the Ethiopian Evangelical Church Mekane Yesus. Addis Ababa, Ethiopia, Feb 02, 2005.

Teka Gebru; member of the Addis Ababa Full Gospel Believers' Church. Addis Ababa, Ethiopia, Jan 22, 2005.

Teklemariam Abera; pastor of the Bethel Tehadisso. Bahir Dar, Ethiopia, Mar 07, 2005.

Teklemariam Gezahegne; senior pastor of the Apostolic Church of Ethiopia. Addis Ababa, Ethiopia, Jan 27, 2005.

Teklu Wolde; general secretary of the Ethiopian Gennet Church. Addis Ababa, Ethiopia, Sep 22, 2003 and Feb 26, 2004. (together with Ashebir Ketema)

Tesfa Derese; elder at the Bahir Dar Ethiopian Heywet Birhan Church. Bahir Dar, Ethiopia, Mar 12, 2005.

Tesfaye Gabbiso; pastor of the Ethiopian Full Gospel Believers' Church. Awasa, Ethiopia, Feb 08, 2005.

Tesfaye Mesfen; spiritual book translator, member of the Meserete Kristos Church. Addis Ababa, Ethiopia, Mar 11, 2004.

Tesfaye Nenko; pastor of the Ethiopian Full Gospel Believers' Church. Awasa, Ethiopia, Feb 24, 2005. (together with Workagene Abera)

Tessema Doyamo; pastor of the Ethiopian Evangelical Church Mekane Yesus. Awasa, Ethiopia, Feb 22, 2005.

Tessema Shapa; pastor of the Heywet Kale Church. Awasa, Ethiopia, Feb 13, 2005.

Tewolde Yohannes; member of the Ethiopian Congregation in Bochum. Bochum, Germany, Aug 16, 2007.

Tolosa Gudina; evangelist and founder of the Truth in Love Gospel Ministries. Addis Ababa, Ethiopia, Mar 30, 2004.

Tsadiku Abdo Alema; general secretary of the Ethiopian Full Gospel Believers' Church. Addis Ababa, Ethiopia, Mar 25, 2004.

Weihmann, Jan; missionary with the Evangelical Lutheran Mission/German Hermannsburg Mission. Hosaina, Ethiopia, Sep 13, 2003.

Wolde Dagnachew; senior pastor of the Assemblies of God in Ethiopia. Addis Ababa, Ethiopia, Mar 03, 2004.

Wondeye Ali Hamza; head of the Literature Section of the Ethiopian Kale Heywet Church. Addis Ababa, Ethiopia, Mar 09, 2004.

Workagene Abera; coordinator at the Southern Regional Office of the Ethiopian Full Gospel Believers' Church. Awasa, Ethiopia, Feb 24, 2005. (together with Tesfaye Nenko)

Woyesa Turalo; pastor of the Assemblies of God. Awasa, Ethiopia, Feb 09, 2005.

Woyita Woza; department head of the Theological and Ministerial Education of the Ethiopian Kale Heywet Church. Addis Ababa, Ethiopia, Jan 31, 2005.

Wubishet Dessalegne; member of the Emaniel Baptist Church. Addis Ababa, Ethiopia, Jan 20, 2005.

Yared Tilahun; evangelist and founder of Golden Oil Ministries. Addis Ababa, Ethiopia, Mar 16, 2004.

Yemaneberhan Endale; senior pastor of the Ethiopian Gospel Deliverance Church. Addis Ababa, Ethiopia, Jan 17, 2005.

Yenina Worku; president of the Ethiopian Heywet Birhan Church. Addis Ababa, Ethiopia, Mar 05, 2004.

Yilma Getahun; general secretary of the Ethiopia Bible Society. Addis Ababa, Ethiopia, Mar 29, 2005.

Yisihak Molla; pastor of the Ethiopian Kale Heywet Church. Awasa, Ethiopia, Feb 16, 2005 and Feb 22, 2005.

Yonatan Takie; director of Youth Impact. Addis Ababa, Ethiopia, Feb 25, 2004.

Yoseph Menna; senior mission expert at the Missions Mobilization, Discipleship and Church Growth Department of the Ethiopian Kale Heywet Church. Addis Ababa, Ethiopia, Feb 03, 2005.

Zekarias Bassa; denominational leader of the Heywet Kale Church. Addis Ababa, Ethiopia, Mar 23, 2005.

Zelleke Alemu; pastor of the Grace Ethiopian Church in Springfield, Virginia, USA. Telephone interview, Sep 04, 2007.

Zenebe Mesfin; deacon of the Orthodox Finote Heywet Mehabir. Awasa, Ethiopia, Feb 22, 2005.

Index